Innovations and Approaches for Resilient and Adaptive Systems

Vincenzo De Florio
PATS Research Group, University of Antwerp & IBBT, Belgium

Information Science
REFERENCE

Managing Director:	Lindsay Johnston
Senior Editorial Director:	Heather A. Probst
Book Production Manager:	Sean Woznicki
Development Manager:	Joel Gamon
Assistant Acquisitions Editor:	Kayla Wolfe
Typesetter:	Nicole Sparano
Cover Design:	Nick Newcomer

Published in the United States of America by
Information Science Reference (an imprint of IGI Global)
701 E. Chocolate Avenue
Hershey PA 17033
Tel: 717-533-8845
Fax: 717-533-8661
E-mail: cust@igi-global.com
Web site: http://www.igi-global.com

Library of Congress Cataloging-in-Publication Data

Innovations and approaches for resilient and adaptive systems / Vincenzo De Florio, editor.
     p. cm.
  Includes bibliographical references and index.
  Summary: "This book is a comprehensive collection of knowledge on increasing the notions and models in adaptive and dependable systems, enhancing the awareness of the role of adaptability and resilience in system environments"--Provided by publisher.
  ISBN 978-1-4666-2056-8 (hardcover) -- ISBN 978-1-4666-2057-5 (ebook) -- ISBN 978-1-4666-2058-2 (print & perpetual access) 1. Adaptive computing systems--Technological innovations. I. De Florio, Vincenzo, 1963-
  QA76.9.A3I56 2013
  621.39'5--dc23
                          2012013061

British Cataloguing in Publication Data
A Cataloguing in Publication record for this book is available from the British Library.

The views expressed in this book are those of the authors, but not necessarily of the publisher.

Editorial Advisory Board

Table of Contents

Section 1
Approaches for Resilient and Adaptive Systems

> *Satyakiran Munaga, IMEC and K. U. Leuven/ESAT, Belgium*
> *Francky Catthoor, IMEC and K. U. Leuven/ESAT, Belgium*

> *Gabriella Carrozza, SESM s.c.a.r.l. - a Finmeccanica Company, Italy*
> *Roberto Natella, Università degli Studi di Napoli Federico II, Italy*

> *Leo Marcus, The Aerospace Corporation, USA*

> *Chi-Yuan Chen, National Dong Hwa University, Taiwan*
> *Han-Chieh Chao, National Dong Hwa University and National I-Lan University, Taiwan*
> *Tin-Yu Wu, Tamkang University, Taiwan*
> *Chun-I Fan, National Sun Yat-sen University, Taiwan*
> *Jiann-Liang Chen, National Taiwan University of Science and Technology, Taiwan*
> *Yuh-Shyan Chen, National Taipei University, Taiwan*
> *Jenq-Muh Hsu, National Chiayi University, Taiwan*

Section 2
Autonomic Behaviors and Self-Properties

Section 3
Middleware and Framework Support for Resilient and Adaptive Systems

Section 4
Algorithms and Protocols for Resilient and Adaptive Systems

Detailed Table of Contents

Section 1
Approaches for Resilient and Adaptive Systems

Chapter 1

   Satyakiran Munaga, IMEC and K. U. Leuven/ESAT, Belgium
   Francky Catthoor, IMEC and K. U. Leuven/ESAT, Belgium

Modern cost-conscious dynamic systems incorporate knobs that allow run-time trade-offs between
system metrics of interest. In these systems regular knob tuning to minimize costs while satisfying
hard system constraints is an important aspect. Knob tuning is a combinatorial constrained nonlinear
dynamic optimization problem with uncertainties and time-linkage. Hiding uncertainties under worst-
case bounds, reacting after the fact, optimizing only the present, and applying static greedy heuristics
are widely used problem simplification strategies to keep the design complexity and decision overhead
low. Applying any of these will result in highly sub-optimal system realizations in the presence of nonlinearities. The more recently introduced System Scenarios methodology can only handle limited form
of dynamics and nonlinearities. Existing predictive optimization approaches are far from optimal as
they do not fully exploit the predictability of the system at hand. To bridge this gap, the authors propose
the combined strategy of dynamic bounding and proactive system conditioning for the predicted likely
future. This paper describes systematic principles to design low-overhead controllers for cost-effective
hard constraint management. When applied to fine-grain performance scaling mode assignment problem in a video decoder design, proposed concepts resulted in more than 2x energy gains compared to
state-of-the-art techniques.

Chapter 2

   Gabriella Carrozza, SESM s.c.a.r.l. - a Finmeccanica Company, Italy
   Roberto Natella, Università degli Studi di Napoli Federico II, Italy

This paper proposes an approach to software faults diagnosis in complex fault tolerant systems, encompassing the phases of error detection, fault location, and system recovery. Errors are detected in the first
phase, exploiting the operating system support. Faults are identified during the location phase, through

a machine learning based approach. Then, the best recovery action is triggered once the fault is located. Feedback actions are also used during the location phase to improve detection quality over time. A real world application from the Air Traffic Control field has been used as case study for evaluating the proposed approach. Experimental results, achieved by means of fault injection, show that the diagnosis engine is able to diagnose faults with high accuracy and at a low overhead.

Chapter 3

Leo Marcus, The Aerospace Corporation, USA

This paper explores the concept of "pure fault tolerance"--when a system can fulfill its computational goal, even though some of its components do not fulfill theirs. This leads to a natural statement of the composition problem for a very general concept of architecture: to what extent are the properties of a system based on that architecture a function of the properties of the components? The author explores several variations on pure fault tolerance, none of which utilize fault detection or error correction.

Chapter 4

Chi-Yuan Chen, National Dong Hwa University, Taiwan
Han-Chieh Chao, National Dong Hwa University and National I-Lan University, Taiwan
Tin-Yu Wu, Tamkang University, Taiwan
Chun-I Fan, National Sun Yat-sen University, Taiwan
Jiann-Liang Chen, National Taiwan University of Science and Technology, Taiwan
Yuh-Shyan Chen, National Taipei University, Taiwan
Jenq-Muh Hsu, National Chiayi University, Taiwan

In recent years, Internet of Things (IoT) and Cloud Computing are the hottest issues of Future Internet. However, there is a lack of common fabric for integrating IoT and Cloud. In telecommunications, the IMS (IP Multimedia Subsystem), based on the All-IP and Open Services Architecture, has been regarded as the trend for Next Generation Network (NGN). The IMS communication platform is the most suitable fabric for integrating IoT and Cloud. This paper focuses on different aspects including Cloud Service Framework, Data Sensing and Communication Technology, Collaborative Authentication and Privacy Protection Mechanism, Operation, Administration, and Maintenance (OA&M), Mobility and Energy-Saving Management, and Application Services. This paper not only provides the discussion of open challenges, but also proposes a possible solution based on the above-mentioned aspects for Future Internet.

Section 2
Autonomic Behaviors and Self-Properties

Chapter 5

M. Leeman, Cisco, Belgium

This paper describes an algorithm for dynamically assigning tasks to processing entities in a world where each task has a set of resource or service requirements and each processing entity a set of resources or service capabilities. A task needs to be assigned to a node that offers all required services and the set of tasks is finished within a minimal execution time frame. Dependability and adaptability are inherent to the algorithm so that it accounts for the varying execution time of each task or the failure of a processing node. The algorithm is based on a dependable technique for farmer-worker parallel programs and is enhanced for modeling the time constraints in combination with the required configuration set in a multidimensional resources model. This paper describes how the algorithm is used for dynamically load balancing and parallelizing the nightly tests of a digital television content-processing embedded device.

Chapter 6

Rémi Sharrock, LAAS-CNRS - University of Toulouse; UPS, INSA, INP, ISAE, France
Thierry Monteil, LAAS-CNRS - University of Toulouse; UPS, INSA, INP, ISAE, France
Patricia Stolf, IRIT and Université de Toulouse, France
Daniel Hagimont, IRIT and Université de Toulouse, France
Laurent Broto, IRIT and Université de Toulouse, France

The growing complexity of large IT facilities involves important time and effort costs to operate and maintain. Autonomic computing gives a new approach in designing distributed architectures that manage themselves in accordance with high-level objectives. The main issue is that existing architectures do not necessarily follow this new approach. The motivation is to implement a system that can interface heterogeneous components and platforms supplied by different vendors in a non-intrusive and generic manner. The goal is to increase the intelligence of the system by actively monitoring its state and autonomously taking corrective actions without the need to modify the managed system. In this paper, the authors focus on modeling software and hardware architectures as well as describing administration policies using a graphical language inspired from UML. The paper demonstrates that this language is powerful enough to describe complex scenarios and evaluates some self-management policies for performance improvement on a distributed computational jobs load balancer over a grid.

Chapter 7

Rocco Aversa, Second University of Naples, Italy
Beniamino Di Martino, Second University of Naples, Italy
Michele Di Natale, Second University of Naples, Italy
Salvatore Venticinque, Second University of Naples, Italy

Compliance with safety standards in constructing sites is a mandatory activity that helps prevent a high number of fatalities during working activities. Unfortunately, because of negligence or limited resources, safety checks are not performed with regularity and this causes a high number of accidents. This paper proposes a distributed solution for automated checking of safety rules, secure logging of violations, and real-time execution of reactions. The constructing site is modeled as a pervasive environment where software agents, executing on smart devices, can detect and interact with people, machineries, and safety equipment to check the compliance of common behaviors with the safety plan designed for that site. The design is presented as a working prototype of a three layered software/hardware architecture.

Autonomous Robots normally perform tasks in unstructured environments, with little or no continuous human guidance. This calls for context-aware, self-adaptive software systems. This paper aims at providing a flexible adaptive middleware platform to seamlessly integrate multiple adaptation logics during the run-time. To support such an approach, a reconfigurable middleware system "ACCADA" was designed to provide compositional adaptation. During the run-time, context knowledge is used to select the most appropriate adaptation modules so as to compose an adaptive system best-matching the current exogenous and endogenous conditions. Together with a structure modeler, this allows robotic applications' structure to be autonomously (re)-constructed and (re)-configured. This paper applies this model on a Lego NXT robot system. A remote NXT model is designed to wrap and expose native NXT devices into service components that can be managed during the run-time. A dynamic UI is implemented which can be changed and customized according to system conditions. Results show that the framework changes robot adaptation behavior during the run-time.

With the next generation of distributed systems, applications become nomad, ubiquitous or ambient. It becomes challenging to dynamically maintain or update functionalities, or to preserve non-functional properties, like the extensibility of the system and the quality of service. This paper describes the CompAA component model. The main contribution introduces the variability concept with the specification of adaptation points integrated by a mixed component/agent approach. The result is the production of self-adaptable entities, including self-discovery and self-composition mechanisms. An experiment in the area of training, based on very scalable services (e-Portfolio), validates these contributions and provides an exemplification of CompAA mechanisms.

Section 3
Middleware and Framework Support for Resilient and Adaptive Systems

Quality-of-service enabled publish/subscribe (pub/sub) middleware provides powerful support for scalable data dissemination. It is difficult to maintain key quality of service properties (such as reliability and latency) in dynamic environments for distributed real-time and embedded systems (such as disaster relief operations or power grids). Managing quality of service manually is often not feasible in dynamic environments due to slow response times, the complexity of managing multiple interrelated quality of service settings, and the scale of the systems being managed. For certain domains, distributed real-time and embedded systems must be able to reflect on the conditions of their environment and adapt accordingly in a bounded amount of time. This paper describes an architecture of quality of service-enabled middleware and corresponding algorithms to support specified quality of service in dynamic environments.

Chapter 11

Hong Sun, University of Antwerp and IBBT, Belgium
Ning Gui, University of Antwerp and IBBT, Belgium & Central South University, China
Chris Blondia, University of Antwerp and IBBT, Belgium

Today, technologies are providing mobile terminals with much more powerful computational abilities. Such improvement has made it possible to run many complex applications on mobile devices. However, many of these new applications are also resource demanding. Lacking sufficient resources would cause performance failures and impact negatively on the users' quality of experience. In order to improve this, it is important to provide the users with an easy access to specifying their requirements. It is also crucial to monitor the system resources and make corresponding adaptation immediately according to the user's specifications. In this paper, the authors propose adaptation strategies that flexibly combine the process of monitoring and adaptation, which provides an easy way to specify user's requirements. By tuning the quality of service, the applications' demand on system resources is reduced, thus decreasing the chances of performance failures and improving the users' quality of experience.

Chapter 12

Stéphane Frénot, University of Lyon, INRIA INSA-Lyon, F-69621, France
Frédéric Le Mouël, University of Lyon, INRIA INSA-Lyon, F-69621, France
Julien Ponge, University of Lyon, INRIA INSA-Lyon, F-69621, France
Guillaume Salagnac, University of Lyon, INRIA INSA-Lyon, F-69621, France

OSGi is a wrapper above the Java Virtual Machine that embraces two concepts: component approach and service-oriented programming. The component approach enables a Java run-time to host several concurrent applications, while the service-oriented programming paradigm allows the decomposition of applications into independent units that are dynamically bound at runtime. Combining component and service-oriented programming greatly simplifies the implementation of highly adaptive, constantly evolving applications. This, in turn, is an ideal match to the requirements and constraints of ambient intelligence computing, such as adaptation to changes associated with context evolution. OSGi particularly fits ambient requirements and constraints by absorbing and adapting to changes associated with context evolution. However, OSGi needs to be finely tuned in order to integrate ambient specific issues. This paper focuses on Zero-configuration architecture, Multi-provider framework, and Limited resource requirements. The authors studied many OSGi improvements that should be taken into account when building OSGi-based gateways. This paper summarizes the INRIA Amazones teamwork (http://amazones. gforge.inria.fr/) on extending OSGi specifications and implementations to cope with ambient concerns. This paper references three main concerns: management, isolation, and security.

Chapter 13

Iacopo Carreras, CREATE-NET, Italy

Andrea Zanardi, CREATE-NET, Italy

Elio Salvadori, CREATE-NET, Italy

Daniele Miorandi, CREATE-NET, Italy

Opportunistic communication systems aim at producing and sharing digital resources by means of localized wireless data exchanges among mobile nodes. The design and evaluation of systems able to exploit this emerging communication paradigm is a challenging problem. This paper presents the authors' experience in developing U-Hopper, a middleware running over widely diffused mobile handsets and supporting the development of context-aware services based on opportunistic communications. The authors present the design of the platform, and describe the distributed monitoring framework that was set up in order to monitor and dynamically reconfigure it at run time. The paper concludes with an experimental evaluation of the framework, showing its practical utilization when monitoring an operational opportunistic communication system.

Section 4
Algorithms and Protocols for Resilient and Adaptive Systems

Chapter 14

Long Vu, University of Illinois, USA

Klara Nahrstedt, University of Illinois, USA

Rahul Malik, University of Illinois, USA

Qiyan Wang, University of Illinois, USA

This paper argues that Dynamic Coalition Peer-to-Peer (P2P) Network exists in numerous scenarios where mobile users cluster and form coalitions, and the relationship between sizes of coalitions and distances from mobile nodes to their Point of Interest (PoI) follows exponential distributions. The P2P coalition patterns of mobile users and their exponential distribution behavior can be utilized for efficient and adaptive content file download of cellular users. An adaptive protocol named COADA (COalition-aware Adaptive content DownloAd) is designed that (a) blends cellular and P2P (e.g., WiFi or Bluetooth) wireless interfaces, (b) leverages the clustering of people into P2P coalitions when moving towards PoI, and (c) utilizes exponential-coalition-size function of the Dynamic Coalition P2P Network to minimize the cellular download and meet content file download deadline. With COADA protocol, mobile nodes periodically sample the current P2P coalition size and predict the future coalition size using the exponential function. In order to decide how much file data is available in P2P coalition channels versus how much file data must be downloaded from the server over the cellular network, Online Codes techniques are used and tune cellular download timers to meet the file download deadline. The simulation results show that COADA achieves considerable performance improvements by downloading less file data from the cellular channel and more file data over the P2P coalition network while meeting the file download deadline.

Flavio Frattini, Institute of High Performance Computing and Networking, Italy
Christian Esposito, Università di Napoli Federico II, Italy
Stefano Russo, Università di Napoli Federico II, Italy

Localization within a Wireless Sensor Network consists of defining the position of a given set of sensors by satisfying some non-functional requirements such as (1) efficient energy consumption, (2) low communication or computation overhead, (3) no, or limited, use of particular hardware components, (4) fast localization, (5) robustness, and (6) low localization error. Although there are several algorithms and techniques available in literature, localization is viewed as an open issue because none of the current solutions are able to jointly satisfy all the previous requirements. An algorithm called ROCRSSI appears to be a suitable solution; however, it is affected by several inefficiencies that limit its effectiveness in real case scenarios. This paper proposes a refined version of this algorithm, called ROCRSSI++, which resolves such inefficiencies using and storing information gathered by the sensors in a more efficient manner. Several experiments on actual devices have been performed. The results show a reduction of the localization error with respect to the original algorithm. This paper investigates energy consumption and localization time required by the proposed approach.

Chapter 16

Muddesar Iqbal, University of Gujrat, Pakistan
Xinheng Wang, Swansea University, UK
Hui Zhang, Swansea University, UK

A gateway node in a WMN acts as bridge between mesh nodes and the external network in order to exchange information between the wireless mesh network operating in a disaster stricken area and remotely located rescue headquarters and government agencies. Using a single gateway, WMN creates huge congestion on the routes to the gateway, as all the data traffic may travel in the same direction using longer routes to access the gateway node, causing channel contention between nodes that operate within carrier sensing range of each other. Therefore a multiple gateway environment is crucial during WMN application in emergency and disaster recovery. This paper presents the design and implementation of a Load-Balanced Gateway Discovery routing protocol called LBGD-AODV, which provides multiple gateway support in Wireless Mesh Network. LBGD-AODV is designed as an extension to the Ad hoc On-Demand Distance Vector (AODV) routing protocol and uses a periodic gateway advertisement scheme equipped with an efficient algorithm to avoid congestion by establishing load-balanced routes to the gateway nodes for Internet traffic. The evaluation tests show that the LBGD-AODV has not compromised the efficiency of basic AODV routing and has improved the performance of the network.

Hui Zhang, Swansea University, UK
Xinheng Wang, Swansea University, UK
Muddesar Iqbal, University of Gujrat, Pakistan

Due to the rapid advancement of mobile communication technologies, the demands for managing mobile devices effectively to fulfill various functionalities are on the rise. It is well known that mobile devices make use of different kinds of modulation approaches to adapt to various channel conditions.

Therefore, in this paper, the authors propose a framework of Modulation Module Update (MMU) for updating the modulation module on the mobile device based on OMA DM. The management object for updating modulation module and the parameters associated with it are defined in the framework, and three operation phases are defined in this framework as well.

When systems are deployed in environments where change is the rule rather than the exception, adaptability and resilience play a crucial role in order to preserve good quality of service. This work analyses methods that can be adopted for the duty cycle measurement of sensor-originated waveforms. These methods start from the assumption that no regular sampling is possible and thus they are naturally thought for an adaptive coexistence with other heterogeneous and variable tasks. Hence, the waveform carrying the information from low-priority sensors can be sampled only at instants that are non-controlled. To tackle this problem, this paper proposes some algorithms for the duty cycle measurement of a digital pulse train signal that is sampled at random instants. The solutions are easy to implement and lightweight so that they can be scheduled in extremely loaded microcontrollers. The results show a fast convergence to the duty cycle value; in particular, a considerable gain with respect to other known solutions is obtained in terms of the average number of samples necessary to evaluate the duty cycle with a desired accuracy is obtained.

Preface

It was with great pleasure that I accepted the kind invitation from my friends at IGI-Global to play again the role of editor for this series of books collecting the papers from the yearly volumes of *IJARAS*, the *International Journal of Adaptive, Resilient, and Autonomic Systems*, established in 2010 and now in its third year of publication. Reflecting on the work done and rearranging the contents into a coherent new "whole picture" provided me again with the chance to get closer and learn once more from the work of so many and diverse contributors. My message here is first and foremost a chance to express my gratitude to them for sharing their lessons learned with me and the readers of IJARAS, as well as for considering our journal for their papers. Some of these contributions are particularly important to me because of their affinity with my own research interests; others for having provided me with new and broader insight and ideas; still others for their innovative character or for the sheer pleasure I had in being shown familiar concepts and approaches from a different angle. Editing this book allowed me also to try and present those contributions under a new light and hopefully better expose their true innovation potential.

The focus of this book is on two fundamental ideas in (computing) systems — resilience and adaptivity. Simply amazing is the number and stature of the scholars who addressed these two intertwined concepts throughout the past centuries. Still more surprising is how much we have yet to understand about resilience and adaptivity, and how actively the scientific and industrial communities are investigating or applying today models, systems, and applications exhibiting resilient and adaptive behaviors. It is my opinion that the common nature of both concepts should be traced back to the Aristotelian concept of *entelechy* (Sachs, 1995; Aristotle & Lawson-Tancred, 1986; De Florio, 2012a). *Entelechy* is in fact one of the main conceptual cornerstones in Aristotle's philosophy — so difficult a concept to be captured in a concise definition that Sachs refers to it as being a "three-ring circus of a word" (Sachs, 1995). Difficulties notwithstanding, it is that very same scholar that in the cited reference provides us with a practical and ingenious translation of entelechy as "being-at-work-staying-the-same." Such a definition obviously consists of the following two parts:

1. "Being at work," which refers to a system's ability to continuously adjust their functions so as to compensate for foreseen and/or unpredicted changes in a given execution environment.
2. "Staying the same," referring to that system's ability to retain their "identity" — in other words, its peculiar and distinctive functional and non-functional features — despite both the above mentioned environmental changes and the adjustments carried out so as to improve the system-environment fit.

As it can be easily realized, the two abilities above are actually adaptivity and resilience — again, the major characters in this book. The common denominator of all articles presented here is in fact their dealing with facets, requirements, and aspects of this "three-ring circus" of a concept that is adaptive-and-resilient computing systems.

Some of the above mentioned aspects and facets are structural and pertain to general approaches towards these "entelechial systems" (De Florio, 2012b). The first section of this book — Approaches for Resilient And Adaptive Systems — presents a number of excellent contributions in that domain. Others aspects are behavioral and focus on the emergence of autonomic properties, e.g. self-safety, self-tuning, self-optimization, self-management, and self-configuration. Accordingly, the interesting articles in our second section all deal with Autonomic Behaviors and Self-Properties. Engineering adaptive and resilient systems in an effective and cost-conscious way calls for practical solutions to common requirements for resilient and adaptive systems. An "accumulation point" of sort for such requirements and solutions is given by middleware and frameworks. Accordingly section 3 offers four valuable contributions dealing with Middleware and Framework Support for Resilient and Adaptive Systems. Operative aspects constitute the subject of the final section of this book, which is entitled Algorithms and Protocols for Resilient and Adaptive Systems and provides excellent examples of ingenious solutions to achieve in practice the emergence of resilience and adaptivity. In what follows I will introduce these sections and their papers.

1. APPROACHES FOR RESILIENT AND ADAPTIVE SYSTEMS

Section 1 includes four very interesting contributions dealing with open problems in quite different domains.

In their excellent paper "Systematic Design Principles for Cost-Effective Hard Constraint Management in Dynamic Nonlinear Systems," authors S. Munaga and F. Catthoor argue that the current system design principles for hardware controllers do not match anymore with current requirements for systems that be able to satisfy hard system constraints while at the same time minimizing costs. The traditional non-predictive approaches privilege simplicity over effectiveness and do not exploit any predictability in the system at hand. Existing predictive or hybrid approaches such as the System Scenarios methodology (Gheorghita et al., 2009) can only handle limited forms of dynamism and nonlinearities, which results in non optimal behaviors that still do not fully exploit the available predictability. The answers of the authors is a number of systematic design principles based on the combined strategy of dynamic bounding and proactive system conditioning for a predicted likely future. This led to more than halving the energy expenditure in a preliminary application in the design of a video decoder. It is my personal conjecture that much more and better results can be expected by engineering the reported approach to the full extent of its potential.

A second very promising work in this section is given by paper "A Recovery-Oriented Approach for Software Fault Diagnosis in Complex Critical Systems," contributed by G. Carrozza and R. Natella. The reported approach is based on the observation that production run failures and field failures cause the software system failure modes to be impossible to define at design time. Then how to be able to match behaviors that continuously change over time? The clever answer of the authors is given by a holistic diagnostic approach in which error detection, fault location, and error recovery have been integrated into one on-line adaptive diagnosis process. When an error is detected, the corresponding fault is located by means of machine learning algorithms, and an error recovery best matching that fault is selected and executed. Teleologic behavior is ensured by including corrective actions to improve dynamically the detection quality. After defining their approach the authors put it to use in a real-life application in the field of Air Traffic Control. Very satisfactory results are observed, including high accuracy and low overhead.

In his brilliant position paper "Abstract Fault Tolerance: A Model-Theoretic Approach to Fault Tolerance and Fault Compensation without Error Correction," L. Marcus explores the concept of "pure fault tolerance," namely the study of a system's emergence of certain desired behaviors despite the fact that not all sub-systems behave as expected. Dr. Marcus discusses this issue and poses several important questions, including:

- What is the degree of resilience intrinsically possessed by a given architecture?
- Given a system modeled after that architecture, to what extent the properties of that system are a function of the same properties in the components of that system? (For instance when we consider reliability and the triple modular redundant (TMR) architecture, a well-known fact is that it is possible to tell precisely how the reliability of the composite is in relation with that of its constituents[2] (Johnson,1989). In this case the formulation is simple and elegant, but when we slightly modify the architecture we get to a much more complex expression[3] (De Florio et al., 1998). Obviously it is very unlikely that analytical formulations such as those may be found for Complex Adaptive Systems!)
- To what extent a system achieves its goals despite misbehaviors of its constituents — a question that makes very much sense also for large collective adaptive systems and even societal systems such as certain governments.

Clearly the focus of this position paper is not in providing an answer to these questions but rather in highlighting their role in understanding the "hidden rules" that govern the emergence of resilience in (adaptive) systems (Holland, 2004). Another contribution of the author is a framework for the expression of the semantics of Pure Fault Tolerance.

Finally, in paper "IoT-IMS Communication Platform for Future Internet" by C.-Y. Chen, H.-C. Chao, T.-Y. Wu, C.-I Fan, J.-L. Chen, Y.-S. Chen, and J.-M. Hsu, the authors point out how the Future Internet is likely to exhibit a convergence of two currently hot topics — Internet of Things and Cloud Computing. A possible common fabric to enable this integration was indicated in the so-called IP Multimedia Subsystem, a communication platform based on All-IP and the Open Services Architecture. The authors discuss corresponding scenarios for the Future Internet based on aspects including cloud services, data sensing and communication technology, authentication and privacy protection mechanisms, and mobility and energy-saving Management. An approach towards the Future Internet based on the above-mentioned aspects is also described.

2. AUTONOMIC BEHAVIORS AND SELF-PROPERTIES

Five excellent papers constitute the section on self-properties and autonomic behaviours.

Self-tuning and *self-optimization* are the key objectives in M. Leeman's paper "A Resource-Aware Dynamic Load-Balancing Parallelization Algorithm in a Farmer-Worker Environment." Built on top of the dependable farmer-worker algorithm described in (De Florio et al., 1997), the system described in this paper is currently being used to dynamically balance the workloads of regression tests of a digital television content-processing embedded device. The proposed resource-aware algorithm automatically compensates for failures in the worker processes as well as in the worker nodes and it ensures that tasks are scheduled according to a policy that minimizes execution time. Most importantly, the algorithm does not assume all the workers to have the same capabilities nor all assignments to include the same set of requirements. Its adoption within CISCO appears to be steadily growing mainly due to the algorithm's ability of reaching its intended design goals with very limited costs.

In "Non-Intrusive Autonomic Approach with Self-Management Policies Applied to Legacy Infrastructures for Performance Improvements," by R. Sharrock, T. Monteil, P. Stolf, D. Hagimont, and L. Broto, the authors address the problem of limiting the time and costs required to operate and maintain large legacy infrastructures. How to let these infrastructure *self-manage* despite their being designed with software engineering principles and practices dating back to long before the advent of autonomic computing? The authors answer this challenge by proposing an outer control loop that does not change the managed system but the environment around it. The state of the managed system is actively monitored and corrective actions are autonomously injected when needed in a non-intrusive way. The approach makes use of administration policies expressed in a graphical language inspired by UML. The authors prove the effectiveness of their approach by evaluating the performance of a distributed load balancer of computational jobs over a grid. They show in particular how the policy description language approach is powerful enough to express self-management of complex scenarios.

The paper "Agents Network for Automatic Safety Check in Constructing Sites" by R. Aversa, B. Di Martino, M. Di Natale, and S. Venticinque represents an interesting example of how information and communication technology may be successfully applied to enhance existing social services and organizations. Often such services and organizations are not "smart" enough and their lock-ins (Stark, 1999) lead to situations where sub-optimal behaviors and properties ultimately emerge. In some cases this even implies endangering human lives, as regrettably enough it is the case in construction processes. Despite a tradition as old as humanity itself and the availability of many and proven safety standards, still such processes are commonly subjected to tragic failures due to e.g. negligence or criminal behavior. Often such failures are the result of bad practice — for instance safety checks missing or not being performed when due or security violations not being filed and persisted. The authors' answer to this matter of fact consists in regarding the construction site as a hybrid environment in which smart devices, software agents, safety mechanisms and human beings cooperate as a collective adaptive system able to produce autonomously *self-safety* behaviors. Such a new social organization automatically performs safety checks by matching observed behaviors with the safety plans and, in case of mismatches, by enforcing secure logging of violations and real-time execution of recovery actions. The authors present their ingenious design as well as a working prototype taking the form of a three layered software/hardware architecture. It is interesting to realize how the consequence of badly constructed software may lead to consequences as catastrophic as those this interesting paper is meant to tackle (Leveson, 1995); it is only natural then to advocate extending the concepts such as the one described in this contribution so as to enhance the processes for *constructing safe software* and avoid what I called the "endangeneer" syndrome in (De Florio, 2009; De Florio 2012a).

In their paper "Run-Time Compositional Software Platform for Autonomous NXT Robots," N. Gui et al. describe an approach towards *self-restructuring and self-configuring* software based on the ACCADA middleware (Gui, De Florio, Sun & Blondia, 2009) (Gui, De Florio, Sun & Blondia, 2011). Here the context does not just drive adaptation but actually the selection of the adaptation logics best matching the current run-time conditions. Such *meta-adaptation* allows the adaptation logic to be dynamically maintained, which paves the way to being able to face autonomously unprecedented environments. Robotic environments are typical cases where such a feature is very attractive — especially when the robot is set to operate in a location that forbids any form of supervision and control. The approach is validated on a Lego NXT robot system: depending on the available energy budget different adaptation logics are dynamically selected, which leads to different quality vs. cost trade-offs.

Last but by no means the least, this section reprints paper "Self-Adaptable Discovery and Composition of Services Based on the Semantic CompAA Approach," by J. Lacouture and P. Aniorté. As in ACCADA, also in the case of the Auto-Adaptable Components approach the aim is reaching *self-adaptation*, which is obtained here through an ingenious combination of components and intelligent agents technologies. A third ingredient to self-adaptation is semantic processing, which is used to express and mechanically manipulate non-ambiguous information about the functional and non-functional properties of the auto-adaptable components. The resulting hybrid entities are shown to exhibit self-discovery and self-composition mechanisms. Auto-Adaptable Components build on top of the Ugatze Component Reuse MetaModeling tool. The authors apply their approach to an e-Portfolio service — namely a "personal digital collection of information describing and illustrating a person's learning, career, experience and achievements" — in the domain of collaborative learning. The authors provide evidence that their approach achieves important key properties to self-adaptation, including robustness, reusability, autonomy, and flexibility.

3. MIDDLEWARE AND FRAMEWORK SUPPORT FOR RESILIENT AND ADAPTIVE SYSTEMS

As already mentioned, middleware and software frameworks are becoming key resources to support the execution of resilient and adaptive systems. In what follows we describe four contributions in this domain.

The first paper is "Timely Autonomic Adaptation of Publish/Subscribe Middleware in Dynamic Environments," by J. Hoffert, A. Gokhale, and D. C. Schmidt. In their excellent article the authors discuss the challenges in providing *middleware support* able to guarantee quality of service properties such as reliability, latency, and timeliness in distributed environments characterized by dynamic variability of resources. The addressed platforms are distributed real-time and embedded systems while typical scenarios for their middleware include safety-critical and mission-critical applications for crisis management or power grids management. Among the challenges addressed by the authors is the hard requirement of a limited and bounded time for reasoning about the context, planning appropriate reactions and taking pointed adaptations.

In their paper "A Generic Adaptation Framework for Mobile Communication," H. Sun, N. Gui, and C. Blondia describe an approach towards the design of user-aware adaptive systems based on coupling aspect orientation and service-oriented architectures. Rather than taking all decisions autonomously, the described system explicitly "wraps" the user in the control loop by means of a simple graphical user-interface. Dynamic trade-offs of quality of service and quality of experience allow resource consumption to be reduced without introducing performance failures or other quality losses. The approach is based on the event-condition-action model and is demonstrated through an adaptive multimedia application that trades off dynamically quality-of-experience and quality of service versus cost. The software platform chosen by the authors is based on OSGi and uses the AspectJ aspect-oriented programming language as well as so-called reflective and refractive variables — an application-level approach to express adaptation concerns in applications written in "good old" C (De Florio & Blondia, 2007).

Considerable attention is being given by both the research and the development communities to OSGi, "a light-weight standardized service management platform that allows for dynamic service provision from multiple providers" (Sun,Gui & Blondia, 2011). The OSGi framework supports the Java programming language and couples the component approach with service-oriented programming, which considerably simplifies the design of applications able to adapt to highly dynamic environments. Ambient specific issues call for specific fine-tuning though, and in their paper "Various Extensions for the Ambient OSGi Framework" S. Frénot, F. Le Mouël, J. Ponge, and G. Salagnac provide their lessons learned on this problem and report on approaches to extend OSGi so as to enhance its ability to cope with ambient-specific concern.

Opportunistic communication is an emerging paradigm based on systematic wireless exchanges of data owned by mobile nodes in proximity of each other. Not only this realizes a greater "social memory," but it allows resources to be economized by intercepting long haul communication requests and translating them into local wireless exchanges when the corresponding data is already available in the memory of nearby nodes.

As can be easily understood, measuring the performance of opportunistic communication systems is vital in order to come up with effective adaptation decisions and it paves the way to autonomic self-adaptation through middleware services. An answer to this need is described by I. Carreras, A. Zanardi, E. Salvadori, and D. Miorandi in their paper "A Distributed Monitoring Framework for Opportunistic Communication Systems An Experimental Approach." The paper reports the lessons learned by the authors while developing the opportunistic communication middleware U-Hopper. The authors present the design of U-Hopper as well as that of the distributed monitoring framework that was set up to monitor U-Hopper's performance and dynamically adapt it to context changes. The paper also demonstrates the practical utilization of the monitoring framework and reports experiments and evaluations.

4. ALGORITHMS AND PROTOCOLS FOR RESILIENT AND ADAPTIVE SYSTEMS

The final section of this book focuses on algorithms and protocols.

In the first paper of this section, entitled "COADA: Leveraging Dynamic Coalition Peer-to-Peer Network for Adaptive Content Download of Cellular Users," L. Vu, K. Nahrstedt, R. Malik, and Q. Wang propose a very interesting theory, namely the spontaneous emergence of dynamic clusters of mobile nodes when users move towards certain points of interest. Such nodes constitute dynamic "coalitions" whose size and distance to target follow exponential distributions. Building on top of this theory and assumption the authors propose the adaptive protocol COADA (COalition-aware Adaptive content DownloAd). As its acronym reveals, COADA aims to reduce to a minimum content download from cellular networks by making use of opportunistic peer-to-peer communication among the nodes in the current coalition. Making use of an exponential coalition-size function COADA nodes periodically monitor the current size of the coalition and make use of this information to predict the future of the coalition. In turn this allows to predict how much data may be acquired within the coalition without resorting to more expansive cellular data transfers. COADA also takes timeliness into account and minimizes the probability to miss content file download deadlines. The effectiveness of COADA is demonstrated by means of simulations, which show how COADA meets its design goals by reducing significantly the transfer of data over cellular networks with no negative impact on transfer deadlines.

The second paper in this section is "ROCRSSI++: An Efficient Localization Algorithm for Wireless Sensor Networks," authored by F. Frattini, C. Esposito and S. Russo. Here the authors investigate optimal localization of sensors in a wireless sensor network. Several important non-functional requirements are typical of this problem, including energy efficiency, high performance and low error rates, but currently available algorithms typically tackle only a few of them. Improving such algorithms is key towards achieving effectiveness in real-life scenarios. The answer of the authors to this problem is an improved version of algorithm ROCRSSI consisting in a better management of the information produced and consumed by the sensors. The new version, ROCRSSI++, is shown to be characterized by reduced localization errors. The paper also describes experiments and reports about the new algorithm's energy consumption and localization latency.

Situation awareness (Ye, Dobson & McKeever, 2012) is an important prerequisite towards efficient and effective performance. An interesting example of this is reported in paper "Load-Balanced Multiple Gateway Enabled Wireless Mesh Network for Applications in Emergency and Disaster Recovery," by M. Iqbal, X. Wang, H. Zhang. The authors observe how the performance of wireless mesh networks is strongly affected by exceptional situations such as crisis management in a disaster stricken area. In such cases a typical group behavior arises in which large amounts of data traffic travel in the same direction to access the same destination, namely the gateway node of the network. The latter is the node acting as bridge between mesh nodes and the external network. In such situation then the gateway node becomes a bottleneck, which translates in chaotic behaviors, strong channel contention of nodes in proximity of each other, and therefore congestions. Redundant gateways is the answer to this problem proposed by the authors. This is achieved through a Load-Balanced Gateway Discovery routing protocol called LBGD-AODV, which extends the Ad hoc On-Demand Distance Vector routing protocol and uses a periodic gateway advertisement scheme with an efficient algorithm that load-balances the routes to the gateway nodes. The authors show that their approach reduces congestion and improves the performance of the network with no penalty with respect to the original routing scheme.

Again situation awareness (Ye, Dobson & McKeever, 2012) and corresponding optimizations are the key topic of the next paper in this section, which is entitled "An OMA DM Based Framework for Updating Modulation Module for Mobile Devices" and authored by H. Zhang, X. Wang, and M. Iqbal. Depending on the current situation and context, the optimal operation of mobile devices calls for specific adaptations. One such adaptation is reported in this paper. in this case it is the condition of the channel that is used to select dynamically among multiple modulation approaches. The corresponding updating protocol is based on OMA DM[1]. The authors describe their protocol as well as the design of a framework to enable its use.

Often algorithm neglect the effects of the interference produced by the concurrent execution of other tasks. An example of this is algorithms for the measurement of the duty cycle of sensor-originated waveforms. When executed on resource constrained microprocessors it becomes very difficult to hold to assumptions such as the possibility to enact samplings at regular intervals. Algorithms requiring such regularity would be "too rigid," which would go to the detriment of the expected accuracy. C. Taddia, G. Mazzini and R. Rovatti answer this problem in their paper "Duty Cycle Measurement Techniques for Adaptive and Resilient Autonomic Systems." There they propose a duty cycle measurement algorithm that is designed so as to coexist adaptively with other concurrent tasks regardless of their nature and duration. Sampling at non-controlled instants can then be regarded as a common event rather than a fault. In this sense, with the terminology introduced in (De Florio, 2010), the solution proposed by the authors constitute an example of an assumption failures tolerant algorithm. Such algorithm is shown to result in lightweight code with a fast and reliable convergence to the duty cycle value.

As a final message before leaving you to the fine contributions in this book I like to focus once more here on the complex and intertwined relationships that characterize entelechial (that is, adaptive and resilient) systems. As suggested by Boulding (1956), mastering such relationships is likely to call for two complementary approaches:

- Extending the research scope to multidisciplinary — actually *inter*-disciplinary domains, such as it is the case for the study of complex socio-ecological systems, and
- Narrowing down our models to some shared nucleus of ideas and concepts able to "directing research towards the gaps which they reveal" — that is, towards what Boulding referred to as gestalts (Boulding, 1956).

Both IJARAS and this book are in fact meant to serve as conceptual and practical tools to aid in the above processes. This goal is pursued by providing researchers and practitioners with a venue designed specifically 1) to disseminate complementary views on a set of problems at the core of disciplines that study the behaviors of adaptive and resilient systems, and 2) to expose theories and approaches aiming to capture the *hidden structures* (Holland, 1995) at the heart of those disciplines. The high quality of the papers being submitted to IJARAS — a remarkable example of which can be found in this very book — as well as the high significance of their scientific innovations and contributions constitute for me a clear indication that we "are moving in the right direction" — which, incidentally, is an alternative concise definition of entelechy.

Vincenzo De Florio
University of Antwerp & IBBT, Belgium
May 9, 2012

REFERENCES

Aristotle, . (1986). *De anima (On the Soul) (H. Lawson-Tancred, Trans.)*. *Penguin classics*. Penguin Books.

Boulding, K. (1956, April). General systems theory—The skeleton of science. *Management Science*, *2*(3). doi:10.1287/mnsc.2.3.197

De Florio, V. (2009). *Application-layer fault-tolerant protocols*. Hershey, PA: IGI Global. doi:10.4018/978-1-60566-182-7

De Florio, V. (2010). Software assumptions failure tolerance: Role, strategies, and visions . In Casimiro, A., de Lemos, R., & Gacek, C. (Eds.), *Architecting Dependable Systems VII* (*Vol. 6420*, pp. 249–272). Lecture Notes in Computer Science Berlin, Germany: Springer. doi:10.1007/978-3-642-17245-8_11

De Florio, V. (2012a). Preface . In De Florio, V. (Ed.), *Technological innovations in adaptive and dependable systems: Advancing models and concepts* (pp. 1–425). Hershey, PA: IGI Global.

De Florio, V. (2012b). *On the constituent attributes of software resilience.* Submitted for publication in "Assurances for Self-Adaptive Systems," Lecture Notes in Computer Science, State-of-the-Art series. Springer.

De Florio, V., et al. (1997). An application-level dependable technique for farmer-worker parallel programs. *Proceedings of the High-Performance Computing and Networking International Conference and Exhibition (HPCN Europe 1997), Lecture Notes in Computer Science, Vol. 1225,* Vienna, Austria (pp. 644–653). Berlin, Germany: Springer.

De Florio, V. (1998). Software tool combining fault masking with user-defined recovery strategies. *IEE Proceedings on Software: Special Issue on Dependable Computing Systems, 145*(6), 203–211. doi:doi:10.1049/ip-sen:19982441

De Florio, V., & Blondia, C. (2007). Reflective and refractive variables: A model for effective and maintainable adaptive-and-dependable software. *Proceedings of the 33rd EUROMICRO Conference on Software Engineering and Advanced Applications* (SEAA 2007), Lübeck, Germany. doi: 10.1109/EUROMICRO.2007.52

Gheorghita, S. V., Palkovic, M., Hamers, J., Vandecappelle, A., Mamagkakis, S., & Basten, T. (2009). System-scenario-based design of dynamic embedded systems. *ACM Transactions on Design Automation of Electronic Systems, 14,* 1–45. doi:10.1145/1455229.1455232

Gui, N., De Florio, V., Sun, H., & Blondia, C. (2009). ACCADA: A framework for continuous context-aware deployment and adaptation. *Proceedings of the 11th International Symposium on Stabilization, Safety, and Security of Distributed Systems (SSS 2009), Lecture Notes in Computer Science, Vol. 5873,* Lyon, France, November 2009 (pp. 325–340). Springer.

Gui, N., De Florio, V., Sun, H., & Blondia, C. (2011). Toward architecture-based context-aware deployment and adaptation. *Journal of Systems and Software, 84*(2), 185–197. Elsevier. Holland, J. H. (1995). *Hidden order: How adaptation builds complexity.* Addison-Wesley.

Johnson, B. W. (1989). *Design and analysis of fault-tolerant digital systems.* New York, NY: Addison Wesley.

Leveson, N. G. (1995). *Safeware: Systems safety and computers.* Addison-Wesley.

Lin, S., Jiang, S., Lin, H., & Liu, J. (2006). An introduction to OMA device management. Retrieved from http://www.ibm.com/developerworks/wireless/library/wi-oma/

Sachs, J. (1995). *Aristotle's physics: A guided study. Masterworks of Discovery.* Rutgers University Press.

Stark, D. C. (1999). Heterarchy: Distributing authorithy and organizing diversity . In Clippinger, J. H. III, (Ed.), *The biology of business: Decoding the natural laws of enterprise* (pp. 153–179). Jossey-Bass.

Sun, H., Gui, N., & Blondia, C. (2011). A generic adaptation framework for mobile communication. *International Journal of Adaptive, Resilient and Autonomic Systems, 2*(1), 46–57. doi:10.4018/jaras.2011010103

Ye, J., Dobson, S., & McKeever, S. (2012). Situation identification techniques in pervasive computing: A review. *Pervasive and Mobile Computing, 8*(1), 36–66. doi:10.1016/j.pmcj.2011.01.004

ENDNOTES

1. OMA, that is Open Mobile Alliance in an initiative started in 2002 and grouping a large set of companies in the mobile industry sector (Lin, Jiang, Lin, & Liu, 2006). OMA's objective are the development of interoperable mobile service enablers able to facilitate Device Management (DM). Self-management, self-optimization, self-diagnosis and self-healing are typical OMA DM design goals.

2. Using Markov models, under the assumption of independence between occurrences of faults, it is possible to show that if $R(t)$ is the reliability of a single, non-replicated component, then the reliability of a triple-modular redundant composite is equal to $R_{TMR}(t) = 3 \times R^2(t) - 2 \times R^3(t)$.

This in particular means that the reliability of the composite is larger than that of its constituents *only when the latter is at least 0.5.*

3. If C is the probability associated with the process of identifying the failed module out of those available and being able to switch in the spare, then the reliability of TMR-plus-one-spare can be expressed in function of the reliability of a single, non-replicated constituent as follows: $R_{TMR+SPARE}(t) = (-3C^2 + 6C) \times (R(t)(1 - R(t))^2 + R_{TMR}(t)$.

Note that in this case the reliability of the composite is larger than that of its constituents when the latter is at least greater than the threshold (De Florio et al., 1998).

Acknowledgment

As I did already for the previous volume in this series — (De Florio, 2012a) — it is only fair that I acknowledge also this time the role played by the members of the IJARAS' Editorial Board and in particular Marcello Cinque, Università di Napoli Federico II, Italy, and Tim Stevens, Ghent University, Belgium, who guest-edited the second issue of IJARAS volume 2. I also would like to express once more my thanks to the people at IGI-Global and especially to Heather Probst for her guidance and friendly support.

My gratitude and love go to my dearest Tiziana and Sandro for explaining me the true meaning of happiness, love, and fulfillment, as well as to Mariella: I was with you from the beginning — you'll be with me to the end.

Section 1
Approaches for Resilient and Adaptive Systems

Chapter 1
Systematic Design Principles for Cost–Effective Hard Constraint Management in Dynamic Nonlinear Systems

Satyakiran Munaga
IMEC and K. U. Leuven/ESAT, Belgium

Francky Catthoor
IMEC and K. U. Leuven/ESAT, Belgium

ABSTRACT

Modern cost-conscious dynamic systems incorporate knobs that allow run-time trade-offs between system metrics of interest. In these systems regular knob tuning to minimize costs while satisfying hard system constraints is an important aspect. Knob tuning is a combinatorial constrained nonlinear dynamic optimization problem with uncertainties and time-linkage. Hiding uncertainties under worst-case bounds, reacting after the fact, optimizing only the present, and applying static greedy heuristics are widely used problem simplification strategies to keep the design complexity and decision overhead low. Applying any of these will result in highly sub-optimal system realizations in the presence of nonlinearities. The more recently introduced System Scenarios methodology can only handle limited form of dynamics and non-linearities. Existing predictive optimization approaches are far from optimal as they do not fully exploit the predictability of the system at hand. To bridge this gap, the authors propose the combined strategy of dynamic bounding and proactive system conditioning for the predicted likely future. This paper describes systematic principles to design low-overhead controllers for cost-effective hard constraint management. When applied to fine-grain performance scaling mode assignment problem in a video decoder design, proposed concepts resulted in more than 2x energy gains compared to state-of-the-art techniques.

DOI: 10.4018/978-1-4666-2056-8.ch001

INTRODUCTION

Highly Dynamic Electronic Systems

Modern electronic systems are highly dynamic with multiple sources of dynamism including user, environment, hardware, input data, and mapping. At hardware implementation level, manufacturing process variability and material degradation are the two most-worried sources in advanced nanoscale device and 3D integration technologies (Borkar, 2005; Groeseneken, 2005; Srinivasan et al., 2004) - they will result in spatial and temporal variation in parametric behavior (such as delay/access-time, active and leakage power) of components (such as functional units, memories, and communication links) (Groeseneken, 2005; Papanicolaou et al., 2008). They can also lead to temporary or permanent unavailability of a whole component or some operational modes of the component. These variations are traditionally hidden under worst-case abstractions (e.g., static clock period and functional failure) and made invisible to higher abstraction levels (typically by using simple redundancy-based techniques (Srinivasan et al., 2005; Constantinides et al., 2006)). With appropriate circuit-level techniques, such as delayed clocking (Ernst et. al., 2003) and measurement-driven adaptation, this dynamism can be propagated through the abstraction layers and made visible to higher levels leading to, what we call, dynamic hardware interface.

Next to this, user inputs (e.g., changing from GPS navigation to video streaming application and changes in quality-of-service requirements such as frame rate, resolution, and level-of-detail) result in a dynamically changing set of applications, algorithms and their workload (Tack et al., 2005). In other words, sharing platform resources among multiple dynamic applications/tasks results in dynamic changes in the resource availability for a given application or task-set. Smart algorithms of future systems which adapt themselves to environment changes (e.g., moving from a WiFi

hotspot area to WiMax/3G coverage area, fluctuating wireless channel state due to fading effects, changing requirements of dynamic active set of users sharing the same frequency spectrum) result in a dynamic workload (Li et al., 2008). In applications like video codec and graphics rendering, input data being processed by the algorithm results in varying workload both within and across the frames (Wiegand et al., 2003). Cost-efficient mapping (e.g., bit-width aware compilation, distributed loop-buffers, etc) of algorithms on architectures further exploits the variations in the control and data signals and thus acts as additional source of dynamism (typical compilation techniques hide this dynamism with abstractions such as worst-case bit-width and predication) (Novo et al., 2008). Although the dynamism introduced by mapping is significantly influenced by other sources of dynamism, its complexity and huge impact on optimality make it worth treating as a separate source.

To summarize, both the physical components of the system (so-called hardware) and their usage (so-called software) are extremely dynamic in most modern system contexts (as conceptually shown in Figure 1). It is important that the system allows the exploitation of dynamism by having not so large load-independent cost as shown in Figure 2. Today many platforms are not designed to expose the underlying true cost

Figure 1. Multi-pronged dynamism in modern system contexts

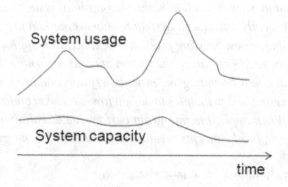

Figure 2. Platforms with large load-independent cost are not fit for exploiting dynamism as there is nothing much to gain from adapting the system to the dynamic situation at hand

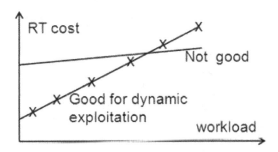

variations. This implies the application designers have to discover the hidden opportunity to push the platform designers towards alternative holistically optimal systems. Similarly we assume that platforms suitable for hard constrained dynamic systems typically incorporate features to enable deterministic application mapping (like software controlled memories, time multiplexed access of shared resources, etc.) (Bekooij et al., 2004).

Design-Time Worst-Case is the Stumbling-Block!

Effectively handling dynamism is a major design challenge of embedded systems where the system-level "quality" constraints (on functionality, timing, quality-of-service, temperature, lifetime, etc.)

are stringent and cost (both design time costs such as chip area, package, & cooling and runtime/operational costs such as energy consumption & QoS-based revenue) sensitivities are high. Dynamism affects, ideally, almost all design abstraction levels including hardware implementation, algorithm design, platform sizing, package design, and application mapping. Unfortunately, conventional system design approaches, either knowingly or otherwise, avoid/hide (and limit the propagation of) dynamism using worst-case abstractions (conceptually shown in Figure 3). This is done partly to reduce the design effort by simplifying mapping complexity and partly due to lack of awareness of such worst-case bounding in the specifications of sub-systems. Worst-case design leads to highly sub-optimal systems when evaluated under real usage conditions (which can only be done retrospectively) - the higher the number of sources and amount of dynamism, the higher the inefficiency. This has already been demonstrated in many instances and better-than-worst-case design techniques are being pursued actively at all design abstraction levels (Keutzer et al., 2002; Austin et al., 2005; Leung et al., 2005; Gheorghita et al., 2008). The worst thing to happen in the worst-case design is mutually conflicting constraints leading to the erroneous conclusion that the desired system is infeasible (and hence not even conceived in the first place!).

Figure 3. Conceptual illustration of hiding dynamism with worst-case abstractions

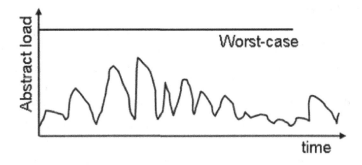

As an example, in prevailing real-time embedded systems the maximum temperature limit and guaranteed reliable lifetime are ensured at design-time using worst-case values for all the influencing dynamic system aspects such as usage, workload, ambient temperature, and process variations (Groeseneken, 2005). In sub-45nm system-in-package era power densities, process variations and material degradation would be so high that such worst-case lifetime assessment will require substantial overdesign of the system, if feasible at all. The penalty of such overdesign would subsume the benefits and become a stumbling block for economically viable systems in nanoscale technologies. We foresee that future systems have to manage temperature and lifetime - both of them require hard-guarantees - at run-time along with other aspects such as timing (today this happens only in soft-guaranty or best-effort contexts without relying on worst-case (Brooks et al., 2001; Srinivasan et al., 2005; Chantem et al., 2008; Karl et al., 2006; Mihic et al., 2004; Sanz et al., 2006; Stavrou et al., 2007)). Once we delegate them to run-time, the system reliability problem translates into cost-efficient execution of dynamic applications on dynamic hardware while satisfying all (functional, timing, thermal, etc.) correctness requirements throughout the assured lifetime.

Run-Time Adaptivity is the First Step

It is widely being accepted that cost-effective handling of dynamism requires continuous run-time system adaptation with the help of "knobs" at many abstraction levels and appropriate monitors, leading to the so-called self-adaptive systems (Adve et al., 2002; Cornea et al., 2003) (see Figure 4). This is evident from the growing amount of recent research in the context of low-power systems, on scalable algorithms (Li et al., 2008; Pollin et al., 2007), dynamic power management (Benini et al., 2000), dynamic voltage scaling (Chen et al., 2007; Venkatachalam et al.,

Figure 4. Conceptual illustration of self-adaptive systems (comprising knobs, monitors and control) for cost-effective realization of dynamic systems

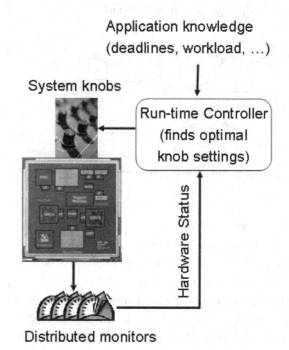

2005), MPSoC mapping (Yang et al., 2001; Zhe et al., 2007), etc. Knobs enable run-time Pareto-optimal (see Figure 5) trade-offs between system metrics of interest (such as performance, power consumption, quality, etc.) which can be utilized to exploit variability in constrained aspects (e.g., execution time) for cost gains (e.g., energy consumption). Examples include circuit-level knobs such as dynamic voltage scaling, mapping knobs such as task/activity migration, and algorithmic knobs. Recent studies have shown that knobs at circuit-level such as run-time configurable buffers also make systems resilient to fabrication process induced variability (Wang et al., 2005; Cosemans et al., 2008). Moreover, ongoing research indicates that once functional and parametric aspects are separated, the reliability problem translates into time-dependent variability and thus can be tackled by knobs at circuit and higher levels in a more cost-effective way than traditional redundancy based techniques by managing lifetime at run-

Figure 5. Example of a pareto-optimal frontier

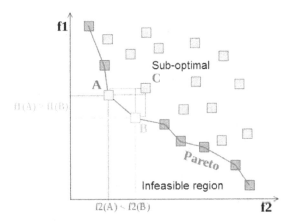

The boxed points represent feasible choices, and smaller values are preferred to larger ones (thus Origin is the best). Point C is not on the Pareto frontier because it is dominated by other feasible choices, namely point A and point B. Points A and B are not strictly dominated by any other, and hence do lie on the frontier (Figure 5).

One of the challenging aspects for the controller is that the systems of interest have large but bounded uncertainties – dynamics (such as computation requirements of tasks, bandwidth requirements of connected users, temperature, etc) that affect the optimal choice (but are not incorporated elsewhere) and that are as yet unknown at the time of decision making. Moreover, our focus is on those systems in which the uncertainties influence not just the cost but the constraints – i.e., blindly relying on not fully correct/assured predictions/estimations of unknowns may result in violation of constraints which is unacceptable. Most of the so-called proactive techniques in the literature (e.g., Yeo et al., 2008) are not suitable for the hard constrained systems (and hence are not discussed further in this article) because they are basically best-effort oriented and do not assure hard guarantees (or rely on design-time worst-case bounds for hard constraints), especially in the presence of conflicting constraints.

time (Groeseneken, 2005; Papanicolaou et al., 2008; Srinivasan et al., 2005; Karl et al., 2006). The more the system aspects (such as deadlines, QoS/QoE, temperature, lifetime) that are managed at run-time, the higher the potential gains from self-adaptivity.

One of the most important aspects of adaptive systems is the control sub-system which is responsible for regularly reconfiguring, in a demand-driven way, the system in such a way that the run-time costs (such as energy consumption, revenue loss due to poor capacity/quality), are minimized while always ensuring that the system is "reliable", i.e., (i) none of the system constraints (such as functional correctness, minimum QoS/QoE, timing deadlines, maximum temperature, assured lifetime, etc) is violated at any time as long as the system is outside the "real over-constrained" regime, and (ii) the system should never be forced into over-constrained regime due to the "retrospectively greedy" (or non-holistic) decisions made by the controller in its effort to minimize the run-time costs. We advocate that the controller uses only those (combinations of) knob settings of components/sub-systems which result in Pareto-optimal operating points – by appropriate filtering at design-time, calibration-time, and even at run-time, if needed, using suitable models and techniques (Geilen et al., 2005; Zhe et al., 2007; Pollin et al., 2007).

Nonlinearity is The Devil

While run-time management is becoming more of a necessity, the systems of interest are rich in nonlinearity which makes the modeling and optimal control of them very challenging. In this context, nonlinearity refers to the temporal asymmetric effects like optimizing the present alone does not lead to optimal solution over the long run, small loss now enables large gain later, decisions of the past strongly affect the costs and viability/stability in the future, and the future strongly influences the present decisions. Figure 6 conceptually illustrates this for the decision moment "Now". Of the three choices that the

Figure 6. Illustration of nonlinearities causing time-linkage. What appears to be optimal at Now is sub-optimal in the long run and the right decision requires analyzing the future in advance.

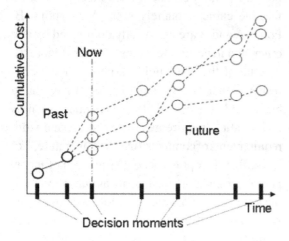

controller has, the locally optimal choice which minimizes the cumulative cost so far will cause the system to evolve in such a way that all the available choices in future incur huge cost penalty and thus making it sub-optimal in the long run. On the other hand, the apparently non-optimal choice at "Now" allows containing more optimal choices in the future and results in significantly better solution over the whole duration.

The sources of such temporal asymmetries include (i) nonlinear evolution of component behavior causing usage history dependence effects – e.g., exponential dependence of leakage on temperature (Zhang et al., 2003), super-linear activity-dependent degradation of platform components (Shin et al., 2007) (ii) overheads involved in switching between the modes of system knobs – e.g., energy and time overheads of changing the voltage and frequency of a processor (iii) modes with nonlinear trade-offs between system metrics – e.g., near quadratic relation between delay & energy of a processor enabled with dynamic voltage scaling, Pareto-optimal application mapping on a heterogeneous platform (iv) discrete modes and non-uniform activities (v) limited window of opportunity to exploit variability of constrained

aspects for cost gains (elaborated further in the illustrative example).

Such nonlinear effects, known as time-linkage in literature (Bosman et al., 2005), deceive the reactive control strategies that are agnostic about or over-simplify the future. This is similar to phase-coupling but the temporal aspect makes it unidirectional or impossible to iterate the decision making process. By the time we know for certain the reaction is too late because the really good options that were available earlier have become obsolete or over constrained (Figure 7).

We refer to a decision making process as *reactive* when it makes use of past/history, present and *only certain/guaranteed future* information (e.g., known future tasks/activities, upper and lower bounds) that is available as is or straightforward (i.e., without any design-time/run-time effort) and assumes worst-case for all the uncertain future that affects the constraints. In practice, this either translates into a worst-case-optimal approach or a react-after-the-fast approach (optimize the present alone after the uncertainties are resolved) or a combination of both. The aforementioned nonlinearities deceive any reactive controller resulting in highly sub-optimal decisions. An ideal controller should try to optimize the system for the real-case, albeit, partly unknown! Towards this goal, a *pseudo-proactive* controller makes use of *both certain and uncertain future* information – both of which is potentially obtained from *simple models* such as look-up tables, equations, and static procedures. A pseudo-proactive control-

Figure 7. Broad classification of control strategies based on how uncertainties are dealt with

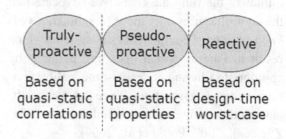

ler thus makes worst-case sub-optimal decisions (still worst-case-safe) using *static strategies/ models* that are based on scenarios and statistics to gain on average in reality. While this is a first step in countering the time-deceptiveness, it is still far from optimal in highly dynamic and strongly nonlinear contexts. We claim that all state-of-the-art controllers that are suitable for the hard constrained systems are only either reactive or pseudo-proactive and are not fully adequate for the dynamic systems of our interest. As proposed and described further in this article, a *truly-proactive* controller dynamically bounds the uncertainties and optimizes for the most-likely future (while still guaranteeing worst-case-safeness) by maximally exploiting the predictability of the system at hand and makes use of intelligent system models in the optimization process for the best trade-off between the cost optimality and the decision overhead. The just described consistent classification of the controllers for hard constrained systems is also a contribution of this text.

The rest of the paper is structured as follows. We first briefly review the state-of-the-art solutions for optimizing hard constrained dynamic systems. We then describe few representative variants of runtime task management problem to exemplify the time-deceptive nonlinearities which raise the need for truly-proactive control. We also illustrate with examples various features to optimally combat/exploit the different types of nonlinearities. Later we present the underlying generalized concepts and strategies of optimal hard constraint management.

RELATED WORK

Mixed Design-Time/Run-Time and System Scenarios

The most recent and rigorous approach for cost-effective handling of nonlinear dynamic embedded systems is based on the concept of design-time identified system scenarios (Gheorghita et al., 2008). It basically relies on automated profiling-based design-time analysis of run-time situations of the entire system from the cost perspective. It then classifies the run-time situations into a few frequently occurring dominant cases/clusters and a backup scenario (as illustrated in Figure 8). Clustering into system scenarios limits the possible dynamic behaviors within a scenario and thus enables simple form of future look-ahead and tighter bounds on uncertainties, which is sufficient in some systems. The system configuration or knob-settings for each of the system scenario is then decided at design-time using traditional design methods. At run-time the scenarios are detected with a low-overhead decision diagram based detector and the system is executed with the predefined and stored knob-settings decided for that scenario. It is also possible that the knob decisions are not necessarily stored in a look-up-table but derived using simple analytical formulae or static parameterized procedure/algorithms with fully pre-defined sequence of actions at design-time. The run-time calibration and adaptation phases can be used to further adapt the parameters, e.g., to changes in frequency of scenario

Figure 8. Clustering of similar run-time situations into few dominant scenarios and a backup scenario in System Scenarios method

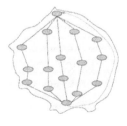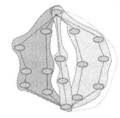

occurrences. Thus System Scenarios increases the scope of design-time preparation to keep the run-time decision overhead very small without much loss of optimality. This is in contrast to the use of simple greedy heuristics for the complex nonlinear optimization which keeps the runtime decision overhead low but at the cost of severe sub-optimality.

While it is a significant first step in the comprehensive treatment of nonlinearity and limited dynamism, unfortunately System Scenarios are not enough for the following reasons: (i) clustering into limited set of dominant scenarios implies still conservative, hence not very tight, worst-case bounds within a scenario, especially in highly dynamic systems (ii) they cannot effectively handle dynamism from multiple sources (e.g., input data, hardware, platform, environment, etc) as the possible run-time situations explode and limited number of dominant clusters can not be identified (iii) another form of dynamism that is too complex for System Scenario analysis is due to intermingled and state-dependent constraints (such as thermal & reliability related) (iv) use of profiling-based bounds improves the cost in comparison with scenario-based design-time predictable worst-case paradigm but not applicable for hard constrained systems.

Model Predictive Control

In contrast to just deciding the current action given the system state, Model Predictive Control (MPC) suggests jointly considering the future control decisions during optimization (Jalali et al., 2006). The optimization is repeated over moving window of time, potentially at every possible decision moment. MPC is used mostly and widely in process control systems. The optimization problem is solved numerically at run-time typically using a dedicated workstation, which is not possible in our context. The time granularity of dynamics in these systems is in the order of seconds or minutes, where-as we are interested

in highly dynamic systems. Typical MPC implementations assume that the uncertainties (such as noise/disturbances and systems modeling errors) are not very dynamic, which is not the case in our systems of interest, and hence they are assumed static in the future. Typical MPC problems do not involve uncertainty dependent hard constraints. In the presence of such constraints it uses worst-case values for the uncertainties (e.g., min-max robust MPC). Most of the MPC work formulates the objective function as quadratic programming in view of efficient solvers. More recent work on explicit MPC to reduce the run-time decision complexity can be seen as combination of MPC and system scenarios concepts. The idea of optimizing present and future together and re-optimizing as uncertainties resolve is also used in electronic systems, e.g., in dynamic task scheduling, but with simple heuristics to solve the optimization problem (Mochocki et al., 2007). As we shall see later brute-force MPC, even if feasible, is situated very far from retrospectively optimal solutions in highly dynamic contexts (Figure 9).

Anticipative Dynamic Optimization

This approach can be seen as generalization of the MPC ideas to any dynamic optimization problem in the presence of uncertainties (Bosman et al., 2005). It suggests considering the predicted/anticipated future during the optimization. Unfortunately only problems where the uncertainties influence just the costs but not the constraints are studied so far. They probably rely on existing techniques in the optimization field to handle uncertainties.

• Robust optimization, minimax, minimax regret, infogap decision theory are nonprobabilistic ways to deal with uncertainty in the optimization problems. These methods try to minimize/avoid the risk – given that in our target optimization problems there always exists a way to avoid the risk,

Figure 9. A discrete model predictive control scheme used in process control

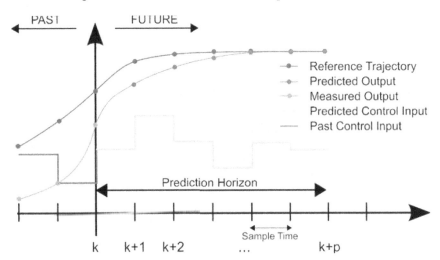

namely the design-time worst-case, they always prefer that solution.

- Stochastic programming is another way of dealing with uncertainty in optimization problems. It exploits probability distributions of the uncertainties with the goal to find a valid solution for all possible data instances but maximizes/minimizes the *expected value* of the objective function. Probability distributions of uncertain parameters are assumed to be given and cannot depend on the decisions taken. In highly dynamic contexts with strong nonlinearities stochastic techniques are inadequate.

Unfortunately all these try to find a single solution, which is valid under all possible cases and optimal on average, for the optimization problem in the presence of uncertainties. We argue that in highly dynamic systems each case will have a different optimal solution and the existence of one optimal solution (or few solutions as in System Scenarios) is a fallacy.

Thus offering hard-guarantees on conflicting constraints (such as timing deadlines, maximum temperature, and assured lifetime) at run-time in a cost-effective way remains a major challenge in highly dynamic nonlinear systems (see Figure 10). Many researchers claim that hard guarantees can only be provided by design-time predictable worst-case design (Bekooij et al., 2004). This strongly discourages delegating more constraints (such as temperature and lifetime) to be handled at run-time in real-time embedded systems. In contrast, managing multiple-constraints at run-time without sacrificing hard-guarantees minimizes system costs significantly. Based on the observations that (i) time-linkage makes look-ahead desirable and (ii) there exist many "correlations" among dynamic aspects, we believe that prediction based optimal control is desirable and feasible. This is the novel core message of this paper and it will be further elaborated in the following sections.

ILLUSTRATIVE EXAMPLE: FINE-GRAIN TASK MANAGEMENT IN LOW-POWER REAL-TIME SYSTEMS

In this section we exemplify the time-deceptive nonlinearities and illustrate the proactive control concepts in the context of dynamic task management problem. In cost-conscious embedded

Figure 10. Systems of interest: run-time control of highly dynamic nonlinear systems with conflicting constraints and costs

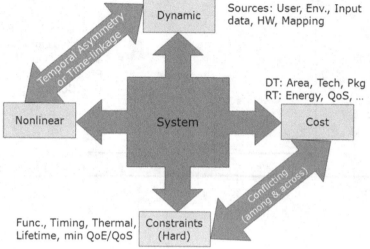

systems, the hardware platform is composed of multiple heterogeneous resources/processors with knobs that allow run-time trade-offs between various metrics such as computational power (say, operations per second) and energy efficiency. The tasks that need to be executed arrive dynamically with varying requirements in terms of computational power, deadlines, etc. These systems have stringent timing requirements due to system functionality/quality (e.g., IO synchronization, response time and display rate) and time-predictability reasons. The role of task management in these systems is to decide where to run (resource allocation and binding), when to run (scheduling or sequencing) and how to run (mode assignment) each of the tasks such that all the constraints are met and the costs are minimized. In practice we find numerous variants of this generic task management problem with variations on the knob types, constraints and cost metrics.

For the purpose of the subsequent discussion, let us consider performance-scaling mode selection/assignment for tasks running on a uniprocessor in a predefined order under hard real-time constraints with the objective of minimizing the overall energy consumption (Chen et al., 2007). The processor is equipped with knobs that offer run-time tradeoffs between energy consumption and execution-time of a given task to enable energy reduction during low workload. Dynamic voltage and frequency scaling (DVFS or DVS) is the most popular knob available in many commercial processors. Adaptive body biasing (along with DVS), partial or full clock-gating and/or power-gating of selective architectural components (such as functional units, register files, instruction fetch, etc.), and size-/delay- configurable memories (Cosemans et al., 2008) are examples of other knobs that can offer useful run-time energy-delay trade-offs (Venkatachalam et al., 2005). Changing the knob settings involves non-negligible switching overhead, both in time and energy, which depends on the type of knobs, system state, and on the desired system configuration. The computational requirement of the tasks varies significantly (>10x) over time. Before executing the task we know the maximum time it may require, i.e., upper-bound, with the given knob setting and the actual time is only known at the completion of the task instance. Typically these upper-bounds are computed at design-time and hence are very loose in highly dynamic contexts. It is guaranteed that the given set of tasks is schedulable on the processor even under worst-case conditions (combination of start-times, deadlines and execution-times) and the corresponding mode settings are known (mode M1 for all tasks in the example of Figure 11). In the absence of a performance scaling mode assignment controller, the tasks will be run with these settings. Also for each deadline the post-deadline mode which guarantees the schedulability of the following tasks is also known (mode M1 for all deadlines in the example of Figure 11). Such information could either come from a task admission controller or a higher level scheduler or even design-time analysis. The goal of the controller is to decide online the mode setting with which the task should be executed such that the total (both active and switching) energy consumption is minimized while ensuring that no task will miss its deadline even under worst-case conditions.

Let us consider the motivational example shown in Figure 11 to better understand the non-linearities in this problem setup and the required features to combat them. At the decision moment t0, tasks T1 and T2 are already in the input queue waiting for execution and their deadlines are 20 and 30 respectively. The processor has 3 modes (M1, M2, and M3) to switch between with the normalized performance and energy scaling factors being (1, 4), (1.5, 3), and (2, 1) respectively. This means, e.g., running the processor in mode M3 doubles the execution time of a task while reducing the energy consumption by 4 times, compared to the mode M1, which is the current mode of the processor at t0. The active energy consumption of a task is also a linear function of its actual load (zero when there is no load, in this example). Mode M1 guarantees that all the tasks can meet their deadlines even in the worst-case. In this example, switching between the modes

Figure 11. Illustrative example with 5 tasks. Each row corresponds to a schedule obtained with a different method. All methods ensure that no deadline is violated even in the worst-case. The numbers below the method name indicate the energy consumption of that schedule, excluding the energy of the optional switching at the end. OW stands for optimization window, the maximum number of tasks analyzed together at the time of decision making. In this example, decisions are made/revised at the end of every task.

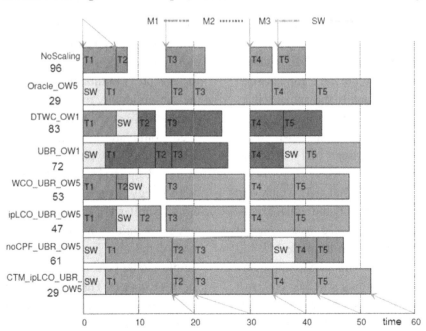

involves 4 units of time overhead and 5 units of energy overhead. For brevity, we assume the energy consumption is zero when the processor is idle. T3, T4, and T5 are the subsequent tasks with release times t15, t30, and t35 and should be completed before t40, t50, and t60 respectively. In this example, we also assume that no knowledge is available beyond the time t60 and hence we should ensure room at the end to switch to mode M1 so that future tasks' schedulability is ensured. The design-time upper-bound on load (and hence execution time with mode M1) of each of these 5 tasks is 10 units. The actual loads at this instance (t0-t60) are 6, 2, 7, 4, and 5 units respectively. As the switching time overhead is of the order of task execution time, we assume that it is not possible to switch between modes during the course of task execution. For the same reason, it is also not possible to generate more Pareto-optimal operating points by combining modes (similar to voltage dithering) and hence we are limited with the available discrete modes.

Huge Gap between Design-Time Worst-Case and Crystal Ball

The NoScaling row shows the schedule of these 5 tasks with the default worst-case mode setting with the corresponding energy consumption of 96 units (= 6*4 + 2*4 +7*4 + 4*4 + 5*4). Note the large idle intervals due to the huge gap between the design-time upper bounds and actual values of uncertain aspects in highly dynamic systems, namely task execution-times and start-times in this case (worst-case start times of T1 to T5 are 10, 20, 30, 40, and 50).

Suppose we have a crystal ball which can predict without any uncertainty the actual execution times and start-times of all 5 tasks – then at t0 we could decide to switch to mode M3 and execute all the 5 tasks without violating any deadlines. The corresponding schedule is shown by the row Oracle_OW5, which only consumes 29 units including the switching energy. This is

3.31 times more energy efficient than the worst-case based schedule. Of course, this is not directly feasible in practice mainly due to the lack of such a crystal ball, i.e. accurate prediction with 100% confidence, but the goal is to close this gap as far as possible. Towards this goal, let us discuss various, both existing and new, strategies that should be combined for just-in-time refinement of the decisions made based on design-time worst-case.

Nonlinearities Deceive Reactive Decision Making

Given the problem setup, the simplest run-time controller to think of acts after the completion of every task and decides the mode setting just for the immediately next task to be executed. It allocates all the available slack to run the current task at hand with the most energy efficient mode possible. The row DTWC_OW1 in Figure 11 shows the corresponding schedule. Note that we could not run the task T1 with mode M2 as we need to leave room for switching time at the end of the task to switch back to default mode M1 to ensure worst-case schedulability of subsequent tasks. Although we could run rest of the tasks with mode M2, the result, in terms of energy gains, is far from the target retrospectively optimal schedule. Note that some of the slack is being wasted as the subsequent tasks are not ready for execution (although it is not contributing to the sub-optimality in this case). If the switching overhead was zero this simple greedy strategy itself would have resulted in reasonably optimal solution in this example (with zero switching overhead, optimal schedule costs 24 units, while this strategy gives a schedule with a cost of 28 units). Similarly if there is no uncertainty in the task's execution time (i.e., we know the exact load of the task just before its execution) this simple strategy results in the optimal solution for this example. Thus the complex combination of uncertainties and effects that hamper slack recovery (such as input/data/control/resource dependencies, switching overhead, discrete modes, nonlinear trade-offs, switching activity variations, etc) causes time-linkage in the decision making process, i.e., a given amount of slack will result in different gains at different moments in time. Time-linkage deceives reactive strategies which try to recover the loss, which is substantial, after the fact. Thus utilizing the right amount of slack at the right moment in time is the key and we need methods which can help towards this.

Refine Upper/Lower Bounds at Run-Time

As we have seen loose upper bounds on the task load is one of the sources of reduced switching opportunities, we advocate run-time refinement to tighten the upper bounds with the help of suitable models. For this we reuse the System Scenarios based method presented in (Gheorghita et al., 2008), where the basic idea is that more information about the task to be executed is known at run-time which can be exploited for this purpose. It exploits the correlations between task's input data and its execution on deterministic/predictable architectures. The method basically clusters frequent task instances which require similar cycles into a few frequently occurring scenarios and the rest into a back-up scenario. Then each scenario is characterized for the required upper-bound information and is stored in a small look-up table (LUT). The LUT is addressed using a customized hash function, called scenario detector, which is developed along with the clustering process. At run-time given the relevant task input data we know the tighter bound of its load by evaluating a small function (typically few comparisons) and accessing a small LUT. Applying such a method, the new upper-bounds for the 5 tasks in the example of Figure 11 are 8, 5, 9, 8, and 7. Note that resulting bounds are tighter but the remaining uncertainty is not negligible. UBR_OW1 shows the schedule obtained by the reactive one-task-at-a-time strategy discussed before with these

refined upper bounds. Note the better modes for T1 and T5, compared to DTWC_OW1.

Optimize the Present and Future Together

Up to now, the switching opportunities are still limited by the conservative assumption that the subsequent tasks might require worst-case mode. Thus it is highly desirable to increase the optimization horizon, i.e., considering the mode decisions of current and future tasks together. This not only increases switching opportunities but also avoids unnecessary switching oscillations and greedy slack usage. For doing this we need information about the subsequent tasks, which in some cases just requires looking at the waiting tasks in the task queue. In some other cases it can be obtained by percolating down the information from higher levels and interacting with local resource managers of other processors. For the example of Figure 11, we assume that at time t0 with appropriate look-ahead mechanism we know the exact release times and deadlines of tasks T1 to T5 and also the input information (such as task headers) required just to refine upper-bounds on their load. Deciding the modes for all 5 tasks at t0 by conventional optimization (with no slack reclaiming as execution progresses) has resulted in a schedule (same as DTWC_OW1) which is poorer than UBR_OW1, in this case. Thus future look-ahead without slack reclaiming may cause more harm than benefit if the remaining uncertainties, even after bound tightening, are still large.

Re-Optimize as Execution Progresses

As the execution-times are uncertain, it is often beneficial to revisit the knob decisions (of the previously considered but yet to be executed tasks) as some of the uncertainties get resolved. Once a task is completed, we know its actual execution time and the resulting slack might enable more optimal knob decisions for the tasks still to be executed. The WCO_UBR_OW5 row in Figure 11 shows the schedule obtained by repeating the optimization at the end of each task for all the remaining tasks together. Note that the optimization is formulated as conventional scheduling problem, but with refined upper bounds instead of design-time worst-case. Note the reduced switching and more optimal slack allocation (less slack for T1 & T2 compared to UBR_OW1 to enable M3 for T3-T5) achieved by the combination of look-ahead and re-optimization. Although getting closer, we are still far from the optimal schedule (1.83 times compared to 3.31) as the optimizer is deceived by the uncertainties due to its inability to realize that more slack will be available as execution progresses.

Typical implementations (e.g., Mochocki et al., 2007) use re-optimization at every possible decision moment (end of every task in this case) to reclaim and redistribute the slack released. To keep the overhead small, e.g., (Mochocki et al., 2007) considers tasks only till the earliest common deadline. In contrast, we advocate to consider multiple tasks beyond a single deadline but to *perform re-optimization dynamically and incrementally*, i.e., repeat only when the resolved uncertainties makes it essential or enable energy gains and repeat only the required steps. Thus the output of the optimization routine is not only the mode list for the tasks optimized together but also the conditions for revising the decisions and pointers to effective methods for doing it along with the data needed for them.

Never Optimize for the Worst-Case

Conventional scheduling problem formulation is conservative, i.e., for uncertain aspects such as execution-time it assumes upper-bounds as the actual values. This ensures that all constraints (e.g., deadlines) are met without rescheduling even when all uncertainties turn out to be their respective worst-case. Thus the resulting mode decisions are

optimal for this rarely occurring case (hence the name worst-case optimal). The re-optimization and upper bound refinement discussed before help to reduce the resulting sub-optimality when the nonlinearities are not so strong and bound refinement is very effective, respectively. As discussed before, in the presence of uncertainties and strong nonlinearities, there exists a time instance when the slack is best utilized and sometimes it was in the past, when the decision making is not proactive enough! Thus playing safe initially and reclaiming the slack later cannot be optimal in dynamic nonlinear systems.

In the light of the possibility to revise decisions as tasks finish their execution, we can opt for alternative slack allocation instead of worst-case optimal allocation. The underlying idea is that before executing a task we need to reserve more slack than it will actually utilize so as to accommodate its worst-case without violating the deadline. Once the task is finished this excess slack is released, when the actual load is less than the upper-bound, and can be utilized by subsequent tasks. Thus we are allocating extra slack only in anticipation that it is not actually consumed and is released by the time it is needed. In other words, if the additionally allocated slack is not released it turns out to be a sub-optimal decision. Such an alternative slack allocation strategy, compared to worst-case optimal slack allocation, sometimes steals more slack from some future (or subsequent) tasks and sometimes reserves more slack for the future, depending upon the nonlinear forces! Note that this results in increased decision freedom (or feasible decision space) compared to traditional conservative scheduling formulation.

Make History the Best in the Likely Future

The scheduler should always ensure that a feasible schedule exists even when the expected slack is not released. However the resulting schedule in some instances may incur an energy penalty that is higher than the expected gains. Worst-case sub-optimal slack management is thus a form of risk-taking and is the underlying concept of speculative speed reduction (Aydin et al., 2004) and look-ahead DVS (Pillai et al., 2001). Aggressive speculative speed reduction of (Aydin et al., 2004; Pillai et al., 2001) uses the maximally available slack to extend the current task at hand. For the example of Figure 11 it results in a schedule same as the one shown in noCPF_UBR_OW5 row. Such aggressive slack stealing enabled to run tasks T1-T3 in mode M3 but the greediness forced T4 and T5 to run in mode M1. The fact that it will be sub-optimal more often than not is acknowledged in (Aydin et. al., 2004) and the authors proposed a scaling factor to control the aggressiveness. But one/few good values for scaling factor does not exist for highly dynamic contexts. We need to know the most likely values for the uncertainties to optimally guide the slack management. Mochocki et al. (2007) recommends the use of the average as likely values. This is again not suitable for highly dynamic contexts. We advocate, instead, the use of good predictors at run-time to predict the likely load of the tasks at hand given the context. The estimates are used to guide the slack allocation and thus to optimize the knob settings for the *expected reality*, in contrast to the statistical optimization and optimizing for the worst-/average-/typical-case. The scheduler is aware that these values are not 100% accurate and they are not safe enough. It still relies on upper-bounds to guarantee all hard constraints.

Use Good Predictors and Play-Forward

Undoubtedly, the better the accuracy of the likely future predictions the better the slack allocation with less surprises and more assured gains. We propose to use highly optimized and adaptive application-, context-, and content-specific predictors for better accuracy with low overhead. It is equally important that these estimates are effectively utilized during the slack allocation to result in optimal knob settings. Safety, i.e., ensuring that deadlines are met even in the worst-case situations, is a concern and can be taken care with the help of safety constraints which limits the maximum slack in view of all future deadlines with the fastest available modes. Note that this slack limit is from the safety but not cost perspective, i.e., consuming all safe slack (which is the case in Pillai et al., 2001) can be very sub-optimal. Poor formulation of the optimization problem may result in excessive slack consumption by earlier tasks even when expected slack is released (i.e., the task load is as expected). This results in insufficient slack for the future task to ensure the deadline with the *desirable mode* and hence forced to switch to costlier mode (T4 and T5 in noCPF_UBR_OW5 row in Figure 11). Propagating and evaluating the effect of mode decisions of earlier tasks on mode decisions of future tasks to avoid sub-optimal future is the key - we call this play-forward mechanism. This can be achieved using explicit play-forward constraints: every task should finish before its deadline with the intended mode even when it requires upper-bound slack but all the previous tasks consume no more than their respective expected slack. Such play-forward constraints are not required if the prediction is 100% confident/assured. The constraints in (Leung et al., 2005), the only comprehensive mathematical formulation of scheduling problem with expected workload, are more conservative than the play-forward constraints and hence will often miss the optimal solution, as in conventional worst-case optimal formulation.

The ipLCO_UBR_OW5 row in Figure 11 shows the resultant schedule with the proposed strategy of optimizing for the likely future with play-forward. It uses an ideal predictor which correctly predicts the actual load of tasks but without 100% guaranty that the predicted values are correct. Thus we still rely on the refined upper bounds to ensure deadline guarantees. We are still unable to run all five tasks in mode

M3 (the optimal solution) as we could not find enough slack to accommodate the upper bounds of T4 and T5. Having known this at time t0 itself, thanks to the look-ahead and the future predictor, the controller decided to run task T1 using mode M1 which enabled running all the remaining tasks T2-T5 with mode M3. In a realistic video decoder design, likely-case optimization based mode-scaling as described here has resulted in more than 2x gains on energy consumption over long video sequences compared to state-of-the-art solutions with a realistic (not ideal) predictor.

The Energy-Hungry Modes Can Help Save More Energy!

Even after applying all techniques discussed so far together – upper-bound refinement, future look-ahead, optimizing for the predicted likely future, re-optimization as uncertainties resolve – we are still away from the optimal solution. The lack of enough virtual slack to accommodate the remaining uncertainty is what holds back in this example. Let us suppose we have another mode M0 with performance and energy scaling factors being 0.5 and 12 respectively. The worst-case optimal schedule would almost never use this mode (definitely for the example in Figure 11) as it incurs significantly high energy penalty. But its performance advantage can bring us the extra slack that we need. As we know that most likely that extra slack is not used, we do not end up using this energy hungry mode eventually and hence no associated energy penalty. The CTM_ipLCO_UBR_OW5 row in Figure 11 shows the resultant schedule in the presence of mode M0 which allows running task T4 in mode M3 without endangering the deadline of T5 in the unlikely event of T4 turning out to be at its maximum load. It is possible that modes like M0 normally do not exist, as it is not essential to support the worst-case load and may involve other dangerous side-effects as discussed further.

Not All Modes Live Long

So far we have dealt with only those modes which are always available, i.e., we can always rely on their availability and the corresponding energy-performance trade-offs. We can imagine modes which are Pareto-optimal, like mode M0 discussed before, but not always available. E.g., a processor can be operated at an over-rated voltage/frequency setting as long as its temperature does not exceed the stated values (disregarding for a moment other factors that influence reliability). As we know that optimal slack allocation is sometimes limited by lack of enough virtual slack (to accommodate the unlikely worst-case), a mode which could give momentary high processing power enhances the opportunities for gainful slack allocation. We call such modes contextual turbo-modes as they are superior on at least one relevant metric but are only available for a limited duration which depends both on the present system state and future evolution.

CONTEXTUAL TURBO-MODES

Complex history/state dependencies of the systems enable novel system operating modes (or knob-settings) which are Pareto-optimal but can only be used for a limited but variable amount of time (see Figure 15). We call them contextual turbo-modes, CTMs (think of a gas-pedal). The available time duration of these modes depends on the system context including the past, present and future. This is in contrast to the regular modes which are always available and can be used for any amount of duration. E.g., running the processor at overrated voltage and frequency results in too much of heat generation (which can lead to detrimental thermal runaway and/or early wear-out if not managed carefully) but can be used for a short time, without any detrimental side-effects, based on current system temperature and application activity. Extremely wide memory interface, temperature- and age- dependent clocking, etc are other examples of CTMs. We can distinguish between four types of contextual-modes: (i) modes which are optimal on all system aspects (i.e., completely dominate some of the existing modes) and hence always better to use if they are available (ii) modes which perform better on some metrics but worse (i.e., incur penalty) only in cost aspects (e.g. higher voltage operation incurs energy penalty) and hence using them when available will not interfere with constraints (iii) modes which perform better on some aspects but worse only in constraint aspects (e.g. temperature) and (iv) modes which perform better on some aspects but worse in both cost and constraint aspects.

Type4 CTMs involve penalty in not just the cost metrics but constrained metrics. Hence continuous usage of such CTM results in violation of other constraints under certain conditions which at design-time cannot be guaranteed not to happen during run-time. In other words, continuous usage of Type3 and Type4 CTMs leads to ridiculously high worst-case bounds on some aspects which influence the design-cost (e.g., package sizing to dissipate away worst-case heat). For this reason and due to lack of effective methods to deal with them, such operating modes are normally excluded during the design space exploration, especially in hard constrained embedded systems. In other words, typical constraints on the valid knob-settings or system configurations are normally based on over-simplified design-time worst-case analysis and hence are artificial. We propose to incorporate CTMs (i.e., increase knob range) in the system and to manage the associated constraints (such as temperature and lifetime) at the run-time. Controlled and efficient use of CTMs helps in closing the gap between retrospectively optimal and practically achievable solutions.

Using CTMs optimally is very intriguing and challenging as the decisions of the optimization

directly influence their duration of availability, but typically with certain time lag and usually with some amount of uncertainty. When a CTM is associated with a cost penalty, the controller may actually use it only in "crisis" (potential constraint violation) situation (either naturally occurring, e.g., in under-designed systems, or artificially created due to over slack consumption in the past) while simultaneously ensuring that such usage will not violate any other constraints. In some cases likely-case optimization may be limited due its inability to find enough virtual slack – CTMs can precisely help in such situations (as seen in the illustrative example of Figure 11). This way CTMs can help close the gap between the crystal ball (or retrospectively-optimal) solution and practically achievable solution. In some cases CTMs can even improve the crystal ball solution further compared to the one that would be derived in the absence of them. CTMs also serve as reserve capacity of the platform. We believe that in most systems CTMs can be built with much less design-time costs (such as silicon area cost, package cost) than traditional over-design to handle the design-time worst-case, as the constraints on the dynamic side-effects such as temperature and reliability are managed at run-time.

The simplest (but far from optimal) way of using CTMs is by reactively exploiting them when they are available based on the present system state and the future bounds. With the help of appropriate models, which take the system state (e.g., current temperature and wear-out) and tightly bounded future evolution as input, we can calculate when and for how long a given CTM is available. This information can be used by the optimizer for performing a better slack allocation. We call these models "*inverse models*" as they perform exactly the opposite of their traditional counterparts which compute the future state given the complete stimuli over time.

SYSTEMATIC DESIGN PRINCIPLES FOR PROACTIVE CONTROL

The novel run-time features discussed in the illustrative task management example can be generalized for optimal run-time knob tuning under hard constraints in dynamic nonlinear systems with significant uncertainties. Some dynamic aspects which are uncertain at design-time (or at a previous time instance) become known at the time of decision making at run-time (reactive controller exploits just these). But we are dealing with systems where there are still significant unresolved uncertainties (reactive controller hides them under design-time worst-case bounds) at the time of decision making. Before further discussion, it is useful to distinguish between various types of uncertainties. Some uncertainties are uncontrollable, i.e., beyond the scope of the decision making controller (e.g., computation requirements of a task). Some are completely and instantaneously under control through the decisions of the controller (e.g., mode switching overhead). Some uncertainties are controllable (partly/fully) but involve time lag, i.e., non-negligible reaction time from the moment of the decision to the desired response (e.g., temperature, aging/degradation). It is also important to note that in our systems of interest, the deterministic architectures and application mapping enable analyzing the uncertainties in one aspect (e.g., resource waiting time, task execution time) from other uncertainty sources with the help of appropriate models.

Intuitively, for optimizing systems with uncertainties we propose/advocate the following concepts:

1. Try to unfold and bound the uncertainties as early as required and possible by maximally exploiting the available information and the system correlations; in highly dynamic systems this needs to be done continuously at run-time and in hard constrained systems we believe it is possible

2. Given that considerable uncertainty will still be remaining even after trying our best to tightly bound it, at run-time continuously predict the most likely future evolution and condition/shape the system such that the decisions are close to retrospectively optimal choices

3. To keep the run-time decision overhead small make maximal use of design-time analysis, reuse, pre-preparation, scenario clustering, and dynamic procedure.

These concepts will be further elaborated throughout this section in the form of multiple features (as shown in Figure 12) using which customized optimal controllers can be designed for the specific system at hand. Some of the features can be discarded depending upon the dominating nonlinear interactions and their frequency of occurrence. For the specific system at hand, we can model the control (or knob tuning) problem as an optimization problem incorporating all the features and strategies described in this section. Each feature can be implemented with different level of complexity/sophistication which we classify into three categories namely reactive, pseudo-proactive, and truly-proactive. Thus a given controller instance, e.g., could be pseudo-proactive in one aspect and reactive in another aspect. The required level of sophistication of a particular feature is again highly dependent on the nonlinearities in the system at hand. Note that most of these features are implemented at run-time with the maximum possible design-time support in the form of appropriate models. The learning, calibration and adaptation are typically meant to effectively deal with the slowly varying dynamic aspects of the system (e.g., quasi-static properties) and thus operate at a coarse-grain time scale. They are not discussed in this article but we emphasize that these are complementary and can be combined with the other features (shown in Figure 12) to enable further gains.

Figure 12. Taxonomy of optimal control for hard constrained dynamic systems

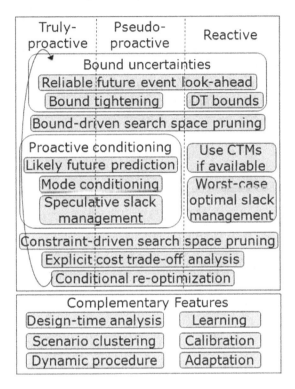

Reliable Future Event Look-Ahead

As mentioned before, we are dealing with systems with time-linkage where the present decisions have strong influence on the future costs and/or viability. In such cases we typically use mechanisms to constrain the present so as to ensure the worst-case future viability. Such techniques are commonly based on the design-time worst-case as it enables design-time analysis and hence reduced run-time decision overhead. These strategies optimize only the present and hence result in sub-optimal systems and sometimes even erroneously conclude that the system is infeasible due to over-constraints. Clearly, in the presence of time-linkage future knowledge while making knob decisions enables better optimization. Thus, we advocate optimizing the knob-decisions of present and future together at run-time to improve cost-efficiency and to proactively avoid/minimize over-constrained situations. Future look-ahead enables exploiting the

potential information that is available at run-time about both certain future (e.g., which subsequent tasks) and uncertain future (e.g., what is potentially (in)feasible, tighter bounds, estimates, etc). Optimizing the present in the knowledge of future events even with design-time worst-case bounds for the unknown aspects may already enable better bounds on controllable uncertainties such as mode switching overheads, data transfer costs, time/resource budgets. Optimizing present and future together ensures that present decisions will not result in over-constrained future and not force sub-optimal choices in the future. Note that the future information obtained in this step (by any of the models discussed below) is 100% reliable and can be safely used for constrained aspects as well.

Very simple future look-ahead, i.e., use of straightforward future information available from instantaneous monitoring, falls under reactive control category. Examples of this include use of subsequent task information by simply looking at the waiting tasks in the task queue. The look-ahead methods in the pseudo-proactive category use additional correlation analysis to obtain future information with the help of simple models and/or static methods based on quasi-static properties of the system at hand, which can be sufficient in some systems. Examples include using group-of-picture order to predict the I/B/P frame type sequence in video, exploiting the meta-data that comes from higher layers or available in the input/control data and scenario-based look-ahead. In some other systems we might benefit even further by exploiting trust-based correlations which shall require a dynamic model to translate such correlations into exploitable future information. Use of such sophisticated dynamic models is the truly-proactive version of future look-ahead.

Bound Tightening

As we should always respect certain hard constraints we should know the upper/lower bounds on the uncertain values which influence them (e.g., task load, switching activity). The tighter these bounds the better the optimality due to increased determinism in the optimization. As design-time bounds are very loose in highly dynamic systems, we advocate run-time bound tightening. Note that the refined bounds are 100% reliable and can be safely used. In this phase we also refine the upper and lower bounds on the availability of CTMs. Figure 13 conceptually illustrates how the future can be tightly bounded as time progresses. The pseudo-proactive version of bound tightening can be implemented with models obtained by reusing the work of System Scenarios or workload curve characterization. These static and potentially parameterized design-time models when used at the run-time with the appropriate inputs (task input data or history) will give tighter bounds. The truly-proactive version will be based on models that exploit additional type of dynamic correlations in the specific system at hand with the help of system invariants identified by domain experts. E.g., quasi-static videos like news do not require more than a certain bit rate for given quality requirement. We believe that for embedded systems with hard constraints, the information required to apply dynamic bound tightening is typically present. There exists a lot of unexploited potential in this topic and worth more research. Incorporating bound tightening feature does not require any special modifications in the optimization problem modeling – we just compute the refined bounds using the appropriate models and pass them to the optimizer. In reactive version, explicit bound tightening by exploiting run-time only available knowledge is not performed and hence design-time bounds are used directly.

Bound-Driven Search Space Pruning

Based on the constraints and dynamic bounding of uncertainties performed in the earlier phases, we could already prune the search space partially, e.g., by eliminating what is infeasible. The purpose of this phase is to reduce the complexity and overhead of the later phases, especially the cost

Figure 13. Conceptual illustration of future look-ahead and bound tightening. Different curves indicate the predictions of future at different time instances t0, t1, and t2. Note that predictions are closer to reality as more correlations become available over time. The range arrows at the bottom indicate the reliable regions of predictions for a given threshold on uncertainty.

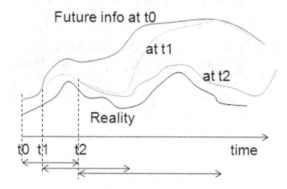

trade-off analysis. Conceptually, this is somewhat similar to the constraint driven search space pruning as in (Mesman et al., 1999; Ku et al., 1991). But the uncertainty awareness of this phase in our context makes it a very different instantiation. Any Pareto-optimal solution for any possible future should not be eliminated during this phase as we are clearly not interested in pruning the search space just for the worst-case.

Likely Future Prediction

Typical optimization problem modeling techniques are always conservative, i.e., they assume safe upper/lower bounds as the actual values for the uncertain aspects in the process of optimization. This ensures that constraints are met without revising any of the decisions made even when all the uncertainties assume their worst-case within the bounds. Thus the resulting decisions are optimal for this rarely occurring case. When the uncertainties cannot be fully bounded and the nonlinearities are strong, re-optimization cannot recover the sub-optimality introduced by playing very safe. The ideal thing to do is to predict what is going to happen, most-likely, in the future and condition the system such that the decisions are optimal for this predicted situation. As mentioned before, when the optimal solution is highly specific to the dynamic situation at hand, trying to find one single safe solution for all possible futures is a fundamental flaw.

We propose to use highly optimized and adaptive application-, context-, and content-specific predictors for better accuracy with low overhead. E.g., one could envisage a predictor which is specialized for video by exploiting the meta-data available in the content headers (pseudo-proactive) and/or the correlations of moving objects across frames (truly-proactive). The pseudo-proactive version of likely future prediction is based on static models such a s ARMA (autoregressive moving average) models, signature-based models (Gu et al., 2006) and parameterized models derived using System Scenarios. The truly-proactive version is based on dynamic exploitation of system correlations, especially the content (e.g., a custom predictor for soccer video). In the reactive version likely future prediction box is empty, i.e., the system is optimized for the worst-case. Design of such specialized predictors is a research topic by itself. Use of sub-optimal models, e.g., design-time average values as run-time predictions, is highly discouraged.

Contextual Turbo-Mode Conditioning

As discussed before, the availability of CTMs depends on the system state which is influenced by the decisions of the controller. The controller can exploit this fact and make decisions in such a way that the CTMs are available for the right amount of duration at the right time which in turn maximizes the objective that the controller is trying to achieve. In short the controller is making decisions which make the history at any given moment the most desirable. We call this feature mode conditioning – this is similar to

speculative slack management discussed later but the difference is in the type of uncertainties dealt with (partly controllable vs. uncontrollable). This difference, in practice, makes mode conditioning implementation very different from the slack conditioning. When CTM usage is not influenced by any other uncontrollable uncertainty (which is rarely the case), or such an uncertainty is ignored (with worst-case bounds), CTM uncertainties are only and completely influenced by the decisions of the controller (and hence fully controllable category, like switching overhead) and the mode conditioning is purely reactive (and is the same as the reactive version of slack conditioning). In the presence of non-negligible uncertainties in the CTM usage, we need to condition/manipulate the system such that CTMs are available for the right amount of duration at the right time, which can be done by making sequence of decisions based on likely future evolution. We can envisage the pseudo-proactive and truly-proactive versions of mode conditioning based on whether it is done by exploiting static properties versus dynamic projection of correlations respectively.

Speculative Slack Management

Given the nonlinearities and the possibility to revise decisions as uncertainties resolve, we can allocate more slack to the present to accommodate its worst-case. As we know that not all of this allocated slack will be consumed, the future will have its own optimal share of slack by the time it is needed. If the present ends up using all the allocated slack, such speculative slack allocation will be clearly sub-optimal. Similarly, due to the nonlinearities, at times it might be more optimal to reserve more slack for the future than we would do in the worst-case optimal allocation. Thus we are essentially conditioning the system's slack (in time/temperature/lifetime/etc), both known and predictive parts, in such a way that the resulting decisions will be optimal (or at least close to it) when the future evolves close enough to what has been predicted. The slack management always ensures that the future is feasible even when all of the allocated slack is consumed by the present. But for that less likely case the resulting decisions incur a cost penalty that is higher than the expected increase in the gains (i.e., the optimizer is taking a risk on the costs).

While it is possible to take blind risks with the hope to perform better on average than being conservative all the time, blind risks are clearly sub-optimal and much better can be done. We advocate use of good predictors for the estimation/prediction of the uncertainties (and thus expected reality) which are in turn used to guide the process of risk taking. The optimizer is aware that these values are not 100% accurate and they are not safe enough. So, it still relies on bounds to guarantee all the hard constraints of present and future. The estimates are used to optimize the knob settings for the expected reality, in contrast to the statistical optimization and optimizing for the worst-case or average-case. Undoubtedly, the better is the accuracy of these predictions, the better the gains.

Modeling the likely-case optimization problem is not that easy: allocate the slack such that it is optimal when evaluated with likely values for the uncertainties while ensuring that there exists a feasible solution for the subsequent future even if all the uncertainties till the next decision moment assume their worst-case. This seemingly optimal strategy is safe but not at all optimal even when the uncertainties turn out to be as predicted. The reason is some instances in future may need more worst-case slack, to be able to safely execute with the intended mode, than is actually available even when everything so far is as expected. We should check for these conditions explicitly during the optimization using play-forward constraints: the maximal available slack (including from the future) at any moment should be able to accommodate the bounded worst-case till the next decision moment with the intended decisions when

all those resolvable uncertainties by then turns out to be as predicted. Such play-forward constraints are not required if the prediction is 100% confident/assured. They over-constrain the search space than bare safety constraints alone and thus prevent the optimizer from making sub-optimal decisions. Thus in combination with reasonably good predictors and play-forward constraints, likely-case optimization strategy *always* performs better on average compared to any other slack allocation strategy.

Constraint-Driven Search Space Pruning

The proactive conditioning phases discussed before imposes additional constraints on the search space by narrowing down the uncertainties. These constraints can be exploited to systematically reduce the search space first before the cost-driven trade-off analysis. This is very similar to the constraint analysis based search space reduction as in (Mesman et al., 1999; Ku et al., 1991). It is possible that this phase is tightly coupled with (often in iterative fashion) or sometimes completely subsumed by the subsequent cost trade-off analysis phase.

Cost Trade-off Analysis

In this phase we perform the explicit cost trade-off analysis and make the final knob decisions. In the absence of explicit cost trade-off analysis, knob decisions are made by evaluating simple analytical formulae or looking up the stored tables. In reactive version, cost trade-off analysis is performed by brute-force/exhaustive search (if the problem size is small or the associated overhead is acceptable) or by using static greedy heuristics. The proactive versions use smarter techniques based on scenario clustering and dynamic procedure (explained later).

Conditional Re-Optimization

While bound tightening helps, most often we will still have significant uncertainties (either due to large uncertainties or strong nonlinearities). Hence it is often beneficial to redo the optimization (or revisit the knob decisions) as some of the uncertainties get resolved or more tightly bounded in the due course of system execution. In other words, the optimization is performed over moving or diminishing time window (known as the receding horizon in systems theory). As execution progresses, future becomes past and some of the uncertainties at the time of previous decision moment are now fully resolved – e.g., computation requirement of a task and its consequences on the resource consumption such as time, energy, degradation/damage and state such as temperature and hardware status are potentially known completely. Also as time progress more inputs and correlation information becomes potentially available which can enable tighter bounds for the still uncertain aspects.

Instead of naïve and complete re-optimization at every decision moment, we propose to perform re-optimization dynamically and incrementally to limit the run-time overhead. Re-optimization should be done in a demand-driven way, i.e., only when the resolved uncertainties make it essential or enable energy gains. We maximally reuse the information from the previous optimization as the changes are often incremental. Basically the optimization process itself also prepares the conditions for when it makes sense to re-optimize and what steps to repeat under different conditions. Thus the optimization procedure not only gives the expected decisions for the future as output but also the conditions for revising these decisions and indication to the effective methods for doing it along with the data needed for them. Dynamic re-optimization can be implemented either using simple and static models (pseudo-proactive) or sophisticated correlation analysis based models (truly-proactive).

Scenario Clustering

As we are dealing with highly dynamic systems the potential run-time situations (RTSs) of the system are very huge. Instead of handling each situation individually, which leads to explosion and hence large decision overhead, we advocate clustering of similar RTSs into scenarios. The similarity of RTSs is largely dependent on the context. E.g., clustering of RTSs for tightening upper-bounds versus predicting the likely-case shall be very different. Thus scenario clustering is complementary to and can be applied for implementing various features discussed above. The pseudo-proactive versions typically use design-time identified parameterized scenarios. The truly-proactive versions create the scenarios dynamically on-the-fly.

Dynamic Procedure

All the features discussed so far aim at improving the quality of optimization result. Some of them, especially future look-ahead, re-optimization, and play-forward, significantly increase the complexity of the optimization. To reduce the overall time and energy overhead of the controller for solving the complex optimization problem at run-time, we advocate the use of a highly customized dynamic procedure. The main idea is that we do not always need to solve the complex optimization with large horizon – even smaller values give decent, sometimes even better results (due to finite horizon deceptiveness typical of uncertain optimization), without negative future consequences, in some cases. If we switch between methods of different complexities at the right moment in time, we can significantly reduce the average run-time overhead of the optimization without noticeable sub-optimality (Figure 14).

Typical algorithms are today implemented as a static procedure, i.e., same computations are repeated each time it is invoked, in other words it is stateless. The reason is that they are not meant for receding horizon optimization and assume

Figure 14. Conceptual example of dynamic procedure

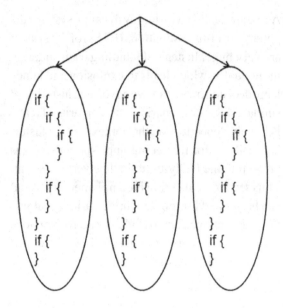

that each time they might get entirely different inputs to process. In contrast, to exploit the inherent incremental nature of proactive control, we first enhance the procedures that we use with state, to reduce their average complexity, by remembering and reusing the computations across repeated invocations of the same procedure. Different major computations of a procedure are gated with simple conditions so that a significant computation is only performed when it is absolute necessary or likely to be beneficial. We associate a complexity model with the procedure which indicates when it would take more computations, e.g., at the initialization or when some of the data (like estimates) used in previous invocation changed significantly. A procedure is always "safe", i.e., it ensures that all the hard constraints are met with the modes recommended by it. The quality of a given procedure is defined as the cost gains (of the system being controlled) achieved by applying this procedure. It is important to note that the quality of a procedure is dynamic, i.e., under certain conditions the quality is very high but poorer in other cases, and hence we maintain a quality model. The complexity and quality

models (typically look-up tables based on generic scenarios concept) will be used at run-time to evaluate a given procedure for the dynamic scheduling instance at hand. We maintain multiple such updating-type procedures each with different quality-complexity trade-offs. A dynamic procedure is the one which uses different state-enhanced gated procedures at different time instances which are selected based on the quality-complexity trade-offs for the given dynamic scheduling instance at hand, within the time available for the decision making. It always tries to use the procedure that potentially maximizes the overall gain for the given complexity. Thus waterfall structure and high reuse are the characteristic features of a dynamic procedure.

The waterfall structure and the type of conditions used in a dynamic procedure, essentially, is the result of the scenario clustering process. The degenerate version of this is use-case scenario version. Use of automated profiling based scenario clustering as in (Gheorghita et al., 2008) to decide (based on a template) the exact structure and conditions results in a pseudo-proactive dynamic procedure. The truly-proactive version involves the structure and/or conditions identified based on sophisticated correlation analysis, which cannot be formalized and hence automated (at least in the near future).

Figure 15. Example to illustrate Contextual Turbo-modes

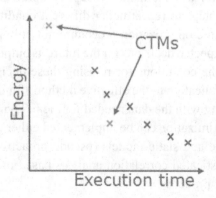

CONCLUSION AND FUTURE WORK

Modern system contexts are becoming highly dynamic with multiple sources of dynamism across all design abstractions from application to hardware. In many cases the dynamism and the associated opportunities are hidden under worst-case abstractions. Cost-consciousness necessitates dynamic systems to incorporate knobs that enable run-time trade-offs to exploit this dynamism, leading to the so-called adaptive systems. Optimal control or knob-tuning of adaptive systems in the presence of conflicting system constraints is highly challenging in the presence of strong nonlinearities. In this article we presented a consistent classification of reactive and proactive controllers for hard constrained systems. We pointed that state-of-the-art controllers are inadequate to handle nonlinear dynamic systems and result in sub-optimal implementations when evaluated for real usage conditions. To bridge this gap, we propose a combined strategy of dynamic bounding and proactive system conditioning for the predicted likely future. Elaborating this strategy, we described systematic principles to design low-overhead proactive controllers. We introduced the notion of and motivated the need for short-term operating points of the system, namely contextual turbo-modes. The proposed strategy also effectively exploits these modes to further close the gap between retrospectively optimal and practically achievable solutions. We used dynamic task management problem to explain the proposed concepts, but we emphasize that the proposed concepts are applicable for a wide variety of problems in a broad range of domains and systems. Instantiation of the proposed concepts to other different problems is future work. This article only presented the "what specification" of truly-proactive versions of various steps in the proposed methodology. The details on how they can be realized/implemented are the subjects of future work as well.

REFERENCES

Adve, S., et al. (2002). The Illinois GRACE Project: Global Resource Adaptation through CoopEration. In *Proceedings of the Workshop on Self-Healing, Adaptive, and self-MANaged Systems*.

Austin, T., & Bertacco, V. (2005). Deployment of better than worst-case design: solutions and needs. In *Proceedings of IEEE International Conference on Computer Design (ICCD)* (pp. 550-555).

Aydin, H., Melhem, R. G., Mossé, D., & Mejía-Alvarez, P. (2004). Power-Aware Scheduling for Periodic Real-Time Tasks. *IEEE Transactions on Computers*, 53, 584–600. doi:10.1109/TC.2004.1275298

Bekooij, M., Moreira, O., Poplavko, P., Mesman, B., Pastrnak, M., & Meerbergen, J. V. (2004). Predictable embedded multiprocessor system design. *In Proceedings of the Software and Compilers for Embedded Systems*. New York: Springer.,*3199*, 77–91. doi:10.1007/978-3-540-30113-4_7

Benini, L., Bogliolo, A., & De Micheli, G. (2000). A survey of design techniques for system-level dynamic power management. *IEEE Transactions on Very Large Scale Integration Systems*, 8, 299–316. doi:10.1109/92.845896

Borkar, S. (2005). Designing Reliable Systems from Unreliable Components: The Challenges of Transistor Variability and Degradation. *IEEE Micro*, 25(6), 10–16. doi:10.1109/MM.2005.110

Bosman, P. A. N. (2005). Learning, anticipation and time-deception in evolutionary online dynamic optimization. In *Proceedings of the workshops on Genetic and evolutionary computation* (pp. 39-47). ACM: New York.

Brooks, D., & Martonosi, M. (2001). Dynamic thermal management for high-performance microprocessors. In *Proceedings of the Seventh International Symposium on High-Performance Computer Architecture* (pp. 171-182).

Chantem, T., Dick, R. P., & Hu, X. S. (2008). Temperature-aware scheduling and assignment for hard real-time applications on MPSoCs. In *Proceedings of the conference on Design, automation and test in Europe* (pp. 288-293). New York: ACM.

Chen, J., & Kuo, C. (2007). Energy-Efficient Scheduling for Real-Time Systems on Dynamic Voltage Scaling (DVS) Platforms. In *Proceedings of Intl. Conference on Embedded and Real-Time Computing Systems and Applications (RTCSA)*.

Constantinides, K., Plaza, S., Blome, J., Zhang, B., Bertacco, V., Mahlke, S., et al. (2006). BulletProof: A Defect-tolerant CMP Switch Architecture. In *Proceedings of the of Intl. Symposium on High Performance Computer Architecture (HPCA)* (pp. 3-14).

Cornea, R., Dutt, N., Gupta, R., Krueger, I., Nicolau, A., Schmidt, D., & Shukla, S. (2003). FORGE: A Framework for Optimization of Distributed Embedded Systems Software. In *Proceedings of International Parallel and Distributed Processing Symposium*.

Cosemans, S., Dehaene, W., & Catthoor, F. (2008). A 3.6pJ/access 480MHz, 128Kbit on-Chip SRAM with 850MHz boost mode in 90nm CMOS with tunable sense amplifiers to cope with variability. In *Proceedings of the Solid-State Circuits Conference* (pp. 278-281). ESSCIRC.

Ernst, D., Kim, N. S., Das, S., Pant, S., Rao, R., Pham, T., et al. (2003). Razor: A Low-Power Pipeline Based on Circuit-Level Timing Speculation. In *Proceedings of the Intl. Symp. on Microarchitecture (MICRO-36)*.

Geilen, M. C. W., Basten, T., Theelen, B. D., & Otten, R. H. J. M. (2005). An Algebra of Pareto Points. In *Proceedings of International Conference on Application of Concurrency to System Design (ACSD)* (pp. 88-97).

Gheorghita, S. V., Basten, T., & Corporaal, H. (2008). Application Scenarios in Streaming-Oriented Embedded-System Design. In *IEEE Des. Test.* (Vol. 25, pp. 581-589). Washington, DC: IEEE Computer Society Press.

Gheorghita, S. V., Palkovic, M., Hamers, J., Vandecappelle, A., Mamagkakis, S., & Basten, T. (2008). System Scenario Based Design of Dynamic Embedded Systems. *ACM Transactions on Design Automation of Electronic Systems*, 14.

Groeseneken, G. (2005). Recent Trends in Reliability Assessment of Advanced CMOS Technologies. In *Proceedings of the IEEE Intl. Conf. on Microelectronic Test Structures* (Vol. 18, pp. 81-88).

Gu, Y., Chakraborty, S., & Ooi, W. T. (2006). Games are up for DVFS. In *Proceedings of the 43rd Annual Design Automation Conference (DAC '06)* (pp. 598-603). New York: ACM.

Jalali, A. A., & Nadimi, V. (2006). A Survey on Robust Model Predictive Control from 1999-2006. In *Proceedings of the International Conference on Computational Intelligence for Modelling, Control and Automation* (p. 207). Washington, DC: IEEE Computer Society.

Karl, E., Blaauw, D., Sylvester, D., & Mudge, T. (2006). Reliability modeling and management in dynamic microprocessor-based systems. In *Proceedings of the 43rd annual conference on Design automation* (pp. 1057-1060). New York: ACM.

Keutzer, K., & Orshansky, M. (2002). From Blind Certainty to Informed Uncertainty. In *Proceedings of the Intl. Workshop on Timing Issues in the Specification and Synthesis of Digital Systems (TAU)*.

Ku, D. C., & De Micheli, G. (1991). Constrained resource sharing and conflict resolution in Hebe. *Elsevier Integration, the VLSI journal, 12*, 131-165.

Leung, L. F., Tsui, C. Y., & Hu, X. S. (2005). Exploiting Dynamic Workload Variation in Low Energy Preemptive Task Scheduling. In *Proceedings of the conference on Design, Automation and Test in Europe* (Vol. 1, pp. 634-639). Washington, DC: IEEE Computer Society.

Li, M., Bougard, B., Novo, D., Van Thillo, W., Van der Perre, L., & Catthoor, F. (2008). Adaptive SSFE Near-ML MIMO Detector with Dynamic Search Range and 80-103Mbps Flexible Implementation. In *Proceeding of IEEE GLOBECOM*.

Mesman, B., Timmer, A. H., Van Meerbergen, J. L., & Jess, J. A. G. (1999). Constraint analysis for DSP code generation. *IEEE Transactions on Computer-Aided Design of Integrated Circuits and Systems, 18*(1), 44–57. doi:10.1109/43.739058

Mihic, K., Simunic, T., & De Micheli, G. (2004). Reliability and Power Management of Integrated Systems. In Proceedings of the Dependable System Design (DSD).

Mochocki, B., Hu, X. S., & Quan, G. (2007). Transition-overhead-aware voltage scheduling for fixed-priority real-time systems. *ACM Transactions on Design Automation of Electronic Systems, 12*, 11. doi:10.1145/1230800.1230803

Novo, D., Bougard, B., Lambrechts, A., Van der Perre, L., & Catthoor, F. (2008). Scenario-Based Fixed-point Data Format Refinement to Enable Energy-scalable Software Defined Radios. In *Proceedings of Design, Automation, and Test in Europe (DATE'08)*.

Papanicolaou, A., Wang, H., Miranda, M., Catthoor, F., & Dehaene, W. (2008). Reliability Issues in Deep Deep sub-micron technologies: time-dependent variability and its impact on embedded system design. In *Proceedings of VLSI-SoC, Research Trends in VLSI and Systems on Chip* (Vol. 249/2008). New York: Springer.

Pillai, P., & Shin, K. G. (2001). Real-time dynamic voltage scaling for low-power embedded operating systems. In *Proceedings of the eighteenth ACM symposium on Operating systems principles* (pp. 89-102). New York: ACM.

Pollin, S., Mangharam, R., Bougard, B., Van Der Perre, L., Moerman, I., Rajkumar, R., & Catthoor, F. (2007). *MEERA: Cross-Layer Methodology for Energy Efficient Resource Allocation in Wireless Networks*. IEEE Trans. on Wireless Communications.

Sanz, C., Prieto, M., Papanikolaou, A., Miranda, M., & Catthoor, F. (2006). System-level process variability compensation on memory organization of dynamic applications: a case study. In *Proceedings of International Symposium on Quality Electronic Design* (pp. 376-382). Washington, DC: IEEE Computer Society.

Shin, J., Zyuban, V., Hu, Z., Rivers, J. A., & Bose, P. (2007). A Framework for Architecture-Level Lifetime Reliability Modeling. In *Proceedings of the 37th Annual IEEE/IFIP International Conference on Dependable Systems and Networks* (pp. 534-543). Washington, DC: IEEE Computer Society.

Srinivasan, J., Adve, S. V., Bose, P., & Rivers, J. A. (2004). Impact of Technology Scaling on Lifetime Reliability. In *Proceedings of the Intl. Conf. on Dependable Systems and Networks (DSN)*.

Srinivasan, J., Adve, S. V., Bose, P., & Rivers, J. A. (2005). Exploiting Structural Duplication for Lifetime Reliability Enhancement. In *Proceedings of the Intl. Symp. on Computer Architecture (ISCA)*.

Stavrou, K., & Trancoso, P. (2007). Thermal-aware scheduling for future chip multiprocessors. *EURASIP Journal on Embedded Systems*, 40–40.

Tack, N., Lafruit, G., Catthoor, F., & Lauwereins, R. (2005). A content quality driven energy management system for mobile 3D graphics. In *Proceedings of the IEEE workshop on Signal Processing Systems Design and Implementation*.

Venkatachalam, V., & Franz, M. (2005). Power Reduction Techniques for Microprocessor Systems. *ACM Computing Surveys*, *37*(3), 195–237. doi:10.1145/1108956.1108957

Wang, H., Miranda, M., Papanikolaou, A., Catthoor, F., & Dehaene, W. (2005). Variable tapered pareto buffer design and implementation allowing run-time configuration for low-power embedded SRAMs. *IEEE Trans. VLSI Syst.*, *13*(10), 1127–1135. doi:10.1109/TVLSI.2005.859480

Wiegand, T., Sullivan, G. J., Bjontegaard, G., & Luthra, A. (2003). Overview of the H.264/AVC video coding standard. *IEEE Transaction on Circuits and Systems for Video Technology, 13*(7).

Yang, P., Wong, C., Marchal, P., Catthoor, F., Desmet, D., Verkest, D., & Lauwereins, R. (2001). Energy-Aware Runtime Scheduling for Embedded-Multiprocessor SOCs. *IEEE Des. Test.*, *18*, 46–58. doi:10.1109/54.953271

Yeo, I., Liu, C. C., & Kim, E. J. (2008). Predictive dynamic thermal management for multicore systems. In *Proceedings of the 45th annual conference on Design automation* (pp. 734-739).

Zhang, Y., Parikh, D., Sankaranarayanan, K., Skadron, K., & Stan, M. (2003). *HotLeakage: A Temperature-Aware Model of Subthreshold and Gate Leakage for Architects* (Tech. Rep. No. CS-2003-05). Charlottesville, VA: University of Virginia, Deptartment of Computer Science.

Zhe, M., & Catthoor, F. (2007). *Systematic Methodology for Real-Time Cost-Effective Mapping of Dynamic Concurrent Task-Based Systems on Heterogeneous Platforms*. New York: Springer.

This work was previously published in the International Journal of Adaptive, Resilient and Autonomic Systems, Volume 2, Issue 1, edited by Vincenzo De Florio, pp. 18-45, copyright 2011 by IGI Publishing (an imprint of IGI Global).

Chapter 2

A Recovery–Oriented Approach for Software Fault Diagnosis in Complex Critical Systems

Gabriella Carrozza
SESM s.c.a.r.l. - a Finmeccanica Company, Italy

Roberto Natella
Università degli Studi di Napoli Federico II, Italy

ABSTRACT

This paper proposes an approach to software faults diagnosis in complex fault tolerant systems, encompassing the phases of error detection, fault location, and system recovery. Errors are detected in the first phase, exploiting the operating system support. Faults are identified during the location phase, through a machine learning based approach. Then, the best recovery action is triggered once the fault is located. Feedback actions are also used during the location phase to improve detection quality over time. A real world application from the Air Traffic Control field has been used as case study for evaluating the proposed approach. Experimental results, achieved by means of fault injection, show that the diagnosis engine is able to diagnose faults with high accuracy and at a low overhead.

INTRODUCTION

Hardware and software technologies are progressing fast, increasing the complexity of modern computer systems significantly. Even in the context of critical scenarios, we are witnessing a paradigm shift from stand-alone and centralized systems toward large-scale and distributed infrastructures and simple monolithic programs are letting the field to modular software architectures, typically based on Off-The-Shelf (OTS) software items. This allows industries to increase market competitiveness by lowering development costs and reducing the time to market. Testing and veri-

DOI: 10.4018/978-1-4666-2056-8.ch002

fication, along with fault tolerance techniques, are used to satisfy dependability requirements. The key for achieving fault tolerance is the ability to accurately detect, diagnose, and recover from faults during system operation.

The great research effort striven in fault tolerant systems has provided good results with respect to hardware-related errors. Recent examples are (Serafini, Bondavalli, & Suri, 2007), (Bondavalli, Chiaradonna, Cotroneo, & Romano, 2004). However, it is well known that many systems outages are due to software faults (Gray, 1985), i.e., to bugs lying into the code which have, then, a permanent in nature. This means that, if a program contains a bug, any circumstances that cause it to fail once will always cause it to fail, and this is the reason why software failures are often referred to as "systematic failures" (Littlewood & Strigini, 2000). However, the *failure process*, i.e., the way the bugs are activated, is not deterministic since (i) the sequence of inputs cannot be predicted, hence it is not possible to establish which are the program's faults (and failures), and (ii) software failures can be due to environmental conditions (e.g., timing and load profile) which let a given fault to be activated. For this reason, it is said that software faults can manifest transiently. By failure we intend the software modules/components failure in which the fault has been activated. This can be viewed as fault from the whole system point of view (Joshi, Hiltunen, Sanders, & Schlichting, 2005). Activating conditions which cause a software fault to surface into a failure have been recognized to be crucial in (Chillarege et al., 1992), where they are defined as "triggers" and where software bugs are grouped into orthogonal, non overlapping, defect types (Orthogonal Defect Classification, ODC). Software faults which manifest permanently, also known as *Bohrbugs*, are likely to fix and discover during the pre-operational phases of system life cycle (e.g., structured design, design review, quality assurance, unit, component and integration testing, alpha/beta test), as well as by means of traditional debugging techniques. Conversely,

software faults which manifest transiently, also known as *Heisenbugs*, cannot be reproduced systematically (Huang, Jalote, & Kintala, 1994), and they have been demonstrated to be the major cause of failures in software systems, especially during the system operational phase (Sullivan & Chillarege, 1991; Chillarege, Biyani, & Rosenthal, 1995; Xu, Kalbarczyc, & Iyer, 1999).

Focus in this work is on recovery oriented software fault diagnosis in complex fault tolerant systems. Little attention has been paid so far to this problem, which plays a key role in maintaining system health and in preserving fault tolerance capabilities. Previous studies on software diagnosis aimed to identify software defects from their manifestations through off-line and/or on-site analysis (Tucek, Lu, Huang, Xanthos, & Zhou, 2007). They aim to discover bugs in the code, by using static/dynamic code screening, in order to perform more effective maintenance operations. Thus, they are not able to catch Heisenbugs since this way the underlying environmental conditions are not easy to localize into the code.

In this work, the aim of diagnosis is twofold. First, starting from outward symptoms we are interested in identifying what are the execution misbehaviors which caused failure occurrence, and where these misbehaviors come from, in order to trigger proper recovery actions. This is crucial in complex, modular and distributed systems, for which the overall failure can be avoided by confining and masking the failures of the parts (nodes, components, processes). Second, we aim to provide information about manifested symptoms that are useful for off-line maintenance activities.

The massive presence of OTS items, whose well-known dependability pitfalls do not hold industries back from their usage in critical systems, further exacerbates the diagnosis problem. In fact, faults can propagate in several ways and among several components, depending on a complex combination of their internal state and of the execution environment. Actually, the failures resulting from unexpected faults, known as production run failures or field failures (e.g., crashes, hangs and incorrect results), are the major contributors to system downtime and dependability pitfalls (Tucek, Lu, Huang, Xanthos, & Zhou, 2007). They cause the system failure modes to be not known at design time, and to evolve over time. To face this problem, we believe that the detection has to be included into the diagnosis process, differently from what existing approaches have proposed so far. As it has been demonstrated in (Vaidya & Pradham, 1994) with respect to distributed systems recovery from a large number of faults, by combing detection and location adaptively, the number of faults diagnosed properly, increases over time at a low additional cost.

Addressed Issues

This work defines a recovery-oriented diagnosis approach, to (i) locate the cause of a system's component failure at run time, and (ii), trigger proper recovery actions, based on an estimate of the fault nature, in the form of fault tolerance via fault masking techniques.

Several issues arise when designing this approach, which have not been addressed before. First, the presence of software faults hampers the definition of a simple, and accurate, mathematical model able to describe systems failure modes (hence, pure model based techniques become inadequate). Second, due to the presence of OTS components, low intrusiveness in terms of source code modifications is desirable. Third, diagnosis has to be performed on-line, i.e., a fault has to be located as soon as possible during system execution and with lack of human guidance. The reason for this is twofold. On the one hand, it is to fulfill strict time requirements, for system recovery and reconfiguration, in the case of a fault. On the other hand, it is to face system complexity with respect to ordinary system management and maintenance operations, whose manual execution would result in strenuous human efforts and long completion times.

Paper's Contributions

This paper proposes a novel approach for on-line software fault diagnosis in complex and OTS based critical systems. To the best of authors' knowledge, this is the first proposal addressing on-line software diagnosis issues of complex and fault tolerant systems, and evaluates in the context of a real world industrial application. Indeed, differently from most of the previous work which proposed off-line/on-site diagnosis approaches aiming to locate bugs in the source code, and sometimes the environmental conditions, we address the diagnosis problem during the system operational phase. Thus, two are the key aspects:

- **Low Intrusiveness:** Since we are addressing OTS-based systems, it is required that target applications is not instrumented at all
- **Holistic Diagnostic Approach:** Detection (D), Location (L), and Recovery (R) have been integrated into one diagnosis process.

More specifically, the approach features:

- A detection strategy in charge of detecting application errors by exploiting OS support, exhibiting high accuracy and low overhead. To face the partial ignorance about the failure modes, the detection strategy is pessimistic and relies on the anomaly detection paradigm. To the best of authors' knowledge, this paradigm has not been applied yet for fault/error detection in critical systems. Experimental results reveal that this approach is promising.
- A novel fault location strategy in charge of (i) locating the cause of system components/modules failures, and (ii) of triggering the most effective recovery action on the basis of the detection output. More important, it is also in charge of solving detection falls and of improving detection

quality over time by means of feedback actions.

- The design of a recovery dictionary in charge of associating automatically the most effective recovery mean to the occurred fault. This is also the main objective of (Joshi, Hiltunen, Sanders, & Schlichting, 2005). Even if it is close in spirit to our work, that work aims to optimize the sequence of recovery actions to be applied, whereas we apply only the best one, by using monitors we implemented by our own.

SYSTEM MODEL AND ASSUMPTIONS

The target systems are assumed to be complex software systems, deployed on several nodes and communicating through a network infrastructure. Each node is organized in software layers and it is made up of several Diagnosable Units (DUs), representing atomic software entities, at it is shown in Figure 1.

In most of the cases, the layered structure of each node encompasses the Operating System (OS), the Middleware and the User Application levels. Since the focus is on software faults, we

Figure 1. System's node model

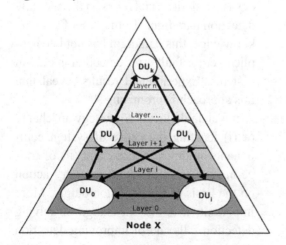

assume this to be the reference system architecture, and we do not pay attention to the underlying hardware equipment. This sounds a reasonable assumption since modern systems are equipped with redundant and highly reliable hardware platforms which are developed and extensively tested in house, especially in the case of mission and safety critical systems. This means that hardware related faults will be not diagnosed by the proposed DLR framework.

DUs are assumed to be processes. This means that a process is the smallest entity which can be affected by a fault and for which it is possible to diagnose faults, as well as to perform recoveries. Of course, the bug which caused the process to fail can be located within an OTS library or module which is being executed in the context of the process; additionally, propagations can occur among different nodes and layers. Look at Figure 2, where the process P1 experiences a failure due to the component C. However, the failure is actually located into the D library, which is running in the context of a different process, P2 and the bug propagates to C through y, e.g., due to an erroneous input from D to y. According to a recovery-oriented perspective, addressing the process as the atomic entity of the system, it is enough to identify the cause which induced the failure of the process, within the context of the process itself. In other words, if a recovery action exists in charge of recovering the failed process by only acting on it, it is unnecessary to go back through the propagation chain out of the context of the process. With respect Figure 2, the failure of P1 will be attributed to y, which is the last link in the propagation within the P1 context.

Once the root cause has been identified the proper recovery action has to be selected. Hence, the final output of diagnosis consists of a couple of vectors (D, R). The former associates the failed node, by means of the IP address, to the failed process which is identified by the Process ID (PID). The latter, instead, associates the experienced failure (f) to the recovery action to be initiated (r). Schematically

Figure 2. Diagnosis at process level

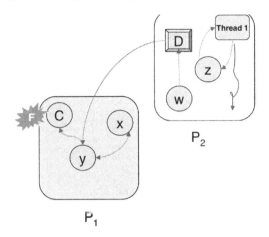

$$D = (IP_{failednode}, PID_{failedprocess})$$

$$R = (Failure_{f}, Recovery_{r})$$

The diagnosis output provides information about the failed process, rather than about the component which caused the failure. This information would not be interesting for the final users. However, it could be helpful for bug fixing and fault removal.

Failure Modes

Crash, hangs and workload failures are encompassed by the proposed approach. A process crash is the unexpected interruption of its execution due either to an external or an internal error. A process hang, instead, can be defined as a stall of the process. Hangs can be due to several causes, such as deadlock, livelock or waiting conditions on busy shared resources. As for workload failures, they depend on the running application. Workload failures can be both value (e.g., erroneous output provided by a function) or timing failures.

Since the target systems are distributed on several nodes, and since faults can propagate, the set of the failures to be encompassed is given by FM=FxDUs, i.e., by the product set of the failure types and of all the DUs (i.e., the processes).

Recovery Actions

Since the focus of this paper is on diagnosis, we assume that some basic Fault Tolerant services are provided by the middleware layer. For instance, in our industrial case study the used middleware implements the standard Fault Tolerant OMG CORBA service (OMG, 2001). Thus, the middleware is able to manage server replication, including issues related to state transfer which usually follows system reconfiguration procedures. The proposed DLR framework encompasses two classes of recovery actions:

- **System Level Recovery**, i.e., actions which aim to repair a failed process by acting at system level. These actions are intended for dealing with crashes and hangs, and they can be more or less costly depending on the size of the system, as well as on the number of processes involved into the failure. Encompassed actions are system reboot, application restart and process kill. Once one of these actions has been performed, the FT middleware service will be able to restore the application.

- **Workload Level Recovery**, i.e., action which aim to repair application failures. These actions are intended for dealing with workload failures; hence a knowledge of the application semantic is required.

THE OVERALL APPROACH

Figure 3 gives an overall picture of the proposed approach, representing how it works from the fault occurrence till system recovery.

During the operational phase of the system, a monitoring system performs continuous detection on each DU, exploiting Operating System (OS) support. Once a failure (*F*) occurs, an alarm is triggered. This initiates the Location phase, aiming to identify the root cause of the failure. Once

33

Figure 3. A time snapshot of the overall DLR approach

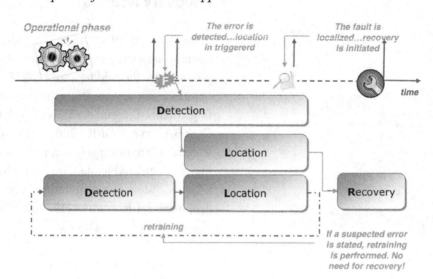

the Location has been completed, the Recovery phase is started in order to recover the failed process(es) and to resume normal activities. The task of detection consists of the alarm triggering when a given process fails. Since if a process fails it is not assured that the system will fail as well, a process failure is conceived as an error for the overall system. For this reason, the task of detection is in fact error detection in the context of this work.

The overall approach is based on the machine learning paradigm, as in many previous papers focusing on diagnosis (Yuan, et al., 2006; Zheng, Lloyd, & Brewer, 2004; Brun & Ernst, 2004). The main reason for this is the presence of field failures, which cannot be known at design/development time. Indeed, such a paradigm makes the DLR engine, and all of its components, able to learn over time. Thus, field failures influence the design of the entire engine, from detection to recovery.

As for detection, an error is defined as a corruption in the state of a *DU*, which can impact in turn on the state of the system. An alarm is triggered each time an anomaly is encountered in system behavior; this is achieved by means of anomaly detection, i.e., all the conditions which deviate from normal behaviors are labeled as errors. This

is quite a pessimistic detection strategy. In fact, not all the anomalies correspond to actual errors, i.e., this way errors can be signaled even when the system is behaving correctly but that working condition has not been recognized as normal. On the one hand, such a pessimistic strategy leads to a non negligible amount of false positives, in that alarms are likely to be triggered which do not correspond to actual errors. On the other hand, it allows minimizing the number of anomalous conditions which are misinterpreted as normal behaviors, thus going unnoticed. This is crucial in the context of critical systems in that not signaled errors are in fact false negatives which may have catastrophic effects. It is worth noting that reducing false positives, i.e., improving detection accuracy, at design time has been the primary requirement of traditional detection system.

Once an alarm has been triggered, the Location phase is initiated to identify its root cause. Along with the aim of pinpointing the actual fault, this phase has also to remedy detection accuracy falls. More precisely, during this phase the presence of an actual fault has to be established, since false positives are likely to be triggered by the detector. This means that the location module behaves ``distrustfully'' to compensate the pessimistic detection. This is achieved via the machine learning paradigm, which underlies this phase in the form of classification. We separate faults into smaller classes, and give criteria for determining whether an occurred fault is in a particular class or not.

Each fault class is represented as a set of features, i.e., a set of measurable properties (which are inferred from OS and produced logs) of the observed *DU*. We adopt a pattern recognition module which gathers observed features during system operation to be classified. Features are determined experimentally; the relation between features and faults is therefore learned (or trained) experimentally as well, and then stored to form an explicit knowledge base. Faults can be identified by comparing the observed values of the features with the nominal ones.

Starting from manifestations (i.e., the errors), the location module has to infer the presence of a fault and to associate it to a class. To design the fault classes properly, three circumstances has to be considered:

1. **SUSPECTED ERROR (SE):** The triggered alarm was not the manifestation of an actual fault, i.e., the detection module triggered a false positive. In this case, there is no need neither for location nor for system recovery;
2. **ERROR:** A fault actually occurred that the location module is able to identify. In this case, recovery actions have to be associated to the fault and initiated as soon as possible;
3. **UNKNOWN FAULT:** The triggered alarm was actually due to a fault which cannot be identified during the location. This is the tricky case of a fault which is *unknown*, i.e., a fault which never occurred before. In this case, the system has to be put in a safe state, and further investigations are needed which can potentially require human intervention.

The location capability of uncovering false positives allows improving the detection accuracy. Actually, this is the aim of the feedback branch,

namely "retraining", depicted in Figure 3: once an alarm has been labeled as a SE, the detection module is upgraded consequently. This allows a reduction of the number of false positives over time, as it will be shown in the following sections.

Recovery actions to be initiated in the case of an ERROR have been associated to the fault classes. This is to perform recovery actions which are tailored for the particular fault that occurred. Since the approach is intended for operational systems, two main phases are encompassed. During the first phase, the DLR engine is trained in order to build a *starting knowledge*. This is leveraged during the second phase, which is in fact the system operational phase.

Figure 4 depicts the training process. In order to train the detection module, which performs anomaly detection; faulty free executions (i.e., correct executions) of the system have to be run in order to model its normal behavior (1). Conversely, fault injection (2) is required in order to allow (i) the definition of the fault classes (3.a) and (ii), the collection and analysis of fault related data to model system behavior in faulty conditions (3.b). DUs running into the system, which are depicted as little triangles in the figure, are the injection target. Once faults have been injected, the supervised training of the location classifier is performed (4), as detailed in section *location*. At the end of the training phase, both the detection and the location classifiers can rely on a starting knowledge about the target system. On the one hand this can be exploited during the operational phase. On the other hand, the base knowledge has to be improved during the system lifetime adaptively in order to take fields failures into account.

DETECTION

Good detection systems have to exhibit low overhead, i.e., they do not have to compromise system resources, as well as low rates of missing and wrong detections. This is in order to reduce

Figure 4. Training of the DLR engine

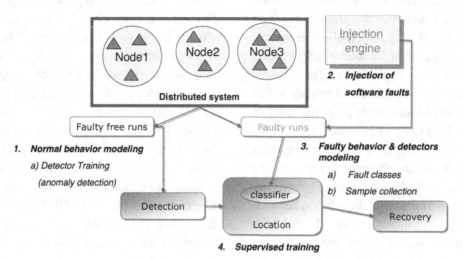

the effects of a not handled fault, and the number of false alarms as well. These requirements represent the most challenging issues when dealing with detection in several fields. As for example, for intrusions detection within networked systems, performance overhead increases with the traffic volume, and users behavior is difficult to characterize (i.e., licit users can behave in unexpected manner thus being misinterpreted as attackers). Anomaly detection is the most common and effective way to detect attacks (Forrest, Hofmeyr, Somayaji, & Longstaff, 1996). However, to the best of authors' knowledge it has not been used yet for error detection in critical, dependable, systems.

In this work we use anomaly detection for error detection. Simply, if the monitored application deviates from the normal behavior (i.e., faulty free executions), it is likely to be faulty. Normal behavior is modeled in two steps. First, the identification of representative and synthetic parameters; second, a training phase during which these are traced and characterized. Since it is influenced by several factors, such as the hardware configuration and usage application profile, the training phase should be repeated (manually or automatically) to take into account their significant

variations. Once the normal behavior has been modeled, the application is let run on the field and it is continuously monitored. When deviations are encountered, i.e., when parameters values differ from the modeled ones, the location phase is initiated aiming at pinpointing the root cause of the error, as well as at uncovering and fixing detection falls, as explained in the previous section.

In fact, DUs are the finest grain for detection, i.e., the above described detection process is applied to all the application DUs. Although the detection process can be applied to several kinds of DUs in principle, the way the detection is actually performed depends on their nature. As stated in section II, in this work DUs are assumed to be OS processes, also seen as "collection" of several threads. This is a very common abstraction used by computer systems. The behavior of a process can be effectively described through its interactions with the OS resources, and with all the other running processes as well. For this reason, we decided to trace these interactions by means of several monitors. Since target systems are OTS based, monitors require neither any internal knowledge of DUs nor their source code availability, i.e., DUs are considered as black boxes.

Parameters and Detection Criteria

The following OS data, which can be to collected and analyzed with a low computational overhead, are monitored to describe *DUs* behavior:

1. **SIGNALS**, i.e., notifications produced by the OS when providing services to the application (e.g., numeric return codes returned by system calls, UNIX signals). Erroneous OS notifications are logged (e.g., return codes different than zero, which represent exceptional conditions and are relatively rare);

2. **TIME EVENTS**, i.e., the timestamp of interesting events for the application execution (e.g., when a given resource becomes available, such as a semaphore). A log entry is produced each time these events do not occur within a given interval, i.e., timeouts are exceeded;

3. **THROUGHPUT**, i.e., the amount of data exchanged by OS processes through I/O facilities (e.g., the throughput of network and disk devices). Upper and lower bounds are associated with the I/O throughput; throughput is periodically sampled, and a log entry is produced when bounds are exceeded.

Architecture and Strategy

The architecture of the detection subsystem implemented in this work is depicted in Figure 5. It is a modular system made up of several, simple, monitors which are combined to provide a detection alarm. This is in order to get the most from each of them, in that monitors exhibit different performances in terms of coverage (i.e., the ability to detect an actual fault) and accuracy (e.g., the ability to avoid false alarms). Additionally, by combining monitors' responses the total number of false positives (e.g., a timeout can be exceeded due to a particular overload condition which is not an actual fault), can be minimized.

Being P the number of processes within the monitored application, monitors are associated to each thread tj of the P processes. Hence they account for a total of P x tjk ∀ k=1..n, where n is the number of monitored parameters. Monitors evaluate a triggering condition periodically (T is the period). An alarm generator (αi) collects the output of all the monitors related to a given parameter p for the i-th process. A counter n is incremented by αi if the monitored thread verifies the triggering condition. The normal behavior of a process (and of a thread as well), is modeled by associating a range of licit values to each alarm generator, specifically ri = [ri-,r_i+] (Figure 5).

Figure 5. Detection architecture

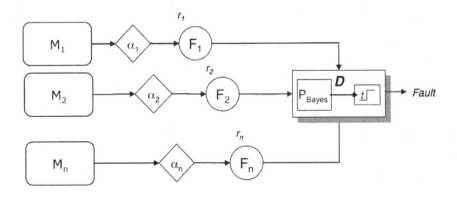

In practice, if the monitored value n for a given parameter p does fall outside ri within a temporal window T, an alarm is triggered. Hence, the output of each αi is a binary variable defined as:

$$F_i = \begin{cases} 1 & \text{if } n \notin r_{in} \text{ in } T \\ 0 & \text{otherwise} \end{cases}$$

The range ri is tuned during the preliminary training phase. The number of events is periodically sampled: the minimum and the maximum values which are experienced during faulty-free runs constitute the limits of the range.

The Bayes' rule has been chosen as the combination rule; hence the probability of a fault is achieved by:

$$P(F \mid \underline{a}) = \frac{P(\underline{a} \mid F)P(F)}{P(\underline{a} \mid F)P(F) + P(\underline{a} \mid \neg F)(1 - P(F))}$$

An alarm is triggered, if the estimated a posteriori probability exceeds a given threshold. In the previous equation, F represents the event "faulty DU", and a is a vector containing the output of the alarm generators αi: if Fi = 1 for L consecutive periods T, then ai = L, in order to take into account the alarm duration and to filter out "transient" false alarms (i.e., alarms triggered for only a short amount of time). Note that we assume that monitors do not fail (i.e., produce false alarms) at the same time. The joint probability distributions P(a | F) and P(a | ¬F), i.e., the probability of detection and the probability of false alarms respectively (Cardenas, Baras, & Seamon, 2006), have to be estimated during the training phase. The former can be estimated using fault injection, by evaluating the number of occurrences of the a vector under faults, over the total number of vectors collected during fault injection. Similarly, the latter can be estimated by counting the number of occurrences of a during faulty-free executions. Finally, the a priori fault probability P(F) has to be known. If field data are available about past fault occurrences, P(F) can be estimated using the ratio T / MTTF (MTTF stands for Mean Time To Failure), i.e., on the average, the DU becomes faulty once every MTTF / T detection periods. Otherwise, P(F) can only be gathered by literature, e.g., by using typical fault rates of complex software systems.

This detection approach reveals to be less intrusive that traditional techniques, such as those based on heartbeat, which also require extra code to be written at application level and can fail in the case of multithreaded applications. Additionally, the proposed approach is able to exploit OS information which would be not available if remote detection were performed: as for example, it allows discerning the nature of a process stuck (e.g., deadlock or I/O waiting).

Monitors

The detection system has been implemented to be compliant with a POSIX operating system. In particular, we developed it under the Linux OS, and the following monitors have been implemented for controlling the detection parameters:

Time-Related Monitors

- Waiting time on semaphores. The delay between time in which a task (a thread in the Linux jargon) requests for a semaphore and the time the semaphore is actually acquired is measured, for each semaphore and task. An exceeded timeout can be symptom of a deadlock between the threads in a process, or between several processes on the same node.

- Holding time on semaphores. The delay between the time in which the task has acquired a semaphore and the time the semaphore is released is measured for each semaphore and task. An exceeded timeout can be due to a process blocked within a critical section.

- Task schedulation timeout. The delay between the preemption of a task (e.g., when its time slice is exhausted and the CPU is granted to another task), and the next schedulation of the same task is measured for each task. This way, blocked tasks due to indefinite wait can be detected. For example, the block can be due to a fault within the task or to the stall of the overall application (hence not only to deadlocks).
- Send/receive timeout on a socket. The delay between two consecutive packets sent on a given socket (both from and to the monitored task) is measured, for each task and socket. This allows detecting stop and omission error of a given task.

Signals Related Monitors

- **UNIX System Calls, UNIX Signals:** Applications use system calls to forward requests to the OS (e.g., access to hardware devices, process communication, etc.). In UNIX systems, each system call can return a given set of codes which reflect exceptions when the system call exits prematurely. Error codes may be both due to hardware faults and to application misbehaviors (e.g., unavailable file or socket is accessed). Similarly, signals are used by the OS to notify exceptional events which are not related to a system call (e.g., memory denied memory access).
- **Task Lifecycle:** The allocation and the termination of a task and its descendants are monitored. In fact, when a task terminates, either voluntarily or forcedly, it is deallocated by the OS, and an error code is returned to the parent process; a common rule is to return a non null code in if there is an error.

Throughput Monitor

- **I/O Throughput:** This monitor takes into account performance failures which may affect the application. In fact, when the application is running in degraded mode (e.g., due to resource exhaustion or overloading), it can be observed an anomalous amount of data (either too low or too high) produced or consumed by the running tasks. In order to keep the overhead low, we considered a simple detection algorithm based on upper and lower bounds for the I/O transfer rate. Bytes read from and written to disks, as well as bytes to and from the network devices were taken into account. Disk and network operations (both in input and output) within the kernel were probed, and the amount of bytes transferred within a second is sampled periodically (we refer to a sample as $X(t)$). The bounds applied to each metric have to be chosen conservatively (i.e., out-of-bound samples are infrequent during normal operation), in order to reduce the amount of false positives. A reasonable way to choose the bounds is to profile the task for a long time period, and to establish the bounds on first-order statistics (i.e., mean and standard deviation) of I/O samples. In this case, the detection algorithm can be described as follows:

$$y = \begin{cases} 1 & \text{if } X(t) > m_X \text{ and } |X(t) - m_X| > k^+ \sigma_X \\ 1 & \text{if } X(t) < m_X \text{ and } |X(t) - m_X| < k^- \sigma_X \\ 0 & \text{otherwise} \end{cases}$$

were m_X and σ_X are the mean and the standard deviation of the profiled samples during the training phase, k^+ and k^- are constants preliminarily set by the user (greater constants will lead to more conservative bounds). In order to take into account bursty and idle periods, a threshold C is chosen such that an error log entry is produced only if C consecutive out-of-bound samples occurs; C can be set to the maximum length of bursty or idle periods occurred during the training phase.

Monitors, which are summarized in Table 1, have been implemented by means of dynamic probing: the execution flow of the OS is interrupted when specific instructions are executed (similarly to breakpoints in debuggers), and ad-hoc routines are invoked to collect data about the execution (i.e., to analyze OS resource usage by monitored applications). Note that dynamic probing was only used for measurement and detection purposes, and no attempt is made to modify kernel and processes execution.

Detection Features for Location

Monitored data have been translated into a vector of real numbers (*features*) in order to be exploited by the location classifier. OS features are provided to the location classifier in order to provide it with insights into the alarms triggered by the detection. This is to allow the discrimination between false positives (i.e., *SE*) and actual faults. Features can be both binary (e.g., they represent the occurrence of an event, like an error of a system call) and real values (e.g., statistics about timeouts within the system, like tasks schedulation times within a DU). Selected features are summarized in Table 2.

LOCATION AND RECOVERY

The machine learning paradigm underlies the location phase in the form of classification. This approach has been used in several works trying to solve different problems, e.g., works focusing on document classification (Manevitz & Yousef, 2002; Jagadeesh, Bose, & Srinivasan, 2005) or aiming to find latent errors in software programs (Brun & Ernst, 2004). The location classifier has been trained in a supervised way, by the means of the pseudo-algorithm in Figure 6.

The basic idea is to associate recovery actions to each experienced fault, thus keeping the classifier aware of the most suitable recovery action to start in the case of actual faults. In fact, for each DU in the system, injected faults are added to the training set, if unknown. This way, a base knowledge is built by exploiting human insights.

Support Vector Machines (SVM) has been used for performing classification. The high-performance algorithm they rely on has been commonly used across a wide range of text classification problems, and they demonstrate to perform effectively for handling large datasets (Joachims, 1998).

SVM classifiers have been mainly introduced to the aim of solving binary problems, where the class label can take only two different values, and which can be solved by discriminating the decision boundary between the two classes. However, real world problems often require to take more complex decisions, i.e., to discriminate among more than two classes, hence SVM have been extended for handling multi-class problems. Multi-Class SVMs (MCSVMs), can be achieved in two ways: (i) by combining several standard, one-class, SVM classifiers, and (ii) by formulating a single optimization criteria for the whole set of available data. The basic idea underlying the SVM classification is to find the maximum margin hyperplane which provides the maximum margin among the classes. For non-linearly separable problems, the original data are projected into a certain high dimensional Euclidean space by means of a kernel function (K). Classification results depend on the proper choice of the kernel function; the (gaussian) Radial Basis Function is a commonly used kernel function. Furthermore, in their original formulation, they do not provide any estimation of their classification confidence; hence they do not allow to leverage any a-priori information which, if available, can be crucial to integrate into the classification process to yield reliable results. A probabilistic SVM variant has been developed to face this issue, even for multi-

Table 1. Monitors running on the Linux Operating System for fault detection

Monitor	Triggering condition	Parameters	Domain
UNIX system calls	An error code is returned	Window length	Syscalls × ErrCodes
UNIX signals	A signal is received by the task	Window length	Signals
Task schedulation timeout	Timeout exceeded (since the task is pre-empted)	Timeout value	$[0, \infty]$
Waiting time on semaphores	Timeout exceeded (since the task begins to wait)	Timeout value	$[0, \infty]$
Holding time in critical sections	Timeout exceeded (since the task acquires a lock)	Timeout value	$[0, \infty]$
Task lifecycle	Task allocation or termination	Window length	Lifecycle event
I/O throughput	Bound exceeded for C consecutive samples	Threshold C	$[0, \infty]$
Send/receive timeout on a socket	Timeout exceeded (since a packet is sent over a socket)	Timeout value	$[0, \infty]$

class problems (MPSVM). It is able to provide a probability value indicating at what extent a given sample belongs to a class; hence, its output is in fact a vector of probabilities whose length equals the number of classes. A formal and thorough discussion about SVM mathematical basis is beyond the scope of this paper. The interested reader can exploit a substantial literature (e.g., Joachims, 1998) can be pursued for an in-depth description.

In this work we use MPSVM variant and we leverage output probabilities to properly diag-

nose Unknown Faults (see section III), as well as to unmask detection of false positives (i.e., SUSPECTED ERRORS in section III). More precisely, we introduce a notion of confidence, C, which is in fact the maximum element of the output probability vector provided by the classifier. A fault is claimed unknown if C is less than a given threshold, t. As for suspected errors, a special class of faults, "No Fault", has been introduced: if the classifier is confident that a given fault belongs to this class, (i.e., $C \geq t$), a suspected

Table 2. Features gathered by OS monitors

Monitor	Number of features	Description
UNIX system calls	1141	For each pair (syscall, error code), there is a binary feature (it is 1 if the pair occurred, 0 otherwise)
UNIX signals	32	For each signal, there is a binary feature (it is 1 if the signal occurred, 0 otherwise)
Task schedulation timeout	4	The mean, the standard deviation, the minimum, and the maximum waiting time for schedulation of DU's tasks
Waiting time on semaphores	4	The mean, the standard deviation, the minimum, and the maximum waiting time for a semaphore of DU's tasks
Holding time in critical sections	4	The mean, the standard deviation, the minimum, and the maximum holding time for a semaphore of DU's tasks
Task lifecycle	2	Binary features representing the occurrence of tasks newly allocated or deallocated, respectively
I/O throughput	1	Binary feature (it is 1 if the throughput exceeded a bound, 0 otherwise)
Send/receive timeout on a socket	2*4*number of nodes	For each node in the system, the mean, the standard deviation, the minimum, and the maximum time since last packet sent over sockets to that node, both in input and in output

Figure 6. Supervised training of the location classifier

```
FOR each node i
      FOR all the processes j running on i
            FOR each fault location k into the code of (i,j)
                  failure= do_injection(fault,k,i,j)
            //do the injection , wait for a while then analyze failed processes
                  IF (failure ==UNKNOWN)    {
                        ADD fault to the set of KNOWN faults
                        ASSOCIATE recovery mean to the injected fault
                  ENDIF
                  COLLECT data from detector related to the last D seconds
                     CREATE the entry (detector_ouput, failure)
                  ADD the entry to the training set
            ENDFOR
      ENDFOR
   ENDFOR

   FOR each collected entry
         do_supervised_training(classifier)
   ENDFOR
```

error is stated. The monitor which triggered the alarm is retrained in this case, by modifying the joint probability distributions in the Bayes' rule. Additionally, no recovery action has to be initiated. Of course, the choice of t impacts on the diagnosis quality, hence we performed a sensitivity analysis, as it will be detailed in the next section. Figure 7 shows diagnosis response with respect to the location output.

EXPERIMENTAL FRAMEWORK AND RESULTS

Case Study Introduction

We evaluate the proposed *DLR* approach on a real case study from the Air Traffic Control (ATC) domain, within the framework of an industrial partnership with Finmeccanica group (COSMIC project, http://www.cosmiclab.it). The case study consists of a complex distributed application for Flight Data Processing. It is in charge of processing aircrafts data produced by Radar Track Generators, by updating the contents of Flight Data Plans (FDPs), and distributing them to flight controllers. The overall (simplified) architecture is depicted in Figure 8; it is based on CARDAMOM (http://cardamom.objectweb.org), i.e., an open-source

CORBA middleware, for mission and safety critical applications which is compliant with OMG FT CORBA specifications. Furthermore, it makes use of OTS software items, such as the Data Distribution Service (DDS) implementation provided by RTI (http://www.rti.com) for publish-subscribe communication among components, and the ACE orb (http://www.theaceorb.com) on which CARDAMOM relies. The architecture is made up of several components:

- **Facade Component**, i.e., the interface between the clients (e.g., the flight controller console) and the rest of the system (conforming to the Facade GoF design pattern); it provides a remote object API for the atomic addition, removal, and update of FDPs. The Facade is replicated according to the warm-passive replication schema. It stores the FDPs along with a lock table for FDPs access serialization.
- **Processing Server:** It is in charge of processing FDPs on demand, by taking into account information from the Correlation Component and the FDPs published on the internal DDS. This component is replicated three times on different nodes, and FDP operations are balanced among servers with a round-robin policy.

Figure 7. Diagnosis response with respect to location output

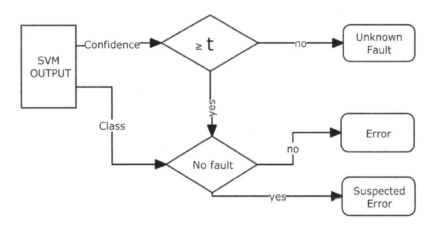

Figure 8. Case study architecture

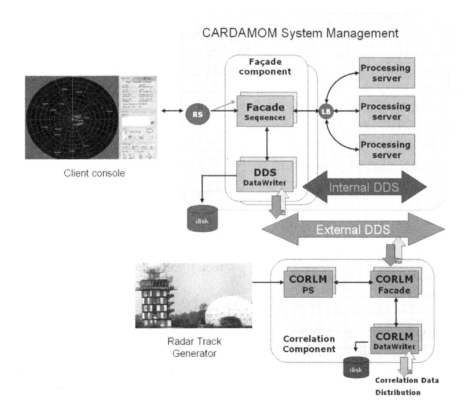

- **Correlation Component:** Which collects flight tracks generated by radars, and associates them to FDPs, by means of Correlation Managers (CORLM in Figure 8).

The workload generates requests to the Facade component, both for flight tracks and FDP updates, in a random way and at a predefined average rate.

Objectives

Conducted experiments aim to demonstrate that:

- The detection approach is able to exploit several low-overhead and inaccurate monitors, by keeping low the false positive rate and the detection latency as well.
- The proposed location and recovery modules are able to correctly locate the root cause of a known fault within the system, and to trigger the proper recovery action in an *on-line* manner.
- The implemented DLR framework is able to partially discover unknown faults within the system. This is useful to trigger off-line maintenance (e.g., by alerting a human operator).

Evaluation Metrics

According to Cardenas, Baras, and Seamon (2006), the following quality metrics have been used to evaluate detection approaches:

- **Coverage:** The conditional probability that, if there is a fault, it will detected. It is estimated by the ratio between the number of detected faults and the number of injected faults.
- **False Positive Rate:** The conditional probability that, if there is not a fault, an alarm will be issued. It is estimated by the ratio

between the number of false alarms and the number of normal events monitored.

- **Latency:** The time between the execution of the fault-injected code, and the time of detection; it is an upper bound of the time between fault activation and the time of detection.
- **Overhead:** We consider the average execution time of remote methods implemented in the Facade remote object; in particular, we focus on the less and the most costly methods, in terms of execution time (respectively, *update_callback*, and *request_return*).

According to (Sebastiani, 2002; Kim, Whitethead, & Zhang, 2008), the following metrics have been used to evaluate the location engine:

- **Accuracy:** The percentage of faults which are classified correctly, with respect to all activated faults. Letting A and B be two classes, it can be expressed as:

$$A = \frac{TP_A + TP_B}{TP_A + FP_A + TP_B + FP_B}$$

- **Precision:** This metric is referred to individual classes; it represents the conditional probability that, if a fault is classified as belonging to class A, the decision is correct. It can be expressed as:

$$P = \frac{TP_A}{TP_A + FP_A}$$

- **Recall:** This metric is referred to individual classes; it represents the conditional probability that, if a fault belongs to class A, the classifier decides for A.

$$R = \frac{TP_A}{TP_A + FN_A}$$

In the previous equations, the quantities TPA, FPA and FNA represent, respectively, the number of True Positives (i.e., the samples of A are classified as A), False Positives (i.e., the samples not of A are classified as A), and False Negatives (i.e., the samples of A are not classified as A).

Faultload

In order to evaluate the proposed fault detection and location techniques, we designed a realistic faultload based on the field data study conducted by Duraes and Madeira (2006). Faults have been injected in the source code of application-level components (i.e., the Facade and the processing servers), using the most common fault operators. Injected faults are detailed in Table 3.

Fault types listed in the table are representative of the most common mistakes made by programmers. In particular, according to the Orthogonal Defect Classification, faults can be characterized by the change in the code that is necessary to correct it. Therefore, in order to emulate a software fault, we have to choose an adequate source code location, which is similar to ones containing faults from the field. Faults operators in (Duraes & Madeira, 2006) describe the rules to locate representative fault locations within source code. The operators were applied to components according to software complexity metrics; in order to choice the source locations containing the most of residual faults (Moraes, Duraes, Barbosa, Martins, & Madeira, 2007). The most complex target components, in term of Lines Of Code (LOCs) and cyclomatic complexity, turned out to be the C++ classes implementing the Facade and Processing Server remote objects; we have injected, respectively, 56 and 16 source-code faults in them.

Before each fault injection campaign, source-code faults are randomly divided in two distinct sets, namely training set and test set. These are characterized by the same size, and the same number of source-code faults. Training sets are used to setup the detection and location techniques, and test sets are used to evaluate their effectiveness. Each fault injection experiment encompasses only one source-code fault at a time.

Table 3. Source-code faults injected in the case study application

ODC DEFECT TYPE	FAULT NATURE	FAULT TYPE	#
Assignment (63.89%)	MISSING	MVIV - Missing Variable Initialization using a Value	8
		MVAV - Missing Variable Assignment using a Value	5
		MVAE - Missing Variable Assignment using an Expression	5
	WRONG	MVAV - Wrong Value Assigned to Variable	26
	EXTRANEOUS	EVAV - Extraneous Variable Assignment using another Variable	2
Checking (6.94%)	MISSING	MIA - Missing IF construct Around statement	2
	WRONG	WLEC - Wrong logical expression used as branch condition	3
Interface (4.17%)	MISSING	MLPA - Missing small and Localized Part of the Algorithm	2
	WRONG	WPFV - Wrong variable used in Parameter of Function Call	1
Algorithm (20.83%)	MISSING	MFC - Missing Function Call	13
		MIEB - Missing IF construct plus statement plus ELSE Before statement	1
		MIFS - Missing IF construct plus statement	1
Function (4.17%)	MISSING	MFCT - Missing Functionality	2
	WRONG	WALL - Wrong Algorithm (Large modifications)	1
Total			72

Adopted Testbed

We used a cluster machine made up of 128 nodes. The system deployment consists of 9 machines (two Facade replicas, one for the CARDAMOM FT service, one for Load Balancing Service, three for the FDP processing servers, and 2 nodes are allocated to the Client and to CORLM component, respectively) wired by Gigabit LAN. In order to have more reliable results, and not be biased by hardware errors, we partitioned the cluster in 10 LANs. Thus, each experiment was launched on the 10 partions, simultaneously. Results are then filtered and averaged. The hardware configuration of testing machines is made up of 2 Xeon Hyper-Threaded 2.8GHz CPUs, 3.6GB of physical memory, and a Gigabit Ethernet interface; machines are interconnected by a 56 Gbps switch, and they are equipped with the Linux OS with kernel v.2.6.25.

DLR in the Case Study

The DLR approach was applied to the considered case study, by defining the features and the classes used for fault diagnosis. In particular, the binaries and the libraries of both the application and OTS libraries (e.g., CARDAMOM, TAO) were inspected to extract potential error messages produced by them (using the *strings* UNIX utility). Several error messages were collected, and a dictionary of words was build on them. The total amount of features from all the monitored DUs and logs was 17171 (see Table 4).

The location classifier was trained using fault injection, and fault classes were identified using the proposed approach (see Table 5). For each class, the root cause is represented by the component in which the fault was injected during the training phase. A proper recovery mean has been associated to each fault class.

Table 4. Features used for diagnosis in the case study application

Number of log file types	8
Number of monitored log files	16
Number of OTS libraries	87
Number of potential log messages	7691
Number of unique tokens within log messages	6043
Number of application keywords	33
Monitored processes by the OS	Façade, 3 Servers
Number of OS features (per process)	1250
Total amount of features	17171

Measurements

Detection

As a basis for comparison, we first evaluated the performance of individual monitors. For each monitor, a sensitivity analysis has been made, letting parameter's value of each monitor vary within the range [1s, 4s] (see Table 1). The best values for all detectors, with respect to the Facade and Server DUs respectively, are shown in Table 6. Different monitors achieve different performances in terms of coverage, since they are suited for different failure modes; actually, monitors are unable to achieve full coverage, except for the *SOCKET* monitor. Furthermore, performances vary with respect to the considered DU. As for example, in the case of the processing server, only crashes (i.e., class 3 in Table 5) have been observed, hence no faults have been identified by monitors controlling blocking conditions (e.g., wait for a semaphore). The reason for which all the monitors experience the same mean latency value, is that they have been triggered all together after the abortion of the processing server DU.

Several monitors provided a small number of false positives, even if there were monitors which provided an unacceptably high false alarm rate.

Table 5. Diagnosis fault classes

	FAULT TYPE	FAULT LOCATION	RECOVERY
Class 0	No fault	None	The system is correctly working.
Class 1	Crash	Façade	Activate the backup replica; a new backup replica is activated.
Class 2	Passive hang	Façade	Free all resources locked by semaphores, and kill the pre-empted transaction. The correctness of this recovery is due to the specific application properties (e.g., the FDP will be correctly updated by the next update operation); another recovery mean would be to kill the hung Façade and treat it as a crashed Façade.
Class 3	Crash	Server	Reboot the server process; add it to the load balanced group.
Class 4	Passive hang (at start time)	Façade	Reboot the whole application. The application start may fail because of transient faults, then the reboot may succeed on the second try. If the application still does not start, human intervention is requested.

For this reason, it is important to filter false positives in order to include those monitors within the system (this is useful to increase the amount of covered faults, and to deliver more information to the location phase).

Table 7 shows the performances achieved by the joint detection algorithm. It can be seen that the joint detector is able to achieve the full coverage of all injected faults, while keeping low the false positive rate (it is comparable to the best rates in Table 6). Another benefit given by the joint detection is the much lower latency: in fact, when one of the individual monitors produce an anomalous value, the other detectors are immediately inspected for anomalies, providing a lower mean detection time.

Finally, the overhead of continuous monitoring DUs at the O.S. level has been measured, by varying the request rate from the client; Figure 9 and Figure 10 show the execution time observed with and without monitors. It should be noted that the overhead was lower that 10% in every case, even during most intensive workload periods.

Location

We evaluated the performance of the location phase with respect to both known faults (i.e., faults similar to ones observed during the training

phase) and unknown faults (i.e., faults completely different than all known ones). First, we excluded faults belonging to class 4 from the training set, and evaluated location capability with respect to the remaining (known) classes, using a low confidence level ($C = 0.9$); in all the cases, the location was able to identify the correct fault class. Moreover, the location was able to identify all false positives produced by detection during faulty-free execution.

Next, faults belonging to class 4 were used for testing location; results are shown in Table 8. It is shown that, although all known faults are correctly classified for $C = 0.9$, only a small amount of unknown faults were identified (represented by the Recall measure for unknown faults); in the most of cases, the locator wrongly classified an unknown fault as a known one. Therefore, we made a sensitivity analysis on the confidence level C in order to discover the confidence level needed for the correct identification of unknown faults. It should be noted that an increase in the required confidence level for location, reduces the amount of known faults correctly identified; therefore, human intervention could be required even for known (but not trustfully classified) faults. Nevertheless, it can be noted that, by increasing the confidence level, a better trade-off between identification of known and unknown faults can

Table 6. Coverage, false positive rate, and latency provided by the individual detectors for the Façade DU

Detector	Parameter	Coverage	False positive rate	Mean Latency (ms)
UNIX semaphores hold timeout	4 s	64.5%	36.08%	1965.65
UNIX semaphores wait timeout	2 s	67.7%	1.7%	521.18
Pthread mutexes hold timeout	4 s	64.5%	4.01%	469.51
Pthread mutexes wait timeout	-	0%	0%	-
Schedulation threshold	4 s	74.1%	3.25%	1912.22
Syscall error codes	1 s	45.1%	0.6%	768.97
Process exit	1 s	45.1%	0%	830.64
Signals	1 s	45.1%	0%	816.57
Task lifecycle	1 s	35.4%	0.05%	375.7
I/O throughput network input	3 s	77.3%	0.4%	4476.67
I/O throughput network output	3 s	77.3%	0.2%	2986.4
I/O throughput disk reads	3 s	70.9%	0.4%	4930
I/O throughput disk writes	2 s	67.6%	0.05%	6168.57
Sockets	4 s	100%	3.47%	469.58
Detector	*Parameter*	*Coverage*	*False positive rate*	*Mean Latency (ms)*
UNIX semaphores hold timeout	2 s	0%	3.61%	-
UNIX semaphores wait timeout	2 s	0%	2.28%	-
Pthread mutexes hold timeout	2 s	0%	4.44%	-
Pthread mutexes wait timeout	-	0%	0%	-
Schedulation threshold	1 s	0%	3.25%	-
Syscall error codes	1 s	100%	0.98%	522.5
Process exit	1 s	100%	0.005%	522.5
Signals	1 s	100%	0.005%	522.5
Task lifecycle	1 s	100%	0.22%	522.5
I/O throughput network input	3 s	100%	0.49%	522.5
I/O throughput network output	3 s	100%	87.35%	522.5
I/O throughput disk reads	3 s	100%	79.31%	522.5
I/O throughput disk writes	3 s	100%	77.77%	522.5
Sockets	2 s	100%	3.14%	522.5

Table 7. Coverage, accuracy, and latency provided by the joint detection approach

	Façade	Server
Coverage	100%	100%
False positive rate	4.85%	6.86%
Mean Latency	100.26±135.76 ms	165.67±122.43 ms

Figure 9. Overhead imposed to the execution of Façade's "update_callback" method

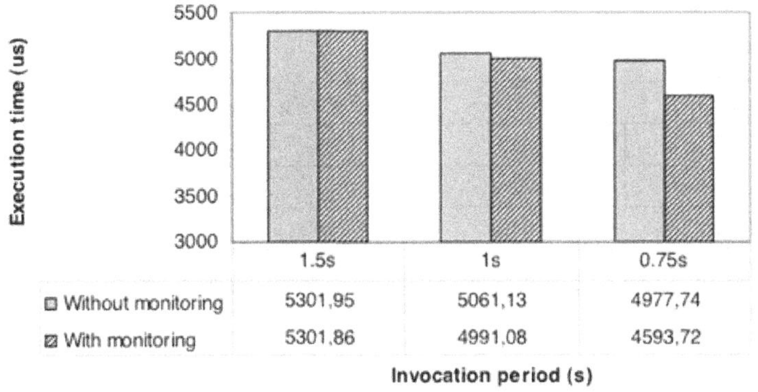

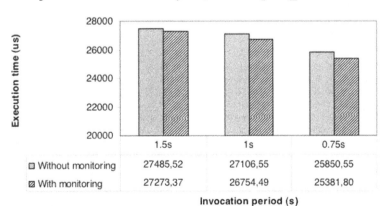

be achieved: a confidence level C = 0.99 or C = 0.995 still provides fully correct known fault classification, with a higher amount of unknown faults identified.

After that, we included in the training set half the samples of class 4, becoming a known fault. Results with the respect to the confidence level are shown in Table 10; known fault classification is still very high for more demanding confidence levels (i.e., C = 0.9, C = 0.99) (Table 9).

In Table 10, the mean time for detection data collection and classification are shown. It can been seen than the total amount of time required to diagnose a fault (the sum of mean detection, collection, and location times on the average) is about 1.2 seconds, which is reasonable for a large class of critical COTS-based systems.

Finally, Figure 11 shows the (cumulative) amount of false positives produced by joint detection during a long period of time. The location has been configured to retrain the detector which erroneously triggered the location, by updating the joint probability distribution $P(a \mid \neg F)$. This produced a dramatic decrease of the false positives rate after less than an hour of execution, by filtering most common false positive patterns occurring during the detection phase.

RELATED WORK

The issue of diagnosis is being faced since a long time, maybe since computers came. The first attempt to formalize the problem is due to Preparata,

Figure 10. Overhead imposed to the execution of Façade's "request_return" method

Table 8. Classification diagnosis evaluation, when deliberately excluding class 4 from the training (UNKNOWN). When a fault was classified as KNOWN, in all cases it was also correctly classified with respect to Table 5

Confidence	ACCURACY	P(KNOWN)	R(KNOWN)	P(UNKNOWN)	R(UNKNOWN)
0.9	60%	59.09%	100%	100%	5.26%
0.99	75.56%	70.27%	100%	100%	42.11%
0.995	77.78%	73.52%	96.15%	90.91%	52.63%
0.999	75.56%	80%	76.92%	70%	73.68%
0.9999	42.22%	n.a.	0%	42.22%	100%

Table 9. Classification diagnosis evaluation, when including all 5 classes in the training. When a fault was classified as KNOWN, in all cases it was also correctly classified with respect to Table 5

Confidence	ACCURACY
0.9	100%
0.99	94.29%
0.995	94.29%
0.999	71.43%
0.9999	25.71%

Table 10. Time measurements for the location phase

Mean time for data collection	84.4 ± 115.11 ms
Mean time for location	917.14 ± 23.63 ms

Figure 11. Cumulative number of false positives during time, using the location output to retrain detection joint probabilities

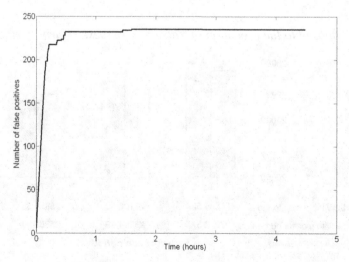

Metze, and Chien (1967) which introduced system level diagnosis. The model they proposed in 1967 (also known as the PMC model) assumed the system to be made up of several units which test one another, and test results are leveraged to diagnose faulty units. Several extensions to this model have been proposed, even recently (e.g., Vaidya & Pradham, 1994, where the safe system level diagnosis has been proposed).

In the last decade or so, there has being an increasing work focusing on diagnosis in order to face the problem by several perspectives and by using quite different techniques. For this reason, we tried to leverage existing solutions to similar problems, as well as to use approaches close to ours which have been rather used to face different issues.

Similar Approaches to Similar Problems (SASP)

The goal of identifying automatically the root cause of a failure is pursued in Yuan et al. (2006). Authors propose a trace-based problem diagnosis methodology, which relies on the trace of low level system behaviors to deduce problems of computer systems. Transient events occurring in the system (e.g., system calls, I/O requests, call stacks, context switches) are traced in order to (i) identify the correlations between system behaviors and known problems and (ii), use the learned knowledge to solve new (i.e., not known) problems. These goals are achieved by means of statistical learning techniques, based on SVMs, similarly to our work. The ultimate aim that authors want to pursue is to make the problem identification fully automatic, thus eliminating human involvement. We have a different goal, in that we also aim to trigger recovery actions. Furthermore, the symptom of the problem needs to be reproduced before the root cause detection.

A decision tree based approach is presented in Zheng, Lloyd, and Brewer (2004) to diagnose problems in Large Internet Services. Similarly to what we do in this work, runtime properties of the system (they record clients' requests) is monitored; automated machine learning and data mining techniques are used to identify the causes of failures. The proposed approach is evaluated by measuring precision and recall, similarly to what we do for evaluating diagnosis quality. However, our work differs from this one for what concerns with detection. In fact, detection is not encompassed in Zheng, Lloyd, and Brewer (2004): authors assume problems to have been already detected and they only concentrate on identifying the root cause, in order to trigger a fast recovery.

Similar Approaches to Different Problems (SADP)

Podgurski et al. (2003) proposes an automated support for classifying reported software failures in order to facilitate the diagnosing of their root causes. The authors use a classification strategy which makes us of supervised and unsupervised pattern classification, as we do for location and detection respectively. Additionally, they also concentrate on the importance of features selection and extraction, as we do. However, the classification performed in this work aims to group failures which are due to the same cause and it is conceived as a mean for helping actual diagnosis. Conversely, we actually perform diagnosis by means of classification.

A very recent work which uses a machine learning approach based on SVM classification is Kim, Whitehead, and Zhang (2008). Its main goal is to predict the presence of latent software bugs in software changes (change classification). In particular, a machine learning SVM classifier is used to determine whether a new software change is more similar to prior buggy changes or clean changes. In this manner, change classification predicts the existence of bugs in software changes. We have in common with this work the classification problem, its formulation and the process of feature extraction.

Machine learning approach has also been used in Brun and Ernst (2004) for identifying program properties that indicate errors. The technique generates machine learning models of program properties known to result from errors, and applies these models to program properties of user-written code to classify the properties that may lead the user to errors. SVMs and decision trees are used for classification. The effectiveness of the proposed approach has been demonstrated with respect to C, C++, and Java programs. However it requires human labor to find the bugs, and the process is not fully automatic.

Aguilera, Mogul, Wiener, Reynolds, and Muthitacharoen (2003) address the problem of locating performance bottlenecks in a distributed system with only internode communication traces. They infer the causal paths through multi-tier distributed applications from message level traces, in order to detect the node causing extraordinary delay. They share with us the great attention which is paid to the presence of OTS items, as well as the fact that the approach requires no modifications to applications and middleware. The major differences with our work are (i) the fact that they pay more attention to performance rather than on faults and (ii), the fact that they perform off-line diagnosis of the problem.

As for Bayesian estimation, a worth noting work to be referred is Chang, Lander, Lu, and Wells (1993) which addresses system diagnosis problems. It refers to comparison-based system analysis to deal with incomplete test coverage, unknown numbers of faulty units, and non-permanent faults. However, only one type of monitor is used in that work and also recovery is not encompassed.

Different Approaches to Similar Problems (DASP)

Closely related to our work in goals are Joshi, Hiltunen, Sanders, and Schlichting (2005), which cares about automatic model driven recovery in distributed systems. Similarly to what we do, au-

thors exploit a set of a limited coverage monitors whose output are combined in a certain way prior to trigger recovery actions. Additionally they also have a Bayesian Faults Diagnosis engine in charge of locating the problem, as well as to pilot a recovery controller that can choose recovery actions based on several optimization criteria. Similarly to the approach we propose, the approach proposed in Joshi, Hiltunen, Sanders, and Schlichting (2005) is able to detect whether a problem is beyond its diagnosis and recovery capabilities, and thus to determine when a human operator needs to be alerted. Despite of these common purposes, we take an opposite perspective in that we do not follow a model based approach since modeling the complex software systems we are addressing could be too difficult and inaccurate. Additionally, our work is different in several points. First, they propose incremental recovery actions whereas we directly start the best one action able to repair the system. Second, we always use the entire set of "always-on" monitors to detect errors instead of invoking additional monitors when needed. Third, we use fault injection to experimentally prove the effectiveness of the approach rather than for making a comparison with a theoretical optimum.

Khanna, Laguna, Arshad, and Bagchi (2007) face the problem of diagnosis in networked environments made up of black-box entities. This goal is achieved by (i) tracing messages to build a causal dependency structure between the components (ii), by tracing back the causal structure when a failure is detected and (iii), by testing components using diagnostic tests. Runtime observations are used to estimate the parameters that bear on the possibility of error propagation, such as unreliability of links and error masking capabilities. The work aims to provide diagnosis of the faulty entities at runtime in a non-intrusive manner to the application. Differently from this work, we do not build causal structure of the system since we do not make any assumption on the structure of the system itself. The main point in common is the fact that we pursue on-line diagnosis as well.

Brown, Kar, and Keller (2001) defines a methodology for identifying and characterizing dynamic dependencies between system components in distributed application environments, which relies on active perturbation of the system. This is in order to identify dependencies, as well as to compute dependency strengths. Even if discovering system dependencies automatically could be a good way for root cause analysis, it is assumed a deep knowledge of system internals. In particular, authors assume to completely know end-users interaction with the system (they use a well known TPC benchmark). We take the opposite position in that we do not require such a knowledge. Furthermore, the Active Dependency Discovery approach which is defined in that work, reveals to be strongly intrusive and workload dependent.

A further worth referring work is Chen, Kiciman, Fratkin, Fox, and Brewer (2002), where the Pinpoint framework is defined. It employs statistical learning techniques to diagnose failures in a Web farm environment. After the traces with respect to different client requests are collected, data mining algorithms are used to identify the components most relevant to a failure. We share with that work the "learning from system behavior" philosophy. However, there is a difference in goals, since we want to detect and diagnose faults in order to determine the cause of the failure and trigger recovery action. Conversely, Pinpoint aims to recognize which component in a distributed system is more likely to be faulty. Fault injection is used also in Chen, Kiciman, Fratkin, Fox, and Brewer (2002) to prove the effectiveness of the approach. The major limitation of this approach is that (i) it is suitable only for small scale software programs, and (ii) it exhibit a significant logging. We differ from that work in two main points: (i) the Pinpoint framework is designed to work off-line and (ii), it is not a recovery-oriented approach.

Finally, on-site failure diagnosis is faced in Tucek, Lu, Huang, Xanthos, and Zhou (2007). The work aims to capture the failure point and conduct just-in-time failure diagnosis with checkpoint-re-execution system support. Lightweight checkpoints are taken during execution and rolls back are performed to recent checkpoints for diagnosis after a failure has occurred. Delta generation and delta analysis are exploited to speculatively modify the inputs and execution environment to create many similar but successful and failing replays to identify failure-triggering conditions. We discard a similar approach since Heisenbugs can be un-reproducible this way: in fact, their conditions of activation are hard to identify (Grottke & Trivedi, 2007). Furthermore, long time is required (almost five minutes) to complete the process: this can be not tolerable for safety critical systems. Table 11 summarizes the related work.

CONCLUSION

In the context of leveraging the dependability of complex and fault tolerant software systems, the paper advocated the need of recovery oriented software fault diagnosis approach, which integrated detection, location, and recovery in one holistic diagnostic framework. This is different from most of the previous work which has been conducted on software failure diagnosis in the last few years in that target systems, in which we also conducted experiments, are very complex. Thus existing approaches, which require human involvement to discover the bug, are not suitable for field failures for a number of reasons. First of all, it is difficult to reproduce the failure-triggering conditions in house for diagnosis. Second, off-line failure diagnosis cannot provide timely guidance to select the best recovery action, i.e., a recovery action which is tailored for the particular fault that occurred.

The experimental campaign has been conducted in the context of a real-world Air Traffic Control system. Results demonstrated that:

- The detection approach is able to exploit several low-overhead and inaccurate monitors at the OS level, by keeping low the false positive rate and the detection latency as well;
- The proposed location and recovery strategies are able to correctly locate the root cause of a known fault within the system, and to trigger the proper recovery action in an on-line manner;
- The implemented DLR framework is able to partially discover unknown faults within the system. This is useful to trigger off-line maintenance (e.g., by alerting a human operator).

REFERENCES

Aguilera, M. K., Mogul, J. C., Wiener, J. L., Reynolds, P., & Muthitacharoen, A. (2003). Performance Debugging for Distributed Systems of Black Boxes. In *Proceedings of the 19th ACM Symposium on Operating Systems Principles* (pp. 74-89).

Bondavalli, A., Chiaradonna, S., Cotroneo, D., & Romano, L. (2004). Effective Fault Treatment for Improving the Dependability of COTS and Legacy-Based Applications. *IEEE Transactions on Dependable and Secure Computing*, *1*(4), 223–237. doi:10.1109/TDSC.2004.40

Brown, A., Kar, G., & Keller, A. (2001). An Active Approach to Characterizing Dynamic Dependencies for Problem Determination in a Distributed Environment. In *Proceedings of the IEEE/IFIP Symposium on Integrated Network Management* (pp. 377-390).

Brun, Y., & Ernst, M. D. (2004). Finding Latent Code Errors via Machine Learning over Program Executions. In *Proceedings of the 26th Conference on Software Engineering* (pp. 480-490).

Cardenas, A. A., Baras, J. S., & Seamon, K. (2006). A Framework for the Evaluation of Intrusion Detection Systems. In *Proceedings of the IEEE Symposium on Security and Privacy* (pp. 63-77).

Chang, Y., Lander, L. C., Lu, H. S., & Wells, M. T. (1993). Bayesian Analysis for Fault Location in Homogenous Distributed Systems. In *Proceedings of the 12th Symposium on Reliable Distributed Systems* (pp. 44-53).

Chen, M. Y., Kiciman, E., Fratkin, E., Fox, A., & Brewer, E. (2002). Pinpoint: Problem Determination in Large, Dynamic Internet Services. In *Proceedings of the IEEE/IFIP Conference on Dependable Systems and Networks* (pp. 595-604).

Chillarege, R., Bhandari, I., Chaar, J., Halliday, M., Moebus, D., & Ray, B. (1992). Orthogonal Defect Classification-A Concept for In-Process Measurements. *IEEE Transactions on Software Engineering*, *18*(11), 943–956. doi:10.1109/32.177364

Chillarege, R., Biyani, S., & Rosenthal, J. (1995). Measurement of Failure Rate in Widely Distributed Software. In *Proceedings of the 25th Symposium on Fault-Tolerant Computing* (pp. 424-433).

Duraes, J., & Madeira, H. (2006). Emulation of Software Faults: A Field Data Study and a Practical Approach. *IEEE Transactions on Software Engineering*, *32*(11), 849–867. doi:10.1109/TSE.2006.113

Forrest, S., Hofmeyr, S. A., Somayaji, A., & Longstaff, T. A. (1996). A sense of self for Unix processes. In *Proceedings of the IEEE Symposium on Security and Privacy* (pp. 120-128).

Gray, J. (1985). *Why Do Computer Stop and What Can Be Done About It?* (Tech. Rep. No. 85.7). Tandem.

Grottke, M., & Trivedi, K. S. (2007). Fighting Bugs: Remove, Retry, Replicate, and Rejuvenate. *IEEE Computer*, *40*(2), 107–109.

Huang, Y., Jalote, P., & Kintala, C. (1994). Two Techniques for Transient Software Error Recovery. In *Proceedings of the Workshop on Hardware and Software Architectures for Fault Tolerance: Experiences and Perspectives* (pp. 159-170).

Jagadeesh, R. P., Bose, C., & Srinivasan, S. H. (2005). Data Mining Approaches to Software Fault Diagnosis. In *Proceedings of the 15th IEEE Workshop on Research Issues in Data Engineering: Stream Data Mining and Applications* (pp. 45-52).

Joshi, K. R., Hiltunen, M. A., Sanders, W. H., & Schlichting, R. D. (2005). Automatic Model-Driven Recovery in Distributed Systems. In *Proceedings of the 24th IEEE Symposium on Reliable Distributed Systems* (pp. 25-36).

Khanna, G., Laguna, I., Arshad, F. A., & Bagchi, S. (2007). Distributed Diagnosis of Failures in a Three Tier E-Commerce System. In *Proceedings of the 26th IEEE Symposium on Reliable Distributed Systems* (pp. 185-198).

Kim, S., Whitethead, E. J., & Zhang, Y. (2008). Classifying Software Changes: Clean or Buggy? *IEEE Transactions on Software Engineering*, *34*(2), 181–196. doi:10.1109/TSE.2007.70773

Littlewood, B., & Strigini, L. (2000). Software Reliability and Dependability: A Roadmap. In *Proceedings of the ACM Conference on The Future of Software Engineering* (pp. 175–188).

Manevitz, L. M., & Yousef, M. (2002). One-Class SVMs for Document Classification. *Journal of Machine Learning Research*, *2*, 139–154. doi:10.1162/15324430260185574

Moraes, R., Duraes, J., Barbosa, R., Martins, E., & Madeira, H. (2007). Experimental Risk Assessment and Comparison Using Software Fault Injection. In *Proceedings of the 37th IEEE/IFIP Conference on Dependable Systems and Networks* (pp. 512-521).

Podgurski, A., Leon, D., Francis, P., Masri, W., Minch, M., Sun, J., et al. (2003). Automated Support for Classifying Software Failure Reports. In *Proceedings of the 25th Conference on Software Engineering* (pp. 465-475).

Preparata, F. P., Metze, G., & Chien, R. T. (1967). On the Connection Assignment Problem of Diagnosable Systems. *IEEE Transactions on Electronic Computers*, *16*(6), 848–854. doi:10.1109/PGEC.1967.264748

Sebastiani, F. (2002). Machine Learning in Automated Text Categorization. *ACM Computing Surveys*, *34*, 1–47. doi:10.1145/505282.505283

Serafini, M., Bondavalli, A., & Suri, N. (2007). On-Line Diagnosis and Recovery: On the Choice and Impact of Tuning Parameters. *IEEE Transactions on Dependable and Secure Computing*, *4*(4), 295–312. doi:10.1109/TDSC.2007.70210

Sullivan, M., & Chillarege, R. (1991). Software Defects and Their Impact on System Availability - A Study of Field Failures in Operating Systems. In *Proceedings of the 21st Symposium on Fault-Tolerant Computing* (pp. 2-9).

Tucek, J., Lu, S., Huang, C., Xanthos, S., & Zhou, Y. (2007). Triage: Diagnosing Production Run Failures at the User's Site. In *Proceedings of the 21st ACM SIGOPS Symposium on Operating Systems Principles* (pp. 131-144).

Vaidya, N. H., & Pradham, D. K. (1994). Safe System Level Diagnosis. *IEEE Transactions on Computers*, *43*(3), 367–370. doi:10.1109/12.272443

Xu, J., Kalbarczyc, Z., & Iyer, R. K. (1999). Networked Windows NT System Field Data Analysis. In *Proceedings of the Pacific Rim Symposium on Dependable Computing* (pp. 178-185).

Yuan, C., Lao, N., Wen, J. R., Li, J., Zhang, Z., Wang, Y. M., et al. (2006). Automated Known Problem Diagnosis with Event Traces. In *Proceedings of the EuroSys ACM Conference* (pp. 375-388).

Zheng, A. X., Lloyd, J., & Brewer, E. (2004). Failure Diagnosis Using Decision Trees. In *Proceedings of the 1st IEEE Conference on Autonomic Computing* (pp. 36-43).

Chapter 3
Abstract Fault Tolerance:
A Model–Theoretic Approach to Fault Tolerance and Fault Compensation without Error Correction

Leo Marcus
The Aerospace Corporation, USA

ABSTRACT

This paper explores the concept of "pure fault tolerance"--when a system can fulfill its computational goal, even though some of its components do not fulfill theirs. This leads to a natural statement of the composition problem for a very general concept of architecture: to what extent are the properties of a system based on that architecture a function of the properties of the components? The author explores several variations on pure fault tolerance, none of which utilize fault detection or error correction.

1. INTRODUCTION

What to do about "errors" or "faults" is an important concern for the design and operation of computer systems, especially for potential quantum computer implementations.[1] Possible mitigation methods include avoidance, correction, compensation, and tolerance. These often involve fault detection.

This whitepaper deals with the latter two mitigations – compensation and tolerance. We were motivated by the desire to explore any potential benefit in tailoring the kind of fault tolerance (FT) employed in a computation to the specification of the computation and its goal, instead of either trying to make all intermediate steps be error-free, by error correction (EC), irrespective of their "role"; or by adding redundancy and "voting". There are two aspects to this: (1) Some computations may be *inherently* fault tolerant, may have "built-in" redundancy – they will "succeed" even with a certain amount of internal error – certainly any kind of fault tolerant system can be considered to be redundant, since it, or a part of it, in a fault-free

DOI: 10.4018/978-1-4666-2056-8.ch003

environment does more than it absolutely has to in order to achieve its declared goal; (2) Error correction, though needed, may fail, and we then need to evaluate the degree to which the goal of the computation has been achieved despite the uncorrected error.

In this paper we speculate on how several issues related to FT could be formulated "abstractly", "semantically". While practical application is a theoretical possibility, and a hoped-for long term goal, that is not attempted here. We do not deal at all with issues of computability or complexity. Rather, we wish to open the discussion at a level of generality that captures the concepts, with as few restrictions based on presumed practical limitations as possible. This could eventually lead to posing the "right" questions—for example, questions whose answers might make possible rigorous reasoning about the trade-offs between EC and FT, or about system fault-state behavior. We believe it is interesting to abstract an application domain to a high enough level where we can see what general reasoning can be brought to bear, and where the assumptions need to be strengthened in order to get anything "useful".

Our approach yields some questions in model theory, perhaps interesting in their own right.

However, one major stumbling block on the path from theory to practice is the potential difficulty of even knowing (calculating) if a given property is true in a given model. We also do not attempt to answer questions whether any "real systems" (e.g., biological) fit this model, or under what circumstances this would be a good way to *design* real systems.

We are interested in the possibility of eliminating error correction altogether – and in some cases, also error detection – and simply do "pure fault tolerance" (which we abbreviate to PFT). In other words, if the errors (or "faults" – we don't differentiate between those for this paper) are sparse enough, or weak enough, then we can actually tolerate them, and the computation will "succeed" (to a specified greater or lesser degree),

"in the presence" of faults. For example, in the case of a fault tolerant computation, this implies that the fault tolerance will have to be an integral part of the algorithm, tailored for each specification. Another way to state this is that we wish to elevate the fault tolerance to the level of the specification, and not leave it to the "implementation details."

For example, it appears that "standard" quantum algorithms, such as those of Shor and Grover, which rely on quantum error correction for their implementation, would have to be rewritten in a major way in order to incorporate PFT, if that were to be at all possible. For example, there may be a quantum factorization algorithm, different from Shor's, say, which even though it is much less efficient in each run, utilizes true PFT, and therefore, perhaps, the tolerable error threshold will be much higher than the current value, and thus it can actually be built sooner.. In order to approach the conditions for potential use in quantum computation, it seems that certain standard fault tolerance techniques – for example, those involving comparisons of values and voting – cannot be used directly. With a better idea of the potential use of PFT in quantum computation, we could then combine that degree of PFT with EC to get an optimal fault tolerant solution.

We also believe that the so-called "threshold theorems" of quantum computation, which guarantee that error correction will prevail over error proliferation if the error rate is small enough, also have analogs in the PFT paradigm.

The real power of the word "prevail" in the above paragraph is that the *cost* of error correction is vastly overpowered by the *benefit* of the resulting fault tolerant computation. Without taking into account the cost/benefit the problem becomes trivial: simply run a (potentially) infinite number of computations in diagonal fashion and check each "result" as it comes out for correctness. (Apparently, not all quantum algorithms are of this type – in which the answers are efficiently checkable.)

All considerations of errors, rates, correction, and tolerance should be "specification-based", so that we could get a theorem of the form:

Given any specification of the (computable) goal **S**, and specification of the threshold E, there is a PFT architecture/algorithm $\mathbf{A}(E)$ that achieves S. (And if that is not true in general, what are the conditions on S and ε that make it true?)

We consider three potential meanings to FT:

1. If the faults fall within the "fault threshold" (number, type, severity, etc.) the right answer/property is achieved exactly.
2. Depending on the nature of the faults, the answer/property is less precise (fault range on processors/components translates into error range on results/system).
3. Depending on the nature of the faults, the right answer/property is achieved with reduced probability.

This paper lays out a framework in which to consider the broader issues. We work under several general principles (the following "rules of the game"):

1. No Error Detection (whatever happens, happens— although it might be difficult to give a satisfactory definition of what that "really" means semantically or information-theoretically. See Weber (1989).
2. No Error Correction (no "actions" taken to "recover" from faults).
3. Search for a threshold (the amount of bad stuff that can happen, but still the desired result is still obtained).
4. Specification-based (the specification is used to structure the algorithm or model so that it does not need EC).
5. The different varieties of faults tolerated are also part of the specification.
6. Study the interaction between the properties being preserved, the properties allowed to be faulty, and the architecture that makes it all hold together.
7. Need for a threshold theorem that formalizes the intuition that if the quality and quantity of things that can go wrong are limited, then the computation will proceed correctly.

We shall try to factor out all but the most basic elements of PFT. The goal would be to see at what point in the abstraction can we get any leverage at all. This leads to the "model-theoretic fault tolerance" (MTFT) formulation below. MTFT seems to be connected to "architecture-based deduction". In MTFT traditional error rate can be specified by making time an explicit part of the language (or via Temporal Logic). Also, the concept of "input" does necessarily play a role. Therefore, the question of how to measure the "cost" (compared to what?) is not obvious. Likewise, if we allow a "degraded" result (compared to the model in which there are no faults at all), then what is the measure of the benefit – how "close" is the achieved state to the desired state?

2. ERRORS, FAULTS, AND FAULT-TOLERANCE: OVERVIEW AND DEFINITIONS

There are many definitions of the terms error, fault, failure, and fault-tolerance in the literature, going back decades. These definitions vary in degrees of abstractness and precision. Even within the same category of abstractness and precision there are differences. We are not concerned with any fault, *qua fault*, but only its effect – to the extent that can be stated/specified by a formula in some logic. We don't define what an error "is", but prefer to say "a component is *in* error" if it satisfies something different (in particular, "less") than what was expected in the context of a given computation.

The kinds of faults we want to be able to specify abstractly are:

1. A component does not satisfy what is expected.
2. The architecture (links, etc.) is faulty.
3. An element (or component) "disappears" or becomes disconnected (this latter condition can possibly be modeled by saying that elements that have disappeared cannot appear in any non-trivial relation with elements from outside the disconnected component).

It is sometimes useful to categorize the causes of faults: internal (bugs or hardware glitches) or external (environmental or adversarial). The type of remedy can be highly dependent on the cause. For example, very detailed assumptions on the types of errors are necessary to evaluate the efficiency of proposed quantum error correction methods.

In our effort to specify what properties can be preserved with faulty components, and what is the level of "granularity" in a system hierarchy (e.g. computer hardware) at which we are considering faults (either for detecting, measuring, correcting, or tolerating them), we note that there is a trade-off between the intuitive meanings of Error Correction (EC) and Fault Tolerance (FT):

- If EC were perfect, no errors would persist past their immediate context (in time and space), they would not be noticed by the outside world, and there would be no need for FT.
- If FT were perfect there would be no need for EC, because all errors, in all quantities, could be tolerated or compensated for.
- If EC were weak in an error-prone environment, there would be a big need for FT.
- If FT were weak in an error-prone environment, there would be a big need for EC.

An open problem is the development of a method to formalize the cost-benefit trade-off between FT and EC and how to measure the net gain and the net cost as a function of the differ-

ent algorithms being implemented. EC and FT are bound explicitly or implicitly because not all errors can be corrected, or are attempted to be corrected, or should be corrected (e.g. only the more common, cheap, potential damaging ones, etc). So we are always left with the possibility that the computation will have to "cope" with uncorrected errors, i.e., tolerate faults. For example, if up to t independent errors can be corrected in an error-correction "block", then an uncorrectable error will occur if (t+1) independent errors occur in the block before recovery is complete.

The main conceptual difference between Error Correction and Fault-Tolerance is that Error Correction is a computation and Fault-Tolerance is a property (a system "does" error correction, but "is" fault tolerant).

2.1. Fault-Tolerant Architectures and Systems Definitions

In this section we describe our formalism for the role of the architecture, the system, and the underlying components. We believe that this direct semantical approach (as opposed to the more technical "architectural connectors" and "institutions" is sufficient for our purposes.

Definition 1: An architecture is a finite relational structure (or "model") $A = <A, R_1, ..., R_n>$, where A is a finite set and the R_i are relations on A, each of its own arity.[2,3]

An "architecture" will serve as a structure on which we can build systems, where a system is essentially an implementation of an architecture:

Definition 2: A system S built on architecture A is a relational structure formed by substituting finite models at each element of A (with their inner relations intact) and extending the definitions of the previous relations R_i of A on S in some natural way. More formally:

S is a system built on architecture A (above) if
$$S = <S, R^*_1, ..., R^*_n, M_a>_{a \epsilon A}$$

where $M_a = <M_a, R^a_1, ... R^a_n>$ are models ("components", in some language, not necessarily the same language as A), $S = \cup_{a \epsilon A} M_a$, and there are several possible ways to define the R^*_i

1. *("Total")* For all $s_1 \epsilon Ma_1, ..., s_k \epsilon Ma_k$ $S|= R^*_i(s_1, ...s_k)$ if and only if $A |= R_i(a_1,.., a_k)$
2. *("Anchored")* Choose one designated $s^*_a \epsilon M_n$ for each $a \epsilon A$ and define $S|= R^*_i(s^*_{a1}, ...s^*_{ak})$ if and only if $A |= R_i(a_1,.., a_k)$

We write such a system built on A as $A(M_a: a \epsilon A)$.

There are other possible definitions of the inter-component relations. For example, there may be utility in choosing *specific* elements (more than one per component) to serve as the "anchors."

The relation between an architecture and a system built on it is hierarchical, in the sense that any system is an architecture on which lower-level systems can be built. (The hierarchy cannot be extended "up" in a useful manner; not every architecture can, nor is it desirable to, be considered as a system built on a higher level architecture.) This hierarchical approach is necessary for composition (see Section 3) where components become architectures in their own right. Actually, this is one of the main goals for this definition: to facilitate compositional reasoning.

Notice that this definition restricts the class of systems under discussion. In particular, relations between two different components must be derived from the architecture, and cannot be added outside of that framework.

The systems built on a given architecture can change over time. As mentioned above, in order that the architecture/system relation be hierarchical, we make no inherent objective distinction between an architecture and a system, only in the relationship between them; and thus architectures also vary over time and are susceptible to errors.

We require that each transition from S_t to S_{t+1} go from a system built on A_t to a system built on A_{t+1} (whatever that perhaps new architecture is, according to our above definition.) Notice that any architecture *is* a system over itself. Also, every architecture is a system over the architecture consisting of a single point (with the appropriate unary relations). In addition to those two trivial architectures (in which either every element is a component, or there is only one component) there are potentially many more ("intermediate architectures") which form an architecture/system pair with the given architecture.

In any given system, there are different kinds and severities of faults. First we have the possibility that even if a given component of the system is faulty, the "property of interest" will still be true, exactly as if the component were not faulty. A similar situation is that even if the ("intermediate") state is faulty, the computation will still continue to the right answer, as if that intermediate state were not faulty. A more general take on the two previous possibilities is that the state is not exactly true, but "almost", depending on the fault, or the computation continues not exactly as it would otherwise, but "almost", depending on the fault. For any of these varieties of fault-tolerance we need the following definition of the concept of correctness:

Definition 3: Let $A = <A, R_1, ..., R_n>$ be an architecture and let P and $\{P_a: a \epsilon A\}$ be consistent properties (sentences) in the language of A.[4] A is *P-correct with respect to* $\{P_a: a \epsilon A\}$ if for any system S built on A with components M_a, $a \epsilon A$, if $M_a |= P_a$ for all $a \epsilon A$, then $S |= P$.

More concisely, A is *P-correct with respect to* $\{P_a: a \epsilon A\}$, if for all $M_a |= P_a$ for all $a \epsilon A$, it holds that $A(M_a: a \epsilon A)|= P$.

The above means that if S is a system constructed from components C_a built on the architecture A, then S will satisfy the property P if all the components satisfy their respective properties.[5]

Theorem 1: If A is P-correct with respect to $\{P_a: a \varepsilon A\}$, and for all $a \varepsilon A$ M_a is P_a-correct with respect to $\{P^a_b: b \varepsilon M_a\}$, then $A(M_a: a \epsilon A)$ (as an architecture) is P-correct with respect to $\{P^a_b: a \epsilon A, b \varepsilon M_a\}$.

The simplest form of fault-tolerance says that in the above context, P will still be true if at most one of the components is faulty, i.e., does not satisfy its respective property. The natural question is: why one? The answer is the "amount" of fault tolerance should be geared to assumptions about the relation between the speed of computation and the error rate, in applications where speed and rate are the relevant concepts.

Here is a simple prototypical example.

Let us assume the underlying architecture A consists of n nodes, and we desire the system built on A to have the property that there are at least *k(n-1)* elements total. If we embed components at each of the n nodes, each of which has k elements, then the resulting system can have one faulty component and still satisfy the desired condition.

This leads us to the next definition:

Definition 4: Architecture A is P-single-fault-tolerant (SFT) with respect to $\{P_a: a \varepsilon A\}$ if A is P-correct with respect to $\{P_a: a \varepsilon A\}$ and for all $a^* \varepsilon A$, A is P-correct with respect to

$$\{P_a: a \neq a^*\} \cup \{\sim P_{a*}\}.$$

In the language of the preceding example, P is "there are at least *k(n-1)* elements," and each P_a is "there are at least k elements."

Notice that we define what it means for an architecture to be fault-tolerant, not a particular system. The reason for doing this is that we want the same fault tolerance "mechanism" to work for whatever kind of faulty components the different systems (computations) bring. For the duration of this work, a system will refer to a particular computation.

Remark

1. Architecture A is P-SFT with respect to $\{P_a: a \varepsilon A\}$ iff for all $a^* \varepsilon A$ and $M_a \models P_a$ for all $a \neq a^*$, $A(M_a: a \varepsilon A) \models P$.
2. Architecture A is *P-SFT* with respect to $\{P_a: a \varepsilon A\}$ iff for all $a^* \varepsilon A$, A is P-correct with respect to $\{P_a: a \neq a^*\} \cup \{\sim P_{a*}\}$.

The above definition naturally lends itself to generalization to P-n-fault-tolerant where n is any integer. Notice that the above simple example of the number of elements can be generalized to an example of P-n-fault-tolerant, not P-(n+1)-fault-tolerant.

The main type of question a designer of fault-tolerance architectures asks is: given a property (or a specification for a computational task), how to design a fault-tolerant architecture for it. Or, to turn the question around, given an architecture A, what is the strongest property P such that A is P-SFT with respect to some chosen $\{P_a: a \varepsilon A\}$? Note that in order to obtain fault tolerance the components may have to satisfy stronger properties than if fault tolerance were not satisfied.

This highlights the possibility that a definition of fault-tolerance that will eventually yield a threshold theorem must also include the algorithm by which the fault is tolerated, not just the model-theoretic statement of the condition of fault-tolerance.

A slightly less-tolerant version of SFT is when the desired system-wide state property P can be achieved if not all of the components M_a satisfy their conditions, P_a, but at most one of them (any one at a time) satisfies a *specified* less strong condition, say P'$_a$. In other words, if all the components satisfied their properties, P would hold system-wide. But P will also hold if at most satisfies its weaker property. This condition is somewhere between pure fault tolerance and error correction: we must take some remedial action, but not total correction of the error.

Definition 5: Architecture A is P-weakly-singly-fault-tolerant (WSFT) with respect to $\{P_a: a \in A\}$ if A is P-correct with respect to $\{P_a: a \in A\}$ and for all $a \in A$, there is P'_a such that for all $a^* \in A$, A is P-correct with respect to $\{P_a: a \neq a^*\} \cup \{P'_{a^*} \& \sim P_{a^*}\}$.

2.2. Severity of Errors

Let us examine the possible utility of differentiating between the severities of errors, with respect to a given specification. Obviously, there are architectures and specifications for which certain errors are more crucial to the correctness of the result of a computation than others. Depending on the severity or type of the error, it may be more easily detected or corrected, or more easily tolerated without correction. This difference could play a role in the cost-benefit analysis of the error-correction / fault-tolerance trade-off. One could imagine a detailed kind of fault-tolerance condition that handles a different number of occurrences of errors for each of the different "types" of error. The criteria for the choice of architecture would be made based on the "efficiency" of the architecture for computing the desired function and the EC/FT trade-off. Some possible criteria for severity include:

1. The difficulty of detecting the error (This means that error detection will "cost" more, or go undetected.)
2. The difficulty of correcting the error, once detected (or not) (This has approximately the same impact as the previous point. However, it may be easily tolerated.)
3. The difficulty of tolerating the error, whether or not detected. (By this last point we mean

how far the system is from its intended specification, if the error goes uncorrected.)
4. "Distance" of error from specification

One reason for the difficulty in formalizing the intuitive idea of severity is that an error that is far away from the component's desired property, or even has damaging "side-effects", may still be more easily corrected than an error which is superficially more benign, but whose effects may be more long-lasting. An architecture designer must carefully evaluate the relation between severity of fault (uncorrected error) and the "cost" of the mechanism to tolerate it.

2.3. Passive Fault Tolerance vs. Active Fault Tolerance

What we have discussed so far is "passive" fault-tolerance – the system operates correctly, to a greater or lesser degree, with the fault, without having to make any dynamic adjustments. There is the possibility of an "active" fault-tolerance, which is still different than error correction. It is more like error compensation. The error is not corrected, but other parts of the system, even in which there was no error, change in response to the fault in order that the system's original specification be achieved.

This implies (perhaps) some degree of error detection, but the architecture does not change.

Definition 6: A is P-single-fault-compensating (SFC) if for all $a^* \in A$ and property P_{a^*} there exist consistent P_a, $a \neq a^*$ such that if $M_a \models P_a$, then $A(M_a: a \in A) \models P$.

In other words, no matter how badly one component might behave, we can, in theory, adjust the other components to compensate, and produce P system-wide.

3. COMPOSITION THEOREM FOR FT

We don't know how to use these methods to construct automatically a fault tolerant architecture for some given predicates, nor "improve" a non-fault tolerant system to a fault tolerant one. But we are able to build larger fault tolerant systems based on smaller ones, and *derive* FT properties of the architecture or system based on the FT properties of the components of that architecture or system. For example:

Theorem 2: If A is P-SFT with respect to $\{P_a: a \varepsilon A\}$, and for all $a \varepsilon A$, M_a (as an architecture) is P_a-SFT with respect to $\{P^a_b: b \varepsilon M_a\}$, then $A(M_a: a \epsilon A)$ (as an architecture) is P-2-Fault-Tolerant with respect to $\{P^a_b: a \epsilon A, b \varepsilon M_a\}$.

*   **Proof:** Assume there are two errors in the lower level predicates. If they are in different components of $A(M_a: a \epsilon A)$, then since each one is single fault tolerant, the "good" predicates hold, get propagated up and all is well. If they are in the same component of $A(M_a: a \epsilon A)$, then that particular component may not satisfy its desired property, but that is okay, since that is the only potential error at that stage, which is also single fault tolerant. -|

Note that attaining SFT at the system (architecture) level is not a lot of value if there are always multiple (e.g. more than one) errors that filter up (to separate component/system interfaces). One needs fault-tolerance together with a low error rate, as provided by error-correction or fault-tolerance at the lower levels. The smaller the n in n-FT is, the lower down in the system hierarchy it has to be pushed to be useful. In other words, it has to be at the level of fewer "basic computing units" that may be susceptible to individual errors. So for example, depending on the (assumed) error rate, a system architecture with n components that are

1-FT should be m-FT for some m in order to maintain the same level of FT as the components. The choice of m relates to the correspondence between the error rate and the number n of components.

4. "GRACEFUL DEGRADATION"

Architectures are usually chosen for their functional or performance characteristics, and then FT is added. In cases where we cannot, or choose not to, achieve the original goal (the property P), we try to do the best we can. This could mean choosing, or evolving to in "real time", properties of the component models such that the net result is "as close" to P as possible, or choosing properties of the component models such that we achieve some other "second-best" specified property. This is the so-called "degradation"; "graceful" simply means the capability to carry on without utter collapse.

This leads to the following general model theory question:

*   Given a model A ("relational structure" in the normal conventional mathematical logic sense of the word), and a bunch of other models M_a, one for each $a \epsilon A$ (assume that the languages of all these models are the same... It doesn't matter....), construct a new model M(A) by "putting" ("embedding") all of M_a "in place of" a, for each $a \epsilon$ A, i.e. the universe of M(A) is the union of the universes of the M_a.

Defining the relations of M(A):

1. Leave all the relations of each M_a as they were.
2. For relations between elements of different models M_a, M_b... there are choices. Here are two:
    2a. "Total": Define $R(m_a, m_b,...)$ for all $m_a \epsilon$ M_a and $m_b \epsilon M_b$.... iff $R(a, b,...)$ in A.

2b. "Anchored": Chose one designated m^*_a in each M_a, and define $R(m_a, m_b....)$ for $m_a \in M_a$ and $m_b \in M_b...$ iff $m_a = m^*_a$, $m_b = m^*_b$,... and $R(a, b,...)$ in A.

In either case the questions are:

Q0: Given A and M_a for each $a \in A$, what is $Th(M(A))$?

Q1: Given $Th(A)$ and $Th(M_a)$ for all $a \in A$, what is $Th(M(A))$?

Q2: Given A and $Th(M_a)$ for each $a \in A$, what is $Th(M(A))$?

Q3: Given A and $Th(M_a)$ for each $a \in A$, if $Th(M(A))$ is not uniquely determined, what is the range?

This type of question could be said to be in "hierarchical model theory" because we can apply the same process to $M(A)$, etc.

5. RELATED WORK

The origin of the modern interest in fault tolerance is probably to be found in von Neumann (1956). More recent work in the same vein is to be found in Gacs (1986) and Pippenger (1990).

Although we have not seen our approach or definitions in the scientific literature, there has been much work in similar issues for particular architectures, e.g. graphs as a model of networks, for particular logics, e.g. monadic second order logic (Courcelle, 2011), and particular model-theoretic methods, e.g. Feferman-Vaught Theorem, direct/reduced product, disjoint sum (Hodges, 2001).

Bernardeschi, Fantechi, and Simoncin (1994), DeFlorio and Blondia (2011), Demirbas (2004), Gaertner (1999), Kulkarni and Ebnenasir (2005), Leal (2001), and Shelton and Koopman (2003) talk about the role of specification in fault tolerance in a more computer science application setting.

Recent work of Whitney (2009) expresses a closely related viewpoint to ours: "We analyze the fault paths through a circuit and determine where error correction sub-circuits are most needed. This technique is in contrast the current common technique of putting error correction "everywhere" in the circuit."

6. QUESTIONS

There are many remaining questions, both theoretical and "practical", in addition to those of Section 4. Here are a few:

1. How/when can you go from a P-SFT with respect to P_i architecture to a P'-SFT with respect to P'_i where either P' is stronger or the P'_i are weaker?
2. Which architectures are "better" than others for P-SFT for a given property P?
3. How about the variation of P-SFT where not all the embedded models are allowed to be faulty, but only certain ones, depending on where they are embedded?

7. CONCLUSION

We have described a framework for expressing the semantics of architectural "pure fault tolerance". The goal was to examine the behavior of systems which have no explicit error correction, but nevertheless achieve their goal, to a greater or lesser degree. We have given definitions for architectural single (and multiple) fault-tolerance and fault-compensation, proved a theorem about composing fault tolerant systems, and presented a very general formulation of the dependence of system properties on component properties.

ACKNOWLEDGMENT

I thank Scott Aaronson, John Baldwin, Bruno Courcelle, Haim Gaifman, Sam Gasster, Wilfrid Hodges, and Setso Metodi for helpful comments.

REFERENCES

Aaronson, S., & Arkhipov, A. (2001). *The computational complexity of linear optics.* Retrieved from http://www.scottaaronson.com/papers/optics.pdf

Bacon, D. (2008). *Self-correcting quantum computers (part II).* Retrieved from http://scienceblogs.com/pontiff/2008/08/selfcorrecting_quantum_compute_1.php

Bernardeschi, C., Fantechi, A., & Simoncin, L. (1994). Formal reasoning on fault coverage of fault tolerant techniques: A case study. In K. Echtle, D. Hammer, & D. Powell (Eds.), *Proceedings of the First European Dependable Computing Conference* (LNCS 852, pp. 77-94).

Courcelle, B. (2011). *Graph structure and monadic second-order logic, a language theoretic approach.* Retrieved from http://www.labri.fr/perso/courcell/Book/TheBook.pdf

De Florio, V., & Blondia, C. (2008). A survey of linguistic structures for application-level fault tolerance. *ACM Computing Surveys, 40*(2), 6.

Demirbas, M. (2004). *Scalable design of fault-tolerance for wireless sensor networks.* Unpublished doctoral dissertation, Ohio State University, Columbus, OH.

Dyakonov, M. I. (2006). *Is fault-tolerant quantum computation really possible?* Retrieved from http://www.ee.sunysb.edu/~serge/ARW-5/ABSTRACTS/DyakonovAbs.pdf

Gacs, P. (1986). Reliable computation with cellular automata. *Journal of Computer and System Sciences, 32*(1), 15–78. doi:10.1016/0022-0000(86)90002-4doi:10.1016/0022-0000(86)90002-4

Gaertner, F. (1999). Transformational approaches to the specification and verification of fault-tolerant systems: Formal background and classification. *Journal of Universal Computer Science, 5*(10), 668–692.

Hodges, W. (2001). *First-order model theory.* Retrieved from http://plato.stanford.edu/entries/modeltheory-fo/

Holzmann, G. J., & Joshi, R. (2008). Reliable software systems design: Defect prevention, detection, and containment. In B. Meyer & J. Woodcock (Eds.), *Proceedings of the First IFIP TC 2/WG 2.3 Conference on Verified Software: Theories, Tools, Experiments.* (LNCS 4171, pp. 237-244).

Kalai, G. (2005). *Thoughts on noise and quantum computation.* Retrieved from http://www.ma.huji.ac.il/~kalai/QN.pdf

Kalai, G. (2007). *How quantum computers can fail.* Retrieved from http://www.ma.huji.ac.il/~kalai/QQT.pdf

Kempe, J. (2006). *Approaches to quantum error correction.* Retrieved from http://www.bourbaphy.fr/kempe.ps

Kulkarni, S. S., & Ebnenasir, A. (2005). Adding fault-tolerance using pre-synthesized components. In *Proceedings of the Fifth European Dependable Computing Conference* (pp. 72-90).

Leal, W. (2001). *A foundation for fault tolerant components.* Unpublished doctoral dissertation, Ohio State University, Columbus, OH.

Pippenger, N. (1990). Developments in the synthesis of reliable organisms from unreliable components. In *Proceedings of the Symposia in Pure Mathematics* (Vol. 50, pp. 311-324).

Shelton, C., & Koopman, P. (2003). Using architectural properties to model and measure graceful degradation. In R. de Lemos, C. Gacek, & A. Romanovsky (Eds.), *Proceedings of the Conference on Architecting Dependable Systems* (LNCS 2677, pp. 267-289).

von Neumann, J. (1956). Probabilistic logic and the synthesis of reliable organisms from unreliable components. In C. E. Shannon & J. McCarthy (Eds.), *Automata studies* (pp. 43–98). Princeton, NJ: Princeton University Press.

Weber, D. G. (1989). Formal specification of fault-tolerance and its relation to computer security. *ACM SIGSOFT Software Engineering Notes*, *14*(3), 273–277. doi:10.1145/75200.7524 0doi:10.1145/75200.75240

Weinstein, Y. (2007). *A universal operator theoretic framework for quantum fault tolerance*. Paper presented at the First International Conference on Quantum Error Correction.

Whitney, M. G. (2009). *Practical fault tolerance for quantum circuits*. Unpublished doctoral dissertation, University of California Berkeley, Berkeley, CA.

ENDNOTES

[1] See the references Aaronson and Arkhipov (2001), Bacon (2008), Dyakonov (2006), Kalai (2005, 2007), Kempe (2006), Weinstein (2007), and Whitney (2009) for a variety of views on quantum computation fault tolerant error correction.

[2] Functions are encoded as the appropriately single-valued relations. We use the convention that the name of the model is in bold italics and the corresponding set on which the model is the same name in regular font.

[3] For a general introduction to model theory, see Hodge's excellent online text.

[4] The question of what language to use to express the "properties" (specifications) is important, but perhaps not necessarily at this stage of abstraction. Of course, standard First Order Logic (FOL) is not in general sufficient for quantum states (see, for example, the logic presented in Baltag), nor for probabilistic computations, nor even for graph properties ....

[5] Note that the architecture does not determine P and the P_a; those can be varied at will, for the same architecture, depending on the context. It is not even clear if A together with the P_a determine P.

This work was previously published in the International Journal of Adaptive, Resilient and Autonomic Systems, Volume 2, Issue 4, edited by Vincenzo De Florio, pp. 25-35, copyright 2011 by IGI Publishing (an imprint of IGI Global).

Chapter 4
IoT-IMS Communication Platform for Future Internet

Chi-Yuan Chen
National Dong Hwa University, Taiwan

Chun-I Fan
National Sun Yat-sen University, Taiwan

Han-Chieh Chao
National Dong Hwa University and National I-Lan University, Taiwan

Jiann-Liang Chen
National Taiwan University of Science and Technology, Taiwan

Tin-Yu Wu
Tamkang University, Taiwan

Yuh-Shyan Chen
National Taipei University, Taiwan

Jenq-Muh Hsu
National Chiayi University, Taiwan

ABSTRACT

In recent years, Internet of Things (IoT) and Cloud Computing are the hottest issues of Future Internet. However, there is a lack of common fabric for integrating IoT and Cloud. In telecommunications, the IMS (IP Multimedia Subsystem), based on the All-IP and Open Services Architecture, has been regarded as the trend for Next Generation Network (NGN). The IMS communication platform is the most suitable fabric for integrating IoT and Cloud. This paper focuses on different aspects including Cloud Service Framework, Data Sensing and Communication Technology, Collaborative Authentication and Privacy Protection Mechanism, Operation, Administration, and Maintenance (OA&M), Mobility and Energy-Saving Management, and Application Services. This paper not only provides the discussion of open challenges, but also proposes a possible solution based on the above-mentioned aspects for Future Internet.

INTRODUCTION

Future Internet is a collection of data communication network technologies in the future. The IoT (Internet of Things) is the most important concept of Future Internet for providing a common global IT Platform to combine seamless networks and networked things. In the future, people will be connected Anytime, Anyplace, with Anything and Anyone, and appropriately utilizing Any network and Any Service. In other words, the IoT addresses the Convergence, Content, Collections, Computing, Communication, and Connectivity between people and things (CERP-IoT, 2009).

DOI: 10.4018/978-1-4666-2056-8.ch004

Cloud Computing (Armbrust et al., 2010) is regarded as the backend solution for processing huge data streams and computations while facing the challenges of everything will be connected with seamless networks in the future. Cloud technologies can provide a virtual, scalable, efficient, and flexible data center for context-aware computing and online service to enable IoT.

Both the IoT and Cloud Computing are the trends of Future Internet. However, the developments of IoT technology are diversity and are not interoperable. On the other hand, the cloud computing solutions are depended on service providers. Since many international organizations are devoted to work out their specifications for providing a common architecture of networks and software. Under this consideration, we regard the IP Multimedia Subsystem (IMS) is the ideal solution for fulfilling the requirements. However, there are still many challenges for IMS being the network and software fabric between IoT and Cloud. In this paper, we will discuss the open challenges and propose the possible solutions for Future Internet.

DISCUSSION OF OPEN CHALLENGES

CERP-IoT has classified the IoT supporting technologies into 13 categories and discussed some possible technologies (CERP-IoT, 2009). However, the possible technologies for enabling IoT are diversity and are not interoperable. Hence we propose the IMS-based possible solutions to fulfill the requirement of these 13 IoT supporting technologies as in Table 1. Furthermore, we also discuss open challenges with different aspects including Cloud Service Framework, Data Sensing and Communication Technology, Collaborative Authentication and Privacy Protection Mechanism, Operation, Administration, and Maintenance (OA&M), Mobility and Energy-Saving Management, and Application Services.

Table 1. IoT supporting technologies and possible solutions

Supporting Technologies	Possible Solutions
Identification Technology	IMS/SIP URI
IoT Architecture Technology	IMS Architecture
Communication Technology	IMS-SIP Protocol
Network Technology	IMS All-IPv6 Transport
Network Discovery	IMS Service Discovery
Software and algorithms	IMS Service Architecture
Hardware	SDR (Software Defined Radio) and CR (Cognitive Radio)
Data and Signal Processing Technology	IMS and Cloud Computing
Discovery and Search Engine Technologies	IMS and Cloud Computing
Relationship Network Management	IMS Architecture
Power and Energy Storage Technologies	SDR, CR, and CN (Cognitive Network)
Security and Privacy Technologies	IMS Security Architecture
Standardization	3GPP (IMS)

Cloud Service Framework

Cloud Computing can be regarded as an enabling technology for processing IoT Services. As mentioned before, cloud computing solutions are depend on service providers and are not compatible with each other. Without a common service framework and communication interface, we will need to implement different access methods between different clouds on IoT. IMS has provided a common service framework based on All-IP transport and SIP (Session Initiation Protocol) for telecommunications. Cloud Computing technologies can be utilized to improve the scalability and efficiency of IMS architecture. However, in order to support IoT services, the following issue should be addressed.

- Redesign the Home Subscriber Server (HSS) database schema for IoT environment.
- Improves the IMS service discovery and search function for IoT.
- Improves the original IMS-URI (Universal Resource Identifier) Naming Architecture for IoT.
- Enabling the 3GPP SCIM (Service Capability Interaction Manager) to achieve the Service Composition and Service Interaction.

Data Sensing and Communication Technology

The future Internet is defined as a dynamical global network infrastructure, in which the IoT is regarded as the most important technology. Differing from the definition and applications of previous RFID-based architectures, the IoT means that all devices can be interconnected by the networks. Nevertheless, without a standardized international standard, the current development of the IoT technology greatly varies. Therefore, it is significant to provide a standard IoT network architecture. To accomplish such a goal requires the data gathered by various identifiers (for example, QRCode, RFID, Barcode, RuBee and so on), which will be encoded into unique identifiers (UID) and written on smart tags. For the integration of ID standards among heterogeneous sensors, the denomination and addressing of smart tags are integrated via the IoT so that different standards can share data through the Internet platform. In addition, to enable the relation among things in the IoT, several challenges must be conquered to enhance the data sensing and communication technology:

- How to design novel encoding methods to integrate the unstandardized WSN (Wireless Sensor Network) ID.

- How to establish a client platform that supports EPC Global code.
- How EPCIS (EPC Information Services) of EPC Global Network enhances the compatibility of smart tags.
- How to establish an All-IP heterogeneous network server and process the messages generated in EPC Network via Local ONS (Object Name System).
- How to construct the relation between the behavior patterns and the things.
- How to construct the relation between the behavior patterns and IMS-URI/UID.
- How to establish the relation between the things.
- How to update the ID relation quickly.

Collaborative Authentication and Privacy Protection Mechanism

Recently, the Internet has become a quite essential part of our lives because the information and communication technologies are developed more quickly than ever. We can obtain internet services by laptops, notebooks, mobile phones, or more modern mobile devices, such as watches, glasses, shoes, and so on to realize the IoT environment in the future. Not only do these devices have the abilities of storage, computing, and communication, but they will bring a great convenience to our lives as well.

Generally, a server must authenticate a user when the user wants to get the service provided by the server. In practice, the authentication is usually completed by verifying the user's ID, password, or smart card over the Internet, which is similar to verifying the ID card in the real world. As to the IoT environment, it is characterized that a user can possess two or more smart "things" such that the user or even every "thing" may need to be authenticated precisely before accessing some designated services. However, we are not able to guarantee that every smart mobile device has sufficient computing and communication capabilities, and it will lead to lack of efficiency when the server authenticates many lower-capability devices of the user at the same time. Thus, the future way of authentication should be more flexible, effective, and convenient than the current way, and it is important to achieve low cost authentication adapted to the devices with different capabilities in the future.

Besides, even though a reliable authentication procedure can be utilized to confirm a user's identity through the devices possessed by the user, there still exists security vulnerability. If the user loses a device, any person who gets the device can obtain the secure information inside or further pass the authentication to impersonate the victim. In order to cope with this problem, we need a solution with stronger reliability and accuracy such that even if a malicious person gets a lost device, he is not capable of impersonating the user successfully.

Moreover, in some situations, it is impractical and time-wasting that the server authenticates all devices of the user simultaneously. Since every device can be regarded as an individual authentic factor, the server can only pick some relative factors to authenticate according to the service type and eventually confirms the user's identity. For example, the hospital authenticates the devices which involve the certificates of identity, health insurance, or body implants while the user goes to see a doctor. In this circumstance, it makes no sense to authenticate other irrelative factors such as sport license. Consequently, it is necessary to design an authentication scheme with flexibility in terms of the security levels and requirements of services. Briefly speaking, the challenge we want to address is how to design an authentication system tailored for the IoT environment to enhance the performance, reliability, accuracy, and the flexibility of the authentication between the service provider and all things.

Operation, Administration, and Maintenance (OA&M)

It's more challenging to use Quality-of-Service (QoS) technique in future Internet because the changing bandwidth and handoff of IoT device communications affect the trans-mission packet seriously. The existing network services can be divided into best effort service and real-time service. The best effort services like FTP and HTTP are just in the work can be completed within a period of time, and the real-time services like voice messages and video streaming are demanded for more real-time requirements so the real-time services are necessary to complete the work in the limited time. Under the current network environment, IoT cannot dynamically different requirements for the provision of appropriate services causes the mechanism cannot satisfy the user QoS requirements. In general wired networks, packet transmissions are in the "best efficiency" of the state, and the state means that the network will try to maintain the required Application bandwidth, but it's not based on band-width availability and network congestion situation to supply any guarantee. This design makes the Internet in the future IoT Real-time Applications Service cannot guarantee QoS

With the future implementation of the Internet, the families, schools and small and medium enterprises are in growing in the using equipment of IoT. These Managed devices are found in every corner, so they require efficient management method. If resource management adopts the management of the proximal, the system will need to visit to each device to be configured IoT object changes and performance monitoring, but it will leads to consume time and labor. If resource management adopts the management of the re-mote, the system will just need access a single point to all of the devices, and the system manager use a simple browser interface to set and control IoT devices with only an Internet connection. The management of the remote significantly improves management performance to consistent with the future Internet era.

Mobility and Energy-Saving Management

IoT (Internet of Things) is an integrated part of future Internet and interoperable communication protocols where physical and virtual "things" have identities, physical attributes, and virtual personalities and are seamlessly integrated into the information network through cloud computing service. To offer the seamlessly switching the IT (Interactive Thing) between different IoT (Internet of Things) environment and provide the high power saving and resource requirements for IT, it is very important to in-depth investigate the mobility and energy-saving manage-ment for IT on the IoT-IMS communication platform. Observe that it is interested that M2M (machine to machine) is the promising and important networking techniques for building the IoT. Some challenges of mobility and energy-saving issues are discussed as follows.

The first challenge is how to investigate the mobility management between the cloud computing service and data sensing service for ITs. M2M communication is one key technique to manage the mobility between IT to pro-vide a seamlessly content switching environment for IT. The customer achieves the high quality of communication anytime and anywhere which is a difficult problem. It is believed that deployment of femtocells which can improves the quality of indoor coverage and network capacity. In addition, the femtocell-assisted technique should be considered to improve the communication quality between ITs. In addition, it obviously needs large energy consumption for service providing while lot ITs provide people a convenient life. The challenge is how to carefully allocate energy usage to ITs based on the property of jobs, which can achieve

the optimal energy distribution. Consequently, the goal is to provide the "user-centric" service and provide terminal mobility, session mobility and service mobility with the femtocell-assisted technique.

The second challenge is how to provide the community service and mobility on the heterogeneous IoT-IMS communication platform. A variety of communication environments is considered to improve the efficient communication between interactive things, while the M2M gateway is built for building the heterogeneous IoT-IMS communication platform. The challenge is how to connect different media interface become a complete IoT network. Conventional research on connection of different interface is to use the conventional handover mechanisms. However, the information of ITs maybe not enough to perform an ideal handover process, because ITs cannot acquire the global information. To achieve the goal of reducing the handover delay and packets loss, the development of the efficient handover mechanism for heterogeneous IoT-IMS communication platform is necessary.

The third challenge is how to investigate the energy-saving management between the cloud computing service and data sensing service for interactive things and the heterogeneous IoT-IMS communication platform. The energy-saving management increases the communication efficiency for ITs to extend the network lifetime. The goal is to achieve the self-aware power allocation and management. ITs can automatically configure the power allocation based on the property of events and environment to build a long life network.

Application Services

In the Internet researches, application services (AS) are often playing the important issues during the evolution of network technologies. The application services usually combine the innovative technologies of mobile and ubiquitous computing to enable the mobile ubiquitous abilities of application services. Besides, the concept of mobile web service, which is based on the location-based (LBS) service, can also provide a user-centric mechanism to find a set of composite services to construct a proper service for people, in order to achieve the goal of resource sharing of the Internet through peer-to-peer and social networking communications. Thus, the application services of the future Internet will provide more connective networking services and smarter living environments for people to effectively work, live, and communicate with others.

It is necessary to modify the layer structures of the existing network architecture in order to integrate the things and the Internet to form the Internet of Things. Tan and Wang (2010) proposed a new layered architecture of IoTs shown in Figure 1. This layered architecture of IoTs consists of six layers, in which the edge technology layer and access layer connect to the existed alone applications to for things communication, the backbone layer is similar to the Today's Internet providing information communicating channel,

Figure 1. A layered architecture of IoTs proposed by Tan and Wang (2010)

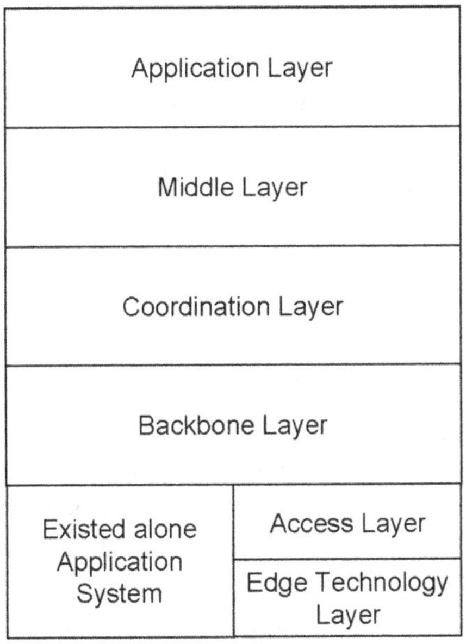

the coordination layer and middle layer response to process the structure of information data from different application systems to reassemble an unified structure for information identification and process of every application system, and the application layer provides the IoT-enable application services for users. Thus, the Internet of Things is not a theory; it is a concept of application technology which our daily lives can benefit from. In fact, many mature IoT application domains, such as retailing (Shen & Liu, 2010), food (Yu et al., 2010), logistics (Hao & Zhang, 2010), and supply chain (Yan & Huang, 2009), have been proposed and act as the development pilots of IoTs application in the future Internet.

Service-oriented architecture (SOA) is a new system architecture model, which can adapt its components and services to fit the individual service demands and composite the proper software components and services for the service users. Therefore, a single and standalone service can not complete the specific needs of independent tasks, many composite services may be combined together and accomplish the task mission in SoA. Guinard et al. (2010) proposed a scheme interacting with the SoA-based Internet of Things for discovery, query, selection, and on demand provisioning of web services. Through this scheme, it will easily blur the IT line between the virtual and real worlds of the IoT. The thing in IoTs is an object or device. It may itself has a number of built-in services, such as network printer providing the printer services and networked TV having the ability of information display. IoT-based things can also adopt the SoA-based Service Composition to construct and build the IoT-enabled application services according to the service abilities and user requirements. Atzori et al. (2010) also proposed a SoA-based architecture for the IoT middleware shown in Figure 2 to provide the proper IoT-enabled application services through object abstraction, service management, and service composition among things in the IoT.

Figure 2. A SoA-based architecture for the IoT middleware proposed by Atzori et al. (2010)

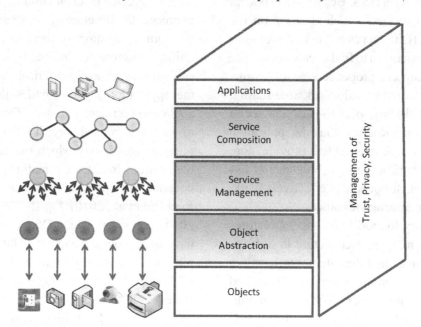

With the rapid development of the IoT, it will be a significant researching challenge to integrate the IoT and the next generation communication platform, such as IMS. In the next section, we will try to stretch out our visions and possible solutions to develop the IoT-IMS communication platform.

IoT-IMS COMMUNICATION PLATFORM

Figure 3 shows the evolution of telecommunication in simple concept. The All-IP architecture was planned promptly after R99 (the forerunner of IMS). Due to the architecture being too complex, the development work was divided into R4 (Release4) and R5 (Release5) in 2000. R4 was expected not to include IMS. It focused on the specification of IP transport, and was released in 2001. R5 was completed in 2002, and brought the IMS formally into the 3GPP standard. Further IMS related functions tend toward stability in R6 (Release 6) and were released in 2005. The

follow-up R7 (Release 7) also adopted the concept of fixed mobile convergence. In the future, more access technologies and service frameworks will be integrated in to 3GPP specification. We believe that IMS will play an important role in Future Internet.

Based on the IMS concept to combine IoT and Cloud, we proposed a common framework for Future Internet as illustrated in the Figure 4 called IoT-IMS Communication Platform. The IoT-IMS can be divided into three layers: 1) Cloud Networks; 2) IMS Core Networks; 3) IoT Networks. We will detail the possible solutions with different aspects as following.

Cloud Service Framework

In order to improve the IMS service framework by utilizing Cloud Computing technologies, the first step is the visualization as illustrated in Figure 5. Infrastructure as a Service (IaaS) is suitable for IMS core network to improving the scalability and performance. We can dynamic allocate the resource for IMS components based the system

Figure 3. The evolution of telecommunication

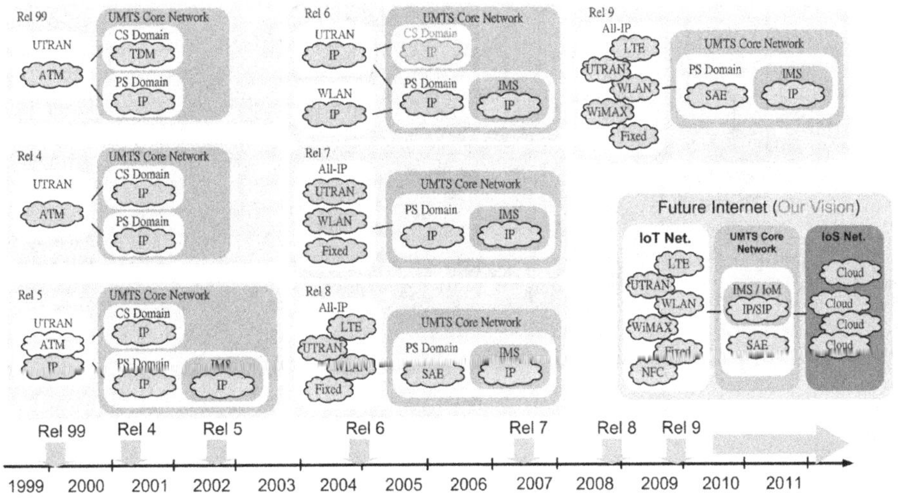

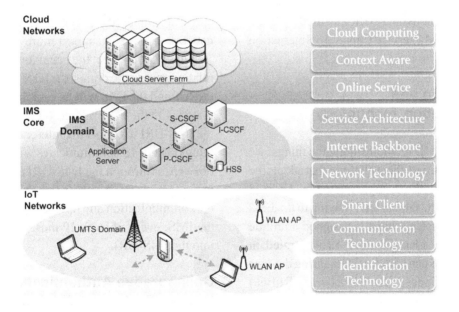

Figure 4. IoT-IMS communication platform

load and component utilization. Furthermore, the IMS HSS database indexing and searching technologies can also be improved by cloud computing technologies for huge users/things and frequent accesses under IoT. The visualization of IMS-AS (Application Server) and Cloud business model are also suitable for IMS service third party providers.

The Identification Technologies is the first challenge for IoT. The IMS-URI naming architecture is suitable for naming everything and every service under IoT, and is also fit for Context-aware Service Discovery and Context-aware

Figure 5. Virtualization for IMS-AS (Application Server)

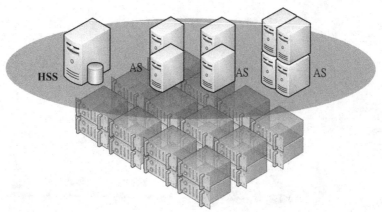

Things/Devices Discovery. The Mapping, Grouping, and Searching of Real/Virtual/Digital Things can be solved by the hierarchical IMS-URI naming architecture. At present, Service Composition and Service Interaction are rarely discussed in IoT. These functions have been specified by 3GPP and called SCIM (Service Capability Interaction Manager).

Data Sensing and Communication Technology

To deal with the ID relation among the things, we first establish a smart client platform that adopts the OSGi service platform implemented by Android and supports EPC Global UID. Owing to the EPC Code, each physical object is assigned a unique identify for the identification. As illustrated in Figure 6, EPCIS can handle EPC-bearing devices (including QRCode, RFID, Barcode, and RuBee) through EPC Global tags.

To integrate UID and All-IP, an All-IP heterogeneous network server that provides global UID and IP redirection will be established. EUI-64 supported by IPv6 is used to correspond to UID and acquire new IPv6 address. Simultaneously, IPv6 redirection among heterogeneous networks, like 6lowPAN, Zigbee, Bluetooth and WiFi, also can be accomplished. In this way, the All-IP het-

erogeneous network server is able to obtain the UID via the IoT and retrieve the IPv6 address to complete the routing and addressing in the cloud network. Moreover, by integrating EPC code with EPC Global technology, we can integrate different WSN standards in the All-IP heterogeneous network server and support more WSN.

Finally, to connect the behavior patterns to the relation among the things, the ID relation between the IoT and the IMS will be established and integrated with the Family Tree-ID Relationship and the IMS-URI to enable the interconnection of the things. The IMS communicates with the destination sensor through the IMS-URI and everything in the IMS. For the establishment of the IoT and the communication and operation of the things in the IMS, every object's IP must be transformed into the IMS-URI.

Collaborative Authentication and Privacy Protection Mechanism

We come up with the concept collaborative authentication by means of using the devices with higher storage and computing capabilities (high-end device) as the role of proxy devices to assist the lower or even no-capability devices (low-end device) to accomplish the authentication effectively and efficiently. In the authentication

Figure 6. Flowchart of data sensing and communication technology

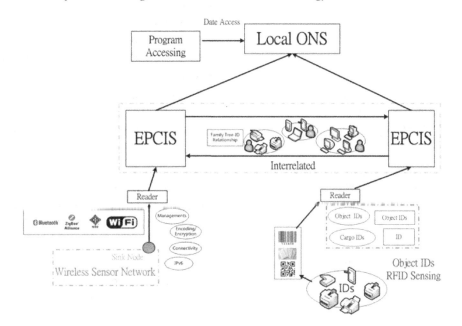

process, public key infrastructure and symmetric encryption are involved to ensure the security and privacy of information exchange during authentication processes, as shown in Figure 7. A user may have several devices where some of them are high-end devices but some are low-end. When a user intends to access a service from the cloud/ network, each of the possessed devices needs to be authenticated by the network in advance. The high-end devices will execute the authentication process with the service provider and if the authentication is successful, then they can act as a proxy to help the low-end devices to accomplish the identity authentication processes as well. By applying this mechanism, all of the devices can complete the authentication processes collaboratively.

Moreover, in order to solve the issues mentioned above, we can extend the collaborative authentication system to provide a threshold mechanism, which can enhance the reliability, accuracy, and flexibility of authentication. First of all, the environment or service provider can set a threshold value of the number of devices needed for authentication according to its require-

ment. If a malicious person gets a lost device of some user, the malicious person cannot be authenticated by the server successfully since the authentication requires more than one device at the same time. Such a mechanism can effectively protect users from being impersonated when they have lost some devices of them. Therefore, it increases the reliability and accuracy of the authentication. On the other hand, we can also set the threshold value according to the importance and privacy degrees of the service, which is going to be accessed. If all of the devices owned by a user have to be authenticated by the server before he is accessing a service, it will be very time-consuming. Therefore, in our threshold idea, services that need a higher security level will have a larger threshold value, and vice versa. For instance, as shown in Figure 8, a user accessing a bank service needs four legal devices in order to be authenticated successfully while he only needs two for accessing a stadium.

Thus, our collaborative authentication with threshold scheme extends the flexibility of the authentication. It is unnecessary to authenticate all of the devices of a user when he is accessing

Figure 7. Authentication processes

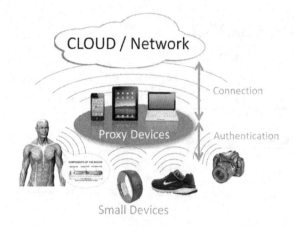

Figure 8. Threshold mechanism

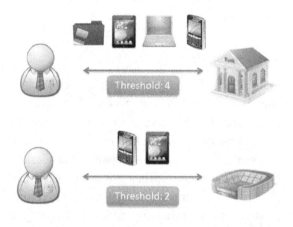

every single service. Collaborative threshold authentication will also be more flexible and efficient for authentication under certain circumstances.

Operation, Administration, and Maintenance (OA&M)

With integrated operation of in the future Internet on issues that may occur, this study proposed an OA&M (Operation, Administrator, and Maintenance) framework to be as a bridge among the various layers to solve the problem of the operation, administration and maintenance issues. Figure

9 shows the basic structure of OA&M diagram that contains OA&M (Operation, Administration, and Maintenance) three layers to proceed with the Internet operation, administration, and maintenance research of IoT-IMS communication platforms. The Operation Plane is responsible for IoT device or network bandwidth and other information and the traffic capture and dynamic bandwidth allocation, so that it ensures that the overall system object with the availability. According to QoS policies defined in Operation Plane, the Administration Plane proceeds with the packet delivery and network services for quality control and ensures that the services be dynamically adjusted according to demand to achieve the best performance system operation and the service with the reliability of the overall system. The Maintenance Plane is in charge of the monitoring and handling of IoT devices and environment to ensure that services run smoothly. And the Charging system is for charging through the other information processing.

The first step is to build IoT-IMS communication platforms and defines related policy module in IoT Networks. With the policy previously adopted the definition of IMS into Codec Policy, QoS Class Policy, Application Classifier and Function Classifier modules, this study integrated IoT Classifier module and IMS Policy to achieve the unity of the whole structure. Through defined QoS policies, importing relevant policy module in IoT-IMS communication platforms to meet the QoS control function related applications. This stage completes the Operation and Administration Mechanism designs of Operation, Administrator, and Maintenance of IoT-IMS communication platforms.

The second step makes use of SNMP (Simple Network Management Protocol) standard to define to meet the Maintenance Plane of IoT-IMS communication platforms. This study defines the part of Communication Domain and Discovery and Search Domain Module in the IoT Networks,

Figure 9. OA&M architecture

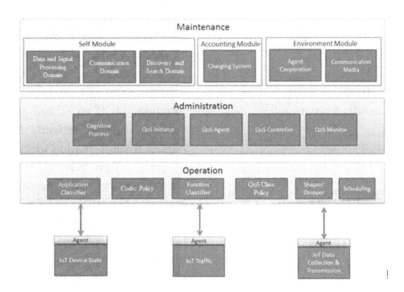

and defines Data and Signal Processing Domain Module in IMS, and exchanges the relevant module information through the Cooperative Agent in Maintenance Plans. The defined module data can use the Cooperative Agent to provide application services, and achieve the purpose of integration. This stage completes the Self and Environment Module Mechanism related designs of Operation, Administrator, and Maintenance of IoT-IMS communication platforms.

The final step is to combine with the first step and second step, and uses the defined Operation Policy and Resource Management Module to import IoT-IMS Charging System. By IoT-IMS Charging System, the charging information will be sent to the cloud system, and the cloud system provides the corresponding service to IoT Terminal device by user permissions. IoT-IMS Charging System can obtain the information of IoT networks and cloud networks. Follow-up billing information in a dynamic way to convey the communications platform in IoT-IMS is to proceed Operation, Administrator, and Maintenance. This final stage completes the Maintenance designs

of Operation, Administrator, and Maintenance of IoT-IMS communication platforms, and uses the results of the first two steps of integration to accomplish building the future Internet IoT-IMS communication platforms.

Mobility and Energy-Saving Management

To provide mobility and energy-saving managements for the IoT-IMS communication platform, we propose a possible mobility and energy-saving framework as shown in Figure 10. The mobility and energy-saving management requires the location information from the M2M gateway. The sensor device always detects a presence of an IoT and responds the UID of the IoT device to M2M gateway. The M2M gateway provides the location and power consumption information for the mobility and energy-saving management function. The mobility and energy-saving management makes the mobility and energy control according to the application requirement in cloud computing. The

Figure 10. System framework

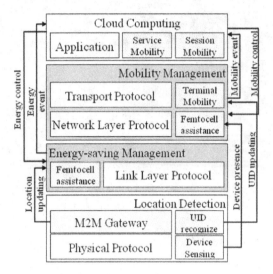

possible functions of mobility and energy-saving management are described as follows.

To provide the mobility management over the IoT-IMS communication platform, a sensor device is used to detect the IT location. Each IT has its own UID as identification. If an IT is within the sensing range of a sensor device, the sensor device sends a message to server via M2M gateway to record the location of the IT as illustrated in Figure 11. For example, one sensor device can be installed at the door to detect an incoming IT in an IoT building. When the IT is detected by the sensor device, the sensor device asks the IT for its UID by self-configured identification. Meanwhile, the sensor device keeps detecting the IT location by self-configured to inform other neighboring sensor devices near to the IT. ITs would maintain the service and the request. When an IT is moving from TV to monitor, sensor devices in TV and monitor can automatically detect its event, and report this event into M2M gateway. Then, a context switching from a TV to the monitor is automatically done through the M2M gateway. On the contrary, when the leave of the IT is de-

tected by a sensor device, it requests the server to stop the IoT service by using self-configured to prevent the server from delivering IoT data.

To provide the community service and mobility on the heterogeneous IoT-IMS communication platform, each IT holds a UID which is mapping to unique IT. If an IT had authenticated and is working in other network, the IT can directly request the information from the M2M gateway of the previous network by the identification technology. For example, the IPv6 state automatic configuration and the IoT automated discovery mechanism can be combined in a heterogeneous environment. When an IT moves to a different network, the IT updates the address table via IoT self-configuration and finally notifies the new location information to its home agent. In the IoT architecture, each UID of IT would be obtained by the identification technology, and use UID to map IT information from the original access network, then the new access network can company setting and not exchanging message with access point as shown in Figure 12. One corresponding node received the new location of the IT. After the IT moves to a different network, if IT wants to communicate with other IT, one useful approach is to use the gateway to exchange data. Therefore, M2M gateway is a key technol-

Figure 11. Mobility scenario through M2M gateway

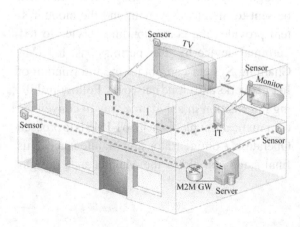

Figure 12. IT mobility in a heterogeneous network environment

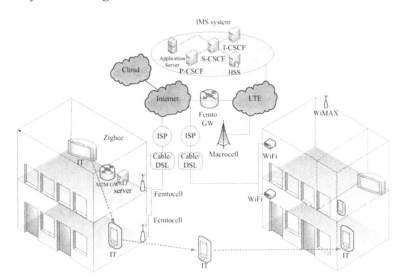

ogy to integrate different IT networks in the heterogeneous network.

To provide the energy-saving management over the IoT-IMS communication platform, the energy state of ITs should be described via an energy event. An IT announces an event for other things to acquire the energy state of other ITs. Based on the energy status information, ITs can re-distribute energy consumption information for communication with other ITs. Note that, ITs deliver the energy consumption information to other by a M2M gateway. Besides, ITs can detect the changes in the environment; then reply a corresponding response. ITs can switch to idle or active modes for events. When the M2M gateway receives the waking up message from the other ITs, the M2M gateway sends a message to ITs for waking up. The M2M gateway manages the power state of ITs for the purpose of the power-saving.

Application Services

We describe a possible solution to deploy the IoT-enabled IMS application services. There are many traditional IMS-based application services, such as voice over IP (VoIP), Instant Message and Pres-ence Service (IMP), push-to-talk over cellular (PoC), video on demands (VoDs), and IPTV. The users can use the application services to communicate with others or enjoy their lives via IMS-based application services. In order to blur the boundary line between IoT and IMS application services, to design the IoT-enable IMS application services are necessary in the next generation network.

Each thing in IoT has a unique identifier (uID). It can use various identification technologies to distinguish them. The most of research issues on IoT identification are often discussed with the RFID identification technology in EPC global network. A thing may accompany a service, when the thing is sensed and identified, and then the corresponding service will be found and triggered. For instance, a RFID-based business card (a thing in IoT) may be linked to a person or a VoIP call contacting that person. In this paper, we will adopt this concept to propose the identification mapping between things of IoT and IMS application services. Thus, we apply the concepts of Object Naming Service (ONS) and Information Service (IS) defined by EPC global network to serve as the application service of thing identification under the integration of IoT and IMS. In the EPC

Figure 13. Identification mapping between things of IoT and IMS application services

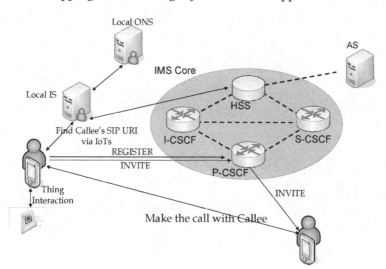

global network, the ONE and IS are responsible for identifying the thing and delivering its corresponding information to the associated application ser-ices. Figure 13 illustrates the design concept of identification mapping between things of IoT and IMS application services. In Figure 13, the IMS user (caller) carrying an IMS-based smart client wants to contact with someone. The user picks up the IoT-enabled business card and interacts with his/her smart client. Through IoT-IMS identification, the uID of IoT-enabled business card will be transmitted to the Local ONS and Local IS to discover and deliver back the associated information of the contacted person (callee). After obtaining the associated contacting information, the caller can make a VoIP with the callee through the identification mapping between things in IoT and IMS application services.

The signaling protocol of IMS usually uses the Session Initiation Protocol (SIP). Thus, we should adopt the SIP messages to design the operational flows of thing identification between the IoT and IMS application services. Figure 14 shows an example of the operational flow of SIP messages to trigger the IOT-enabled VoIP service. From step (1) to step (5), the smart client queries the corresponding uID of the IoT-enabled business

card through Local IS and Local ONE services. The following steps, from step (6) to step (8), are the standard procedure of making a VoIP call through the corresponding SIP messages. Thus, it can provide a possible solution to integrate the thing identification between IoT and IMS. In order to carry the corresponding information of the thing in IoT via SIP signaling messages, such as the uID of IoT thing and its associated contacting information. We should extend the part of SIP message for storing them. Figure 15 illustrates an extended example of SIP signal message car-rying the uID of IoT thing and its associated contacting information. We apply the SIP message, which type is MESSAGE, to encapsulate the identified uID in the XML (Extensible Markup Language) fashion, send the home subscriber server (HSS), and query the corresponding SIP URI (uniform resource identifier). If the HSS has the SIP URI associated the uID, it will send back the responding message, 200K, which contains the contacting information of uID formed in XML. In this way, the caller can obtain the contacting information of the callee to make the VoIP call via the thing interaction of the IoT-enabled business card. That is, IoT-enabled technology can make the IMS-based service environment smarter.

Figure 14. SIP operational flows between the things interaction of IoT and service invocation of the IMS VoIP call

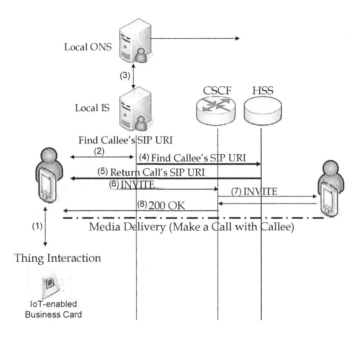

Figure 15. SIP operational flows between the things interaction of IoT and service invocation of the IMS VoIP call

```
MESSAGE sip:user2@domain.com SIP/2.0
  Via: SIP/2.0/TCP user1pc.domain.com;branch=z9hG4bK776sgdkse
  Max-Forwards: 70
  From: sip:user1@domain.com;tag=49583
  To: sip:user2@domain.com
  Call-ID: asd88asd77a@1.2.3.4
  CSeq: 1 MESSAGE
  Content-Type: text/plain
  Content-Length: 18
  Event:uID

<?xml version="1.0" encoding="UTF-8"?>
<IoTThing>
<uID>18799010123459</uID>
</IoTThing>


SIP/2.0 200 OK
  Via: SIP/2.0/TCP user1pc.domain.com;branch=z9hG4bK776sgdkse; received=1.2.3.4
  From: sip:user1@domain.com;;tag=49394
  To: sip:user2@domain.com;tag=ab8asdasd9
  Call-ID: asd88asd77a@1.2.3.4
  CSeq: 1
  MESSAGE Content-Length: 30

<?xml version="1.0" encoding="UTF-8"?>
<IoTThing>
<uID>18799010123459</uID>
<Name>alice@domain.com</Name>
  ...
```

As mentioned above, through our proposed methodology, it will provide a simple and direct mapping mechanism combining both features of the IMS and IoT to build the IoT-IMS communication platform and the corresponding IoT-enabled IMS application services in the future Internet.

RELATED WORKS

According to the report of CERP-IoT (2009), the Future Internet is defined as a dynamic global network infrastructure. It must have self-configuring capability based on standard and interoperable communication protocols to seamlessly integrate physical and virtual things in to information network. Besides the network and protocol, the Future Internet is composed of IoT (Internet of Things), IoM (Internet of Media), IoS (Internet of Services), and IoE (Internet of Enterprises).

The IoT was proposed by the Auto-Id Labs more than ten years ago. It has been dedicated to using RFID to the logistics value chain. In the ITU Internet Reports 2005 (ITU, 2005), the definition and applications are quite different from RFID (Radio Frequency Identifier) approach (Hancke et al., 2010). In recent years, the more communication technologies and applications (Presser et al., 2009; Broll et al., 2009; Hong et al., 2010) are developed to facilitate the concept of IoT (Atzori et al., 2010).

The concept of IMS is to merge telecommunication technologies, wireless networks and wired networks under the All-IP environment to provide more extensible, real-time and interactive multimedia services for next generation networks (Chang et al., 2010). IMS uses modified IETF SIP (Session Initiation Protocol) to establish the service session. In IMS, the contents are not limited by the access medium but become more extensible to offer more value-added services to users (Wiljakka et al., 2004; Bari et al., 2009).

The IMS architecture can be divided into three tiers: the Media/Transport plane, Control/Signaling plane and Service/Application plane. The Media/Transport plane refers to a wide range of different access technologies. Within the IP transport layer, users go through Wireless LAN, GPRS (General Packet Radio Service) or UMTS (Universal Mobile Telecommunication Systems) to acquire network connectivity. Once connected to IMS, users can access a variety of multimedia services. There is a set of IMS core components in the Control/Signaling plane–CSCFs (Call Session Control Functions), which includes Proxy-CSCF (P-CSCF), Interrogating-CSCF (I-CSCF) and Serving-CSCF (S-CSCF). The SIP signaling will be processed and routed to the destination through this plane. In the Service/Application plane, there are various application servers. The application servers provide users a wide range of IMS service. Operators can use the standard IMS architecture to build up their application servers.

CONCLUSION AND FUTURE WORK

The goal of IoT-IMS communication platform is to provide a common framework for Future Internet based on the existing IoT, Cloud Computing, and IMS technologies. IMS is the ideal solution to combine IoT networks and Cloud networks and maximize the benefit of each other. In this paper, we not only discuss the integration issues of Cloud Service Framework and Data Sensing and Communication Technology but also include the Collaborative Authentication and Privacy Protection Mechanism, Operation, Administration, and Maintenance (OA&M), Mobility and Energy-Saving Management, and Application Services. In the future, we will implement our proposed IoT-IMS communication platform to realize IoT services.

ACKNOWLEDGMENT

This research was partly funded by the National Science Council of the R.O.C. under grant NSC 99-2219-E-197-001, NSC 99-2219-E-197-002, NSC 99-2219-E-110-001, NSC 99-2219-E-011-006, NSC 99-2219-E-305-001, NSC-99-2219-E-415-001, and NSC 99-2221-E-032 -040. The authors would like to thank Whai-En Chen, Chao-Hsi Huang, Jun-Cheng Chen, Shih-Wei Huang, Hoi-Tung Hau, Pei-Jen Tsai, Wei-Zhe Sun, Pei-Jia Yang, Yan-Fang Li, Yi-Wei Ma, Ching Hsien Chou, and Yun-Wei Lin for their valuable contribution to this study.

REFERENCES

Armbrust, M., Fox, A., Griffith, R., Joseph, A. D., Katz, R., & Konwinski, A. (2010). A view of cloud computing. *Communications of the ACM, 53*(4), 50–58. doi:10.1145/1721654.1721672

Atzori, L., Iera, A., & Morabito, G. (2010). The Internet of things: A survey. *Computer Networks, 54*, 2787–2805. doi:10.1016/j.comnet.2010.05.010

Bari, F., & Leung, V. C. M. (2009). Architectural aspects of automated network selection in heterogeneous wireless systems. *International Journal of Ad Hoc and Ubiquitous Computing, 4*(5), 282–291. doi:10.1504/IJAHUC.2009.027478

Broll, G., Rukzio, E., Paolucci, M., Wagner, M., Schmidt, A., & Hussmann, H. (2009). Perci: Pervasive service interaction with the Internet of things. *IEEE Internet Computing, 13*(6), 74–81. doi:10.1109/MIC.2009.120

Chang, K.-D., Chen, C.-Y., Chen, J.-L., & Chao, H.-C. (2010). Challenges to next generation services in IP multimedia subsystem. *Journal of Information Processing Systems, 6*(2), 129–146. doi:10.3745/JIPS.2010.6.2.129

de Saint-Exupery, A. (2009). *Internet of things: Strategic research roadmap.* Retrieved from http://ec.europa.eu/information_society/policy/rfid/documents/in_cerp.pdf

Guinard, D., Trifa, V., Karnouskos, S., Spiess, P., & Savio, D. (2010). Interacting with the SOA-based Internet of things: Discovery, query, selection, and on-demand provisioning of web services. *IEEE Transactions on Service Computing, 3*(3), 223–235. doi:10.1109/TSC.2010.3

Hancke, G. P., Markantonakis, K., & Mayes, K. E. (2010). Security challenges for user-oriented RFID applications within the "Internet of things.". *Journal of Internet Technology, 11*(3), 307–313.

Hao, Z., & Zhang, M. (2010). Management optimization of tangible goods for e-commerce logistics process in Internet of things era. In *Proceedings of the International Conference on on Management and Service Science.*

Hong, S., Kim, D., Ha, M., Bae, S., Park, S. J., Jung, W., & Kim, J. (2010). SNAIL: An IP-based wireless sensor network approach to the Internet of things. *IEEE Wireless Communications, 17*(6), 34–42. doi:10.1109/MWC.2010.5675776

International Telecommunication Union (ITU). (2005). *Internet reports 2005.* Retrieved from http://www.itu.int/osg/spu/publications/internetofthings/

Presser, M., Barnaghi, P. M., Eurich, M., & Villalonga, C. (2009). The SENSEI project: Integrating the physical world with the digital world of the network of the future. *IEEE Communications Magazine, 47*(4), 1. doi:10.1109/MCOM.2009.4907403

Shen, G. C., & Liu, B. W. (2010). Research on application of Internet of things in electronic commerce. In *Proceedings of the International Symposium on Electronic Commerce and Security* (pp. 13-16).

Tan, L., & Wang, N. (2010). Future internet: The Internet of things. In *Proceedings of the International Conference on Advanced Computer Theory and Engineering* (pp. 376-380).

Wiljakka, J., Soininen, J., Sundquist, J., & Sipilä, T. (2004). IPv6 enabling IMS-based peer-to-peer services in 3GPP and 3GPP2 cellular networks. *Journal of Internet Technology*, 5(2), 67–73.

Yan, B., & Huang, G. W. (2009). Supply chain information transmission based on RFID and Internet of things. In *Proceedings of the International Colloquium on Computing, Communication, Control and Management* (pp. 166-169).

Yu, L., Li, X. M., Zhong, J., & Xiong, Y. N. (2010). Research on the innovation of strategic business model in green agricultural products based on Internet of things (IOT). In *Proceedings of the International Conference on e-Business and Information System Security* (pp. 1-3).

This work was previously published in the International Journal of Adaptive, Resilient and Autonomic Systems, Volume 2, Issue 4, edited by Vincenzo De Florio, pp. 54-73, copyright 2011 by IGI Publishing (an imprint of IGI Global).

Section 2
Autonomic Behaviors and Self-Properties

Chapter 5

A Resource-Aware Dynamic Load-Balancing Parallelization Algorithm in a Farmer-Worker Environment

M. Leeman
Cisco, Belgium

ABSTRACT

This paper describes an algorithm for dynamically assigning tasks to processing entities in a world where each task has a set of resource or service requirements and each processing entity a set of resources or service capabilities. A task needs to be assigned to a node that offers all required services and the set of tasks is finished within a minimal execution time frame. Dependability and adaptability are inherent to the algorithm so that it accounts for the varying execution time of each task or the failure of a processing node. The algorithm is based on a dependable technique for farmer-worker parallel programs and is enhanced for modeling the time constraints in combination with the required configuration set in a multidimensional resources model. This paper describes how the algorithm is used for dynamically load balancing and parallelizing the nightly tests of a digital television content-processing embedded device.

INTRODUCTION

In environments where processing power is limited or where continuously increasing processing power is needed, parallelization is the main method for speeding up tasks. These tasks can be divided into equally sized subtasks. Through the application of multiple instruction stream, multiple data stream (MIMD) techniques, the subtasks are assigned in parallel to available processing entities (Hennessy & Patterson, 2003). When processing a subtask fails or when processing is delayed due to decreased performance, the subtask can be reassigned. Processing nodes can be added when they become available or can be removed upon failure.

DOI: 10.4018/978-1-4666-2056-8.ch005

In some applications, however, neither subtasks nor processing entities are mirrors of each other. Some subtasks can be executed only on one or more processing nodes, as only these nodes offer the services or configuration the subtask requires. In this respect, subtasks are recognized as having certain requirements, and each processing entity as offering a set of capabilities. Subtasks need to be assigned to nodes meeting the subtask's requirements. If no node offers the required capabilities, the subtask cannot be executed.

Furthermore, the complete set of subtasks often needs to be completed as soon as possible. Some subtasks are more time-consuming than other ones, and even the processing time of one subtask can differ between two executions. Hence the varying execution length requires a dynamic assignment process. Assigning these subtasks is multidimensional: one dimension for each requirement, and another for the time constraints.

The next section describes the basic algorithm for parallelizing tasks with a farmer-worker dependable model. Afterward, a new algorithm is described that assigns tasks dynamically, such that the requirements of each subtask are met and the complete set of subtasks is finished with minimal delay, even if some processing nodes fail. A test case is covered in which this algorithm assigns nightly tests to devices that process digital television streams in the telecom domain. Finally, some future work is described.

THE FARMER-WORKER ALGORITHM AND ITS DEPENDABLE EXTENSION

The dependable multiresource dynamic algorithm is based on an elaboration of the traditional farmer-worker algorithm. In the most commonly known basic farmer-worker model, a "farmer" processing entity grabs the input data or tasks, divides the tasks into subtasks, and feeds the subtasks in parallel to processing entities called "workers."

The farmer collects the results and glues them together to one resulting processed output.

The farmer needs to go through quite some sequential processing between two runs. The input data needs to be grabbed, divided, and dispatched to the workers, and afterward the worker's processing output needs to be collected, merged, and finalized to one result. In video processing, where video is received from a camera and images extracted and divided for further processing, real-time behavior is important. Furthermore the failure of one worker endangers the processing of the complete task.

Therefore a dependable extension of the farmer-worker model has been proposed (De Florio, Deconinck, & Lauwereins, 1997) and, later, a corresponding framework library, RAFT-net (Leeman, Leeman, De Florio, & Deconinck, 2003). This extension describes a "dispatcher" and a "collector." The workers subscribe themselves for processing with the dispatcher. The farmer grabs the input data and sends the list of subtasks to the dispatcher, which assigns them to idle workers. While these workers are processing subtasks and the dispatcher is assigning them, the farmer can grab the input data for the next run.

Once a worker has processed a subtask, it notifies the dispatcher of its idle state so that a new subtask can be assigned to it. The output is sent to the collector. This entity collects the output from each worker and notifies the dispatcher that this subtask has been processed. From the moment a subtask is finished, the dispatcher also notifies the farmer, which sends as a response the corresponding subtask from the next run to the dispatcher.

Other algorithms have been proposed by similarly introducing an additional farmer or collector process in a flat (Chan & Abramson, 2001) or a hierarchical model (Aida, Futakata, & Tomotaka, 2006; Berthold, Dieterle, Loogen, & Priebe, 2008). Further improvement can be achieved by exploiting algorithm characteristics like dynamic grain size, denoting the task can be split up in subtasks of a dynamic – larger – size. This reduces the potential bottleneck of the dispatcher when a lot of workers become available and are sending messages to the dispatcher (Goux, Linderoth, & Yoder, 2000).

The dependable extension of the farmer-worker model also handles worker failure (De Florio, Deconinck, & Lauwereins, 1997; Leeman, Leeman, De Florio, & Deconinck, 2003). The freshness grade of a subtask denotes the number of times it has been assigned to a worker. When all subtasks have been assigned once, but not all results collected yet, each unfinished subtask is reassigned whenever a worker becomes idle. Consequently, its freshness grade is increased. In this way, a failing or delayed worker does not affect the overall result as long as there are remaining available workers. There is only a certain delay for reprocessing a failed subtask.

Once all subtasks are finished, the collector performs some final processing, merges the output of all subtasks, and saves the result to permanent storage. Meanwhile the farmer has already sent all the subtasks of the next run to the dispatcher; only the notification for starting this new cycle is still to be sent to the dispatcher.

A worker can be dynamically added to the parallelization process by sending its worker ID to the dispatcher. At that time, the new worker is treated as a worker that has become idle, and the dispatcher sends it a new subtask to process. When a worker leaves the farm, the subtask it was processing will be reprocessed by another worker.

This extended farmer-worker algorithm adds further parallelization, dependability, and dynamic allocation of subtasks to the original model. However, for certain applications, there are some shortcomings of this model.

First of all, the algorithm supposes all subtasks have the same requirements and all workers possess the same basket of services or capabilities, which are sufficient for any subtask. This means that any subtask can be assigned to any worker. In many applications, however, this is not the case. Workers might offer a diverse set of capabilities, and subtasks might use or even need some of the services available only on a subset of the workers. Hence, not all subtasks can be assigned to any worker.

Second, the priority of subtasks is used only for subtasks with the same freshness grade. A subtask for which processing has failed or which has been assigned to a failing worker has a higher freshness grade than unassigned subtasks. It is reassigned only when all the other subtasks have at least the same freshness grade. This procedure might be sufficient when all the subtasks have more or less the same processing time. However, if the failed subtask has a significantly longer processing time, the overall result is delayed once all the other subtasks are finished.

Furthermore, when a worker fails to process a subtask, and all the other subtasks have been assigned but are not all finished, the failed subtask is not given priority for reassignment over the unfinished subtasks, as the dispatcher is not aware which subtask has failed. This might mean further delay until the failed subtask is reassigned.

Finally, in the algorithm each worker is volunteering as a processing entity. This principle is not applicable to all domains. For instance, embedded devices are typically not "polluted" with knowledge of the overall algorithm or the required algorithm's communication flow concerning the worker. Also when third-party devices or entities are used for processing tasks, direct communication between these devices and the dispatcher or collector would most often not be possible.

In the next section, the farmer-worker algorithm is extended so that it is aware of resources and other constraints while ending the task with minimal delay. The model is adapted to use processing entities that are not aware of the algorithm's communication flow.

A DEPENDABLE RESOURCE-AWARE FARMER-WORKER MODEL

All workers offer a set of services or capabilities that might, but do not necessarily, overlap. On the other hand, some subtasks have weak requirements or none at all, so that they can be executed by any or almost any worker. Other subtasks have a well-defined set of requirements that might be met by the capability of only one worker or a very limited set of workers. The resource-aware farmer-worker model assigns subtasks to workers based on a measure of resource scarcity or the level of availability of these resources. The model is extended for monitoring the worker's available services and adapting the assignment process accordingly when a worker loses a capability or extends its list of services.

Adding Resource Scarcity

A subtask with a strict set of requirements that can be processed by a limited set of workers should have preference in assignment above subtasks that can be processed by any worker. In other words, when a worker offering a scarce capability or a scarce set of capabilities becomes idle, it should be given to a subtask that needs this scarce set of capabilities the most. The reason is twofold.

1. This worker or another one offering the required capabilities may be idle again soon, as subtasks have different execution times. Hence, to minimize the total execution time of the run, this task has to be assigned before subtasks that can be executed by any worker.
2. If this worker fails permanently during the course of the run cycle, there may not be another chance to allocate the subtask to any other worker offering the required but scarce resources. In this case, this subtask will not be executed at all if no other worker offers the same required capabilities.

Subtask requirements that must be matched with a well-defined and scarce set of worker capabilities or resources are hard requirements. Hard requirements are binary: Either the worker matches the subtask's set of requirements, or it does not.

Subtasks can also have soft requirements. These are scarce resources that workers possess in a certain nonbinary quantity or resources that subtasks require in a certain nonbinary quantity. One such example is the execution time of a subtask. In this respect, time is treated as a scarce resource.

All these scarce resources, the hard and soft requirements, are combined. Subtasks are ordered according to their joint scarcity. Two definitions are introduced; the resource set availability and the resource scarcity grade.

The resource set availability (RSA) is the level of congruity between a subtask's set of requirements and a worker's capabilities. The RSA takes into account the following facts:

1. The combination of requirements for a subtask is more important than the individual requirements of the subtask. For instance, if a subtask needs requirements A and B, then the subtask can be processed only when there is a worker offering both capabilities at the same moment.
2. If a subtask's set of requirements is not met on a worker, the RSA for this subtask is zero.
3. If a subtask's set of requirements is met by a certain worker, then the RSA for this subtask on this worker is nonzero.

The RSA for a subtask s on a worker w is the combination of resource availabilities (RAs) for each requirement r of this subtask. The RA is the level at which requirement r is met by a worker's capabilities. It is either 0 or 1 for a hard requirement, and might be a value in between for a soft requirement. For instance if the duration of a subtask s is marked as soft requirement r, the

RA can be measured based on the duration D of the subtask as:

$$RA(r, s_i, w_j) = \frac{1}{D(s_i)}$$

The RSA for a subtask s on worker w is defined as the product of the RAs for each requirement r of this subtask on this worker, multiplied by a weighted resource availability measure. The product in the RSA formula results in an RSA of 0 if at least one of the requirements is not met at all. The importance factor i denotes the relative importance of resource availabilities. Typically, hard requirements have a larger importance factor than soft requirements.

$$RSA(s_i, w_j) = $$
$$\prod_{r \in s_i} RA(r, s_i, w_j) \times \sum_r i_r \times RA(r, s_i, w_j)$$
$$\forall r \in s_i : 0 \leq RA(r, s_i, w_j) \leq 1$$
$$\forall r \notin s_i : RA(r, s_i, w_j) = 0$$
$$\sum_r i_r = 1$$

The resource set availability is the level of congruity between a subtask's set of requirements and a worker's capabilities and can have values in the range $(0,1)$. The resource scarcity grade (RSG) is a relative score assigned to each subtask, for all workers. It denotes a subtask's need for scarce resources or their level of scarcity. That is, it ranks subtasks according to the relative scarcity of the resources needed for processing each subtask in the pool of workers. Subtasks needing a widely available set of requirements have a lower resource scarcity grade. Subtasks with a long execution time have a higher resource scarcity grade. A subtask's combination of requirements is scarcer when fewer workers offer the combination of required capabilities. For instance, if requirement set A is met by workers M and N, and requirement set B is met by worker M, then requirement set B is scarcer than requirement set A. Hence, the resource scarcity grade of subtasks requiring B is higher than the resource scarcity grade of subtasks requiring A but not B.

The resource scarcity grade is defined as follows:

$$RSG(s_i) = N(w) - \sum_w RSA(s_i, w_j)$$

$N(w)$ denotes the number of active workers in the pool. The resource scarcity grade is higher when fewer workers offer the subtask's set of capabilities. A farm of workers in which no worker offers a subtask's set of requirements results in an RSG of $N(w)$. If a subtask's requirements are all hard requirements, and all workers offer those required capabilities, the RSG equals 0. This means the subtask can be assigned to any worker.

Each time a worker is added to or removed from the pool, the resource scarcity grades need to be recomputed. This is a limited computation, as the RSG can be computed incrementally. For each subtask, adding a worker boils down to computing the RSA for this worker and then taking the subtask's former RSG and adding 1 minus that value; removing a worker means subtracting 1 minus that value:

$$RSG(s_i, N+1) = RSG(s_i, N) + (1 - RSA(s_i, w_t))$$
$$RSG(s_i, N-1) = RSG(s_i, N) - (1 - RSA(s_i, w_t))$$

$RSG(s_i, N)$ denotes the RSG for subtask s_i for N workers in the pool. w_t is the worker that is added to or removed from the farm. This computation time is more significant for a larger number of subtasks or at startup with a large pool of workers. In most cases, however, a dedicated suboptimal resource scarcity grade computation can be sufficient to achieve or approach the required level of load balancing.

Once the subtasks are ordered by decreasing resource scarcity grade, the subtasks can be assigned to workers starting at the top of the list.

Only subtasks with a resource scarcity grade smaller than $N(w)$ can be processed by the current pool of workers. The moment a worker becomes available, it receives the subtask with the highest resource scarcity grade whose requirements match the worker's capabilities. This is performed for each worker that becomes idle and awaits a new subtask.

Embracing Dependability

One difference between the traditional and the dependable farmer-worker model is in handling the possibility that a worker can fail during processing. However, as described earlier, there are several performance drawbacks with the dependable model. These drawbacks can be dealt with in two ways:

1. Giving priority to a subtask's resource scarcity grade above its freshness grade.
2. Making the dispatcher aware of the failed processing of a subtask.

In this section, these enhancements are explained.

With the Notion of Resource Scarcity...

Once the processing of a subtask has failed due to, say, a deficient worker, the subtask is reassigned. It is reinserted in the list of subtasks according to its resource scarcity grade. In practice, the subtask is inserted somewhere at the top of the list of subtasks because the failing worker received during the previous assignment the subtask with the highest requirements it could process. With this adaptation, the performance pitfalls are drastically limited.

To avoid reassigning a subtask too often, a maximum freshness grade is introduced. For instance, if the maximum freshness grade is defined as 3, the subtask can be assigned only three times, in most cases to a different worker each time. If

three different workers fail to process the subtask, there is a significant possibility that no worker will ever successfully process the subtask. Taking this maximum freshness grade into account is especially important when the pool of workers gets larger, because it avoids an extreme delay if there is an insurmountable problem in the network or the subtask itself.

And the Introduction of Supervisors...

The dispatcher should be kept informed whenever a worker fails, so that the subtask can be rescheduled and reinserted as soon as possible in the list of subtasks. This is the task of a supervisor.

A supervisor is initialized for each active worker. The first task of the supervisor is to find out the capability set C of the worker and to send this information together with its worker ID w to the dispatcher. Based on this capability list, the dispatcher can compute the resource scarcity grades and assign a subtask to this worker via the supervisor. The supervisor delegates the subtask it receives to the worker, monitors the worker's state, and notifies any events to the dispatcher. From the moment the supervisor has processed a subtask, it transfers the output o to the collector and resends the worker ID w to the dispatcher, so that a new subtask can be assigned.

The supervisor plays an active role for obtaining a higher level of fault tolerance in three types of events:

1. The worker loses one of its capabilities, or (re)gains an extra service.
2. The worker becomes nonresponsive or responsive again.
3. The worker fails to process a subtask.

The worker might lose one of its capabilities or (re)gain an extra service. It is the task of the supervisor to notice such a change in the worker's capability list. He resends this updated capability list C to the dispatcher. As a result, the resource scarcity grades of all unfinished subtasks are updated. New tasks can be assigned to this worker only according to the updated capability list. This means a subtask cannot be assigned to a worker that has lost one of the capabilities the subtask requires.

In most cases, processing a current subtask fails when the worker loses a capability. The supervisor sends not only the output o to the collector but also the state T, which denotes whether processing the subtask is finished or not. The collector stores the output of the subtask, performs some final processing, and notifies the dispatcher about the final state of the subtask T', which is the same as T if collecting, merging and storing the output have succeeded, and which is unfinished otherwise. If the state is unfinished, and the subtask's freshness grade has not reached the maximum freshness grade, the dispatcher reinserts this subtask into the list of unfinished subtasks so that it can be reassigned to another worker. If on the other hand the maximum freshness grade is already reached, the subtask will not be reassigned anymore. Note that in this model, the introduction of supervisors brings along concurrent error handling instead of preemptive error handling (Avizienis, Laprie, & Randell, 2001).

A similar flow happens when a worker becomes nonresponsive. The supervisor notifies the dispatcher that this worker has lost all its capabilities. As a result, the dispatcher does not assign a new task to this worker until further notice. The resource scarcity grades of the remaining subtasks are updated.

The collector is also notified about the partial processing. Once the collector has collected the output of the unfinished task, it notifies the dispatcher that the subtask has not been properly completed. If its freshness grade has not yet reached the maximum, the subtask is reinserted into the list of unfinished subtasks to get reassigned to another worker.

The final event is when the worker is correctly processing and does not miss any of its capabilities, but a subtask has failed due to an unexpected result. This indicates an error in the worker's processing or in the expected result. The supervisor should notice this as it receives the output from the worker and analyzes it.

Handling a failed subtask is not dealt with by this model, but has been the subject of the N-version programming approach (Avizienis, 1985), the recovery block method (Randell, 1975) or other methods (Randell, Xu, & Zorzo, 1996). Hence the failed subtask is not to be reprocessed and the supervisor marks it FINISHED. This finished state is sent to the collector and forwarded to the dispatcher once the output is stored. As the subtask is marked finished, the dispatcher does not reschedule it.

In this respect a worker becomes a dumb processing node, not aware of the specific farmer-worker model communication. The supervisors are polling the workers for their capabilities and send this information and any updates to the dispatcher. The supervisor also delegates the subtask to the worker and is aware when the worker has finished and can trigger the collector. When the collector receives the output, it notifies the dispatcher whether this subtask has been finished or whether it needs rescheduling if the freshness grade has not yet reached the maximum.

And a Planner

In the original dependable farmer-worker model, the workers notify a central dispatcher to start participating in processing the subtasks. In this model, the workers are dumb processing entities, not aware of the algorithm communication. Still, the dispatcher needs to know the list of active workers. Controlling the list of registered workers is the role of the planner.

The planner has knowledge of which workers are currently available for joining the farm. This knowledge can be attained through configuration, through network scans, or by any other means.

Whenever a nonparticipating worker becomes available, the planner initializes a supervisor for the worker. The supervisor sends the worker's capability list and its worker ID w to the dispatcher in order to start the worker's contribution to the farm. The planner can also remove a worker by destroying the supervisor. The supervisor ends the worker's processing, notifies the dispatcher of the empty capability list, and sends the subtask's output and its UNFINISHED state to the collector. After the collector has received the output, the dispatcher is notified about the unfinished state. The dispatcher in turn reschedules this subtask.

ACTORS IN THE DEPENDABLE RESOURCE-AWARE FARMER-WORKER ALGORITHM

Bringing together these enhancements and integrating them with the original dependable farmer-worker model, produces the following actors (Figure 1).

Planner

The list of active workers w forms the farm and contains the workers ready to participate in the parallelization process. On startup, the initial list of active workers is defined and the corresponding supervisors initialized. The planner continuously keeps track of the inactive worker list and moni-

tors whether one should be added to the farm of active workers. In this case it initializes a supervisor for a newly active worker. On the other hand, when an active worker should be removed from the farm, the planner sends a STOP message to the supervisor.

Also note that the task of the planner is not to monitor the requirements, nor to keep track of a worker failure like non-responsiveness. The planner has knowledge only about the moment a worker starts participating or the moment it should be retrieved, independent of the state or failure of these workers. Still, the planner can monitor the responsiveness of the supervisors and hence can contribute to a higher fault-tolerance level in the system.

Farmer

The farmer grabs the input data and divides the task into a series of subtasks s with ID k. This list of subtasks is sent to the dispatcher. The farmer also notifies the dispatcher via a NEW_RUN message that all subtasks of one input data run have been sent to the dispatcher and the dispatcher can start the run by allocating subtasks to workers. With a STOP message the dispatcher and consequently all the other players are notified that the whole process should be terminated.

Figure 1. The dependable resource-aware farmer-worker algorithm

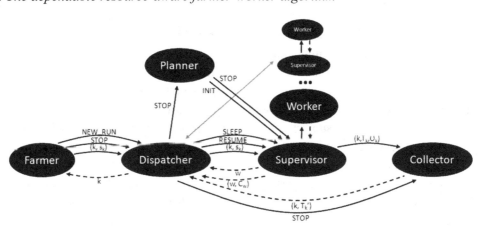

Dispatcher

The dispatcher receives the list of subtasks s with ID k from the farmer. On receiving the capabilities from the supervisors, it computes the resource scarcity grades and sorts the subtasks accordingly. The subtasks requiring the most limited combination of resources are given priority in the parallelization process. Once the farmer has sent the NEW_RUN message, the dispatcher starts allocating the subtasks to idle workers in the farm in the form of a (k, s) message.

The dispatcher can send two other types of messages to the supervisor. A SLEEP message denotes that the dispatcher has new subtasks at its disposal but cannot assign these yet as it is awaiting the farmer's NEW_RUN message. Such a SLEEP message is always followed by a RESUME message before new subtasks are allocated to the active workers.

When no more input data is available, the farmer sends a STOP message to the dispatcher. The dispatcher in turn propagates this STOP message to the planner and the collector. The whole process is then terminated.

Supervisor

At initialization the supervisor sends its worker ID w to the dispatcher, denoting that a new subtask can be assigned, together with the worker's list of capabilities C. The dispatcher calculates the resource scarcity grades and assigns a subtask s by sending the combination of this subtask and its ID k. This supervisor forms the communication link between the worker and all the other actors in this model.

The supervisor can send the subtask as a whole to the worker, or it can divide the subtask into smaller commands, depending on the interface the worker offers. The supervisor also keeps track of the worker's correct functioning. If a worker becomes unresponsive, the supervisor sends an empty capability list C to the dispatcher; if the worker's capabilities have changed, the supervisor sends a new capability list. The dispatcher then recalculates the resource scarcity grades.

The final task of the supervisor is notifying the collector when a subtask has finished. In addition to the worker ID k, the resulting output o and the subtask's state T are sent to the collector. This state is either FINISHED or UNFINISHED.

Worker

The worker is a dumb device, not aware of the farmer-worker algorithm's communication. It processes commands received from the supervisor. The supervisor is the only communication partner of the worker in this model.

Collector

When a subtask has been processed, the supervisor notifies the collector by sending the subtask ID k, the output o, and the subtask's state T. The collector grabs and merges the output of all the subtasks and performs some final processing on the output. The collector notifies the dispatcher about the subtask's final state T', indicating whether this subtask is finished or not and whether collecting, merging, and postprocessing have succeeded. Based on this, and on the subtask's freshness grade, the dispatcher reschedules the subtask if marked UNFINISHED.

THE TEST CASE

The extended resource-aware model adds optimization through dynamic load balancing based on resource scarcity. Furthermore, it removes performance degradation upon the failures or state changes of the workers. This model has been applied to the test environment of the Cisco Digital Content Manager (DCM), a content-processing device that receives digital television streams, processes them, and sends the processed streams out.

The digital television market is a fast-changing environment with more and more functionality continuously added to processing devices. Because of the number of features being developed, automated testing is a necessity to keep the quality of the product high. For each feature developed on the device, a test plan is set up and the corresponding test script written and added to a list of automated test scripts. Each evening, a new build is made of the package. After an automated upgrade, all test scripts are run on a list of available content-processing devices. The results are stored on a server, and an e-mail report is sent out to the engineers, preferably before the first engineer arrives at work the following day.

As the device feature list grows, the nightly automated test runtime increases. When tests are run on one device, the results appear after days. In the current fast-changing world, this is unacceptable. Therefore test scripts are run on several devices in parallel, and if the capacity of the pool is insufficient to get the results the following day, new devices are added to the pool (Figure 2).

Each device typically has another layout. The current and future configuration possibilities are very diverse. Several possible degrees of freedom are taken into account.

1. **Hardware:** One device takes a main board and one to four processing boards. The most obvious type of processing board is an I/O (input/output) board, which can receive streams and send them out again. The market defines several types of physical interfaces, or ports, for receiving or sending out streams via satellite, cable, and terrestrial transmission (Fischer, 2004; Lundstrom, 2006). There are several types of I/O boards, which vary in the number and the type of interface or combination of interfaces they are offering.

I/O boards are typically set up with "loopback" cables between ports, so that the output stream on one port serves as an input stream on another port. As a result, this input stream can be used for further analyzing, processing, and testing. There is a well-determined layout of loopback cables on the several types of I/O boards. Still, this layout can vary, for example, either by connecting ports on different I/O boards or connecting ports

Figure 2. The increasing number of automated scripts over two years of Cisco DCM package releases

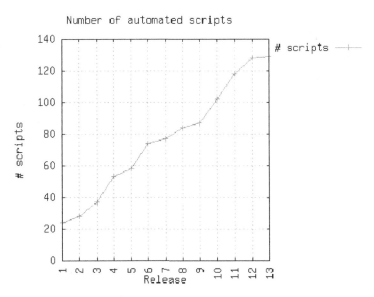

with routers or other equipment for thorough or integrated testing.

In addition to I/O boards, there are also several types of dedicated pure processing boards, which do not have any I/O interfaces. Furthermore, some I/O boards and dedicated processing boards can be extended with co-processing boards.

2. **Input:** The second degree of freedom comprises the list and type of incoming digital content, or streams. Tests are run with a combination of test streams and real-life streams. There are several types of transport-stream standards. In Europe, the DVB Standard Information (SI) is used (Fischer, 2004; Lundstrom, 2006). In North America, PSIP (Program and System Information Protocol) is the standard (Eyer, 2003; Fischer, 2004). Japan uses the ARIB SI (Association of Radio Industries and Businesses, 2007).

All these degrees of freedom can be combined. It requires no further explanation to say that the number of combinations is vast and increases over time. On the other hand, each test script requires one or more of these configuration options. Matching and dividing test scripts over the devices manually is very time-consuming. Furthermore, it needs to be done on a regular basis, because the list of test scripts is steadily growing, and because the test scripts must be finished as quickly as possible. For this reason, the resource-aware farmer-worker algorithm described above has been applied to this test environment.

Resource Scarcity Grade

Two factors define the resource scarcity grade. First of all, for each test script, a list of devices is set up on which the test script can be run. This is the list of devices offering the script's set of hard requirements. The scripts that can be run on only one device are inserted at the beginning

of the list. Hence, if a device becomes available for processing, the dispatcher first assigns it test scripts that can be run only on this device. If none are present, a script is taken that can be run on only two devices, of which one is the newly available device. Subtracting the number of devices that the script can run on from the total number of active test devices in the pool forms the first factor F_1 of the resource scarcity grade, with the largest values at the beginning of the script list.

Second, within the list of test scripts that can be run on the same number of devices, the scripts are ordered in decreasing predicted processing time. The predicted processing time is measured by taking the time previously needed for running the script successfully. This duration can be initiated to a large value. The predicted processing time forms the second factor F_2 of the resource scarcity grade.

In short, the following formula has been used for computing the resource scarcity grade:

$$RSG(s_i) = F_1 << 16 + F_2$$

The first factor is shifted 16 bits in order to model its absolute preference above the duration factor F_2. The duration is measured in seconds and is assumed not to be larger than 16 bits. This formula is similar to the formerly mentioned formula for the *RSG,* with the hard requirements receiving importance factors that are much larger than the importance factor of the subtask's duration (Figure 3).

The current focus is on dynamically assigning test scripts in one execution run, that is, in testing one build at a time. Testing more than one build is done sequentially. The algorithm's actors are translated in this test case as follows.

The task is one test run, comprised of testing all test scripts once on one of the available devices for one nightly build. Each test script forms a subtask that can be assigned to a worker. A script is a set of interface definition language, or IDL

Figure 3. The Cisco DCM's test environment

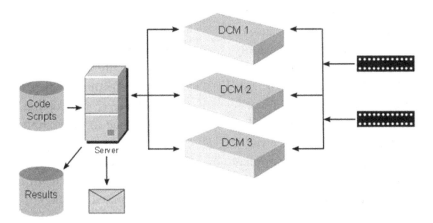

(Vogel, Vasudevan, Benjamin, & Villalba, 1999) calls to the worker.

The planner, farmer, dispatcher, supervisors, and collector are processes on a server. The planner is limited to a configured pool of workers. The list of active workers is revised for each run. The farmer grabs the input; in other words, it extracts the latest version of the scripts for this build from a version control system. The list of scripts to be executed is passed on to the dispatcher. The dispatcher sorts the list of scripts according to the above formula for the resource scarcity grade and assigns a script to a supervisor whenever a worker becomes idle again.

Each worker is a DCM communicating with the outside world through IDL. The supervisor consists of a framework that handles the script's execution. Each IDL call in the script is sent to the worker sequentially, and the response is analyzed. When processing a script has ended, the supervisor analyzes the result and marks the script as SUCCESS, FAIL, or CONFIG_ERROR, which is part of the script's output o. In the case of FAIL, debugging output is retrieved from the device for the engineers. For all cases, logs are retrieved. Finally, the supervisor notifies the collector about the state T of the script, which is FINISHED or UNFINISHED.

The collector collects the output received from the supervisor and stores it to permanent storage. Statistics are set up based on the script's output and the logs. The dispatcher is notified about whether the script's final result is FINISHED or UNFINISHED.

As mentioned, the three possible results of an executed test script are SUCCESS, FAIL, and CONFIG_ERROR. This is important information for deciding the steps to be taken next.

- **SUCCESS:** The script receives a final state of FINISHED. This means the script succeeded completely and the dispatcher does not need to reschedule it.
- **FAIL:** The script fails. This means the device's output of the IDL command did not match the expected result. Upon failure, the script is ended sooner, as no further processing is done. A script failure can be due to a bug in the device, or due to an error in the expected results of the script. The collector receives the output of the script and notifies the dispatcher that this subtask has been FINISHED, so the subtask is not reassigned and no retries are scheduled. Still, the collector extracts the result FAILED from the subtask's output o,

and sends an e-mail with the failure to the script's responsible engineer. The engineer is assumed to analyze and fix the cause of the failure as soon as possible, preferably by the start of the next build or test run.

- **CONFIG_ERROR:** The supervisor polls the worker for setting up the list of worker capabilities and sends this to the dispatcher. When the supervisor receives a new subtask or script, or when a script has failed, it tries to match the script's list of requirements with a worker's capabilities. As scripts are assigned only to workers offering these capabilities, this matching step should not fail. If it does, it means that the worker has lost at least one of its capabilities, either temporarily or permanently. The dispatcher is notified about this change in the worker's capability list. The supervisor also notifies the collector about the script ending with the state UNFINISHED. The collector in turn notifies the dispatcher about this subtask's state. Upon arrival at the dispatcher, the subtask is rescheduled, unless the subtask's freshness grade has reached the maximum.

DISCUSSION AND RESULTS

The introduction of this extended resource-aware farmer-worker model brings considerable improvements:

- **Dynamic Load Balancing:** No more time has to be spent on manually load balancing the scripts, a task that would have become more and more difficult with the current explosion of features, capabilities, and scripts added to the devices. Even more, a failing script can end earlier than it would have as a successful one. With static load balancing, the remaining scripts were not redivided among the devices. Dynamic load balancing ensures that the total duration of the tests is shorter, as the scripts are dynamically divided.

- **Faster Testing:** With static load balancing, there is a suboptimal division of the scripts due to the complexity and number of capabilities. With dynamic load balancing, all workers end within ten minutes of each other. This small difference is a result of the limited duration of some scripts that require widely available capabilities. The only exception is a test device with a very limited but dedicated set of capabilities. This device ends early in the test run.

- **A Larger Pool of Workers:** The pool of devices is easily extended between runs. Each new device only needs to be added to the planner's list of workers. As testing times drastically increased, a bunch of engineers' development devices were added to the pool of workers in the nightly tests, as they were mostly idle anyway at night. When approaching and finalizing a certain release, tests must be executed very often. However, parallel development of the next release has already started, which also requires test runs. Adding devices to the pool of workers ensures that several releases can be tested in sequence at night and if needed continued during the day.

- **Faster Debugging:** The short e-mail report upon the failure of a script is interesting if tests are run during the day. The error can be dealt with immediately, and fixes can be performed by the next nightly build and test run. Errors reported by the scripts are more quickly documented, and captured bugs are more quickly solved. As a consequence, development is more stable with regard to existing functionality, and fixes are available faster.

- **Flexibility and Reduced Cost:** Adding engineers' development devices to the pool of workers, instead of extending the pool of dedicated test devices, reduces the cost of testing. Fewer new devices need to be reserved purely for testing purposes. Furthermore, when for instance a new board is developed, the first ones are typically assigned to developers implementing the embedded software or firmware. Using these engineers' development devices for testing reduces the initial number of hardware parts needed early in the development cycle (Figure 4).

There are also some risks involved with introducing this model. As the test environment gets more intelligent, daily management must also be dealt with and has to grow at the same pace.

First of all, redundancy is necessary in any case. It also shortens the test runtime, and if a device fails, the scripts can still be executed if another device in the pool of active test devices meets the same necessary requirements.

Second, a best practice is to split up scripts if needed. A script should not combine tests needing a scarce set of capabilities with a large set of tests that can be run on any device. Independent of the length and number of tests that can be run on any device, such a script has to be scheduled on a device offering the scarce resources. Furthermore, if a script's runtime is shorter, the impact of rescheduling it is smaller, and load balancing is more easily achieved. On the other hand, if this *grain size* is too small, the dispatcher can be overwhelmed by workers requesting a new subtask (Goux, Linderoth, & Yoder, 2000).

Managing the pool of active devices also needs to be easy and transparent to everyone whose device is participating. Centralizing the configuration of this pool brings along a certain overhead if the pool is steadily growing and several releases are developed concurrently.

Figure 4. The RSG values of assigned scripts over time. An RSG value of zero for a device denotes there are no more scripts to be assigned to it. Device 3 becomes a bottleneck when the pool of test devices further enlarges.

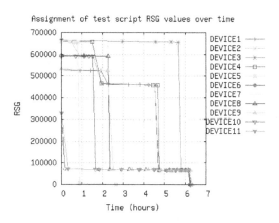

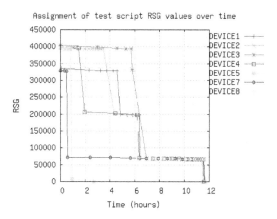

The short e-mail reports of a script failure trigger the engineers' analysis of the problem earlier. Still, the results of their analysis need to be collected and centralized. In this respect, not only are the tests to be automated but also, as much as possible, the management surrounding them. In the ideal case, one engineer pushes the button for starting the tests. When e-mails notify engineers that a script has failed, they should conduct a dispersed effort to analyze the errors and fill in a report. A central point should be available for them to check in the results of these analyses and reports, which might also be sent out once all script failures are analyzed. A reminder can be sent if any failures are not analyzed after a certain time.

Last but not least, this dynamic load balancing does not solve all load-balancing issues. The list of scripts requires that configuration decisions be made on the test devices. Some requirements need to be combined for certain scripts, others do not. Some combined requirements need more processing time than other requirements. This is an optimization problem on its own, and might be solved with existing static optimization tools like LINDO, LINGO or CPLEX (Sarker & Newton, 2007). Still, this configuration is not always changed with the addition of scripts or devices, and if the most needed requirements are widely available in the farm, a suboptimal division is sufficient. In practice, the largest bottlenecks are monitored over time, and the configuration is rescheduled over the devices if one of the bottlenecks has gone over a certain runtime threshold.

FUTURE WORK

The application of this extended farmer-worker model is still in progress. The following phases have been set up at Cisco.

Phase 1: Dynamic load balancing and adding workers flexibly between test runs

This phase comprises applying resource scarcity grades, sorting the scripts accordingly, and assigning scripts dynamically to workers. The goal of this phase is speeding up nightly tests by offering a flexible way to add scripts or test devices, and by letting engineers receive the results as soon as possible with minimal effort.

Phase 2: Dynamically adding and removing workers during a test run

This is more important if the nightly tests are slightly evolving toward continuous testing, es-

pecially when a release is near. A test run started during the day cannot use the engineers' test devices before 7 p.m., because these are used for development and testing by the engineers during the day. However, once the engineers have left the lab, these devices should be added to the pool of workers in order to speed up the test run.

The same holds for test runs started at night but not finished yet in the morning. The engineers' test devices can be added to the pool at night, but automatically removed from the pool in the morning.

Phase 3: Enhanced planning

As more engineers' development devices are used for testing, planning gets more and more important. On most occasions, engineers' devices can be used at night. However, engineers are performing regular personalized tests on their development devices at night, during which time these devices cannot be added to the pool of automated test devices. Enhanced planning involves a system of either statically determining the active worker pool through configuration or reservation, or dynamically through polling, scanning, or monitoring. The advantage of dynamically defining the pool of active workers is the flexibility and very limited management involved in order to plan test runs. For instance, it would be the responsibility of the engineers to change the configuration to include or exclude their devices at a certain moment in time. The advantage of configuring the active pool is the much more accurate estimated time of arrival of a certain test run in which management is interested. Probably the best approach is a combination of both.

Phase 4: Runtime capability-list changes

This phase determines at runtime the capability set of the devices and handles any state changes (the addition or removal of capabilities at runtime). It opens the door for reassigning scripts upon configuration errors. A script can be rerun on other devices if the device it has run on does not possess the necessary capabilities anymore.

Phase 5: Partial testing

The last phase involves the global picture. Devices should be occupied as much as possible and continuous testing introduced. This, however, requires a system to allow a test run to be paused and resumed — and to enable another, more urgent, test run of a pending release to be run between those two commands. Also the notion of a test *preview* should be defined. There can be full or core tests. *Full tests* would execute all the test scripts; *core tests* would execute a selection or preview of test scripts. The question is whether the list of core tests can be extended to full tests, and how the scripts requiring more resources should be handled.

For the moment, the first phase has ended at Cisco and the second one is in progress. Already – quite soon after the first phase was introduced – it is seen as a necessity in further speeding up the test runs.

CONCLUSION

The farmer-worker algorithm and its dependable extension offer a model for parallelization and the dynamic load balancing of subtasks within a pool of workers. However, in some cases not all workers have the same capabilities, and not all subtasks to be executed contain the same set of requirements. For these applications, the resource-aware farmer-worker algorithm describes how to order the subtasks based on the scarcity of their requirements, and how to set up these scarcity grades for each subtask or deal with failing workers.

Furthermore, the model is extended to deal with the fact that embedded devices do not participate in the algorithm's communication process.

This resource-aware farmer-worker algorithm has been applied to the test environment of the Cisco DCM, a digital television content-processing device. The introduction of this algorithm has already contributed to the dynamic load balancing, automated management, and speeding-up of nightly tests. Furthermore, this model proposes enhanced error handling and fault tolerance in the test setup. As a result, more test runs are being executed, which contributes to a more stable development and an expedited tracking down of faults in the system. And all this despite a world where functionality is continuously added to the device at a fast pace.

REFERENCES

Aida, K., Futakata, Y., & Tomotaka, O. (2006). Parallel branch and bound algorithm with the hierarchical master-worker paradigm on the grid. *Transactions on High Performance Computing Systems, 47*(12), 193–206.

Association of Radio Industries and Businesses. (2007). *ARIB Standard, Service Information for Digital Broadcasting System.* Retrieved December 14, 2009, from http://www.arib.or.jp/english/html/overview/doc/6-STD-B10v4_4-E1.pdf

Avizienis, A. (1985). The N-version approach to fault-tolerant software. *In Proceedings of the IEEE Transactions on Software Engineering, 11*(12). Washington, DC: IEEE Computer Society. 1491–1501. doi:10.1109/TSE.1985.231893

Avizienis, A., Laprie, J. C., & Randell, B. (2001). *Fundamental concepts of dependability* (Tech. Rep. No. 1145). Paris: LAAS-CNRS.

Berthold, J., Dieterle, M., Loogen, R., & Priebe, S. (2008). Hierarchical master-worker skeletons. In P. Hudak & D. S. Warren (Eds.), *Proceedings of the 10ᵗʰ International Symposium on Practical Aspects of Declarative Languages* (Vol. 4902, pp. 248-264). New York: Springer.

Chan, P., & Abramson, D. (2001). NetFiles: A novel approach to parallel programming of master/worker applications. In *Proceedings of the 5th International Conference and Exhibition on High Performance Computing in the Asia-Pacific Region (HPC Asia 2001)*, Queensland, Australia. Retrieved December 14, 2009, from http://messagelab.monash.edu.au/Publications

De Florio, V., Deconinck, G., & Lauwereins, R. (1997). An application-level dependable technique for farmer-worker parallel programs. In B. Herzberger & P. Sloot (Eds.), *Proceedings Of the High-Performance Computing and Networking International Conference And Exhibition. Lecture Notes in Computer Science* (Vol. 1225, pp. 644-653). Berlin: Springer Verlag.

Eyer, M. K. (2003). *PSIP: Program and system information protocol*. New York: McGraw-Hill.

Fischer, W. (2004). *Digital television: a practical guide for engineers*. Berlin: Springer Verlag.

Goux, J. P., Linderoth, J., & Yoder, M. (2000). *Metacomputing and the master-worker paradigm*. Retrieved December 14, 2009, from http://www.cs.wisc.edu/condor/mw/papers.html

Hennessy, J. L., & Patterson, D. A. (2003). *Computer architecture: a quantitative approach*. San Francisco: Morgan Kauffmann.

Leeman, M., Leeman, M., De Florio, V., & Deconinck, G. (2003). A flexible library for dependable master-worker parallel programs. In A. Clematis (Ed.), *Proceedings of the Eleventh Euromicro Conference on Parallel, Distributed and Network-Based Processing* (pp. 299-307). Washington, DC: IEEE Computer Society.

Lundstrom, L. (2006). *Understanding digital television: an introduction to DVB systems with satellite, cable, broadband and terrestrial TV distribution*. Focal Press.

Poldner, M., & Kuchen, H. (2008). On implementing the farm skeleton. In []. New York: World Scientific Publishing.]. *Proceedings of the International Workshop on High-Level Parallel Programming and Applications, 18*(1), 117–131.

Randell, B. (1975). System structure for software fault tolerance. In []. Washington, DC: IEEE Computer Society.]. *Proceedings of the International Conference on Reliable Software, 10*(6), 437–449. doi:10.1145/800027.808467

Randell, B., Xu, J., & Zorzo, A. (1996). Software fault tolerance in object oriented systems: approaches, implementation and evaluation. In *First year report of Design for Validation* (pp. 213–226). DeVa.

Sarker, R. A., & Newton, C. S. (2007). *Optimization modelling: a practical approach*. Boca Raton, FL: CRC Press. doi:10.1201/9781420043112

Vogel, A., Vasudevan, B., Benjamin, M., & Villalba, T. (1999). *C++ programming with CORBA*. New York: John Wiley & Sons, Inc.

This work was previously published in the International Journal of Adaptive, Resilient and Autonomic Systems, Volume 2, Issue 1, edited by Vincenzo De Florio, pp. 1-17, copyright 2011 by IGI Publishing (an imprint of IGI Global).

Chapter 6

Non–Intrusive Autonomic Approach with Self–Management Policies Applied to Legacy Infrastructures for Performance Improvements

Rémi Sharrock
LAAS-CNRS - University of Toulouse; UPS, INSA, INP, ISAE, France

Thierry Monteil
LAAS-CNRS - University of Toulouse; UPS, INSA, INP, ISAE, France

Patricia Stolf
IRIT and Université de Toulouse, France

Daniel Hagimont
IRIT and Université de Toulouse, France

Laurent Broto
IRIT and Université de Toulouse, France

ABSTRACT

The growing complexity of large IT facilities involves important time and effort costs to operate and maintain. Autonomic computing gives a new approach in designing distributed architectures that manage themselves in accordance with high-level objectives. The main issue is that existing architectures do not necessarily follow this new approach. The motivation is to implement a system that can interface heterogeneous components and platforms supplied by different vendors in a non-intrusive and generic manner. The goal is to increase the intelligence of the system by actively monitoring its state and autonomously taking corrective actions without the need to modify the managed system. In this paper, the authors focus on modeling software and hardware architectures as well as describing administration policies using a graphical language inspired from UML. The paper demonstrates that this language is powerful enough to describe complex scenarios and evaluates some self-management policies for performance improvement on a distributed computational jobs load balancer over a grid.

DOI: 10.4018/978-1-4666-2056-8.ch006

INTRODUCTION

Autonomic Computing Principles

Autonomic computing aims to provide methods and tools to answer the exponentially growing demand in IT (Information Technologies) infrastructures. These IT systems are getting increasingly complex while using a wide variety of technologies. Huebscher (2008) compares the actual situation to the one experienced in the 1920s in telephony: automatic branch exchanges finally supplanted trained human operators. Nowadays, large IT facilities involve important time and effort costs to operate and maintain hardware and software. Numerous new technologies are emerging and they consume considerable human resources in learning how to run, tweak, or configure. One of the challenges facing large companies that use such IT infrastructures is that of reducing their maintenance and operating costs (David, Schuff, & St. Louis, 2002) in order to increase their dependability (Sterritt & Bustard, 2003) and assurance levels to help them being more confident.

Here are some of the issues raised in this field of research:

- First of all, managing large scale infrastructures requires describing the global system in a synthetic way. This involves describing a deployment objective, a picture of what to deploy and how to deploy it. This picture represents what the system should look like upon deployment, the intended construction. Indeed, it is necessary to have an automatically orchestrated deployment process due to the huge number of machines (at least hundreds, and up to thousands) that are potentially involved. It has been shown that large deployments cannot be handled by humans, because this often leads to errors or inconsistencies (Flissi, Dubus, Dolet, & Merle, 2008).

- Once deployed, the system has to be configured and started. These multiple tasks are ordered (some parts of the system have to be configured or started before others), which also imply an automatic process. Indeed, Kon and Campbell (1999) argue that it is hard to create robust and efficient systems if the dynamic dependencies between components are not well understood. They found common issues were some parts of the system fail to accomplish their goals because unspecified dependencies are not properly resolved. Sometimes, failure of one part of the system could also lead to a general system failure.

- During runtime, human system operators tend to have slow reaction times and this can result in unavailability of critical services. For example, Gray (1986) clearly shows that human mistakes made during maintenance operations or reconfigurations are mainly responsible for failures in distributed systems. The need here is to introduce a rapid system repair or reconfiguration so that critical services are kept at an acceptable level (Flaviu, 1993). Moreover, new services (large audience services like social networks, video services) tend to follow heavy fluctuations in demands (Cheng, Dale, & Liu, 2008). Thus, these services experience scalability issues and need fast rescale mechanisms.

Raised Problematics

Exploring the autonomic computing principles lead us to the following questions:

- How to describe deployment objectives, repairs, reconfigurations or rescaling? This raises the need for easy to use, high-level policies to describe the management of distributed systems.

- How to administrate proprietary system components (also called legacy), even those that do not include their own built-in management capabilities, within another management system? This points out the need for a non-intrusive, generic framework that does not require modification of the proprietary components.

In this paper, we deal with these problems and present an approach for an autonomic computing platform that uses high level policies specification for dynamic reconfiguration of legacy software. Our work is based on an existing prototype called TUNe (Broto, Hagimont, Stolf, De Palma, & Temate, 2008), implemented in java, and introduces dynamic performance adaptation capabilities.

This paper is structured as followed: first, we compare our approach to related works and introduce our prototype; we continue with the description of the hardware and software models, and the management policies model. To finish, we experiment the policies on a real system and some results are presented.

Principles of our Approach

Our approach aims at managing in an autonomous way distributed systems composed of legacy software elements and probes (the environment) while optimizing simultaneously their performance. These elements are automatically deployed and configured on different hardware resources. During runtime, we enable the environment to evolve (for example, by adding/removing components, restarting, reconfiguring or repairing them). Our autonomic closed control loop therefore encompasses:

1. Event detection by generic probes, proprietary probes or even the software elements themselves if the legacy includes its own

probing system. The detection of one or many events can generate one or more notifications depending on the probe's integrated intelligence.
2. Notification dispatching to the autonomic manager that gathers information (how to identify the faulty elements, probing metrics).
3. Reaction: the autonomic manager can then react on the system, given the high-level behavior specification (the intelligence). This description is both used to analyze the information and to carry on actions on legacy software pieces or probes.

Each administration facet (deployment, configuration, reconfiguration, optimization) has a specific description need. Four types of Domain Specific Modeling Language (DSML) are introduced for their specification: one for the Hardware Description (HD), one for the Software Description (SD), one for the Software Wrapper Description (SWD), and one for the Policy Description (PD). The DSML used for SWD is based on a simple XML syntax. The DSML used for HD, SD and PD are inspired from a subset of UML graphical language (Dobing & Parsons, 2006), and the resulting graphical diagrams are called Hardware Description Diagram (HDD), Software Description Diagram (SDD) and Policy Description Diagram (PDD). These diagrams describe the global view of the system and its management in a high level of abstraction. TUNe (Toulouse University Network) deploys applications in various domains: web architecture (like a J2EE service (Chebaro, Broto, Bahsoun, & Hagimont, 2009), grid computing (like electromagnetic simulations (Sharrock, Khalil, Monteil, Stolf, Aubert, Cocccetti, Broto, & Plana, 2009)), or middleware architecture (like a DIET service (Hagimont, Stolf, Broto, & De Palma, (2009))). The input diagrams (HDD, SDD and PDD) may be created with graphical UML editors, are being automatically parsed by TUNe, and executed using a multithreaded deamon.

One possible use case for TUNe would be:

1. System preparation and description: creation of the diagrams, TUNe starting.
2. TUNe enters the initial deployment phase of the system: hardware and software are mapped together; software and input files are being installed on machines.
3. TUNe configures (creates the dynamic configuration files), initializes, and launches the system during the starting phase.
4. TUNe manages the system autonomously without any human intervention during the management phase.
5. When the entire system wants to stop or if the user orders to do so, TUNe enters the ending phase.

RELATED WORKS

Autonomic Computing Approach

Some software programs have their own general-purpose facilities to automate problem detection and/or problem correction. For example, some new operating systems include engines to automate the collection of crash data (like windows XP and its crash report (Ganapathi, 2005)); other tools help detect anomalous behavior by monitoring system, network or application logs like nagios (Harlan, 2003) or ganglia (Massie, Chun, & Culler, 2004). However, these tools do not analyze how and what the system should be doing (or not doing). They leave this task to human administrators, who must then determine if something is going wrong, to eventually plan and carry out a reconfiguration or repair process.

Several research works have been conducted in addressing the challenges of autonomic computing. In Kephart and Chess (2003), the authors call a system autonomic if it takes care of some "four-Self" concepts, like: Self-configuration, Self-optimization, Self-healing or Self-protection.

As a result, different autonomic systems have been developed. These systems can be broadly classified as

1. Systems that incorporate autonomic mechanisms for problem determination, monitoring, analysis, management (e.g., OceanStore (Kubiatowicz, Bindel, Chen, Czerwinski, Eaton, Geels, & Gummadi, 2000), Oceano (Appleby, Fakhouri, Fong, Goldszmidt, Kalantar, Krishnakumar, & Pazel, 2001), AutoAdmin (Agrawal, Bruno, Chaudhuri, & Narasayya, 2006), QFabric (Poellabauer, Abbasi, & Schwan, 2002)).
2. Systems that investigate models, programming paradigms and development environments to support the development of autonomic systems and applications (e.g., Kx (Kinesthetics eXtrem) (Kaiser, Parekh, Gross, & Valetto, 2003), Astrolable (Van Renesse, Birman, & Vogels, 2003), Autonomia (Dong, Hariri, Xue, Chen, Zhang, Pavuluri, & Rao, 2003), AutoMate (Parashar, Liu, Li, Matossian, Schmidt, Zhang, & Hariri, 2006)).

Our approach falls in the second category and Kx is closely related to it. We both provide autonomic capabilities onto legacy systems, by relying on specific wrapping mecanism (Effectors in Kx) to adapt a proprietary software. However, we will see that our approach is more high-level since it actually uses a graphical language and it hides the low-level difficulties to the end user, especially the way to describe an execution flow, or the way to describe architectural modifications. Also, Autonomia implements the *self-configuring* and *self-healing* concepts with mobile agents; our approach implements the *four-self* concept, and is contextually aware by automatically deploying small agents on each nodes. Autonomia also provides check-pointing and migration solutions that are currently being developed in our tool.

Intrusive vs. Non-Intrusive Legacy Management

Most approaches described in the literature for developing autonomic software are intrusive. Indeed, they use framework interfaces that need to be implemented within the system to be managed, like Autonomic Management Toolkit (Adamczyk, Chojnacki, Jarzqb, & Zielinski, 2008), or Policy Management Autonomic Computing (Agrawal, Lee, & Lobo, 2005). This means that the components have to be modified, becoming framework-dependent, and also implies that the administrators have access to all source codes to rebuild them. This assumes that the developer of the components will be willing and able to migrate to these frameworks, which is usually not an option because it costs too much (Claremont, 1992).

Some other solutions in the autonomic computing field have relied on a component model to provide a generic, non-intrusive system support (Bouchenak, De Palma, Hagimont, & Taton, 2006; Garlan, Cheng, Huang, Schmerl, & Steenkiste, 2004; Oreizy, Gorlick, Taylor, Heimbigner, Johnson, Medvidovic, & Quilici, 1999). The idea is to encapsulate the managed elements (the legacy software) in software components (called wrappers) and to administrate the environment as a component architecture. This way, the source codes do not have to be modified and the wrapped elements are controlled via the wrappers interfaces.

However, we rapidly observed that the interfaces of a component model are too low-level and difficult to use. This led us to explore and introduce higher level formalisms for all the administration tasks (wrapping, configuration, deployment, and reconfiguration). Our main motivation was to hide the details of the component model we rely

on, and to provide a more abstract and intuitive graphical specification interface.

DSML USED FOR THE DEPLOYMENT PHASE

Hardware Description Diagram

When deploying a distributed system, multiple sets of computers may be used, like directly accessible machines or managed resources (accessible via a resource scheduler). The latter include grid platforms and their Virtual Organizations (VOs) (Foster, Kesselman, & Tuecke, 2001) or cloud computing platforms (Buyya, Yeo, Venugopal, Broberg, & Brandic, 2009; Hayes, 2008). These represent the hardware layer (resource layer) of the system.

In our approach, the hardware platform is described with a DSML inspired from the UML class diagram. In the resulting HDD, each class represents a set of computers, making them members of a same family (called host-family). We eventually found that a minimum of two properties for a family have to be specified:

- **How to get resources:** direct access, or using a specialized resource scheduler.
- **How to access them:** which protocol to use to copy the files, execute commands.

These properties are defined using the attributes of the HDD classes. A typical HDD class would include a *user* attribute (the user to use on the machines), a *DirLocal* attribute (the automatically created working directory on the machines), a *javahome* attribute (the jdk location used by TUNe), a *type* attribute (either *local* or *cluster* that uses *nodefile* attributes pointing to a file containing all machines addresses, or a name of a TUNe scheduler plugin), and the *protocole* attribute (either *rcp*, *ssh*, or any other protocol developed in a TUNe protocol plugin). The actual

HDD diagram do not support links between HDD classes, and we consider that all machines of all classes using the same protocol can communicate.

To illustrate our approach, we made some experiments using the French national grid Grid'5000 (Cappello, Caron, Dayde, Desprez, Jegou, Primet, & Jeannot, 2005). Grid'5000's architecture is distributed among 9 sites around France (dispatched in all major cities), each one hosting several clusters. Grid'5000 software set provides, among others, a reservation tool: OAR (Capit, Da Costa, Georgiou, Huard, Martin, Mounié, & Neyron, 2005), and a deployment tool: Kadeploy2 (Georgiou, Leduc, Videau, Peyrard, & Richard, 2006). Resource allocation is managed at two levels: a cluster level (with the *oar* command) and a grid level (with the *oargrid* command), and provides most of the important features implemented by other batch schedulers such as priority scheduling by queues, advanced reservations, backfilling and resource match making.

Figure 1 (a) shows a HDD example with two classes representing two families of nodes on the Grid'5000 platform. Specialized attributes are used to fit the OAR resource allocation manager. For this specific grid, the *type* is either *oar* for cluster-level (*toulouse* class), *oargrid* for multiclusters on multi-sites reservations (*allsite* class) or *kadeploy* for specifying what operating systems to deploy during reservation. The *sites* is a scheduler-specific parameter representing the city names and the number of nodes to reserve for each site, and the *walltime* is the duration of the nodes reservation, here 2 hours. The *keypath* facilitates the remote login with ssh keys on the grid to avoid password typing. Finally, there is a specific *protocol* to access the nodes called "oarsh" within Grid'5000, instead of the standard *ssh* protocol.

Other specific properties for managed machines are described in the same way. For instance, the user is able to describe hardware-specific

Figure 1. (a) up: HDD for Grid'5000 (b) down: SDD for DIET

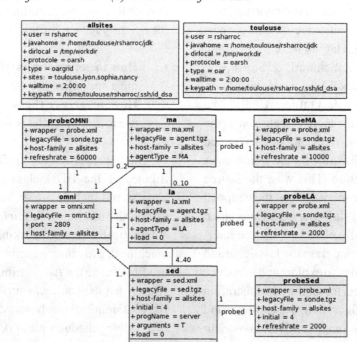

constraints like the minimum amount of memory, CPU speed, or minimum disk space within specific attributes.

Software Description Diagram

The software infrastructure (legacy layer or application layer) is also composed by multiple sets of software pieces. TUNe provides generic software probes that the user can attach to its application, and it is possible to develop proprietary probes as long as their notifications follow a specific syntax (reaction identifier and a set of arguments: names of faulty elements, names and values of probing metrics). Usually, the overall design of a software organization can be described using architecture schemas. They outline the *intended* structure to be deployed initially, but one important aspect of autonomic computing is that the system may evolve during runtime. Indeed, certain parts of the system may grow following the demands, according to the self-optimization recommendation (for example, adding new servers to fit the growing incoming flows of requests). Therefore, it is necessary to introduce a framework for the evolution of the system.

As for the HD, the intended initial deployment of the application and its evolution framework is described using a DSML inspired from the UML class diagram.

As an example, we chose to deploy and manage a middleware named DIET (Caron & Desprez, 2006). DIET stands for Distributed Interactive Engineering Toolbox and is used as a hierarchical load balancer for dispatching computational jobs over a grid. DIET architecture consists of a set of agents: some Master Agents (MA) are linked to Local Agents (LA) that manage a pool of computational SErver Deamons (SED). These servers can achieve specialized computational services. Communications between agents are driven by the omniORB system (OMNI). MAs listen to client requests and dispatch them through the architecture to the best SED that can carry

out this service. We attached generic probes to the OMNI, MA, LA and SED to monitor the CPU load average and if the process is alive. For single-CPU systems that are CPU-bound, the CPU load average (output of the *uptime* command) is a percentage of system utilization during the last minute. For systems with multiple CPUs, the probe divides by the number of processors in order to get a comparable percentage.

Figure 1 (b) is the SDD for this architecture where each class corresponds to a software which can be instantiated in several instances (components). Also, maximum and minimum cardinalities between each class have been introduced to limit the number of instances. Predefined attributes are used for the initial deployment, like the *initial* number of instances (1 by default if it is not set), which set of computers to use (*host-family*), the archive containing the software binaries and libraries (*legacyFile*, TUNe comes with scripts to automatically construct these archives). The *wrapper* attribute gives the name of the SWD which interfaces the software (see Figure 1 (b)). This SDD shows that initially, one MA, two LA and four SED are deployed, as well as their respective attached probes. Moreover, cardinalities show that one MA can be linked up to 10 LA, and each LA can be linked up to 40 SED. Note that the link with the probes is named *probed* to facilitate the use of generic method calls in the SWD. Also, specialized attributes have been introduced to configure the agents (*agentType*, *progName*, *arguments*), and one attribute will be used to store a dynamic values for a metric called (*load*).

Software Wrapper Description

In our approach, each managed software is automatically wrapped into a Fractal component (Bruneton, Coupaye, Leclercq, Quéma, & Stefani, 2006). To simplify and hide the complexity of this underlying component model, the wrapper is described using a SWD based on the XML syntax, which contains methods defining how to start, stop, configure or reconfigure the software deployed. TUNe comes with a predefined set of generic SWD containing start, stop and configure methods that can be reused. Most of the needs should be met with this provided finite set of generic methods. Furthermore, other legacy specific methods or proprietary operations can be defined according to the specific management requirements of the wrapped software.

Here is an example for the SWD of the SED in the DIET architecture:

```xml
<?xml version='1.0'
encoding='ISO-8859-1' ?>
<wrapper name='sed'>
  <method name="start"
key="extension.GenericUNIXMethods"
      method="start_with_pid_
linux" >
    <param value="$dirLocal/$progName
$dirLocal/$srname-cfg $arguments
$srname"/>
    <param value="LD_LIBRARY_
PATH=$dirLocal"/>
    <param value="OMNIORB_
CONFIG=$dirLocal/$omni.srname-cfg" />
  </method>
  <method name="configureOmni"
key="extension.GenericUNIXMethods"
      method="configure_plain_
text">
    <param value="$dirLocal/$omni.
srname-cfg"/>
    <param value=" = "/>
    <param value="InitRef:NameServi
ce=corbaname::$omni.nodeName:$omni.
port"/>
    <param value="DefaultInitRef:corb
aloc::$omni.nodeName" />
  </method>
...
```

This SWD shows the methods *start* and *configureOmni* for the SED SDD class. The *key* determines a package location that contains imple-

mented methods. For each method, parameters are given with the *param* tag. The character *$* allows to get the different attribute values from the SDD, and the character allows to navigate through the links between SDD classes. Thus, values are dynamically interpreted for each instance of one class of the SDD. Specific keywords allows to get the name of the instance (*srname*, which by default is the name of the SDD class followed by an incremented number), or the node name on which it is deployed (*nodeName*).

DSML USED FOR THE POLICIES DESCRIPTION

DSML Principles and Definitions

Each characteristic of the four-self concept has a particular need on the managed system. At deployment time, self-configuration of the elements needs a contextually aware environment. Indeed, some elements need to know the configuration of others elements to auto-configure. Self-healing needs a probing system to detect failures, and a way to diagnose and repair them (an example is given in (Broto, Hagimont, Stolf, De Palma, & Temate, 2008). Self-optimization needs a way to adapt the system (modifying the number of instances running) and to apply reconfiguration procedures. Finally, self-protection involves two points of view: external protection to defend against malicious attacks, and internal protection to maintain the system's consistency and to avoid its explosion. In our approach, we consider the "four-self" entirely, but we limit the self-protection to the internal protection.

Policies for the autonomous management of the system are modeled using a DSML inspired from UML activity diagrams (part of the behavioral set of UML). These diagrams are created using the Topcased editor (Farail, Gaufillet, Canals, Le Camus, Sciamma, Michel, & Crégut, 2006) that creates uml files following the UML 2.0 standard description in XML. Our tool parses these files and creates runnable objects that are executed following the sequential or parallel flow descriptions of the diagram.

In the following section, we focus on the meta-model for this DSML. We also give examples for the *self-configuring, self-optimizing* and *self-protecting* mechanisms.

DSML Meta-Model for the Policy Description Diagram

Figure 2 illustrates our DSML meta-model for the policy description diagram. This meta-model is composed by multiple *nodes* and eventually some input/output *parameters*. *Nodes* are linked with *edges* also called transitions. We can see that our DSML consists of two different stereotypes for the *Node* metaclass, namely *Action* and *Control*. The stereotype *Action* describes the specific tasks related to the managed system while the stereotype *Control* is used to control the global execution path of execution for the PDD.

The *structural modification* extends the *Action* metaclass, meaning that it has an impact on the managed system. Indeed, creating or destructing a component modifies the running architecture. The same goes for link creation/destruction actions to create or delete bindings between components. Moreover, *SWD method call* are used to call SWD methods like starting, stopping or reconfiguring the components during runtimes, thus modifying the system's behavior. The *Component modification and selection* stereotype provides actions to create or modify attribute values with the *Attribute value creation* and *Attribute value modification*. The *Component selection* filters lists of components depending on the values of their attributes. The *PDD reference* action executes another PDD (references another PDD).

The stereotype *Control* can be classified as *Fork / Join* nodes, they are used to parallelize the PDD execution flow by creating Threads and synchronizing them. Furthermore, within one PDD, there is a unique entry point which is called the *Initial node* and one unique ending point called the *Final node*. Eventually, at the end of the execution, the diagram can return a code with a *return code* node. The *timer* controls the execution flow

Figure 2. Metamodel of the DSML for the PDD

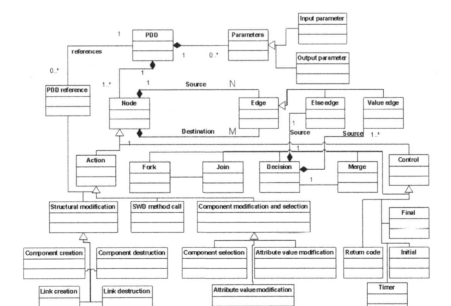

by pausing the diagram. Finally, *Decision* and *Merge* nodes are used to create mutual exclusive paths crossed under conditions, and to merge them before the end of the PDD. Note that a Decision node is a source for some *Value edge* and a source for a minimum of one *Else edge*. Indeed, if all conditions of the *Value edge* are not satisfied, this forces the PDD to continue the execution on the *Else edge* to avoid a dead lock. The cardinality between one node and one edge (N,M) depends on the type of the node: Fork(2..*,1), Join(1,2..*), Decision(2..*,1), Merge(1,2..*), Action(1,1), Initial(1,0), and Final(0,1).

Each of the actions is represented by a node that contains its particular expression following a specific syntax. Here are some of these syntaxes, written in the Extended Backus-Naur Form (Scowen, 1993):

```
component creation = list, "=",  SDD
class name, "++", [ "[", number of
instances to create, "]" ] ;
PDD reference = [ outs ], "=", PDD
name, "(", [ ins ], ")" ;
outs = out, { ",", out } ;
out = list, { " ", variable } ;
ins = in, { ",", in } ;
in = list, { " ", input } ;
input = variable | attribute ;
```

For example, the component creation is a SDD class name followed by ++ and optionally the number of instances to create in brackets.

Another example is the PDD reference consisting of optional input and output parameters (*ins* and *outs*): *ins* are a succession of *in* with a, separator, *in* is a list name followed by a succession of *input* with a space separator, and *input* is either a variable name or an attribute. In the next section, we introduce a simple PDD example consisting of only actions on components (SWD method calls) and standard fork and join nodes. The grammar of the SWD is given below:

```
method call = list | SDD class name,
".", SWD method name ;
```

PDD for Self-Configuring and Starting of DIET

The Figure 3 represents a particular PDD for starting the DIET software architecture. This PDD is named *start* and is automatically executed upon the starting phase (see the principles of our approach section). To simplify, we do not consider starting errors in this case, and introduce failure cases with the self-protecting case in the section related to self-protection. We can see that actions on components used for starting and configuration (SWD method calls like *ma.configure*) are executed in parallel thanks to fork nodes creating different threads. Moreover, SDD class names are used which means that methods are invoked on all instances of the SDD class, also in a parallel way.

Threads are then synchronized with the join node and the execution follows a specific sequen-

Figure 3. PDD for self-configuring and starting of a DIET architecture

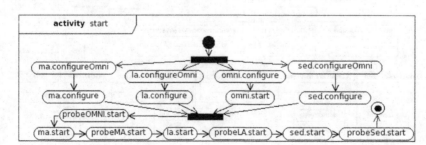

tial flow. Indeed, it is necessary to start all MAs before all LAs, so that they can connect to their parent MAs. The same goes for the SEDs that have to be started after their parent LA, and probes that have to be started after the element they are probing.

PDD for Self-Optimizing of the DIET Architecture

The DIET architecture is designed to be a multi-client platform, meaning that clients can arrive at any time asking for a computational service. Thus, the SEDs may encounter heavy fluctuations of their load that depends, among others, on the number of clients they have to treat in parallel. Furthermore, the LAs dispatching clients to SEDs may also encounter heavy loads that depend, among others, on the clients' requests rate, and the number of SEDs they are in charge of.

For this example (Figure 4 (b)), the PDD describes how overloaded SEDs are managed (the average load of all SEDs exceeds a maximum threshold). The goal is to create a calculated number of new SEDs, using the following equation (second action of the PDD): $x = \left\lceil \dfrac{\sum_{i=1}^{n} C_i}{T} - n \right\rceil$

with x: the number of SEDs to create, C_i: the load of SED number i, n: the actual number of SEDs, and T: the targeted average load.

In Figure 4 (b), the targetted average load is the optimum uptime: 100%. The new SEDs are connected to the appropriate LA. Indeed, *list_la = min(LA.load)* creates a list of filtered LAs minimizing their CPU load. As multiple LAs could have the same minimum CPU load value, at binding time (*bind list_newsed list_la*) the ones that are already binded to a minimum of SEDs are chosen. If all LAs have reached their maximum cardinality (Figure 1 (b)), then some others are created (the bind action fails and continues on the *else* transition). All the new SEDs are binded to the newly created LAs in the *create_la_bind_sed* referenced PDD. Finally, all new components are configured (dynamic configuration files are created), and started using the *configure_start* referenced PDD.

Figure 4. (a) up: global PDD for the experiments (b) down: PDD for self-optimization of DIET

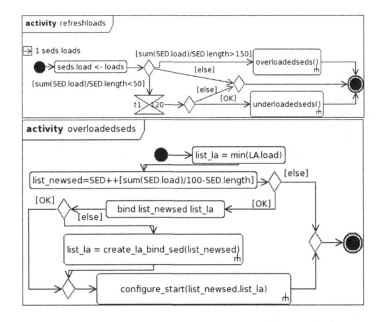

Self-Protecting within the Autonomic Manager

Structural modifications of the managed architecture raise difficult problems to maintain the system's consistency, thus our approach also includes static and dynamic verification mechanisms. Indeed, adding and removing components or bindings between them could lead to system inconsistencies, like exceeding the cardinalities between classes in the SDD (Figure 1 (b)). The SDD introduces an architectural pattern and all reconfigurations during runtime must follow the pattern constraints. This ensures the internal protection mechanism, thus making the global system *self-protected*. At first, the autonomic manager includes a static consistency verifier that checks HDD, SDD, SWD and PDD consistencies. These include:

- The DSML consistency, each diagram/ SWD must follow the correct DSML syntaxes and constraints.
- The initial deployment consistency, meaning that the initial number of components is consistent with cardinalities between classes in the SDD.
- The management policies consistency, meaning that all PDD actions refer to existing SDD classes and links between classes, that input/output parameters can be mapped within PDD reference calls, and that the execution flow is correct: fork nodes are joined and decision nodes are merged before the final node, and decision nodes placed in-between fork and join nodes are merged before the join node.
- Various consistencies, like the return codes use, and all the expression syntaxes conformity within PDD actions.

If the static consistency verification fails, then the initial deployment will not occur and the diagrams/SWD files have to be modified.

The dynamic consistency verifier acts during runtime, checking if during the PDD execution, the modifications lead to a system inconsistency. For instance, when a new component is created and linked to another, cardinalities between the corresponding SDD classes must be verified.

As shown by Figure 5, three automatic processes are activated to maintain the system consistency. These processes are hidden to the end user, which makes the final PDD much lighter (Figure 5 (a) compared to (b)), but the user is still able to describe manually any other scenarii, overwriting some of the automatic processes. These processes are:

- Automatic binding creation process (the *bind list_newla OMNI* and *bind list_newla MA* actions in Figure 5 (b)): this process is activated at two levels. The first level is when a reconfiguration action needs to navigate through bindings that do not exist. That is, when a reconfiguration action needs to know a configuration parameter of another component it is linked to, but the binding does not exist yet, the binding is automatically created. The second level is when the PDD finishes, and some components do not verify the minimum cardinality of the SDD.
- Automatic component creation process (all actions related to the *probeLA* or the *list_ newprobe*): this process is activated when the second level of the automatic binding creation process fails. This means that a component needs to be linked to another type of component but all instances of that type already have reached their maximum capacity defined by the maximum cardinality. Then some new instances are created, binded, configured and started automatically, but only if these new components do not involve another creation, thus avoiding creation loops.

Figure 5. PDD for creating some LA (a) left: user PDD (b) right: visible automatic actions

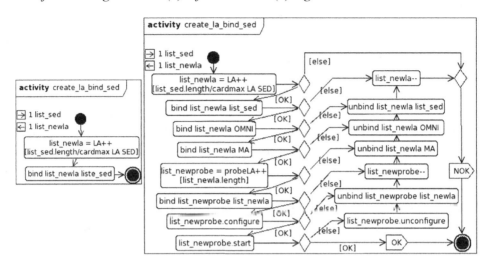

- Automatic rollback process (actions on else edges in Figure 5 (b)): this process is activated when all of the above fail. In the worst case, and if the system is still inconsistent, then all previous actions are cancelled in the exact reverse order. If parallel actions (executed in thread after join nodes) have to be cancelled, the absolute time of execution is considered. This is achievable only for actions that have their reverse action. This is the case for component creation/destruction, link creation/destruction, and generic actions on components like starting/stopping or configuring/unconfiguring.
- At the end of the PDD, return codes like OK or NOK are automatically propagated to the caller PDD.

EXPERIMENTS RESULTS

Experiments Preparation

For these experiments, we use and run the policies described by the PDD for self-optimizing. The generic probes send the load of the probed elements periodically (*refreshrate* attribute of Figure 1 (b), in ms) in a *refreshloads* notification. The global policy described with the corresponding PDD (See Figure 4 (a)) is executed when TUNe receives this notification. The first input parameter *1 seds loads* contains the name of the probed element(s) and the new value(s) for their load. The attribute value modification action *seds.load <- loads* updates the load attribute of the components with these fresh values. If the average load of all SEDs exceeds 150, the *overloadedseds* PDD is executed. If it goes under 50, the t1 timer is started for 120 seconds and the *underloadedseds* PDD is executed. The timer ensures that the *underloadedseds* PDD is executed once every 120 seconds at maximum, otherwise the execution continues on the else edge after the timer action.

Underloaded and Overloaded Experiments

We created a load injector that sends computational client requests to the DIET architecture like matrix multiplications. To simplify, we fixed here one request every fourteen seconds, and each request takes about 2 minutes of CPU time (with two Quad Core Intel Xeon 2.83 GHz CPUs).

Figure 6 (a) shows how the average load of all SEDs if affected when the overloadedseds policy is applied. During the first six minutes, the average load of all SEDs is increasing rapidly and exceeds the maximum threshold three times. As shown by Figure 4 (b), a calculated number of new SEDs is created so that the average load targets the optimum uptime of 100%. Three new SEDs are created the first time, four the second time and six the third time. We can see that the average load goes a little bit over the maximum threshold because it takes a few seconds to create and start all the new SEDs. From t=7 to t=15 minutes, seventeen servers are running and absorbing the client requests, and their load average is stabilizing around 60% at t=10 minutes. The little overshoot of the target threshold at six minutes is due to the fact that the default internal DIET scheduling is a round robin that do not prioritizes newly created SEDs. Thus, some requests are still dispatched to the loaded SEDs until the round robin reaches the new ones.

Figure 6 (b) shows an example of the under-loadedseds PDD execution. We first loaded thirteen SEDs and then decreased the number of requests so that their average load goes under the minimum threshold (one request every second with a calculation of about six seconds of CPU time). The number of SEDs to disconnect is calculated the same way as for the *overloadedseds* PDD, but rounded to the smaller integer, here six

SEDs are disconnected. When a SED is disconnected, it does not receive more requests and finishes the running ones. Once all requests are finished, TUNe stops all processes, cleans files and makes the hardware available again. We see that the average load stabilizes around 95% from t=2 to t=4 minutes. Indeed, the requests are redirected to the remaining SEDs, and this load transfer and stabilization could take more time depending on the request rate and the calculation time. The t1 timer (Figure 4 (a)) waits two minutes for the next *underloadedseds* PDD execution if the average load stays under the minimum threshold (which is not the case here).

Constrained Load Balancing Experiments

For this experiment, we deployed a DIET architecture with two LAs (added attribute initial=2 in Figure 1 (b) or the LA SDD class). We forced the first Local Agent (LA_1) to be placed on a fast computer, and the second one (LA_2) on a slow computer (Intel Xeon EM64T 3GHz versus Intel Xeon 5110 1.6 GHz). To do this, we created a new host-family in Figure 1 (a) with fixed values for the two computer addresses, and we changed the host-family attribute for the LA SDD class in Figure 1 (b).

Figure 6. Results after applying the PDD (a) left: overloadedseds (b) right: underloadedseds

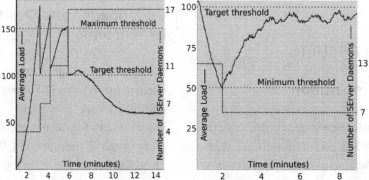

The first experiment consists in creating ten new SEDs every minute, with a numerical load balancing: the SEDs are connected to the LA with the lowest number of SEDs it manages. To do this, we replaced the first action of the PDD for self-optimization of the DIET architecture with *list_la = min(LA.SED)* (Figure 4 (b)) Figures 7 (a) and (b) demonstrate that a numerical load balancing is not always optimal. Indeed, the LA on the slowest computer cannot handle the incoming request rate (fixed at twenty requests per seconds) when the number of children SEDs reaches thirty (its load overpasses 100% and explodes), whereas the LA

on the fastest computer is loaded around 70%. The second experiment constrains the SED binding by choosing the LA that minimizes its CPU load (first action of Figure 4 (b)).

Figures 8 (a) and (b) show that, as a result, the LA on the fastest computer has to manage more SEDs than the one on the slower computer. Indeed, both LA reach an average load of 80%, but the first one manages forty SEDs, whereas the second one manages twenty SEDs. This demonstrates that, in this case, a constrained balancing for the number of SEDs under LAs is more efficient than a more natural numerical load balancing.

Figure 7. Numerical load balacing of SEDs under LAs (a) left: Local Agent 1, fast computer (b) right: Local Agent 2, slow computer

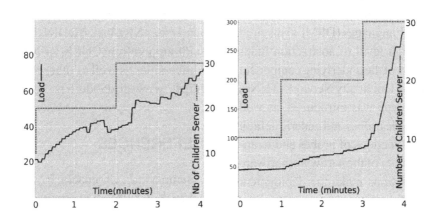

Figure 8. Constrained load balancing of SEDs under LAs (a) left: Local Agent 1, fast computer (b) right: Local Agent 2, slow computer

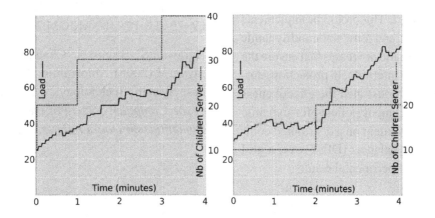

CONCLUSION AND FUTURE WORKS

Large IT facilities are increasingly complex and difficult to manage. They consume a lot of human resources that tend to have slow reaction times. To address this issue, much research projects related to autonomic computing give a new approach in designing distributed architectures that are able to manage themselves. However, existing systems do not necessary follow this new approach. Also, autonomic frameworks and APIs used for developing autonomic software are intrusive. We proposed an approach that is non-intrusive using automatic wrapping of software in a component architecture. This approach takes into account the hardware description, software description and autonomic policies description. These descriptions are modeled using Domain Specific Modeling Languages (DSMLs) inspired from UML, this high level of abstraction hides the usual complexity of the underlying component model. The Toulouse University Network (TUNe) implemented prototype was introduced, as well as connectable generic probes and generic default wrappers. These collections of probes and wrappers, and the reusability of the hardware, software and policies descriptions make the deployment and management of distributed legacy systems a lot easier for the final user. Indeed, TUNe takes into account the entire life-cycle of the software by autonomously reserving hardware resources, mapping software and hardware, deploying, starting, configuring and managing (optimizing, repairing) the software. This prototype implements the four-self concept, and some static and dynamic verifiers with automatic processes that ensure the system consistency (internal self-protection) during runtime. We demonstrated the effectiveness of some self-management policies for dynamic performance improvement on a distributed computational jobs load balancer (DIET) over a grid (Grid'5000), with experimental results.

As a perspective, we would like to work on a specific extension for TUNe to manage Quality of Service (QoS) within datacenters. Indeed, management needs of networks and applications in datacenters are increasing while customers are asking to meet more QoS needs. This extension would dynamically reconfigure network-level hardware like routers or switches, thus enabling TUNe to manage not only the software layer but also the hardware layer during runtime.

Acknowledgments: The work reported in this paper benefited from the support of the French National Research Agency through projects Self-ware (ANR-05-RNTL-01803), Scorware (ANR-06-TLOG-017), Lego (ANR-CICG05-11) and the French region Midi Pyrenees. Experiments presented in this paper were carried out using the Grid'5000 experimental testbed, being developed under the INRIA ALADDIN development action with support from CNRS, RENATER and several Universities as well as other funding bodies (see https://www.grid5000.fr).

REFERENCES

Adamczyk, J., Chojnacki, R., Jarzqb, M., & Zielinski, K. (2008). *Rule Engine Based Lightweight Framework for Adaptive and Autonomic Computing* (LNCS 5101, pp. 355-364).

Agrawal, D., Lee, K. W., & Lobo, J. (2005). Policy-based management of networked computing systems. *IEEE Communications Magazine, 43*(10), 69–75. doi:10.1109/MCOM.2005.1522127

Agrawal, S., Bruno, N., Chaudhuri, S., & Narasayya, V. (2006). AutoAdmin: Self-Tuning Database Systems Technology. *A Quarterly Bulletin of the Computer Society of the IEEE Technical Committee on Data Engineering, 29*(3), 7–15.

Appleby, K., Fakhouri, S., Fong, L., Goldszmidt, G., Kalantar, M., Krishnakumar, S., et al. (2001). Oceano-SLA based management of a computing utility. In *Proceedings of the 7th IFIP/IEEE International Symposium on Integrated Network Management,* Seattle, WA (Vol. 5).

Bouchenak, S., De Palma, N., Hagimont, D., & Taton, C. (2006). Autonomic management of clustered applications. In *Proceedings of the IEEE International Conference on Cluster Computing,* Barcelona, Spain.

Broto, L., Hagimont, D., Stolf, P., de Palma, N., & Temate, S. (2008). Autonomic management policy specification in Tune. In *Proceedings of the ACM Symposium on Applied Computing,* Fortaleza, Ceara, Brazil (pp. 1658-1663).

Bruneton, E., Coupaye, T., Leclercq, M., Quéma, V., & Stefani, J. (2006). The FRACTAL component model and its support in Java. *Software, Practice & Experience, 36*(11-12), 1257–1284. doi:10.1002/spe.767

Buyya, R., Yeo, C. S., Venugopal, S., Broberg, J., & Brandic, I. (2009). Cloud computing and emerging IT platforms: Vision, hype, and reality for delivering computing as the 5th utility. *Future Generation Computer Systems, 25*(6), 599–616. doi:10.1016/j.future.2008.12.001

Capit, N., Da Costa, G., Georgiou, Y., Huard, G., Martin, C., Mounié, G., Neyron, P., et al. (2005). *A batch scheduler with high level components.* Arxiv preprint.

Cappello, F., Caron, E., Dayde, M., Desprez, F., Jegou, Y., Primet, P., et al. (2005). Grid'5000: a large scale and highly reconfigurable grid experimental testbed. In *Proceedings of the 6th IEEE/ACM International Workshop on Grid Computing,* Seattle, WA (pp. 99-106).

Caron, E., & Desprez, F. (2006). DIET: A Scalable Toolbox to Build Network Enabled Servers on the Grid. *International Journal of High Performance Computing Applications, 20*(3), 335–352. doi:10.1177/1094342006067472

Chebaro, O., Broto, L., Bahsoun, J. P., & Hagimont, D. (2009). Self-TUNe-ing of a J2EE clustered application. In *Proceedings of the 2009 Sixth IEEE Conference and Workshops on Engineering of Autonomic and Autonomous Systems,* San Francisco (pp. 23-31).

Cheng, X., Dale, C., & Liu, J. (2008). Statistics and social network of youtube videos. In *Proceedings of the IEEE 16th International Workshop on Quality of Service,* Enschede, The Netherlands.

Claremont, B. (1992). *Understanding the Business Aspects of Software Migration.* Migration Specialties.

David, J. S., Schuff, D., & St. Louis, R. (2002). Managing your total IT cost of ownership. *Communications of the ACM, 45*(1), 101-106. doi:http://doi.acm.org/10.1145/502269.502273

Dobing, B., & Parsons, J. (2006). How UML is used. *Communications of the ACM, 49*(5), 113. doi:10.1145/1125944.1125949

Dong, X., Hariri, S., Xue, L., Chen, H., Zhang, M., Pavuluri, S., & Rao, S. (2003). Autonomia: an autonomic computing environment. In *Proceedings of the 2003 IEEE International Performance, Computing, and Communication Conference* (pp. 61-68).

Farail, P., Gaufillet, P., Canals, A., Le Camus, C., Sciamma, D., Michel, P., et al. (2006). The TOPCASED project: a toolkit in open source for critical aeronautic systems design. In *Proceedings of the European Congress on Embedded Real Time Software,* Toulouse, France (pp. 54-59).

Flaviu, C. (1993). Automatic reconfiguration in the presence of failures. *Software Engineering Journal, 8*(2), 53–60. doi:10.1049/sej.1993.0009

Flissi, A., Dubus, J., Dolet, N., & Merle, P. (2008). Deploying on the Grid with DeployWare. In *Proceedings of the 2008 Eighth IEEE International Symposium on Cluster Computing and the Grid (CCGRID)* (p. 177-184).

Foster, I., Kesselman, C., & Tuecke, S. (2001). The anatomy of the grid: Enabling scalable virtual organizations. *International Journal of High Performance Computing Applications, 15*(3), 200. doi:10.1177/109434200101500302

Ganapathi, A. (2005). *Why does Windows Crash?* Berkeley, CA: Berkeley University.

Garlan, D., Cheng, S. W., Huang, A. C., Schmerl, B., & Steenkiste, P. (2004). Rainbow: Architecture-based self-adaptation with reusable infrastructure. *Computer,* 46–54. doi:10.1109/MC.2004.175

Georgiou, Y., Leduc, J., Videau, B., Peyrard, J., & Richard, O. (2006). A tool for environment deployment in clusters and light grids. In *Proceedings of the Second Workshop on System Management Tools for Large-Scale Parallel Systems,* Rhodes Island, Greece (Vol. 4).

Gray, J. (1986). Why do computers stop and what can be done about it. In *Proceedings of the Symposium on reliability in distributed software and database systems,* Los Angeles (Vol. 3).

Hagimont, D., Stolf, P., Broto, L., & De Palma, N. (2009). Component-Based Autonomic Management for Legacy Software. *Autonomic Computing and Networking,* 83-104.

Harlan, R. C. (2003). Network management with Nagios. *Linux Journal,* (111), 3.

Hayes, B. (2008). Cloud computing. *Communications of the ACM Journal, 51*(7), 9–11. doi:10.1145/1364782.1364786

Huebscher, M. C., & McCann, J. A. (2008). A survey of autonomic computing—degrees, models, and applications. *ACM Computing Surveys, 40*(3), 1–28. doi:10.1145/1380584.1380585

Kaiser, G., Parekh, J., Gross, P., & Valetto, G. (2003). Kinesthetics eXtreme: an external infrastructure for monitoring distributed legacy systems. In *Proceedings of the Autonomic Computing Workshop Fifth International Workshop on Active Middleware Services,* Seattle, WA (pp. 22-30).

Kephart, J. O., & Chess, D. M. (2003). The vision of autonomic computing. *Computer,* 41–50. doi:10.1109/MC.2003.1160055

Kon, F., & Campbell, R. H. (1999). Supporting Automatic Configuration of Component-Based Distributed Systems. In *Proceedings of the USENIX Conference on Object-Oriented Technologies and Systems,* San Diego (Vol. 5, p. 13).

Kubiatowicz, J., Bindel, D., Chen, Y., Czerwinski, S., Eaton, P., & Geels, D. (2000). Oceanstore: An architecture for global-scale persistent storage. *ACM SIGARCH Computer Architecture News, 28*(5), 190–201. doi:10.1145/378995.379239

Massie, M. L., Chun, B. N., & Culler, D. E. (2004). The ganglia distributed monitoring system: design, implementation, and experience. *Parallel Computing, 30*(7), 817–840. doi:10.1016/j.parco.2004.04.001

Oreizy, P., Gorlick, M. M., Taylor, R. N., Heimbigner, D., Johnson, G., & Medvidovic, N. (1999). An Architecture-Based Approach to Self-Adaptive Software. *IEEE Intelligent Systems, 14*(3), 54–62. doi:10.1109/5254.769885

Parashar, M., Liu, H., Li, Z., Matossian, V., Schmidt, C., Zhang, G., & Hariri, S. (2006). AutoMate: Enabling Autonomic Applications on the Grid. *Cluster Computing, 9*(2), 161–174. doi:10.1007/s10586-006-7561-5

Poellabauer, C., Abbasi, H., & Schwan, K. (2002). Cooperative run-time management of adaptive applications and distributed resources. In *Proceedings of the tenth ACM international conference on Multimedia* (pp. 402-411).

Scowen, R. S. (1993). Extended BNF-a generic base standard. In. *Proceedings of the Software Engineering Standards Symposium, 3*, 6–2.

Sharrock, R., Khalil, F., Monteil, T., Stolf, P., Aubert, H., Cocccetti, F., et al. (2009). Deployment and management of large planar reflectarray antennas simulation on grid. In *Proceedings of the 7th international workshop on Challenges of large applications in distributed environments*, Munich, Germany (pp. 17-26).

Sterritt, R., & Bustard, D. (2003). Autonomic Computing - a means of achieving dependability? In *Proceedings of the 10th IEEE International Conference and Workshop on the Engineering of Computer-Based Systems*, Huntsville, AL (pp. 247-251).

Van Renesse, R., Birman, K. P., & Vogels, W. (2003). Astrolabe: A robust and scalable technology for distributed system monitoring, management, and data mining. [TOCS]. *ACM Transactions on Computer Systems, 21*(2), 164–206. doi:10.1145/762483.762485

This work was previously published in the International Journal of Adaptive, Resilient and Autonomic Systems, Volume 2, Issue 1, edited by Vincenzo De Florio, pp. 58-76, copyright 2011 by IGI Publishing (an imprint of IGI Global).

Chapter 7
Agents Network for Automatic Safety Check in Constructing Sites

Rocco Aversa
Second University of Naples, Italy

Beniamino Di Martino
Second University of Naples, Italy

Michele Di Natale
Second University of Naples, Italy

Salvatore Venticinque
Second University of Naples, Italy

ABSTRACT

Compliance with safety standards in constructing sites is a mandatory activity that helps prevent a high number of fatalities during working activities. Unfortunately, because of negligence or limited resources, safety checks are not performed with regularity and this causes a high number of accidents. This paper proposes a distributed solution for automated checking of safety rules, secure logging of violations, and real-time execution of reactions. The constructing site is modeled as a pervasive environment where software agents, executing on smart devices, can detect and interact with people, machineries, and safety equipment to check the compliance of common behaviors with the safety plan designed for that site. The design is presented as a working prototype of a three layered software/hardware architecture.

INTRODUCTION

Safety in construction sites is today a relevant problem because of an increase of *white deaths*, that is the high number of fatalities during working activities. Even if the risk depends on the specific kind of job, it grows up exponentially when the safety standards are violated. Although the legislation provides for the establishment of a Safety Plan, which regulates the working activities, and at the same time safeguarding the health of workers, the attention about the compilation of

DOI: 10.4018/978-1-4666-2056-8.ch007

this document, and especially the implementation of measures are at least neglected in almost all cases. There are currently no resources or tools that help to ensure compliance with the measures prescribed by law, to warn in real time the staff about dangers, due to the violation of the specified rules, or allowing a posteriori verification of the correct implementation of the plan for the specific site. We aim at designing and implementing a service that monitors the compliance of workers' activities with the safety standards. Misconducts by workers, accidents and critical situations must be detected, notified, traced and eventually corrected.

Such scenario is characterized by the presence of many mobile workers and machines, by many pervasive objects whose presence affects the correct development of human activities. The complexity of the system is due to the heterogeneity and to the high number of elements to be monitored in a dynamic changing environment. The dependability of the designed solution must be guaranteed because it affects safety of involved people and infrastructures.

- Security is relevant because privacy of monitored people must be granted. Furthermore nobody should be able to tamper the system and the integrity of the logged history.
- Performance affects the time necessary to detect a dangerous situation and to provide necessary reactions in real-time.
- Reliability is necessary to prevent a period meanwhile we miss the detection of a dangerous situation and we do not activate reactions.
- Availability is important to get the required response when we notify the occurrence of a relevant situation and there are not resources to activate necessary countermeasures.
- Scalability must be provided because dimension of working area, number of peo-

ples and objects can increase a lot between one scenario to another one. It can affect not only performance but also the cost of the infrastructure.

In the following we model the application scenario as an ubiquitous system where pervasiveness of sensors and mobile devices can be exploited to design and develop an effective solution. We provide details about the designed architecture and describe a prototypal implementation which works to detect the violation of some significant rules as it is already required by our government and it is (should be) currently done manually by dedicated people.

The proposed distributed solution is based on autonomous agents which represent the connection between a centralized control service and its extensions, implemented by pervasive sensors and actuators. Agents will check the compliance of detected situations with a set of rules which compose a global plan that regulates common activities. When a failure has been detected, agents can execute some actions. They can react proactively to handle specific events using pervasive actuators, services or supporting users in doing it. An agent here is a software entity that is able to sense the environment, to evaluate the context and to react according its configuration profile.

In a prototypal implementation we use smart devices to estimate relative positions of pervasive objects worn by workers (e.g., special clothes and safety accessories such as helmets, shoes and glasses), in order to check safety rules, to apply needed local reactions and to notify violations to adopt centralized countermeasures.

The next section presents application context and requirements. We then introduce the problem formulation and provide our proposal for modeling the safety plan and a language to define its rules. Next, we give an overview of the architectural design of our solution and some details about its prototypal implementation. Finally related work and conclusion are due.

SIGNIFICANT SCENARIOS AND SAFETY PLAN

In Italy the relevant safety rules to be checked for protection of workers in constructing sites are defined in D.Lgs 81/2008 of Italian Law.

Among these we chose some which are representative of common situation and can easily implemented and checked by our solution.

- **Falling Objects:** A safety helmet is required to be worn for every worker and visitor which stand or move in the site, in outdoor and indoor environments. As it is shown in Figure 1, it is used to protect the head in case of collision with falling objects or also with protruding elements.
- **Protection of Feet:** Safety shoes, which have steel mid-sole and aluminum toe-cap, are used to protect the feet against nails and sharp points in transit areas and against falling objects.
- **Metal and Mobile Scaffolds: Safety belt must be used to avoid falls (Figure 2).**
- **Exposure to Chemicals:** Safety face mask, glasses and gloves must be used to protect against chemicals (Figure 2).
- **Ejection of Resulting:** Materials: safety glasses and gloves must be used, above all during demolition, grinding or cutting operations, to protect eyes and hands against ejection of resulting materials. In Figure

Figure 1. Protection against falling objects and nails

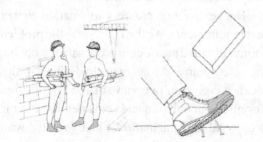

Figure 2. Safety belt against falls. Gloves and mask to protect against chemicals.

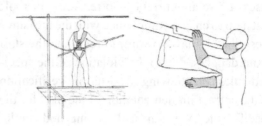

3 it is shown how the need to wear these equipments can be related to the simultaneous presence of working tools for cutting or grinding.

- **Noise Exposure:** Personal ears noise protection must be used when the daily exposure to noise is above 85 dBA.
- **People Moving within the Range of Working Machine:** People cannot stand within the range of dangerous machineries which are moving. The arm of crane should be halted if the presence of a worker is detected.

All these rules compose a safety plan that must be personalized for the specific site. It must be automatically checked its violation to prevent, or to recover dangerous situations.

PROBLEM FORMULATION AND REQUIREMENTS

We can model the working site as wide area where people move and can interact with distributed sensors and actuators. We aim at deliver in this space a monitoring and control service which, interacting with users, can use any embedded devices as their extension spread in the environment. User must be able to define a set of rules which will be periodically verified. Necessary reactions must be activated when one rule fails.

Figure 3. Protection against ejected materials and noise

Of course beyond the model a dedicated analysis must be performed in order to choose the suited technology and for implementing an effective solution. It will depend on the particular problem and on the specific environment.

In order to pursue this goal it is necessary to:

- Define a representation of the environment;
- Provide the on-line characterization of objects and users with spatial and temporal parameters;
- Model relevant situations;
- Define rules to be checked during services exploitation.

Additional properties must be granted when the environment changes dynamically such as adaptivity and reconfigurability of service delivery and exploitation. Security, traceability and certification of events can be required in critical applications.

First and second requirements listed above deal with the dynamic localization and identification of users and objects. We mean with localization the capability to know at any time the position of a user/object in the environment. Localization is here both spacial and temporal. We mean with identification the capability to associate the localized entity to a class or to a specific instance of that class (the specific user or object). Eventually the identification is able also to describe the status of that entity (it could be standing, or moving).

We can describe at any time an entity of our environment with the triple [p,i,s] (position, identity, status). We need to define and associate to each entity a set of rules to be satisfied. By means of rules we aim at monitoring the correctness of mutual interactions among users/objects. This means that a rule can refer to *n* entities standing or moving in a common environment.

Let us represent a situation, that means also a mutual interaction, at time *t* with X(t):

$$X(t) = [p,i,s]_1, \cdots, [p,i,s]_n$$

X(t) is a set of triples which have been detected at a specific time. A rule can be described as a function evaluated on X(t):

$$f: \quad X(t) \rightarrow \left\{TRUE, FALSE\right\}$$

The set of rules

$$P: \left\{f: f(X(t)) = TRUE\right\}$$

represents the global plan that grants the correct execution of activities into the environment.

Of course we need:

- A language to define rules and situations;
- A technology to localize and identify objects;
- A mechanism to verify the rules and to notify violations.

Furthermore, as we want to activate necessary reactions when some rules fail, we need to associate a set of actions to be executed to any detected failure.

Technical and technological issues to be addressed already in this phase are related to:

1. The kind of environment: indoor, outdoor, with obstacles which are standing or moving;
2. Dynamic changes and lack of fixed points of reference;
3. Heterogeneity of objects, entities, devices;
4. An eventual high number of objects/users and situation to be handled. Because of this the complexity of the problem increases and it can be not possible to detect entities and to verify rules with the necessary frequency and to execute reactions in real-time.

MODELING AND EDITING THE SAFETY PLAN

A safety plan is modeled as a set of assertions which must be always true when checked.

Each assertion has the following syntax:

```
<ID_Assertion>;<ID1,...,IDn>
[:comment_1,...,comment_n];
<expression> ; <parser> ; <action>
[,action]
```

- **<ID_Assertion>** represents a unique identifier that is communicated to the server in order to notify what specific rule has been violated;
- **<ID1,ID2,...,IDn>** represent the identifiers of the objects referenced by the assertion. ID-i can identify a class of objects if it matches just with the first part of the detected one;
- **[:comment_1,...,comment_n]** are labels related to the identifiers. They are not considered when the assertion is parsed;
- **<expression>** represents the condition to be evaluated. It can involve constants, implicit variables and available operators;
- **<parser>** is a Java class, dynamically loaded, that is able to interpreter and to evaluate the current expression. We provide a

default parser for the sintax described in the following;
- **<action> [,action]** represents a list of action to be executed when the assertion is evaluated false.

Actually an expression can use the following operators:

- Arithmetic operators: *, /, -, +
- Relational and for string comparison: <, >, =, #, @
- Logic: !(NOT), & (AND), — (OR)

Terms of an expression are constant values or keywords, which identify objects and the information they provide. Round brackets can be used to define precedence or to improve readability. In the Table 1 keywords which refer to scanned objects are showed.

When more IDs are referenced in the second field of an assertion, an index must be used to associate keywords to related sensors (es: VALUE1,..., VALUEn). Another set of keywords, which can be used to refer to the fields of the assertion, is listed in Table 2. They can be useful for logging purposes but not just for it. In fact each action class, that has been activated on an occurrence of violation, can access to all information related to the assertion.

Let us consider two reference scenarios depicted in Figure 4.

Table 1. Keywords to refer to object properties

Keywords	Meanings
IDVALUE	RFID identifier
VALUE	Value provided by the sensor
PRESENCE	Its true if the ID has been detected
CONTPRES	Number of IDs belonging to the referenced group
IDREADER	Reader identifier

Table 2. Keywords to refer rules properties

Keywords	Meaning
CODE	Assertion ID
DEVTYPE	Object ID
DEVNAME	Object name (optional part of the second field)
EXP	Expression (third field)

1. People who works on a scaffold must wear helmet, gloves, protective shoes and safety belt.
2. People cannot stand or move within a certain range when the arm of a crane is in motion.

In the first case it is necessary to know about the contemporary presence of some objects at any time when a worker is nearby a scaffold. It could be possible, with suited sensors to know if the object is really worn or not. A smart device is worn by the worker. It use a reader to scan RFIDs which are reachable in a significant range. An RFID tag can be used to identify helmets, gloves and other objects. Passive short range tags can be used. The following assertion is an examples that describes this situation

```
125;001,2390,007;
(!PRESENCE3) | (PRESENCE3 & PRESENCE1
&PRESENCE2);
default; action.Beep
```

It says that if a sensor whose ID starts with 001 (a scaffold) it is necessary also to detect an ID that starts with 2390 (an helmet) and an ID that starts with 007 (safety belts). Of course if we specify a full ID (Es. 239000022) we are meaning that we want the user wears its own helmet. If the assertion results false a beeper alerts the worker.

In the second case it is necessary to know the relative positions of the crane and of the worker, and to know the status of the arm (moving or not moving). A smart device can be installed on the crane and it can react stopping the crane. Active tags or Bluetooth technology can be used to detect presence of workers or of their devices.

The correspondent rule of the safety plan will be:

```
126;010;
(!PRECENSE)
|((PRESENCE1)&(VALUE1=OFF));
default;action.Beep,action.Halt
```

A crane (010) should not be present, or if present, it must be off. If the assertion results false two action are performed. A beeper alerts the worker, and a message is sent to ask for halting the crane.

With a further rule we want to assert that if a specific temperature sensor (4450) is detected, the temperature value that is read should be below 40 degrees otherwise that failure should notified to the server and logged. The correspondent expression is:

Figure 4. Representation of two significant scenario in construction sites

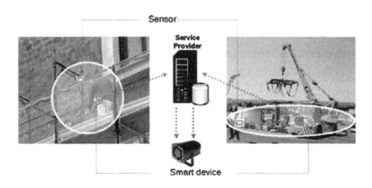

```
127;200103482;(FVALUE1<40);default;
action.Log
```

DECENTRALIZED LAYERED SOLUTION FOR AUTOMATION OF SAFETY CHECKS

Many issues arise when we look for an affordable and effective technology that supports the localization of all objects in the site to build a global knowledge of the working site, that means all the situation $X(t)$ at a certain time. Beyond the complexity of handling a huge number of objects over a wide area, many limitations are due to the heterogeneity of the sites (indoor and outdoor areas), the dynamic changing which do not allow to have fixed landmark, the interference due to static and mobile metal infrastructure and machines.

Starting from these consideration, we decided neither to get a global and complete knowledge of the system, nor to localize in absolute way the entities.

We adopted a decentralized solution based on autonomy of agents which are able to detect other agents and objects nearby, and to verify locally a subset of rules (their profile). This approach allows also to reduce the complexity and to grant scalability when the size of the site is increasing.

Our decentralized solution delegates the verification to independent entities, configured to interact with *close objects* and to communicate with a central system that can have one vision of all detected failures. The conceptual model is organized according a three layered architecture. At higher layer (layer III) we have a centralized service provider that communicates with agents of layer II. Sensors and actuators can be seen as services extensions, exploited by users through agents, which execute on embedded devices. Agents use sensors and actuators of layer I automatically or interactively, on behalf of users or of the centralized service. This choice allows also to

use at Layer I very simple and cheap sensors like RFID. In fact sensors do not need to self organize or to be directly connected to the server. As it can seen in Figure 5 information flows across the layers, but interactions could be supported also among entities at the same layer. Let us imagine a sensor network at Layer I, social capabilities of agents at Layer II or services composition at Layer III. A prototypal implementation has been developed using java and off the shelf devices to have rapidly a working proof of concept to be reengineered.

Service Layer

At service layer we designed and developed some facilities which allow to handle entities and communication.

Facilities to be provided are:

1. Editing and configuration of the safety plan.
2. Secure communication with agents which monitor the correctness of activities in within the working area.
3. Secure logging of violations of the safety rules which are notified by agents.
4. Automatic activation of necessary reaction to notified violations.

The application we developed provides a registry of objects, agents, rules and actions. Rules can be grouped in order to build profiles. A Profile is a set of rules that can be associated to an agent in order to specify its behavior. Rules are expressed as assertions which must be always true. It is possible to associate a set of actions to be performed when a violation of an assertion has been notified. Action can be performed at this layer or by agents at Layer II. All violations are logged by the server. A secure mechanism for certification of logs is being to be designed and developed. Our Java implementation allows to develop new actions, which can be automatically integrated into the system and used, by inheritance and reflection.

Figure 5. Layered architecture for a distributed solution of automated safety checks

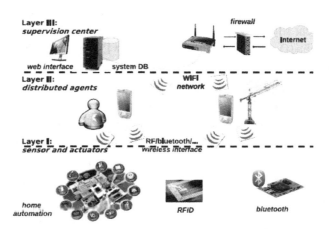

Notifications are received from agents by HTTPS messages. At this layer is also possible to manage agents, in order to reconfigure profiles at any times, to recognize, through log analysis, relevant patterns which cannot be detected by agents who have only a local view about what is happening. Temporal evolution of events can be monitored. Finally, even if our decentralized solution is based on a local view of close objects by agents, if a marker is used to identify a fixed point of reference in the environment, at this level a log of its detection allows for localization of the absolute position of an agent.

A web application implements the functionalities provided at this layer. It allows to register objects and workers. It allows to register and associate RFID, to define rules, to configure profiles and to associate remote actions to assertion failures. It has implemented by the Apache-tomcat application server.

Even if the utilization of an embedded hardware secure storage is planned, actually we provide a software implementation of the secure logging based on public key technology.

The administrator starts the service providing his RSA private key. The application generates a random symmetric key, stored in un-swappable memory, that will be used to write an encrypted version of the log. The symmetric key is signed with the administrator private key and is encrypted with is public key.

Each asserted violation is numbered, encrypted with the symmetric key and written in a log file.

No one can delete, add, or modify a record into the file because the symmetric key is secret. The symmetric key cannot be replaced and a new file cannot be generated because the secret key has been also signed by the administrator at the start-up.

The integrity of the log will be checked only by the administrator who will use its private key to get the symmetric key for decrypting the log. If the plain version will be consistent it will be signed and stored.

Layer II: Autonomous Agents

The second layer is composed of smart embedded devices which are able to localize close entities.

Here we provide:

1. Autonomous rules checking.
2. Notification of violations.
3. Local reaction to detected violations.

Agents periodically scan the environment in order to detect and identify objects. Their profile is composed by a set of assertions, that is checked according to the presence or the absence of a set

131

of objects. When the assertion results *false* the corresponding set of reactions are activated.

At each scanning an agent fills a table of record. Each record contains the ID of a sensor and, eventually, the value provided. Of course it will store in the table only those sensors which are in the area covered by the reader. For each assertion listed into the agent profile, the referenced sensor is searched in the table in order to verify its presence or a more general expression.

An agent profile is a text file with different lines, each for a different assertion to be evaluated. In Figure 6 the UML architecture of an agent is showed. *Execute* represents the interface implemented by all actions to be performed when an assertion is false. *Parser* is an abstract class that must be inherited by the provided *Default* parser and by all new parsers would be developed. The class Reader is the main one. It instantiates the ReaderProc thread that scans the environment and invokes parsers and action on each assertion listed into the agent profile.

As all the configurable components (actions, and parsers) are loaded dynamically, an agent could be reconfigured with a new software and a new profile at any time. Violations are notified to the server by a specific action that sends an https request with information about the detected failure. A java implementation of the agent works on

a HTC TyTn handheld device with Myisaifu JVM and the bluecove library.

Layer I: Pervasive Actuators and Sensors

Sensor or actuators belong to the lowest level (Level I). Here we find simple devices, which can just communicate their presence and their identity, or can communicate and interact in a more complex way with agents of Layer II. They are associated to any physical entities whose interaction with agents and services is relevant to be enabled for the application of the safety plan.

The minimal functionalities to be provided at this layer are:

1. Detection.
2. Identification.
3. Eventually communication.

We mean that it could be sufficient to detect the presence of the helmet, or of a particular helmet close to the worker. A sensor can be exploited to deactivate the helmet transmitter when it is not worn. Another sensor could be read to evaluate temperature or some other information. An actuator could receive some command to turn off a machinery in a dangerous situation. We could

Figure 6. UML agent architecture

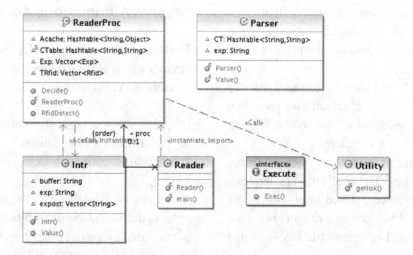

imagine a complex sensor networks that act as a whole at this layer and behave as one sensor that is detected nearby the agent of the upper layer.

An abstraction of simple sensors has been described by a Java interface that provides the following functionalities:

- **void connect(int p):** Connects to the reader p.
- **int getArraySize():** Returns the number of tags detected by the reader.
- **int getID(int i):** Returns the ID of the reader *i*.
- **void writeTag(String t,String s,int p):** Writes a String *s* as parameter *p* of the tag *t*.
- **String readTag(String k,int p):** Returns a String *s* that represents the *p* value stored into the tag *k*.
- **boolean scanTag():** Executes a new scan and updates the list of detected Tag, returns true if some information have been updated.
- **boolean scanTag(int n):** Updates only the information of the sensor *n*. It returns true if the tag *n* has been detected again.

At Layer II an agent is able to detect and manage heterogeneous sensors by this unique interface with several implementations. Many implementations can be necessary to use more than one technology, at the same time or in different applications.

A cheap solution, when there are not special requirements, suggested us to investigate the exploitation of RFID (Radio Frequency Identification Devices). These kind of devices are cheap and are characterized by low power consumption. On the other hand we have exploited Bluetooth technology to implement more complex interactions. Microcontrollers with Bluetooth interface can be interfaced with more complex sensors or devices. Above all they can perform pre-computations on acquired information.

To localize and identify objects at Layer I we experimented three active tags which communicate their ID as an integer value. A RFID-UHF reader has been used to detect tags. To use the functionalities of the reader the vendor provides a set of api which can be used by linking a shared native library to the user application. Another implementation of the abstract sensor at this layer uses Bluetooth technology. With demonstration purpose we used a microcontroller with a Bluetooth interface to sense a load cell and to control a DC motor which have been connected to a simple model of a crane that has been built using Lego Mindstorm.

RELATED WORK

Many application contexts nowadays are characterized by pervasiveness of embedded systems in crowded environments of everyday life. Among embedded devices let us cite cellular phones, RFID readers for product identification, any kind of electronic guides in museums, traffic and environmental sensors, and so on. Different models to develop and deliver advanced services in these contexts can be conceived such as sensor networks and context aware systems. Common issues are communication among users, services and sensors, security, interoperability, collection of information and context representation.

Relevant applications could be monitoring of working areas, home automation, social networks of mobile users, collaborative environments, value added services such as location based ones. In this scenario we aim at supporting monitoring, traceability, on-line interaction between users and pervasive devices. Many hardware and software architectural solutions have been proposed to support development and delivery of services in ubiquitous contexts. Some differences deal with where and how information is collected, who can use information to take decisions, what technological infrastructure is needed to satisfy application requirements.

Effective utilization of low-cost, low-power, multifunctional sensor nodes that are small in size and communicate untethered in short distances has become feasible (Akyildiz, Vuran, Akan, & Su, 2005). The ever-increasing capabilities of these tiny sensor nodes, which consist of sensing, data processing, and communicating components, enable the realization of wireless sensor networks (WSN) based on the collaborative effort of a large number of nodes. WSNs represent both a technique and a technological solution that can be applied in many application contexts such as environmental monitoring, home automation, healtcare applications. A WSN is composed of simple devices with limited capability, which use sensors to collect and communicate information to a base point through a wireless ad-hoc network.

Ubiquitous healthcare refers to the disposition of any type of health services such that individual consumers through mobile computing devices can access them (Kirn, 2002). In Giorgino (2009) a remote rehabilitation system, which can be employed both at home and in the hospital, supporting motor rehabilitation for post-stroke patients is presented. A garment, which embeds kinesthetic sensors, is provided with a wireless connection to a computer (the patient station). The station detects in real time whether the patient is performing the exercises correctly or not, and provides feedback through an easy visual representation on the screen. In Kirn (2002) authors propose in an ubiquitous healthcare infrastructure to use local systems as cooperative problem solvers. They focus on interaction patterns among agents. Bae (2007) describes an embedded monitoring systems that collects information about the status of distributed sensors by hub nodes in embedded equipments. Agents which execute on hub nodes are responsible just to collect data and transmit it to the server. SmartFieldTM Hockey (Cefriel, n.d.) is a platform that allows for real-time tracing health condition and position of a single player. It

exploits UWB-RFID (Ultra Wide Band - Radio Frequency Identification) worn by players. A set of readers collects the information from sensors and communicates with a process unit that reconstructs movements of players. The position is computed by a triangulation of signals received form more RF readers. In Muldoon, Hare, Phelan, Strahan, and Collier (2009), authors introduces the Agents Channeling ContExt Sensitive Services (AC-CESS) architecture, an agent-based architecture that supports the development and deployment of context sensitive services. It focus on intelligent agent modeling and users' profiling. Among context properties, localization is described with a low resolution (for examples shop area and business hours). About context detection, in Intille, Bao, Munguia Tapia, and Rondoni (2004), authors focus on context information that can be acquired from a personal physical activity, as opposed to other types of context (e.g. location-based, emotional). Wearable mobile computing sensors such as accelerometer are used to feed with data classification algorithms that can often robustly detect activities such as walking, running, scrubbing, and vacuuming. The approach adopted by SmartFieldTM Hockey is based on the global and centralized vision of the system and aims at localize and identify each sensor at any time in the space. Let us observe that the feasibility of the approach depends on the fixed topology of the field of play and to absence of interference sources. Kang, Song, Kim, Park, and Cho (2007) focuses on monitoring of ubiquitous collaborative environments. However mobility and autonomy of monitoring agents is not addressed. We aim at investigating a solution that is robust respect of dynamic change in the environment, whose implementation can be cheap even if when a lot of sensors must be used, that does not suffer of interferences in hostile environment when a specific technology can be chosen, that can dominate complexity. In Lorentz (2005) authors present a model for designing an agents-based architecture that supports distributed users in ubiquitous computing, however a technological solution is not provided. Furthermore they do not make assumptions about what kind of distributed sensors can be handled and how it can be done in a general way. We provide a solution that is completely decentralized, and, by the second and the third level, is compliant with that model. Agents can act autonomously and use the facilities by the server just when they are available. There is a number of contributions focusing on the problem of localization and monitoring, also using RFID in construction sites. Chae and Kano (2005) and Delizadana, Azlz, Anumbab, and Kamata (2008) focus on absolute localization and use a centralized approach. The first one uses heterogeneous technologies to localize users in indoor and outdoor environments. The second one installs fixed readers in specific positions of the site. Some other works (Wing, 2006) offer facilities such as object tracking, product life cycle tracking, location of buried cables, but do not address issues related to dynamic changes in the environments. Furthermore they do not assist users in services exploitation by a proactive interaction with local sensors and actuators. Added values we are able to provide, exploiting our approach for provisioning of ubiquitous services in pervasive environments (Aversa, Di Martino, & Venticinque, 2009), are reconfigurability of the system, automatic assistance to workers, proactivity of software agents.

CONCLUSION

We proposed a distributed model, for monitoring and control of safety in a constructing site, which exploit pervasive extension composed of different kind of sensors and actuators. Our solution uses a network of autonomous agents which execute on embedded devices. They can be configured to collect information from close sensors and to check the compliance of user activities with a set of rules. We experimented the automatic monitoring of safety standards in a constructing site. We provided a prototypal implementation that monitors presence and status of UHF-RFID nearby an user device. A set of assertion allows to detect presence of sensors and to check the truth of simple assertion that express arithmetical and logical relationships on received data. Violations are communicated to a supervision center. Reaction can be configured locally and on remote. In the proposed model the information flows across the three levels. Agent can communicate among them by an ad-hoc connection when the network connection is not available to forward notifications or to contact nearby workers, e.g. to ask for help. We developed a Bluetooth message transfer protocol to support connection and communication among them. However collaboration among entities at the same layer will be exploited in future works to support adaptivity as well reactivity. Experimental activities have been done in our laboratory with technologies which allowed as to realize a proof of concept but are not suited for production and cannot provide significant quantitative performance information.

We are investigating the utilization of different technology that implements the common abstract model of a sensor at Layer I. A whole wireless sensor network can be seen as a sensor that can be read or written to interact with the surrounding environment.

REFERENCES

Akyildiz, I. F., Vuran, M. C., Akan, O. B., & Su, W. (2005). Wireless sensor networks: A survey revisited. *Computer Networks Journal, 38*(4), 393–422. doi:10.1016/S1389-1286(01)00302-4

Aversa, R., Di Martino, B., & Venticinque, S. (2009). Distributed agents network for ubiquitous monitoring and services exploitation. In *Proceedings of the 7th IEEE/IFIP International Conference on Embedded and Ubiquitous Computing* (Vol. 1, pp. 197-204).

Bae, J.-H., Lee, K.-O., & Park, Y.-Y. (2006). MONETA: An embedded monitoring system for ubiquitous network environments. *IEEE Transactions on Consumer Electronics, 52*(2), 414–420. doi:10.1109/TCE.2006.1649658

Behzadana, A. H., Aziz, Z., Anumbab, C. J., & Kamata, V. R. (2008). Ubiquitous location tracking for context-specific information delivery on construction sites. *Automation in Construction, 17*(6), 737–748. doi:10.1016/j.autcon.2008.02.002

Cefriel. (n. d.). *Cefriel: Forging innovation*. Retrieved from http://www.cefriel.it/

Chae, S., & Kano, N. (2005, September). *A location system with RFID technology in building construction site*. Paper presented at the ISARC 22nd International Symposium on Automation and Robotics in Construction, Ferrara, Italy.

Giorgino, T., Tormene, P., Maggioni, G., Capozzi, D., Quaglini, S., & Pistarini, C. (2009). Assessment of sensorized garments as a flexible support to self-administered post-stroke physical rehabilitation. *European Journal of Physical and Rehabilitation Medicine, 45*(1), 75–84.

Intille, S., Bao, L., Munguia Tapia, E., & Rondoni, J. (2004). Acquiring in situ training data for context-aware ubiquitous computing applications. In *Proceedings of the Conference on Human Factors in Computing Systems* (pp. 1-8).

Kang, K., Song, J., Kim, J., Park, H., & Cho, W.-D. (2007). USS monitor: A monitoring system for collaborative ubiquitous computing environment. *IEEE Transactions on Consumer Electronics, 53*(3), 911–916. doi:10.1109/TCE.2007.4341565

Kirn, S. (2002). Ubiquitous healthcare: The OnkoNet mobile agents architecture. In M. Aksit, M. Mezini, & R. Unland (Eds.), *Proceedings of the International Conference on Objects, Components, Architectures, Services, and Applications for a Network World* (LNCS 2591, pp. 265-277).

Lorentz, A. (2005). Agent-based ubiquitous user modeling. In L. Ardissono, P. Brna, & A. Mitrovic (Eds.), *Proceedings of the 10th International Conference on User Modeling* (LNCS 3538, pp. 512-514).

Muldoon, C., O'Hare, G., Phelan, D., Strahan, R., & Collier, R. (2003) ACCESS: An agent architecture for ubiquitous service delivery. In *Cooperative Information Agents VII*, (LNCS 2782, pp. 1-15).

Wing, R. (2006). RFID applications in construction and facilities management. *ITcon, 11*, 711–721.

This work was previously published in the International Journal of Adaptive, Resilient and Autonomic Systems, Volume 2, Issue 2, edited by Vincenzo De Florio, pp. 23-36, copyright 2011 by IGI Publishing (an imprint of IGI Global).

Chapter 8
Run–Time Compositional Software Platform for Autonomous NXT Robots

Ning Gui
University of Antwerp, Belgium

Vincenzo De Florio
University of Antwerp, Belgium

Chris Blondia
University of Antwerp, Belgium

ABSTRACT

Autonomous Robots normally perform tasks in unstructured environments, with little or no continuous human guidance. This calls for context-aware, self-adaptive software systems. This paper aims at providing a flexible adaptive middleware platform to seamlessly integrate multiple adaptation logics during the run-time. To support such an approach, a reconfigurable middleware system "ACCADA" was designed to provide compositional adaptation. During the run-time, context knowledge is used to select the most appropriate adaptation modules so as to compose an adaptive system best-matching the current exogenous and endogenous conditions. Together with a structure modeler, this allows robotic applications' structure to be autonomously (re)-constructed and (re)-configured. This paper applies this model on a Lego NXT robot system. A remote NXT model is designed to wrap and expose native NXT devices into service components that can be managed during the run-time. A dynamic UI is implemented which can be changed and customized according to system conditions. Results show that the framework changes robot adaptation behavior during the run-time.

DOI: 10.4018/978-1-4666-2056-8.ch008

INTRODUCTION

Autonomous robots can perform their intended tasks in unstructured environments without (or with minimal) human guidance. An autonomous robot may also learn or gain new capabilities like adjusting strategies for accomplishing its task(s) or adapting to changing surroundings. Such a high degree of autonomy is particularly desirable in fields such as space exploration, cleaning floors, mowing lawns, and waste water treatment.

A basic concept that is applied in autonomous robot control is the closed control loop. Each autonomic system consists of managed resources (controllable hardware or software components) and an autonomic manager for steering the underlying managed resources. Normally, this system includes automated methods to collect the details it needs from the system (Sensor); to analyze those details and determine if something needs to change (Analyzer); to create a plan, or sequence of actions, that specifies the necessary changes (Planner); and to perform those actions (Actuator). As we can see, in such system, Analyzer and Planner play a key role in such a control loop. These adaptation modules can greatly influence robot adaptation behavior. Several approaches have been proposed to provide a more flexible adaptation strategy – examples include (Hashimoto, Kojima, & Kubota, 2003), which uses evolutionary computation and fuzzy systems, or (Inamura, Inaba, & Inoue, 2000), using Bayesian networks. However, these works focused on designing certain adaptability algorithms for autonomous robots. Their control logics are statically linked and mingled with other system modules such as sensors and actuators. This static nature makes it very hard for autonomous robots to change their adaptation strategies. Most of these approaches can only effectively adapt within certain known environments or under certain predefined conditions.

A typical example is given by the Nasa Mars Rovers (Jet Propulsion Laboratory, n. d.). These robots, 170 to 320 million kilometers away from the Earth, are able to receive and send quite some information, either directly or via the Mars Orbiter (satellite around Mars). However, the downside of this communication is that their latency is very high (about 20 minutes), which obviously means that the robots cannot be remotely controlled. To perform their mission for NASA these robots had a software system that ran over a list of actions that were uploaded during the communication moment. A problem with this software is the static nature of its software platform. When the software needs an update to fix some problem or when some new features are needed to face unprecedented conditions, the robot software needs to be completely replaced.

The work described in this paper applies a new approach to implementing the adaptation loop in autonomous robot systems. In a nutshell, our architecture model realizes an adaptation loop which can be run-time revised so as to better match the current context. This strategy allows the application configuration to be modified outside of the application business logics. In order to deal with changing environments or/and robot status, our adaptation framework is designed to systematically support multiple adaptation logics. An adaptation plan is generated by run-time selected adaptation modules according to context to date. Robot applications, built from individual component instances, are composed and reconfigured by these run-time generated policies. This work is based on our ACCADA framework proposed in (Gui, De Florio, Sun, & Blondia, 2009b).

In order to seamlessly integrate the NXT robot into the ACCADA framework, a remote NXT model is designed to expose native NXT sensors and actuators as run-time manageable components. This remote NXT model allows future more advanced sensors/actuators to be easily plugged into our framework. Our modular middleware solution can effectively support adding/removing context-specific Planners during run-time, selecting the right adaptation Planner according to context by e.g. using a battery oriented adaptation scenario. Other adaptation strategies, such as fault-tolerant adaptation, can be injected into the system during the run-time to provide other adaption features to the existing adaptation capabilities.

The rest of the paper is organized as follows: First we describe the definition of our run-time reconfiguration framework as well as its key modules. Then we focus on software system design in implementing such framework and some adaptation scenarios. Finally we discuss related work in and provide our conclusion.

RUN-TIME ADAPTION MODEL

The model presented in this paper is an extension of the concept of adaptation manager in Autonomic Computing (AC) (Kephart & Chess, 2003) with a new idea: the management systems are driven by a run-time composited adaptation module rather than a predefined adaptation scheme. In a sense, they constitute an adaptive meta-system. Here, we will firstly introduce this adaptation framework.

Adaptation Framework

Figure 1 shows our ACCADA framework. As can be clearly seen from that picture, compared to typical AC control loop, our approach makes use of an extended control loop, consisting of

five basic modules – *Event Monitor*, *Adaptation Actuator*, *Structural Modeler*, *Context-specific modeler* and *Context Reasoner.*

The Event Monitor observes and measures various system states. It triggers the adaptation processes. Possible sources of a new round of the adaptation may include, for example, a new component being installed or the CPU reaching a status that may have a significant effect on the existing system configuration. It could also be a simple Timer that triggers periodically. The Adaptation Actuator carries out the actual system modification. In our current framework implementation, a set of basic actions are provided, including component lifecycle control, attribute configuration, and component reference manipulation. Adaptation actions might also trigger another adaptation process and create step-wise adaptation until the system reaches its new preferred state. The above two modules provide an interface to manage the installed component instances and form our Management Layer. The other three modules – Context-specific modeler, Structural Modeler and Context Reasoner, constitute what we call the Modeling Layer. This layer builds the system's global adaptation model according to the changing context (Gui, De Florio, Sun, & Blondia, 2009a).

Figure 1. Adaptation framework with multiple context-specific modelers

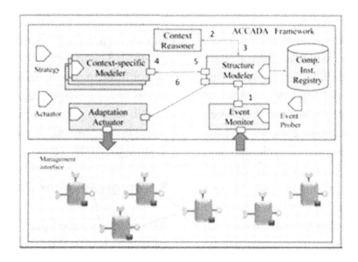

In order to make correct run-time adaptation, a software system adaptation model requires handling constraints from different aspects – this includes handling design-time knowledge such as interfaces or constraints as well as other domain-specific optimization aspects such as security, user's preference, performance etc. We identify that the software system adaptation needs to provide support for two main aspects – software architecture management and domain-specific adaptation knowledge. Such aspects are managed respectively by two specific modules – Structural Modeler and Context-specific modeler.

The Structural Modeler handles functional dependence between components. Compared to the Context-specific modeler, its major function is to manage the software architecture. By checking composition compatibility, it decides whether a component is "structure-satisfied" (that is, all its functional requirements are met). A component can only be initialized when functional requirements are fulfilled, no matter which context it is in. This characteristic gives it the uppermost priority in all the software adaptation aspects of our architecture. At the same time, such modeler is rather stable; in particular, it is invariant to context. That is why, in the software design, Structural Modeler is separated from the modeler selection process. It is always included in the adaptation process no matter what the external context is. As shown in Figure 2, for a system run-time, only one instance of this modeler will be installed.

In contrast, a Context-specific modeler takes care of those adaptations which are triggered by specific context changes. It does not need to deal with component functional dependence check or with dynamic reference managements between components. Rather, its major task is to set the right configuration, including lifecycle state and properties values, towards its components of interest. As our objective is to support multi-context adaptation and run-time context switching to cope with dynamically changing environments, more than one context-specific modeler can be supported. With many candidate context-specific modelers installed, a selection process is needed to determine the subset of the context-specific modeler(s) that are appropriate for the current adaptation. According to the current value of various system metrics, Context Reasoner selects the set of modelers matching the current context.

Service Component Model

According to Mazeir Salehie's recent review (Salehie & Tahvildari, 2009) of 16 projects on self-adaptive systems, all of the surveyed projects use certain level of external approach, which supports separation of the adaptation mechanism from the application logic. However, systematic supports for dynamically changing context are missing in many of their implementations. The source of this problem lies partially with the approach followed in their implementation – the adaptation modules are statically linked with system run-time. As the adaptation module is tightly coupled with other system run-time services, it is very hard to change system adaptation strategy during the run-time.

In order to achieve more reusability and flex-ibility, our framework is designed according to the service-oriented model. Each module is designed and implemented as a service component, such as sensors, actuators and adaptation strategies, etc. Modules implement and register their interfaces into the system service registry. Thanks to such loosely coupled structure, candidate adaptation modules can be easily interchanged during system run-time. This architecture enables many existing and/or future more sophisticated context-specific modelers to be easily plugged into our framework. Details of this service component model can be found in our previous work (Gui, De Florio, Sun, & Blondia, 2008, 2009a).

Sponsor-Selector Pattern

As several context-specific modelers may co-exist in a specific time, only one of them will be selected according to current system context. Context reasoner and context-specific modelers are implemented through a revised Sponsor-Selector pattern (Riehle, Buschmann, & Martin, 1998), as the context reasoner selects the best context-specific modeler from a set of candidates that changes dynamically. By separating three kinds of responsibilities: 1) knowing when a modeler is useful, 2) selecting among different modelers, and 3) generating an adaptation plan, our software platform integrates different modelers and various knowledge into the system during the run-time in an extensive way, while being transparent to system managed applications.

As described in Figure 2, the selection process works as follows. The System run-time reaches a point at which certain adaptation needs to be taken. It then asks the context reasoner for a context-specific adaptation plan. The selector checks the meta-data from all registered context-specific modelers (sponsors), then it rates these modelers for applicability in the current context. The modeler which is most appropriate for current context is selected and its reference is returned by selector. Then, system run-time begins working with this modeler for constructing a context-specific adaptation plan.

PLATFORM IMPLEMENTATION

As our ACCADA framework is abstract and universal, it can be used to implement various types of system optimization goals (such as fault-tolerance, security, application reconstruction, etc) to applications in a transparent way. In what follows we focus on a reference implementation deployed upon LEGOs MindStorm NXT robots to demonstrate how robots can be reconfigured during run-time. Each context-specific modeler can be individually installed, used, removed from the system run-time.

The presented case study demonstrates the most important features of our systems, which is based on our modular middleware implementation. This includes application run-time composition, context switching, context-specific modeler switching, as well as run-time deployment of new context-specific modelers. By using scenarios based use cases we demonstrate how context-specific modelers are switched during context changes. Two different scenarios are shown: one is to reconstruct according to system context a robot explorer application and another shows how to provide/remove fault-tolerant capability into this robot system.

Figure 2. Sequence diagram for context-specific modeler selection

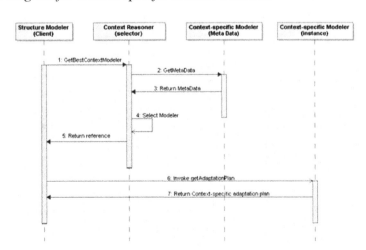

The implementation of such system is based on OSGi platform, with Equinox (Eclipse, 2010) v.3.3.1. As target robot system, the Lego's NXT robot was selected due to its off-the-shelf availability and low cost. This NXT robot' firmware was reprogrammed to support Java virtual machine by using the LeJOS system (LeJOS, 2009).

Remote NXT Model

The LeJOS system runs a special JVM known as Micro JVM. This JVM supports only a subset of the minimum requirements for OSGi. It is therefore not feasible to run the ACCADA framework directly on the NXT as our ACCADA framework is built upon OSGi framework. To tackle this problem, the robot software is split into two parts. The robot itself runs a static part while another more powerful computing device that supports OSGi runs the ACCADA adaptation part. A standard PC was select for the latter.

In Figure 3 the left block represents the NXT robot, which runs a static program whose major goal is to expose most of the devices of the NXT over the network. To do this a remote NXT model is created. A program that runs on top of the NXT robot executes a custom design protocol to receive commands and send corresponding responses. On the PC side, represented by the right block, we created a set of proxy service components which represent exactly the same functional parts of the

NXT robot. By using the remote NXT protocol, all devices of the NXT become available in the PC side too.

As the proxy devices are implemented as service components, these components can be directly used to compose a robot application by using the ACCADA run-time. This remote NXT model lets the remote devices, such as sensors and motors of a remote NXT, be managed as local OSGi service components. Although this model is used in NXT robot, this design can be easily extended to support more complex external sensors and/or actuators that are not natively supported by a NXT robot. In this way, we can easily increase a robot's capability without the need to redesign/buy a robot. In order to enhance NXT robot's sensor capabilities, by using this model, we successfully integrated a video camera sensor from a Sony Ericsson K750 Smartphone into our autonomous robot control platform.

We would like to remark here that we designed this remote NXT model in a layered way. This means that users can easily change their underlying transport medium with another transmission protocol. Currently, Bluetooth and USB transmission can be used.

Of course, if the targeted robot is powerful enough to run OSGi upon, then, this structure might not be needed. But it can still be used to extend that robot's set of supported sensors and actuators.

Figure 3. Remote NXT model

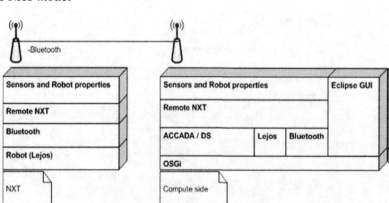

SIMPLE EXAMPLE: TOUCH SENSOR

The easiest way to fully understand the protocol and to place all components involved is by means of a very simple example. Next section describes how the remote NXT robot model is implemented so as to make the touch sensor remote controllable. A simple device – the touch sensor – is used. In the robot side, the TouchSensor class provided by Lejos has one method to test if a touch sensor was pressed. Since we want to expose the class over the network, touch sensor developer needs to implement the ICommandable interface. A ITouchSensor interface is introduced that allows multiple versions of component implementations. In the later self-healing scenario, the NXT robot light sensor is constructed as a virtual back-up touch sensor. Figure 4 shows the class diagram structure from both PC side as well as Robot side.

The Class Hierarchy of Touch Sensor Implementation

In order to facilitate the development of the robotic component, we provide one abstract class that can be extended by using class inheritance. Besides realizing the *IManagement* interface which enables

the middleware to make "reversion of control", the *AbstractCommandable* class also provides predefined methods for business logics code, which provide the session management support to get latest sensor values from connection. This sensor also implemented serializable IsPressed class to send sensor-specific inquiry command to the robot side. Details of this part can be found in (Pintens, 2010)

The TouchSensor component and its position in the class hierarchy are shown in Figure 5. The implementation of TouchSensor is completed by realizing the logics that collect the sensor data from remote NXT robot side and process the response to generate sensor-specific values.

The Touch Sensor component and its hierarchy are shown in the class diagram in Figure 5. The implementation of a Touch Sensor is to design a sensor-specific "operation" class. In the case at hand, the IsPressed class was created. In order to effectively communicate with remote NXT, such class needs to have the communication session available. Only when the communication is successfully built, the touch sensor can effectively send its command to its NXT robot counterpart. This dependence is managed by the system run-time.

Figure 4. Remote NXT model – touch sensor

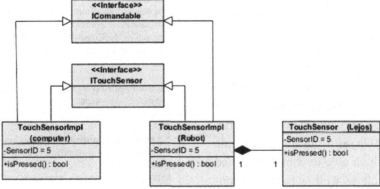

Figure 5. Class hierarchy of touch sensor implementation

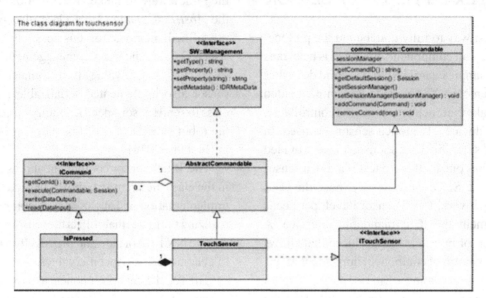

Sample Context-Specific Modeler Implementation

As shown in the previous section, robot key elements such as sensors, actuators can be developed individually by using NXT remote model. These key elements, together with robot control module – denoted as strategy module, can be used to build robot exploration program. It gets sensors' monitored data and drive robot actuators. (motor for control ultrasonic sensor direct and pilot actuator to control robot movements). Figure 7a, 7b shows two different exploration application configurations. As different exploration strategies might fit for different environments, one nature requirement is how to constructe the exploration application by using the most appropriate composition for current environment. In our ACCADA framework, context-specific model is used to express such contextual adaptation knowledge.

A context-specific modeler (Gui, De Florio, Sun & Blondia, 2009b) is a run-time pluggable adaption module which able to control installed components' lifecycle as well as perform property configuration. Box 1 shows the code for one

simple modeler implementation. Such modeler selects as its preferred exploration strategy one matching higher battery environment and disables other exploration strategy components designed for other environments. It used *resolveSatisfied* methods to control which strategy component can

Box 1. Context-specific modeler for battery based application reconstruction

```
  public AdaptationPlan resolveAdaptationPlan (ISystemCon-
text systemcontext, ContextChangeEvent ev)
  {
AdaptationPlan plan = new AdaptationPlan(systemcontext);
List newCompsProps =new ArrayList();
List newlyenabledComps = resolveSatisfied(systemcontext.
getInstalledComponents());
 plan.setEnabledComps(newlyenabledComps);
 plan.setCompProps(newCompsProps)
 return plan;
 }
  resolveSatisfied (List enabledComponentConfigurations)
 if (enabledComponentConfigurations.isEmpty()) {
 return Collections.EMPTY_LIST;
 }

   List resolvedSatisfiedComponentConfigurations ;
   Select the right components and put them into resolvedSat-
isfiedComponentConfigurations ;
 return resolvedSatisfiedComponentConfigurations.isEmpty()
? Collections.EMPTY_LIST : resolvedSatisfiedComponent-
Configurations;
 }
```

be enabled, so as the application composition. As context-specific modeler is contextual selected to control installed component states, so exploration application will be (re) composed during run-time.

As our structure modeler provides component dependence managements so implementation of a context-specific modeler can be rather concise.

Dynamic User Interface

To visualize certain parts of the application on the computing side, some extra components were designed to have better control and debug capabilities. This user interface is also designed based on our ACCADA framework. For each sensor, an optional UI component can be deployed into the system to visualize its control interface. User can directly monitor sensor's data and set its properties, for instance, through calibration. Each UI component is designed corresponding to functional sensor/motors in our application.

Box 2 is an excerpt of meta-data attached to a Light Sensor UI component. This component provides the *be.ac.ua.gui.view.View* service to the system, while it requires LightSensor service.

If functional dependence is satisfied which means the LightSensor is activated, its corresponding UI component will be shown. In other words,

Box 2. Excerpt of LightSensorUI component meta-data declaration

```
<reference bind="setLightSensor" unbind="unsetLightSensor"
cardinality="1..1" interface="be.ac.ua.robot.lightsensor. Light-
Sensor" name="LightSensor" policy="dynamic" />
  <service>
  <provide interface="be.ac.ua.gui.view.View"/>
  </service>
```

when its required sensor/actuator is disabled, the corresponding UI component will be automatically disabled. This dynamicity is automatically managed by the structure modeler. In resource-scarce environments, a context-specific modeler can selectively disable certain sensor/actuator components to save resources. The structure modeler will then disable corresponding related UI components. Figure 6 shows the screenshots of our UI. When NXT application has not built the connection with NXT robot yet, no required connection service provider exists. As sensors and actuators declare their dependence on the connection services, they will not be activated by system run-time as they do not have all the required services. As UI components depends on their corresponding sensors and actuators, these UI will not be shown, just as seen in Figure 6a. While the connection is built, the UI for the activated sensors will be initialized and shown as illustrated in Figure 6b.

Figure 6a. UI before connection Figure 6b. UI after connection

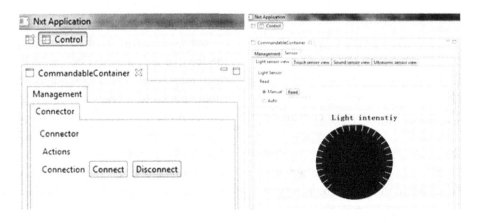

Figure 7a. Application structure (high battery) b. Application structure (medium)

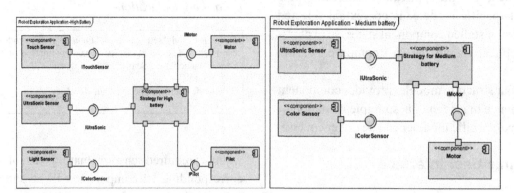

Another benefit of this approach is that we decouple the functional codes from their presentation. The same sensor – similarly to actuator, or exploration strategy – can have different UI that can be installed or removed during the run-time. This approach can effectively reduce UI interface implementation complexity and reduce errors generated by human erroneous inputs.

ADAPTATION SCENARIOS

In this scenario, we introduce how applications are constructed according to run-time selected context-specific adaptation modelers. These adaptation modelers are executed outside the application business domain. This adaptation experience also shows how a context-specific modeler is chosen on the basis of two system basic metrics.

Battery-Based Adaptation

For most autonomous robot systems, battery life plays a very important role. Switching robot behaviors according to different battery modes can be very useful and perhaps could be considered as a must on some battery-energized robots.

The basic idea is simple: depending on current battery state, a robot will perform different actions. When the batteries are high loaded and plenty of power is available the robot should try to run the most complex and energy costly strategies. When the batteries are low and are not recharging, for instance at night, the robot must not deplete its batteries by executing heavy duty tasks, as complete depletion would make the robot shut down and abort its possibly very expensive mission. Normally, a typical implementation is to incorporate all these strategies into one application; however, this solution makes the application difficult to adapt to new environments and impossible to revise with new adaptation models.

In this scenario, context knowledge is represented by the current battery voltage level. When the robot performs its tasks, the battery will gradually discharge its power. Thus the context will change. However, unlike in the traditional approaches, which statically link the adaptability strategy into the adaptation modules, our platform enables run-time addition/removal of robot adaptation strategies.

In this scenario, two different context-specific modelers are designed. Each modeler carries its own adaptation logics to build context-specific robot application. They are also tagged with two service properties, namely "robot.context.battery.low" and "robot.context.battery.high" to indicate their preferred application environments The corresponding modeller is selected when battery is in between 'low' and 'high'For instance, the High battery modeler is deployed with robot.context.battery.low=9 and robot.context.battery.high=12 which means this modeler will be selected when battery voltage is among this range [9,12]. By checking these meta-data attached to its services as well as the system current battery level, the Context Reasoner will select the most appropriate modeler.

In what follows we briefly sketch the adaptation logics in each modeler.

- **High Battery:** This application drives robot around in a circle while polling sound, light as well as ultrasonic sensors. This modeler uses touch sensor, ultrasonic sensor and light sensor, as well as motor actuator and pilot actuator. The constructed application has a good data fetching rate, with high power consumption though.
- **Low-Medium Battery:** The robot is stationary; it rotates the motor over 360 degrees scanning its environment with the ultrasonic sensor. It uses comparably less power as it only needs one motor. Results are less accurate.

Figure 7 shows how applications are constructed according to two different modelers. In this demo, only battery is used to represent the system's current context; however, it can be easily extended to support more complex context metrics. Adaptation videos can be downloaded from http://www.win.ua.ac.be/~ninggui/video/configuration_switch_battery.wmv

Fault-Tolerant Scenario

In this section the ACCADA framework is used to improve the fault tolerance of the robot. A backup touch sensor was built into the robot by reconstructing the light sensor with other mechanical modules, based on the change of light sensor value. It is placed at back-side of the robot. Detailed mechanic configuration can be seen in reference (Pieter-Jan, 2010). However, the backup touch sensor is not as responsive and accurate as the regular touch sensor.

The goal of this experiment is to show that the ACCADA framework can independently deploy new adaptation modelers during run-time to increase the fault tolerance of a robot. To do this, a developer only needs to implement a simple context-specific modeler with two different actions. Firstly, it needs to select to select the most appropriate touch sensor available in the system. Secondly, the backup touch sensor is located at the opposite side of this robot. Although the backup touch sensor provides the same service interface, changes of touch sensor provider actually change the configuration of the robot: in the case at hand, in order to keep the robot working correctly, the robot needs to take a 180 degree turn and reverse its navigation direction. Although we can take context-specific adaptation actions which include properties changes and compositional adaptation, separation of application structure maintenance makes the development of a new context much more concise than the standalone solution. That is because the ACCADA functional modeler and system run-time (Gui, De Florio, Sun, & Blondia, 2009b) will do vast parts of management work, such as components lifecycle control, component instance dependence injection, etc.

This scenario demonstrates three major adaptations. (1) When no error is detected, context-specific modeler always selects the primary touch sensor to compose the application. (2) When errors are detected on the primary touch sensor the context-specific modeler will activate the backup touch sensor and reconstruct accordingly the application as well as pilot actuator's direction. (3) After a fix is introduced for the primary touch sensor, such sensor is reintegrated. Adaptation modeler will reconstruct the application, switching back the primary sensor. In order to let the application continue working its task, the pilot actuator's configuration needs to restore to its original configuration). The last switch is done because the primary touch sensor is preferable with respect to the backup version as explained before. Adaptation videos can be downloaded from http://win.ua.ac.be/~ninggui/video/faulty-sensor.wmv

RELATED WORK

Currently, the researches of autonomous robot focused on developing those algorithms that can introduce autonomic behavior for existing robot, such as avoiding local obstacles and reaching goal points ahead. Evolutionary computation and fuzzy system or Bayesian networks are used to equip robot with some basic intelligence (Hashimoto et al., 2003; Inamura et al., 2000). However, these solutions cannot answer the question on how to provide systematic support on dealing with changing/evolving strategies.

In order to deal with component dynamicity, Cervantes and Hall (2004) propose a service-oriented component based framework for constructing adaptive component-based applications. The key part of their framework is the Service Binder which automatically controls the relationship between components. However, such an approach lacks the key part on how to incorporate external context knowledge into adaptation process and how to deal with context switches.

Garlan, Cheng, Huang, Schmerl, and Steenkiste (2004) propose a general architecture-based self-adaptation framework. Their Rainbow framework uses software architectures and a reusable infrastructure to support self-adaptation of software systems. The use of external adaptation mechanisms allows the explicit specification of adaptation strategies for multiple system concerns and domains. However, their approach lacks of component composition support which is also important in building applications.

Sicard, Boyer, and De Palma (2008) identify novel requirements on reflective component models for architecture-based management systems.

Their construct layer is designed for the meta-data checkpoint and replication. Interfaces and processes for self-repairing are defined, such as lifecycle management, setter/ getter interface as well as the meta-data based configuration. A faulty component can be repaired by restoring its state and all the meta-data information outside of the component instance. However, their approach lacks a clear definition and separation between system services. Their hard-wired architecture makes it very hard to reuse their framework across different contexts.

CONCLUSION

This paper describes our work in providing run-time adaptation support to autonomous robot systems. In our approach, rather than predefining adaptation logics in the robot system itself, we enable the system to run-time select the best adaptation modules according to the current context. In order to integrate ACCADA framework into an NXT Mindstorm robot, a remote NXT model is designed and implemented in a layered way. Our platform is implemented based on service oriented structure, which makes run-time adaptation possible.

Our ongoing work is in adding more refined custom event support to improve the efficiency of the adaptation loops.

It is worth remarking how our achievements are consistent with Boulding's vision on General Systems Theory (Boulding, 1956). There, "systems" are classified according to their ability to self-adapt. Current robotic systems would fall in Boulding's categories of "Plants" or "Animals" class – adaptive systems with limited introspection capability, The extra features granted by ACCADA allow robotic systems to be designed which are indeed able to revise their own adaptation strategies – which places them a step higher in Boulding's classification.

REFERENCES

Boulding, K. E. (1956). General systems theory - the skeleton of science. *Management Science, 2*(3), 197–208. doi:10.1287/mnsc.2.3.197

Eclipse. (2010). *Equinox platform.* Retrieved from http://www.eclipse.org/equinox/

Garlan, D., Cheng, S. W., Huang, A. C., Schmerl, B., & Steenkiste, P. (2004). Rainbow: Architecture-based self-adaptation with reusable infrastructure. *Computer, 37*(10), 46–49, doi:10.1109/MC.2004.175

Gui, N., De Florio, V., Sun, H., & Blondia, C. (2008). *A framework for adaptive real-time applications: The declarative real-time OSGi component model.* Paper presented at the the 7th Workshop on Adaptive and Reflective Middleware (ARM), Leuven, Belgium.

Gui, N., De Florio, V., Sun, H., & Blondia, C. (2009a). An architecture-based framework for managing adaptive real-time applications. In *Proceedings of the Euromicro Conference on Software Engineering and Advanced Applications* (pp. 502-507).

Gui, N., De Florio, V., Sun, H., & Blondia, C. (2009b). ACCADA: A framework for continuous context-aware deployment and adaptation. In R. Guerraoui & F. Petit (Eds.), *Proceedings of the 11th International Symposium on Stabilization, Safety, and Security of Distributed Systems* (LNCS 5873, pp. 325-340).

Hall, R. S., & Cervantes, H. (2004). Challenges in building service-oriented applications for OSGi. *IEEE Communications Magazine, 42*(5), 144–149. doi:10.1109/MCOM.2004.1299359

Hashimoto, S., Kojima, F., & Kubota, N. (2003). Perceptual system for a mobile robot under a dynamic environment. In *Proceedings of the IEEE International Symposium on Computational Intelligence in Robotics and Automation* (pp. 747-752).

Inamura, T., Inaba, M., & Inoue, H. (2000). *User adaptation of human-robot interaction model based on Bayesian network and introspection of interaction experience.* Paper presented at the the IEEE/RSJ International Conference on Intelligent Robots and Systems.

Jet Propulsion Laboratory. (n. d.). *Nasa Mars rover.* Retrieved from http://marsrover.nasa.gov

Kephart, J. O., & Chess, D. M. (2003). The vision of autonomic computing. *Computer, 36*(1), 41–50. doi:10.1109/MC.2003.1160055

LeJOS. (2009). *Java for LEGO mindstorms.* Retrieved from http://lejos.sourceforge.net/

Pieter-Jan, P. (2010). *An adaptive OSGi robotic application.* Unpublished doctoral dissertation, University of Antwerp, Belgium.

Riehle, D., Buschmann, F., & Martin, R. C. (1998). *Pattern languages of program design 3.* Reading, MA: Addison-Wesley.

Salehie, M., & Tahvildari, L. (2009). Self-adaptive software: Landscape and research challenges. *ACM Transactions on Autonomous and Adaptive Systems, 4*(2), 14–55.

Sicard, S., Boyer, F., & De Palma, N. (2008). Using components for architecture based management. In *Proceedings of the 30th International Conference on Software Engineering* (Vol. 1-2, pp. 101-110).

This work was previously published in the International Journal of Adaptive, Resilient and Autonomic Systems, Volume 2, Issue 2, edited by Vincenzo De Florio, pp. 37-50, copyright 2011 by IGI Publishing (an imprint of IGI Global).

Chapter 9

Self–Adaptable Discovery and Composition of Services Based on the Semantic CompAA Approach

J. Lacouture
Université de Toulouse, France

P. Aniorté
Université de Pau et des Pays de l'Adour, France

ABSTRACT

With the next generation of distributed systems, applications become nomad, ubiquitous or ambient. It becomes challenging to dynamically maintain or update functionalities, or to preserve non-functional properties, like the extensibility of the system and the quality of service. This paper describes the CompAA component model. The main contribution introduces the variability concept with the specification of adaptation points integrated by a mixed component/agent approach. The result is the production of self-adaptable entities, including self-discovery and self-composition mechanisms. An experiment in the area of training, based on very scalable services (e-Portfolio), validates these contributions and provides an exemplification of CompAA mechanisms.

INTRODUCTION

During the last years, distributed systems have known a rapid development with new technologies (Services Oriented Architectures, Grid computing, nomad and ubiquitous computing). Within such environments, the software architecture of the system evolves at runtime. Some critical systems have to be maintained, updated and improved without service discontinuation. Consequently, the persistence of the services and dynamic aspects establish new challenges and bring to reconsider inherent problems that are the reuse of the existing services and their adaptation. This dynamic

DOI: 10.4018/978-1-4666-2056-8.ch009

adaptation deals with the constant evolution of systems (evolution in terms of availability of services, updates, failures, or evolution of needs at runtime).

The CompAA (Auto-Adaptable Components) approach is proposed to deal with this kind of contextual adaptation. It tries to produce systems with the most dynamic and most autonomous properties, among other things by the discovery of the available services.

An original method that we promote with CompAA, inspired by related works (Briot, 2005; Krutisch et al., 2003), is the idea to combine components and agents advantages in a mixed approach. The idea to use the component paradigm is motivated by results obtained, on the one hand in the field of re-use, and on the other hand in the area of the modeling and the deployment of distributed applications. Components present limits in terms of flexibility and autonomy, which are intrinsic characteristics of software agents. Indeed agents are often used to automate systems but they have not the same assets to produce reusable and reconfigurable entities. That's why, we find a real interest in mixing these two complementary paradigms to take the benefits of both.

For that purpose, our contributions get organized around two main propositions:

- A model of adaptable components, leaning on the principles of abstraction and variability, and also leaning on a semantic definition in terms of functional and non-functional properties allowing an automatic interpretation by software agents;
- A process of dynamic adaptation implementing the proposed model. The specified process covers stages going from the analysis of needs to the adaptation of components, as well as stages of discovery and selection of components. Various policies of adaptation allow a level of adaptability increased within the process.

This paper is organized as follows. Next section gives an overview of related works and another section defines the area of our experiments, the e-learning (with the use of e-Portfolios), in order to give an exemplification throughout the paper. Then, we specify the CompAA component model introducing the variability principle to develop adaptable entities. Another section is devoted to CompAA agents and the CompAA process of self-adaptation. Afterward, we present first experimental results concerning the self-adaptation of e-Portfolios using the CompAA approach. Finally, we conclude giving an outlook on future works.

RELATED WORKS

With many approaches proposing adaptable solutions for opened distributed systems, (a non-exhaustive shortlist: Sirac, AGIL or Accord), some relevant elements are pointed out:

- The use of components (software components, web/grid services, ...) which reusable quality modeling reduces time and cost in the development cycle;
- The use of software agents to automate the processes of discovery, selection or adaptation of provided services;
- The use of semantic models like ontologies to describe "contextual" data and to allow to autonomously interpret them;
- Sometimes, the use of peer-to-peer communication mechanisms to improve autonomous and dynamic interactions thanks to a decentralized management.

As we emphasize in the introduction, components and agents are often used to manage the adaptation of services. Agents and multi-agents systems are convenient tools for designing complex systems, in particular in the context of ubiquitous computing and ambient intelligence

(Cabri et al., 2005; Satoh, 2004). Software agents (Nwana & Heath, 1996) are autonomous artifacts which are set in an environment, able to interact with it and to communicate with other agents. Autonomy refers to proactivity and to the ability of agents to make adapted decisions by themselves with their own decision procedures, knowledge, and perception data. Adaptation is essential in multi-agent systems (Marin & Mehandjiev, 2006) and their use helps in decentralizing knowledge, decision and control.

Krutish (2003) distinguishes two ways of combining agents and components: "agentifying" sees component technology as the starting point and tries to include agent properties into existing components; and "componentifying" considers agent technology as the starting point and tries to add component features to existing agent technology).

Most often, components and architectural description languages (ADL) are used to manage adaptation at a structural level (e.g., the proposition of Fractal (Bruneton et al., 2006) and its extension toward adaptability (Safran) (David & Ledoux, 2006), the proposition of the JavaPod platform within the Sirac project (Bruneton & Riveill, 2001), works around the Madcar model (Grondin et al., 2006) or plugin approaches (Bako et al., 2006; Tu et al., 1998). We observe that the flexibility of the adaptation of these approaches is not obvious, far from it. Safran doesn't take into account non-functional properties, and JavaPod and others approaches are too oriented on (re) configuration and too far from our concern of autonomy.

Agents allow introducing an interesting level of flexibility to adaptation methods at the inter-actions level, and also in terms of automation. Thus, works around JavAct and MAY (Arcangeli et al., 2004; Noel et al., 2010) or DIMA (Guessoum, 2000) propose the construction of software agents thanks to components. The substitution of

components allows changing the agent behaviour in order to adapt the application to the needs and context evolution.

However, components are quite equivalent to COTS components, predefined, that is quite far from our idea of assembling and dynamically adapting services (based on runtime discovery, selection and adaptation, and the dynamic analysis of semantic services).

Works around the Accord framework (Agarwal et al., 2003; Liu & Parashar, 2006) are very close to our approach, concerning the idea of combining agents and components. But, in Accord, works are oriented toward autonomic computing, drawing inspiration from the biological model, and aim at adapting components to environmental context. The targeted applications are critical situation from the chemistry domain or forest fire management. Software entities are automated and more far from human factor than our matters of concern (like e-learning, e-training) where suggestive require-ments must taken into account.

The novelty of our approach is especially accentuated with the way of combining agents and components in order to take into account advantages of both paradigms:

- Software components, proposed as web services abstraction, are designed to be dynamically adapted, contrary to DIMA or JavAct/MAY which are based on a "componifying" approach and contrary to Accord where "services" and "abstraction" concepts are dismissed;
- Software agents, evolving as peers, are allocated to each component to introduce a level of autonomy. Services specifica-tion, including their functional and non-functional properties, thanks to semanti-cal interpretable standards is a natural and necessary condition to make possible the approach.

Moreover, it is now admitted that enabling the Web for software components can be ideally supported through the use of Semantic Web technologies (Kagal et al., 2006). The Semantic Web aims to introduce meaning to the Web using ontologies (DeRoure & Sure, 2006). Ontologies can create a shared understanding of application domain and development process knowledge that is crucial for component development activities such as matching and connecting requesters and providers of component services.

According to this statement, our approach tries to define semantic services allowing to self-interpret services descriptions. The CompAA contributions, detailed in this paper, are voluntarily linked to service oriented architectures works and advances in this domain (use of semantic services, ontologies and standards like OWL-S).

Figure 1 places the novelty of our contribution in relation with well known paradigms and tools, and also in relation to quoted works. The CompAA approach draws inspiration from service oriented computing and its technological breakthroughs (XML, WSDL, WSRF, OWL, OWL-S), from software components with well-known properties of reuse or interoperability and with works like fractal, Madcar or plug-in, and from software agents with the need to be flexible and autonomous, and approaches providing an interesting and approved background like MAY, Accord or AGIL (Jonquet et al., 2007).

E-PORTFOLIO AS A SELF-ADAPTABLE SERVICE

The European project ELeGI (European Learning Grid Infrastructure) (Gaeta et al., 2003) represents our main application area. The project aims at developing an infrastructure for collaborative learn-

Figure 1. Place of CompAA in comparison to related works

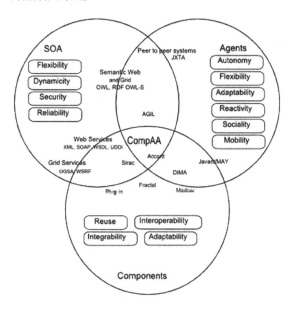

ing on the grid, based on a learning paradigm shift. The idea is to focus on knowledge construction using experiential-based and collaborative learning approaches in a contextualized, customized and ubiquitous way, and to replace the current information transfer paradigm based on content and on the key authoritative figure of the teacher who provides information.

Our contribution to the project aims at providing a process for learners qualification, we call the "e-Qualification process" (Gouarderes et al., 2005), to support collaborative learning, and more particularly formal/informal learning. We illustrate this kind of activities specifying collaborative fly-training activities between trainees sharing knowledge and performing procedures on a fly simulator.

In this context, we introduce a central tool to manage the e-Qualification process, in the shape of an e-Portfolio service. An e-Portfolio is a personal digital collection of information describing and illustrating a person's learning, career, experience and achievements (Grant, 2005). Inspired by IMS e-portfolio specifications (http://www.imsglobal.org/ep/index.html), the objectives of our e-Portfolio are to:

- Evaluate formal and informal learning;
- Provide information on individual and collective development;
- Allow learners to acquire knowledge, to practice and to attest new abilities;
- Promote collaborative learning between trainees and knowledge sharing among communities (Communities of Practice (Wenger, 2000) and Communities of Competencies (Smith, 2005)).

More than a simple repository of data, our e-Portfolio (Lacouture & Mansour, 2007) is the support of collaborative knowledge sharing between users. It evolves with the competencies' acquisition, the needs' evolution and the services' availability (other connected trainees with their e-Portfolio). For us, it illustrates what we present in the introduction as a concern of dynamic adaptation. We define how to specify e-Portfolios as an adaptable service. Then, we introduce agents and a process managing e-Portfolio to dynamically adapt them. Thus, e-Portfolios will help the reader to understand how CompAA can be concretely implemented with a practical example of service adaptation.

ADAPTABLE DISTRIBUTED COMPONENTS

Toward an Adaptable Component Model

Two essential principles must ideally underlie these models (Cauvet & Semmak, 1999): the principle of abstraction and the principle of variability (Figure 2).

Abstraction in a component consists in distinguishing explicitly reusable knowledge (the realization of the component) and knowledge useful to its realization (the specification of the component). Realization is the "hidden" part. Specification is the "visible" part. This principle is necessary to build effective infrastructures of re-use. Indeed, the specification part of a component can play an essential role in the exploitation of the re-use architecture, in particular at the time of the search and the integration of components.

The principle of variability results in distinguishing a fixed part and a variable part in the specification of a component. Both parts are visible and they introduce the generic character of the component. At the re-use time, it is by fixing the variable part that we choose a particular realization and that we adapt the component according to the specificities of the system under development.

The CompAA component model is based on the Ugatze component model (Seyler & Aniorté, 2004) developed for the static integration of

Figure 2. Abstraction and variability principles - graphical view

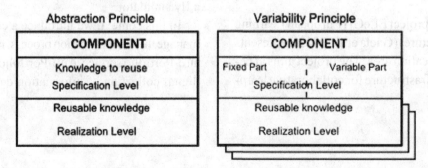

autonomous, heterogeneous and distributed software components. Ugatze components have been related to the principle of abstraction and rest on two essential concepts: the interface of the component and the interaction between components.

We integrate the variability extending Ugatze component model interface with new specification points (Lacouture & Aniorté, 2008). We call this kind of specification points: adaptation points. Thus, an adaptation point is associated to each subservice of a component. It is the selection (or the no selection) of an adaptation point which allows to select subservices and adapt the component to specific needs producing a particular reuse case (Figure 3).

The description of adaptation point in the component interface is not new and we find some ways of thinking adaptation in literature. For instance Bracciali et al. (2005) provides a kind of formalized adaptation points extending components interfaces with a description of the behavior of the component. However descriptions rely on functional properties and do not integrate semantics. That's what differentiates our definition of adaptation points which exhibit functional and non-functional properties and requirements of the components.

Adaptable Components Description

Figure 4 describes an e-Portfolio designed thanks to the CompAA component model. An e-Portfolio component is divided into two parts (abstraction principle): the realization with a core and subservices and the specification with specification points, notably adaptation points linked to each subservice. In the core of an e-Portfolio, we can find personal data (Curriculum Vitae with personal information) and basic elements (history of his learning activities, goals...). Various subservices are proposed by the e-Portfolio of the figure. Particularly, it provides subservices to share information about landing procedure, take off procedure, flaps handling or reactions to alarms.

In order to produce adaptable components manageable by software agents, we describe e-Portfolio components with functional and non-functional properties.

Functional Properties

Functional properties represent the subservices offered by a trainee, when his skills are sufficient to provide some help and advice. In Figure 4, a trainee has obtained good results during the simu-

Figure 3. The CompAA component model - specification point of view

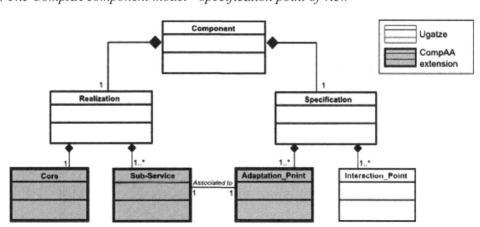

Figure 4. E-Portfolio designed with the CompAA component model - graphical point of view

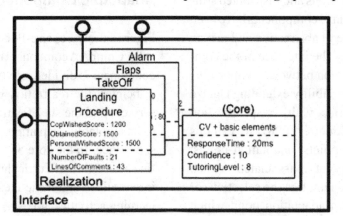

lation concerning various procedures (Landing, TakeOff, Flaps and Alarm) and he can provide subservices to give information and tips to other connected trainees. So in order to produce a functional description of these provided subservices semantically interpretable by software entities, we lean on a domain ontology. The advantages of using ontologies are multiple, especially in terms of interoperability (Gruber, 1993). As regards to our field of experiment, the ontology we use is an OWL ontology from the VET (Vocational and Educational Training) domain. It provides common semantics for the subservices description of all components of the system and it plays the role of a common vocabulary for the communication between software agents. The ontology we use to describe functional properties is an OWL file (an

extract is presented in Figure 5). Among others things, it gives a common support for knowledge shared between e-Portfolios, which is necessary for self-interpretation and self-adaptation.

In addition, each adaptation point is functionally valuated with a triplet of values to estimate the relevance of the information provided with regard to the obtained results and assigned objectives.

Thus, a procedure, like the landing procedure, performed on the simulator is monitored by three values:

- CoPWishedScore, instructor assigned objectives to the whole of the CoP (Community of Practice);

Figure 5. Extract of the ontology describing various procedures (knowledge) shared by trainees

```
<owl:Class rdf:ID="Procedure"/>
  <rdfs:subClassOf rdf:resource="#"/>
<owl:Class rdf:ID="TakeOfProcedure">
  <rdfs:subClassOf rdf:resource="#Procedure"/>
</owl:Class>
<owl:Class rdf:ID="HeadingTakeOfProcedure">
  <rdfs:subClassOf rdf:resource="#TakeOfProcedure"/>
</owl:Class>
<owl:Class rdf:ID="LandingProcedure">
  <rdfs:subClassOf rdf:resource="#Procedure"/>
</owl:Class>
<owl:Class rdf:ID="HeadingProcedure">
  <rdfs:subClassOf rdf:resource="#Procedure"/>
</owl:Class>
```

- ObtainedScore, acquired scores after procedure realization on the simulator, results fall with reported errors;
- PersonalWishedScore, personal assigned objectives that can be different from those of the instructor. Assigning personal objectives is relevant for "ree-play session". The default value of personal objectives is the same as the CoPWishedScore's.

The representation of needs in CompAA components uses the same triplet of values. Results evolve from a perfect score and fall with reported errors. The idea is to adapt the service offering according to detected needs (results less than objectives), to the evolution of its own knowledge (results) and to automatically propose interesting answers to the user (knowledge, advices, comments...). Discovering an interesting adaptation point means discovering a subservice that functionally provides the necessary information (ontology matching between concepts, procedure) and that also provides satisfying results ("ObtainedScore" superior than "CoPWishedScore").

Non-Functional Properties

With the rapid development of distributed systems, services sharing have to take into account of main criteria like QoS, reliability, security, performance… These examples of non-functional properties are usually assessed when the system is assembled (Zschaler, 2004). With CompAA, we give this kind of information to individual components to improve the way of choosing them during the discovery and the selection of components.

Many approaches (Petri nets, stochastic process...) exist to instantiate non-functional properties, often focusing on a property or a family of properties. However, metrics provide a simple way for the representation of various non-functional properties and allow comparing various values. The use of metrics allows an additional degree for

an automation and a self-adaptation managed by an agent-directed process.

Our approach draws its inspiration from the specification of this kind of properties thanks to a software quality model and metrics. Due to its qualities and its general use, we choose to lean on the ISO 9126 software quality model from the range of existing models.

Thus, a non-functional property is represented by a set of quality criteria (fault tolerance, interoperability, learnability, accuracy...). And each criteria is valuated by a set of metrics. A metric is defined by a type (integer, float, char...), a unit (second, octets...) and a variance indicating how to read the metric value (*variance: 0* if the lowest value is the best and *1* if the best value is the highest).

To specify adaptable components thanks to this type of representation we develop an OWL ontology to represent and instantiate non-functional properties. Figure 6 gives the structure of the OWL ontology we use. We refer the reader to works around the QoSOnt ontology that inspires our approach (Dobson et al., 2005). QoSOnt is particularly interesting with the opportunity to convert units and thus to compare them (for instance, for time units: to allow comparing seconds and minutes). With regard to the e-learning context, we only develop an ontology allowing to directly compare values expressed with the same unit.

Thus, the examples of non-functional properties specified in an e-portfolio, which refer to various criteria of quality, are illustrated in Figure 7 ("reliability", "understandability" or "performance"). The properties associated to each of these criteria are instantiated (variance, value…). For instance, the "NumberOfFaults" is a metric of the "reliability" quality criterion, its value is "21" and its variance is set to "0", which means that the lowest value will be the best. In the same way, the "Confidence" is also a metric of the "reliability" quality criterion, its value is "10" (max value) and its variance is set to "1", which means that the highest value will be the best.

Figure 6. OWL ontology for non-functional properties

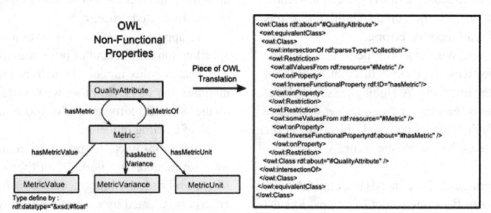

Figure 7. Non-functional properties in an adaptation point and in the core of an e-Portfolio

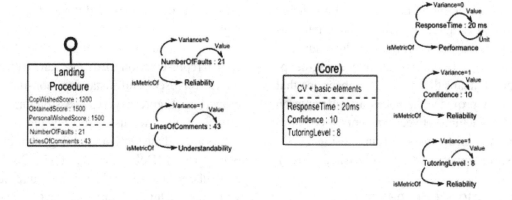

Moreover, non-functional properties are instantiable at two levels:

- In the core of a compaa component, when non-functional properties are not specific to a particular subservice and are factorisable to the whole component. For instance, the level of "Confidence" is a non-functional property ("Reliability") we specify in the core of e-Portfolios that indicates if its owner has shared efficient knowledge in past activities. The value of "10" (max value) decreases with bad sharing experiences and increases with successful ones;

- In the description of adaptation points, when non-functional properties are specific to a particular subservice and give

information about this one. For instance, the number of "linesofcomments" is a non-functional property ("Understandability"). We specify in the description of the "landingprocedure" an adaptation point that indicates if its owner is able to provide a significant quantity of information about this procedure.

SELF-ADAPTABLE PROCESS

The CompAA Agents

In Lacouture and Aniorté (2008), we give a first idea of how to specify a process managed by agents allowing self-adapting CompAA specified components. The originality of our approach consists in its mixed nature. CompAA components, with adaptation points and interpretable and sharable descriptions of subservices, give the support of adaptable entities. In order to make them self-adaptable, we associate to each CompAA component an agent in charge of dynamically adapting services to unpredictable events. In highly distributed and dynamic systems, many problems have to be taken into account: breakdowns, services failures, services availability and so on. Agents, thanks to their autonomy and flexibility properties, are able to react and find adapted solutions to maintain such systems.

Figure 8 describes the CompAA approach. An agent is associated to a component (one-to-one) in order to manage interactions. Agents, when they observe the components' evolution or when they react to specific events and act as peers (sometimes client, sometimes server), use peer-to-peer mechanisms (see an approved definition of peer-to-peer in Schollmeier, 2001). The traditional client/server model is more and more seen as a constraint and peer-to-peer solutions are increasingly evolving to an expanded use in distributed networks. In client/server mode, most of the information resides on one side (server) and most of the intelligence on the other (client). In

Foster and Iamnitchi (2003), Foster underlines that peer-to-peer is an adapted technology for open environments, like the Grid, P2P allowing to virtualize resources. Many contributions are developed relating to P2P technologies allowing to use P2P systems to improve scalability (wide-scale) and to access dynamically to heterogeneous resources. For an overview of P2P technologies, we invite the reader to refer to Milojicic et al. (2002). However, we point out that Peer-to-peer communication mechanisms are interesting for CompAA agents because they offer advantages in terms of:

- Decentralization and extensibility; each peer has alternately functions of consumer and provider. As a result, the traditional client-server architecture bottleneck is reduced;
- Fault tolerance; several peers can assume the same functionalities, the same data can be stored on multiple nodes. This mechanism guarantees the consistency of an application;
- Dynamics and adaptability; the system's configuration can evolve with breakdowns, availability, or adding and deleting peers. Peer-to-peer systems propose strategies to

Figure 8. General aspect of the CompAA approach - agents managing the interaction level

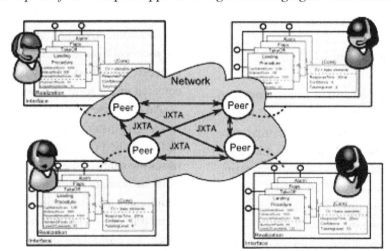

self-organize nodes of the infrastructure. Moreover, P2P systems assume that the computing environment is highly dynamic. That is, resources, such as compute nodes, will be entering and leaving the system continuously. When an application is intended to support a highly dynamic environment, the P2P approach is a natural fit.

Therefore, communications tools and protocols are integrated in CompAA agents. Agents developed for e-Portfolios management use the JXTA platform (JXTA, 2003) and protocols. JXTA provides P2P facilities (creation, search, add peers, delete peers, advertisement, discovery, and so on). All the agents are considered as equal and especially have a common task: managing component interactions. An agent has a description of its capabilities that will be published as a JXTA advertisement, so that it can easily be discovered by other members of the network. We take advantage of the JXTA protocols for simplicity and efficiency.

In the field of the adaptation of e-Portfolios, the CompAA process is developed to provide to each trainee an adapted learning context, taking into account his own needs and on time environmental constraints (availability of services). Needs are detected in the e-Portfolio of their owner and the goal of the process is to provide e-Portfolios of other trainees containing competencies (subservices) capable of helping the user in his learning.

The CompAA Process

Four main steps are identified in the CompAA adaptation process managed by CompAA agents (Figure 9). They form a cycle of an iterative process. Indeed, the described process is adaptable and iterative. Agents are continuously operating allowing more flexibility: if an error feedback occurs (i.e., no peers providing functionalities) or if some improvements can be done (i.e., new available competencies), corrections will be taken

Figure 9. Nominal CompAA process for adaptation of components

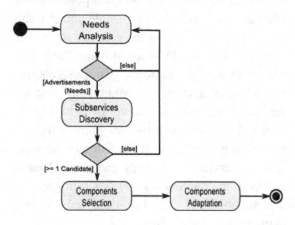

into account in the next iterations. The process is also adaptable because various policies of detecting needs or of selecting components are available and allow to self-adapt to the behavior of the process. The CompAA adaptation process steps are described below.

Needs Analysis

This first step assumes that a part of a component is observable, interpretable, by software agents. It is the developer's responsibility to define what to observe and how to report it.

Agents observe continuously components concerning their achievement (checks are done at the end of each adaptation process cycle). For our application, they simply observe the gap between learning objectives assigned by instructors and the user's effective results. When the difference between these two values is positive, a need is detected in the form of required subservice.

An advertisement describing the required subservice (for instance: LandingService) is produced and published (Figure 10). Functionally, it publishes the name of the skill, here LandingService, from the domain ontology and an ObtainedValue (candidates have to exhibit better results than the client trainee). As regards to non-functional properties, it is possible to specify some requirements.

Figure 10. Piece of a JXTA advertisement produced to find peers

```
<SubService>
    LandingProcedure
    <ObtainedResult>
        300
    </ObtainedResult>
    <Qual i tyAttribute >
        <Metric="LinesOfComments " Variance="1" Value="2">
    </QualityAttribute >
</SubService>
<QualityAttribute >
    <Metric="TutoringLevel " Variance="1" Value="8">
</QualityAttribute >
```

The default specification of non-functional needs is to discover subservices with a minimum of two lines of comments concerning the researched skill (LinesOfComment, non-functional property of the subservice) and an assessment level at least equal to the client trainee one (TutoringLevel, non-functional property instantiated in the core of the e-Portfolio).

Of course, we propose a very simple interpretation of need analysis with this context. To generalize the approach, various ways are possible. We plan various representations for needs, from simple XML files to UML statecharts diagrams.

Sub-Service Discovery

Agents have peer-to-peer communication mechanisms (JXTA) allowing to find peers providing required services, available via advertisements (representing adaptation points).

Figure 11 gives an example of request using the JXTA discovery protocol.

In the context of learners having to improve their knowledge, agents search instructors or other trainees publishing interesting competencies on their e-Portfolios.

When other peer agents are candidates for providing subservices, the agent checks published adaptation points in terms of functional and non-functional properties. A first simple verification of functionalities is facilitated by the use of a common ontology.

Figure 12 shows an example of response (advertisement) received when searching peers (Figure 10). It indicates the provided subservice ("LandingProcedure"), the "ObtainedScore" and non-functional properties specific to the subservice ("LinesOfComment") or peculiar to the provided component core ("TutoringLevel").

In the next sections, we will see how policies are implemented to improve the services discovery when no responses are received. The relaxation of constraints concerning functional and non-functional requirements or composition and decomposition strategies, are introduced to enhance the approach.

Component Selection

This step deals with the selection of the best composition with the best candidate. For existing configurations, the question is to know if new e-Portfolio components are available on the network.

In our experimentation, if several components (server e-Portfolios) are able to share interesting knowledge suitable to help the trainee, the five most adapted are selected and form a list of the best candidates. It is conceivable, especially with collaborative situation, that several solutions are

Figure 11. Example of use of the JXTA discovery protocol to find a trainee providing a Landing subservice

```
grp . ge tDi s cove rySe rvi c e ( ) . getRemoteAdvertisements ( nul l ,
Di scoveryService .ADV," SubService ","*"+" LandingService "+"*" ,10 , thi s ) ;
```

Figure 12. Piece of a received JXTA advertisement describing a provided subservice

```
<!DOCTYPE PeerAdv>
<GroupName>trainee1 </GroupName>
<SubService>
    LandingProcedure
    <ObtainedResult>
        1000
    </ObtainedResult>
    <QualityAttribute >
        <Metric="LinesOfComments " Variance="1" Value="5">
    </QualityAttribute >
</SubService>
<QualityAttribute >
    <Metric="TutoringLevel " Variance="1" Value="10">
</QualityAttribute >
<SiteAgent>JLac : K1184795976014</SiteAgent>
</PeerAdv>
```

proposed to a trainee allowing him to improve his understanding of the given problem in one way or another.

To classify received advertisements, we introduce a function ("EvalPeer()") to compare two advertisements with their non-functional properties. A matching between them allows to compare two identical properties and to decide which one is the best. The default policy doesn't give a priority to a particular property but alternative strategies can be established to emphasize some properties to obtain a different classification. (The EvalPeer() function compares two advertisements using the DOM package allowing to process XML documents. The algorithm consists in sequentially reading the first file and searching in the other file similar elements (properties type) and compares them when properties are found. The better values allow to score and rank advertisements).

Following the discovery step, three cases are possible.

No candidate found. When no candidate is found after three iterations of the cycle, successive strategies are implemented. A policy of constraints relaxation is processed by compaa agents. To hope to discover more results in future cycles, after three iterations we can relax non-functional

requirements. An example we implement is to find subservices with tutoringlevels lower than those researched. After five iterations, we also give the opportunity to relax functional requirements. An example is to decrease obtainedresults by 20 percent to broaden the research and the number of candidates.

Only one candidate. In this case, if the received advertisement matches with the one which is sent, the candidate is directly selected.

Two or more candidates. In this case, the selection step has to compare and classify candidates. For our experimentation we choose to classify candidates and to present the five best ones to the (client) trainee (Figure 13, the "BestCandidatesList"). The "evalPeer()" function is used to successively compare received advertisements and to establish a qualitative ranking.

Component Adaptation

After the selection of adaptation points providing required subservices, the last step consists in adapting components and composing them. Reuse cases are produced with their core and selected subservices. The Figure 14 gives a graphical illustration of this adaptation. The "LandingService" is selected and a reuse case is produced to be integrated. The produced adapted e-Porfolio is directly made available on (client) trainee e-Portfolio interface. It allows the trainee to access to a useful view of an e-Portoflio with interesting knowledge helping him in his learning. E-Portfolios are available in the list of online users thanks to CompAA agents that guarantees the transparency of the process.

Subservices Decomposition and Composition Scenarios

We implement other ways to improve the services discovery when no candidate is found. The constraints relaxation is one of these ways. The subservices decomposition or composition is another

Figure 13. Selection and classification of received candidates

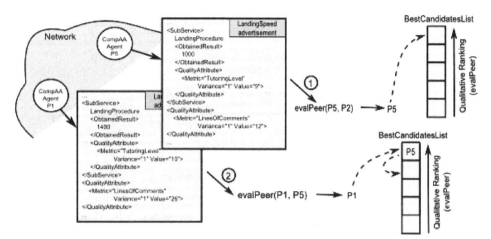

Figure 14. e-Portfolio component adaptation

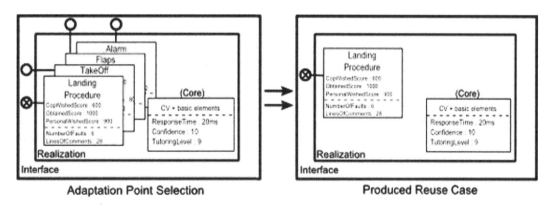

one, also allowing improving existing solutions. The idea is to compose a subservice or decompose it when it's possible. This strategy is based on the provided domain ontology and on the "HasChild" properties (for the decomposition mechanisms) and "isChildOf" properties, the inverse property (for the composition mechanisms).

In Figure 15, the "LandingProcedure" has two children: "LandingSpeed" and "LandingGear". The idea is to broaden the research of provided adaptation points.

The discovery of "LandingProcedure" information is extended to fine-grained subservices for a subservice decomposition. Inversely, the "LandingSpeed" discovery can be replaced by a

coarse-grained research (about "LandingProcedure" information) for a subservice composition.

As regards the subservices decomposition, additional mechanisms are developed to allow an assessment of fine-grained results. When a decomposition policy is introduced, the subservices discovery returns a set of subservices, to form a configuration (the whole children of the initial researched subservice, in our example a configuration, is a pair: "LandingSpeed/LandingGear"). The assessment of a configuration is made in two stages. First of all, a virtual peer is created. The goal is to specify only one peer, combining all (functional and non-functional) properties of the configuration peers.

Figure 15. Part of the domain ontology allowing to decompose subservices into child subservices

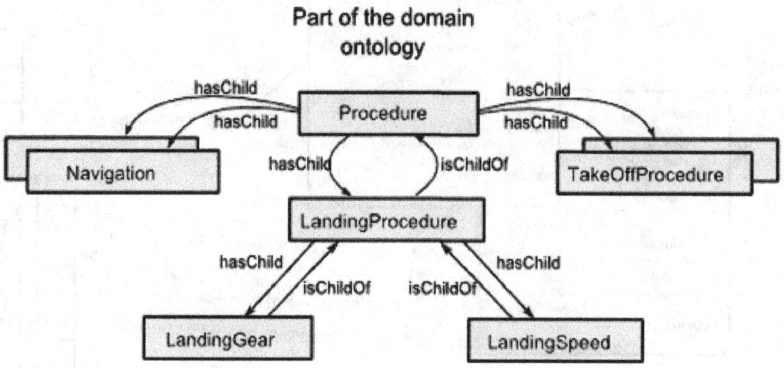

$$VirtualPeer(P_1,...,P_n) = \sum_{i=1}^{n} \text{Pr}\, operties\,(P_i)$$

Then, after the virtual peers creation, we are in the same situation of the classical components selection. We use the "evalPeer()" function to assess and classify candidates. Figure 16 gives a general overview of the decomposition process. Candidates of the "BestCandidatesList" are integrated thanks to the adaptation step that we have presented.

Note that the subservices decomposition uses the same kind of mechanisms, therefore we choose to don't describe it in this paper.

EXPERIMENTAL RESULTS

Experiments were done to evaluate the level and the quantity of shared knowledge in collaborative situations. It allows, for us, to test the feasibility and the relevance of the introduction of CompAA mechanisms (the design of e-Portfolios by the way of CompAA components and the use of CompAA agents to dynamically adapt interactions between e-Portfolios to improve collaborative learning). Collaborative situations remain possible if e-Portfolios offer is adapted to the evolution of the needs. When e-Portfolios become unsuitable

in terms of provided services (knowledge and competencies not adapted to user requirements), interactions become unexciting and the number of exchanged messages drop.

Within the scope of the ELeGI project, trainees are making exercises on a simulator to improve their capabilities. After a first simulation session, they are placed in collaborative situations. The acquired knowledge will be assessed within future simulation sessions.

After performing a first step of simulation, trainees can interact directly with each other by the way of their e-Portfolios (designed as CompAA components).

Figure 17 gives an idea of the benefits of the CompAA approach in terms of self-adaptability.

Measures are realized observing a group of 11 trainees cooperating on different nodes of a network. We chose to observe the quantity of exchanged data (number of data messages exchanged between the different e-Portfolios of each trainee). The number of messages allows to assess that e-Portfolios content/services are adapted to requirements and that an efficient cooperation is preserved. We measure this metric with two similar groups with similar objectives. The main objective is to check that CompAA adaptation actions allow to preserve adapted interactions longer.

Figure 16. Subservices decomposition mechanisms

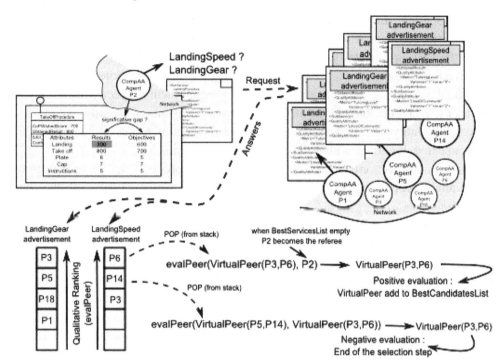

Figure 17. Data exchange observation between 11 trainees improving their knowledge after simulation

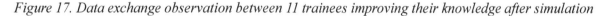

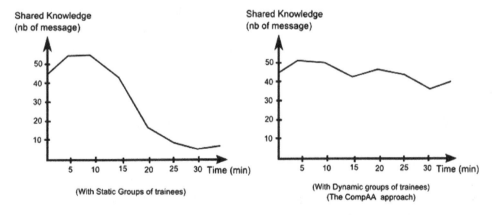

The left part of the figure presents interactions between the 11 trainees that are initially statically grouped with regards to their results. After 15 minutes of collaborative learning the number of exchanged data decreases considerably because trainees' knowledge evolves and groups become not adapted for sharing. This learning situation is optimal at the beginning of the collaboration, but this sharing context becomes unsuitable to the new requirements of the trainees.

The right part of the figure presents results obtained introducing the CompAA model and process. Agents are in charge of discovering, adapting and presenting adapted e-Portfolios (content and services) to trainees. After 15 minutes of interaction, the sharing of data is preserved thanks to the iterative property of the CompAA discovery mechanisms, taking into account the evolution of needs. When the knowledge of the trainees evolves, the quality criteria of researched e-Portfolio are updated. It allows, with different strategies of research and selection of components, to find best available collaborative situations/ partners.

The CompAA process has allowed replacing static groups of trainees by a dynamic discovery of trainees. It efficiently improves the quality of collaborative sessions and the acquired knowledge is assessed with better results in the next simulation sessions.

These conclusions are the result of first experiments. Accurate measures will be conducted to improve the assessment of the approach and to improve the CompAA contributions. Large scale experiments will certainly highlight some improvements to be done concerning, for instance, potential bottlenecks of analysis and selection steps of the CompAA process (e.g., the need to define when begins the selection step? When it finishes? When we decide to relax constraints or to change the current strategy?).

DISCUSSION

Regarding our propositions of software components adaptation based on semantic descriptions, a natural open question relates to the adaptability of the approach in terms of how generic is the methodology when applied to other domains. In this paper, we illustrate our propositions thanks to experiments around e-training, the specification of e-Portfolios and an agent-directed process in charge of adapting trainee behaviors. Some of the propositions are directly linked to experiments like the use of a domain ontology to define functional

subservices. Another specific point rests with our way to specify needs in CompAA components: the instantiation of a triplet of values (ObtainedScore, CoPWishedScore, PersonalWishedScore). The only one advice we note to replace this triplet is the requirement to specify interpretable needs by software agents. Currently, we are working on other ways of representing needs, for instance with state machine diagrams.

In our propositions, some aspects are already generic or nearly generic. At the specification level, we use standards (OWL, OWL-S...) to guarantee a first form of adaptability. Except for a required implementation effort, the approach could, easily, be used for other domains than e-learning. The non-functional description of components (ontology and metrics) is generic and a large number of non-functional properties are insatiable (Dobson et al., 2005).

However, a limit could be pointed out concerning state management. The services that are currently used are stateless. Indeed, concerning our e-learning applications, e-portfolios' discovery and composition is done dynamically, but the user does not need to manage states. When an e-portfolio service becomes unavailable, agents track other solutions by using various strategies (new research, relaxing constraints, composition and decomposition). For other research areas, the same techniques are not always applicable and solutions have to be proposed to manage services with states to introduce mechanisms to dynamically stop and restart services saving the execution parameters of the current service. With our current approach, we don't take into account this kind of considerations but we're thinking of introducing some elements of states management for the specification of each component subservice. Often enough, states machine approaches are foreseen. For instance, in Ballagny et al. (2007) states machines (UML 2.0 state diagrams) are developed to compose dynamically autonomic components behaviors.

CONCLUSION AND FUTURE WORK

In this paper, we have presented an original approach for adaptability by mixing component and agent paradigms. Components are used to specify adaptable services and agents manage them. The CompAA component model is based on Ugatze methodology. We have extended Ugatze with the variability principle and the proposition of adaptation points that we defined with functional and non-functional properties. Then, we have introduced agents for their properties of autonomy and flexibility. The idea is to be able to discover available components and customize them to detected needs.

As well as components and agents benefits, the approach seems very interesting to us thanks to the transparency of the agent's activity for the user.

Some technology choices are also recommended in the CompAA approach: the use of ontology to make easier agents discovery and verification process, the use of metrics to select the most relevant services and also the use of peer-to-peer communication mechanisms for extensibility and adaptability benefits.

Moreover, we propose a nominal agent-directed scenario for the management of a dynamic adaptation and we develop alternative scenarios allowing adapting policy of need analysis and selection of component to find newer or better candidates or to classify them in another way.

In the field of the ELeGI European Project, our approach has been tested through the development of adaptable and dynamic grid services called e-Portfolios. The results highlight the relevance of the approach in terms of flexibility with an interesting personalization of services relative to on-demand specified needs.

Future works will be devoted to the production of new scenarios increasingly integrating non-functional properties and more complex mechanisms of evaluation and selection of components. A large-scale validation will allow sorting out undetected problems like potential bottlenecks during services discovery and more detailed mechanisms for steps succession.

More generally, we hope to encourage the development of mixed approaches. With the CompAA approach, components combined with agents provide a set of qualities for a dynamic adaptation: robustness, reuse, autonomy and flexibility. It would be surely interesting to experiment if this kind of approaches provides viable results for other concerns with dynamic constraints. With this idea, works are in progress, in our labs, to define how it is possible to mix components and agents, using a model driven engineering approach to design service oriented architectures.

ACKNOWLEDGMENT

Work partially supported by the European Community under the Innovation Society Technologies (IST) programme of the 6th Framework Programme for RTD - project ELeGI, contract IST-002205. This document does not represent the opinion of the European Community, and the European Community is not responsible for any use that might be made of data appearing therein.

REFERENCES

Agarwal, M., Bhat, V., Liu, H., & Matossi, V. (2003). Automate: Enabling autonomic applications on the grid. In *Proceedings of the Fifth Annual International Autonomic Computing Workshop on Active Middleware Services* (pp. 48-57). Washington, DC: IEEE Computer Society.

Arcangeli, J.-P., Leriche, S., & Pantel, M. (2004). Development of flexible peer-to-peer information systems using adaptable mobile agents. In *Proceedings of the DEXA Workshops* (pp. 549-553).

Bako, B., Borchert, A., Heidenbluth, N., & Mayer, J. (2006). Linearly ordered plugins through self-organization. In *Proceedings of the International Conference on Autonomic and Autonomous Systems* (p. 8). Washington, DC: IEEE Computer Society.

Ballagny, C., Hameurlain, N., & Barbier, F. (2007). Endowing software components with autonomic capabilities based on modeling language executability. In *Proceedings of the 1st Workshop on Model-driven Software Adaptation* (pp. 55-60).

Bracciali, A., Brogi, A., & Canal, C. (2005). A formal approach to component adaptation. *Journal of Systems and Software, 74*(1), 45–54. doi:10.1016/j.jss.2003.05.007

Briot, J.-P. (2005). Foreword. In Choren, R., Garcia, A., Lucena, C., & Romanovsky, A. (Eds.), *Software Engineering for Multi-Agent Systems III (LNCS 3390)*.

Bruneton, E., Coupaye, T., Leclercq, M., Quéma, V., & Stefani, J.-B. (2006). The fractal component model and its support in java: Experiences with auto-adaptive and reconfigurable systems. *Software, Practice & Experience, 36*(11-12), 1257–1284. doi:10.1002/spe.767

Bruneton, E., & Riveill, M. (2001). An architecture for extensible middleware platforms. *Software, Practice & Experience, 31*(13), 1237–1264. doi:10.1002/spe.412

Cabri, G., Ferrari, L., Leonardi, L., & Zambonelli, F. (2005). The laica project: Supporting ambient intelligence via agents and ad-hoc middleware. In *Proceedings of the 14ᵗʰ International Workshop on Enabling Technologies: Infrastructure for Collaborative Enterprise* (pp. 39-46). Washington, DC: IEEE Computer Society.

Cauvet, C., & Semmak, F. (1999). La réutilisation dans l'ingénierie des systèmes d'information: Etat de l'art. In *Génie Objet: Analyse et conception de l'évolution d'objet*. Paris, France: Hermés.

David, P.-C., & Ledoux, T. (2006). An aspect-oriented approach for developing self-adaptive fractal components. In W. Löwe & M. Südholt (Eds.), *Proceedings of the 5ᵗʰ International Symposium on Software Composition* (LNCS 4089, pp. 82-97).

DeRoure, D., & Sure, Y. (2006). Semantic grid - The convergence of technologies. *Journal of Web Semantics, 4*(2), 82–83. doi:10.1016/j.websem.2006.03.004

Dobson, G., Lock, R., & Sommerville, I. (2005). Qosont: A qos ontology for service-centric systems. In *Proceedings of the 31st EUROMICRO Conference on Software Engineering and Advanced Applications* (pp. 80-87). Washington, DC: IEEE Computer Society

Foster, I. T., & Iamnitchi, A. (2003). On death, taxes, and the convergence of peer-to-peer and grid computing. In M. F. Kaashoek & I. Stoica (Eds.), *Proceedings of the Second International Conference on Peer-to-Peer Systems II* (LNCS 2735, pp. 118-128).

Gaeta, M., Ritrovato, P., & Salerno, S. (2003). Elegi: The European learning grid infrastructure. In *Proceedings of the 3ʳᵈ LeGE-WG Workshop*.

Gouardères, G., Mansour, S., Nkambou, R., & Yatchou, R. (2005). The grid-e-card: Architecture to share collective intelligence on the grid. *Applied Artificial Intelligence, 19*(9-10), 1043–1073. doi:10.1080/08839510500304108

Grant, S. (2005). Clear e-portfolio definition: A prerequisite for effective interoperability. In *Proceedings of the First International ePortfolio Conference*.

Grondin, G., Bouraqadi, N., & Vercouter, L. (2006). MaDcAr: An abstract model for dynamic and automatic (re-)assembling of component-based applications. In I. Gorton, G. T. Heineman, I. Crnkovic, H. W. Schmidt, J. A. Stafford, C. Szyperski, & K. Wallnau (Eds.), *Proceedings of the 9th International SIGSOFT Symposium on Component-Based Software Engineering*, Vasteras, Sweden (LNCS 4063, pp. 360-367).

Gruber, T. R. (1993). Towards principles for the design of ontologies used for knowledge sharing. *International Journal of Human Computer Studies, 43*(5-6), 907–928. doi:10.1006/ijhc.1995.1081

Guessoum, Z. (2000). A multi-agent simulation framework. *Transactions of Computer Simulation, 17*(1), 2–11.

Jonquet, C., Dugenie, P., & Cerri, S. A. (2008). Agent grid integration language. *Multiagent and Grid Systems, 4*(2), 167–211.

JXTA. (2003). *Project jxta v2.0.* Retrieved from http://www.jxta.org

Kagal, L., Berners-Lee, T., Connolly, D., & Weitzner, D. J. (2006). Using semantic web technologies for policy management on the web. In *Proceedings of the AAAI Conference on Artificial Intelligence* (pp. 1337-1344).

Krutisch, R., Meier, P., & Wirsing, M. (2003). The agent component approach, combining agents, and components. In M. Schillo, M. Klusch, J. Müller, & H. Tianfield (Eds.), *Proceedings of the First German Conference on Multiagent System Technologies* (LNCS 2831, pp. 1-12).

Lacouture, J., & Aniorté, P. (2008). Compaa: A self-adaptable component model for open systems. In *Proceedings of the 15th IEEE International Conference on Engineering of Computer-Based Systems* (pp. 19-25). Washington, DC: IEEE Computer Society.

Lacouture, J., & Mansour, S. (2007). E-portfolio, an auto-adaptable grid service with components using peer-to-peer agents. In *Proceedings of the 4th International Conference on Grid Engineering and Management*, Leipzig, Germany (pp. 51-65).

Liu, H., & Parashar, M. (2006). Accord: A programming framework for autonomic applications. *IEEE Transactions on Systems, Man, and Cybernetics, 36*(3), 341–352. doi:10.1109/TSMCC.2006.871577

Marin, C. A., & Mehandjicv, N. (2006). A classification framework of adaptation in multi-agent systems. In *Proceedings of the Conference on Cooperative Information Agents* (pp. 198-212).

Milojicic, D. S., Kalogeraki, V., Lukose, R., Nagaraja, K., Pruyne, J., Richard, B., et al. (2002). *Peer-to-peer computing* (Tech. Rep. No. HPL-2002-57R1). Palo Alto, CA: Hewlett-Packard.

Noel, V., Arcangeli, J.-P., & Gleizes, M.-P. (2010). Component-based agent architectures to build dedicated agent frameworks. In *Proceedings of the International Symposium on From Agent Theory to Agent Implementation*, Vienna, Austria (pp. 483-488).

Nwana, H. S., & Heath, M. (1996). Software agents: An overview. *The Knowledge Engineering Review, 11*(3), 1–40. doi:10.1017/S026988890000789X

Satoh, I. (2004). Software agents for ambient intelligence. In *Proceedings of the International Conference on Systems, Man and Cybernetics* (pp. 1147-1152). Washington, DC: IEEE Computer Society.

Schollmeier, R. (2001). A definition of peer-to-peer networking for the classification of peer-to-peer architectures and applications. In *Proceedings of the First International Conference on Peer-to-Peer Computing.* (pp. 101-102). Washington, DC: IEEE Computer Society.

Seyler, F., & Aniorté, P. (2004). A model driven integration process to manage component interoperability. In *Proceedings of the Conference on Software Engineering Research and Practice* (pp. 104-110).

Smith, E. A. (2005). Communities of competence: New resources in the workplace. *Journal of Workplace Learning*, *17*, 1. doi:10.1108/13665620510574423

Tu, M. T., Griffel, F., Merz, M., & Lamersdorf, W. (1998). A plug-in architecture providing dynamic negotiation capabilities for mobile agents. In *Proceedings of the Second International Workshop on Mobile Agents* (pp. 222-236).

Wenger, E. (2000). Communities of practice: The key to knowledge strategy. In Lesser, E. L., Fontaine, M. A., & Slusher, J. A. (Eds.), *Knowledge and communities*. Boston, MA: Butterworth Heinemann. doi:10.1016/B978-0-7506-7293-1.50004-4

Zschaler, S. (2004). Formal specification of non-functional properties of component-based software. *Software and Systems Modeling*, *9*(2), 161–201. doi:10.1007/s10270-009-0115-6

This work was previously published in the International Journal of Adaptive, Resilient and Autonomic Systems, Volume 2, Issue 4, edited by Vincenzo De Florio, pp. 54-73, copyright 2011 by IGI Publishing (an imprint of IGI Global).

Section 3
Middleware and Framework Support for Resilient and Adaptive Systems

Chapter 10
Timely Autonomic Adaptation of Publish/ Subscribe Middleware in Dynamic Environments

Joe Hoffert
Vanderbilt University, USA

Aniruddha Gokhale
Vanderbilt University, USA

Douglas C. Schmidt
Vanderbilt University, USA

ABSTRACT

Quality-of-service enabled publish/subscribe (pub/sub) middleware provides powerful support for scalable data dissemination. It is difficult to maintain key quality of service properties (such as reliability and latency) in dynamic environments for distributed real-time and embedded systems (such as disaster relief operations or power grids). Managing quality of service manually is often not feasible in dynamic environments due to slow response times, the complexity of managing multiple interrelated quality of service settings, and the scale of the systems being managed. For certain domains, distributed real-time and embedded systems must be able to reflect on the conditions of their environment and adapt accordingly in a bounded amount of time. This paper describes an architecture of quality of service-enabled middleware and corresponding algorithms to support specified quality of service in dynamic environments.

DOI: 10.4018/978-1-4666-2056-8.ch010

INTRODUCTION

Emerging Trends and Challenges

The use of publish/subscribe (pub/sub) technologies for distributed real-time and embedded (DRE) systems has grown in recent years due to the advantages of performance, cost, and scale as compared to single computers (Huang, 2006; Tarkoma, 2006). In particular, pub/sub middleware has been leveraged to ease the complexities of data dissemination for DRE systems. Examples of pub/sub middleware include the CORBA Notification Service (Ramani, 2001), the Java Message Service (JMS) (Monson-Haefel, 2000), Web Services Brokered Notification (Niblett, 2005), and the Data Distribution Service (DDS) (Pardo-Castellote, 2003). These technologies support the propagation of data and events throughout a system using an anonymous publication and subscription model that decouples event suppliers and consumers.

Pub/sub middleware is used across a wide variety of application domains, ranging from shipboard computing environments to cloud computing to stock trading. Moreover, the middleware provides policies that affect the end-to-end quality of service (QoS) of applications running in DRE systems. Policies that are common across various middleware technologies include grouped data transfer (*i.e.*, transmitting a group of data atomically), durability (*i.e.*, saving data for subsequent subscribers), and persistence (*i.e.*, saving data for current subscribers).

Even though tunable policies provide fine-grained control of system QoS, several challenges emerge when developing pub/sub systems deployed in dynamic environments. Middleware mechanisms used to ensure certain QoS properties for one environment configuration may be ineffective for different configurations. For example, a simple unicast protocol, such as the User Datagram Protocol (UDP), may address the specified latency QoS when a publisher sends to a small number of subscribers. UDP could incur too much latency, however, when used for a large number of subscribers due to its point-to-point property, leaving the publisher to manage the sending of data to each subscriber.

Challenges also arise when considering multiple QoS policies that interact with each other. For example, a system might need low latency QoS and high reliability QoS, which can affect latency due to data loss discovery and recovery. Certain transport protocols, such as UDP, provide low overhead but no end-to-end reliability. Other protocols, such as the Transmission Control Protocol (TCP), provide reliability but unbounded latencies due to acknowledgment-based retransmissions. Still other protocols, such as lateral error correction protocols (Balakrishnan, 2005), manage the potentially conflicting QoS properties of reliability and low latency, but only provide benefits over other protocols in specific environment configurations.

It is hard to determine when to switch from one transport protocol to another or modify parameters of a particular transport protocol so that desired QoS is maintained. Moreover, manual intervention is often not responsive enough for the timeliness requirements of the system. DRE systems operate within strict timing requirements that must be met for the systems to function appropriately. The problem of timely response is exacerbated as the scale of the system grows, *e.g.*, as the number of publishers or subscribers increases.

This article describes how our work (1) monitors environment changes that affect QoS, (2) determines in a timely manner which appropriate transport protocol changes are needed in response to environment changes, (3) integrates the use of multiple supervised machine learning techniques to increase accuracy, and (4) autonomically adapts the network protocols used to support the desired QoS. We have prototyped this approach in the ADAptive Middleware And Network Transports (ADAMANT) platform (as briefly outlined previously (Hoffert & Schmidt, 2009) that supports environment monitoring and provides timely autonomic adaptation of the middleware. ADA-MANT provides the following contributions to research on autonomic configuration of pub/sub middleware in dynamic environments:

- Leveraging anonymous publish and sub-scribe middleware based on the DDS specification. DDS defines topic-based high-performance pub/sub middleware to support DRE systems. ADAMANT le-verages the middleware to provide envi-ronment monitoring information that is disseminated throughout the DRE system (*e.g.*, change in sending rate, change in net-work percentage loss) to provide updates occurring in the operating environment.
- Multiple supervised machine learning (SML) techniques as a knowledge base to provide fast and predictable adapta-tion guidance in dynamic environments. ADAMANT provides timely integrated machine learning (TIML), a novel ap-proach to provide high accuracy and time-ly determination of which SML technique to use for a given operating environment.
- Configuration of DRE pub/sub middle-ware based on guidance from supervised machine learning. Our ADAMANT mid-dleware uses the adaptive network trans-ports (ANT) framework (Hoffert, Gokhale, & Schmidt, 2009) to select the transport protocol(s) that best addresses multiple QoS concerns for given computing re-sources. ANT provides an infrastructure for composing and configuring transport protocols using modules that provide base functionality (*e.g.*, an IP multicast mod-ule that handles multicasting the data to the network). Supported protocols include Ricochet, which uses a variation of forward error correction called lateral error correc-tion that exchanges error correction infor-mation among receivers (Balakrishnan, 2007), and NAKcast, which uses negative

acknowledgments (NAKs) to provide reli-ability. These protocols enable trade-offs between latency and reliability to support middleware for enterprise DRE pub/sub systems.

This paper extends our prior work (Hoffert et al., 2010a, 2010b) on ADAMANT by exploring the architecture and control flow for autonomic adaptation of QoS-enabled pub/sub DRE systems. Moreover, this paper (1) empirically evaluates TIML as an approach to increase accuracy and maintain constant-time complexity, (2) leverages the DDS pub/sub infrastructure to disseminate environment changes to all data senders and receivers, (3) empirically evaluates the bounded response times of the ANT framework when adapting transport protocols, and (4) provides an autonomic controller that manages the adaptation of transport protocols to support QoS as the envi-ronment changes and details how the controller manages the adaptations. The paper is organized as follows. We start by describing a motivating example and highlighting the challenges. Next, we present the structure and functionality of the ADAMANT framework. We then detail and ana-lyze our experimental results. We compare our work with related research in autonomic adapta-tion. Finally, we conclude with lessons learned.

MOTIVATING EXAMPLE: AMBIENT ASSISTED LIVING IN A SMART CITY ENVIRONMENT

This section describes Smart City Ambient Assisted Living (SCAAL) applications, which combine Ambient Assisted Living (AAL) in the context of a smart city. It also presents research challenges associated with SCAAL applications. SCAAL applications help motivate the need for managing QoS interactions and providing timely adjustments of transport protocols for QoS-enabled pub/sub middleware deployed in dynamic environments. The objective for smart cities is to meld computational infrastructure into the surrounding environment and establish ubiquitous, context-aware services in a metropolitan area (Chandy, 2007). The purpose of AAL is to increase the independence and quality of life for elderly people, while decreasing the need for direct interaction of healthcare workers so they are freed up for other concerns.

As an example SCAAL scenario depicted in Figure 1, imagine an elderly person is navigating a large metropolitan area equipped with multiple technological devices. These devices aid in various aspects of the person's ability to be aware of her environment, *e.g.*, mobility, sensory enhancement, communication, and monitoring devices. In particular, the elderly person has a history of heart disease and 3-dimensional high-resolution heart monitoring equipment is periodically transmitting data. A personal datacenter publishes and subscribes to the data being managed by the personal devices including the heart monitoring data, and interfaces with the smart city by publishing and subscribing to data from the ambient environment. More specifically, health care workers, hospitals, and emergency medical services specialists are subscribing to the heart monitoring information that is being published.

The personal datacenter operates in a dynamic environment since (1) the elderly person moves through space in the smart city and updates personal information in time and (2) the smart city enhances and updates the amount and kind of data that it provides as it moves through time. Our research focuses on (1) composite metrics to evaluate transport protocols in support of multiple QoS concerns (such as reliability and low latency for high-resolution 3D heart monitoring information), (2) evaluations of multiple transport protocols in different operating environments using the composite metrics, (3) support for monitoring the environment, (4) supervised machine learning techniques to determine transport protocols that best support the QoS that a personal datacenter device must manage in a SCAAL application, and (5) autonomically adapting the transport protocols to provide the best QoS given the changes in the environment. Supporting autonomic adaptation of the personal datacenter presents the following challenges:

Challenge 1: Managing Interacting QoS Requirements

The personal datacenter must manage multiple interacting QoS requirements, *e.g.*, data reliability so enough data is received and low latency

Figure 1. Smart City Ambient Assisted Living (SCAAL) example

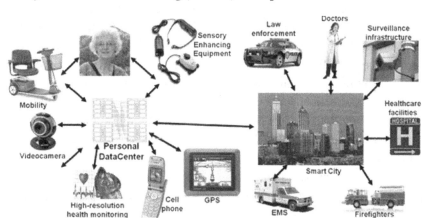

and jitter for soft real-time data so that detailed 3-dimensional heart monitoring data arrive before they are needed. For example, the streamed data must be received soon enough so that successive dependent data can also be used, such as dependent MPEG B and P frame data being received before the next I frame makes them obsolete. Moreover, the personal datacenter must balance the interacting QoS requirements with an environment that varies dynamically, *e.g.*, number of data senders and receivers, network bandwidth, network packet loss. Section *Addressing Challenge 1: Managing Interacting QoS Requirements* describes how we address this challenge by supporting runtime migration and reconfiguration in bounded time of transport protocols used as the QoS mechanisms to provide needed QoS.

Challenge 2: Accurate Adaptation

The personal datacenter must be able to adjust to changes in the environment accurately. As changes in environment occur (*e.g.*, increases in heart data updates, decreases in networking capability, requests for data from additional senders and receivers), the personal datacenter must accommodate data needs for data producers and consumers, take advantage of additional resources, or provide access to additional data producers and consumers while maintaining QoS. For a given environment configuration, the SCAAL application must accurately implement adjustments that are appropriate to the operating environment. If the personal datacenter cannot make accurate adjustments as the environment changes then situation awareness and critical health information could be lost or delayed causing loss of orientation or injury to the elderly person. Section *Addressing Challenge 2: Accurate Adaptation* describes how we address this challenge by leveraging DDS to disseminate the environment monitoring information needed to determine an accurate adaptation and TIML to accurately determine the appropriate transport protocol.

Challenge 3: Timely Adaptation

Due to timeliness concerns of DRE systems such as SCAAL applications, the personal datacenter must adjust in a timely manner as the environment changes. If the personal datacenter cannot adjust quickly enough it will fail to perform adequately and critical data such as 3-D heart information will not be received in time. As the amount of data relevant to the SCAAL application fluctuates and the demand for information varies with a corresponding change in the data update rate, the personal datacenter must be configured to accommodate these changes with appropriate responsiveness to maintain the specified quality of service. Configuration changes must not only be timely in general but they must also be bounded – and ideally constant time – so that critical information updates (such as health monitoring) are not lost or received too late to be of use. Section *Addressing Challenge 3: Timely Adaptation* describes how we address this challenge by using constant-time complexity machine learning techniques, constant-time integration of these techniques, and constant-time migration of transport protocols.

Challenge 4: Reducing Development Complexity

Many elderly people can use a personal datacenter to improve their independence. Likewise, the health care industry can benefit from the decreased workload for health care providers. A personal datacenter that is developed for one particular elderly individual in a particular operating environment, however, might not work well for a different elderly individual in a different operating environment with different personal equipment. For example, one elderly person might have a cell phone, visual enhancing equipment, and a heart monitor in a smart metropolitan area where police officers, firefighters, and healthcare workers can subscribe to and publish information relevant to the city. Another elderly person might have a PDA, a GPS device, a video camera, and a personal monitoring screen that is able to display video of what is behind the person in a smart metropolitan area where ambulances, hospitals, and traffic monitoring cameras can subscribe to and publish information relevant to the city. These two different scenarios impose different pub/sub demands (*e.g.*, the number of publishers and subscribers, the data sending rates)

The personal datacenters used to manage the information between the elderly person and the smart city therefore need to be developed and configured readily for any one particular operating environment accounting for different metropolitan areas, differences in personal equipment, and differences in the data needs of various individuals to leverage the personal datacenters across a wide range of individuals and locales. Section *Addressing Challenge 4: Reducing Development Complexity* describes how we address this challenge by leveraging DDS to disseminate environment updates, and using machine learning to map environment configurations to the appropriate transport protocols.

STRUCTURE AND FUNCTIONALITY OF ADAMANT

This section presents the structure and functionality of the ADAMANT middleware platform, focusing on its software architecture and control flow. It also describes how ADAMANT addresses the challenges of SCAAL applications presented in section *Motivating Example: Ambient Assisted Living in a Smart City Environment*.

Architecture of ADAMANT

Figure 2 shows ADAMANT's control flow and logical architecture. This section details the architecture of ADAMANT while the following section *Control Flow of ADAMANT* describes how autonomic adaptation is manifested in ADAMANT in each one of the steps illustrated in Figure 2. ADAMANT integrates and enhances the following technologies and innovative techniques to provide autonomic adaptation of DRE pub/sub middleware in dynamic environments and address the challenges listed in the motivating example section:

Figure 2. ADAMANT architecture and control flow

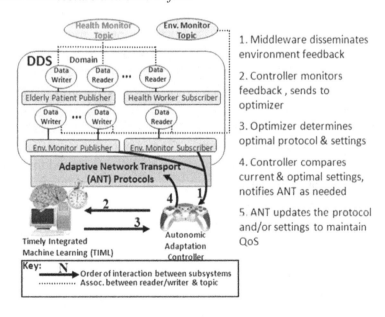

1. Middleware disseminates environment feedback

2. Controller monitors feedback, sends to optimizer

3. Optimizer determines optimal protocol & settings

4. Controller compares current & optimal settings, notifies ANT as needed

5. ANT updates the protocol and/or settings to maintain QoS

- The OMG Data Distribution Service (DDS) is standards-based QoS-enabled pub/sub middleware for exchanging data in event-based DRE systems. It provides a global data store in which publishers and subscribers write and read data, respectively. ADAMANT uses DDS to provide the infrastructure for disseminating environment monitoring information needed to determine accurate adaptations, as well as normal application data, such as the health monitoring information in SCAAL applications. DDS enables applications to communicate by publishing information they have and subscribing to information they need in real time.

DDS enables *flexibility* and *modular structure* by decoupling: *location*, via anonymous publish/subscribe; *redundancy*, by allowing any numbers of readers and writers; *time*, by providing asynchronous, time-independent data distribution; and *platform*, by supporting a platform-independent model that can be mapped to different languages (*e.g.*, Java and C++).

The DDS architecture consists of two layers: (1) the data-centric pub/sub (DCPS) layer that provides APIs to exchange topic data based on chosen QoS policies and (2) the data local reconstruction layer (DLRL) that makes topic data appear local. Our work focuses on DCPS since it is more broadly supported than the DLRL. Moreover, DCPS provides finer grained control of QoS.

The DCPS entities in DDS include *topics*, which describe the type of data to write or read; *data readers*, which subscribe to the values or instances of particular topics; and *data writers*, which publish values or instances for particular topics. Moreover, *publishers* manage groups of data writers and *subscribers* manage groups of data readers. Various properties of these entities can be configured using combinations of the 22 DDS QoS policies. DDS' rich support for QoS can be applied for application data and for the environment monitoring topic that ADAMANT provides (*e.g.*, prioritization for transporting and managing the operating environment updates as well as the application data).

- TIML provides a novel integration of multiple supervised machine learning techniques as a knowledge base. This knowledge base, in turn, provides fast and predictable adaptation guidance in dynamic environments. TIML also uses machine learning techniques to manage the inherent complexity of providing the appropriate transport protocol recommendation for a given operating environment. TIML utilizes perfect hashing (Brodnik, 1994) on the mapping of environment configurations to transport protocols to provide constant-time determination of which supervised machine learning technique to use for a given environment configuration. In particular, TIML utilizes the GPERF (Schmidt, 2000a) open-source implementation of perfect hashing.

For our ADAMANT prototype TIML uses several supervised machine learning techniques, including Artificial Neural Networks (ANNs) (Patterson, 1998) to determine in a timely manner the appropriate transport protocol for the QoS-enabled pub/sub middleware platform given an environment configuration that is known a priori (i.e., used for training). It also uses Support Vector Machines (SVMs) (Meyer, 2003) to determine in a timely manner the appropriate transport protocol for an environment configuration unknown until run-time (i.e., not used for training).

An ANN is a supervised machine learning technique modeled on neuron interactions in the human brain. As shown in Figure 3, an ANN has an input layer for aspects of the operating environment, *e.g.*, percent network loss and sending rate. An output layer represents the solution generated based on the input. A hidden layer connects the input and output layers. As the ANN is trained on inputs and correspondingly correct outputs, it strengthens or weakens connections between layers to generalize based on inputs and outputs.

Figure 3 also shows how an ANN can be configured statically in the number of hidden layers and the number of nodes in each layer that directly affects the processing time complexity between the input of operating environment conditions and the output of an appropriate transport protocol and settings. This static configuration structure supports constant response times.

SVMs are supervised learning techniques used for classification and prediction. An SVM is first given a set of training examples where each example is denoted as belonging to a particular class or grouping. An SVM next builds a model that predicts into which grouping a new example should be categorized. As shown in Figure 4, the SVM creates classification boundaries between the different classification groupings to maximize the differences between the groupings. Leveraging the heuristic of locality, this maximization helps to correctly classify new examples that have not been used in training the SVM model, *i.e.*, examples in the same group are deemed fairly close to each other in the classification space. Like ANNs, SVMs are configured offline during training to exhibit constant response times at runtime.

- ADAMANT uses the ANT framework to select the transport protocol(s) that best address multiple QoS concerns for a given operating environment. ANT provides infrastructure for composing and configuring transport protocols via base modules, such as the IPMulticastModule that supports sending out and receiving data using IP Multicast. These modules can flexibly and dynamically be connected together by publishing and subscribing to event types (*e.g.*, SEND_PACKET_EVENT, GOT_PACKET_EVENT, SEND_NAK_EVENT, and GOT_NAK_EVENT).

ANT supports transport protocols that balance the need for reliability and low latency. For example, Ricochet enables trade-offs between latency and reliability to support middleware for DRE pub/sub systems involved with dissemination of multimedia data. The ANT framework allows ADAMANT to change and reconfigure transport protocols (including protocol parameters) while an application is running. The time complexity for ANT to reconfigure protocols is bounded as needed for DRE systems.

- A QoS monitoring topic defines the data for environment information relevant to adapting transport protocols. ADAMANT

Figure 3. Artificial neural network for determining appropriate transport protocol

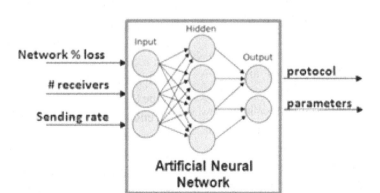

Figure 4. Maximizing grouping differences in a support vector machine

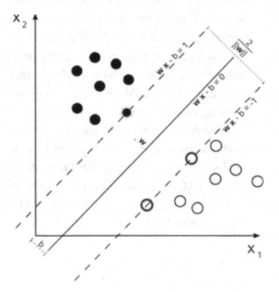

leverages DDS to provide this topic dedicated to describing the operating environment of an application. This environment information is used to determine appropriate adaptation of the QoS mechanisms in ADAMANT, namely, the transport protocols. Moreover, since ADAMANT leverages DDS to create the environment monitoring topic, DDS QoS policies can also be applied to the dissemination of this topic data providing fine-grained control as to when and how environment configuration updates are propagated in the SCAAL application (*e.g.*, applying DDS' transport priority QoS policy to health monitoring data to ensure the data has priority over other data on the network).

• Autonomic control manages the adaptation process. ADAMANT provides an autonomic controller that responds to changes in the operating environment. Whenever environment changes are communicated via ADAMANT's environment monitoring topic, the controller passes the changes to TIML to determine the appropriate re-

sponse. The controller then passes TIML's recommended adaptation to the ANT framework to change the transport protocols while the system is running.

Control Flow of ADAMANT

ADAMANT supports the *Monitor, Analyze, Plan, Execute – Knowledge* approach (Kephart, 2003; Huebscher, 2008), which abstracts the management architecture into the four needed functions of collecting data, analyzing the data, creating a plan of action based on the updated data and corresponding analysis, and executing the plan. Undergirding these functions is knowledge extraction which raises the level of abstraction from data collection and analysis to determining the behavior and state of the system along with the appropriate high level adaptations. ADAMANT components are physically distributed across the computing platforms in the system, *e.g.*, each computing platform has its own identical instantiation of TIML and the autonomic adaptation controller. Since environment configuration changes are published to all subscribers via DDS, all local ADAMANT components receive the same updates. Since components are deterministic, they generate the same transport protocol to use and initiate the same protocol modifications. This distributed architecture enables scalability in the number of publishers, subscribers, and computing platforms.

The first step in ADAMANT's control flow (shown as Step 1 in Figure 2) is receiving changes to the environment configuration. ADAMANT creates and supports an environment monitoring topic to which various application data senders and receivers can publish and subscribe, respectively. For example, the heart monitoring portion of the SCAAL application can publish changes to the environment monitor topic when it adjusts its data sending rate based on requests from health workers subscribing to the data. Likewise, data subscribers can query the environment monitor topic for the periodic sending rate of the data and then calculate the loss percentage in the network by dividing the expected number of data updates for a given period with the actual number of updates received.

Figure 5 shows the data described in environment monitor topic. The data is described in the platform-independent interface definition language (IDL) as defined by the OMG. Our prototype is interested in the attributes of the environment information shown in Table 1 since the data values for these aspects are used to determine the most appropriate transport protocol.

After updates have been made to the environment monitor topic, the autonomic controller receives the updated environment configuration (outlined as Step 2 in Figure 2). The autonomic controller then compares the new and previous environment configurations. If the configurations are different the controller invokes TIML to determine which transport protocol and parameter values best support the desired QoS. If the configurations do not differ the autonomic controller simply returns since no adaptation is needed.

Step 3 in Figure 2 shows how TIML receives the new environment configuration and determines if the configuration is one on which the machine learning techniques have been trained. If the machine learning techniques have previously been trained off-line using the configuration, TIML uses an ANN to determine the appropriate transport

Figure 5. Environment monitor topic

```
struct QosMonitoring {
    long receiver_count;
    long percent_network_loss;
    long send_rate_in_Hz;
    string cpu_speed;
    string ram;
    string network_speed;
    string dds_impl;
    string composite_metric;
};
```

protocol and parameter settings. Since we over-fitted the ANN to our experimental training data, the ANN produces 100% accurate determinations for these known environment configurations as illustrated in our previous work (Hoffert et al., 2010b; Hoffert, Mack, & Schmidt, 2010). Overfitted ANNs are specialized for the environments they have seen—and on which they have been trained—which reduces development complexity and increases accuracy (Dietterich, 1995).

If machine learning techniques have not previously been trained on an environment configuration, however, TIML uses an SVM to determine the appropriate transport protocol and parameter settings. Our prior work (Hoffert, Mack, & Schmidt, 2010) shows how an SVM will provide higher accuracy for determining the appropriate protocol and parameters than an ANN when the input environment configuration was not used during off-line training (*i.e.*, unknown until run-time). The overall accuracy of ADAMANT is enhanced by combining the 100% accuracy of an overfitted ANN for environment configurations known *a priori* with the higher accuracy of an SVM for environment configurations unknown until run-time. In particular, we see an increase in accuracy of 8.6% combining both an ANN and an SVM, compared to only using an ANN (*i.e.*, 77.69% average ANN accuracy for environments unknown until run-time compared to 86.29% for the SVM).

Both ANNs and SVM provide constant-time complexity for determining protocols and parameters. The mechanism used to determine if the environment configuration have been known *a priori* must therefore also provide constant-time complexity to maintain this time complexity for the entire protocol optimization process. TIML utilizes perfect hashing for the environment configurations to determine in constant time whether or not an environment configuration is known *a priori* (*i.e.*, used for training) or unknown until run-time. Since the environment configurations used for training the ANN are known *a priori* TIML uses this

Table 1. QoSMonitoring attributes

Attribute	Description
receiver_count	The number of receivers currently receiving application data (*e.g.*, value 5 indicates that 5 receivers are receiving application data).
percent_network_loss	The percent packet loss in the network (*e.g.*, value 3 indicates that a 3% loss of packets occurs in the network).
send_rate_in_Hz	The data sending rate for the heart monitoring data in Hz (*e.g.*, value 50 indicates a sending rate of 50 Hz, *i.e.*, 50 times a second).
cpu_speed	The speed of the CPU being used in MHz (*e.g.*, "2992.883" indicates a CPU speed of 2.992883 GHz). For clarity and simplicity, the ADAMANT prototype assumes common CPU speeds for all machines used.
RAM	The amount of random-access memory available on the machines being used in kilobytes (*e.g.*, "2062172" indicates 2 GB of RAM). Again, for clarity and simplicity, the ADAMANT prototype assumes common amount of RAM for all machines used.
network_speed	The speed of the network being used in Mb/sec (*e.g.*, "1000" indicates a 1 Gb/sec network).
dds_impl	The DDS implementation being used (*e.g.*, "OpenSplice" indicates the use of PrismTech's OpenSplice DDS implementation). For simplicity as a proof of concept, the ADAMANT prototype only currently supports the OpenSplice DDS implementation, though support for the other DDS implementations (*e.g.*, OpenDDS or RTI DDS) can easily be added.
composite_metric	The composite metric of interest to the application, *e.g.*, "ReLate2". The ReLate2 composite metrics quantitatively evaluate multiple QoS properties. For example, the ReLate2 metric combines data reliability and latency to produce a single value used for quantitative comparison. Other composite metrics include ReLate2Jit that quantitatively evaluates data reliability, latency, and jitter; ReLate2Net that evaluates reliability, latency, and network bandwidth usage; and ReLate2Burst that evaluates reliability, latency, and network data burstiness (Hoffert et al., 2010a).

information to construct the perfect hash which can be thought of as a constant-time table lookup. TIML provides the environment configurations on which the ANN has been trained as keys to the perfect hashing to map to the corresponding scaled environment configuration data. If the key is found via the perfect hash the TIML knows that the environment configuration has been seen before in off-line training and then uses the ANN since it will provide perfect accuracy. If the key is not mapped, then TIML will use the SVM since it provides the highest accuracy for environment configurations that are unknown until runtime.

Once the appropriate transport protocol has been decided, TIML returns this result to the autonomic controller (Step 4 in Figure 2). The controller then compares the recommended transport protocol and protocol parameters with the current transport protocol and protocol parameters. If there is no difference, the controller need not take any further action. If there are differences between the

current protocol and the recommended protocol, the controller passes the new protocol settings to ANT to make the needed adaptation.

Our ADAMANT prototype uses the OpenSplice DDS implementation, which uses a networking daemon on each machine to send and receive data across machine boundaries. The ANT framework resides in the networking daemon since the ANT protocols are used to disseminate the application data across the network. The autonomic controller resides in the application executable since it needs to respond to updates in the environment as facilitated by the environment monitor topic. For a single computer platform, OpenSplice uses shared memory to communicate between the SCAAL application executable and the OpenSplice daemon. Since the daemon runs as a separate process from the application executable, some form of interprocess communication (IPC) is needed to have the controller inform ANT of the needed protocol changes.

The form of IPC used when communicating between the autonomic controller and ANT can vary depending upon the needs of the application and the IPC mechanisms supported by the operating system. In our ADAMANT prototype the autonomic controller residing in the application executable sends a signal to ANT residing in the networking daemon. The OpenSplice networking daemon is enhanced to include a signal handler. In particular, when the controller determines the transport protocol must be modified it sends a signal (*e.g.*, SIGUSR1) to the networking daemon. When the networking daemon processes the signal, the daemon invokes ANT to reconfigure. ADAMANT utilizes the Component Configurator pattern (Schmidt, 2000b) for ANT to reconfigure itself by constructing the appropriate configuration file and then signaling ANT to reconfigure.

The need for IPC depends upon the DDS implementation. For example, rather than using a network daemon, the OpenDDS DDS implementation supports direct point-to-point network connectivity between application executables residing on different machines. For ADAMANT using OpenDDS, intra-process communication would be needed rather than IPC. ADAMANT would set a variable accessible across threads using appropriate locking mechanisms. ANT would then wait until the variable was set (*e.g.*, using a condition variable) and reconfigure the transport protocol as needed.

After ANT receives the signal to reconfigure (Step 5 in Figure 2) it determines whether to modify an existing transport protocol or switch to a new protocol. ANT keeps track of the current transport protocol being used for comparison. If the current protocol must be modified then ANT invokes the appropriate methods on the relevant protocol modules to change the protocol parameters. If a new protocol must be used ANT first disables the existing protocol and enables the new protocol.

The modules in the ANT framework use pub/sub communication to consume and supply events of interest. This approach allows for flexibility in the way modules are connected together to create the functionality needed for a particular transport protocol. This approach also allows the enabling/disabling of transport protocols simply by registering and unregistering for particular events. ANT thus unregisters events for the old protocol to disable the old protocol and registers events for the new protocol to enable the new protocol.

Addressing Challenges of SCAAL Applications

This section describes how ADAMANT addresses the challenges of SCAAL applications presented in the section *Motivating Example: Ambient Assisted Living in a Smart City Environment*.

Addressing Challenge 1: Managing Interacting QoS Requirements

ADAMANT addresses the challenge of managing interacting QoS requirements by using the transport protocols provided by the ANT framework. ANT supports transport protocols that address interacting QoS requirements. In particular, it provides the NAKcast and Ricochet transport protocols that balance the contentious QoS requirements of data reliability and low latency. As shown in previous work (Hoffert, Gokhale, & Schmidt, 2009), these protocols ameliorate the loss of network data packets while imposing low latency overhead. In particular, the NAKcast protocol uses negative acknowledgments (that is, NAKs) that the receiver sends to the sender for notification of lost data packets. NAKcast provides a tunable timeout parameter to determine when NAKs should be sent. The Ricochet protocol supports error correction information that the receivers send to each other to recover from lost data packets. Ricochet provides a tunable parameter to determine how many data packets need to be received before error correction is sent out. Ricochet also provides a tunable parameter to determine how many other receivers receive the error correction information from a single receiver.

Addressing Challenge 2:
Accurate Adaptation

ADAMANT addresses the challenge of accurate adaptation in several ways. First, it leverages the use of DDS to provide the infrastructure to disseminate the environment monitoring information needed to determine an accurate adaptation. Second, it uses TIML to provide an integration of multiple supervised machine learning techniques to provide high accuracy for both operating environments known *a priori* and operating environments unknown until runtime. TIML supports accurate adaptation guidance in dynamic environments by using the most accurate machine learning technique for operating environments known *a priori* (*i.e.*, ANNs) integrated with the most accurate technique for operating environments unknown until runtime (*i.e.*, SVMs). Our previous work presents experimental results illustrating the accuracy of ANNs and SVMs (Hoffert, Mack, & Schmidt, 2010). In particular, the SVM accuracy results use n-fold cross validation where n is the number of mutually exclusive training and testing data sets (Liu, 2006). Third, ADAMANT's autonomic controller ensures accuracy by managing the adaptation process of receiving environment updates, delegating this information to TIML to provide guidance, and passing the recommended transitions to ANT.

Addressing Challenge 3:
Timely Adaptation

ADAMANT addresses the challenge of timely adaptation in several ways. First, as already mentioned for Challenge 2, it uses DDS to disseminate the environment monitoring information needed to determine an accurate adaptation. Second, since the monitoring information is realized as a DDS topic, the DDS QoS policies can be applied to the topic and the applicable entities involved with the topic (*e.g.*, data readers, data writers). For example, the transport priority QoS policy

can be applied to the environment monitoring data to ensure the environment updates have priority over other data on the network.

ADAMANT supports constant-time runtime transition and reconfiguration of transport protocols used as the QoS mechanisms to provide needed QoS, as discussed in the section *Experimental Results and Analysis*. In particular, TIML utilizes an ANN to provide adaptation guidance in constant time for operating environments known *a priori*. TIML uses an SVM to guide adaptation in constant time for operating environments unknown until runtime. Moreover, TIML uses constant-time perfect hashing to integrate the machine learning techniques and determine the appropriate technique to use.

Addressing Challenge 4: Reducing Development Complexity

ADAMANT addresses the challenge of reducing development complexity by using machine learning techniques that manage the inherent complexity of providing the appropriate transport protocol recommendation for a given operating environment. The machine learning techniques can also be used directly in the ADAMANT implementation. These techniques thus reduce development complexity by eliminating the accidental complexity of transforming the mapping of environments to protocols from design to implementation (Hoffert et al., 2010a). Moreover, ADAMANT provides an environment monitoring topic that disseminates and handles the environment information updates relevant to adapting the QoS mechanisms of transport protocols.

EXPERIMENTAL RESULTS AND ANALYSIS

This section describes the setup, design, and analysis of results from experiments we conducted to identify the need for autonomic adaptation of transport protocols and evaluate the timeliness of the adaptations in dynamic environments representative of the SCAAL applications presented in the section *Motivating Example: Ambient Assisted Living in a Smart City Environment.* These results quantify (1) the effect of changes in the operating environment on the QoS provided by ADAMANT as measured by the composite QoS metrics defined below, (2) the timeliness of TIML's determination of an appropriate transport protocol, and (3) the timeliness of ADAMANT's adaptation of transport protocols via the ANT framework.

Experimental Setup

We conducted our experiments using the Emulab testbed (http://www.emulab.net) at the University of Utah. Emulab allows the configuration of various types of computing and networking platforms. For our experiments highlighting the need for adaptation, we held the computing and networking platform constant (*i.e.*, 3 GHz CPU, 1 Gbps LAN). We used the Redhat Fedora Core release 6 OS with real-time patches across all the computing nodes.

The points of variability for the experiments were indicative of dynamic environments. In particular, we varied the number of data receivers, the percent loss in the network, and the data sending rate as outlined in section *Control Flow of ADAMANT.* By adjusting these variables we were able to highlight scenarios where changes in the environment mandated changes to the transport protocols being used to provide the highest level of QoS for the multiple QoS properties involved.

Composite QoS Metrics for Reliability and Timeliness

Our previous work on QoS-enabled pub/sub middleware performance (Hoffert, Gokhale, & Schmidt, 2009; Hoffert & Schmidt, 2010) showed that some transport protocols provide better reliability (as measured by the number of network packets received divided by the number sent) and lower data latency for particular environments while other protocols provide better reliability and lower latency for other environments. We therefore developed several composite QoS metrics to quantitatively evaluate multiple QoS aspects simultaneously. These composite metrics provide a uniform and quantitative evaluation of ADAMANT in dynamic environments. Our family of composite metrics are based on the QoS concerns of reliability and average latency and optionally include the QoS aspects of (1) jitter (*i.e.*, standard deviation of the latency of network packets), (2) network bandwidth usage, and (3) burstiness (*i.e.*, the standard deviation of average bandwidth usage per second of time).

In particular, we defined the ReLate2 family of composite QoS metrics. The ReLate2 metric is defined by the product of the average data packet latency and the percent loss that the transport protocol provides + 1 (to account for 0% loss) which implies an order of magnitude increase for 9% loss. Based on previous research which evaluated percent data loss for multimedia applications (Bai, 2006, 2007; Ngatman, 2008), this adjustment is relevant for multimedia data such as the high-resolution 3-D health data in our SCAAL example. For example, if for a given protocol the average packet latency is 1,000 μs and the percent loss is 0 (*i.e.*, no packets lost) then the ReLate2 value is 1,000. Having 9% and 19% loss with the same average latency produces the ReLate2 values of 10,000 and 20,000, respectively. ReLate2Jit is a product of the ReLate2 value and the jitter of the data packets to quantify the multiple QoS concerns of jitter, reliability, and average latency. Each of these composite metrics provides a single quantitative value that can be objectively compared when using different transport protocols in various operating environments.

Experiments Highlighting Need for Autonomic Adaptation

We now present the results of experiments for autonomic adaptation of the QoS mechanisms of transport protocols. We apply the composite metrics defined in the previous section to several different operating environments to highlight how differences in the environment trigger differences in the transport protocols used to support QoS. Figure 6 shows a change in the sending rate corresponding to a change in the protocol that provides the best QoS.

In particular, for an operating environment using the OpenSplice DDS implementation, machines with 3 GHz CPUs, 5 data receivers, and 5% network packet loss, we see that for a data sending rate of 25Hz, the NAKcast protocol (with a timeout parameter to determine NAK transmissions of 0.001 seconds) performs better (*i.e.*, has lower ReLate2Jit values) than Ricochet (with an *R* value of 4 and a *C* value of 3).

Ricochet's *R* value determines how many data packets are received before error correction data is sent (*e.g.*, 4 packets received before one error correction packet is sent) and Ricochet's *C* value determines how many other receivers this receiver sends error correct data (*e.g.*, 3 receiv-

ers receive error correction data from any one receiver). When the sending rate is changed to 50Hz, however, Ricochet performs better. Finally, when the sending rate is further increased to 100Hz NAKcast again performs better (*i.e.*, has lower ReLate2Jit values).

Timeliness of TIML

We next describe the timeliness of TIML as it decides the most appropriate transport protocol for a given environment configuration. As described in Challenge 2 (timely adaptation), the personal datacenter for the SCAAL application needs to have timely adaptations. We now provide timing information based on the responsiveness of TIML when queried for an optimal transport protocol. We used the Emulab configuration as described in the section *Experimental Setup*. A high resolution timestamp was taken right before and right after each call was made to TIML.

TIML combines and integrates the use of ANN and SVM machine learning techniques. These techniques present different response times (although the times for each technique remain constant). We therefore conducted experiments with operating environment configurations that would use the ANN (*i.e.*, the configurations that were

Figure 6. Changing data sending rate

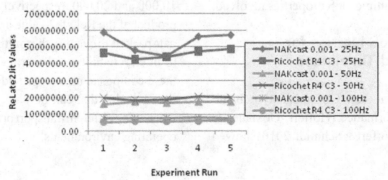

known *a priori*) and configurations that would use the SVM (*i.e.*, the configurations that were unknown until run-time). Since these techniques provide constant-time performance, their compute times are invariant to the specific environment configuration, so we did not run timing test for all different environment configurations.

Figure 7 presents the response times for TIML in ADAMANT for 1,000 iterations when TIML selects and uses either an ANN or the SVM. The figure highlights the times used within the integrated machine learning techniques when the environment configuration is (1) known *a priori* and thus triggers the use of an ANN and (2) unknown until run-time triggering the use of an SVM. On average TIML when using the ANN presents the lower response time of 11.161 μs while TIML using the SVM presents an average response time of 11.996 μs. The bound on TIML is then the maximum between the two (*i.e.*, 11.996 μs). The figure also appears to show that TIML using the ANN has more jitter than TIML using the SVM. The jitter is within the resolution of the timers (*i.e.*, 1 μs) used for collecting the times, however, since the times only vary by +/- 1 μs from the median values (*i.e.*, 11 μs for the TIML when the ANN is used and 12 μs when the SVM is used).

Timeliness of ANT Reconfiguration

We now describe the experiments we conducted to show the timeliness of the ANT framework as it transitions from one transport protocol to another. As described in Challenge 2 (timely adaptation), the personal datacenter for the SCAAL application needs to have timely adaptations. In the previous section we presented timing results for determining the appropriate transport protocol. In this section we provide timing information on the reconfiguration of transport protocols supported in the ANT framework portion of ADAMANT. We used the same experimental environment as described in the section *Experimental Setup*. A high resolution timestamp was taken right before and right after each call made to ANT to reconfigure transport protocols.

Figure 8 shows the times taken for transport protocol reconfiguration across 1000 iterations. The figure includes times for three different scenarios. Two of the scenarios are most relevant for the transport protocols that best handle reliability and latency (*i.e.*, the NAKcast and Ricochet protocols). The third scenario presents a baseline when checks are performed to determine if a protocol transition is needed but no transition is needed.

Figure 7. Integrated supervised machine learning response times

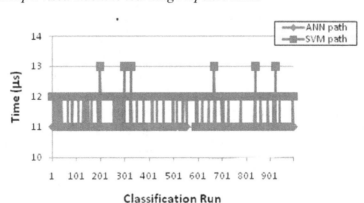

Figure 8. Transport protocol reconfiguration times within ANT

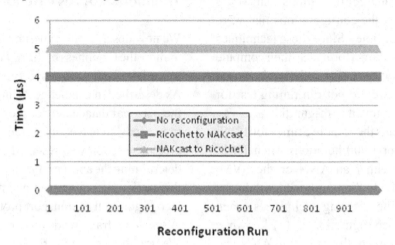

The baseline times for no reconfiguration shows 0 μs taken to determine that no protocol reconfiguration is needed. Obviously, some time is taken to make the determination that no reconfiguration is needed but this time is smaller than the resolution of the timestamps taken (*i.e.*, < 1 μs). These times provide an idea of the overhead required in making any protocol reconfiguration.

The remaining two scenarios are when (1) the NAKcast protocol is running and a transition is made to the Ricochet protocol and (2) when the Ricochet protocol is running and a transition is made to the NAKcast protocol. The times for these transitions should be constant since, when reconfiguring, ANT registers a constant number of events and event handlers for the new protocol and unregisters a constant number of events and event handlers for the old protocol. The number of event and event handlers is known *a priori* at development time. Registering and unregistering events and event handlers correspond to inserting and removing items from a queue which are constant time operations.

It should be noted that the transport protocols that are a focus of this research do not have state that needs to be transferred from one protocol to another. Therefore, transitioning from one

protocol to another did not require quiescence of the system for transferring state. There are trade-offs between having either both transport protocols running during the transition (*i.e.*, when transitioning from the NAKcast protocol to the Ricochet protocol, start up the Ricochet protocol before stopping the NAKcast protocol) or having neither protocol running during the transition (*i.e.*, when transitioning from the NAKcast protocol to the Ricochet protocol, stop the NAKcast protocol before starting up the Ricochet protocol. Running both protocols during the transition will temporarily increase reliability and processing while running neither protocol will decrease reliability and processing. Evaluating these trade-offs in detail is left as future work.

In particular, for the NAKcast and Ricochet protocols we know *a priori* the number and kinds of events and event handlers that each protocol uses. ADAMANT first unregisters all the relevant events and event handlers for an old protocol and then registers all the relevant events and event handlers for the new protocol. Since ADAMANT controls how and in what order events and event handlers are registered and unregistered in ANT, managing the lists for these events and event handlers can be done in constant time. The Ricochet to

NAKcast transition consistently takes 4 μs while the NAKcast to Ricochet transition consistently takes 5 μs. For the ADAMANT prototype using the OpenSplice DDS implementation, these transitions are happening within the single network daemon per computing platform. As noted in section *Control Flow of ADAMANT*, ANT's transitions are deterministic with the DDS middleware ensuring that all the computing platform see the same updates and therefore make the same transitions. These empirical transition times verify that ANT protocol transitions are made in a constant amount of time.

Summary of Results

The results of experiments presented in this section show that there are scenarios where a change in the operating environment requires a change in the QoS mechanisms (*e.g.*, transport protocols) that ADAMANT is utilizing. Based on this information, the experiments show that ADAMANT delivers constant-time decision-making regarding the appropriate transport protocol to use as well as constant-time transitioning from one transport protocol to another. For QoS-enabled DRE pub/sub applications ADAMANT provides the constant-time complexity needed for detecting environment changes, determining the appropriate course of action, and executing that plan.

RELATED WORK

This section compares our work on ADAMANT with related work.

Support for Adaptive Middleware

The Mobility Support Service (MSS) (Caporuscio, 2003) provides a software layer on top of pub/sub middleware to enable end host mobility. The purpose of MSS is to support the movement of clients between access points of a system using pub/sub middleware. In this sense, MSS adapts the pub/sub middleware used in a mobile environment. Mobile clients notify MSS when mobility starts and ends. MSS buffers messages and manages connections while the client moves to a different access point. MSS is designed to support multiple pub/sub technologies, *e.g.*, implementations of JMS, and adapt to the technology-specific characteristics.

MSS is solely focused on supporting mobility of pub/sub, however, and therefore does not address Challenge 1 (managing interacting QoS). Moreover, MSS is not focused on DRE systems and therefore does not address Challenge 2 (timely adaptation). Finally, MSS does not address operating environments where aspects of the environment change and impact QoS.

Gridkit (Grace, 2005) is a middleware framework that supports reconfigurability of applications dependent upon the condition of the environment and the functionality of registered components. Gridkit focuses on grid applications which are highly heterogeneous in nature. For example, these applications will run on many types of computing devices and across different types of networks.

To register components, application developers use Gridkit's API, which is based on binding contracts. Gridkit then uses the contract information along with a context engine to determine which components to include in the application. The context engine takes into account the context of the host machines, *e.g.*, battery life, network connectivity.

Gridkit focuses on reconfiguration for installing an application and does not address Challenge 2 (accurate adaptation) or Challenge 3 (timely adaptation) for systems operating in dynamic environments. Within Gridkit no consideration is given to making timely and accurate adaptations based on the environment changing for a single application installation. Moreover, Gridkit fails to address Challenge 1 (managing interacting QoS) as it does not address QoS concerns.

David and Ledoux have developed SAFRAN (David, 2006) to enable applications to become context-aware themselves so that they can adapt to their contexts. SAFRAN provides reactive adaptation policy infrastructure for components using an aspect-oriented approach. SAFRAN follows the structure of a generic AOP system by supporting (1) a base program which corresponds to a configuration of components, (2) point-cuts which are invoked in response to internal events (*e.g.*, invocations on interfaces) and external events (*e.g.*, change in system resources), (3) advices which define functionality to be executed for point-cuts, and (4) adaptation which uses adaptation policies to link join points to advices.

The SAFRAN component framework, however, only provides development support of maintaining specified QoS. The adaptive policies and component implementation are the responsibility of the application developer. Therefore, SAFRAN does not address Challenge 2 (accurate adaptation) and Challenge 3 (timely adaptation).

Machine Learning in Support of Autonomic Adaptation

Vienne and Sourrouille (Vienne, 2005) present the Dynamic Control of Behavior based on Learning (DCBL) middleware that incorporates reinforcement machine learning in support of autonomic control for QoS management. Reinforcement machine learning not only allows DCBL to handle unexpected changes but also reduces the overall system knowledge required by the system developers. System developers provide an XML description of the system, which DCBL then uses together with an internal representation of the managed system to select appropriate QoS dynamically.

DCBL's use of reinforcement learning, however, does not address Challenge 3 (timely adaptation) as reinforcement learning is unbounded in its time complexity. DCBL also focuses on single computers rather than addressing scalable DRE

systems and therefore does not address Challenge 4 (development complexity) for DRE systems. Moreover, DCBL requires developers to specify in an XML file the selection of operating modes given a QoS level along with execution paths, which leaves handling Challenge 1 (managing interacting QoS) to developers.

Tock *et al.* (2005) utilize machine learning for data dissemination in their work on Multicast Mapping (MCM). MCM hierarchically clusters data flows so that multiple topics are mapped onto a single session and multiple sessions are mapped onto a single reliable multicast group. MCM's approach manages the scarce availability of multicast addresses in large-scale systems. MCM leverages machine learning to adapt as user interest and message rate change during the day. MCM is designed only to address the scarce resource of IP multicast addresses in large-scale systems, however, rather than Challenge 1 (managing interacting QoS).

Autonomic Adaptation of Service Level Agreements

Herssens *et al.* (2008) describe work that centers on autonomically adapting service level agreements (SLAs) when the context of the specified service changes. This work acknowledges that both offered and the requested QoS for Web services might vary over the course of the interaction and accordingly modifies the SLA between the client and the server as appropriate. However, this work does not address Challenge 2 (accurate adaptation) or Challenge 3 (timely adaptation) in dynamic environments but rather negotiates the QoS agreement to fit the dynamic environment.

Autonomic Adaption of Networks

The Autonomic Real-time Multicast Distribution System (ARMDS) (Brynjulfsson, 2006) is a framework that focuses on decreasing excessive variance in service quality for multicast data across the Internet. The framework supports the autonomic adaptation of the network nodes forming the multicast graph so that the consistency of service delivery is enhanced. However, ARMDS does not address Challenge 1 (managing interacting QoS).

CONCLUSION

Developers of systems that utilize DRE pub/sub middleware face a number of challenges when developing and deploying their systems in dynamic environments. To address these challenges, we developed ADAMANT to integrate and enhance (1) QoS-enabled pub/sub middleware, (2) an environment monitoring topic, (3) a flexible transport protocol framework, (4) a novel integration of supervised machine learning techniques, and (5) an autonomic controller to provide fast and predictable reconfiguration of middleware and transport protocols for enterprise DRE pub/sub systems. This paper presents the results of experiments that show how ADAMANT can adapt autonomically to changing conditions in operating environments to support QoS in a fast, constant-time, and accurate manner.

The following is a summary of lessons learned from our experience evaluating ADAMANT's autonomic adaptation performance in various operating environments:

- **Several trade-offs exist when using machine learning in dynamic environments:** There are several trade-offs between having machine learning that (1) is completely accurate for environments known at training time, (2) highly accurate for environments unknown until run-time, (3) can accommodate new data on which to train as the system is running, and (4) can expend the appropriate amount of time interactively training machine learning tools while the system is running.

Since overfitting an ANN to environment configurations known *a priori* provides perfect accuracy and low response times, it is preferable to incorporate new operating environment configurations unknown until runtime into the ANN training set while the system is running. A low-priority thread could be used to constantly re-train the ANN and swap in the updated ANN at appropriate times. While this approach would incorporate new environment configurations, our future work is addressing trade-offs between when to migrate to using the updated ANN versus how to determine the importance of the low-priority training thread so it will not be starved.

- **Preparing environment information for use in machine learning tools is time consuming and tedious:** A large amount of data can be generated based on the number and types of environment variables (*e.g.*, number of receivers, data sending rate, percent loss in the network, CPU speed, QoS metric used). In addition to the raw data, the data can be scaled (*i.e.*, transformed to be within minimum and maximum values such as between -1 and 1). Some machine learning techniques provide better results when the data are scaled. For our experimental data, scaling the data produced the best results. When scaling the data produces the best results, the environment data received from ADAMANT's monitoring topic also needed to be scaled as well which adds some overhead and complexity. The scaling factors used on the data for training the machine learning tools need to be managed and applied to the data collected from the environment during runtime.

- **Multiple machine learning approaches can be integrated to handle configurations known *a priori* and environment configurations not known until runtime:**

Some machine learning techniques provide higher accuracy than others for operating environments known *a priori*. In particular, ANNs can be overfitted to the data to provide 100% accuracy for these kinds of environments. Other techniques provide higher accuracy for environments unknown until runtime. An integration of multiple machine learning techniques can provide higher overall accuracy than can be provided by any single machine learning technique. If timeliness is a concern, then when integrating multiple techniques, care must be taken to ensure that the integration itself does not change the time complexity characteristics. ADAMANT incorporates TIML to increase its overall accuracy for both operating environments known *a priori* and environments unknown until runtime while also ensuring that the integration itself maintains the constant-time complexity needed by DRE systems.

- **Transport protocols need to be selectively used based on the QoS specified:** While several DDS implementations (*e.g.*, OpenDDS and OpenSplice) provide pluggable transport frameworks to leverage standard and custom transport protocols the properties of these protocols must be dictated by application-specified QoS policies. The focus on transport protocols is a starting point for research into classifying QoS mechanisms (which is a far richer space than just transport protocols) and mapping application specified QoS policies to these QoS mechanisms in an automated way. For example, in our work we wanted to specify that the environment monitoring topic information be sent and received reliably. DDS implementations, however, provide no infrastructure for mapping between the transport protocols (*e.g.*, Ricochet and NAKcast) used and the QoS properties (*e.g.*, reliable data com-

munication, or "best-effort") specified. Our future work is therefore developing a transport protocol taxonomy that QoS-enabled middleware can leverage to determine which protocol to apply based on QoS specified at the application level using DDS QoS policies. The properties that transport protocols provide can be used to classify the protocols with respect to QoS. The middleware can then select (1) the most appropriate transport protocol based on the QoS properties needed and (2) different transport protocols for different QoS properties.

- **QoS-enabled middleware provides a fairly coarse-grained approach to reliability:** Utilizing transport protocols such as Ricochet and NAKcast allows QoS-enabled middleware to provide finer-grained reliability as well as considering latency. Reliability is typically only supported, however, as the binary choice of either best-effort reliability (which implies no reliability support) or *perfect reliability* (which implies reliability support for every individual network packet) with no consideration of highly probabilistic reliability (where the probability of receiving any one network packet is high but is not intended to be 100%). Moreover, the semantics of combining multiple QoS aspects (*e.g.*, reliability and latency) are not clearly defined at the middleware level. Transport protocols, such as Ricochet and NAKcast, capture the finer-grained reliability property of high probability of reliability and low data latency which need to be specified, for example, in applications transmitting multimedia data.

- **High-level metrics are useful to quickly differentiate the performance of various configurations:** The use of metrics—even coarse-grained metrics—helps explore a large configuration space efficiently.

Developing composite metrics (*e.g.*, ReLate and ReLate2) helps ameliorate navigating a configuration space with several points of variability.

All the source code and documentation for ADAMANT is available in open-source form at www.dre.vanderbilt.edu/~jhoffert/ADAMANT.

REFERENCES

Bai, Y., & Ito, M. (2006). A study for providing better quality of service to VoIP users. In *Proceedings of the 20th International Conference on Advanced Information Networking and Application* (pp. 799-804). Washington, DC: IEEE Computer Society.

Bai, Y., & Ito, M. (2007). A new technique for minimizing network loss from users' perspective. *Journal of Network and Computer Applications*, *30*(2), 637–649. doi:10.1016/j.jnca.2006.01.003

Balakrishnan, M., Birman, K., Phanishayee, A., & Pleisch, S. (2007). Ricochet: Lateral error correction for time-critical multicast. In *Proceedings of the Fourth Usenix Symposium on Networked Systems Design and Implementation* (pp. 73-86). New York, NY: ACM Press.

Balakrishnan, M., Pleisch, S., & Birman, K. (2005). Slingshot: Time-critical multicast for clustered applications. In *Proceedings of the Fourth IEEE International Symposium on Network Computing and Applications* (pp. 205-214). New York, NY: ACM Press.

Brodnik, A., & Munro, J. (1994). Membership in constant time and minimum space. In J. van Leeuwen (Ed.), *Proceedings of the Second Annual European Symposium on Algorithms* (LNCS 855, pp. 72-81).

Brynjulfsson, B., Hjalmtysson, G., Katrinis, K., & Plattner, B. (2006). Autonomic network-layer multicast service towards consistent service quality. In *Proceedings of the 20th International Conference on Advanced Information Networking and Applications* (pp. 494-498). Washington, DC: IEEE Computer Society.

Caporuscio, M., Carzaniga, A., & Wolf, A. (2003). Design and evaluation of a support service for mobile, wireless publish/subscribe applications. *IEEE Transactions on Software Engineering*, *29*(12), 1059–1071. doi:10.1109/TSE.2003.1265521

Chandy, M., Etzion, O., von Ammon, R., & Niblett, P. (2007). *DROPS 07191 summary – event processing*. Paper presented at the Dagstuhl Seminar on Event Processing, Schloss Dagstuhl, Germany, David, P.-C., & Ledoux, T. (2006). An aspect-oriented approach for developing self-adaptive fractal components. In W. Löwe & M. Südholt (Eds.) *Proceedings of the 5th International Symposium on Software Composition* (LNCS 4089, pp. 82-97).

Dietterich, T. (1995). Overfitting and undercomputing in machine learning. *ACM Computing Surveys*, *27*(3), 326–327. doi:10.1145/212094.212114

Grace, P., Coulson, G., Blair, G., & Porter, B. (2005). Deep middleware for the divergent grid. In G. Alonso (Ed.), *Proceedings of the ACM/IFIP/USENIX International Conference on Middleware* (LNCS 3790, pp. 334-353).

Herssens, C., Faulkner, S., & Jureta, I. J. (2008). Context-driven autonomic adaptation of SLA. In A. Bouguettaya, I. Krueger, & T. Margaria (Eds.), *Proceedings of the 6th International Conference on Service-Oriented Computing* (LNCS 5364, pp. 362-377).

Hoffert, J., Gokhale, A., & Schmidt, D. (2009). Evaluating transport protocols for real-time event stream processing Middleware and applications. In *Proceedings of the 11th International Symposium on Distributed Objects, Middleware, and Applications* (pp. 614-633).

Hoffert, J., Mack, D., & Schmidt, D. (2010). Integrating machine learning techniques to adapt protocols for QoS-enabled distributed real-time and embedded publish/subscribe Middleware. *Network Protocols and Algorithms, 2*(3), 37–69. doi:10.5296/npa.v2i3.429

Hoffert, J., & Schmidt, D. (2009). Maintaining QoS for publish/subscribe middleware in dynamic environments. In *Proceedings of the 3rd International Conference on Distributed Event-based Systems* (pp. 1-2). New York: ACM Press.

Hoffert, J., Schmidt, D., & Gokhale, A. (2010a). Adapting and evaluating distributed real-time and embedded systems in dynamic environments. In *Proceedings of the 1st International Workshop on Data Dissemination for Large Scale Complex Critical Infrastructures* (pp. 23-28). New York, NY: ACM Press.

Hoffert, J., Schmidt, D., & Gokhale, A. (2010b). Adapting distributed real-time and embedded pub/sub middleware for cloud computing environments. In I. Gupta & C. Mascolo (Eds.), *Proceedings of the ACM/IFIP/USENIX 11th International Middleware Conference* (LNCS 6452, pp. 21-41).

Huang, Q., Freedman, D., Vigfusson, Y., Birman, K., & Peng, B. (2010). Kevlar: A flexible infrastructure for wide-area collaborative applications. In I. Gupta & C. Mascolo (Eds.), *Proceedings of the ACM/IFIP/USENIX 11th International Middleware Conference* (LNCS 6452, pp. 148-168).

Huang, Y., & Gannon, D. (2006). A comparative study of web services-based event notification specifications. In *Proceedings of the International Conference on Parallel Processing Workshops* (pp. 7-14). Washington, DC: IEEE Computer Society.

Huebscher, M., & McCann, J. (2008). A survey of autonomic computing—degrees, models, and applications. *ACM Computing Surveys, 40*(3), 1–28. doi:10.1145/1380584.1380585

Kephart, J., & Chess, D. (2003). The vision of autonomic computing. *Computer, 36*(1), 41–50. doi:10.1109/MC.2003.1160055

Liu, Y. (2006). Create stable neural networks by cross-validation. In *Proceedings of the International Joint Conference on Neural Networks* (pp. 3925-3928). Washington, DC: IEEE Computer Society.

Meyer, D., Leisch, D., & Hornik, K. (2003). The support vector machine under test. *Neurocomputing, 55*(1-2), 169–186. doi:10.1016/S0925-2312(03)00431-4

Monson-Haefel, R., & Chappell, D. (2000). *Java message service*. Sebastopol, CA: O'Reilly Media.

Ngatman, M., Ngadi, M., & Sharif, J. (2008). Comprehensive study of transmission techniques for reducing packet loss and delay in multimedia over IP. *International Journal of Computer Science and Network Security, 8*(3), 292–299.

Niblett, P., & Graham, S. (2005). Events and service-oriented architecture: The OASIS web services notification specifications. *IBM Systems Journal, 44*(4), 869–886. doi:10.1147/sj.444.0869

Pardo-Castellote, G. (2003). OMG data-distribution service: Architectural overview. In *Proceedings of the 23rd International Conference on Distributed Computing Systems* (pp. 200-206). Washington, DC: IEEE Computer Society.

Patterson, D. W. (1998). *Artificial neural networks: Theory and applications*. Upper Saddle River, NJ: Prentice Hall.

Ramani, S., Trivedi, K. S., & Dasarathy, B. (2001). Performance analysis of the CORBA notification service. In *Proceedings of the 20th IEEE Symposium on Reliable Distributed Systems* (pp. 227-236). Washington, DC: IEEE Computer Society.

Schmidt, D. C. (2000). GPERF: A perfect hash function generator. In Martin, R. (Ed.), *More C++ gems* (pp. 461–491). Cambridge, UK: Cambridge University Press.

Schmidt, D. C., Stal, M., Rohnert, H., & Buschmann, F. (2000b). *Pattern-oriented software architecture: patterns for concurrent and networked objects* (*Vol. 2*). New York, NY: John Wiley & Sons.

Tarkoma, S., & Raatikainen, K. (2006). *State of the art review of distributed event systems* (Tech. Rep. No. C0-04). Helsinki, Finland: University of Helsinki.

Tock, Y., Naaman, N., Harpaz, A., & Gershinsky, G. (2005). Hierarchical clustering of message flows in a multicast data dissemination system. In *Proceedings of the International Conference on Parallel and Distributed Computing Systems* (pp. 320-326).

Vienne, P., & Sourrouille, J.-L. (2005). A middleware for autonomic QoS management based on learning. In *Proceedings of the 5th International Workshop on Software Engineering and Middleware* (pp. 1-8). New York, NY: ACM Press.

This work was previously published in the International Journal of Adaptive, Resilient and Autonomic Systems, Volume 2, Issue 4, edited by Vincenzo De Florio, pp. 1-24, copyright 2011 by IGI Publishing (an imprint of IGI Global).

Chapter 11
A Generic Adaptation Framework for Mobile Communication

Hong Sun
University of Antwerp and IBBT, Belgium

Ning Gui
University of Antwerp and IBBT, Belgium and Central South University, China

Chris Blondia
University of Antwerp and IBBT, Belgium

ABSTRACT

Today, technologies are providing mobile terminals with much more powerful computational abilities. Such improvement has made it possible to run many complex applications on mobile devices. However, many of these new applications are also resource demanding. Lacking sufficient resources would cause performance failures and impact negatively on the users' quality of experience. In order to improve this, it is important to provide the users with an easy access to specifying their requirements. It is also crucial to monitor the system resources and make corresponding adaptation immediately according to the user's specifications. In this paper, the authors propose adaptation strategies that flexibly combine the process of monitoring and adaptation, which provides an easy way to specify user's requirements. By tuning the quality of service, the applications' demand on system resources is reduced, thus decreasing the chances of performance failures and improving the users' quality of experience.

INTRODUCTION

With the development of technologies, the functions of the mobile terminals are becoming more and more powerful; access to pervasive services is available in many areas. Users with powerful mobile terminals are granted with the ability to access information and multimedia services from almost anywhere at any time.

However, there are still some restrictions impacting on the user's quality of experience (QoE) due to the limitation of the available resources: examples include a high CPU usage impacting

DOI: 10.4018/978-1-4666-2056-8.ch011

the system's ability to support burst computation requirements; or an environment that is changing when the user is roaming, thus affecting the available bandwidth, etc. In order to increase the user's QoE and avoid performance failures (also known as late timing failures [Cristian, 1991]), the mobile terminal should intelligently detect the changes of environment (battery capacity, bandwidth usage, CPU usage, etc.), and take proper adaptations promptly.

Many adaptation strategies are already developed in different domains, such as switching transcoding methods, or adjusting the tasks' priorities. However, adaptations are highly application-specific or domain-specific, which may bring conflicts between different application domains. For instance, in the power consumption domain, reducing the power could obtain a longer battery life, while in the communication domain, increasing the power may guarantee a better communication quality. Another feature of these application-specific adaptations is that they are normally hard bound with the application code and lack of flexibility to make reconfigurations in different environments.

Rather than scattering the adaptation logics in different applications and represent them as low-level binary code, architecture-based adaptation uses external models and mechanisms in a closed-loop control fashion to achieve various goals by monitoring and adapting system behavior across application domains. A well-accepted design principle in architecture-based management consists in using a component-based technology to develop management system and application structure (Kon, Costa, Blair, & Campbell, 2002; Sylvain, Fabienne, & Noel, 2008; Costa et al., 2007). However, in most of the above mentioned approaches, the configurations of applications and components are generally carried out before runtime; these systems still need to improve their ability to take runtime reconfigurations according to the change of system status.

In this paper, we are proposing an adaptation model to flexibly assemble the monitoring process of system resources, and provide an easy access for the users to specify their preferences. Adaptation logics are separated from applications and controlled by the system, while the reactions are still carried out on applications. Such a framework could flexibly implement, modify, and execute adaptation policies through users' preferences, thus helping avoid the performance failure and increase the users' QoE.

The rest of this paper is organized as follows: we will firstly introduce some design issues of the mobile adaptation frameworks; then we will present our adaptation model. Experiments of such an adaptation model will be given in and conclusions will be made.

DESIGN ISSUES

Many design issues need to be considered in developing adaptation framework for mobile systems, among which, we deem the following to be the most important ones:

When to take the adaptations:

- Choices here include deploying the adaptation policies in the installation phase, and adaptations at execution time (Houssos, Gazis, & Alonistioti, 2003). Our view is that if the adaptation schemes are solely configured in the setup time, they would lack of flexibility, while if there are too many operations during the runtime, this will also introduce extra costs such as extra time to switch the policies, and make the system too complex to design. In our design, we set our adaptation policies in the deployment time, however, still provide our users with access to switch adaptation policies and modify adaptation parameters during the runtime. Such runtime modifications can be implemented in a simple way and without introducing an excessive amount of design complexity.

Where to carry out the adaptation:

- Three models are widely used to take adaptations: centralized, application-transparent adaptation; decentralized, application-specific adaptation; and integrated model (Edmonds, Hopper, & Hodges, 2001). The centralized model performs adaptation at operating system level, which avoids the competition between applications, makes decisions concerning the best adaptation strategy on system level and aids efficiency in resource usage. However, the drawback is that lacking the knowledge from specific applications, adaptation actions are not efficient in such a model. The decentralized model performs adaptation solely within the application. Monitoring and adaptations are glued together in certain applications without any support from the system. Such a solution is effective to solve a particular adaptation facet; however, it is scarcely efficient system wide. Furthermore there might be conflicts between different decentralized adaptations. The integrated adaptation model takes the advantage of the two above mentioned approaches: it combines the system management of resources with the application specific knowledge of exactly what is required and how to execute the adaptations. The integrated approach is much more difficult to implement compared with the other two approaches: it requires especially tight cooperation between the applications and the operating system, and existing applications need to be modified to run effectively under such model. In our adaptation model, we use the integrated approach. Monitoring and applications are scattered through the

system, however, the monitoring results, adaptation analysis and adaptation instructions are processed in a centralized way. We will explain how we execute the adaptations on applications in later sections.

How to carry out the adaptation:

- There are many ways to take adaptations; however, here we generally categorize them into three levels based on granularity: the highest level is switching adaptation policies according to different locations, targets, etc.; the second one is adaptation of services, e.g. switching the coding method of a video encoder, etc; the last one is setting key parameters, e.g. resetting the frame dropping rate of a mobile video player, etc. In our previous research (Sun, De Florio, Gui, & Blondia, 2007), we built up an adaptation framework combining adaptations on both services and parameters. However, the drawback here is that these two adaptations are carried out separately through service oriented architectures (SOA) and so-called reflective-and-refractive variables (RR vars) (De Florio & Blondia, 2007). In this paper, we will combine Aspect Oriented Programming and SOA to integrate the above mentioned approaches together.

RELATED WORKS

Autonomic Computation

Approaches such as autonomic computation (AC) are developed to construct self-governing computing systems that can manage themselves given high-level objectives from administrators (Kephart, & Chess, 2003). The target systems of autonomic computation, as shown in Figure 1, are single or networked devices. Techniques such as

Figure 1. Structure of an autonomic element

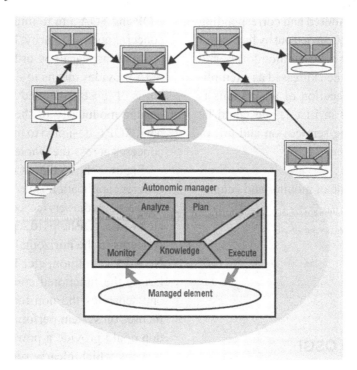

context aware computing and ambient intelligence are also widely applied here nowadays in monitoring the changes of the application environment and either adapting the devices or changing the surrounding environments so as to improve users' quality of experience. In this paper, the general logic of the adaptation framework for the single or connected devices is quite similar with those presented in the AC autonomic manager.

OSGi Framework

OSGi (OSGi, 2008) is a light-weight standardized service management platform that allows for dynamic service provision from multiple providers. The OSGi platform supports the Java programming language and implements a complete and dynamic component model. Applications or components can be remotely installed, started, stopped, updated and uninstalled without requiring a reboot.

Adopting the OSGi framework allows the applications to be organized according to the service oriented approach (they are built as OSGi bundles); this allows the components/applications to be managed flexibly in loosely coupled way. The adaptation framework to be presented in the following sections makes use of the OSGi framework to wrap and organize the applications as OSGi bundles.

Aspect Oriented Programming (AOP)

Aspect Oriented Programming (AOP) is a technique to design and address the cross-cutting concerns (Kiczales et al., 1997; Kislev, 2002). AOP attempts to realize scattered concerns as elements of a separated Aspect class, and eject them horizontally from the object structure.

The AOP technique could well support the adaptations by monitoring and processing the cross-cutting concerns. Sensitive (or interested) attributes scattered around the system could be gathered together and processed. Changes of these attributes could be monitored and corresponding adaptations could also be carried out by the Aspect class. The relationship between monitoring and adaptation in AOP can be expressed as exemplified in List 1. The execution of adaptations is symbolized as advices in List 1, and could be carried out as switching services on and off, or resetting their parameters.

List 1. A simple example of monitor and adaptation

```
pointcut CPUMonitor(float value) :
    call (float DisplayCPU(float))
    && args(value);

after(float value) : CPUMonitor(value){
    /*
     Advice, specify adaptation policy here
    */
}
```

Binding AOP with OSGi

The digital systems around us are becoming more and more powerful; meanwhile, the complexity of the systems is also increasing on and on, which may result in system bottlenecks. The above mentioned problem could be addressed by improving the separation of system concerns and the modularity of the system (Parnas, 1972). Both AOP and SOA aim to improve the separation of concerns and modularity; however, these two approaches appear to be orthogonal to each other: SOA provides means to develop applications in terms of loosely coupled services, thus improving the modularity of the system; on the other hand AOP is designed to modularize crosscutting concerns across the whole system.

Figure 2 shows that SOA helps to separate the different applications into services in the vertical axis, e.g., media service, communication service, etc.; while AOP helps to separate different system concerns in the horizontal axis, e.g. CPU usage, Network Condition, etc. The former one modularizes the functional concerns while the latter one separates the non-functional concerns and focuses on system performance. Their combination could provide a powerful solution to build systems which clearly separate both functional and non-functional concerns thus well addressing the issue of bottleneck avoidance.

There are many research efforts aiming at integrating AOP with OSGi. Examples include AJEER (Lippert, 2004) and AOSGi, which were merged into the Equinox Aspect project [Equinox Aspect, 2008]. Such efforts integrated the As-

Figure 2. Improving separation of concerns and modularity with AOP and SOA

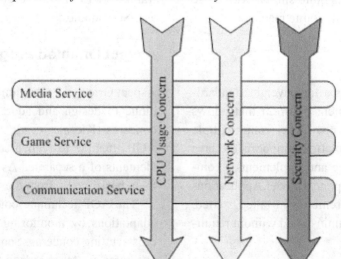

pectJ programming language into the OSGi platform (Equinox); using a load-time weaving extension Equinox is able to add AspectJ aspects to bundle-based systems just by putting them into general OSGi bundles. There are also other approaches to realize such integration, such as Jadabs (Frei & Alonso, 2005), which uses dynamic proxies to implement the aspects into the OSGi platform. Some other effort was carried out in integrating the JBoss AOP into the OSGi platform (Irmert et al., 2007). The adaptation framework reported in this paper adopts Equinox Aspect as it is a mature product still continuously updated, easy to use and characterized by a wide spread target system (Equinox).

ADAPTATION FRAMEWORK

Global Adaptation Framework

In our previous work (Sun, De Florio, Gui, & Blondia, 2007) we proposed a so-called global adaptation framework to realize the adaptation. We deem that in order to make correct adaptations in mobile applications, there is a stringent requirement for the system to be aware of the environmental changes. The proposed adaptation strategies are thus constructed as an event-condition-action model (Etter, Costa, & Broens, 2006; De Florio & Blondia, 2005). The system

is context aware, and adaptations are taken when the context changes. The event module detects the changes of the surrounding environment. The detected events trigger the reasoning of the rule engine; depending on the conditions, specific adaptation rules will be fired and the adaptations will be held in the action module.

In Figure 3 (Sun, De Florio, Gui, & Blondia, 2007), the event module is designed to monitor the environment around the mobile terminal, availability of applications and the system status of the mobile terminal. Services and reflective variables are used to separate different kinds of information. Services are developed as OSGi bundles, and changes of the services are detected by the service listener. In order to better indicate the system status, so-called "reflective variables" (De Florio & Blondia, 2008) are used to represent some of the key system state parameters reified as variables of a programming language. Adaptation decisions are made in the condition module, where certain rule engines can be implemented, and adaptation decisions are to be deduced based on predefined rules. The action module in the framework executes the adaptations when certain adaptation rules are fired in the condition module. Adaptations in the action module are executed as adjustments on service, such as start/stop/update OSGi bundles; or by setting some system parameters, which is done through so-called "refractive variables".

Figure 3. Architecture of global adaptation framework

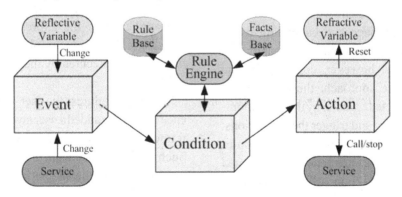

The above mentioned solution provides an agile way to detect the change of context by the combination of service change detection and the reflective/refractive variables. It also provides fine grained adaptation by the combination of changing services and resetting the refractive variables. The drawback is that firstly, the monitoring and adaptations of services and variables are processed separately by SOA and RR variables, which increases system complexity and reduces efficiency; and secondly, the adaptation policies are all stored as predefined rules in deployment, which lacks of flexibility to carry out runtime changes.

The adaptation strategies we propose in this paper are developed from the structure shown in Figure 3; however, the above mentioned drawbacks are solved in our proposed adaptation strategies here. The adaptation model that we propose in this paper is shown in Figure 4.

Generic Context Aware Global Adaptation Framework

Figure 4 shows our generic context aware adaptation framework. Such framework is divided into three layers. In the service layer, applications are wrapped as services to ease adaptations in the later stage. Applications such as media players or different types of monitors are wrapped as OSGi service bundles.

In the adaptation layer, the event monitor module collects the detected changes from different monitor bundles. Information of the interested resources are collected system-widely: for instance, the value of CPU usage and bandwidth usage are reported by the CPU monitor and bandwidth monitor separately; however, contrarily to the application-specific approach, these monitored values will be collected together by the event monitor module to analyze and trigger the adaptations.

The relationship between the monitor modules and adaptation modules are generally expressed as aspect weavings in Equinox Aspect (Equinox

Figure 4. Context aware global adaptation framework

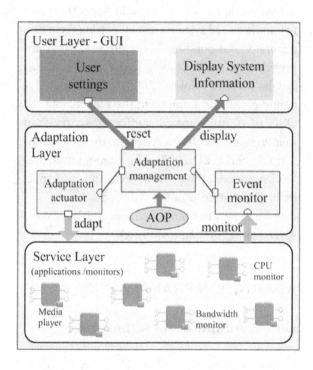

Aspect, 2008), which is shown in Figure 5 (Lippert, 2008). Concerns in different bundles, e.g. CPU usage, are monitored by a separate aspect bundle. Adaptation policies are also resident in the same aspect bundle written with AspectJ language in the advice area. An independent GUI is also attached to this adaptation bundle.

Adaptation decisions are deduced in the adaptation management module, based on the adaptation policies and the system resources. The relationship between monitoring and adaptation in AOP can be expressed as shown in List 1. In real-life applications, the expression of adaptation logics could be very complex, and such adaptations will be executed by the adaptation actuator module.

In order to address the user's quality of experience (QoE), we added a user layer to our adaptation framework, which hosts a graphical user interface. Such GUI is connected to the adaptation management module in the adaptation layer; the system

Figure 5. Aspect weaving for OSGi

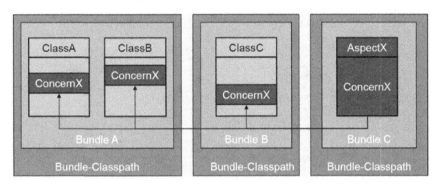

information received by the monitor module is sent and displayed on the GUI. Most importantly, the GUI provides the users with an access to switching between the predefined adaptation policies, or resetting some key parameters, such as applications priorities, during the runtime. An instance of the GUI is shown in Figure 7, which is used and further explained in next section.

EXPERIMENTS

The following application was developed as an experiment to validate how our proposed adaptation framework could monitor the system information and guide the adaptations on video playing.

The structure of the experiment is shown in Figure 6. A videoclip is played by the Mplayer (an open source media player) in the client side as an application. The sources of the displayed videos are stored in the server side, and the server provides the videos with three different resolutions upon decisions from the client side. The monitor module in the client side monitors the information of CPU usage, bandwidth, and memory exchange rate; such information is displayed in the GUI in Figure 7. The adaptor bundle retrieves the system information from the monitor bundle; meanwhile, it also retrieves MPlayer objects, which describe and control the video that is being played by the MPlayer. According to the system status, the adaptor bundle takes corresponding adaptations on the Mplayer objects, and selects the appropriate resolutions. When the system is meeting restrictions on resources, such as low CPU, or limited bandwidth, it is still possible to avoid performance failures by trading off quality of service that least affects QoE. In this case performance failures are avoided by reducing the resolution of the videos.

The thresholds that we defined to take the adaptations are shown in Figure 8. There is no particular reason to choose these figures, which are to be considered here merely a proof of concept for our adaptation framework. There are two adaptation policies in our experiment: either considering the combined value of CPU and Bandwidth usage, or considering the combined value of CPU and Memory usage. Users have to choose one of these policies; it is also possible for user to change the adaptation policies during the runtime through the GUI (see the User settings buttons in Figure 7.). In the adaptation log in Figure 7, it is shown that the adaptations are woven by the change of the values on CPU and bandwidth at the beginning, while later on we switched to adaptations based on the combination of CPU and memory usage. It is also possible to switch the priorities between different videos when more than one video is being displayed.

The results of the experiments proved that our proposed adaptation framework could flexibly organize the adaptations, while also being able to

Figure 6. Experiment structure

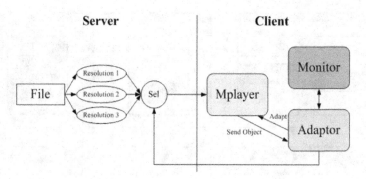

Figure 7. Graphic user interface

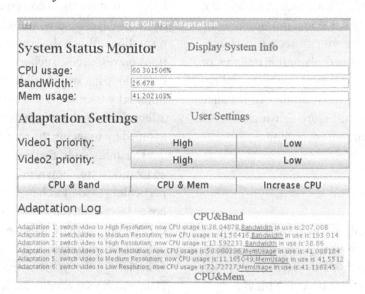

Figure 8. Adaptation thresholds

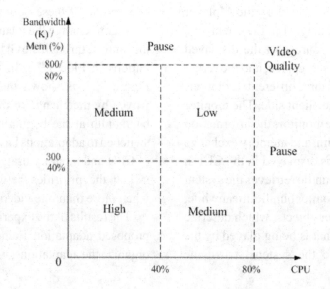

meet the user's requirements, and even change adaptation policies at runtime. Thus it could best meet the users' QoE and reduce the performance failure in mobile computations. In our demonstration, the video could be broadcast with minimal impact on quality of experience by reducing resolutions in stringent computation environments.

Our demo here is worked out as a proof of concept to show that our adaptation framework is able to switch adaptation policies at runtime and it is also capable to orchestrate adaptations on different applications. Thus the adaptation policies that we listed above are merely a proof of concept of our adaptation framework – finding efficient adaptation policies is out of the research scope of this paper.

CONCLUSION

This paper proposed a framework to organize adaptation in mobile terminals with the design goal of improving the user's QoE and reducing the performance failures. The framework is organized according to the event-condition-action model, which flexibly allows adaptations acting upon the changes of environment context. By coupling AOP and SOA in an OSGi environment, the architecture proposed in this paper achieves the following improvements:

- The proposed architecture provides a flexible way to detect the changes and take adaptations. Changes and adaptations include modifications of both services and parameters; however, both are treated in a uniform way.
- Through the GUI of our proposed architecture, users can easily discover system changes, and more importantly, they are made able to change the adaptation policies at runtime, thus best improving their QoE.

Further work will be carried out on embedding such a framework in the thin-client application architecture (Simoens et al., 2006) to assist the adaptation at the client's side. Applications of such an adaptation framework in homecare environment will be investigated aiming at constructing safety ambient assisted living environments for the elderly people in their surrounding environments (Sun, De Florio, Gui, & Blondia, 2010).

ACKNOWLEDGMENT

The authors would like to thank IBBT for supporting this work, and also our colleagues in the "End-to-End Quality of Experiences"[1] project for their cooperation.

REFERENCES

Costa, P., et al. (2007). The RUNES middleware for networked embedded systems and its application in a disaster management scenario. In *Proceedings of the 5th Annual IEEE Int. Conf. on Pervasive Computing and Communications*.

Cristian, F. (1991). Understanding Fault-Tolerant Distributed Systems. *Communications of the ACM, 34*(2), 56–78. doi:10.1145/102792.102801

De Florio, V., & Blondia, C. (2005). A System Structure for Adaptive Mobile Applications. In *Proceedings of the IEEE International Symposium on a World of Wireless, Mobile and Multimedia Networks 2005 (WOWMOM 2005)*, Giardini Naxos, Italy.

De Florio, V., & Blondia, C. (2007). Reflective and Refractive Variables: A Model for Effective and Maintainable Adaptive-and-Dependable Software. In *Proceedings of the 33rd Euromicro Conference on Software Engineering and Advanced Applications (SEEA 2007)*, Luebeck, Germany.

Edmonds, T. (2002). Pervasive Adaptation for Mobile Computing. In A. Hopper & S. Hodges (Eds.), *Proceedings of the 15th International Conference on Information Networking (ICOIN'01)*.

Equinox Aspect. (2008). Retrieved from http://www.eclipse.org/equinox/incubator/aspects/index.php

Etter, R., Costa, P., & Broens, T. (2006). A Rule-Based Approach Towards Context-Aware User Notification Services. In *Proceedings of the IEEE International Conference on Pervasive Services 2006*, Lyon, France (pp. 281-284).

Frei, A., & Alonso, G. (2005). A Dynamic Lightweight Platform for Ad-Hoc Infrastructures. In *Proceedings of the Third IEEE International Conference on Pervasive Computing and Communications* (pp. 373-382). Washington, DC: IEEE Computer Society.

Houssos, N., Gazis, V., & Alonistioti, N. (2003). A Novel Mechanism for Mobile Service Adaptation. In *Proceedings of the 57th IEEE Vehicular Technology Conference*.

Irmert, F., et al. (2007). Towards Runtime Adaptation in a SOA Environment. In *Proceedings of the 4th ECOOP Workshop on Reflection, AOP and Meta-Data for Software Evolution*.

Kephart, J., & Chess, D. (2003). The Vision of Autonomic Computing. *Computer, 36*(1). doi:10.1109/MC.2003.1160055

Kiczales, G., Lamping, J., Mendhekar, A., Maeda, C., Videira Lopes, C., Loingtier, J.-M., & Irwin, J. (1997). Aspect-Oriented Programming. In *Proceedings of the European Conference on Object-Oriented Programming (ECOOP)*, Finland.

Kiselev, I. (2002). *Aspect-Oriented Programming with AspectJ*. Indianapolis, IN: Sams.

Kon, F., Costa, F., Blair, G., & Campbell, R. (2002). The case for reflective middleware: building middleware that is flexible, reconfigurable, and yet simple to use. *Communications of the ACM, 45*(6), 33–38.

Lippert, M. (2004). AJEER: An AspectJ-Enabled Eclipse Runtime. In *Proceedings of Conference on Object Oriented Programming Systems Languages and Applications (OOPSLA '04)*, Vancouver, Canada. New York: ACM.

Lippert, M. *(2008). Aspect weaving for OSGi. In* Proceedings of Conference on Object Oriented Programming Systems Languages and Applications, Companion to the 23rd ACM SIGPLAN conference on Object-oriented programming systems languages and applications.

OSGi Alliance. (2008). *OSGi Service Platform* (Release 4.1).

Parnas, D. (1972). On the criteria to be used in decomposing systems into modules. *Communications of the ACM, 15*.

Sicard, S., Boyer, F., & De Palma, N. (2008). Using components for architecture-based management: the self-repair case. In *Proceedings of the 30th International Conference on Software Engineering*, Germany.

Simoens, P., Deboosere, L., De Winter, D., De Turck, F., Dhoedt, N., & Demeester, P. (2006). Optimization Models for Application Migration to Support Mobile Thin Clients. In *Proceedings of EuroNGI Workshop*.

Sun, H., De Florio, V., Gui, N., & Blondia, C. (2007). Global Adaptation Framework for Quality of Experience of Mobile Services. In *Proceedings of the 2007 IEEE Three-Rivers Workshop on Soft Computing in Industrial Applications*.

Sun, H., De Florio, V., Gui, N., & Blondia, C. (2010). The missings ones: Key ingredients towards effective ambient assisted living systems. *In the Journal of Ambient Intelligence and Smart Environments, 2,* 1-12.

ENDNOTE

1   Official website of End-to-end Quality of Experience: https://projects.ibbt.be/qoe/

This work was previously published in the International Journal of Adaptive, Resilient and Autonomic Systems, Volume 2, Issue 1, edited by Vincenzo De Florio, pp. 46-57, copyright 2011 by IGI Publishing (an imprint of IGI Global).

Chapter 12
Various Extensions for the Ambient OSGi Framework

Stéphane Frénot
University of Lyon, INRIA INSA-Lyon, F-69621, France

Frédéric Le Mouël
University of Lyon, INRIA INSA-Lyon, F-69621, France

Julien Ponge
University of Lyon, INRIA INSA-Lyon, F-69621, France

Guillaume Salagnac
University of Lyon, INRIA INSA-Lyon, F-69621, France

ABSTRACT

OSGi is a wrapper above the Java Virtual Machine that embraces two concepts: component approach and service-oriented programming. The component approach enables a Java run-time to host several concurrent applications, while the service-oriented programming paradigm allows the decomposition of applications into independent units that are dynamically bound at runtime. Combining component and service-oriented programming greatly simplifies the implementation of highly adaptive, constantly evolving applications. This, in turn, is an ideal match to the requirements and constraints of ambient intelligence computing, such as adaptation to changes associated with context evolution. OSGi particularly fits ambient requirements and constraints by absorbing and adapting to changes associated with context evolution. However, OSGi needs to be finely tuned in order to integrate ambient specific issues. This paper focuses on Zero-configuration architecture, Multi-provider framework, and Limited resource requirements. The authors studied many OSGi improvements that should be taken into account when building OSGi-based gateways. This paper summarizes the INRIA Amazones teamwork (http:// amazones.gforge.inria.fr/) on extending OSGi specifications and implementations to cope with ambient concerns. This paper references three main concerns: management, isolation, and security.

DOI: 10.4018/978-1-4666-2056-8.ch012

INTRODUCTION

Using OSGi technology in ambient environments requires focusing on specific problems such footprint of the run-time framework, zero configuration of the application and service provisioning for multi-provider environments. Because ambient intelligence is, and will remain, based on hardware with limited resources, the size and complexity of the framework have to be kept under control. The kind of platform we address is that of middle-sized devices, like smart phones, set-top boxes or automotive embedded systems. They have much more computing resources than tiny embedded systems like micro-controllers, but much less then commodity PCs or traditional servers. We call these platforms gateway devices, since most of the time they act as intermediaries between a local network of services and the Internet. As an illustration, the platforms we used in our experimentations were ARM-based devices as the LinkSys NSLU2 (266Mhz CPU, 32MB RAM, 8MB Flash) or sheeva PC plugs (1.2Ghz CPU, 521MB RAM, 512MB flash).

Devices for ambient environment should work in an autonomic way without any user interaction apart from network and electrical connections and hardware factory resets. They should address many kinds of concurrent applications from many providers. Each of them shall have its own running space, where he is able to manage its own local information and interact with local equipments. This management model is similar to the Apple and Android store model where the end-user has the ability to choose its hosted applications, and where each of them may have its own autonomy. This implies a dynamic architecture where each service provider may have an application life-cycle that is neither bounded nor constrained by the gateway system and hardware life-cycle. Furthermore, various external constraints such as costs and environmental issues distinguish gateway hardware from data-centers. The former has resource constrains both in memory and processing power that are not compliant with full best-effort developed applications.

In this article, we compiled most of our current OSGi-related proposals in order to have a synthetic view of the investigated extensions. The paper is divided in three sections. First we summarize the OSGi framework and focuses on our specific concerns. Next, we present each provided extension as a walkthrough of our various publications. The last section synthesizes our proposed extensions.

OSGi Context

OSGi (http://www.osgi.org/Main/HomePage) is a container framework built on top of the Java platform. It hosts deployment units called *bundles*, which contain Java resources such as compiled classes, properties files or dynamically linked native libraries. Each bundle features an *Activator* class, which is the entry point to be notified when the bundle is started or stopped. A descriptor, expressed as a regular Java manifest, details meta-data such as the *Activator* qualified name, or the various requirements the bundle expects, such as the presence of another bundle exposing a specific Java package.

The OSGi platform automatically checks dependencies between bundles and controls the life-cycle of each bundle. One key feature of the OSGi framework is the seamless support of application deployment: new applications can be installed, updated and uninstalled at runtime without requiring a restart of the Java virtual machine itself, thanks to classloaders native isolation. This streamlines administration enables multiple hosted applications installed as independent deployment units.

Bundles are typically materialized as JAR archives that can even be fetched by the OSGi framework from a remote HTTP server. Each bundle is associated with a dedicated Java class loader that provides resource isolation with respect to the other bundles. Unlike the local, closed classloader hierarchies found in standard Java applications, OSGi provides a dynamic hierarchy of classloaders with a fine control of which classes and resources should be exposed or not. At deployment time, the bundle manifest indicates which packages are made public and which packages the bundle depends on.

The OSGi underlying programming model focuses on Service-Oriented Programming (SOP) (http://openwings.org/). The driving motivation for SOP is to minimize coupling among software elements of an application. A service is an interface that describes what a software entity provides in terms of API binding requirements. In turn, several implementations can be provided for the same interface and their details remain hidden to the service requesters. Combining dynamic bundle management and SOP awareness enables continuous application evolution at run-time within the same virtual machine instance.

OSGi Extensions

Ambient architectures we studied so-far exposed three main concerns: gateway autonomy, multi-provider application hosting and security. Also OSGi provides many ways to help develop and enforce ambient application in a generic and standard way, it still presents limitations. Since 2004, we provided many extensions to the OSGi framework to cope with these limitations. Most of them focus on the bundle management layer and aim at providing sound answers to the next three questions:

1. How can we improve bundle management and deployment?
2. How can we optimize the run-time environment for bundles?
3. How can we enforce security for the deployed bundles?

Deployment and security concerns influence autonomic behavior. Deployment, Run-time optimization and Security are of high consideration when building a multi-provider architecture. Run-time optimization and Security enforcements directly impacts limited resource equipments where resource control is a matter of importance. In the three next sections, we detail the various OSGi extensions trying to answer those questions.

Bundle Management and Deployment.

When dealing with ambient environments we consider that the gateway is remotely managed by providers and end-user and that it performs as many autonomous activities as it can on low cost, low energy, low noise electronic device. Although OSGi enables software management within gateways, it initially has a very primitive way of handling service deployment and management. An initial remote console to interact with bundle was the only provided management solution. Service providers must be able to install new applications on remote gateways and be able to both manage their behaviors and monitor their execution (Royon & Frénot, 2007). In this purpose we provided two extensions: the first is a full implementation of OSGi remote management specification and the second one focuses on an efficient bundle deployment layer.

MOSGi

Management was one of the OSGi specification concerns, which were not implemented in the first place. We developed and donated to the Apache Felix community (http://felix.apache.org/site/index.html) the MOSGi framework that mainly consists in a wrapper around the JMX management protocol (Fleury & Frénot, 2003). We provided an end-to-end management layer that covers both the gateway and the client-side part of the architecture. One can find both a run-time for the gateway handling local probes and a run-time manager for the client.

It is worth noting that the manager was also developed as an OSGi bundle and thus provides a really interesting dynamic use-case. When a probe is started on the gateway side, it provides two facets: (1) the MBean facets that provides the management API compliant with the JMX protocol, (2) a specific MOSGi facet that is used by the client side to get a graphical user interface interacting with the remote probe. The client is dynamic: when it connects to the gateway, it requests for the list of installed probes that correspond to the JMX facet integration. Then, for each probe it checks whether it complies with the specific MOSGi facet. If so, it asks the probe for an URL that provides a bundle that brings the graphical user interface. This dynamically discovered graphical bundle is plugged into the manager and starts interacting with the gateway. As an example, the running use-case of the MUSE project (D'Haeseleer, 2008) was that of a user buying a fridge. When the fridge is installed at the home environment, the set-top box gateway downloads a fridge management probe. When the fridge vendor has to remotely access the fridge, its local manager downloads a graphical user interface that can communicate with the fridge probe and provides a dedicated management user interface.

When we developed the MOSGi framework in a multi-provider environment, one issue was to understand the management limits. If any provider can ask for probing information, the management layer can overload the gateway. If the remote manager asks for the fridge temperature every tenth of a second the gateway can fall in some kind of Denial of Service state and not be able to do other things. We developed a monitoring scheduling process for gateway devices (Frénot et al., 2008) through which we wondered if we could anticipate the increase in CPU load when a new probe is inserted into the gateway. The provided approach

is a specific bench generator that measures every installed JMX probe and stores its response time. We showed that the targeted gateway CPU loading curve was regular, and that the combination of the various curves leads to good CPU load schedules. If the equipment provider indicates the probe and the pace he wants to query, we can anticipate the CPU load increment. By way of consequences, we can make a distinction between normal behavior and a probe failure since we can observe and anticipate a homogeneous load activity.

POSGi

Traditionally, OSGi bundles are installed from a remote web server using an HTTP URL such as *start* http://www.somehost.com/abundle.jar. But in ambient environment, simultaneous deployment of the same software component onto a large number of devices may overwhelm the server behind www.somehost.com. The server behind www.somehost.com may host many bundles and can be overwhelmed by a peak in installation requests.

Our Peer-to-Peer (P2P) OSGi extension focuses on efficient and resilient deployment of OSGi bundles. The goal of this system is to substitute the traditional centralized bundle repositories with a P2P architecture. By using a P2P approach, we can avoid server failure during peak installation request period since every gateway can be part of the global, distributed repository. We used Freepastry (http://www.freepastry.org/) as a Distributed Hash Table (DHT) overlay network where every gateway and every bundle obtains a specific Freepastry id. DHT yields an efficient routing algorithm between two ids. When sending a new bundle to the network of gateways, it is routed towards the gateway that has the nearest Freepastry id from its own id. When one gateway needs to install a bundle, its request is routed hop-by-hop towards the root gateway that handles the initial archive. On the way back, each gateway on the route can locally store the initial archive. If, later, another gateway needs the same bundle, it can be provided either by the root gateway or by any gateway that handles the bundle on the route. POSGi (Frénot & Royon, 2005) enables URL installation schemes such as *p2p://abundle.jar*. The implementation impacts the OSGi URL scheme handler, adds an alternate local cache where bundles are stored from the Freepastry overlay and a bundle that offers the P2P management.

Discussion

Ambient environments are directly influenced by both deployment and management layers. When dealing with multiple providers acting on the same equipment, each one must have their own management vision of it. If for instance the home gateway manages a specific fridge and a specific vacuum cleaner, each provider may remotely manage these equipments without interfering with others. The MOSGi architecture is a first direction that enables this function. If one of the providers must upgrade to a new version all its bundles a P2P approach such as POSGi presents many advantages in regards to efficiency. For the end-user, an autonomic deployment and management layers are very important, since the end-user equipment should be as simple and standard as other legacy ones. For instance, in a home gateway, there should be no user interface at all. MOSGi and POSGi frameworks bring autonomic and multi-provider support for deploying and managing applications in ambient environments without any user interaction.

This section described the early phases of bundle life-cycle; the next section focuses on the main execution phase through various run-time extensions.

Run-Time Extensions

Java virtual machines combined with the OSGi framework is the operating system solution for handling multi-provider, multi-applications within a heterogeneous hardware environment. Neverthe-

less Java was not designed with a multi-session philosophy in mind. OSGi is a direction in providing component isolation, but it still has the best-effort scheme imposed by Java. Bundle isolation is not as perfect world as we can imagine, if a bundle does not behave in the proper manner it can stop the virtual machine. By specifications, OSGI, it's all sweetness and light. In a multi-provider and autonomic approach, unless a global manager holds everything, we need to be much more on our guards. A stopped bundle may be effectively stopped, which implies that al reserved resources during bundle execution should be released when stopped. As it is not the case, Amazones observed this issue through many directions.

OSGi Sandboxing

OSGi sandboxing aims at isolating bundle execution and management one from each other. The sandboxing issues we initially investigated were related to the MUSE multi-provider architecture. Indeed, if we host many bundles from various providers on the same gateway, they should be isolated one from each other as they could be in competition. One bundle should not interfere with the one from the other providers. Sandboxing has many levels of granularity on virtual machines: (1) bundle naming isolation, (2) coding design for proper isolation, and (3) low-level resources isolation within a virtual machine. We investigated all these three level of isolation.

Virtual OSGi. VOSGi (Royon et al.,2006) is a rather naive implementation where we provide OSGi itself as a service. The service provides a single start/stop interface that instantiates or nullifies a brand new OSGi implementation within the first one. With this, we can assign a specific provider to an OSGi gateway that virtually runs within another OSGi gateway. We provide a start/stop gateway management shell command available from the main gateway, which is in turn called the *core gateway*. When running multiple OSGi instance in the same management shell, commands are not associated with a specific gateway. In order to interact with each virtual gateway, we developed a specific MOSGi probe that enables to remotely manage the virtual instances.

Although running new OSGi instance within one instance is rather straightforward, difficulties raise when these instances need to communicate with each other. A virtual gateway may use services provided by another gateway, either the core gateway or another virtual gateway. Our current implementation only enables service exchanges from the core gateway to virtual gateways. When starting a virtual gateway, it declares the service interfaces it wishes to access from the core gateway. At virtual gateway bootstrap time, it receives references to the various corresponding implementations and registers each transmitted implementation within its own registry. Hence, each service exchanged between a core and a virtual gateway is declared in both registries and points to the same implementation.

Nevertheless, one remaining problem in the VOSGi approach is that the OSGi ``standard'' behavior does not enforce ``true'' bundle isolation: bundles can obtain as many system resources as they want such as network connections, threads, and so on. There is no way to constrain a bundle contract within the framework. Moreover, any class can stop the entire virtual machine through a call to *java.lang.System.exit(0)*. This is a serious issue when hosting multi-provider bundles that may not be ``honest''. We focused on two developments to improve bundle isolation. The first one is based on development contract conformance enforcement, while the second one is based on a dedicated virtual machine.

Suspend and Resume (Dunklau & Frénot, 2009). This INRIA technical report raises one simple problem linked to the bundle lifecycle. In the OSGi specifications, bundles can be in the following states: Installed, Resolved and Active. Although this life cycle seems complete, we believe that it lacks a Suspended state. Considering that ambient equipment may be paused and

resumed and not systematically rebooted, the Suspended state is a real ambient need as bundle may be suspended in order to free its resource, in case of exhaustion. For instance, the gateway manages run-time profiles, such as *"high-priority"*, *"standard,"* or *"night supervision"*. It may have to pause bundles when switching to specific profiles. This suspend state necessity arises each time we need to reconfigure partially the gateway. At present, the only way of doing it is by managing an internal state when stopping and starting the bundle. It is impossible to distinguish between rebooting and suspending a bundle. One problem raised by introducing the Suspended state is that it impacts mostly the run-time model. The Suspended state needs to suspend threads, network connections and all running activities.

When dealing with the programming model, accessing resources is restricted to some kind of dispatcher. It allocates resources to requesters and maintains a whiteboard associating requesters to resources. When suspension time occurs, the dispatcher knows exactly which resource i.e. bundle is associated to each requester. In this approach, every direct call to a specific resource allocation should be transferred to a dispatcher that manages identifications. Our implementation adds a specific Apache Felix shell command that integrates the *suspend #bundleid* action and a specific *Bundle-SuspendableActivator* Java interface that adds two hooked methods for suspending and resuming a bundle. Our architecture currently focuses on the threading architecture and only provides a dispatcher to allocate threads and suspend them automatically. A similar work should be done for network connections.

Although this architecture is rather simple to put under operation, it is still dependent on the good will of bundle developers: if they provide only standard OSGi bundle, these can still be hosted on the gateway, but may present unmanageable behavior. The only workaround for this issue is to constrain bundle behavior at the virtual machine level.

iJVM Project. The iJVM (Geoffray et al., 2009) project aims at designing a virtu al machine for constrained environment that enforces resource control mechanisms. Even though iJVM had security issues in mind, its main goal is to provide an efficient isolation layer for bundle requesting resources while preserving an efficient communication layer between isolated bundles. iJVM provides three main features for OSGi bundles: (1) memory isolation, (2) resource accounting and (3) isolates termination.

Discussion

VOSGi, Suspend and Resume, and iJVM projects target run-time isolation for bundle code. The OSGi bundle paradigm offers the appropriate granularity level to enforce isolation. Depending on the desired isolation guarantees, each approach offers different level ranging from simple naming isolation, to a hard, resource constrained, environment. But the harder the constraints are enforced, the lesser standard and generic the architecture is.

While trying to enforce isolation and since target hardware platforms have limited resources, we also addressed run-time code optimization.

Run-Time Code Optimization

Most of the time bundle life-cycle is human driven either by the end-user or the remote provider. In our run-time optimization investigations, we tried to find more automated ways for handling those updates. Two directions were developed for tackling them: the ROCS architecture and the AxSel framework.

ROCS. The Remotely Provisioned OSGi framework for Ambient Systems (Frénot et al., 2010) project leverages a very simple standard Java principle, which is that of remote classes loading. Before starting the activator of a bundle, the OSGi framework performs the following activities. It downloads the bundle from a remote location, extracts the jar file on a local cache, extracts the

bundle descriptor to control bundle coherence with the current running environment and, provided everything is right, it loads the activator class and invokes its *start* method. ROCS proposes to manage all these activities through a remote approach. The gateway relies on a remote server that hosts the bundles and responds to gateway remote queries. Exploiting the Java remote class loading is straightforward with the OSGi framework. The usage scenario is the following.

When installing a new bundle, it is downloaded from the repository to a remote server and the gateway obtains a local proxy to interact with the remote server. It asks for the bundle manifest, downloads the file from the remote Jar and controls the meta-data to see if every dependency is satisfied. If so, it remotely loads into memory the corresponding *BundleActivator* byte-code and starts the bundle. Then, all subsequent required classes are downloaded on-demand through the *RemoteClassLoader*.

This remote architecture has also been applied to the standard Java runtime classes (i.e., *java.** and *javax.** packages) such that it is considered as a plain bundle. We put the necessary classes to bootstrap a minimal OSGi/Java stack into a local classpath classloader. Once started, all remaining standard classes are downloaded from the remote location. Trough our approach, we build an entire OSGi/Java run-time stack that can be hosted on small equipments, less than 8MB of flash, since all loaded classes come from remote locations and are directly brought into memory. ROCS demonstrates that, provided we are connected, we have the same kind of response time as if, we locally cached all bundle classes.

AxSel. Whereas ROCS focuses on loading classes contained in remote bundles, AxSel (Ben Hamida et al., 2008) aims at optimizing class loading at the service granularity level. The Service-Oriented Programming feature of OSGi specifications enables the description of an applications as a composition of services. One application can have implementation variations, depending on the environment. For instance, when using a standard OSGi bundle repository, all dependent bundles are automatically downloaded into the gateway, and then started. A local service maintains a dependency graph from *Package-Import* and *Package-Export* statements of the bundle manifest. We exploit the *ImportService* manifest property to also maintain a dependency graph between parts of the application. The AxSel framework holds an internal representation of the run-time and regularly polls remote repositories to find new or alternate implementations. When the gateway is in idle mode, it triggers a reconfiguration process that calculates for every dependent element, bundle or service, if it can find a better implementation. If so, bundles are updated and services are automatically reconfigured.

Discussion

AxSel and ROCS are complementary approaches: the ROCS system enables a minimal run-time where everything is downloaded on-demand within the main memory, and AxSel brings automatic reconfiguration and optimization of the running environment.

Ambient environments need to cope with autonomy, multi-providers and some resource control issues. The various sandboxing frameworks we studied so far aim at empowering application autonomy and multi-provider integration within ambient environments. They enable providers behave as if they were using the system alone. Achieving autonomy is much easier as you can do whatever you want without disturbing your neighbors. Although sandboxing enable application to feel isolated, the underlying system still has to cope with its limited resources. Axsel and ROCS are a first proposal toward dynamic resource management in ambient environment. ROCS focuses on getting the minimal quantity of execution code into memory, whereas Axsel

aims at continuously finding better configuration opportunities. They both influence autonomy and resource awareness of ambient systems.

Most of the dynamic features of OSGi framework presented so far, load byte-code into memory from remote locations or from downloaded bundles. We identified many security issues when dealing with isolation. All these concerns led to consider security as specific and generic concern that needs dedicated attention.

Security around OSGi

Most of the time security in ambient environment is a primary concern, and most of the time security in constrained environment is disabled since it has a very high cost. OSGi mostly extends Java security elements without considering their run-time cost. Amazones felt that OSGi component and service paradigms bring new clues for improving application security while also bringing new ways of disturbing an environment. We started a security activity around OSGi to identify both new breakages and design new ways of handling security.

Security issues in the OSGi/Java stack are spanning across many points. They arise both at low-level (e.g., bundle code signing) and high-level parts of the OSGi stack (e.g., deployment). The overall OSGi picture reveals many points where security needs enforcements. Our overall approach identified the following elements.

• **Deployment:** Bundles are downloaded from remote locations. Thus, we need some strong guarantees from those locations regarding the origins and integrity of the bundles. The OSGi specification proposes a signing process that identifies bundle sources and providers, but when we started our study, no implementation was available.

- **Bundle:** Downloaded bundles can lead to two kinds of security breaches. Indeed, they can contain code that directly harms the system, or they can contain code that weakens the framework. We need to consider the two issues to decide whether a bundle is a threat to the framework, and whether it opens security flaws that could be locally / remotely exploited.

- **Framework:** The OSGi specification does not enforce security constraints, as they are mainly implementation issues. Most of current framework implementations are subject to instability if malevolent bundles are installed.

A preliminary work has been conducted to design a bundle signing architecture. This work has been achieved in the context of the MUSE European project where we designed a tool-chain to sign bundles and verify their validity at deployment time. The architecture is detailed in Parrend and Frénot (2006, 2007b). An implementation is available with the SFelix project (http://sfelix.gforge.inria.fr/).

After having designed this tool-chain, we worked on a bundle threats catalog aimed at identifying OSGi security weaknesses. The catalog elements and summary are detailed in Parrend and Frénot (2007a, 2008a, 2008c).

We applied those catalogs to design a hardened OSGi / Java framework. The Parrend and Frénot (2009) article stresses OSGi open-source framework vulnerabilities and expresses guidelines to develop hardened implementations. Yet, some vulnerabilities cannot be controlled at the OSGi framework layer and need to be addressed at the Java Virtual Machine layer. The iJVM (Geoffray et al., 2009) virtual machine for isolating threads was mainly designed for this purpose.

The last track we followed when dealing with security concerns was to be able to statically analyze the code of bundles. We developed an install-time analyzer that introspects bundles compiled code to detect vulnerabilities. CBAC (Parrend & Frénot, 2008b) describes the proposal. The CBAC control is triggered at the same time as the digital verification signature process, thus only inducing an overhead at deployment time. Unlike the standard Java permissions built-in framework, the CBAC security model does not have any runtime overhead.

Discussion

Security improvement within ambient environment is a primary concern. Autonomic computing, multi-provider and limited Resources concerns are all influenced by security issues. When installing, managing, upgrading applications, one has to guarantee that the system still behaves as before, that it does not consume much more resources and that it does not break provider isolation by trying to transfer private data throughout the system. Limited resource architecture influence security architecture since they all come with a non negligible cost and most of the time they need to be disabled in order to have a viable system. Amazones proposals cover many directions to easy security management. They all converge to some kind of benchmark tools to control ambient system security conformity but both metrics and levels still need proper definitions.

Synthesis

The OSGi extensions that we presented address issues such as management, run-time optimization and security. We summarized our contributions in Table 1.

All our extensions have been developed under the Apache Felix project. Some of them, VOSGi, MOSGi, Unsecured Bundle Catalog have also been validated on Concierge (Rellermeyer & Alonso, 2007). They all run on standard Intel-based architectures, but many of them, MOSGi, VOSGi, ROCS, SFelix, have also been validated on a NSLU2 (http://en.gentoo-wiki.com/wiki/

Table 1. Extensions to the OSGi space

Extension	Domain	References
MOSGi	Management	(Royon & Frénot, 2007; Fleury & Frénot, 2003; Frénot et al., 2008)
POSGi	Management	(Frénot & Royon, 2005)
VOSGi	Runtime	(Royon et al., 2006)
Suspend & Resume	Runtime	(Dunklau & Frénot, 2009)
iJVM	Runtime	(Geoffray et al., 2009)
ROCS	Runtime	(Frénot et al., 2010)
AxSel	Runtime	(Ben Hamida et al., 2008)
SFelix	Security	(Parrend & Frénot, 2006, 2007b)
Unsecured Bundle Catalog	Security	(Parrend & Frénot, 2007a, 2008a, 2008c)
Hardened OSGi	Security	(Parrend & Frénot, 2009; Geoffray et al., 2009)
CBAC	Security	(Parrend & Frénot, 2008b)

Gentoo/_on/_NSLU2) ARM board, with a dedicated JamVM / GNU Classpath execution stack. All the code that we developed is available from the INRIA GForge project and can be obtained by sending us an email. All code is provided under either the Apache Software License version 2.0 (http://www.apache.org/licenses/), or one of the CeCill licenses (http://www.cecill.info/).

The provided extensions impact various elements of the OSGi specifications and implementations as summarized in the Table 2.

- **Specification Implementation:** MOSGi and SFclix propose implementation of OSGi specifications that are not included in the open-source implementations.

- **Framework Patch:** VOSGi, Suspend & Resume, ROCS, Hardened OSGi need patching some specific version of Apache Felix to operate. Most of the time, the patches correspond to very few lines of code and some extended classes.

- **Bundle Lifecycle Modifications:** Some of our extensions point out the necessity of extending the standard bundle lifecycle (*Resolved, Installed, Active*) through new status. *Suspended* for Suspend & Resume, *Invalid* for SFelix.

- **Tools:** Tools are elements that do not interfere with the standard OSGi/Java stack. They provide non-intrusive additional services to the framework.

Since iJVM impacts the underlying virtual machine it does not directly concern the OSGi framework.

OSGi is a very interesting environment. Its simplicity and pragmatism are keys to build efficient run-time systems. The INRIA Ama-

Table 2. Impacted OSGi elements conclusion

Extension	Specification	Patch	Lifecycle	Tool
MOSGi	X	O	O	X
POSGi	O	O	O	X
VOSGi	O	X	O	O
Suspend & Resume	O	X	X	O
iJVM	O	O	O	O
ROCS	O	X	O	O
AxSel	O	O	O	X
SFelix	X	O	X	X
Unsecured Bundle Catalog	O	O	O	X
Hardened OSGi	O	O	O	O
CBAC	O	X	X	O

zones team focuses on ambient environments and provides extensions that cope with ambient constraints such as limited memory size, remote access, dynamism, context awareness and energy efficiency. Our extensions depend on framework implementations, and as such, they are rather difficult to keep up-to-date with upstream codebase changes. Our current policy is to keep those extensions alive for specific upstream project versions, and to provide upgrades when needed. At present, and due to limited resources within our team, only the MOSGi framework has been donated to the main Apache Felix codebase, under the *mosgi* submodule in the project Subversion repository.

We are still working on various extensions to the framework in different directions. We integrate device mobility concerns in some of our projects and log management features to enhance fault management. However, those projects are still under development and need further validation before publication.

ACKNOWLEDGMENT

Most of this work would not have been made without PhD students and research engineers. PhD works, mostly in French, of Ben Hamida (2010), Ibrahim (2008), Parrend (2008) and Royon (2007) had direct impacts on our extensions and we gratefully thank them all.

REFERENCES

Ben Hamida, A. (2010). *AxSeL: Un intergiciel pour le déploiement contextuel et autonome de services dans les environnements pervasifs*. Unpublished doctoral dissertation, INSA de Lyon, Villeurbanne, France.

Ben Hamida, A., Le Mouël, F., Frénot, S., & Ben Ahmed, M. (2008). A graph-based approach for contextual service loading in pervasive environments. In R. Meersman & Z. Tari (Eds.), *Proceedings of the Federated International Conferences of On the Move to Meaningful Internet Systems*, Monterrey, Mexico (LNCS 5331, pp. 589-606).

D'Haeseleer, S. (2008). *DB 3.1: Detailed requirement-based functional specification of gateway: Part 1: Private network (Tech. Rep. No. MUSE IST-6thFP-507295)*. Brussels, Belgium: MUSE.

Dunklau, R., & Frénot, S. (2009). *Proposal for a suspend/resume extension to the OSGi specification* (Tech. Rep. No. RR-7060). Le Chesnay, France: INRIA.

Fleury, E., & Frénot, S. (2003). *Building a JMX management interface inside OSGi* (Tech. Rep. No. RR-5025). Le Chesnay, France: INRIA.

Frénot, S., Ibrahim, N., Le Mouël, F., Ben Hamida, A., Ponge, J., Chantrel, M., et al. (2010). ROCS: A remotely provisioned OSGi framework for ambient systems. In *Proceedings of the Symposium on Network Operations and Management*, Osaka Japan (pp. 503-510). Washington, DC: IEEE Computer Society.

Frénot, S., & Royon, Y. (2005). Component deployment using a peer-to-peer overlay. In A. Dearle & S. Eisenbach (Eds.), *Proceedings of the Third International Working Conference on Component Deployment*, Grenoble, France (LNCS 3798, pp. 33-36).

Frénot, S., Royon, Y., Parrend, P., & Beras, D. (2008). Monitoring scheduling for home gateways. In *Proceedings of the Symposium on Network Operations and Management*, Salvador de Bahia, Brazil (pp. 411-416). Washington, DC: IEEE Computer Society.

Geoffray, N., Thomas, G., Muller, G., Parrend, P., Frénot, S., & Folliot, B. (2009). I-JVM: A java virtual machine for component isolation in OSGi. In *Proceedings of the International Conference on Dependable Systems and Networks*, Estoril, Portugal (pp. 544-553).

Ibrahim, N. (2008). *Spontaneous integration of services in pervasive environments*. Unpublished doctoral dissertation, INSA de Lyon, Villeurbanne, France.

Parrend, P. (2008). *Modèles de Sécurité logicielle pour les plates-formes a`composants de service (SOP)*. Unpublished doctoral dissertation, INSA de Lyon, Villeurbanne, France.

Parrend, P., & Frénot, S. (2006). *Secure component deployment in the OSGi(tm) release 4 platform* (Tech. Rep. No. RT-0323). Le Chesnay, France: INRIA.

Parrend, P., & Frénot, S. (2007a). *Java components vulnerabilities - an experimental classification targeted at the OSGi platform* (Tech. Rep. No. RR-6231). Le Chesnay, France: INRIA.

Parrend, P., & Frénot, S. (2007b). Supporting the secure deployment of OSGi bundles. In *Proceedings of the International Symposium on a World of Wireless, Mobile and Multimedia Networks*, Helsinki, Finland (pp. 1-6). Washington, DC: IEEE Computer Society.

Parrend, P., & Frénot, S. (2008a). Classification of component vulnerabilities in java service oriented programming (sop) platforms. In M. R. V. Chaudron, C. Szyperski, & R. Reussner (Eds.), *Proceedings of the 11th International Symposium on Component-Based Software Engineering*, Karlsruhe, Germany (LNCS 5282, pp. 80-96).

Parrend, P., & Frénot, S. (2008b). Component-based access control: Secure software composition through static analysis. In C. Pautasso & E. Tanter (Eds.), *Proceedings of the 7th International Symposium on Software Composition*, Budapest, Hungary (LNCS 4954, pp. 68-83).

Parrend, P., & Frénot, S. (2008c). *More vulnerabilities in the Java/OSGi platform: A focus on bundle interactions* (Tech. Rep. No. RR-6649). Le Chesnay, France: INRIA.

Parrend, P., & Frénot, S. (2009). Security benchmarks of OSGi platforms: Towards hardened OSGi. *Journal of Software Practice and Experience, 39*(5), 471–499. doi:10.1002/spe.906

Rellermeyer, J. S., & Alonso, G. (2007). Concierge: A service platform for resource-constrained devices. In *Proceedings of the European Conference on Computer Systems* (pp. 245-258). New York, NY: ACM Press.

Royon, Y. (2007). *Environnements d'exécution pour passerelles domestiques*. Unpublished doctoral dissertation, INSA de Lyon, Villeurbanne, France.

Royon, Y., & Frénot, S. (2007). Multiservice home gateways: Business model, execution environment, management infrastructure. *IEEE Communications Magazine, 45*(10), 122–128. doi:10.1109/MCOM.2007.4342834

Royon, Y., Frénot, S., & Le Mouël, F. (2006). Virtualization of service gateways in multi-provider environments. In I. Gorton, G. T. Heineman, I. Crnkovic, H. W. Schmidt, J. A. Stafford, C. Szyperski et al. (Eds.), *Proceedings of the 9th International Symposium on Component-Based Software Engineering*, Stockholm, Sweden (LNCS 4063, pp. 385-392).

This work was previously published in the International Journal of Adaptive, Resilient and Autonomic Systems, Volume 2, Issue 3, edited by Vincenzo De Florio, pp. 1-12, copyright 2011 by IGI Publishing (an imprint of IGI Global).

Chapter 13
A Distributed Monitoring Framework for Opportunistic Communication Systems:
An Experimental Approach

Iacopo Carreras
CREATE-NET, Italy

Andrea Zanardi
CREATE-NET, Italy

Elio Salvadori
CREATE-NET, Italy

Daniele Miorandi
CREATE-NET, Italy

ABSTRACT

Opportunistic communication systems aim at producing and sharing digital resources by means of localized wireless data exchanges among mobile nodes. The design and evaluation of systems able to exploit this emerging communication paradigm is a challenging problem. This paper presents the authors' experience in developing U-Hopper, a middleware running over widely diffused mobile handsets and supporting the development of context-aware services based on opportunistic communications. The authors present the design of the platform, and describe the distributed monitoring framework that was set up in order to monitor and dynamically reconfigure it at run time. The paper concludes with an experimental evaluation of the framework, showing its practical utilization when monitoring an operational opportunistic communication system.

DOI: 10.4018/978-1-4666-2056-8.ch013

1. INTRODUCTION

The proliferation of mobile technologies such as mobile phones, gaming consoles and MP3 players, equipped with short-range wireless communication technologies (e.g., Bluetooth and WiFi) has encouraged the development of applications that allow users to produce, access and share digital resources in a wide number of everyday occasions without relying on a fixed telecommunication infrastructure. The communication paradigm behind these application scenarios is referred as "opportunistic communications" (Pelusi et al., 2006), and is based on the possibility of exchanging data whenever in mutual communication range. The applications behind this communication paradigm have addressed the possibility for users to access data from certain locations (location-based) or to share contents with other users in proximity (mobile peer-to-peer). Examples include mobile social networking (Aka-Aki), where users exploit opportunistic communications to share information, distributed computing scenarios (Tan et al., 2007), where the opportunistic replication of data is used to, e.g., recovery data in case of a device failure, or Delay Tolerant Networks (DTNs) (Fall, 2003), where the nodes of network act as data carriers in order to let messages reach the intended destinations.

In this work we focus on mobile social computing. The importance of these application scenarios is mainly determined by two factors. On the one hand, it is a direct consequence of the widespread diffusion of mobile devices (e.g., smartphones or PDAs). On the other, such devices are constantly increasing their computing, communication and storage power. Several mobile phones are in fact equipped with Bluetooth and Wi-Fi technologies, which are directly accessible for programmers through freely available and easy-to-use APIs. Furthermore, mobile phones are now capable of intensive processing operations and of storing and processing large amounts of data in their internal memory. This is significantly changing the use that people make of mobile phones: originally conceived for making calls, they are becoming nowadays platforms for entertainment, for running data and communication intensive mobile applications. This has led to creative and innovative application scenarios, mobile social computing being one of the most popular ones.

Opportunistic communication systems have been deeply investigated from a theoretical viewpoint. Such studies explored the many tradeoffs existing between the performance of the system, and the resources allocated for running it (Zhang et al., 2007). Typically, the performance of an opportunistic system (e.g., end-to-end delay) is inversely proportional to the resources utilized for running the system (e.g., number of copies introduced for each message): the more copies are generated for each message, the faster it will reach the intended destination. Congestion is generally not an issue, since we are dealing mostly with sparse scenarios, where nodes are assumed to be isolated most of the time.

Most of the research in opportunistic networking has been devoted to the definition of forwarding mechanisms capable of optimally exploiting such trade off. Conversely, limited work has been done in the literature to study the many challenges related to the design, engineering and operation of such systems.

Following these considerations, we have developed a User-centric Heterogeneous Opportunistic Middleware (Create-Net, 2008), which is a middleware platform running over any Java-enabled smartphone and leveraging Bluetooth connectivity for exchanging data. Such platform provides all the necessary programming abstractions for developing opportunistic mobile services, and transparently handles all the necessary operations that are needed in order to dynamically program data gathering tasks.

In this paper, we present an overview of the U-Hopper platform and describe our experience in developing, evaluating and testing opportunistic mobile applications running over commercially available platforms. We describe the distributed monitoring framework that is part of the U-Hopper platform and allows to gather system information such as, e.g., memory usage, data exchange success rate, etc., from all nodes of the network. This information is then post-processed in order to extract system-wide performance figures. This is of paramount importance in order to fine-tune the operations of the opportunistic communication system, and permits to monitor the existing tradeoff between the resources allocated for running the system and the overall performance.

We validated both the U-Hopper middleware and the distributed monitoring framework in a small-scale field trial. This consisted in 11 co-workers carrying around for three days a mobile phone running the U-Hopper platform. Messages were exchanged opportunistically and the overall system performance (e.g., end-to-end delay vs. number of copies) was measured thanks to the monitoring framework running on the U-Hopper platform and regularly collecting system information.

The remainder of this paper is organized as follows. In Section 2 we provide a general overview of opportunistic communication systems, including a description of the most promising application scenarios and of the main challenges that developers need to address when designing such systems. In Section 3 we describe the main choices behind the design of the U-Hopper system. In Section 4 we present the methodology and the testbed we set up in order to evaluate the performance of the system. Finally, Section 5 draws the conclusions of this work, and outlines some promising research directions to pursue.

2. OPPORTUNISTIC COMMUNICATION SYSTEMS

Opportunistic communications (Pelusi et al., 2006) initially emerged as a communication paradigm to provide connectivity in intermittently con-

nected scenarios, such as the cases of Interplanetary Internet (Fall, 2003; Jain et al., 2004) and developing regions (Burleigh et al., 2003). In all the cases where connectivity could not be taken for granted, nodes should be able to temporarily buffer data, and forward it at the next communication opportunity. The paradigm applied was therefore a "store-and-forward" one, where nodes were expected to first store, and then forward any information destined outside the local network.

The same communication paradigm was later on extended to more commercial application scenarios. Examples include urban sensing (Lee & Magistretti, 2008), where the sensing capabilities of mobile devices are exploited to collect and diffuse "living memories" of places or moments; vehicular sensor networks (Lee & Magistretti, 2008), where vehicles become at the same time sensing devices and mobile nodes of the network; distributed context provisioning applications, where information is shared in an ad-hoc fashion among mobile users running context-aware applications (Riva, 2006).

Recently, significant attention has been devoted to mobile application scenarios, where the carriers of information are represented by people with their personal hand-held device (Chaintreau et al., 2006). In this case, the user's device itself is a node of the mobile network and proximity communication wireless technologies such as, e.g., Bluetooth or Wi-Fi, are exploited in order to "opportunistically" exchange data whenever in mutual communication range. This is raising an increasing interest in the area of mobile peer-to-peer applications (Riva & Toivonen, 2007; Su et al., 2007), where the proximity of mobile nodes is exploited for exchanging personal or contextual information such as e.g., pictures, music, personal interests, etc.

2.1. Design Space

The design of an opportunistic communication system is tightly coupled to the specific application scenario being supported (Ibrahim et al., 2009). This is due to the fact that the diffusion of data relies primarily on the mobility nodes, which act as carriers of information. It is then clear that nodes' density and mobility pattern strongly affect the performance of the system, and the specific application scenario being supported determines these variables.

As an example, we can consider the following two reference application scenarios. The first is that of a trade show, or conference environment, where the opportunistic communication system is exploited in order to diffuse information about, e.g., changes in the schedule or personalized advertisements. This application scenario is characterized by a large density of nodes (the attendees) and by a limited dynamism, as nodes will always be moving in a confined area. In this case, it is reasonable to assume a certain level of redundancy in the system, which makes scalability the primary issue to be addressed: it is important to design the system in such a way that the various communication protocols scale well with density of nodes in the network.

A second example is that of mobile social computing (Bedd), (Imity), (Aka-Aki) where nodes are moving in an urban setting and sharing information on-the-move. In this case, nodes are extremely sparse, and the environment over which nodes are moving can be very large. Furthermore, there is limited redundancy in the system and it is important to ensure a sufficient level of circulation of data, despite the limited carriers of information.

From these considerations it is clear that the design space, especially in terms of networking, is mostly centered around these two dimensions: nodes density and mobility pattern. Depending on these two parameters, one forwarding scheme can be more suitable than another, where a forwarding mechanism determines how any two nodes meeting exchange messages. As an example, epidemic routing (Vahdat & Becker, 2000) implements a message flooding, which performs best in terms

of end-to-end delivery, but, at the same time, is also the most demanding in terms of resources. A more conservative mechanism is the two–hop routing (Groenevelt et al., 2005), where the source node—upon encountering a potential relay node—generates a new copy of the message with a given probability; relay nodes forward it to the intended destination whenever they get within mutual communication range. The probability with which a source node generates a new copy of a message can be regarded as the control variable of the routing scheme. There are many other variants (Al Hanbali et al., 2008), which depend on the target tradeoff between resources and performance, or on the knowledge on the network structure such as the mobility pattern of nodes.

2.2. EVALUATING OPPORTUNISTIC COMMUNCATION SYSTEMS

Opportunistic communication systems have been deeply investigated from a theoretical point of view (Neglia & Zhang, 2006). Such studies explored the many tradeoffs existing between the performance of the system, and the resources allocated for running it. The typical approach used for studying DTNs follows either an analytical approach, or a simulative/emulative one. In both cases, starting from a given assumption on the mobility pattern of nodes and on the forwarding mechanism utilized for relaying messages, the end-to-end delay – the time needed for a message to reach the intended destination – is measured as a function of the number of copies generated (Groenevelt et al., 2005; Neglia & Zhang, 2006).

The mobility pattern of nodes can be characterized statistically, as in the case of stochastic modeling (Groenevelt et al., 2005), simulated (Musolesi & Mascolo, 2007) or gathered from real-world traces (Pietilainen & Diot, 2009). In this last approach, experiments are run in order to measure nodes "contacts" (Chaintreau et al., 2006; Miklas et al., 2007) where a contact is defined as the communication opportunity deriving from the physical proximity of nodes. Once gathered, such contacts can be "played back" in order to reproduce the sequence of nodes meetings, and combined with a given routing scheme in order to emulate the diffusion of data in the DTN.

Despite the great amount of research dedicated to the modeling and performance evaluation of DTNs, only limited work has been devoted to the study of the many challenges related to the design, engineering and operation of such systems in a real-world setting. The work that most closely relates to these aspects is concerned mostly with aspects related to realistic mobility pattern of nodes, and follows a hybrid approach, where nodes proximity is first recorded and then utilized for (1) emulating the spreading of data (Pietilainen & Diot, 2009; Miklas et al., 2007; Legender et al., 2008) or (2) understanding the social dynamics behind such contacts (Hui et al., 2007; Miklas et al., 2007; Musolesi & Mascolo, 2007). This approach, while providing important insights into social dynamics regulating the nodes' contacts, greatly simplifies the many real-world constraints related to the design, implementation and operation of such systems. As an example, the PHY medium utilized for exchanging data greatly affects the overall system performance. Furthermore, many cross-layer aspects play an important role when operating such systems and are not taken into account when focusing on nodes proximity only.

Following these considerations, we have developed a *User-centric Heterogeneous Opportunistic Middleware* (Create-Net, 2008), which is a middleware platform running over any Java-enabled smartphone and leveraging Bluetooth connectivity for exchanging data. This platform was used to understand the many challenges related to the engineering of such systems, and to their operation and monitoring in a real-world setting.

3. U-HOPPER

U-Hopper (Carreras et al., 2007) is a User-centric Heterogeneous Opportunistic Middleware platform for enriching personal communication devices with means for supporting context-aware opportunistic content delivery. It is implemented as a software running over Java-enabled mobile phones (covering a large share of the overall smart-phones market), and exploits proximity-based wireless communications (Bluetooth in the current implementation) for diffusing content (1) from dedicated devices, for example, throwboxes (Ibrahim et al., 2009), totems) to users and (2) among users.

U-Hopper has been developed for supporting the delivery of information with a limited scope in space and time (e.g., special sales in a shop, happy hour in a bar, etc.): such kind of "transient" information is badly handled by Web-based applications and requires a different approach, based on a push model, where it is not the user searching for relevant contents, but vice-versa.

The focus has been put on designing a system easy to use, cheap and fast to deploy, which runs on devices most people own (mobile phones) and that can address the security issues common people feel. The core is provided by a middleware platform, which handles all the necessary data management and communication tasks. The communication is driven by the user profile, which is expressed as a set of interests/topics the user is interested in. The profile is dynamically updated to reflect changes in interest and/or situations. Only content relevant to the user (as expressed by interests in the profile) is collected and stored locally. Content can be propagated from device to device (from user to user) using Bluetooth or other kinds of short-range wireless communications. In such a way, only content of interest is delivered and propagated in the system. The middleware provides all the necessary programming abstractions for supporting different application scenarios, and provides an engine for requesting, transmitting and managing contents in the system.

3.1. System Design

The U-Hopper middleware platform is briefly summarized in Figure 1 and is composed by (1) the Controller, (2) the Interest Manager, (3) the Content Manager and (4) the Opportunistic Communication Unit. All modules are then monitored by the Monitoring Framework. More in detail:

- A U-Hopper Service implements a specific application that is provided to the end-user. Each service is responsible of handling any interaction with the end-user, displaying the proper User Interfaces (UIs) and implementing the needed business logic for running the service. Each service is linked to the U-Hopper middleware through the Controller component;

Figure 1. U-Hopper system architecture

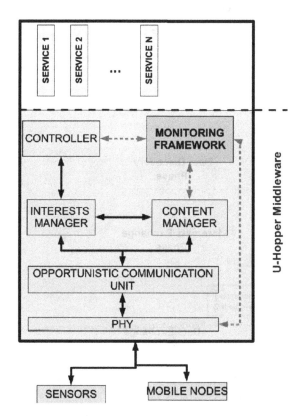

- The Controller is the component through which services access the U-Hopper middleware functionalities. In particular, it manages the service life cycle (registration, deprecation) and allows any pervasive service currently deployed over the mobile node to seamlessly (1) access the data stored in the internal memory and (2) program data gathering tasks. The controller is also responsible for issuing service callbacks, whenever data matching some search criteria is retrieved;
- The Interest Manager (IM) defines the way according to which information is exchanged between any two mobile nodes. In particular, data exchange is regulated through the concept of "interests", which is a description of the information requested by the service. When two nodes meet, they first exchange the set of interests. Such interests are then used for matching the data currently stored in the permanent storage. If a match exists, the matched data is sent to the requesting node. Further details can be found in (U-Hopper, 2010);
- The Content Manager (CM) manages the persistent storage available on mobile devices. In particular, it provides a SQL-like environment to facilitate the querying of data. It also runs routines, which are necessary in order to preserve the limited resources available on mobile devices. Such routines implement appropriate "data aging" techniques that, starting from the user interests and from the metadata associated with content, discarding outdated information (Carreras et al., 2007). As an example data is typically associated with a Time To Leave (TTL), which defines the temporal validity of a content, starting from when it was initially generated. Once this TTL expires, the CM discards the corresponding item, and avoids to forwarding it further. This is extremely important, especially

when it comes to communication. Indeed, although it might be not critical to store large amounts of data in the permanent storage of a mobile device, it can become crucial exchanging it in short periods of time;

- The Opportunistic Communication Manager (OCM) handles all the networking operations that are needed to gather data from data sources or exchange data with other mobile nodes. This includes (1) beaconing functionalities for discovering neighboring peers (2) appropriate device caching techniques for improving the efficiency of data exchanges (3) data exchange protocols, for obtaining the desired interests-based data exchange (U-Hopper).

Figure 2 depicts the communication handshake between any two nodes meeting. A beacon message is periodically sent by nodes in order to detect neighboring devices. Once a neighboring device is found, an *interests exchange* phase is triggered. During this phase, nodes exchange (1) a list of interests, which are a description of the

data searched by nodes (2) an aggregated cache of the data stored, in order to avoid redundant transmissions. Starting from the interests, each node determines whether there is relevant data to send to the encountered node and, if so, it sends it during the data exchange phase.

- The Monitoring Framework (MF) handles all the necessary operations for the monitoring of single nodes as well as the system as a whole. It collects general device status information (e.g., memory utilization, device load, etc.) and information on the specific forwarding algorithm implemented by the *OCM*. The information stored by the *MF* is stored locally and can be dynamically downloaded by a base station upon request. Furthermore, the *MF* can be adaptively and dynamically re-programmed by means of active messages that are received and interpreted at run time by the U-Hopper middleware. As an example, it is possible to reconfigure the frequency according to which data is collected by the MF.

Figure 2. The three phases of the communication handshake run by any two nodes meeting

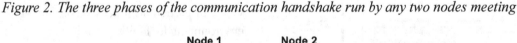
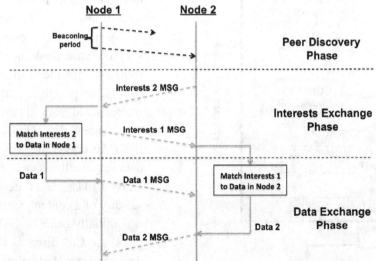

3.2. Implementation Details

One of the main objectives of the U-Hopper system design is to support the most widely diffused software/hardware platforms. In order to embrace a sufficiently large number of "potentially available" mobile devices, we selected smartphones as our target. Indeed, smartphones have reached a sufficiently large computing and communication power to perform very complex operations. At the same time, these devices are typically carried around by users during their daily activities and represent therefore the ideal platform candidate for running context-aware pervasive services.

In order to leverage on a widely diffused and standardized computing environment, we chose to develop the mobile version of U-Hopper as a Java MIDlet running over J2ME (MIDP profile 2.0), which is currently available on a large share of smartphones shipped today. By implementing U-Hopper as a Java component, we guarantee that the software shall be portable over a large set of mobile devices.

Furthermore, we assumed Bluetooth as the networking interface for achieving localized peer-to-peer data exchanges among mobile nodes. While not being the most appropriate networking technology for opportunistic networking, it is the only one which is available on a broad range of devices, and that can be easily programmed thanks to the J2ME programming APIs (such as the well-known JSR 82).

Another issue we had to face was to design a proper persistent storage on each device. Typically, in smartphones data is saved locally using the Record Management Store (RMS), where information can be easily stored as an array of bytes and retrieved using easy-to-use matching methods. We implemented a user-friendly interface to store and retrieve data. This is based on a SQL-like programming abstraction which allows developers to easily query the data in the internal memory of the device.

In order to interface with legacy systems, we implemented a laptop-based version of the U-Hopper middleware. It runs the same software components, except for the Content Manager, which now relies on a MySQL database for permanently storing data. The Opportunistic Communication Manager is the same as its mobile version and is based on the Avetana Bluetooth library, an open source Bluetooth stack that allows applications designed for JSR-82 to run on a J2SE environment.

4. EVALUATION AND DISTRIBUTED MONITORING OF AN OPPORTUNISTIC COMMUNICATION SYSTEM

Developing embedded applications is a non-trivial task and requires a deep understanding of the many parameters involved in the system design. In particular, mobile software development follows a life-cycle that is briefly summarized in Figure 3. The first step consists in developing the mobile application. In this, developers are facilitated by the use of appropriate software development IDEs. Once this first step is completed, the software is ready for offline testing. This is typically performed by exploiting emulators, which reproduce the functioning of mobile devices. Existing software products can be used to this aim.

The following steps regard the testing of the application over mobile devices, where real hardware and software constraints are present and where the peculiarities of the different devices can play a major role in terms of portability. For this, it is important to set up a dedicated testing environment, which allows to easily develop and evaluate the performance of the various algorithms and protocols that are part of the distributed system. In a fixed environment there are many tools, which help developers in this task. Differently, in an embedded and fully distributed environment

Figure 3. Mobile application development life-cycle and applied software development tools

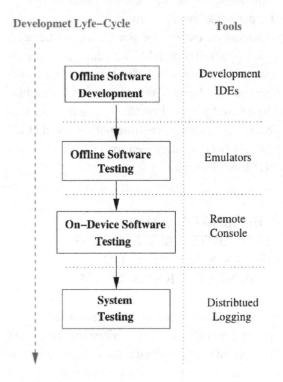

this can only be done by developing instruments that allow to easily (1) monitor, from remote, the correct functioning of single mobile devices (2) run system-wide experiments, collecting data from the whole system, and post-processing it in order to extract the most interesting performance figures. We have then developed two different tools, which facilitate the work of developers for the on-device prototyping: a remote console service and a distributed monitoring mechanism. The former tool is useful for the third phase of the software development process, where the application is run over real mobile devices and developers need to verify the correct operations of the mobile application. The latter tool comes into help when evaluating how the system "as a whole" behaves, and is particularly important in the case of opportunistic communication systems.

4.1. Remote Console

The first component we developed is a remote console mechanism, which allows to remotely log into a device and issue queries on its status. As an example, developers can exploit the SQL-like querying interface of the Content Manager to verify the data that is stored in the internal memory of the device, or can verify the internal status (e.g., memory usage, permanent storage usage, etc.). Such console service runs in the background of the mobile application and can be easily enabled or disabled. It uses Bluetooth connectivity for retrieving data and delivering it to a remote user interface, over which is then displayed.

4.2. Distributed Monitoring Framework

Once the mobile application has been tested over the single device, it is important to perform system-wide measurements. The reasons for this are twofold: first, system scalability and system dynamic behavior can only be verified when running the system on a large scale. As outlined in Section 2, opportunistic communication systems may span very different operating conditions and it is therefore important to reproduce, where possible, the target scenario and perform measurements in such conditions. With this respect, appropriate tools are needed for running different experiments, tailored to the verification of how the system behaves when, as an example, the number of devices increases (scalability) or when devices join and leave the network (dynamism).

Second, many real-world constraints emerge only when running the mobile application over real hardware and software platforms. An example is the usage of memory: smartphones are still limited in the available RAM. The Nokia E65 smartphone that we used in our experiments runs with an internal memory of 20 MB, which can be easily exceeded if the system is not designed or implemented properly. A simple query loading a large number of data items can suffice to saturate the limited device memory. When this occurs, unpredictable behavior can happen, including the reboot of the smartphone. It is therefore extremely important to monitor the usage of memory in order to identify those operations, which are the most memory consuming.

Permanent storage is another limited resource, even though this constraint is being reduced with modern smartphones. However, besides its availability, memory access still requires a non-negligible amount of time and can be responsible for large delays in the operation of the mobile application. It is therefore mandatory to always verify that the items in the permanent storage are limited, or that queries always regard a limited portion of the device permanent storage.

Finally, the scarcest resource is communication. In the current implementation of U-Hopper, Bluetooth is assumed as the default communication medium. Although there are all the necessary APIs for accessing it, its functioning is related to the communication protocol that regulates how information is sequentially exchanged between any two nodes. Moreover, Bluetooth was designed for different application scenarios, where a communication channel is first established and then maintained over time. Differently, we are addressing scenarios where nodes are in proximity for limited periods of time, and need to maximally exploit such data exchange "opportunity". This requires the use of smart caching techniques, combined with appropriate data exchange mechanisms that ensure that only the minimal necessary information is transferred between any two meeting nodes.

Clearly, the utilization of the Bluetooth communication medium is also linked to the consumption of batteries. In particular, the more often a Bluetooth discovery is triggered for searching for neighboring nodes, the higher the consumption of energy. Vice-versa, the less often a device discov-

ery is triggered, the longer the battery life-time but also the higher the chance to miss nodes close by. In order for the system to perform efficiently, this tradeoff must be monitored and regulated dynamically at run-rime.

In order to address all these issues, we developed a distributed monitoring framework, which allows the gathering of status information from all the nodes. We developed our own distributed probing mechanism in order to obtain a higher degree of flexibility, and to design such mechanism so as to minimally interfere with the normal operation of the system.

Monitoring messages are generated by all nodes of the system and collected by a dedicated base station, which saves such information into a permanent storage (e.g., a MySQL database) for later post-processing. The monitoring mechanism supports the message types in Table 1.

Once the monitoring information is gathered, a dedicated software is then in charge of analyzing it offline, and of extracting appropriate performance figures. Such figures can be aggregated over all system nodes, or can be specific to single ones. In both cases, it is possible to extract:

- **Memory Utilization:** This performance figure provides insights into the memory utilization over time. In particular, it is important to monitor the memory utilization of the device over long periods of time, since single (time-limited) on-device experiments may hinder memory leaks, or specific operations that are performed only when the number of nodes increases;
- **Peer Discoveries:** This is an important metric to measure, especially when addressing the scalability of the system. Indeed, the number of peer discoveries of the system is supposed to scale with the number of nodes: the higher the number of nodes, the lower the required peer discoveries thanks to the higher redundancy in the system;

Table 1. STATUS, COMMUNICATION and FORWARDING monitoring information currently supported by the distributed monitoring framework

Parameter	Description
core.status (STATUS)	*Core.status* monitoring messages regularly trace the overall status of a single node. This includes the free memory (expressed in bytes), the number of data items stored in the permanent storage, the occupation (expressed in bytes) of the permanent storage. Core status information is traced into each device at regular time intervals;
peer.discovered (COMMUNICATION)	*Peer.discovered* messages are generated at any Bluetooth peer discovery performed by the device and trace the number of devices found in proximity. This is an important metric, since it provides an important heuristic for estimating how dynamic the environment is. As an example, the number of new peers discovered over some reference time interval is strongly related to how fast the surrounding environment is changing;
peer.servicedisc (COMMUNICATION)	*Peer.servicedisc* monitoring message is related to the Bluetooth service discovery phase, which follows the peer discovery. This information is important in order to record the nodes that are associated to specific services.
peer.dataexch (COMMUNICATION)	*Peer.dataexch* message is related to a data exchange between two nodes meeting. It contains aggregated information on the data exchange being performed. This includes, e.g., the data (expressed in bytes) exchanged, the number of data items exchanges and the time elapsed for the data exchange to conclude.
message.hops (FORWARDING)	*Message.hops* messages store the number of hopes traversed by each message received by a node. This is an important information for understanding the diameter of the network.
message.received (FORWARDING)	*Message.received* messages contains information on the time instant at which a given message was received. This allows to extract the dynamics of the system, and the time it takes for a message to circulate in the network.

- **Data Exchange Rate:** As emerged from the description of the system, communication is the most critical aspect to be considered when designing opportunistic communication systems. This is particularly true when using Bluetooth connectivity, where data rate is limited and it takes a non negligible time to set up a communication channel with another mobile device. Furthermore, there are many dependencies among the U-Hopper software components, which can interfere with the data exchange rate. As an example, depending on the time needed for querying data from the Content Manager, the data exchange can be more or less efficient. It is therefore important to trace how various implementation solutions impact the exchange of data among mobile nodes.

- **Caching Performance:** Caching is an important mechanism of the U-Hopper OCM, since it allows to regulate when to exchange data with a discovered mobile node. Depending on the application scenario, it allows to set how often two devices will exchange information. As an example, in extremely dynamic environments, where new data items are injected into the system at a very high rate, caching needs to be maintained low. This increases the likelihood that two nodes meeting will verify if they have information to exchange. Conversely, in more static scenarios it is possible to avoid unnecessary data exchanges, thus preserving devices resources (e.g., battery);

4.3. Experimental Validation

In order to experiment the performance of the U-Hopper platform and of the developed monitoring tools, we have set up a testbed composed by 11 smartphones and 2 base stations. We deployed the U-Hopper middleware on each smartphone, together with a traffic generator that was injecting a new message with a rate distributed according to a Poisson distribution with mean *10* minutes. Each message was characterized by a given size of the payload, and a given Time-To-Leave (TTL). The TTL determined the time validity of a certain message in the network starting from the instant in time the message was generated. Once expired, the message is no longer forwarded by nodes. The choice of the TTL is very important since it allows avoidance of useless data exchanges, thus preserving the limited resources of the system. Furthermore, the choice of the TTL is typically linked to the specific application scenario being supported. As an example, in an application scenario where information is related to events going on in the city center, there is no need to disseminate contents related to the past.

The U-Hopper middleware was running both the remote console for specific on-device debugging, and the distributed monitoring framework for collecting system status information. The monitoring information was gathered by the two base stations and processed offline in order to extract both system-wide and node-specific performance figures.

We have run a field trial within an office environment, where *11* workers - with different roles within the organization and working on *4* floors of the same building - were equipped with a mobile phone running the software. The experiment lasted for *2* days and a different system configuration was assigned to each day of the experimentation. Each configuration consisted in a different size of the messages that were injected by the mobile nodes. In particular, the first day each message contained a payload of *10* Kb, with a total load of the network of *10 * 11* Kb/hour. The second day the payload was increased to *100* Kb.

Table 2 provides a summary of the parameters used for the experimentation.

Given the limited scale of the experiment, epidemic routing (Vahdat & Becker, 2000) was assumed as the forwarding strategy. Different

Table 2. Summary of the settings used for the 2 days field trial

Number of Users	11
Duration of the Trial	2 days
Devices Used	Nokia N80, E65
Wireless Comm. Technology	Bluetooth 1.2
Message Generation Rate	1 msg / 10 min.
Payload size	10 and 100 Kb
Time to Leave (TTL)	8 hours

schemes can be easily supported by varying the policy according to which messages are relayed by the OCM of the U-Hopper platform (Figure 1).

4.4. Experimental Results

We first analyzed the performance of the forwarding mechanism. We measured this in terms of Broadcast Diffusion Time, Network Diameter and Infection Ratio in the case of nodes generating 6 messages/hour with payload 10 and 100 Kb.

The Broadcast Diffusion Time (BDT) represents the time required by a message to reach all nodes. This is an important indication of the system dynamics and load of the network, since it reflects the time needed to achieve system-wide communications. Clearly, this performance parameter strongly depends on the mobility pattern of the nodes of the network: a higher degree of mobility results in a lower BDT.

The Network Diameter (ND) measures the maximum number of hops traversed by each message, and reflects the diameter of the network. This is an important parameter as it is tightly coupled with the level of redundancy present. Indeed, a low diameter indicates a clustered network, where messages can be delivered through many alternative paths.

The Infection Ratio (IR) measures the total number of nodes reached by a given message before its expiration.

Table 3 presents the mean and the variance of the *BDT*, *ND* and *IR* in the case of messages with a payload of *10* and *100* Kb. As it is possible to observe, a lower load of the network leads to a reduced *BDT* (*3.07* hours) and to a higher *IR* (*10.52* nodes). In other words, the system is able to deliver messages to almost all nodes in approximately *3* hours. The *ND* tells us the average number of nodes traversed by each message. In the case of 10Kb payload this resulted to be *4* nodes, meaning that the network is not particularly clustered. This can be explained by the fact that the users were distributed over *4* floors and is therefore very likely that the network was partitioned into *4* groups, with a few nodes acting as carriers across such groups.

In the case of 100 Kb payload, the load of the network is ten times higher. This means that the limited time that nodes have to exchange messages is not enough, and that nodes need more than one contact opportunity to exchange all messages they are storing. As a result, it takes more time to disseminate messages to all nodes, with an average *BDT* of 3.59 hours. Accordingly, the diameter of the network is reduced to 2,76 hops. The IR is also reduced to 7,56, which means that on average only 7 nodes out of 11 are reached by the messages. This is mostly due to the expiration time of messages, which occurred before such messages were delivered to all nodes.

Table 3. Broadcast Diffusion Time, Network Diameter and Infection Ratio in the case of 11 mobile nodes distributed over a 4 floors office environment, generating 6 messages/hour with payload of 10 and 100 Kb, respectively

	10 Kb Payload		100 Kb Payload	
	Mean	Variance	Mean	Variance
Broadcast Diffusion Time (hours)	3.07	1.26	3.59	1.65
Network Diameter	4.18	0.98	2.76	1.44
Infection Ratio	10.52	1.18	7.56	3.19

Figure 4 depicts the distribution of the number of data exchanges throughout the hours of the first day of experimentation. The *2* peaks of the distribution correspond to those hours where all users participating to the experimentation were in the office. During (1) lunch break, (2) early morning and (3) later afternoon the number of data exchanges was significantly lower due to absence of the users from the office environment. It is worth noticing that the distribution of data exchanges over time is extremely important as it can be used for augmenting predictive routing algorithms, where the probability of nodes meetings is used in order to optimize the forwarding mechanisms (Zhao et al., 2005).

Figure 5 reports nodes centrality, which measured the number of times a node was in the delivery chain of a message. This is an important metric for determining the *hubs* of the opportunistic network - the nodes that mostly contribute to the dissemination of data. Also this information is extremely important as it allows to exploit the social dynamics of the people carrying the mobile device for maximizing the diffusion of data (Hui et al., 2007; Miklas et al., 2007; Musolesi & Mascolo, 2007). From the histogram it is possible to observe that node *6* presents the highest centrality, while node *6* the lower one. Indeed, node *6* was assigned to a member of the administrative stuff which works at strict contact with different people distributed over the *4* floors.

Figure 6 reports the dynamics of the message diffusion over the opportunistic network, in the case of 10 and 100 Kb payload messages. Messages take a relatively short time to reach 8 nodes of the network, while it takes much longer to reach the remaining nodes, in particular the last one. This is justified by the fact that only one participant to the field trial was residing on the fourth floor, and was therefore meeting other nodes only in rare occasions (e.g., coffee breaks, lunch, etc.).

Accordingly with the results of Table 3, the payload of messages affects the dynamics of the messages diffusion. In particular, message diffu-

Figure 4. Distribution of the number of data exchanges throughout the hours of the first day of experimentation

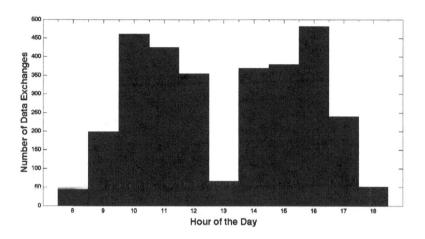

Figure 5. Nodes centrality during the two days of experimentation in the case of a 10 Kb payload traffic

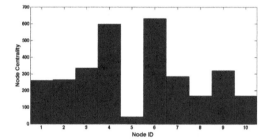 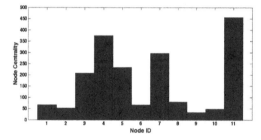

sion for 100 Kb messages take a longer time to diffuse. This is particularly evident in the "long tail" of the diffusion process, where the diffusion time is almost double with respect to the 10 Kb payload messages.

Figures 7 through 9 present an example of the performance figures that is possible to extract from the status information. It depicts the memory utilization and number of content items stored in the device database of node 3 during the first day of the field trial. This is an important information to extract from the opportunistic communication system, as it allows to identify the current load of the system and to fine tune the parameters of the forwarding mechanism. As an example, in

case of heavy load of the network it is possible to reduce the *TTL* of messages in order to limit their time validity and free some node resources. In the experiment carried out, the effect of the *TTL* parameter is evident on the right hand side of Figure 7, where around *16* PM the number of items stored in the device decreases due to their time expiration. In fact, this is due to the *8* hours of *TTL* used for the messages generated in the field trial and, considering that the experiment started around *9* AM in the morning, messages started to be removed around 17 PM.

Clearly, nodes are in communication range only for limited periods of time and the opportunities to exchange data are more rare. Each ex-

Figure 6. Dynamics of the network infection ratio

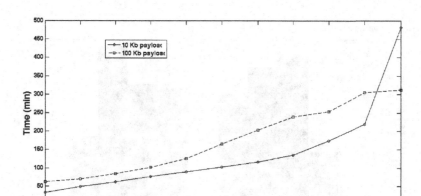

Figure 7. Memory utilization and number of content items stored in node 3 during the first day of the field trial

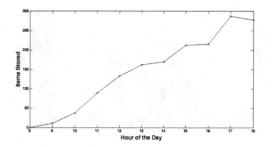 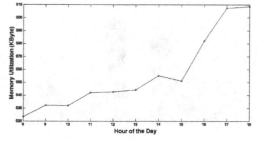

periment last a predefined amount of time and we measured, for each message, the number of mobile nodes reached. We performed this experiment for various settings of the system, trying to understand how well the system reacts to dynamic environments. This provided us with a useful mapping of the system parameters to desired system behavior.

5. CONCLUSION

In this paper we presented our experience in developing and evaluating U-Hopper, a middleware platform supporting opportunistic communication based services. We developed the platform as a Java MIDlet and implemented a testbed environment for testing the performance of the distributed system. Such environment permits to monitor and dynamically reconfigure the opportunistic communication system in real-time.

The U-Hopper platform development and experimental evaluation confirmed the challenges in developing opportunistic mobile applications, and the need to support software development with instruments for testing software on target platforms. With this respect, the implemented tools proved to be very useful means to dimension the system and to determine the proper set of system parameters, given the application scenario being supported.

REFERENCES

Al Hanbali, A., Ibrahim, M., Simon, V., Varga, E., & Carreras, I. (2008, October). A survey of message delivery protocols in mobile ad hoc network. In *Proceedings of the INTERPERF Conference*, Athens, Greece.

Burleigh, S., Torgerson, L., Fall, K., Cerf, V., Durst, B., & Scott, K. (2003). Delay-tolerant networking: An approach to interplanetary internet. *IEEE Communications Magazine, 41*(6), 128–136. doi:10.1109/MCOM.2003.1204759

Carreras, I., Chlamtac, I., De Pellegrini, F., & Miorandi, D. (2007). BIONETS: Bio-inspired networking for pervasive communication environments. *IEEE Transactions on Vehicular Technology, 56*(1), 218–229. doi:10.1109/TVT.2006.883762

Carreras, I., Tacconi, D., & Miorandi, D. (2007, October). Data-centric information dissemination in opportunistic environments. In *Proceedings of the International Conference on Mobile Adhoc and Sensor Systems*, Pisa, Italy (pp. 1-3).

Chaintreau, A., Hui, P., Crowcroft, J., Diot, C., Gass, R., & Scott, J. (2006, April). Impact of human mobility on the design of opportunistic forwarding algorithms. In *Proceedings of INFOCOM*, Barcelona, Spain.

Create-Net. (2008). *U-Hopper: User centric - heterogeneus opportunistic middleware.* Retrieved from http://u-hopper.create-net.org

Fall, K. (2003, March). A delay-tolerant network architecture for challenged internets. In *Proceedings of the ACM SIGCOMM Conference on Applications, Technologies, Architectures, and Protocols for Computer Communications*, Karlsruhe, Germany (pp. 27-34).

Groenevelt, R., Nain, P., & Koole, G. (2005). The message delay in mobile ad hoc networks. *Performance Evaluation, 62*(1-4), 210–228. doi:10.1016/j.peva.2005.07.018

Hui, P., Yoneki, E., Chan, S.-Y., & Crowcroft, J. (2007, August). Distributed community detection in delay tolerant networks. In *Proceedings of the 2nd ACM/IEEE International Workshop on Mobility in the Evolving Internet Architecture*, Kyoto, Japan (p. 7).

Ibrahim, M., Nain, P., & Carreras, I. (2009, June). Analysis of relay protocols for throwbox equipped DTNs. In *Proceedings of the 7th International Symposium on Modeling and Optimization in Mobile, Ad Hoc and Wireless Networks*, Seoul, Korea (pp. 1-9).

Jain, S., Fall, K., & Patra, R. (2004, March). Routing in a delay tolerant network. In *Proceedings of the ACM SIGCOMM Conference on Applications, Technologies, Architectures, and Protocols for Computer Communications*, Portland, OR (pp. 145-158).

Java Community Process. (n. d.). *JSR82: Javatm apis for bluetooth.* Retrieved from http://jcp.org/aboutJava/communityprocess/final/jsr082

Lee, U., & Magistretti, E. (2008). Dissemination and harvesting of urban data using vehicular sensing platforms. *IEEE Transactions on Vehicular Technology, 99*, 1.

Legendre, F., Lenders, V., May, M., & Karlsson, G. (2008, September). Narrowcasting: An empirical performance evaluation study. In *Proceedings of the Third ACM Workshop on Challenged Networks* (pp. 11-18).

Miklas, A. G., Gollu, K. K., & Saroiu, S. Gummadi, K. P., & de Lara, E. (2007, September). Exploiting social interactions in mobile systems. In *Proceedings of the 9ᵗʰ International Conference on Ubiquitous Computing*, Innsbruck, Austria.

Musolesi, M., & Mascolo, C. (2007). Designing mobility models based on social network theory. *ACM SIGMOBILE Mobile Computing and Communication Review, 11*(3).

Neglia, G., & Zhang, X. (2006, September). Optimal delay-power tradeoff in sparse delay tolerant networks: A preliminary study. In *Proceedings of the SIGCOMM Conference on Challenged Networks*, Pisa, Italy (pp. 237-244).

Nicolai, M., Behrens, N., & Yoneki, E. (2006, March). Wireless rope: An experiment in social proximity sensing with bluetooth. In *Proceedings of the PerCom Conference*, Pisa, Italy.

Pelusi, L., Passarella, A., & Conti, M. (2006). Opportunistic networking: Data forwarding in disconnected mobile ad hoc networks. *IEEE Communications Magazine, 44*(11). doi:10.1109/MCOM.2006.248176

Pietilainen, A.-K., & Diot, C. (2009, June). Experimenting with opportunistic networking. In *Proceedings of the MobiArch Conference*, Kraków, Poland.

Riva, O. (2006, November). Contory: A middleware for the provisioning of context information on smart phones. In M. van Steen & M. Henning (Eds.), *Proceedings of the 7ᵗʰ International Conference of Middleware*, Melbourne, Australia (LNCS 4290, pp. 219-239).

Riva, O., & Toivonen, S. (2007). The dynamos approach to support contextaware service provisioning in mobile environments. *Journal of Systems and Software, 80*(12), 1956–1972. doi:10.1016/j.jss.2007.03.009

Su, J., Scott, J., Hui, P., Crowcroft, J., de Lara, E., Diot, C., et al. (2007, August). Haggle: Seamless networking for mobile applications. In J. Krumm, G. D. Abowd, A. Senevirante, & T. Strang (Eds.), *Proceedings of the 9ᵗʰ International Conference on Ubiquitous Computing*, Innsbruch, Austria (LNCS 4717, pp. 391-408).

Tan, F., Ardon, S., & Ott, M. (2007). UbiStore: Ubiquitous and opportunistic backup architecture. In *Proceedings of the Fifth Annual IEEE International Conference on Pervasive Computing and Communications*, White Plains, NY (pp. 71-78).

Vahdat, A., & Becker, D. (2000). *Epidemic routing for partially connected ad hoc networks* (Tech. Rep. No. CS-2000-06). Durham, NC: Duke University.

Zhang, X., Kurose, J., Levine, B. N., Towsley, D., & Zhang, H. (2006, September). Study of a bus-based disruption tolerant network: Mobility modeling and impact on routing. In *Proceedings of the Mobicom Conference*, Montreal, QC, Canada (pp. 195-206).

Zhao, W., Ammar, M., & Zegura, E. (2005, April). Controlling the mobility of multiple data transport ferries in a delay-tolerant network. In *Proceedings of the IEEE Annual Joint Conference INFOCOM*, Miami, FL (pp. 1407-1418).

This work was previously published in the International Journal of Adaptive, Resilient and Autonomic Systems, Volume 2, Issue 3, edited by Vincenzo De Florio, pp. 45-62, copyright 2011 by IGI Publishing (an imprint of IGI Global).

Section 4
Algorithms and Protocols for Resilient and Adaptive Systems

Chapter 14
COADA:
Leveraging Dynamic Coalition Peer-to-Peer Network for Adaptive Content Download of Cellular Users

Long Vu
University of Illinois, USA

Klara Nahrstedt
University of Illinois, USA

Rahul Malik
University of Illinois, USA

Qiyan Wang
University of Illinois, USA

ABSTRACT

This paper argues that Dynamic Coalition Peer-to-Peer (P2P) Network exists in numerous scenarios where mobile users cluster and form coalitions, and the relationship between sizes of coalitions and distances from mobile nodes to their Point of Interest (PoI) follows exponential distributions. The P2P coalition patterns of mobile users and their exponential distribution behavior can be utilized for efficient and adaptive content file download of cellular users. An adaptive protocol named COADA (COalition-aware Adaptive content DownloAd) is designed that (a) blends cellular and P2P (e.g., WiFi or Bluetooth) wireless interfaces, (b) leverages the clustering of people into P2P coalitions when moving towards PoI, and (c) utilizes exponential-coalition-size function of the Dynamic Coalition P2P Network to minimize the cellular download and meet content file download deadline. With COADA protocol, mobile nodes periodically sample the current P2P coalition size and predict the future coalition size using the exponential function. In order to decide how much file data is available in P2P coalition channels versus how much file data must be downloaded from the server over the cellular network, Online Codes techniques are used and tune cellular download timers to meet the file download deadline. The simulation results show that COADA achieves considerable performance improvements by downloading less file data from the cellular channel and more file data over the P2P coalition network while meeting the file download deadline.

DOI: 10.4018/978-1-4666-2056-8.ch014

1. INTRODUCTION

Besides the traditional cellular communication interface, smart phones currently come equipped with ad hoc wireless interfaces such as Bluetooth and Wifi (i.e., peer-to-peer) enabling creation of mobile P2P networks. This offers a novel opportunity in which smart phones can collaboratively communicate in a peer-to-peer (P2P) fashion to improve performance of network protocols. As a result, recent research in designing content distribution protocols for smart phones starts to take the P2P communication into consideration (Luo et al., 2007; Jung et al., 2007; Yoon et al., 2008; Stiemerling & Kiesel, 2009). However, leveraging P2P communication remains challenging since the P2P communication is limited by a short transmission range and thus becomes broken under mobility of cellular users.

More importantly, cellular users may not have the intermediate incentive to communicate in the P2P channel, which is highly energy-consuming. Let us consider a shopping street scenario where customers walk to their interested shops and download the product preview video to their cell phones using the cellular connectivity, and at the same time they exchange the video via the Bluetooth or 802.11 wireless interfaces of the phones. Given two co-located customers *A* and *B*, according to previous protocols (Luo et al., 2007; Jung et al., 2007; Yoon et al., 2008), *A* and *B* are required to collaboratively exchange/forward messages. However, *A* and *B* may have different targeted shops, so they may move towards different directions in very near future, causing their wireless connection to break. Further, if *A* is interested in jewelry and *B* is interested in digital cameras, what is the immediate incentive for *A* to disseminate the packet about digital cameras from *B*, and vice versa? We therefore believe that sharing mutual content interest is crucial to motivate people (with their smart phones) to collaboratively exchange content messages.

Interestingly, we observe numerous scenarios where co-located people motivate themselves to collaborate since they share mutual content interests. For example, smart phones of co-located audiences or co-located soccer fans may form coalitions to exchange data via the P2P channel, while these mobile users are heading towards the same Points of Interest (PoI) such as the concert theater or the soccer stadium. In this context, these smart phones form a communication network called *dynamic coalition P2P network*.

In this paper, we exploit the transition of coalition pattern when the nodes move from the sparse areas to the dense areas in the dynamic coalition P2P networks to design an adaptive content download protocol named COADA. Particularly, we first study the relationship between the size of coalitions formed by mobile nodes and the distance from the mobile nodes to the PoI on three real maps taken from Google Map (Google, n. d.). Our study shows that the coalition size distribution follows an exponential function with respect to the distance from the mobile nodes to the PoI. This result is further confirmed by our model of coalition pattern using Mobius modeling tool (Deavours et al., 2007). Relying on this exponential coalition size distribution, we present COADA, a novel adaptive protocol that blends cellular and P2P interfaces of the mobile devices to improve content distribution. COADA uses the Online Codes (Maymounkov & Mazieres, 2003) technique to estimate the available data in P2P channel so that we can efficiently plan the download in cellular channel. We evaluate our protocol using simulation and the results show that COADA achieves considerably better performance than the current state of the art protocol, meets the file download deadline, and reduces message overhead significantly.

In this paper, we first present the dynamic coalition P2P networks in Section 2. Then, we study the coalition pattern on three realistic maps taken from Google Map in Section 3. In

Section 4, we use the Mobibus modeling tool to model the movement of people in different street configurations and find that the coalition size follows an exponential function. This motivates us in designing COADA protocol to exploit the exponential-coalition-size function in Section 5. Then, we present the simulation results in Section 6 and conclude the paper in Section 7.

2. DYNAMIC PEER-TO-PEER COALITION NETWORK

In the Dynamic Peer-to-Peer Coalition Network, mobile nodes move towards the same PoI. When heading towards that PoI, co-located mobile nodes may cooperatively form coalitions to share data. Since at the closer distance from the PoI, there are more mobile nodes heading towards that PoI, the coalition size may grow. In our context, a coalition is considered as a "Communication Coalition", which is defined recursively as follows:

1. Nodes are connected in collaborative one-hop manner: If mobile nodes n_1 and n_2 are in the communication of each other via the P2P channel, they are moving towards the same Point of Interest, and they share the same PoI mutual content interest (exchange the same file), then n_1 and n_2 belong to the same communication coalition. In this case, n_1 and n_2 are one-hop neighbors of each other.
2. Nodes are in transitive relation: If nodes n_1 and n_2 belong to the communication coalition C, and n_2 and n_3 belong to the coalition C, then n_1 and n_3 belong to the communication coalition C. This transitive property means that communication coalition can be expanded to multiple hop networks.
3. The coalition is per topic content/interest, so one mobile node n may belong to multiple coalitions at the same time. For example, if n is downloading two content files in the topics of soccer and classical music at the

same time, then n may belong to two different coalitions of "soccer fan" and "classical music fan". Also, one cluster of co-located people may form multiple coalitions if these people exchange content of different interests.

Henceforth, we use the terms *communication coalition* and *coalition* interchangeably. In our context, the dynamic coalition P2P network consists of two concepts: Point of Interest and mobile node. Point of Interest (PoI) represents a fixed place destination such as a soccer stadium, a concert theater, a shopping mall, etc., where people move towards. While moving towards the mutual PoI, these mobile users may share the mutual content interest about the PoI and thus they may use the cell phone to collaboratively download and share the content. The mobile node concept represents the cell phone of pedestrians or drivers, who are heading towards the PoI. These mobile nodes form the dynamic coalition P2P network with following important properties: (1) only mobile nodes in the same coalition collaborate to exchange data via the P2P channel, and (2) the size of coalitions formed by mobile nodes becomes bigger at closer distance from the PoI. In other words, closer to the PoI, the density of nodes heading to the PoI increases thus the communication coalition expands. Figure 1 shows a dynamic coalition P2P network with three Points of Interest and mobile nodes in which the shading pattern represents the node's content interest. In this figure, at closer distance from a PoI, there are more mobile nodes heading towards the PoI. We find that the dynamic coalition P2P network exists in numerous scenarios as presented below.

The first class of scenarios can be found in the context of location-dependent event. For example, pedestrians move towards the location of the same Points of Interest for *social events* such as an outdoor concert or a costume festival. When they walk towards the event location, people may use cell phones to download video files about the

Figure 1. A dynamic coalition P2P network

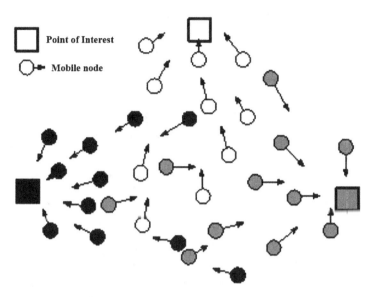

event from a server via the cellular channel. Closer to the event location, there are more people going towards the event location and downloading the event content. In this case, a dynamic coalition P2P network can be formed by these cell phones that exchange downloaded data via the P2P channel to speed up the download process. Similar scenario exists when the drivers drive towards these Points of Interest and want to access the event content using their cell phones.

The second class of scenarios exists when pedestrians or cars move towards the same Point of Interest and download a location-dependent content. For example, when customers go to the shopping malls and shopping street, they may use cell phones to download video files such as product preview video, local commercial advertisement. Closer to these Points of Interest, there are more people going to these areas and their cell phones form a dynamic coalition P2P network to download the videos. In this case, some clients download video file from the server via the cellular channel and then share/exchange downloaded file data via the P2P channel with the other peers. Similar phenomenon exits if these customers move towards these Points of Interest by car.

We believe that this coalition pattern frequently occurs in reality and offers a novel opportunity to improve the performance of content distribution service. In this paper, we focus on the formation of coalition and exploit the transition of coalition size when the nodes move from the sparse areas to the dense areas of the network to design an adaptive content distribution protocol. Particularly, we first study the coalition pattern on three real maps taken from Google Map and the coalition pattern modeled by Mobius tool. Then, we exploit the result of the study to design the content distribution protocol.

3. VALIDATION STUDY OF COALITION PATTERN ON REAL GOOGLE MAPS

To understand the coalition pattern of mobile nodes in realistic scenarios, we perform the following experiment. First, we select a real map M_p from Google Map with a Point of Interest P at the center of the map. Second, we select N nodes at random locations on M_p in the surrounding areas of P. Let these selected locations of N nodes be their initial locations. We simulate two different scenarios for pedestrians and cars. If the map M_p is for the pedestrians, the distance from N nodes to P is shorter than that of the map M_p, which is used for cars. Third, we use Google Map APIs (Google, n.d.) to find the routes, which we call Google routes, for nodes from their initial locations to P. We observe that the routes returned by Google Map APIs usually represent the shortest routes. Fourth, we assume that all nodes arrive at P at approximately the same time and thus nodes closer to P will depart towards P later than nodes farther from P. In the simulation, N nodes will start at their initial locations and then they follow their Google routes to move towards P. While these nodes are moving towards P, we calculate the average coalition size at different distances from P. Here, the communication range of the nodes is 200 (m). In other words, if the distance between two nodes n_1 and n_2 is less than 200 (m) while they are moving towards P, n_1 and n_2 are one-hop neighbors of one coalition. The coalition can be expanded to multiple hops as presented in the definition of Coalition in Section 2.

We perform our simulation on three real maps for three realistic scenarios. The first map is for the Assembly Hall, a stadium in Champaign, Illinois (i.e., longitude=40.096327, latitude=-88.238583) where the basket ball matches or concert events are held. For this map, we select 320 pedestrians (e.g., basket ball fans) at random locations as shown in Figure 2. When the simulation starts, these 300 nodes move from their initial locations to the Assembly Hall (i.e., PoI) along with their Google routes. Similarly, we select 300 pedestrians at random locations in the surrounding area of the Times Square (i.e., longitude=40.759903, latitude=-73.984294) in New York City as shown in Figure 3. When the simulation starts, these 300 nodes move from their initial locations to the Times Square (i.e., PoI) along with their Google routes. The third map is the Market Shopping Mall, a shopping center in Illinois (i.e., longitude=40.142927,

Figure 2. This figure shows the initial positions of mobile nodes before the simulation. During the simulation mobile nodes move from their initial positions towards the Assembly Hall location and co-located mobile nodes form coalitions.

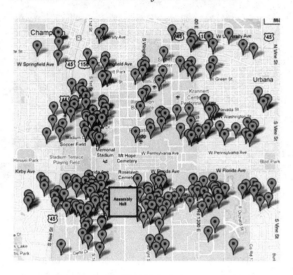

latitude=-88.244419) as shown in Figure 4. Here, we select 350 cars at random locations with farther distances than those in Assembly Hall and Times Square simulations. When the simulation starts, these 350 nodes move from their initial locations to the Market Mall (i.e., PoI) along with their Google routes. For this simulation, the speed of the cars (i.e., from 8 to 10 (m/s)) is much higher than that of pedestrians (i.e., from 1 to 2 (m/s)) in the two previous simulations for Assembly Hall and Times Square.

Although the value of the coalition size depends on the street configuration of the selected map, Figures 5 and 6 show that the coalition size increases significantly at the closer distance from the Point of Interest. More interestingly, we found that the coalition size fits very well to the exponential function. In particular, the exponential fitting functions of Assembly Hall, Times Square, Market Mall experiments are $y(d) = 300e^{-0.006d} + 7$, $y(d) = 300e^{-0.003d} + 25$, and $y(d) = 350e^{-0.0008d} + 10$, respectively.

Figure 3. This figure shows the initial positions of mobile nodes before the simulation. During the simulation mobile nodes move from their initial positions towards the Time Square area and co-located mobile nodes form coalitions.

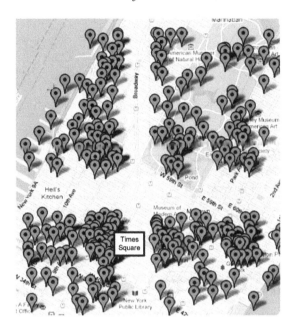

Figure 4. This figure shows the initial positions of mobile nodes before the simulation. During the simulation mobile nodes move from their initial positions towards the Market Mall location and co-located mobile nodes form coalitions.

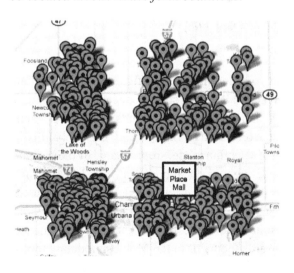

In conclusion, the simulations of three real maps with Google routes show that the coalition size exhibits an exponential function in which the coalition size increases exponentially with respect to the distance from the PoI. We observe that the routes returned by Google Map APIs (n. d.) usually are the shortest routes. Meanwhile, recent studies stated that people with different socioeconomic characteristics may prefer different routes (Millonig & Gartner, 2009) when they move from the same starting location to the same destination. Therefore, in the next section we investigate a further study to confirm whether the shortest routes returned by Google Map APIs create the exponential coalition size or this coalition size distribution is common in reality and independent of the shortest route selection. If the coalition size is common, then we can exploit it to design a new content distribution protocol.

4. MODELING THE COALITION PATTERN IN MOBIUS MODELING TOOL

4.1. Motivation

As we discussed in Section 3, the Google routes returned by Google Map APIs are usually the shortest routes. However, the analysis of the pedestrian movement trace in Koblenz city shown that given the same pair of starting location and destination, different people may choose different routes when they move from the starting location towards the destination (van der Spek, 2009). Particularly, people only prefer the shorter route towards the destination and they do not always select the shortest route. Another recent study claimed that people with different socioeconomic characteristics may prefer different routes (Millonig & Gartner, 2009) when they move from the same starting location towards the same destination. In other words, people usually select the shorter route towards the destination with a

Figure 5. Coalition size distribution of pedestrians moving to Assembly Hall or Times Square

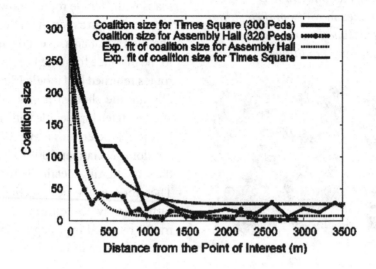

Figure 6. Coalition size distribution of cars moving to Market Place Mall

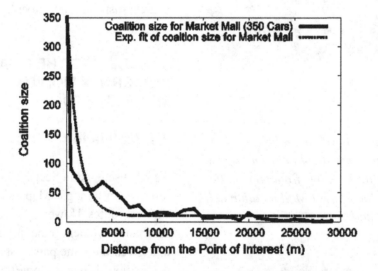

higher probability, which depends on the person's socioeconomic characteristics such as age, gender, etc. and environmental factors such as weather, social events, time of day, etc.

In order to represent the aforementioned route selection behavior of people, we present a probabilistic model of route selection, in which a shorter route towards the PoI is selected with a higher probability. Then, we use this route selection model as the mobility model of mobile nodes in two different street configurations: Manhattan street and Random street. For each configuration (or map), we have two Points of Interest. Then, the street configurations and the probabilistic route selection model are simulated by the Mobius modeling tool (Deavours et al., 2007), which has been extensively used to model various stochastic systems. Finally, we study the coalition patterns resulted from the movement of mobile nodes towards their PoI in the Mobius modeling tool.

4.2. The Probabilistic Model of Route Selection

We present a probabilistic route selection model, which assigns a higher probability to the shorter route from the starting location to the PoI. We believe our probabilistic model represents the route selection behavior of people better than previous mobility models (Nain et al., 2005; Hong et al., 1999; Johansson et al.. 1999) since it introduces the flexibility into the route selection and represents the realistic movement behavior as studied in (Millonig & Gartner, 2009; van der Spek, 2009). Particularly, we use the probability to represent the uncertainty of the route selection and the impacts of socioeconomic factors in people's route selection as presented below.

We consider a mobile node n moving within a physical movement area, which consists of multiple street segments and intersections. Each street segment has two intersections at two ends. To simplify the model, we assume that the PoI is also an intersection. From its current location, node n follows consecutive street segments towards the PoI. We use an undirected graph $G =<V, E>$ to present the movement area as follows. The ith intersection in the movement area is represented by a vertex $v_i \in V$. Meanwhile, a street segment connecting the ith and j^{th} intersections is represented by an edge $(v_i, v_j) \in E$. An edge $(v_i, v_j) \in E$ has a weight d_{ij} representing the physical distance between v_i and v_j. So $d_{ij} = d(v_i,$ $v_j)$ and we assume that the distance from v_i to v_j is equal to that from v_j to v_i (i.e., $d_{ij} = d_{ji}$ and G is an undirected graph). Further, each vertex $v_i \in V$ has a value D_i representing the shortest distance from v_i to the PoI. Figure 7 shows an example of the graph representation of a movement area. In this figure, v_6 is the PoI and mobile nodes from other vertices will move towards v_6, and each vertex maintains the shortest distance to v_6. In our model, a route towards the PoI consists of vertices in V. We define the transition probability p_{ij} as the probability that the node n selects v_j as the next vertex in the route towards the PoI if n currently stays at vertex v_i. The next step is to calculate p_{ij}. Let A_i be the set of adjacent vertices of v_i, and each vertex of A_i has a shorter distance to the PoI than v_i. Formally, $A_i = \{v_j; D_j < D_i, (v_i, v_j) \in E\}$, and we have:

$$
p_{ij} = \begin{cases} \dfrac{d_{ij} + D_j}{\sum_{v_k \in A_i}(d_{ik} + D_k)} , \forall v_j \in A_i \\ 0 , \qquad Otherwise \end{cases} \tag{1}
$$

In Figure 7, if node n stays at v_2 and its PoI is v_6, then n selects v_3 as the next vertex with the probability $p_{23} = (d_{23}+D_3)/(d_{23}+D_3+d_{24}+D_4)$. Given a street configuration with intersections and a PoI, we can construct a graph G to represent this street configuration, in which each intersection is represented by one vertex in $v \in G$. The next step is to study the coalition patterns formed

Figure 7. Sample Street Configuration with the PoI at v_6

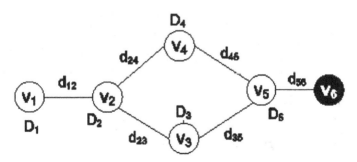

by nodes moving in a specific street configuration, in which each node uses the probabilistic model to select the route towards the PoI. For this study, we use the Mobibus modeling tool as presented in the following section.

4.3. Exponential Coalition Size of the Probabilistic Route Selection

We use the Mobius modeling tool (Deavours et al., 2007) to study the coalition patterns of the Manhattan and Random street configurations as shown in Figure 8 and Figure 9. Mobius modeling tool is the Stochastic Activity Network, which has been used extensively for modeling the behavior of distributed systems and networking systems. We study the coalition size distribution at the steady state of the system since we believe the steady state provides insightful movement characteristics of the system.

Figure 8 shows the Manhattan street configuration, in which $l = 100(m)$ is the length of distance. Figure 9 shows the Random street configuration where we specify the distance with the street segment. For each movement area, we have 1000 mobile nodes moving towards the two PoIs v_1 and v_{25} with a random speed s in the range [1.0, 2.0]

Figure 8. Manhattan Street Configuration with two PoIs at v_1 and v_{25}

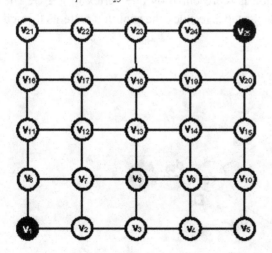

Figure 9. Random Street Configuration with two PoIs at v_1 and v_{25}

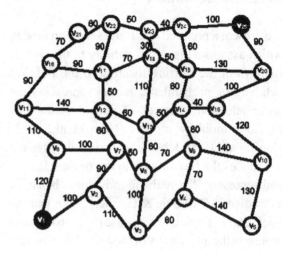

(m/s). We select the movement speed in the range of [1.0, 2.0] since this is the normal walking speed of pedestrians in reality.

First, we use an undirected graph $G = <V, E>$ to represent the street configuration. Then, for each vertex $v_i \in V$, we create one atomic model in Mobius and specify the transition probability of the case activity in this atomic model as the probability calculated by the Equation (1). The duration a node n stays in the activity of the atomic model follows an exponential distribution with the mean $\lceil l/s \rceil$ seconds. Notice that $\lceil l/s \rceil$ is the traveling time node n spends to travel the street segment of length l. By using the exponential distribution with the mean $\lceil l/s \rceil$ as the traveling time of n on the street segment of length l, we use Mobius to model the movement of n. On arriving at one PoI, nodes stay for a random period, which follows an exponential distribution. For each street configuration, we have two different cases: the first case has staying period t_1 (i.e., nodes stay at PoI for t_1 period) and the second case has staying period t_2 (i.e., nodes stay at PoI for t_2 period), in which $t_1 > t_2$. After staying at the PoI, nodes start moving towards the other PoI, again by following the probabilistic route.

Figure 10 and Figure 11 show the coalition size distribution in two above movement areas in which $t_1 = 5t_2$. From these figures, the coalition size gets maximized at the PoI and decreases when the distance to the PoI increases. Moreover, with the staying period t_1, nodes are more clustered at the PoI since the staying period is longer than the staying period of t_2. We further fit the coalition size distribution to the exponential function in the form of $y(d) = ae^{-cd} + b$ with $d > 0$, $a > 0$, $c > 0$, $b \geq 0$. We see that the coalition size distributions of these two movement areas fit very well with the exponential function. Here, $y(d)$ is the coalition size, d is the distance from the PoI, and a, b, c are coefficients.

In conclusion, when the route to PoI is selected such that the shorter route has a higher probability to be selected, the nodes form coalitions in which the coalition size follows an exponential function with respect to the distance from the PoI. This result confirms the results obtained in Section 3 from the simulation on three real Google Maps. In following sections, we leverage this exponential-coalition-size function to design COADA, a Coalition-aware Adaptive content DownloAd protocol for cellular users.

5. COADA: COALITION-AWARE ADAPTIVE CONTENT DOWNLOAD PROTOCOL

5.1. System Models

We focus on a dynamic coalition P2P network where the coalition size follows the exponential function. We assume that each mobile node has a cellular interface and a P2P interface (e.g., Bluetooth, Wifi). We consider the scenario where a mobile user moves towards a PoI, requests download of files from the content server, sets the deadlines for these downloads, and uses multiple connectivity interfaces to download the file. The mobile node (i.e., cell phone) then downloads data blocks from the file server via the cellular communication, sends its own and receives other downloaded data blocks via the P2P communication to/from other nodes in the same coalition to expedite the download. Henceforth, we use "mobile user" and "mobile node" interchangeably.

We use Online Codes (Maymounkov & Mazieres, 2003) to encode files at the server. Particularly, the file server divides the original file into B equal-sized message blocks. B is a large number

Figure 10. Manhattan Street Configuration (Here ``destination'' is the PoI). Coalition size exhibits an exponential increase with respect to the distance from the PoI.

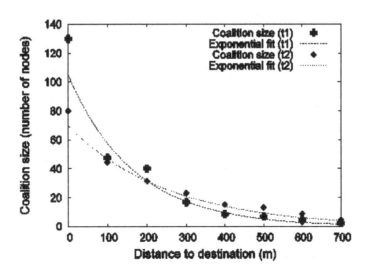

Figure 11. Random Street Configuration (Here "destination" is the PoI). Coalition size exhibits an exponential increase with respect to the distance from the PoI.

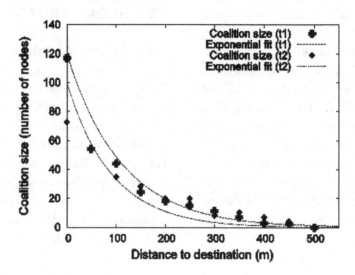

so that duplication in block generation can be avoided. As shown in (Maymounkov & Mazieres, 2003), the B message blocks will be decoded in linear-time as long as n receives at least $(1-\delta)$B' check blocks (either from the server via cellular channel or from other nodes via P2P channel). In this paper, we use the terms "check-block" and "block" interchangeably.

5.2. Design Objective and COADA Protocol Overview

The objective of COADA is to minimize the amount of downloaded data blocks from the cellular channel and meet the file download deadline. Each mobile node n has a cellular download timer T, which specifies how often n downloads a content block from the content server via the cellular interface (i.e., at each T interrupt, a file data block is downloaded via cellular network from the file server). Our objective is to tune T adaptively to the coalition pattern of the network so that n can minimize the cellular download while meeting the file download deadline.

Particularly, n predicts the coalition pattern of the network and tunes the download timer T

adaptively. Since nodes choose different routes to the PoI, coalition sizes observed by different nodes may be different, and thus the actual shapes of their exponential-coalition-size functions are different. Therefore, each mobile node n will periodically obtain and keep the coalition sizes in a coalition size list. Then, n predicts the future coalition size function by fitting the coalition size list to an exponential function (i.e., curve fitting) and uses this function to estimate the data availability in P2P channel based on Online Codes (Maymounkov & Mazieres, 2003) (See Section 5.6 for calculation of data availability). Given the estimation of data availability in P2P channel, n tunes the cellular download timer T to meet the download deadline. The protocol is adaptive since n predicts the coalition size function and tunes the cellular download timer T on the move. Notice that one download timer T is for one file download. If the user has two concurrent downloads for different files, we use two different timers T. Since the number of people downloading each of the two files is different or the coalition pattern for each file is different (See the definition of coalition in Section 2), the download timer for each file should be adaptively tuned separately. Table 1 shows notations used in COADA protocol design.

5.3. Bootstrapping

In the COADA protocol, we divide time into equal-sized periods Δ. The length of the period Δ depends on node's speed. For example, for the network formed by cellular phones of pedestrians, Δ is longer than that of the network formed by mobile phones of drivers. This is intuitive since when nodes move faster, the coalition size changes faster and thus Δ should be smaller. So, Δ specifies how frequently n needs to sample the coalition size.

When the mobile user starts her file download, node n is moving towards the PoI, n sets a deadline for the file download and switches both cellular and P2P channels on. Initially, n has a default cellular download timer T (with $T < \Delta$) and when T expires, n requests a check-block of the file from the content server via the cellular channel.

Table 1. Notations used in COADA protocol design

Name	Description
F	Number check-blocks n must download to decode the original file, $F = (1 - \delta) B'$
T_D	Deadline at which n must finish downloading the file
T_C	Current time
T	Cellular download timer. After one T, n downloads a check-block from content server
g(t)	The predicted exponential-coalition-size function, $g(t) = ae^{\lambda t} + b$
$G(t_k)$	Set of nodes in the same coalition with n at time t_k, including n. Size of $G(t_k)$ is $g(t_k)$
M	Number of check-blocks n is carrying throughout the current time T_C
Δ	The protocol time period. For each period Δ, n samples coalition size once
B_p	Estimated # of check-blocks n obtains from the P2P channel during period $[T_C, T_D]$
B_c	Estimated # of check-blocks n downloads from the server during period $[T_C, T_D]$

At the same time, n exchanges downloaded data with other peers within n's P2P one-hop communication range.

To avoid wrong prediction of its coalition size function, the node n first samples several coalition sizes, one sample per period Δ, and put these coalition sizes into the list of coalition sizes. Then, for each period Δ, n performs 4 following actions: (1) predicts the future coalition size function using the list of coalition sizes, (2) downloads data from cellular channel when T expires, (3) tunes T to meet the file download deadline, and (4) exchanges data via the P2P channel. Next, we present in detail these actions of n.

5.4. Predicting the Coalition Size Function

As shown in Section 3 and 4, in our network the coalition size follows an exponential function with respect to the distance d from the node's current location to the PoI as follows:

$$y(d) = a_1 e^{-c_1 d} + b_1 \tag{2}$$

In Equation 2, $a_1 > 0$, $b_1 > 0$, $c_1 > 0$, and $y(d)$ decreases when d increases. Let t_0 be the time at which the node n starts downloading the file content from the content server via the cellular channel. Let d_0 be the distance from the location of n to the PoI at time t_0. Since the node n is moving towards the PoI, the distance d is the decreasing function of time. Here, we use $d(t)$ to denote the distance from the location of n to the PoI at time $t > t_0$. Assuming that the movement speed of n is v, for a time $t > t_0$, we have $d(t) = d_0 - v \cdot (t - t_0)$ with $d(t) > 0$. Or we have:

$$d(t) = d_0 + vt_0 - vt \tag{3}$$

By replacing d in Equation 2 with d(t) in Equation 3, we have:

$$y\big(d(t)\big) =$$

$$a_1 e^{-c_1(d_0 + vt_0 - vt)} + b_1 = (a_1 e^{-c_1(d_0 + vt_0)})e^{(c_1 v)t} + b_1$$

Let g(t) = y(d(t)) = $ae^{\lambda t}$ + b. Then, we have a $=(a_1 e^{-c_1(d_0 + vt_0)})$, $\lambda = (c_1 v)$, and b = b_1.

The intuition of the above analysis is as follows. Since the file download deadline is T_D, the file downloading period is $[t_0, T_D]$. At time t, where $t_0 < t < T_D$, the node n is downloading the file and n is also moving towards the PoI. We see that the distance d decreases if the time t increases since when t increases, n moves closer to the PoI (i.e., d decreases). Therefore, while $y(d)$ is a decreasing function with respect to d, $g(t)$ is an increasing function with respect to t. Intuitively, when the node n gets closer to the PoI, there are more other mobile nodes moving towards the same PoI, so the coalition size increases. As a result, we have $g(t) = ae^{\lambda t} + b$, in which $g(t) > 0$, and $\lambda > 0$, a, b are coefficients. The next step is to obtain the coefficients a, b, λ for the function $g(t)$ of the mobile node n.

For each period Δ, the node n obtains a new (current) coalition size and puts this new coalition size into n's list of coalition sizes. To obtain the coalition size, n broadcasts a membership message, and nodes in n's coalition respond to this membership message. n can obtain the coalition size based on the responsive messages. Then, n fits the list of coalition sizes to an exponential function in the form of $ae^{\lambda t} + b$ to obtain coefficients a, b, λ of $g(t)$. Since nodes choose different routes to the destination, coalition sizes observed by nodes may be different. However, notice that at a specific time t, nodes in the same coalition will observe the same coalition size. Node n will use its predicted exponential-coalition-size function $g(t)$ to estimate the amount of data node n can obtain from the P2P channel (to be shown in Section 5.6).

5.5. Downloading Data from Cellular Channel

The node n has a cellular download timer T. When this timer T expires, n requests new data from the server. Upon receiving the request from n, the server creates a check-block (an encoded block from the original blocks) and sends it to n (Maymounkov & Mazieres, 2003). Since Online Codes is applied at the server side and the number of message blocks B is large, the server will not create duplicate check-blocks with high probability (Maymounkov & Mazieres, 2003). Therefore, any check-block returned by the server is useful for n (and its peers if n sends the downloaded blocks to them) to decode the original file.

5.6. Tuning the Cellular Download Timer

Given the predicted coalition size function $g(t)$, the next step is to calculate the data availability in P2P channel (i.e., B_p in Table 1) and tune the cellular download timer T adaptively. In our protocol, when the two nodes n_1, n_2 first meet at time t, they exchange all new check-blocks via the P2P channel. For the node n_2, the blocks of n_1 are new if the blocks are not carried by n_2 at time t. After that, when they stay in one coalition, n_1 and n_2 only exchange check-blocks, which are newly downloaded during the last period Δ. Then, B_p is estimated as follows.

Since n only knows its current cellular download timer T, n assumes all nodes in n's current coalition have the similar cellular download timer T. The reason for the similar timers T is as follows: intuitively, nodes in one coalition carry the same set of check-blocks and observe similar coalition size, so their cellular download timers should be similar or at least close. For a future time $t_k > T_C$, the coalition size $g(t_k) = ae^{\lambda t_k} + b$ can be predicted by using the function $g(t)$ of n.

Further, the number of check-blocks a node in $G(t_k)$ can download via the cellular channel for the period $[t_k; t_k + \Delta]$ is $\frac{\Delta}{T}$. The total number of check-blocks downloaded via the cellular channel by all nodes in $G(t_k)$, including n, for the period $[t_k; t_k + \Delta]$ is $g(t_k)\frac{\Delta}{T}$. Notice that this calculation holds since the server will not create duplicate check-blocks with high probability by using On-line Codes as presented in (Maymounkov & Mazieres, 2003). As a result, all new check-blocks downloaded by other nodes in $G(t_k)$ are useful for n to decode the original file. The number of periods Δ between the current time T_C and the file download deadline T_D is $\delta = \frac{T_D - T_C}{\Delta}$. So, we have:

$$B_p = \sum_{i=0}^{\delta} g\left(T_C + i\Delta\right)\frac{\Delta}{T} \qquad (4)$$

Let M be the number of check-blocks carried by node n since the download starts until the current time T_C. Therefore, $M + B_p$ is the number of check-blocks n can potentially obtain by the file download deadline T_D, using the unchanged cellular download timer T for the duration $[T_C; T_D]$. To make the protocol adaptive, n updates the cellular download timer T as follows:

1. If $M + B_p < F$, then $B_c = F - (M + B_p)$. The number of check-blocks that n needs to download from the cellular channel for each period Δ is $\frac{B_c}{\delta}$. As a result, the new cellular download timer is $T = \frac{\delta\Delta}{B_c}$. If $T > \Delta$, then n sets $T = \Delta$.
2. If $M + B_p > F$, then that means n can potentially download all needed check-blocks

from the P2P channel to decode the original file. However, n conservatively sets $T = T + \frac{T}{2}$ to prepare for a sudden change of coalition pattern in the future. If $T > \Delta$, then n sets $T = \Delta$.

Given the new value of the cellular download timer T obtained by these above steps, the node n uses the new T to download check-blocks via the cellular channel from the next Δ onward.

5.7. Exchanging Data via P2P Communication

Since the neighbor list may change over time, node n uses timestamp to avoid duplicate data exchange with its neighbors as follows. Any time n receives a block from the content server or the peer, if the block is new to n, n marks the block with n's current time. Any time n wants to send a block to n_1 via the P2P channel, n sends the oldest block b that n has not sent to n_1, based on the timestamp of b marked by n. Upon sending b to n_1, n records the timestamp of b as the oldest time n sends a block to n_1. As a result, n can use the timestamp to avoid duplicate data exchange.

5.8. Protocol Discussion

Since the fitting function of the coalition size is an exponential function, which is more expressive than a linear function, we believe COADA works even better for other scenarios (with different street configurations and node densities) where the coalition size distribution exhibits a linearly increasing function. COADA is also not limited to the combination of cellular and Wifi/Bluetooth communications. We believe that COADA is applicable for other communication combinations such as cellular and ZigBee.

6. EVALUATION

6.1. Simulation Settings

We write our own simulator in C++ to evaluate COADA. Nodes in our simulation move in a Manhattan street area with 100 intersections as shown in Figure 12, in which v_{100} represents the PoI. Table 2 shows the details of simulation settings. For the cellular channel, we use 1xEV-DO (Evolution-Data Only) with a peak data rate of 2.4Mbps and implement the Proportional Fair Scheduler of the cellular network as presented in (Bender et al., 2000). Initially, a node n is randomly placed at one of intersections v_6, v_{15}, v_{24}, v_{33}, v_{42}, v_{51}. We start nodes at these intersections to give them the similar distance from v_{100}. Then, n moves towards the destination v_{100}. To avoid the wrong coalition size sampling, initially n has the initial coalition size 1 and after the first 100(s), n starts sampling the coalition size. n starts to predict the coalition size function at 200(s). At each intersection, n selects the next intersection towards v_{100} by following the probabilistic route selection model presented in Section 4.

We simulate two different types of dynamic coalition P2P networks named Pedestrian and Car networks. The Pedestrian network represents to the scenario where football fans are walking towards the football stadium to attend a football match as mentioned in Section 2, where they download the video of match preview via the cellular channel and exchange data via the Bluetooth channel. Meanwhile, Car network corresponds to the scenarios where shoppers drive towards the shopping malls and download videos of product preview via the cellular channel and exchange downloaded data via the Wifi channel. For the Car network, we use 75 (m) for the transmission range since the transmission range in practice is much shorter than the theoretical range (i.e., 250 m) due to the fading of the Wifi channel and the obstacles on streets. The deadline of the file download is set to 1200 (s) since a node n is about to arrive at v_{100} with this deadline, which is set based on the movement speed and the distance from the initial location of n towards v_{100} in Table 2. Notice that different mobile nodes have different movement speeds. However, they download the same file in our simulation. We run the ex-

Figure 12. Simulation Area. Nodes start at v_{51}, v_{42}, v_{33}, v_{24}, v_{15}, v_6 and move towards the PoI at v_{100}

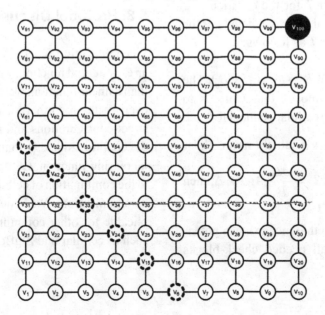

Table 2. Simulation settings

Parameter	Description
Number of nodes	[75,100,150,200]
Street seg. length (v_1; v_2)	Pedestrian:100, Car:500 (m)
Destination (i.e., PoI)	v_{100}
Download deadline	1200 (s)
Start locations	v_6; v_{15}; v_{24}; v_{33}; v_{42}; v_{51}
File length	[5000,10000,15000,20000] (block)
Block size	2KB
Cellular download rate	2 (Mbps) (Bender et al., 2000)
P2P transmission range	Pedestrian:10, Car:75 (m)
Node speed	Pedestrian:[1.0,2.0], Car:[8.0,10.0] (m/s)
Δ	Pedestrian:50(s), Car: 40(s)

periments 10 times and plot the average of the two metrics: (1) the percentage of downloaded blocks via the cellular link, and (2) the peer-to-peer message overhead. These two metrics are chosen to evaluate the performance of COADA since we want to reduce the expense from cellular download and save the node energy.

6.2. Simulation Results

6.2.1. Comparison of COADA with Non-Adaptive Protocol

We first describe the non-adaptive protocol and then compare the performance of COADA protocol with the non-adaptive protocol.

Non-adaptive Protocol: for the non-adaptive protocol, a mobile node uses the cellular channel to download random message blocks from the content server and at the same time uses the P2P channel to exchange downloaded message blocks. Here, no networking coding is used to encode the file at the content server and no coalition pattern of the network is considered. Notice that the non-adaptive protocol is the current state of the art protocols (Hanano et al., 2009; Luo et al., 2007;

Yoon et al., 2008; Aly & Elnahas, 2008; Hsieh & Sivakumar, 2004; Stiemerling & Kiesel, 2009; Kang & Mutka, 2004; Ioannidis et al., 2005; Park & Kasera, 2005).

Comparison: Figures 13, 14, and 15 compare the performance of COADA with the above non-adaptive protocol. In our simulation, using the COADA protocol, all nodes meet the file download deadline. These figures show that the adaptive protocol outperforms the non-adaptive protocol in both Pedestrian and Car networks. Particularly, COADA reduces the cellular download from 20% to 25% compared to the non-adaptive scheme. In Figure 13, when the file size increases, COADA works better for Car network since when the network is more dynamic, nodes may meet more peers, create coalitions, and have a higher chance to obtain more missing check-blocks. Figure 14 shows that when the number of nodes in the network increases, both COADA and non-adaptive protocol perform better since the nodes have more peers to exchange data. Again, COADA works better for the Car network due to the increases of network dynamics. Figure 15 shows that compared to the non-adaptive protocol, the use of timestamp in peer to peer data exchange significantly saves the message overhead of COADA. Notice that the y-axis of this figure is in log-scale.

6.2.2. Fitting Error

Figure 16 shows that when the nodes get closer from the destination, COADA can predict the exponential coalition function $g(t)$ more accurately. In this figure the average normalized error is calculated as follows.

The analysis in this paragraph is for a mobile node n. Let Y denote the set of all predicted coalition size functions $g(t)$ of n for the entire simulation. Notice that for each Δ period, we have one predicted function $g(t)$ for a mobile node n. For the ith Δ period, let $g_i(t)$ be the exponential coalition function predicted for the ith Δ period. So, we have $Y = \{g_i(t)\}$, which is the set of all these $g(t)$

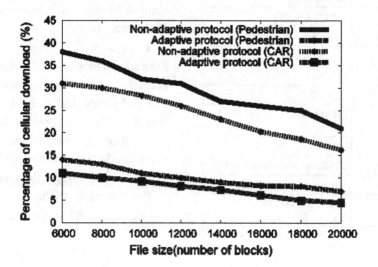

Figure 13. Variation of file size and its impact on % of file downloaded from the cellular network. The adaptive protocol is COADA. COADA outperforms non-adaptive protocol from 15% to 20%.

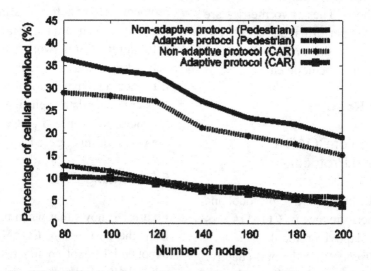

Figure 14. Variation of number of nodes its impact on % of file downloaded from the cellular network. The adaptive protocol is COADA. COADA outperforms non-adaptive protocol from 15% to 20%.

functions obtained since the starting time of the download t_0 until the file download deadline T_D. At the time of file download deadline T_D, the obtained function $g(t)$ should be the most accurate coalition size function since in our simulation the node is very close to or stays at PoI at the file download deadline. Let α be the last Δ period before the file download deadline T_D. Let $g_\alpha(t)$ be the predicted function obtained during the period

α, we have $g_\alpha(t) \in Y$. For one function $g_i(t) \in Y$, we calculate the sum of absolute difference, E_i, between $g_i(t)$ and $g_\alpha(t)$. Let E_{max} denote the maximum value of E_i for all functions $g_i(t) \in Y$, or $E_{max} = \text{argmax}_i \{E_i\}$. Then, we normalize E_i (i.e., $E_i = E_i / E_{max}$), hence we have $0 \le E_i \le 1$ for all functions $g_i(t) \in Y$. As a result, for each node n we have a set of normalized sum errors of all functions $g_i(t) \in Y$.

Figure 15. The adaptive protocol is COADA. COADA outperforms non-adaptive protocol significantly in terms of message overhead.

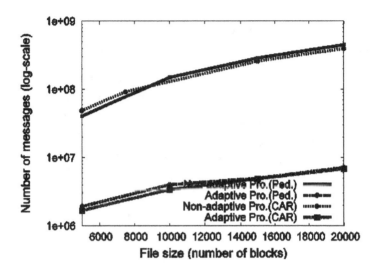

Figure 16. When nodes get closer to the PoI, the coalition size function is estimated more accurately. The adaptive protocol is COADA.

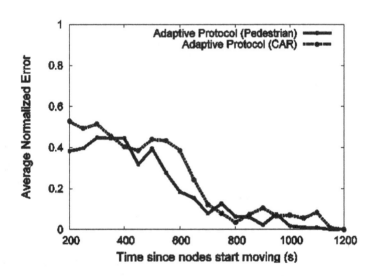

Figure 16 is obtained by averaging the normalized sum errors E_i of all 1000 nodes in the simulation of Pedestrian network and Car network. In Figure 16, the average normalized error decreases when time is closer to the file download deadline or node is closer to the PoI. That means, the coalition size function is predicted more accurately when node is closer to the PoI since the node obtains more "knowledge" about the coalition pattern of the network.

7. CONCLUSION

We exploit the transition of coalition size when the nodes move from the sparse areas to the dense areas of the Dynamic coalition P2P Network to design an adaptive content distribution protocol. In order to understand the coalition pattern of nodes, we study the relationship between the size of coalitions and the distance from the mobile nodes to the Point of Interest on three real maps taken from Google Map. Our study shows that the coalition size distribution follows an exponential function with respect to the distance from the PoI. This result is further confirmed in our model of the coalition pattern in the dynamic coalition P2P Network using the Mobius modeling tool. Given the exponential-coalition-size, we present a novel adaptive protocol named COADA that blends cellular and P2P communications of the mobile devices and leverages the exponential-coalition-size function to improve content download. The simulation results show that COADA considerably outperforms the non-adaptive protocol and adapts well to network dynamics.

REFERENCES

Aly, S. G., & Elnahas, A. A. (2008). Sustained service lookup in areas of sudden dense population. *Wireless Communications and Mobile Computing, 8*, 61–74. doi:10.1002/wcm.427

Bender, P., Black, P., Grob, M., Padovani, R., Sindhushayana, N., & Viterbi, A. (2000). CDMA/HDR: A bandwidth-efficient high-speed wireless data service for normadic users. *IEEE Communications Magazine, 38*(7), 70–77. doi:10.1109/35.852034

Deavours, D. D., Clark, G., Courtney, T., Daly, D., Derisavi, S., & Doyle, J. M. (2007). The mobius framework and its implementation. *IEEE Transactions on Software Engineering, 28*(10), 956–969. doi:10.1109/TSE.2002.1041052

Gkantsidis, C., & Rodriguez, P. (2005). Network coding for large scale content distribution. In *Proceedings of the 24th Annual Joint Conference on INFOCOM* (Vol. 4, pp. 2235-2245).

Google. (n. d.). *Geolocation API*. Retrieved from http://code.google.com/apis/gears/api_geolocation.html

Hanano, H., Murata, Y., Shibata, N., Yasumoto, K., & Ito, M. (2009). Video ads dissemination through wifi-cellular hybrid networks. In *Proceedings of the International Conference on Pervasive Computing and Communications* (pp. 1-6).

Hong, X., Gerla, M., Pei, G., & Chiang, C. C. (1999). A group mobility model for ad hoc wireless networks. In *Proceedings of the 2nd International Workshop on Modeling, Analysis and Simulation of wireless and mobile systems* (pp. 53-60).

Hsieh, H.-Y., & Sivakumar, R. (2004). On using peer-to-peer communication in cellular wireless data networks. *IEEE Transactions on Mobile Computing, 3*.

Ioannidis, I., Carbunar, B., & Nita-Rotaru, C. (2005). High throughput routing in hybrid cellular and ad-hoc networks. In *Proceedings of the International Symposium on the World of Wireless Mobile and Multimedia Networks* (pp. 171-176).

Johansson, P., Larsson, T., Hedman, N., Mielczarek, B., & Degermark, M. (1999). Scenario-based performance analysis of routing protocols for mobile ad-hoc networks. In *Proceedings of the 5th Annual International Conference on Mobile Computing and Networking* (pp. 195-206).

Jrv, O., Aasa, A., Ahas, R., & Saluveer, E. (2007). Weather dependence of tourist's spatial behavior and destination choices: case study with passive mobile positioning data in Estonia. In Matzarakis, A., de Freitas, C. R., & Scott, D. (Eds.), *Developments in tourism climatology*. Milwaukee, WI: International Society of Biometeorology.

Jung, S., Lee, U., Chang, A., Cho, D.-K., & Gerla, M. (2007). Bluetorrent: Cooperative content sharing for bluetooth users. *Pervasive and Mobile Computing, 3*, 609–634. doi:10.1016/j.pmcj.2007.06.003

Kang, S.-S., & Mutka, M. (2004). Efficient mobile access to internet data via a wireless peer-to-peer peer network. In *Proceedings of the 2ⁿᵈ Annual Conference on Pervasive Computing and Communication* (pp. 197-205).

Lee, U., Park, J.-S., Lee, S.-H., Ro, W. W., Pau, G., & Gerla, M. (2008). Efficient peer-to-peer file sharing using network coding in manet. *Journal of Communications and Networks, 10*, 422–429.

Luo, H., Ramjee, R., Sinha, P., Li, L., & Lu, S. (2007). The design and evaluation of unified cellular and ad hoc networks. *IEEE Transactions on Mobile Computing, 6*(9), 1060–1074. doi:10.1109/TMC.2007.1035

Mansfeld, Y., & Ya'acoub, K. (2004). Patterns of tourist destination-choice and travel behavior among members of the urban and rural arab community of israel: A comparative study of haifa and ibilin. *GeoJournal, 35*(4), 459–470. doi:10.1007/BF00824356

Maymounkov, P., & Mazieres, D. (2003). Rateless codes and big downloads. In *Proceedings of the International Workshop on Peer-to-Peer Systems.*

Millonig, A., & Gartner, G. (2009). Ways of walking - developing a pedestrian typology for personalised mobile information . In Gartner, G., & Rehrl, K. (Eds.), *Location based services and telecartography II: From sensor fusion to context models* (pp. 79–94). Berlin, Germany: Springer-Verlag. doi:10.1007/978-3-540-87393-8_6

Nain, P., Towsley, D., Liu, B., & Liu, Z. (2005). Properties of random direction models. In *Proceedings of the 24ᵗʰ Annual Joint Conference of INFOCOMM* (Vol. 3, pp. 1897-1907).

Papatheodorou, A. (2001). Why people travel to different places. *Annals of Tourism Research, 28*(1), 164–179. doi:10.1016/S0160-7383(00)00014-1

Park, J. C., & Kasera, S. (2005). Enhancing cellular multicast performance using ad hoc networks. In . *Proceedings of the Wireless Communications and Networking Conference, 4*, 2175. doi:10.1109/WCNC.2005.1424854

Stiemerling, M., & Kiesel, S. (2009). A system for peer-to-peer video streaming in resource constrained mobile environments. In *Proceedings of the 1ˢᵗ Workshop on User-Provided Networking: Challenges and Opportunities* (pp. 25-30).

van der Spek, S. (2009). Mapping pedestrian movement: Using tracking technologies in Koblenz . In Gartner, G., & Rehrl, K. (Eds.), *Location based services and telecartography II: From sensor fusion to context models* (pp. 95–118). Berlin, Germany: Springer-Verlag. doi:10.1007/978-3-540-87393-8_7

Wang, M., & Li, B. (2007). R2: Random push with random network coding in live peer-to-peer streaming. *IEEE Journal on Selected Areas in Communications, 25*.

Yoon, H., Kim, J., Tany, F., & Hsieh, R. (2008). On-demand video streaming in mobile opportunistic networks. In *Proceedings of the 6ᵗʰ Annual International Conference on Pervasive Computing and Communication* (pp. 80-89).

This work was previously published in the International Journal of Adaptive, Resilient and Autonomic Systems, Volume 2, Issue 2, edited by Vincenzo De Florio, pp. 1-22, copyright 2011 by IGI Publishing (an imprint of IGI Global).

Chapter 15

ROCRSSI++:
An Efficient Localization Algorithm for Wireless Sensor Networks

Flavio Frattini
Institute of High Performance Computing and Networking, Italy

Christian Esposito
Università di Napoli Federico II, Italy

Stefano Russo
Università di Napoli Federico II, Italy

ABSTRACT

Localization within a Wireless Sensor Network consists of defining the position of a given set of sensors by satisfying some non-functional requirements such as (1) efficient energy consumption, (2) low communication or computation overhead, (3) no, or limited, use of particular hardware components, (4) fast localization, (5) robustness, and (6) low localization error. Although there are several algorithms and techniques available in literature, localization is viewed as an open issue because none of the current solutions are able to jointly satisfy all the previous requirements. An algorithm called ROCRSSI appears to be a suitable solution; however, it is affected by several inefficiencies that limit its effectiveness in real case scenarios. This paper proposes a refined version of this algorithm, called ROCRSSI++, which resolves such inefficiencies using and storing information gathered by the sensors in a more efficient manner. Several experiments on actual devices have been performed. The results show a reduction of the localization error with respect to the original algorithm. This paper investigates energy consumption and localization time required by the proposed approach.

DOI: 10.4018/978-1-4666-2056-8.ch015

INTRODUCTION

Wireless Sensor Networks (WSNs) consist of a massive number of low-cost, low-power and multi-functional small sensors, capable to communicate with other neighbours by means of wireless networks. One of the fundamental issues to efficiently realize a WSN in a real case scenario is *Localization*, i.e., identifying the position of a certain sensor. In fact, there are several real use cases where location-awareness in data dissemination among sensors within a WSN is crucial. Let us consider the case of a WSN used for environmental monitoring, e.g., controlling the occurrence of fire within a forest. The mere information of the presence of fire is not useful if it is not correlated with information on where such fire is present. This is made by attaching to the exchanged messages the location of the sender, e.g., the sensor that detected the fire. Therefore, it is important to be able to determine the location of sensors, so to realize location-aware data dissemination in WSNs.

Localization in WSNs has to satisfy some requirements (Akyildiz, Su, Sankarasubramaniam, & Cayirci, 2002). It is common that sensors are deployed in inaccessible areas, so the substitution of the batteries is very difficult. Moreover, due to the small size of sensors, batteries are small and characterized by short life, and then, energy efficiency is one of the main requirements for these devices. The solution to avoid battery consumption is to use algorithms with low communication and computation overhead without requiring any particular hardware. Moreover, the use of sensors in critical situations implies that localization has to be fast and robust, so that countermeasures can be triggered when a critical situation is detected. In addition, WSN are usually deployed in challenging environments and sensors make use of wireless network for communicating among each other. Therefore, the adopted algorithm must properly handle phenomena, such as message losses and

signal interference, that may compromise localization. Last, it is required a low localization error.

Most common solutions for localization have been proved to be unsuitable for WSNs, since they are unable to satisfy such requirements (Mao, Fidan, & Anderson, 2007). For instance, the market offers small GPS modules for sensors, but their costs and energy consumption preclude their use in the field of WSNs. Therefore, in recent years, both academia and industry have developed several localization algorithms tailored on the characteristics of WSN. They can be broadly classified in *range-based* or *range-free* localization algorithm, depending if the location is computed by estimating the absolute point-to-point distances among the sensors or relative distances. Another adopted classification is based on how localization is performed. It can be centralized, i.e., a single sensor is responsible of localizing all the other sensors, or distributed, i.e., each sensor will take care of computing its own position by properly interacting with other neighbouring sensors. In this work, we have preferred to use a range-free and fully-distributed algorithm. This is motivated by the consideration that range-free algorithms do not require complex hardware, and centralized ones are difficult to be realized in a real case WSN due to the resource limitation of sensors in terms of computation power, memory and communication overhead.

In this work, we have adopted "Ring Overlapping Based on Comparison of Received Signal Strength Indicator" (ROCRSSI) (Liu, Wu, & He, 2004), which estimates sensors location by considering the overlap of rings of finite definite thickness by comparing RSSI values received by some neighbouring sensors. This algorithm has been proved in previous works, such as (Liu & Wu, 2005), to require few computations, to exhibit low communication overhead, and to achieve the best localization accuracy among the range-free algorithms. However, such algorithm is affected by (*1*) inconsistency, (*2*) variable RSSI, (*3*) channel asymmetry, (*4*) memory and communication inefficiency. The main contributions of the work described in this paper are twofold. On one hand, we propose ROCRSSI++, which addresses ROCRSSI inefficiencies, unmanaged by another refined version of the algorithm, called ROCRSSI+ (Crepaldi, Casari, Zanella, & Zorzi, 2006). On the other hand, we have evaluated the proposed algorithm using a real case WSN in order to assess its localization error, energy consumption and localization time.

This paper is organized as follows. The next section introduces the issue of localization in WSN briefly; then some general concepts on localization are presented and related works are illustrated. The section *ROCRSSI* introduces the homonym localization algorithm, while in the *ROCRSSI++* section our refinements are presented. Subsequently, experimental results are discussed. Finally, we conclude this paper by summarizing paper contributions, and outlining future work.

PROBLEM STATEMENT

The use of WSNs in real case scenarios implies several different issues that need to be carefully addressed when designing a localization algorithm:

1. Sensors adopted in WSN have limited size, and are equipped with short-life batteries. In addition, in most of the application scenarios, such as monitoring of landslides or fires, battery substitution is impossible. Then, low energy consumption is needed. This can be obtained if the adopted algorithm is simple, i.e., it does not require many and/or complex computations, or it does not exchange many messages. Table 1 shows power consumption of typical operations performed by a generic WSN application for Mica2 motes. From these data it is evident that GPS can not be used because of its high energy consumption. However, also power consumption of the radio module is not negligible, so the number of transmitted and received messages has to be kept as low as possible.

2. Sensors are characterized by limited resources, e.g., mostly all the sensors used in devising WSN have about 8KB RAM (Crossbow Technology, 2009). This implies avoiding algorithms that exhibit high computational complexity and heavy use of the memory.

3. Hardware of sensors for WSN is relatively simple, so most of them are only equipped with RF technologies as communication means and any particular additional hardware component is avoided (Crossbow Technology, 2009; BeanAir, 2010; Wireless Sensors, 2010).

4. Time needed to locate a sensor has to be within a temporal constraint imposed by the given application scenario, e.g., in fire detection, the temperature information. Therefore, localization estimation needs to be received before a proper deadline, based on specific application requirements, has expired.

5. Messages among sensors are conveyed by wireless networks, which are known to exhibit a faulty behaviour. Moreover, the environment where the WSN has been deployed can be affected by signal pollution, which can alter the RSSI measurements. The adopted localization algorithm has to tolerate such phenomena, so that its outcomes are not strongly affected by them.

6. WSNs are often used in scenarios which require a precise estimation of the location where data have been obtained, e.g., in fire monitoring within a building, it is crucial that the room where the fire started is exactly located. Otherwise, if the correct point where the fire spread is not reported, the fireman will not arrive on time to extinguish it before it expands in other rooms.

In summary, localization in WSN is characterized by the following requirements: (*1*) efficient energy consumption, (*2*) low communication or computation overhead, (*3*) no use of particular hardware, (*4*) fast localization, (*5*) robustness, and (*6*) high positioning accuracy.

BACKGROUND AND RELATED WORK

Localization is the issue of determining the position of a given device by using a combination of technologies, methods and techniques, as illustrated in Figure 1 (Hightower & Borriello, 2001).

Technologies represent the ICT infrastructure adopted to perform raw measurements. These technologies can be classified as *dedicated*, which are specifically designed for positioning purpose, e.g., ultra-sound or satellite infrastructures, or *integrated*, which can be used also for communication purposes, e.g., Radio Frequency (RF) technologies such as Wi-Fi or ZigBee.

Methods represent the features measured by using the adopted technologies:

1. **Time of Arrival (ToA):** Time that a signal emitted by a source takes to reach its destination, and it can be evaluated only if clocks of sender and receiver are synchronized;
2. **Time Difference of Arrival (TDoA):** Difference among reception instances of a signal at two, or more, spatially separated

receiver devices, and as previously, it can be computed only if there is clock synchronization among the devices;
3. **Angle of Arrival (AoA):** Estimation of the direction from which a device receives a signal emitted by a given source;
4. **Received Signal Strength Indicator (RSSI):** Power of signals received by a given device.

On top of the methods, there are the techniques, i.e., algorithms transforming raw measures into canonical position information. The most important techniques can be summarized as follows:

1. **Triangulation:** The user location is computed from given measures of angles and sides of one or more triangles formed by the point where the user is located and two, or more, so-called beacons, i.e., sensors at known location;
2. **Scene analysis**: Features of a scene observed from a particular point of view are used to infer the user location;
3. **Proximity Sensing**: The user location is equal to the location of the closest reference point at a known location.

Then, a localization system is characterized by selecting a combination of technologies, methods and techniques.

Figure 1. Localization stack, consisting of technologies, methods and techniques

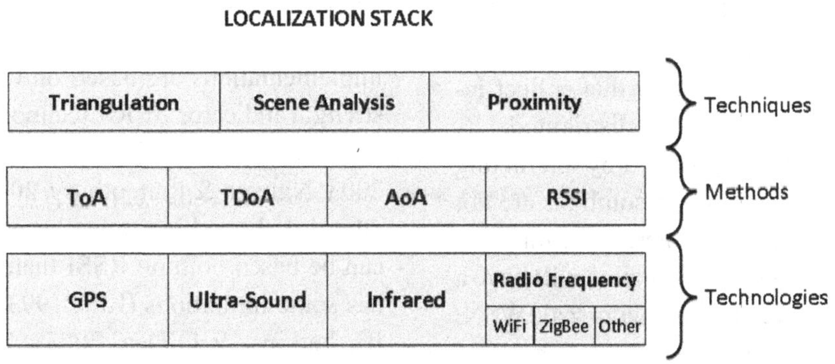

Referring to Figure 1, most wireless sensors manufacturers provide sensors equipped with RF technologies based on IEEE 802.15 standard for Wireless Personal Area Network (WPAN) (Crossbow Technology, 2009; BeanAir, 2010; Wireless Sensors, 2010). Indeed, other technologies are too expensive and/or have high battery consumption, as in the case of GPS. Moreover, most of the methods in the figure require special hardware components, e.g., AoA requires special antennas, such as multidirectional ones, while ToA and TDoA require particular hardware for clock synchronization. Instead, RSSI is typically defined in the specifics of most RF technologies, such as Bluetooth, Wi-Fi, ZigBee, and does not require additional hardware for its detection. Scene analysis cannot be used in WSNs since they are usually deployed in environment that are unknown beforehand, e.g., in fire monitoring in National Parks, sensors can be randomly deployed by dropping them from an aircraft. Besides, localization based on knowledge of the graph of the network has a high computational cost and requires centralized computation, as in the case of MDS-MAP technique (Shang, Ruml, Zhang, & Fromherz, 2003). Last, proximity does not allow having good localization accuracy with a scarce density of sensors. However, in WSN it is not possible to have a suitable density to have an accepted accuracy when using proximity. Therefore, the only combination that is suitable for WSNs is the following one: (*1*) a given RF technology, such as ZigBee, (*2*) RSSI and (*3*) triangulation.

The literature of localization in WSN is rich of solutions that realize such combination, and they can be classified as centralized, i.e., localization is carried out by a single sensor that collect information from the other ones, or distributed, i.e., each sensor estimates its location by interacting with other sensors. Centralized solutions are not able to guarantee an efficient energy consumption and low overhead, since computation will have a strong complexity even for a medium-scale WSN, and are vulnerable to the failure of the centralized

Table 1. Current draw and power consumption for Mica2 Motes by Crossbow Technology (adapted from Davis & Miller, 2009)

Component	Current (mA)	Power (mW)
Empty Program	7,5	.02325
Leds	2	.006
Radio Idle	16	.0496
Radio On/Off	4	.0124
Radio Trasmit	21	.0651
Radio Receive	16	.0496
GPS	110,106	.3413
EEPROM Read	11,971	.0371
EEPROM Write	32,871	.1019

sensor, which is probable to happen due to the fast consumption of its battery. Therefore, only distributed algorithms can be viable solutions to the problem described in the previous section. Such algorithms can be further classified as range-based or range-free, depending if the location is estimated by using the absolute point-to-point distance among sensors or not.

Range-based RSSI algorithms are known to be strongly affected by errors due to the unpredictable radio propagation behaviour, so they present poor localization accuracy (Elnahrawy, Li, & Martin, 2004). Among the range-free RSSI algorithm, we have selected ROCRSSI due to its simplicity in terms of computation and communication cost and for its high localization accuracy (Liu & Wu, 2005).

Table 2 summarizes main characteristics of some localization approaches. Min-Max and Multilateration are range-based algorithms, whose implementations are based on the use of signal strength indicator of RF technologies and their accuracy is very limited (Langendoen & Reijers, 2003; Nguyen & Rattentbury, 2003). Also Maximum Likelihood is a range-based algorithm that can be based both on RSSI than on ToA, and it has some limitations (Kay, 1993; Patwari, Hero III, Perkins, & O'Dea, 2003). MDS-MAP is a

Table 2. Main characteristic of some localization algorithms for Wireless Sensor Networks; the symbol (-) means that we have not information about that characteristic of the algorithm

Algorithm	Communication & Computation	Hardware	Robustness	Accuracy
Min-Max	simple	simple	affected by noise	Limited
Multilateration	simple	simple	affected by noise	Limited
Maximum Likelihood	complex	simple if based only on RSS and not on ToA too	-	asymptotically optimum
MDS-MAP	complex	simple if based only on RSS and not on ToA too	yes	High
ROCRSSI	very simple	simple	affected by reflection and refraction	Limited

centralized algorithm that has high accuracy, but it is very complex with respect to other localization algorithms for WSNs (Shang et al., 2003; Ji & Zha, 2004). Last, ROCRSSI is a range-free, distributed algorithm.

ROCRSSI

Ring Overlapping based on Comparison of Received Signal Strength Indication (ROCRSSI) (Liu, Wu, & He, 2004) distinguishes nodes in two distinct categories: beacons and unknown nodes. The former ones have a known position, while the location of the latter ones is not available and needs to be estimated by using the RSSI

values obtained from the messages received from the beacon nodes.

To explain how to localize sensors with ROCRSSI, we present here a concrete example, which is illustrated in Figure 2. There are three beacons, namely A, B and C, and an unknown sensor, namely S. All the sensors exchange beaconing messages, so that each of them have achieved RSSI estimations. Such estimations are indicated as $RSSI_{xy}$, i.e. the RSSI value defined as the strength of a signal emitted by x and received by y, and assumed to do not change if the measure is computed backward. Let us consider that the following inequalities are verified:

$$RSSI_{AC} < RSSI_{SA} < RSSI_{AB}$$
$$RSSI_{BC} < RSSI_{SB} < RSSI_{AB} \qquad (1)$$
$$RSSI_{AC} < RSSI_{SC}$$

The first inequality in Equation 1 implies that S estimates to be in the ring (drawn with an unbroken line in Figure 2) with its center in sensor A with inner and outer radius respectively equal to the distance between sensors A and B, and between sensors A and C. The second inequality defines another ring (drawn with a dashed line in

Figure 2. Localization using ROCRSSI

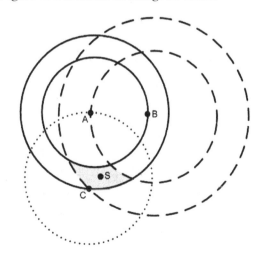

Figure 2) centered in sensor B with inner and outer radius equal to the distance between sensors B and A, and between sensors B and C. Last, the third inequality indicates that S is placed within a circle (drawn with a dotted line in Figure 2) centered in sensor C and with radius equal to the distance between sensors C and A. The center of gravity of the intersection area of the rings and the circle represents the estimated position of S.

Grid Scan Algorithm

In order to simplify the computation of the intersection areas and discretize the set of possible positions in which an unknown sensor is located, the Grid Scan Algorithm is used (He, Huang, Blum, Stankovic, & Abdelzaher, 2003). It considers a WSN as deployed on a grid, where a given sensor is assumed to be positioned in the center of a cell, and the grid is considered as a Cartesian coordinate plane, as in Figure 3. Each cell has associated a counter, whose value could be updated at every iteration of the localization

Figure 3. Grid with five sensors

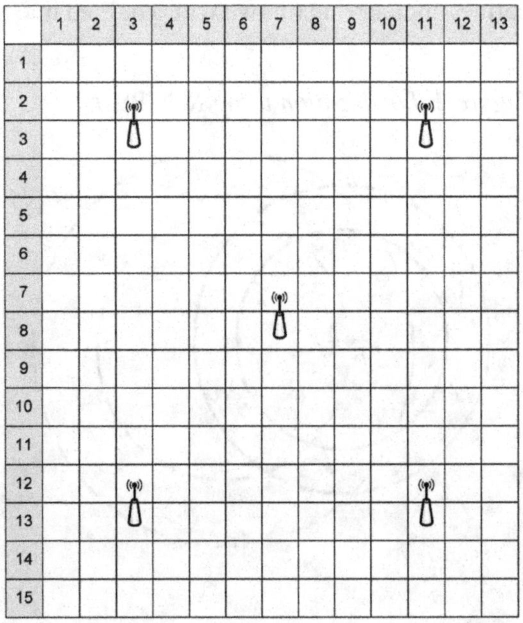

algorithm. If the cell is within one of the areas defined by the inequities produced during the localization algorithm, such as in Equation 1, its counter is incremented. The intersection area is defined as the set I of cells whose counter assumes the maximum value; the coordinates x and y of the center of gravity of such area are obtained according to the following formula:

$$x = \frac{1}{n}\sum_{i=1}^{n} x_i; \quad y = \frac{1}{n}\sum_{i=1}^{n} y_i \qquad (2)$$

where x_i and y_i are the coordinates of a generic cell of set I, and n is the cardinality of I.

ROCRSSI+

ROCRSSI is affected by an accuracy reduction due to a severe drawback. In fact, it assumes that nodes are located inside an unbounded area, i.e., normal nodes are surrounded by beacons, as illustrated in Figure 2. However, it is not rare that in Equation 1 there may be the following inequity:

$$RSSI_{SC} < RSSI_{AC} \qquad (3)$$

Such situation is shown in Figure 4, where sensor S is located outside the range of beacon A and B. In this case the application of ROCRSSI will assign to S the position of sensor C. In fact, information obtained by sensors whose range does not contain sensor S, such as A and B in Figure 4, are not considered during the location estimation.

An improvement, named ROCRSSI+, has been proposed by (Crepaldi et al., 2006) to resolve this drawback; such version of the algorithm also considers for the location estimation RSSI values assigned to sensors whose range does not contain the unknown sensor.

Figure 4. Localization using ROCRSSI+

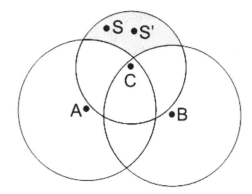

Table 3. Comparison of ROCRSSI and ROCRSSI+ (adapted from Crepaldi et al., 2006)

	ROCRSSI		ROCRSSI+	
# Beacons	Avr.	Std. dev.	Avr.	Std. dev.
3	437	216	427	210
4	414	245	402	266
5	403	254	388	217

In fact, the position of the unknown sensor *S* is equal to the center of gravity of the intersection among rings and circles of sensors whose range contains the sensor *S*, and the areas outside the range of sensors whose range does not contain the sensor *S*. This allows achieving a greater accuracy then basic ROCRSSI. For instance, considering Figure 4, ROCRSSI+ will not consider all the range of sensor S, but only its area outside the coverage of *A* and *B* (depicted in gray within the Figure 4). Such estimated area has a center of gravity, indicated as *S'*, that is closer to the real location of the sensor *S* than the position of sensor *C*. An empirical evidence of the improvement achieved by ROCRSSI+ is illustrated in Table 3. Such table shows average localization error (indicated as Avr. in table) and its standard deviation (indicated as Std. Dev. in table) with respect to ROCRSSI and ROCRSSI+ algorithms in three different experiments in the same environmental conditions, and increasing the number of the beacons.

ROCRSSI++

Despite the improvement of ROCRSSI+, RO-CRSSI still exhibits some inefficiencies:

1. Inconsistency, i.e., results may change depending on the order of the inputs provided to the algorithm;
2. Variable RSSI, i.e., RSSI values slightly fluctuate when they are measured at different instances, due to the unstable nature of the wireless connections;
3. Channel asymmetry, i.e., the RSSI computed by measuring a signal emitted by sensor A and received by sensor B could be dissimilar to the value computed vice-versa;
4. Memory and communication inefficiency, e.g., RSSI values need to be exchanged when a sensor needs to be located for the first time, or a variation in the WSN topology takes place, and they need to be persistently stored within each sensor.

The rest of this subsection is organized in four different parts, each one proposing a solution to each of the previous inefficiencies.

Figure 5. Example of RSSI and distance values among three beacons and an unknown sensor

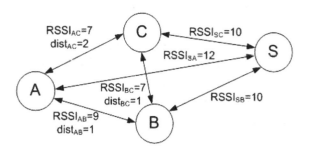

CONSISTENCY OF ROCRSSI

An algorithm is defined as consistent if it returns the same result regardless of the order in which inputs are processed. We observed that ROCRSSI algorithm, and its refinement, result inconsistent since the estimated location depends on the order in which RSSI values are considered. Let us consider the case of three beacon nodes of Figure 5. Distance between beacons A and B is 1[1] and RSSI is equal to 9. While, distance between beacons A and C is 2 and the RSSI is 7. Last, distance between beacons B and C is 1 and RSSI is 7. Now let us consider RSSI values of unknown sensor S with the beacons A, B and C to be equal respectively to 12, 10, and 10. Due to inequities such as the one expressed in Equation 3, when considering the beacons in the order A-B-C the algorithm will locate the node in the intersection of (*1*) a circle with center in A and radius equal to 1, (*2*) a circle with center in B and radius equal to 1, and (*3*) a circle with center in C and radius equal to 2. Instead, if the algorithm considers the beacons in the order B-A-C, it will locate the node in the intersection of (*1*) the circle with center in B and radius equal to 1, (*2*) the circle with center in A and radius equal to 1, and (*3*) the circle with center in C and radius equal to 1. So, the difference is the radius of the circle with center in C.

This inconsistency occurs in case of two channels with equal RSSI values but at different distances. To avoid this issue, the distance value to be assigned to a certain RSSI value, i.e., the radius of the circle in which an unknown sensor is located, has to be chosen using the following rule: we consider more reliable the RSSI value estimated on the longest distance. In fact, RSSI values depend on the attenuation faced by signals on their path from emitter to receiver, which is function of the distance, but also of possible obstacles. If same RSSI values are related to beacons at distinct distances, there must be more obstacles between beacons at lower distance, than the ones

at higher distance. So, the RSSI associated to the greatest distance is surely to be more dependent only on distance and less on possible met obstacles. A ROCRSSI++ pseudo-code is shown in Figure 6.

RSSI EVALUATION

If RSSI is computed at different time instances, we can observe a variation in the measures, i.e., RSSI values are not stable but can vary over the time. This is caused by the several phenomena that affect wireless communications, such as reflection, refraction and interferences. To address this issue, we have decided to compute RSSI not considering the exchange of a single message, but a succession of messages. Therefore, RSSI is computed as the average of the RSSI measured per each exchanged message. However, if measures present a strong standard deviation, we also apply a weighted mean by assigning greater weights to greater RSSI values. The reason for this choice is similar to the case described in the previous subsection: the strong sudden reduction of RSSI is not related to the distance, so such values are less considered.

Symmetry of Channels

The RSSI is measured by exchanging a message between an emitter and a receiver, so that the receiver can analyze the strength of the signals conveying the message and compute the RSSI value. If we consider a pair of two beacons, namely A and B, the RSSI values obtained when A plays the role of emitter and B the receiver can be dissimilar to the value when B is the emitter and A the receiver. This is due to asymmetry of wireless communication links. ROCRSSI algorithm considers communication channels between sensors to be symmetric in order to simplify the evaluation of RSSI. Such asymmetry is common

Figure 6. Pseudo-code of ROCRSSI++

```
1 Sn : set of beacons close to the unknown node S;
2 ROCRSSIplus ( ) {
3       R = {};
4       while (Sn has elements) {
5             step 1:    beacon A = Sn.nextElement();
6                        SA: set of beacon closest o A;
7             step 2:    divide SA in two sets
8                        SA1: ∀ I in SA1 RSSIAI > RSSIAS;
9                        SA2: ∀ J in SA2 RSSIAJ < RSSIAS;
10            step 3:    if (SA == empty set) go to step 1;
11                       else {
12                            d1 = d2 = 0;
13                            if (SA1 != empty set) {
14                                 I = element with maximum distance
15                                 among ones with the smallest RSSI in
16                                 SA1;
17                                 d1 = distance between I and A;
18                            }
19                            if (SA2 != empty set) {
20                                 J = element with maximum distance
21                                 among ones with the greatest RSSI in
22                                 SA2;
23                                 d2 = distance between J and A;
24                            }
25                            if (d1 != 0 e d2 != 0) {
26                                 r = ring with center A, inner radius
27                                 d1, outer radius d2;
28                            }
29                            if (d1 = 0) {
30                                 r = circle with center A and radius
31                                 d2;
32                            }
33                            if (d2 = 0) {
34                                 r = out of circumference with center
35                                 A and radius d1;
36                            }
37                            R = R + {r}; // insert r in R;
38                       }
39       }
40       step 4:    evaluate intersection of areas in R;
41       step 5:    return {center of gravity of intersection area};
42 }
```

in low-power wireless sensors, such as the ones used in WSN, even if all sensors have the same hardware and transmit power. This issue needs to be addressed by the algorithm so that sensors can have the same reciprocal estimation of RSSI. In order to handle this issue, the solution is to solve a simple problem of consensus. Specifically, after an exchange of messages, one of the two nodes sets the RSSI value and sends it to all other nodes. Then, its reciprocal node along the channel stores the received value, and compares it to the one that it has evaluated itself. If the two values are

not equal, it chose as its RSSI value the biggest, and notifies of the variation the other sensors. It is simple to verify that this procedure satisfies the requirements of a consensus algorithm: (1) Termination, eventually each correct node sets its RSSI value for a channel; (2) Agreement, the RSSI value assigned to a channel is the same for the two nodes of the channel if they are both correct; and (3) Integrity, if both nodes propose the same RSSI value than both of them will assign that value to the channel.

Store RSSI Values

In order to perform a given RSSI-based localization algorithm, a node has to know RSSI values relative to pairs of beacon nodes, apart from their distances, and RSSI between itself and each beacon. Therefore, it is necessary to communicate and store these values. In case of N beacon nodes, each node would have a matrix $N \times N$, where the element $a(i, j)$ represents the RSSI value evaluated for beacons i and j and their distance. However, methods to reduce the size of such a matrix can be applied: due to the achieved symmetry in RSSI values, element $a(i, j)$ is equal to $a(j, i)$, and a node does not need to know the RSSI to itself. The same is valid for distance values between each couple of beacons. Then, the matrices used to store these data are strictly triangular, and we can use packed storage matrix. In case of N beacon nodes we can use a vector whose dimension

is $\left(N - 1 + N - 2 + ... + 1\right) = \dfrac{N \cdot (N - 1)}{2}$.

Therefore, the memory saving is $\dfrac{N \cdot (N + 1)}{2}$, or $50 \cdot \left(1 + \dfrac{1}{N}\right)\%$, always greater than 50%.

Because of small payload of packets used in WSN, this storage technique also contributes to reduce the total number of messages exchanged among nodes so to lower battery consumption, as it will be shown later.

EXPERIMENTAL EVALUATION

In order to evaluate the proposed refinements we have implemented ROCRSSI++ in nesC for TinyOS 2.1 and flashed it on the ROM of Iris Motes, sensors commercialized by Crossbow Technology. We have also used other devices and software provided by the same manufacturer, such as MIB520 programming board to flash the ROM of the sensors, a Base Station and a software, XSniffer, to capture all the radio traffic on a specified ZigBee channel. Sniffed traffic helped to control messages and information exchanged among sensors in order to verify the correctness of the implementation and execution of our algorithm. Using such prototype, we have conducted an experimental campaign both in indoor that in outdoor environments. Specifically, the indoor environment is a computer laboratory with the shape of a rectangle, whose dimensions are 497 cm as length and 622 cm as width, which corresponds to an area of about 31 square meters. In this environment there are no obstacles among

Table 4. Planning of the experimental campaign both in indoor and in outdoor environment

Configuration Name	Environment	# Beacons	Grid granularity	Beacons' Disposition		Interferences
				Wall	Grid	
config 1	Indoor	3-5	fixed	near	no	medium/low
config 2	Indoor	3-5	fixed	nar	yes	medium/low
config 3	Indoor	3-5	fixed	near	yes	medium/low
config 4	Indoor	3-5	fixed	far	no	medium/low
grid 83	Indoor	5	variable	-	-	medium/low
grid 41	Indoor	5	variable	-	-	medium/low
grid 10	Indoor	5	variable	-	-	medium/low
Outdoor	Outdoor	5	fixed	-	yes	Null

sensors, however, environment is polluted by Wi-Fi interference. In this scenario, we have performed 60 experiments using four configurations, each characterized by keeping a certain distance between beacons and walls, and by deploying sensors according to a specific disposition. The adopted disposition can be either random or grid aligned (i.e., beacons are placed within the workspace so that imaginary lines linking them draw regular geometric shapes, as in Figure 3). The campaign has been conducted varying the number of beacons from three to five. Moreover, further 27 indoor experiments were carried out in order to assess performance at different grid granularity. On the other hand, the outdoor environment is a rectangle whose dimensions are 583 cm as length and 1770 cm as width, with an area of about 103 square meters. In this case there are not neither obstacles nor perimeter walls or Wi-Fi interferences. In such environment we have performed 9 experiments using a grid aligned configuration and five beacons. Each experiment of the campaign has been repeated 20 times in the indoor environment, while 10 times in the outdoor one, so to obtain statistically relevant information. Table 4 resumes the configurations of the experimental campaign. In the indoor environment "near the wall" means that sensors are less than

70 centimeters far from walls, while "far from wall" means that the distance from each sensor to walls is grater than 100 centimeters.

In our experiments we have quantified the localization error in centimeters and defined it as the distance of the estimated position from the real position. We also provide a percentage characterization of the error by comparing it to the maximum distance detectable in the environment, e.g., the diagonal when the environment has a rectangular shape.

Indoor Results

In the indoor scenario, we obtained the best results with beacons deployed a meter away from the walls and with grid alignment. In this case, average error is 17.23%, which is about 137.18 centimeters. On the contrary, the worst case is obtained when beacon nodes are placed very close to the walls, less than 21 centimeters. In this case, average error has been 24.74%, which is equal to 196.93 centimeters. This is probably due to signal reflection and refraction caused by the walls, making RSSI values less stable. Indeed, the trend of RSSI values varying the distance between emitter and receiver does not have a decreasing curve when increasing the distance; this is shown in Figure 7,

Figure 7. RSSI and distance in indoor environment, config3, with beacon nodes deployed near walls and grid aligned

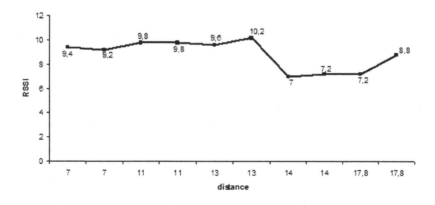

Figure 8. Average error and number of beacon nodes used for indoor localization

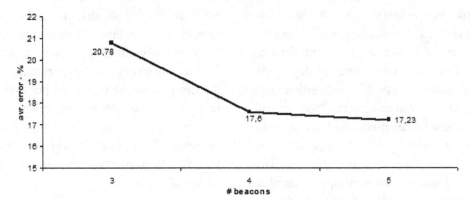

which is relative to the indoor environment with beacons deployed near the walls and grid aligned, in whose case the distance of sensors from walls is always less than 21 centimeters. Furthermore, grid alignment has resulted better than random one because of a more uniform coverage of the workspace.

Accuracy of a localization algorithm is strictly related to the number of adopted beacons. Specifically, if more beacons are used, the error results to be smaller. In fact, when having more beacons, each unknown sensor could obtain more information useful for localization, i.e., the algorithm will be able to build more rings and circles so that the intersection area would be smaller. This consideration is confirmed by our experimental results shown in Figure 8: average error has a decreasing trend when increasing the number of beacons.

However, we have noticed that after using 4 beacons within the environment, the improvement in accuracy is quite marginal. The number of beacons used for localization is a crucial parameter not only to achieve good localization accuracy. In fact, when the number of beacons is increased, also the number of messages to be exchanged among sensors grows, with a resultant increase of battery consumption and time to localize, as it will be shown in following subsections. Therefore, we cannot choose the number of beacons with the only scope to maximize the localiza-

tion accuracy, but we have to consider a trade-off among localization error, battery consumption and time to localize.

Outdoor Results

Outdoor experiments provide better results. When using the same number of beacons, localization error is less than the one obtained in the indoor environment. In fact, average error is 313.15 cm, which corresponds to 16.80%. Let us note that we have used the same number of beacon nodes as in the previous experiments, but in a three-time larger environment. The absence of walls, which causes reflection and refraction of the radio signal, and interferences allows obtaining more stable and less compromised RSSI values, i.e., such values often respect inverse proportionality with distances and fluctuates less varying the time of measurement. Figure 9 shows the trend of RSSI values varying the distance between emitter and receiver in an outdoor environment, and except for few distances, we have a decreasing curve when we increase distance.

Grid Scan

Grid granularity, i.e., the length of cells within the grid, is a parameter on which localization quality may depend. Smaller is cell dimension, greater is localization precision. However, our experiments

Figure 9. RSSI and distance in outdoor environment

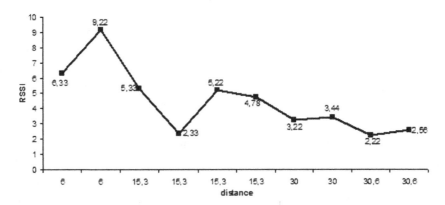

Figure 10. Average error varying cell size

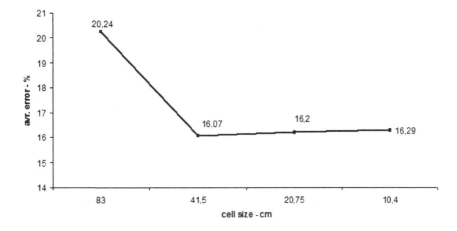

have proved that using fine-grained grids does not always provide better results: as shown in Figure 10, average error exhibits a decreasing behaviour when grid granularity is reduced, but after a certain value of granularity, i.e., 41.5 centimeters, we could not see a sensible localization improvement.

Our experimental results showed that the Grid Scan algorithm may also introduce an error due to iterations that involve few cells. For example, in Figure 11 the intersection area is the one in the top right of the grid with six dark-gray cells, whose counter is equal to 3; these cells locate the unknown sensor far from its real position in (6;7), the cell

with the thick border. Instead, if we also consider cells whose counter is equal to 2 we achieve a better localization, locating the node in (7;6), the cell with the circle. However, the lowest number of cells that have to be in the intersection area to correctly locate the sensor is not *a-priori* known. Then, we propose to take into account how many counters are modified at each iteration and to compare their mean value, *mean*, with the umber of cells with the maximum counter, *num*. If *num* is less than a percentage of *mean* also cells whose counter is equal to *maximum*-1 are considered for the evaluation of the center of gravity.

Figure 11. Example of Grid Scan algorithm execution

	1	2	3	4	5	6	7	8	9	10	11	12
1	2	1	1	1	1	1	2	3	3	3	2	2
2	2	1	1	1	1	2	2	2	2	3	3	2
3	2	1	1	1	2	2	2	2	2	2	3	2
4	1	1	1	2	2	2	2	2	2	2	2	2
5	1	1	1	2	2	2	2	2	2	2	2	1
6	1	1	2	2	2	2	2	2	2	2	2	1
7	1	1	2	2	2	2	2	2	2	2	1	1
8	1	2	2	2	2	2	2	2	2	2	1	1
9	1	2	2	2	2	2	2	2	2	1	1	1
10	1	2	2	2	2	2	2	2	1	1	1	1
11	0	2	2	2	2	2	1	1	1	1	1	1
12	0	1	1	1	1	1	1	1	1	1	1	1
13	0	1	1	1	1	1	1	1	1	1	1	1
14	0	1	1	1	1	1	1	1	1	1	1	1
15	0	0	1	1	1	1	1	1	1	1	1	1

Using such correction to the Grid Scan Algorithm, the error in the case of indoor localization decreases from 17.23% to 12.02%, and this percentage corresponds to an error of 95.70 centimeters.

Comparison with Previous Versions

To assess the improvement achievable by using the proposed refinements, this subsection compares the localization error obtained by ROCRSSI+ with the error of ROCRSSI++ by varying the number of beacons in the network. The error values for ROCRSSI+ have been taken from (Crepaldi et al., 2006), while values for ROCRSSI++ are obtained by the experiments described in subsection *Indoor Results*. Such values are shown in Table 5, which contains estimated average error (indicated as Avr. in table) in centimeters and also in percentage due to the different dimensions of the experimental environments. It is evident that the refinements proposed in this paper improve the localization accuracy than ROCRSSI+.

Power Consumption

One of the most important parameters for an application for WSN is energy consumption. As shown in Table 1, battery consumption for a mote is mainly due to the use of the radio module; then networking operations are the main cause of consumption, while CPU operations can be neglected (Davis & Miller, 2009; Shnayder, Hempstead, Chen, Werner Allen, & Welsh, 2004). Considering values from Davis and Miller (2009) and Shnayder et al. (2004) and current draw for Iris Mote (Crossbow Technology, 2009), we can consider with good approximation values in Table 6, which shows the estimated power consumption for sending and receiving a message.

Let m be the number of exchanged messages to evaluate RSSI and n the number of beacon nodes in the network; the evaluation of power consumption will be different for beacons and for unknown sensors.

Beacon Nodes

Let us consider a beacon node A; in order to make possible to each other beacon node in the network to evaluate RSSI of its channel to A, in the worst case A has to send $m \cdot (n-1)$ messages; besides it has to send two other messages to an unknown node, one with RSSI values and distances among beacons, the other one with its position and the estimated RSSI value of the channel with the unknown node. If it sends a message per second, the battery consumption in mJ is $0.0495 \cdot (m \cdot (n-1) + 2)$. Furthermore, the node

Table 5. Comparison of ROCRSSI+ and ROCRSSI++

	ROCRSSI+ avr. error		ROCRSSI++ avr. error	
# beacons	(cm)	(%)	(cm)	(%)
3	427	31.75	165.44	20.78
4	402	29.89	140.13	17.60
5	388	28.25	137.18	17.23

Table 6. Power consumption for Iris Mote (evaluated using data by Davis & Miller, 2009; Shnayder et al., 2004; Crossbow Technology, 2009)

Operation	Power consumption (mW)
Transmission	0.0495
Reception	0.048

A will receive $m \cdot (n-1)$ messages by other beacon nodes and at least m messages by an unknown node, so the total is $m \cdot n$ messages, and consumption for received messages is $0.048 \cdot m \cdot n$. Total energy consumption for the beacon node is:

$$0.0495 \cdot \left(m \cdot (n-1) + 2 \right) + 0.048 \cdot m \cdot n.$$

Table 7 shows mJ consumption when increasing the number of beacon nodes. Linear growth is due to the increase of the number of messages needed to determine the values of RSSI of the channels. So, when selecting the number of beacons, it should also take account of energy consumption. The number of exchanged messages among sensors to evaluate RSSI values

between them is another parameter that influences energy consumption. Fixing the number of beacons in the network, the energy consumption has a linear growth trend when increasing the number of exchanged messages.

Unknown Nodes

Now, let us consider unknown nodes; in the worst case this kind of node has to transmit m messages to each of n beacon nodes in order to evaluate RSSI values, then an unknown node sends $m \cdot n$ messages and energy consumption for transmission is $0.0495 \cdot m \cdot n$. Besides, an unknown node receives two messages by each beacon node, one with information about RSSI and distances between beacons, the other one with

the position of the beacon and RSSI value from the unknown node to the beacon node, for a total of $2n$ messages. Total energy consumption for the unknown node is:

$$0.0495 \cdot m \cdot n + 0.048 \cdot 2n.$$

Also in this case energy consumption has an increasing trend when increasing the number of beacon nodes, as shown in Table 8; furthermore, as in the case of beacon nodes, energy consumption has a linear growth trend when increasing the number of exchanged messages too. Then, the number of beacon nodes and the number of messages used to evaluate RSSI are two main parameters to define in the setup phase of the network on which battery consumption and time for localization depend. Besides, as shown in subsection *Indoor Results*, not always it is possible to improve localization increasing the number of beacon nodes or the number of messages for RSSI evaluation; sometime that only increases costs, wastes energy and requires more time to locate sensors.

In the subsection *Store RSSI Values* we introduced a technique for storing RSSI and distance values between beacon nodes; such technique has a memory saving greater than 50%, and it also contributes to reduce the number of messages exchanged among nodes so to lower battery consumption. Indeed, ROCRSSI/ROCRSSI+ require a matrix *NxN*, while ROCRSSI++ a vector whose

Table 7. mJ energy consumption for a beacon node when increasing the number of beacon nodes in the network using one message to evaluate RSSI of channels (m=1)

# Beacons	Energy consumption (mJ)
3	0.34
4	0.44
5	0.54

Table 8. mJ energy consumption for an unknown node when increasing the number of beacon nodes in the network using one message to evaluate RSSI of channels (m=1)

# Beacons	Energy consumption (mJ)
3	0.44
4	0.58
5	0.73

dimension is $\dfrac{N \cdot (N-1)}{2}$; if each position of the matrix and of the vector stores a RSSI value and a distance value, and each of them requires 1 byte, in the former case the algorithms require $N^2 \cdot 2$ bytes, in the latter $N \cdot (N-1)$. The IEEE Standard 802.15.4 (IEEE Standards Association, 2003) indicates as maximum dimension of the payload 104 bytes; than, ROCRSSI and ROCRSSI+ require $\left\lceil \dfrac{N^2 \cdot 2}{104} \right\rceil 2$ messages, while ROCRSSI++ requires $\left\lceil \dfrac{N \cdot (N-1)}{104} \right\rceil$ messages. As expected, the saving of exchanged messages is equal to memory saving, i.e. $50 \cdot \left(1 + \dfrac{1}{N}\right)\%$.

Time for localization

Localization has to be as fast as possible, and then time for localization is another important feature. In this subsection we want to evaluate the time required for the localization of an unknown node in a network that has just been initialized.

The time required by CPU for data processing is negligible. In fact, in our experiments we noticed that after receiving data from beacon nodes, the unknown node was able to communicate its estimated position in a very short time. Therefore, the time required for the localization of a node mainly depends on the time required for exchanging messages for collecting data and

evaluating RSSI values and then on the number of such messages.

As shown in previous subsection, the localization of an unknown node requires that each beacon node sends $m \cdot (n-1)$ messages to other beacons and receives $m \cdot (n-1)$ messages from other beacons; besides a beacon also receives m messages by an unknown node, which has to receive $2n$ messages by beacon nodes. Then the total number of exchanged messages is $2 \cdot m \cdot (n-1) + m + 2n$, and in the worst case they are sent each one in a different instant. The time required for exchanging these messages also depends on the frequency with whom each sensor sends messages, i.e. the time interval between two messages. This time is a variable that we call t. If t is equal to 1 second and 10 messages are used for the evaluation of RSSI values of the channels, the localization requires 56 seconds using 3 beacon nodes, 78 seconds using 4 beacon nodes and 100 seconds with 5 beacon nodes.

As expected, time for localization has an increasing trend when increasing the number of beacons in the network and, similarly, the number of messages exchanged to evaluate RSSI values of channels between nodes. Since the number of messages used by ROCRSSI++ is less than or equal to the number of messages used by ROCRSSI and ROCRSSI+, the time for localization of ROCRSSI++ is equal to or less then time for localization of the older versions of the algorithm.

CONCLUSION

This paper deals with localization in Wireless Sensor Networks, and proposes an algorithm, called ROCRSSI++, to satisfy their requirements in terms of energy efficiency, low overhead, hardware simplicity, fast localization, robustness and low error. The proposed algorithm consists of further improvements of a technique known in literature as ROCRSSI+, which is a range-free method based on RSSI. The proposed improvements do not require additional hardware or sensors with particular equipment. We have presented experimental results showing that ROCRSSI++ achieves better localization than the algorithms present in literature. In fact, ROCRSSI+ exhibits an average error in indoor environments of 28.25% and in outdoor environments of 22.30%, while ROCRSSI++ average errors are respectively 17.23% and 16.80%. Moreover, we have also proposed variations to the Grid Scan Algorithm, which allow us to achieve a further improvement of about 5%. In fact, ROCRSSI++ with modified Grid Scan and five beacons reaches an error of 12,02%, which is lower than the one in case of ROCRSSI++ with original Grid Scan. Besides, thanks to the reduction of information exchanged among sensors, it is also possible to reduce energy consumption and the time necessary to locate a sensor.

There are still many interesting issues to investigate as future work. The trend of RSSI with respect to distance between nodes may be corrected. In fact, if we consider the interpolation with a cubic spline of the points in Figure 7 and in Figure 9, instead of linear interpolation, it will have a decreasing trend, as should be in the ideal case. Besides, further information may be obtained using additional range estimation parameters which do not require particular hardware, such as Link Quality, or varying the Power of Transmission of the signal transmitted by each sensor.

ACKNOWLEDGMENT

This work was partially supported by Regione Campania, in the framework of the REMOAM project (REti di sensori per il MOnitoraggio dei rischi AMbientali), misura 3.17 POR Campania 2000/06.

REFERENCES

Akyildiz, I. F., Su, W., Sankarasubramaniam, Y., & Cayirci, E. (2002). Wireless sensor networks: A survey. *Computer Networks: The International Journal of Computer and Telecommunications Networking, 38*(4), 393–422.

BeanAir. (2010). *BeanDevice TH version datasheet*. Retrieved from http://www.beanair.com/English-docs/Flyer%20BeanDevice%20TH.pdf

Crepaldi, R., Casari, P., Zanella, A., & Zorzi, M. (2006). Testbed implementation and refinement of a range-based localization algorithm for wireless sensor networks. In *Proceedings of the Third International Conference on Mobile Technology, Applications & Systems* (Vol. 270, p. 61).

Crossbow Technology. (2009). *Iris OEM datasheet*. Retrieved from http://bullseye.xbow.com:81/Products/Product_pdf_files/Wireless_pdf/IRIS_OEM_Datasheet.pdf

Davis, H., & Miller, R. (2009). *Power management for Mica2 motes*. Retrieved from www.cs.etsu.edu/

Elnahrawy, E., Li, X., & Martin, R. (2004). The limits of localization using signal strength: A comparative study. In *Proceedings of the First IEEE International Conference on Sensor and Ad Hoc Communications and Networks* (pp. 406-414).

He, T., Huang, C., Blum, B., Stankovic, J., & Abdelzaher, T. (2003). Range-free localization schemes for large scale sensor networks. In *Proceedings of the 9th Annual International Conference on Mobile Computing and Networking* (pp. 81-95).

Hightower, J., & Borriello, G. (2001). A survey and taxonomy of location system for ubiquitous computing. *IEEE Computer, 34*(8), 57 66.

IEEE Standards Association. (2003). *802.15 WPAN Low Rate Alternative PHY Task Group 4a*. Retrieved from http://www.ieee802.org/15/pub/TG4a.html

Ji, X., & Zha, H. (2004). Sensor positioning in wireless ad-hoc sensor networks using multidimensional scaling. In *Proceedings of the Twenty-Third Annual Joint Conference of the IEEE Computer and Communications Societies* (Vol. 4, pp. 2652-2661).

Kay, S. M. (Ed.). (1993). *Fundamentals of statistical signal processing: Estimation theory*. Upper Saddle River, NJ: Prentice Hall.

Langendoen, K., & Reijers, N. (2003). Distributed localization in wireless sensor networks: A quantitative comparison. *Computer Networks: The International Journal of Computer and Telecommunications Networking, 43*(4), 499–518.

Liu, C., & Wu, K. (2005). Performance evaluation of range-free localization methods for wireless sensor networks. In *Proceedings of the IEEE International Conference on Performance, Computing, and Communications* (pp. 59-66).

Liu, C., Wu, K., & He, T. (2004). Sensor localization with ring overlapping based on comparison of received signal strength indicator. In *Proceedings of the IEEE International Conference on Mobile Ad-hoc and Sensor Systems* (pp. 516-518).

Mao, G., Fidan, B., & Anderson, B. D. O. (2007). Wireless sensor network localization techniques. *Computer Networks: The International Journal of Computer and Telecommunications Networking, 51*(10), 2529–2553.

Nguyen, X., & Rattentbury, T. (2003). *Localization algorithms for sensor networks using RF signal strength* (Tech. Rep. No. CS252). Berkeley, CA: University of California.

Patwari, N., Hero, A. O. III, Perkins, M., Correal, N. S., & O'Dea, R. J. (2003). Relative location estimation in wireless sensor networks. *IEEE Transactions on Signal Processing, 51*(8), 2137–2148. doi:10.1109/TSP.2003.814469

Shang, Y., Ruml, W., Zhang, Y., & Fromherz, M. P. J. (2003). Localization from mere connectivity. In *Proceedings of the 4th ACM International Symposium on Mobile Ad Hoc Networking & Computing* (pp. 201-212).

Shnayder, V., Hempstead, M., Chen, B., Werner Allen, G., & Welsh, M. (2004). Simulating the power consumption of large-scale sensor network applications. In *Proceedings of the 2nd International Conference on Embedded Networked Sensor Systems* (pp. 188-200).

Wireless Sensors. (2010). *SB110-T datasheet*. Retrieved from http://www.wirelesssensors.com/pdf/WSI%20SB110-T%20v4.5.pdf

ENDNOTES

[1] This can be either a dimensionless measure or be relative to a given unit, such as meters or yards.

[2] $\lceil x \rceil$ is the *ceiling* function of x which gives the smallest integer greater than or equal to x.

This work was previously published in the International Journal of Adaptive, Resilient and Autonomic Systems, Volume 2, Issue 2, edited by Vincenzo De Florio, pp. 51-70, copyright 2011 by IGI Publishing (an imprint of IGI Global).

Chapter 16
Load–Balanced Multiple Gateway Enabled Wireless Mesh Network for Applications in Emergency and Disaster Recovery

Muddesar Iqbal
University of Gujrat, Pakistan

Xinheng Wang
Swansea University, UK

Hui Zhang
Swansea University, UK

ABSTRACT

A gateway node in a WMN acts as bridge between mesh nodes and the external network in order to exchange information between the wireless mesh network operating in a disaster stricken area and remotely located rescue headquarters and government agencies. Using a single gateway, WMN creates huge congestion on the routes to the gateway, as all the data traffic may travel in the same direction using longer routes to access the gateway node, causing channel contention between nodes that operate within carrier sensing range of each other. Therefore a multiple gateway environment is crucial during WMN application in emergency and disaster recovery. This paper presents the design and implementation of a Load-Balanced Gateway Discovery routing protocol called LBGD-AODV, which provides multiple gateway support in Wireless Mesh Network. LBGD-AODV is designed as an extension to the Ad hoc On-Demand Distance Vector (AODV) routing protocol and uses a periodic gateway advertisement scheme equipped with an efficient algorithm to avoid congestion by establishing load-balanced routes to the gateway nodes for Internet traffic. The evaluation tests show that the LBGD-AODV has not compromised the efficiency of basic AODV routing and has improved the performance of the network.

DOI: 10.4018/978-1-4666-2056-8.ch016

1. INTRODUCTION

Natural disasters such as earthquakes, tsunami, hurricanes and cyclones can affect large geographical areas resulting in significant impact on the network infrastructures, such as water, electricity, transport and communications. A quick response to provide the disaster rescue operation in affected areas is very critical to saving many lives. For example, people trapped under collapsed buildings and landslides in the disastrous stricken areas may have a greater chance of survival if they are rescued within 72 hours. As these disasters are increasingly becoming common threat facing mankind, ensuring effective disaster response, mitigation and recovery has become an important and growing topic for the research community worldwide. One of the major aftermaths of these disaster situations is the destruction of the traditional infrastructure of communications. The loss of communication systems makes rescue and relief operations extremely difficult which results in heavy loss of lives. Therefore establishing a temporary alternative communication network to support emergency communications is one of the most urgent tasks in a disaster rescue mission.

The nature of Wireless Mesh Network (WMN) makes them suitable to be deployed as an alternative communication network to facilitate an emergency and disaster recovery operation. WMN provides a useful and feasible solution for communication services in extreme emergency situations where the fast and effective deployment of a communication network infrastructure is impossible.

Rescue teams in each stricken area consist of a few trained professional squads: police, army, fire fighters, medical professionals and potentially many hundreds or thousands of disorganized volunteers. During large scale disasters these rescue teams have to work simultaneously at different disaster affected geographical locations as shown in the example scenario Figure 1. Therefore an emergency response usually requires a central control to coordinate the rescue efforts being carried by different teams at different locations. WMN provides that central control through gateway nodes which connect to the backbone external network, thus building a bridge between the WMN and external networks in order to share and exchange the critical information via www, email and FTP. It enables the command centers to learn about on-going situations to allocate and guide the rescue teams.

A mobile truck or van with satellite terminals can be used as an onsite command post at the scene of disaster to provide a gateway Internet connection for disaster areas and enable communication between the disaster site and headquarters. In a WMN, all the nodes on the network route packets destined for external networks to the gateway node, thus maintaining a good throughput to a gateway node becomes a primary goal for each mesh router to efficiently provide data services such as www, email and file transfer between the WMN and external network. Topology design and routing play a vital role when it comes to performance challenges such as maintaining an efficient throughput. Since the WMN is a multihop network, in order to reach a gateway node on the network the mesh nodes have to depend on routing protocols operating in the network layer.

Most of the routing protocols use the shortest path between source node and destination node as main routing criteria. The performance of data exchange between mesh routers and a single gateway node in a WMN decreases as the hop distance increases. A packet travelling on longer routes requires more intermediate nodes to forward the packet between the source and gateway nodes. This results in network congestion due to channel contention among the nodes operating within carrier-sensing range of each other. Application of WMN in disaster recovery may require the network to cover a larger stricken area. If a single gateway node is used to cover a larger network then all the traffic originated within the network

Figure 1. A WMN application in emergency and disaster recovery application scenario

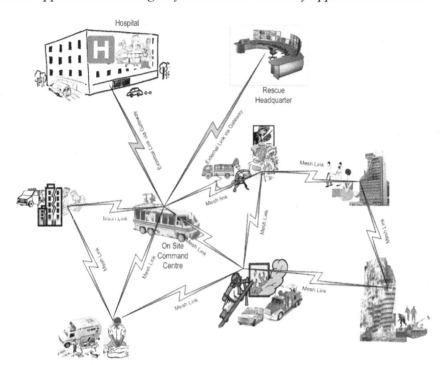

will go through the gateway node. This may result in huge congestion. Therefore a multiple gateway environment is crucial for WMN deployment to provide network coverage in a large scale disaster stricken area.

We have used improved AODV (Iqbal et al., 2009) as a routing protocol in our previously developed SwanMesh testbed (Iqbal et al., 2009; Zhou et al., 2009; Wang et al., 2008; Iqbal, Li, Wang, & Ellis, 2009; Iqbal, Wang, & Wertheim, 2009; Iqbal, Li, Wang, & Ellis, 2009). AODV uses the shortest path as its routing criteria, but AODV does not provide support for multiple gateways. Studies conducted in (Das et al., 2000; Johanson et al., 1999) show that the performance of AODV protocol drops as the network size increases. A multiple gateway topology with an efficient gateway discovery and load balancing approach can help maintain required throughput to the gateway and enhance the performance in these situations. Many load balancing algorithms using different criteria (Lee et al., 2001; Song et

al., 2003; Yi et al., 2001; Kim et al., 2003; Lee et al., 2005; Pearlman et al., 2000; Zhang et al., 2002) and gateway discovery techniques (Wakikawa et al., 2006; Broch et al.,1999; Belding-Royer et al., 2001; Jonsson et al., 2000; Sun et al., 2002; Jelger et al., 2004; Ratanchandani et al., 2003) have been presented in ad-hoc networks. The gateway discovery approaches are mainly categorized as reactive (Wakikawa et al., 2006; Broch et al.,1999) and proactive (Belding-Royer et al., 2001; Jonsson et al., 2000; Sun et al., 2002; Jelger et al., 2004). In the reactive approach, when a router node needs a gateway it broadcasts a solicitation to the network in order to find the gateway and in the proactive approach the gateway node broadcasts a periodic message to the network to inform other nodes of its existence. (Ratanchandani et al., 2003; Lee et al., 2003) proposed a hybrid approach which makes use of a combination of both reactive and proactive approaches. In a multiple gateway enabled mesh network, the knowledge of a gateway's existence is not enough for a node to make a right choice between selecting one gateway among multiple available gateways. This is because apart from distance to the gateway, the load on a gateway and network congestion on available routes to it also affects the performance. Thus a multiple gateway scheme also needs to be equipped with an appropriate load-balancing algorithm to balance the traffic load among the multiple gateways within the entire network. Otherwise the network resources cannot be utilized efficiently and unbalanced load on certain routes and gateways could result in congestion. This paper will propose a new load balanced gateway discovery approach to avoid congestion in multiple gateway enabled WMN.

In the remainder of this paper, in section 2 we look at major limitations within the existing schemes to provide multiple gateway support. In section 3, we describe the detailed design and implementation of the proposed solution to provide load-balanced multiple gateway support in a WMN. Section 4 presents the evaluation tests and finally the paper is concluded in section 5.

2. SUMMARY OF PROBLEMS WITH EXISTING SCHEMES

Several solutions to provide and support Internet connectivity in wireless networks have been proposed. All these solutions have different problems at different levels while providing Internet connectivity in a multiple gateway environment. These problems can be summarized as follows:

- The first challenge is to find the location of the destination. Most of the schemes mentioned in Introduction section flood the network with a Route Request and if no reply is received at the end of route discovery process the packet destination is assumed to be an Internet destination. This introduces delay while routing Internet

packets. Jelger et al. (2004, 2006) used the concept of prefix continuity to build a multiple logical spanning tree, where each tree acts as a sub-network. The network is organized automatically into a sub-network in terms of prefixes when multiple gateways are available.

- WMNs are multihop networks therefore a gateway node on the network needs to either advertise its existence to the network, or a network node needs to send an explicit request to find a gateway node by broadcasting a solicitation. Both of these methods are widely used and some approaches have combined the two methods in adopting a hybrid approach. According to the performance evaluation of Gateway Discovery schemes presented by Ruiz et al. (2005) and Rosenschon et al. (2004), the proactive IGW selection approach produces a greater amount of control traffic due to the periodic broadcast of Gateway Advertisement messages but compared to re-active approach it shows the highest performance in terms of data throughput because the node always has the information of all the available gateways when it needs to route Internet packets. The knowledge of a gateway's existence is not sufficient for a node to make the right choice while selecting one gateway among multiple available gateways. This is because apart from distance to the gateway, the load on a certain gateway and network congestion on available routes to it will also affect the performance. In order to perform load-balancing the network topology information needs to be available locally for each node. If this information is collected using a separate scheme this could prove costly in terms of overheads. Thus if the task of performing load-balancing is integrated with the gateway discovery process, this could solve the problem by performing a load-balanced gateway discovery using a single process.

• WMN application in disaster recovery requires the network to support Internet data traffic in the presence of real-time multimedia traffic. Real time multimedia communication uses UDP which has strict quality of service requirements compared to TCP Internet traffic. The real-time multimedia streaming may create congestion on the limited wireless network resources, therefore while selecting a gateway in the multiple gateway environment, apart from hop count distance and Internet traffic load on the gateway, local congestion on the intermediate nodes should also be considered to avoid congested routes.

• The default route scheme for packet forwarding has issues operating correctly in some situations especially in multiple gateway environments (Nordström et al., 2010). During an active transmission the default routes can be re-directed to a different gateway as shown in Figure 2.

As shown in the Figure 2, Source Node 1 has an active transmission with Gateway 1 but when Source Node 2 originates a RREQ to find a gateway, it receives an RREP from Gateway 2 via Router Node which is currently pointing to Gateway 1 as the default route. At the end of the route discovery process Source Node 2 establishes a communication with Gateway 2 and as a result Router Node starts pointing to Gateway 2 as the default route. Source Node 1 is unaware of this change in the default route at Router Node and assumes that it is still communicating to the Internet via Gateway 1.

Tunneling the packets between the source and a gateway node is an alternative to a default route in order to forward the packets (Perkin, 1996). The tunnel approach takes address the problems described in Figure 2 as tunnels only require modifications at source and gateway nodes routing table, which makes it possible to implement forwarding without having to modify the routing state at intermediate nodes. The problem with tunneling is that it carries overheads as it requires the source node to insert an outer IP header into the packet before the datagram's IP header. Both the default route and tunneling have drawbacks. Therefore a packet forwarding scheme is required to overcome the limitations of the default route and tunneling schemes.

3. LBGD-AODV: A LOAD BALANCED GATEWAY DISCOVERY

We have proposed a load-balanced gateway discovery scheme called LBGD-AODV. As discussed before, in a multiple gateway enabled mesh network, the knowledge of gateway exis-

Figure 2. Default route mismatch problem in a multiple gateway environment

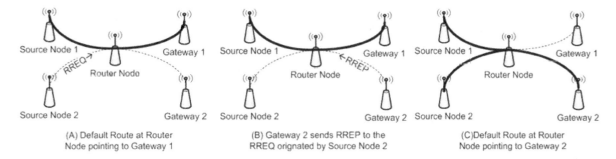

tence may not be sufficient for a node to make a right choice while selecting one gateway among multiple available gateways. A multiple gateway scheme needs to be equipped with an appropriate load-balancing algorithm to balance the Internet traffic load among the multiple gateways within the entire network. Otherwise the network resources cannot be utilized efficiently and an unbalanced load on certain route and gateway could result in congestion. LBGD-AODV provides a load-balanced gateway discovery mechanism to address these problems.

We have designed and implemented LBGD-AODV as an extension to the AODV protocol. It uses a periodic gateway discovery advertisement method, where each gateway node broadcasts a periodic Gateway Hello control message to make itself known to the network. As the Gateway Hello message travels through the network, it not only helps advertise the gateway to the network but also helps each node to learn about all the available routes to the gateway and load information on the gateway. Thus LBGD-AODV helps each node to proactively maintain the information on all the available routes to gateways and the corresponding load on each gateway. When a node generates an Internet packet, LBGD-AODV uses this information during the reactive route discovery process of AODV to provide a load balanced route to the Internet packet in multiple gateway environment.

Furthermore, we have also proposed a QoS scheme (Iqbal, Wang, & Ellis, 2009) LBGD-AODV co-ordinates with the proposed QoS scheme to share the congestion information to avoid congested routes to the available gateway nodes. The congestion information is stored locally into Bandwidth Information table at each node which is maintained by the proposed QoS scheme.

3.1. Software Architecture of LBGD-AODV

The proposed LBGD-AODV protocol uses two control messages called Gateway Hello (GWH) message and Route Activation message to support its operation. It also maintains a Gateway Information (GI) table to store route information on all the available gateway nodes and the corresponding load on them. This information about the network is delivered by a GWH message to each node as it travels through the network to advertise a gateway. Further in this section, we describe the format of these control messages and Gateway Information table.

A. Gateway Hello (GWH) Message

The GWH message is broadcast periodically. Figure 3 shows the size and format of the message. The GWH gathers and exchanges network topology information as it travels through the network. Thus the proposal relies on a periodic

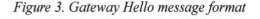

Figure 3. Gateway Hello message format

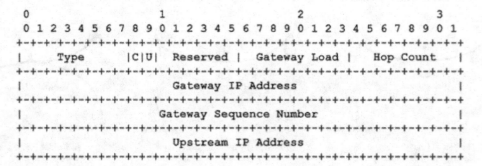

hop-by-hop exchange of information via a GWH message as it travels through each node. It delivers all the information to the network that is required to perform load balanced gateway discovery.

- **Gateway IP Address:** While generating the GWH message the gateway node adds its own IP address to the Gateway IP Address field.
- **Gateway Sequence Number:** The gateway sequence number is a unique number assigned by the gateway node while creating the GWH message.
- **Upstream IP Address:** LBGD-AODV maintains the knowledge of the two hop upstream nodes on the route to each available gateway. When a node rebroadcasts the GWH message it adds the IP address of its upstream next hop node on the route to the gateway into the Upstream IP Address field of GWH. So when a node receives the GWH message, the IP SOURCE header of the GWH message carries the address of next hop upstream node from which it has received the message, and Upstream IP Address field of GWH message carries the second next hop upstream node on the route to the gateway. This enables each node to maintain two hop upstream nodes information on each gateway through which the gateway node can be reached.
- **Gateway Load:** Gateway Load field is a count of the total number of active routers and the member nodes that a gateway is currently serving.
- **Hop Count:** Hop Count field carries the number to describe the hop distance to the corresponding gateway node.
- **Flags:** GWH has two flags UPSTEAM CHANGED (C) and UPDATE(U). UPDATE flag is used when a gateway changes its location so that other nodes can adapt to the change. The UPSTREAM_ CHANGED flag is used when an inter-

mediate node starts pointing to a different gateway and it wishes to inform its DOWNSTREAM nodes about the change.

The GWH message is a periodic control message which is broadcast by the gateway node with the TTL setting to a value to accommodate all the nodes on the network. The value of TTL is decreased by one every time a node re-broadcasts GWH message.

We propose setting the value of the TTL based on hop count up to which a gateway node could serve the clients. This is because a gateway node can only serve up to a limited number of hops due to noticeable throughput drop after each hop. Thus there is no point informing the entire network about the gateway's existence. On receiving the GWH message each node logs the network topology and load information it carries into the Gateway Information table and then re-broadcasts the GWH message.

B. . Gateway Information (GI)Table

The Gateway Information (GI) table keeps a record of all the information gathered through group hello messages. The following are the fields of the Gateway Information Table:

- Gateway IP Address
- Gateway Sequence Number
- Gateway Load
- Next Hop*

*Next Hop is a linked list structure which maintains information about all the next hop neighbours which are nodes on the potential routes to the gateways. It has the following fields:

- Next Hop IP Address
- Upstream Node
- Activation Flag
- Link Direction
- Hop Count

The GI table maintains an entry against each gateway on the network. Whenever a node receives a GWH message from a new gateway or from an existing gateway with updated information, the node updates its GI table against that gateway. The Gateway IP Address, Sequence number and Gateway Load fields from GWH message are entered into the corresponding fields of GI table.

The next Hop field is used to record all the next hop neighbor nodes from which a node receives the GWH message. The GWH message carries the IP address of the next hop neighbor in its IP SOURCE header. Therefore we refer the next hop neighbor from which a node receives the GWH message as GWH's IP SOURCE.

Each entry in the Next hop linked list structure records GWH's IP SOURCE address into Next Hop IP Address field. The GWH message carries the second upstream node address on the route to the gateway which is saved into the Upstream Node field of the Gateway Information table. The Activation Flag field is set to indicate the activation of the route. If a node is part of an active route to forward Internet packets generated by a DOWNSTREAM node to the gateway, the Activation flag in its next hop entry for UPSTREAM link direction is set to indicate the node as a router node, but if the node is part of an active route to the gateway to forward locally generated Internet packets, then the activation flag is set to indicate it as a registered member node.

If Activation flag is not set, it indicates that this Next Hop entry is for a non-active next hop neighbor node on the potential route to the gateway from which the node has received a GWH message. Link Direction is used to indicate the direction of next hop neighbor as UPSTREAM or DOWNSTREAM. UPSTREAM node is the next hop node on the route to the gateway and DOWNSTREAM is the next hop node on the route to the gateway which is further away from the gateway. The hop count field is used to log the hop count distance to a particular gateway via each next hop UPSTREAM neighbor node.

C. Route Activation Message

A node sends a Route Activation message with procedure control flags when it wishes to activate a selected route to the gateway. It is also used by a node when it wishes to deactivate the active route to a gateway at the end of transmission. Figure 4 illustrates the format of the message.

The Downstream Load field is used to carry new load information on the selected route to the gateway. J is a join flag which is set when a node wishes to activate the route to a selected gateway during reactive route discovery process. P is a prune flag which is set when a node wishes to prune itself from a gateway. The Q and T flags are used by QoS scheme described by (Iqbal, Wang, & Ellis, 2009). The size of Downstream Load field is kept to 2 bytes based on the QoS scheme operation requirement which also shares the use of Route Activation Message. Flag C is a procedure control flag which is set along with J or P to update the nodes on the new load, for those that are part of an existing active route to the gateway. The use of Route Activation message and use of all these flags are explained in detail in LBGD-AODV Operation section.

Figure 4. Route activation message format

```
 0                   1                   2                   3
 0 1 2 3 4 5 6 7 8 9 0 1 2 3 4 5 6 7 8 9 0 1 2 3 4 5 6 7 8 9 0 1
+-+-+-+-+-+-+-+-+-+-+-+-+-+-+-+-+-+-+-+-+-+-+-+-+-+-+-+-+-+-+-+-+
|      Type       |J|P|C|Q|T|       |       Downstream Load     |
+-+-+-+-+-+-+-+-+-+-+-+-+-+-+-+-+-+-+-+-+-+-+-+-+-+-+-+-+-+-+-+-+
```

D. LBGD-AODV Operation

We designed and implemented LBGD-AODV as an extension to the AODV protocol. It proactively maintains the information on each gateway and corresponding network load to it using proactive Gateway Discovery process. During the route discovery process a node makes a prefix check to ensure the location of the packet. If it is an Internet packet, the node selects an appropriate route to an appropriate gateway using the proactively maintained information in the Gateway Information table on routes available to all gateway nodes and the corresponding network load on them. The information is used during the route discovery process by each intermediate node to select the most appropriate node from one of its neighbors to reach the gateway.

Once an appropriate gateway is selected LBGD-AODV activates the route between source and gateway nodes. The selected next hop neighbor then becomes what we defined as its UPSTREAM next hop neighbor on the route to the gateway. The route becomes inactive once the communication between source node and gateway is finished.

In LBGD-AODV Re-active Route Discovery Process section, we describe how LBGD-AODV selects and activates the route between source and gateway nodes using the proactively maintained route and load information on the gateway. How LBGD-AODV proactively maintains all the potential routes to all the gateways and corresponding load information with the help of Gateway Hello.

E. LBGD-AODV Re-Active Route Discovery Process

We have integrated the LBGD-AODV route discovery for Internet destination within AODV's existing route discovery process. Further in this section we explain how a node selects an appropriate route to an appropriate gateway for Internet destination and how it activates it.

Gateway Route Selection

When a source node initiates the reactive route discovery process for an Internet destination, it selects an appropriate gateway using the hop count and loads information stored in the Gateway Information table on all the available Gateways. It then unicasts the RREQ to the selected gateway using the Gateway Information table selected route's corresponding next hop UPSTREAM node to the gateway. All intermediate nodes on the selected route forward the RREQ using the route information stored in the Gateway Information table on the corresponding gateway node. AODV always creates or updates a reverse route as described in (Perkins et al., 2008) which is eventually used if needed to send a RREP back to the originator of the RREQ.

Once the source node receives the RREP it confirms the route details by comparing the RREP information with the GI table entries before selecting and activating the route.

Gateway selection is made based on the hop count distance to the gateway node, network load information on the gateway and local congestion load on intermediate nodes on the route.

Hop Count Criteria

The hop count distance between a mesh router and the gateway is the factor which affects the throughput most; therefore we have set hop count to the gateway as highest priority to keep each node at a minimum possible distance from the gateway either in single or in a multiple gateway scenario.

Gateway Load Criteria

If in situations where all the choices available to establish a route between the mesh router and gateway node have the same hop count distance then the gateway load is used as a secondary criterion to make a decision. Gateway load is the total number of active routers and members routing via a gateway node. This information is gathered with the help of a proactive gateway discovery process described in Proactive Gateway Discovery section.

Local Congestion Load on Intermediate Nodes Criteria

Local congestion load on each intermediate node on the route to the gateway also affects performance. Application of WMN in disaster and emergency requires the network to support Internet TCP traffic in the presence of real-time multimedia UDP traffic. Multimedia streaming may result in heavy network congestion. The QoS scheme described by Iqbal, Wang, and Ellis (2009) gathers the congestion information each node which is maintained in the Bandwidth Information table. LBGD-AODV shares this information during its route discovery process to avoid the congested routes during the gateway route selection process. While selecting a gateway, when a node originates or forwards a RREP message in response to the RREQ as described above, it checks if the route indicated by RREP has enough bandwidth available to support the TCP flow. A node can calculate its bandwidth consumption using information available in the Bandwidth Information table maintained by the QoS scheme. The details on our proposed bandwidth calculation scheme are described by Lee et al. (2005). If the current available bandwidth is being fully utilized by a multimedia flow then the node discards the RREP message without forwarding it back to the source node. Therefore the source node only receives the RREP with routes to the available gateway nodes that can accommodate the TCP traffic. Thus it helps to avoid the congested routes to the gateway nodes.

If the node does not receive the RREP after the wait time expires, it means that either the gateway does not exist anymore or the route is fully congested or it has broken.

In a second attempt to find a gateway route, the source node may unicast the additional route requests to all the available routes to all the gateways in its GI table. All the intermediate nodes repeat the process by forwarding the RREQ to all the route entries in their GI table which are corresponding to the destination gateway nodes. Through this second attempt each gateway node will receive several RREQs via different available routes maintained by the proactive Gateway Discovery process. In a second attempt several RREPs may travel back to the source node via reverse route entries. The source node would select the best gateway with the best route based on the available hop count and load information.

In case there is no entry for a gateway in the Gateway Information table or there is no RREP received for any gateway listed in GI table during the process explained above, then instead of unicast, the node broadcasts the RREQ for the Internet destination, to which only a gateway node can reply with a unicast GWH message. As the GWH message travels back to the source node, it creates GI table entries on each intermediate node for the gateway. If GWH message is not received after RREQ_RETRIES additional RREQs, the node may assume that no gateway node exists within the connected portion of the network. If a node has received one or more than one GWH from one or multiple gateways, it selects a gateway and sends the RREQ as described above.

F. Gateway Route Activation

Once the source node has selected an appropriate gateway with an appropriate route at the end of route discovery process, the next step is to explicitly activate that route between the source node and the gateway node to forward the Internet packets. The source node generates and sends a Route Activation message with J flag and Downstream Load field set to 1. Each intermediate router node updates the Downstream Load field by adding 1 to count itself as an active DOWNSTREAM node, then forwarding it to the next UPSTREAM neighbor. The Route Activation message travels via selected next hop on each intermediate node, effectively establishing a route between itself and next hop UPSTREAM node to the gateway. When the UPSTREAM node receives the Route Activation message, it activates the route with the DOWNSTREAM node. It then forwards the message after updating the Downstream Load field. If an intermediate node which already has an active route to the selected gateway receives the Route Activation message, the node also sets the C flag and simply forwards the message to the active upstream next hop without updating the Downstream Load field. When the next hop node receives the message with the J and C flags set it understands that this message has been sent to provide an update on the additional gateway load. When the gateway node receives the Route Activation message it has the total number of active nodes on a given route which are either originating or forwarding Internet packets destined for the gateway. The gateway node adds the entire DOWNSTREAM local load to calculate the gateway load, which it adds to the Gateway Load field while generating a new GWH message.

The source node which is actively originating the Internet packets joins the gateway as a registered member. All the other nodes on the route that are not actively generating the Internet packets join the gateway as a router node. This is because these nodes are only taking part in forming the route to forward the packets generated by the registered members.

When a node wishes to deactivate a route at the end of a communication session, it sends a Route Activation message with the P flag. It sets the local load to 1 and unicasts the Route Activation message in a similar way to the J flag described above in this section. When the next hop node receives the Route Activation message with the P flag set, it deactivates the route with DOWNSTREAM node. If the next hop UPSTREAM node is not a registered member and is just a router node then on receiving a Route Activation message with the P flag set, it also deactivates the route to its UPSTREAM next hop node and forwards the

message to the next hop UPSTREAM node after updating the local load information. This way the Route Activation message with the P flag travels all the way to the gateway deactivating all the active routes and finally at the gateway node updates its gateway load information.

If an intermediate node which is taking part in forming the route tree is also a registered member of the gateway or is acting as an intermediate node for another active DOWNSTREAM node on the route to the gateway, it needs to keep the route active between itself and gateway node. In this case when it receives a Route Activation message with the P flag set, it removes the active route to the DOWNSTREAM node from which it has received the PRUNE request but it does not remove the UPSTREAM route to the next hop UPSTREAM node. Instead it sets the C flag before forwarding the message to the next active UPSTREAM node. This way when the UPSTREAM next hop receives a Route Activation message with the P and C flags set, it understands that the active downstream node has sent this message to only update it on the new decreased local load. The message travels all the way up to the Gateway node and informs it of the new decreased load information.

G. Proactive Gateway Discovery

LBGD-AODV uses a proactive gateway discovery mechanism. This mechanism advertises a new gateway to the network by broadcasting a periodic Gateway Hello control message after every GATEWAY_HELLO_INTERVAL milliseconds. The architecture of the Gateway Hello message is described in Gateway Hello (GWH) message section. When a node receives the GWH broadcast, it updates the Gateway Information table using the information carried by the GWH message and rebroadcasts the GWH message. As the GWH travels hop-by-hop, each node updates the GWH information such as Upstream IP Address and Hop count field before it re-broadcasts the GWH message after processing it.

Each node increments the Hop count field by 1. The Upstream IP Address field maintains the knowledge of the two hop upstream nodes on the route to each available gateway. When a node re-broadcasts the GWH message it adds the IP address of its upstream next hop node on the route to the gateway into the Upstream IP Address field of GWH. So when a node receives the GWH message, the IP SOURCE header of the GWH message carries the address of the next hop upstream node from which it has received the message, and the Upstream IP Address field of the GWH message carries the second next hop upstream node on the route to the gateway. This enables each node to maintain the two hop upstream node information on each gateway through which the gateway node can be reached.

The GWH message travels through the network and helps all mesh nodes on the network to learn more information about the network topology. The GI table architecture is shown in Gateway Information (GI)Table section. It is a routing table which is maintained by each mesh node to store the network topology information to support the LBGD-AODV functions. When a mesh node needs to send data to an Internet destination, it uses the GI table information to select an appropriate gateway with an appropriate load-balanced route during the reactive route discovery process.

H. Packet Destination Locality Checks

When a node originates a packet, it confirms the locality of the packet to find out that either packet destination exists locally within the mesh network or it is an Internet destination. The node does this through a prefix check. Therefore all the nodes in a WMN must share a prefix (e.g., 192.168.0.0/16).

I. Packet Forwarding

If the originator node does not have an active route to the gateway, it selects and activates the route as described in LBGD-AODV Re-active Route

Discovery Process section. If the originator node is part of an active route to the gateway as a router node, it starts transmitting the data packets along the path to the gateway node and changes its status flag as member node in the GI table.

All the Internet data packets are transmitted using normal IP forwarding to the Gateway node. Once the Gateway node receives the data packets, it also uses normal IP forwarding to route the data packets to their intended destinations. Since each node maintains two hop upstream node information on each gateway through which the gateway node can be reached. This helps to avoid the packet forwarding problems described in Figure 2.

4. EVALUATION TESTS

We have performed performance tests using the SwanMesh testbed to evaluate the LBGDAODV implementation. During the validation tests we used debugging reports and cross referenced them with the route table entries to ensure the correct functionality of the algorithm. we used IxChariot [Ixia, Calabasas, USA] which uses performance endpoint software running on two client laptops to perform client to client throughput tests. The SwanMesh node hardware used during all the evaluation tests is shown in Figure 5.

We used IxChariot to perform the client to client throughput test. We used two laptops during the tests. Laptop 1 remains connected to the gateway node as a client and acts as an end point for IxChariot. We used Laptop2 to connect to the mesh router as client during the test at each hop to perform the tests. We executed the high performance throughput script on laptop2 after connecting it to each mesh router as a client. This script is designed to be used with TCP. For transaction it sends 10 Mbytes from Endpoint Laptop 2 to Endpoint Laptop 1, then waits for an acknowledgment. The script runs 100 transactions in total during each test at each hop.

Figure 5. SwanMesh hardware used for performance tests

4.1. Tree Topology Performance Test Scenario

In this stage of the performance evaluation we performed tests using the emulated tree topology shown in Figures 6 and 7. The test results of throughput for single gateway tree topology are shown in Figure 6. The results shown on the client laptop screen labeled as Laptop 2 indicate the throughput in Mbps between the gateway node and each router node.

We have performed another test using the tree topology shown in Figure 7 with two Gateway nodes.

The results show that the multiple gateway environment has enabled mesh routers to gain higher throughput to their associated gateway especially routers R5, R6, R7 and R8. The performance tests show the LBGD-AODV extension implementation has not compromised the efficiency of basic routing and has enhanced the performance of the network by providing a load-balanced multiple gateway environment. In Basic AODV and LBGD-AODV performance Comparison section we compare the LBGD-AODV performance with basic AODV.

4.2. Basic AODV and LBGD-AODV Performance Comparison

First we performed tests using basic AODV without the LBGD-AODV extension implementation and only a single gateway node was used during the test. We perform another test using a similar chain topology but two gateway nodes to test the performance of the Load-Balanced Gateway Discovery extension implementation.

AODV uses tunneling to forward the Internet packets between a source and destination which requires the source node to insert an outer IP header into the packet before the datagram's IP header. The source and destination addresses in the outer IP header identify the endpoints of the tunnel, whereas the inner IP header source and destination addresses identifies the sender and recipient of the datagram. LBGD-AODV enables the transmission of Internet packets to the gateway using the proactively maintained gateway routing information. It uses normal IP forwarding. Once the Gateway node receives the data packets, it also uses normal IP forwarding to route the data packets to their intended destinations. The topology and test results of the performance tests conducted using basic AODV are shown here again in Figure 8.

Similar to basic the AODV test topology shown in Figure 8, to test LBGD-AODV, we used 5 router nodes in chain but with two gateway nodes instead of one. The second gateway is placed next to Router 5 in the chain topology. During both basic AODV and LBGD-AODV tests a ping command was run to ping an Internet destination on each router node while performing the throughput test between itself and the associated gateway. AODV has a single gateway; therefore the ping packets were transmitted via Gateway G1. During LBGD-AODV performance tests, the routers R1, R2 and R3 transmitted the ping packets via G1 whereas routers R4 and R5 transmitted the ping

Figure 6. Single gateway performance test scenario

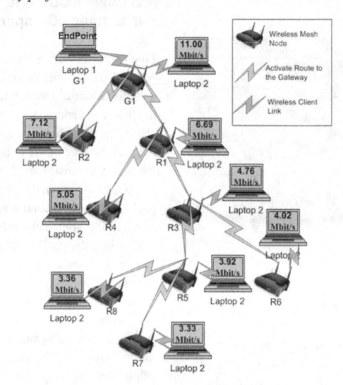

Figure 7. Multiple gateway performance test scenario

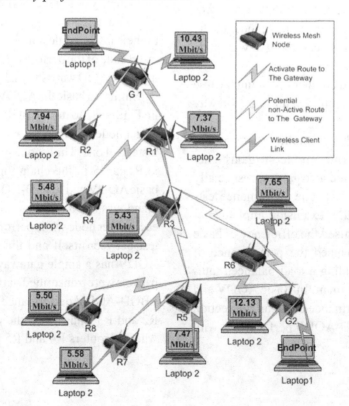

Figure 8. Basic AODV single gateway chain topology tests

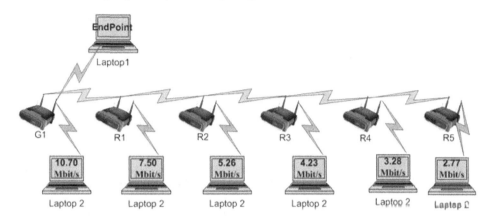

packets via G2 as shown in Figure 9. The green link represents an active route to the gateway whereas the yellow link represents a potential nonactive route to the gateway node. We confirmed this with the debugging reports. Therefore in order to measure the throughput between each mesh router and its associated gateway, we connected Laptop1 endpoint to G2 while performing IxChariot throughput tests on routers R4 and R5 and Laptop 1 to G1 during the throughput tests on routers R1, R2 and R3. The throughput results in Mbps between each router and its associated gateway at each hop are shown in Figure 9 on the client laptop screen labeled as Laptop 2. We used the same script as used during the previously performed basic AODV performance tests shown in Figure 8.

It is noted, that due to the multiple gateway environment, routers 4 and router 5 joined gateway 2; which results in higher throughput for routers 4 and 5 as a result of decreased hop count distance. Table 1 shows the comparison between the AODV single gateway and LBGD-AODV multiple gateway environment tests.

As shown in Table 1, S represents the basic AODV test readings a using single gateway and M represents the LBGD-AODV test readings in a multiple gateway environment. R1, R2 and R3 have the same hop count to the gateway during both the AODV and LBGD-AODV tests, therefore these readings present a good performance com-

parison. We have Gray shaded the area to indicate the test results using the same hop distance to the gateway. The results show that LBGD-AODV has a better response time and has higher throughput compared to the basic AODV protocol. Routers R4 and R5 have much higher throughput and shorter response time as they have lower hop distance in the multiple gateway scenario compared to the single gateway scenario.

The comparison between basic AODV and the LBGD-AODV extension implementation shows that the LBGD-AODV performs better both in terms of throughput and response time compared to basic AODV.

5. CONCLUSION

An ideal application of WMN is intended to be in emergency and disaster recovery in order to provide video surveillance and broadband services. SwanMesh could provide a means to exchange important information via multimedia and data (email, www etc.) communications during a disaster rescue operation. Disaster situations destroy the traditional infrastructure for communications; therefore organizing a reliable communication infrastructure is important for the rescue and first response teams. The self-organized, self-managed and self-healing technology of the SwanMesh would allow the deployment of an efficient net-

Figure 9. LBGD-AODV dual gateway chain topology throughput test

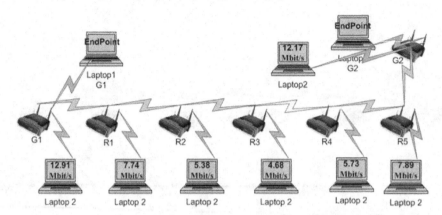

Table 1. Comparison of throughput in basic AODV single and LBGD-AODV two gateways test scenarios

	Router R1		Route R2		Route R3		Router R4		Router R5	
	S1Hop	M1Hop	S2Hop	M2Hop	S3Hop	M3Hop	S4Hop	M2Hop	S5Hop	M1Hop
Response Time (Seconds)	10.67	10.34	15.20	14.87	18.89	17.08	24.42	13.95	28.87	10.13
Throughput (Mbps)	7.50	7.74	5.26	5.38	4.23	4.68	3.28	5.73	2.77	7.89

work within minutes at a disaster site A gateway node in a WMN acts as bridge between mesh nodes and the external network in order to exchange information between the wireless mesh network operating in disaster stricken area and remotely located rescue headquarters and government agencies. Using a single gateway WMN creates huge congestion on the routes to the gateway; as all the data traffic use the same route to access the gateway node. A large number of mesh nodes may be required to cover a larger disaster stricken area. In a single gateway environment an Internet packet may have to travel on longer routes to reach the destination. Longer routes require more intermediate nodes to forward the packets between the source node and destination gateway to enable multihop communication path. This results in congestion due to channel contention between nodes that operate within carrier sensing range of each other. Therefore a multiple gateway

environment is crucial during WMN application in emergency and disaster recovery.

In this paper we have presented the detailed design and implementation of LBGD-AODV, a load balanced gateway discovery routing protocol which provides self-organized, self-managed, self-healing and load-balanced multiple gateway environments for SwanMesh. The proposed algorithm works as an extension to the AODV routing protocol. We have integrated LBGD-AODV route discovery for an Internet destination within AODV's existing reactive route discovery process. Thus when a node needs a route for an Internet destination, it uses the topology and load information available on all the gateways to select an appropriate gateway with an appropriate route for an Internet destination in an on-demand fashion. All these data packets are transmitted using normal IP forwarding to the gateway node. Once the gateway node receives the data packets, it also uses normal IP forwarding to route the data packets to their intended destinations. The packet forwarding scheme used in LBGD-AODV overcomes the limitations of default routes and tunneling schemes.

The performance tests show that the LBGD-AODV extension implementation has not compromised efficiency of basic routing and enhances the performance of the network by providing a load-balanced multiple gateway environment. The comparative analysis of the tests conducted using basic AODV with LBGD-AODV tests show that the LBGD-AODV implementation performs better than basic AODV both in terms of throughput and response.

REFERENCES

Belding-Royer, E., Sun, Y., & Perkins, C. E. (2001). *Global connectivity for IPv4 mobile ad hoc networks*. Retrieved from http://tools.ietf.org/id/draft-royer-manet-globalv4-00.txt

Broch, J., Maltz, D., & Johnson, D. (1999). Supporting hierarchy and heterogeneous interfaces in multi-hop wireless ad hoc networks. In *Proceedings of the IEEE International Symposium on Parallel Architectures, Algorithms, and Networks*, Perth, Australia (pp. 370-375).

Das, S. R., Perkins, C. E., & Royer, E. M. (2000, March). Performance comparison of two on-demand routing protocols for ad hoc networks. In *Proceedings of the IEEE Conference on Computer Communications*, Tel Aviv, Israel (pp. 3-12).

Iqbal, M., Li, S., Wang, X. H., & Ellis, T. S. (2009, October 12-14). Bandwidth calculation scheme to provide cross layer rate adaptive admission control in wireless mesh networks. In *Proceedings of the Conference on Next Generation Wireless Systems*, Melbourne, Australia.

Iqbal, M., Shancang, L., Wang, X. H., & Ellis, T. (2009). A QoS scheme for multimedia multicast communications over wireless mesh networks. *IET Communications*, *4*(11), 1312–1324. doi:10.1049/iet-com.2009.0413

Iqbal, M., Wang, X. H., & Wertheim, D. (2009). Reliable multimedia multicast communications over wireless mesh networks. *IET Communications*, *4*(11), 1288–1299. doi:10.1049/iet-com.2009.0134

Iqbal, M, Wang, X. H., Wertheim, D., & Zhou, X. (2009). SwanMesh: A multicast enabled dual-radio wireless mesh network for emergency and disaster recovery services. *The Journal of Communication*, *4*(5), 298–306.

Jelger, C., & Noel, T. (2006). Algorithms for prefix continuity in IPv6 ad hoc networks. *Ad Hoc & Sensor Wireless Networks, 2*(2).

Jelger, C., Noel, T., & Frey, A. (2004). *Gateway and address autoconfiguration for ipv6 adhoc networks*. Retrieved from http://tools.ietf.org/html/draft-jelger-manet-gateway-autoconf-v6-02

Johanson, P., Larsson, T., Hedman, N., Mielczarek, B., & Degermark, M. (1999). Scenario-based performance analysis of routing protocols for mobile ad-hoc networks. In *Proceedings of the 5th Annual ACM/IEEE International Conference on Mobile Computing and Networking*, Seattle, WA (pp. 195-206).

Jonsson, U., Alriksson, F., Larsson, T., Johansson, P., & Maguire, G. Q., Jr. (2000). MIPMANET - Mobile IP for mobile ad hoc networks. In *Proceedings of the 1st ACM International Symposium on Mobile Ad Hoc Networking and Computing*.

Kim, B. C., Lee, J. Y., Lee, H. S., & Ma, J. S. (2003). An ad-hoc routing protocol with minimum contention time and load balancing. In *Proceedings of the IEEE Global Telecommunications Conference* (pp. Vol. 1, 81-85).

Lee, J., Kim, D., Garcia-Luna-Aceves, J. J., Choi, Y., Choi, J., & Nam, S. (2003, April). Hybrid gateway advertisement scheme for connecting mobile ad hoc networks to the Internet. In *Proceedings of the 57th IEEE Semiannual Vehicular Technology Conference*, Jeju, Korea (pp. 191-195).

Lee, S. J., & Gerla, M. (2001). Dynamic load-aware routing in ad hoc networks. In *Proceedings of the IEEE International Conference on Communications*, Helsinki, Finland (pp. 3206-3210).

Lee, Y. J., & Riley, G. F. (2005, March 13-17). A workload-based adaptive load-balancing technique for mobile ad hoc networks. In *Proceedings of the IEEE Wireless Communications and Networking Conference* (pp. 2002-2007).

Nordström, E., Gunningberg, P., & Tschudin, C. (2010). *Design of Internet connectivity for mobile ad hoc networks*. Retrieved from http://user.it.uu.se/~erikn/papers/adhoc-internet.pdf

Pearlman, M. R., Haas, Z. J., Sholander, P., & Tabrizi, S. S. (2000). On the impact of alternate path routing for load balancing in mobile ad hoc networks. In *Proceedings of the 1st ACM International Symposium on Mobile Ad Hoc Networking & Computing*, Boston, MA (pp. 3-10).

Perkins, C. E. (1996). *IP encapsulation within IP*. Retrieved from http://tools.ietf.org/html/draft-ietf-mobileip-ip4inip4-00

Perkins, C. E., Royer, E. M., & Das, S. R. (2008). *Ad hoc on demand distance vector routing*. Retrieved from http://tools.ietf.org/html/rfc3561

Ratanchandani, P., & Kravets, R. (2003). A hybrid approach to internet connectivity for mobile ad hoc networks. In *Proceedings of the IEEE Conference on Wireless Communications and Networking*, New Orleans, LA (pp. 1522-1527).

Rosenschon, M., Mänz, T., Habermann, J., & Rakocevic, V. (2004, March). Performance analysis of Internet gateway discovery protocols in ad hoc networks. In *Proceedings of the IEEE Conference on Wireless Communications and Networking* (pp. 120-125).

Ruiz, P. M., & Gomez-Skarmeta, A. F. (2005). Adaptive gateway discovery mechanisms to enhance internet connectivity for mobile ad hoc networks. *Ad Hoc & Sensor Wireless Networks, 1*, 159–177.

Song, J.-H., Wong, V., & Leung, V. C. M. (2003, April 22-25). Load-aware on-demand routing (LAOR) protocol for mobile ad hoc networks. In *Proceedings of the 57th IEEE Semiannual Vehicular Technology Conference* (pp. 1753-1757).

Sun, Y., Belding-Royer, E. M., & Perkins, C. E. (2002). Internet connectivity for ad hoc mobile networks. *International Journal of Wireless Information Networks, 9*(2), 75–88. doi:10.1023/A:1015399632291

Wakikawa, R., Malinen, J., Perkins, C., Nilsson, A., & Tuominen, A. (2006). *Global connectivity for IPv6 mobile ad hoc networks*. Retrieved from http://tools.ietf.org/html/draft-wakikawa-manet-globalv6-05

Wang, X. H., Iqbal, M., & Zhou, X. (2008, May 30-31). Design and implementation of a dual-radio wireless mesh network testbed for healthcare. In *Proceedings of the 5th International Conference on Information Technology and Applications in Biomedicine*, Shenzhen, China.

Yi, Y., Kwon, T. J., & Gerla, M. (2001). A load aWare routing (LWR) based on local information. In *Proceedings of the 12th IEEE International Symposium on Personal, Indoor and Mobile Radio Communications*, San Diego, CA (Vol. 2, pp. 65-69).

Zhang, L., Zhao, Z., Shu, Y., Wang, L., & Yang, O. W. W. (2002). Load balancing of multipath source routing in ad hoc networks. In *Proceedings of the IEEE International Conference on Communications* (Vol. 5, pp. 3197-3201).

Zhou, X., Wang, X. H., Iqbal, M., & Yan, L. (2009). A handheld mobile device for wireless mesh networks in healthcare. In *Proceedings of the 2nd IEEE International Symposium on IT in Medicine & Education*, Jinan, China (pp. 1070-1073).

This work was previously published in the International Journal of Adaptive, Resilient and Autonomic Systems, Volume 2, Issue 4, edited by Vincenzo De Florio, pp. 36-53, copyright 2011 by IGI Publishing (an imprint of IGI Global).

Chapter 17
An OMA DM Based Framework for Updating Modulation Module for Mobile Devices

Hui Zhang
Swansea University, UK

Xinheng Wang
Swansea University, UK

Muddesar Iqbal
University of Gujrat, Pakistan

ABSTRACT

Due to the rapid advancement of mobile communication technologies, the demands for managing mobile devices effectively to fulfill various functionalities are on the rise. It is well known that mobile devices make use of different kinds of modulation approaches to adapt to various channel conditions. Therefore, in this paper, the authors propose a framework of Modulation Module Update (MMU) for updating the modulation module on the mobile device based on OMA DM. The management object for updating modulation module and the parameters associated with it are defined in the framework, and three operation phases are defined in this framework as well.

INTRODUCTION

Mobile wireless technology has gained tremendous popularity due to its ability to provide ubiquitous information access to users on the move (Sandeep et al., 2004; Siddiqui & Zeadally, 2006). With the rapid advancement of the mobile communication technologies, mobile device gains more

functionalities and higher intelligence. However, the development of these technologies has also raised a range of requirements such as the firmware update over-the-air (OTA) (Hoffmeyer et al., 2004). Furthermore, as the demand of high quality services in next generation wireless communication systems increases, high performance of data transmission requires an increase of spectrum

DOI: 10.4018/978-1-4666-2056-8.ch017

efficiency and an improvement of error performance in wireless communication systems (Choi & Lajos, 2001; Seshadri Sastry & Prasad Babu, 2010). Generally, mobile devices make use of different kinds of modulation approaches to adapt to channel conditions. Therefore, update of the modulation module by downloading modulation modules over-the-air can be an effective way to satisfy the requirement. In this paper, we propose a framework for the update of the modulation module on the mobile devices based on Open Mobile Alliance Device Management (OMA DM) (http://www.openmobile alliance.org).

The remainder of this paper is arranged as follows. First we describe the OMA DM standards and latest developments of applying OMA DM in updating software in mobile devices. Next we present the design of a framework to update the modulation module based on OMA DM. Finally we show the details of the design and implementation of the framework and conclude this paper.

OMA DEVICE MANAGEMENT

OMA DM is developed by Open Mobile Alliance (OMA) primarily to standardize the device management functions, which is intended to support the typical uses, such as configuring devices, enabling and disabling features, updating software packages or fixing bugs, reporting error of the device, and so on (Steinke & Strohmenger, 2007; Lim et al., 2008; Ma et al., 2008). The DM working group of OMA is mainly responsible for the revision and publication of OMA DM specifications (Husain et al., 2008).

OMA DM Architecture and FUMO

A simple architecture of OMA DM for firmware update is shown in Figure 1. As shown in Figure 1, DM Server is the server-side implementation of the OMA DM protocol. Its task is to manage OMA DM compliant devices using different management operations, e.g., provisioning, con-

Figure 1. OMA DM architecture

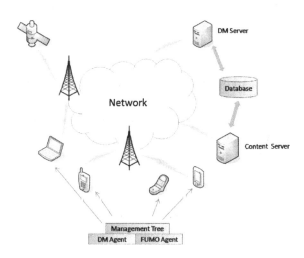

figuration of device, updating software, and fault management (Shi et al., 2007). Content Server is in charge of providing and managing the software packages and multi-media contents for the software upgrades and bug fix of the mobile device.

The device to be managed is composed of hardware components, software modules for managing the hardware components, and device management agent that performs software updates/managements and firmware updates by connecting to the OMA DM server (State et al., 2004).

Each device that supports OMA DM contains a Management Tree. The Management Tree organizes all available management objects in the device in a hierarchical tree structure where all nodes can be uniquely addressed with a Uniform Resource Identifiers (URI) (OMA, 2008; IETF, 1998). DM Server realizes the management actions by manipulating the nodes in a device management tree.

DM Agent is a software component that resides in the mobile device. It is used to process the messages received from the DM Server, including parsing messages from DM Server, interpreting OMA DM commands, and executing relevant actions in the device. In addition, the DM agent can also generate relevant responses and send them back to the DM Server.

Firmware Update Management Object (FUMO) is an OMA specification for updating the firmware of mobile devices over-the-air, which allows mobile devices to be updated over-the-air using the industry-standard protocol OMA DM (2009). Additionally, FUMO also specifies a range of standard commands with relevant parameters and management objects that can be used for OTA firmware updates. Figure 2 shows a simple procedure of the firmware update.

Generally, FUMO Agent and other special purpose agents can coexist to provide additional functions on a managed device. FUMO Agent coexists with the DM Agent to provide firmware downloading and updating functions on the managed device.

OMA DM Process

OMA DM process is composed of two phases. One is the setup phase that takes charge of the authentication and device information exchange, the other is the management phase which is used for realizing the management operations (OMA, 2005, 2007). Figure 3 depicts the two phases.

Related Works

In Shi et al. (2007) the authors presented the work on a demonstration platform for a Software Defined Radio proof-of-concept and how OMA DM protocol and Functional Description Language can be used to support Radio Access Technology (RAT) reconfiguration on SDR terminals.

In Chakravorty and Ottevanger (2002), the Smart Box Management (SBM), an end-to-end remote management framework for Internet enabled device, is proposed. The SBM server provides the basic set of services to the SBM clients over the Internet, such as remote activation, remote configuration, dynamic updates (downloads), and device diagnostic uploads, based on a set of protocols like device registration protocol, configuration protocol, upload protocol, and download protocol. The SBM realizes these management functions by using their own protocols defined for the system which limits the generality of the system.

Mobile Device Management Agent (Shin et al., 2008) is designed and implemented based on OMA DM, which provides more effective device management functions with small amount of network traffic by using Tree and Description

Figure 2. Firmware update

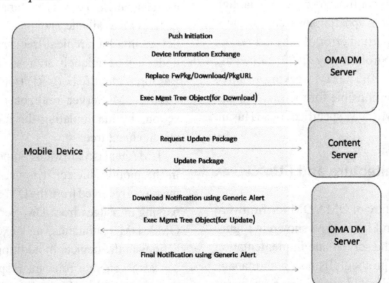

Figure 3. Setup phase and management phase

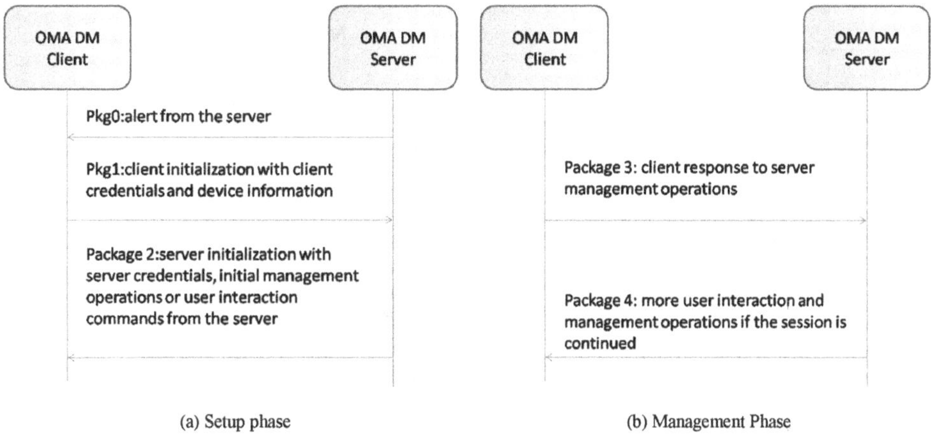

(a) Setup phase   (b) Management Phase

Serialization Specification for acquiring, adding, and editing management objects in mobile devices. This system is a client side implementation of the OMA DM protocol and does not realize the operation mechanism of firmware update.

Software fault management method (Kang et al., 2009) mainly concentrates on remotely determining and correcting problems of mobile devices based on OMA DM with the definition of management objects and a method to collect them from mobile devices. This method focuses on data gathering and correcting but not the firmware download and update.

This paper aims to develop a framework in connection with the modulation module update in mobile devices. The Modulation Module Update (MMU) proposed in this paper is a framework for updating the modulation module on the mobile device based on OMA DM. The management object for updating modulation module and the parameters associated with it as well as three operation phases are defined in this framework. The client side of MMU downloads new version of modulation module over-the-air, then updates the modulation module on the device by the firmware update interface which is provided for simulating the update procedure. Currently, the utilization of OMA DM and FUMO is generally for high layer

software update or bug fixing over-the-air, but rarely focuses on lower layer firmware update such as modulation module. For this reason, we propose this framework to combine OMA DM and the update of lower layer firmware.

MANAGEMENT ARCHITECTURE

This section describes the logical layer structure of the MMU. Figure 4 shows the management architecture of the framework we proposed.

Management Object

Virtual tree structure built with the management objects is used for efficient device management. Through the DM Agent, DM Server may access individual node of the virtual management tree, or, by accessing the parent node, it may reach all its children nodes (Oommen, 2001; Krishnaswamy et al., 2007). We define the firmware update management object in the device management tree for the update of the modulation module based on FUMO. Figure 5 shows how the management object is defined, including its format, Access Control List (ACL) and Scope, and how they relate to other nodes.

Figure 4. Management architecture

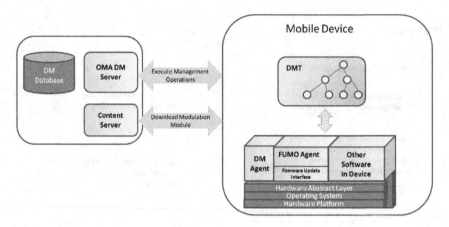

Figure 5. Management Object for modulation module update

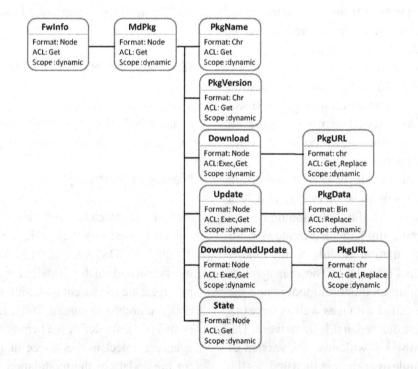

FwInfo (./FwInfo), an interior node expanding the root node, acts as the entrance of the firmware management object.

MdPkg (./FwInfo/MdPkg) is an interior node acting as a placeholder for the modulation module's unique identifier.

PkgName(./FwInfo/MdPkg/ PkgName) is a leaf node that specifies the name associated with the modulation module.

PkgVersion(./FwInfo/MdPkg/ PkgVersion) is a leaf node that specifies the version information associated with the modulation module.

Download(./FwInfo/MdPkg/ Download) is an interior node, acting as the target of an "Exec" command. Server operates the node to perform the initialization of the modulation module download.

PkgURL(./FwInfo/MdPkg/ Download / PkgURL) is a leaf node specifying the URL where the modulation module is located.

Update(./FwInfo/MdPkg/ Update) is an interior node, acting as the target of an "Exec" command. Server operates the node to perform the update operation of the modulation module.

PkgData(./FwInfo/MdPkg/ Update / PkgData) is a leaf node acting as the target of a 'Replace'

command when DM is used to directly provide the binary firmware update module.

DownloadAndUpdate(./FwInfo/MdPkg/ DownloadAndUpdate) is an interior node and the target of an 'Exec' command. The update takes place as soon as the downlaod finishes.

State(./FwInfo/MdPkg/ State) is a leaf node that contains a value indicating the current state of the update of the modulation module.

Management Operations

The update procedure is composed of following management operation phases: initialization phase, modulation module download phase, and modulation module update phase.

- **Initialization Phase:** At the beginning of the setup phase, the server sends the Notification to the client to make the client connect to the server. After the client receives the notification message, it sends the initialization message with the device information to the server to identify itself with the server. When all these identifica-

Figure 6. Initialization phase

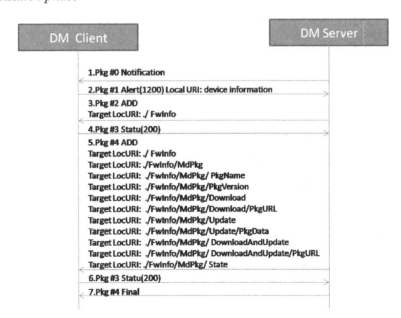

tions are completed, the server executes management operation for the initialization of the modulation module update. First, the DM Server sends operation message with "Add" command to create FwInfo as the entrance of the firmware management object. Then, the rest nodes related to the update management object are added by the "Add" commands within the next package. In the framework we proposed, the commands of adding the management objects are all in one operation message rather than the respective messages for higher efficiency. Figure 6 shows the details of the initialization phase.

Download Phase: The download of the modulation module phase is mainly based on Download and the PkgURL. By handling the two nodes, DM Server achieves the control of the download operation. Server sends operation message with "Replace" command to operate the./Download/ PkgURL for specifying the download descriptor of the modulation module. After that, the download procedure is started by the message with "Exec" command on Download node received from the server.

The client in the device connects to the content server for downloading the modulation module after analyzing download descriptor by HTTP. Figure 7 shows the details of the download phase.

- **Update Phase:** Update phase is commenced by the message with "Exec" command on the update from the server. This phase is right after the client sends the message back to the server to notice the server that the download is finished. Client provides firmware update manager to manage the update operation of the modulation module on the device. Meanwhile, the interface related to the firmware layer is provided as well, which can be invoked to complete the modulation module update operation. Figure 8 shows the details of the update phase.

DESIGN AND IMPLEMENTATION

The framework proposed in this paper is composed of server side and client side. Moreover, the client side located in the device is a vital part

Figure 7. Download phase

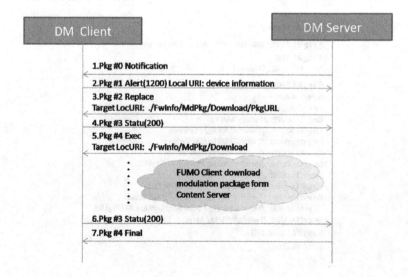

Figure 8. Update phase

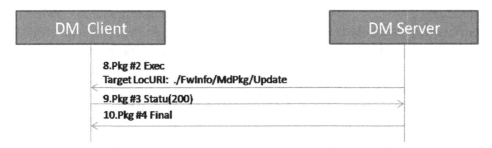

Figure 9. Structure of client agent

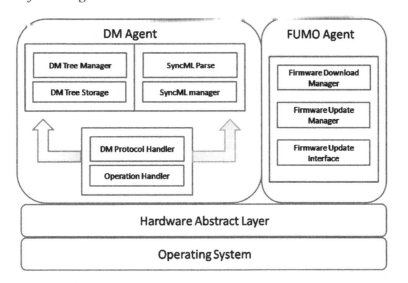

Figure 10. Screenshot of MMU

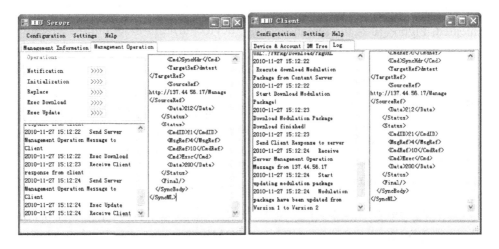

for MMU. Figure 9 details structure of the client side in the device.

DM Agent is composed of DM Tree Manager, DM Tree Storage, SyncML Parser, SyncML Manager, DM Protocol Handler, and Operation Handler. DM Tree Manager is used for managing the device management tree in the device. DM Tree Storage acts as the entity of the management tree including the information of the management objects. SyncML Parser is in charge of parsing the SyncML messages. SyncML Manager is responsible for the generation of the SyncML messages. DM protocol Handler manages sessions between the DM server and the DM client. Operation Handler handles all the management operations as well as management commands, such as Add, Delete, Replace, Exec, and so on.

FUMO Agent is composed of Firmware Download Manager, Firmware Update Manager, and Firmware Update Interface. Firmware Download Manager aims to analyze download descriptor and download modulation module to the device by HTTP. Firmware Update Manager manages firmware update nodes on the device management tree and is in charge of the modulation module update procedure. Firmware Update Interface is the interface that can be invoked by the higher layer for the update of modulation module.

The sever side and client side of MMU has been implemented. Figure 10 is the screenshot of MMU.

CONCLUSION

As the demand of high quality services in wireless communication systems increases, mobile device makes use of different kinds of modulation approaches to adapt to different channel conditions (Mohammed et al., 2006). In this paper, we proposed a framework for the modulation module update on the mobile device based on OMA DM. Three phases are defined for the framework, which are initialization phase, download phase, and update phase. In addition, we have developed the DM server, the content server and the client to validate the framework.

REFERENCES

Berners-Lee, T. (1998). *Uniform resource identifiers (URI): Generic syntax.* Retrieved from http://www.ietf.org/rfc/rfc2396.txt

Chakravorty, R., & Ottevanger, H. (2002). Architecture and implementation of a remote management framework for dynamically reconfigurable devices. In *Proceedings of the 10th IEEE International Conference on Networks* (pp. 375-381).

Choi, B.-J., & Lajos, H. (2001). Optimum mode-switching assisted adaptive modulation. In *Proceedings of the Global Telecommunications Conference* (pp. 3316-3320).

Hoffmeyer, J., Il-Pyung, P., Majmundar, M., & Blust, S. (2004). Radio software download for commercial wireless reconfigurable devices. *IEEE Communications Magazine, 42*(3), 26–32. doi:10.1109/MCOM.2004.1273771

Husain, S., Alonso, T., Midani, M., & Jung, K. (2008). Remote device management of WiMAX devices in multi-mode multi-access environment. In *Proceedings of the IEEE International Symposium on Broadband Multimedia Systems and Broadcasting* (pp. 1-14).

Kang, J. M., Ju, H.-T., & Choi, M.-J., Won-ki Hong, J., & Kim, J.-G. (2009). OMA DM-based remote software fault management for mobile devices. *International Journal of Network Management, 19*(6), 491–511. doi:10.1002/nem.724

Krishnaswamy, D., Pfeifer, T. et al. (2007). OMA DM based remote RF signal monitoring of mobile devices for QoS improvement. *Real-Time Mobile Multimedia Services,* 76-87.

Lim, H.-J., Park, S.-H., & Chung, T.-M. (2008). u-MoDEM: Ubiquitous mobile device environment manager based on OMA-DM. In *Proceedings of the 10th International Conference on Advanced Communication Technology* (pp. 283-287).

Ma, J., Liao, J., & Zhu, X. (2008). Device management in the IMS. *Journal of Network and Systems Management*, *16*(1), 46–62. doi:10.1007/s10922-007-9092-7

Mohammed, H. K., Tripathi, R., & Kant, K. (2006). Performance of adaptive modulation in multipath fading channel. In *Proceedings of the 8th International Conference on Advanced Communication Technology* (pp. 1277-1282).

Oommen, P. (2001). A framework for integrated management of mobile-stations over-the-air. In *Proceedings of the IEEE/IFIP International Symposium on Integrated Network Management* (pp. 247-256).

Sandeep, A., Sangita, M., & Vasudevan, V. (2004). Universal manager: Seamless management of enterprise mobile and non-mobile devices. In *Proceedings of the IEEE International Conference on Mobile Data Management* (pp. 320-331).

Seshadri Sastry, K., & Prasad Babu, M. S. (2010). Adaptive modulation for OFDM system using fuzzy logic interface. In *Proceedings of the IEEE International Conference on Software Engineering and Service Sciences* (pp. 368-371).

Shi, Z., Dolwin, C., Steinke, B., & Droege, A. (2007). A OMA DM based software defined radio proof-of-concept demonstration platform. In *Proceedings of the IEEE 18th International Symposium on Indoor and Mobile Radio Communications* (pp. 1-5).

Shin, J., Chung, Y., Sun Ko, K., & Ik Eom, Y. (2008). Design and implementation of the management agent for mobile devices based on OMA DM. In *Proceedings of the 2nd International Conference on Ubiquitous Information Management and Communication*.

Siddiqui, F., & Zeadally, S. (2006). Mobility management across hybrid wireless networks: Trends and challenges. *Computer Communications*, *29*(9), 1363–1385. doi:10.1016/j.comcom.2005.09.003

State, R., Fester, O., & Zores, B. (2004). An extensible agent toolkit for device management. In *Proceedings of the IEEE/IFIP International Symposium on Network Operations and Management Symposium* (pp. 845-858).

Steinke, B., & Strohmenger, K. (2007). Advanced device self management through autonomics and reconfigurability. In *Proceedings of the 16th Mobile and Wireless Communications Summit* (pp.1-4).

This work was previously published in the International Journal of Adaptive, Resilient and Autonomic Systems, Volume 2, Issue 3, edited by Vincenzo De Florio, pp. 13-23, copyright 2011 by IGI Publishing (an imprint of IGI Global).

Chapter 18
Duty Cycle Measurement Techniques for Adaptive and Resilient Autonomic Systems

Chiara Taddia
University of Ferrara, Italy

Gianluca Mazzini
University of Ferrara, Italy

Riccardo Rovatti
University of Bologna, Italy

ABSTRACT

When systems are deployed in environments where change is the rule rather than the exception, adaptability and resilience play a crucial role in order to preserve good quality of service. This work analyses methods that can be adopted for the duty cycle measurement of sensor-originated waveforms. These methods start from the assumption that no regular sampling is possible and thus they are naturally thought for an adaptive coexistence with other heterogeneous and variable tasks. Hence, the waveform carrying the information from low-priority sensors can be sampled only at instants that are non-controlled. To tackle this problem, this paper proposes some algorithms for the duty cycle measurement of a digital pulse train signal that is sampled at random instants. The solutions are easy to implement and lightweight so that they can be scheduled in extremely loaded microcontrollers. The results show a fast convergence to the duty cycle value; in particular, a considerable gain with respect to other known solutions is obtained in terms of the average number of samples necessary to evaluate the duty cycle with a desired accuracy is obtained.

DOI: 10.4018/978-1-4666-2056-8.ch018

1. INTRODUCTION

One of the options for the deployment of systems able to sense and react to environment changes exploiting some redundancy to possibly provide robust and dependable behaviors is the creation of a network of simple nodes with both sensing, processing and communication abilities. In such a framework, the limited energy budget of every node (Rao, Vrudhula, & Rakhmatov, 2003; Moragrega, Ibars, & Geng, 2009) often implies large sleeping times with asynchronous wake-ups (Vigorito, Ganesan, & Barto, 2007) stimulated by high priority tasks due to communication or coordination.

To be environment-aware, wake-ups must be also used to monitor available sensors whose readings can be collected in those short time-slices of the microcontroller that are left idle from higher-priority tasks.

This configuration may easily cope with sensors whose reading is immediately available at a digital or analog port. Yet the deployment of such sensors can be over killing when extremely slowly varying physical quantities have to be monitored and/or when the number of wires that can be employed for the connection between the sensing and processing units must be kept to a minimum. For example, sensors exist that communicate their output by modulating a square wave so that its duty cycle is proportional to the measured physical quantity. TMP03 (http://www.analog.com) and SMT160-30 (http://www.smartec.nl/pdf/DSSMT16030.PDF) are among these and may be used to sense temperature in sensor networks for environmental monitoring (Lach, Evans, McCune, & Brandon, 2003; Lan, Qilong, & Du, 2008).

The most common method for duty cycle measurements is to read high and low periods by means of a timer/counter port (de Jong & Toth, n.d.) of the microcontroller. An alternative idea is introduced in (Bhatti, Denneau, & Draper, 2005) and is based on random sampling and on the ap-

plication of the Law of Large Numbers (Spiegel, 1975): the state of the square wave is repeatedly sampled at the edges of a random clock; if the duty cycle of the signal is D, then the probability of sampling a high signal level in each trial is equal to D; the duty cycle is then calculated as the ratio between the number H of the high samples and the total number of samples N; since we have $\lim_{n \to \infty} \dfrac{H}{N} = D$; the accuracy increases arbitrarily as the number of samples increases. In the rest of the paper we refer to this algorithm with the term Count Active Algorithm, CAA.

The random sampling technique is particularly interesting for our scenario. In fact, since both the wake-ups and the idle time-slices within the working intervals cannot be predicted at design-time, information about the signal status can be inherently collected only in a random set of time-instants. Note that, in this sense, the random occurrence of the samples is something that our approach has to cope with and not some working hypothesis that we impose to the system: the random behavior of the sampling activity is naturally dictated by the operating system that collects the samples only during its idle periods of time.

In Taddia and Mazzini (2006) we have proposed three novel algorithms based on a random sampling approach to calculate the duty cycle of a square wave. We suppose to know the signal period and the temporal instants in correspondence of the signal rising edges; furthermore we suppose to work with a signal that maintains a constant period. All these are solutions that can be easily implemented on microcontrollers. In Taddia and Mazzini (2006) we have presented simulation results that show a considerable gain in terms of number of samples necessary to obtain a desired error level: our solutions can estimate the duty cycle with an average error of 10^{-2} after N = 50 samples, while the (Bhatti, Denneau, & Draper, 2005) would require N = 1000 samples. In our previous works (Taddia & Mazzini, 2006; Taddia, Mazzini, & Rovatti, 2010) we have calculated through an analytical framework the mean error that can be obtained by the proposed algorithms with the knowledge of the first two collected samples, irrespective of their statistical distribution and with a generic number of collected sampled, provided that they are independent and uniform distributed. Furthermore we have proved the feasibility of the proposed techniques with a test-bed implementing the algorithms.

In this work we enrich the description of the mathematical model by presenting several numerical and mathematical evidences that corroborate the analytical framework describing the mean error and the deviation of this error after the collection of a generic number of samples. Overall, a good match between theoretical trends and simulation results can be observed.

The rest of the paper is organized as follows: Section 2 describes the four proposed algorithms and introduces some metrics to evaluate the performances of the algorithms, such as mean error between actual and estimate duty cycle and its variance; Section 3 shows the results obtained through simulations; Section 4 studies the actual memory of the sampling process considered and the correlation between the collected samples; Section 5 presents a result concerning the behavior of the P DF of a quantized sum of random variables. Section 6 describes the analytical framework related to the algorithms.

2. DESCRIPTION OF THE ALGORITHMS AND METRICS

We consider a square wave $w(t)$ of period T with duty cycle D; we remember that the duty cycle of a pulse train of rectangular pulses is defined as the ratio between the pulse duration (Z, time in which the signal has a high logic level) and the pulse period T (Figure 1a). Without loss of generality we proceed by considering a period $T = 1$: therefore the duty cycle D coincides with the pulse duration Z. In the rest of the paper we will refer

to these quantities with the single term D. We are interested in the signal duty cycle measurement by using a random sampling technique, i.e., by sampling the signal at random temporal instants. We suppose that the signal maintains a duty cycle at least for a number of periods sufficient to perform the duty cycle measurement; this is the case, for example, of the digital output of a sensor measuring a slow variable quantity, such as the temperature. The samples succession is described by the temporal instants at which the samples occur: the i-th sample occurs at the time instant t_i, with $t_i = t_{i-1} + g_i$ where t_{i-1} is the instant of arrival of the previous sample and g_i is the time elapsed between the two samples collected respectively in t_{i-1} and in t_i. The interarrival time, $g \geq 0$, between two successive samples, is described by the probability density function $f_g(\cdot)$. We suppose to know the signal period and the temporal instants in correspondence of the signal rising edges: with these information and from the knowledge of the absolute temporal instant of a sample occurrence we can derive the position of the sample inside a single period width $[t_i]$, by performing a modulus 1 operation (operator $[\cdot]$): for each sample we calculate therefore $[t_i] = t_i \bmod 1$ (Figure 1b). In the following, we will define three algorithms that can estimate the duty cycle (Equation 1, 2, and 3) thanks to modulus 1 operation, therefore thanks to the period and rising edges instants of the signal $w(t)$. In case these information were not available, the three algorithms we propose would still be applicable, after a start-up phase in which the period length and the rising edges instants are estimated. By referring to the first N gathered samples and, with 1 and 0, being respectively the high and low logic level of $w(t)$, we indicate with $\pm_N^+$ the maximum element of the collection of $[t_i]$ smaller than D and $i \leq N$ and with $\pm_N^-$ the minimum element of the set of $[t_i]$ and $i \leq N$ (Figure 1c):

Figure 1. Definition of some parameters: a) duty cycle; b) and c) variable used in the algorithms definitions

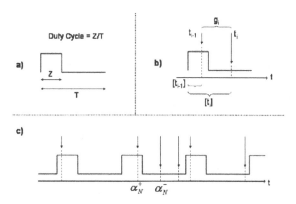

$$\pm_N^+ = \max\{[t_i] \mid w(t_i) = 1, i \le N\}$$
$$= \max\{[t_i] < D, i \le N\}$$

$$\pm_N^- = \min\{[t_i] \mid w(t_i) = 0, i \le N\}$$
$$= \min\{[t_i] > D, i \le N\}$$

Note that the left is related to the signal while the right one regards its mathematical and semantic definition. We describe here four low-complexity and easy to implement algorithms, to calculate the duty cycle of the signal w(t) by exploiting the samples obtained from the random sampling activity described by the pdf $f_g(\cdot)$.

A. Active Time Algorithm, ATA

This algorithm takes into account only the samples gathered in correspondence of the high level of the square wave; therefore it exploits the set of t_i defined by
$$\{[t_i] \mid w(t_i) = 1, i \le N\} = \{[t_i] < D, i \le N\}.$$
The duty cycle is estimated as the largest $[t_i]$ between the set of $[t_i]$ less than the actual duty cycle D and with $1 < i < N$; therefore D_N^{EST} is defined as follows:

$$D_N^{EST} = \max\{[t_i] \mid w(t_i) = 1, i \le N\} = \pm_N^+ \tag{1}$$

In case that all the N samples happen in the interval [D,1] the estimate D_N^{EST} remains equal to the initialization value 0.

B. Inactive Time Algorithm, ITA

A variant consists in taking into account only the samples in correspondence of the low pulse of the square wave, $\{[t_i] \mid w(t_i) = 0, i \le N\} = \{[t_i] > D, i \le N\}$. The duty cycle is estimated as the smallest element of the set of samples corresponding to a low logic level signal w(t), i.e., the lowest $[t_i]$ between the set of $[t_i]$ greater than the actual duty cycle D and with $1 < i < N$; therefore D_N^{EST} is defined as follows:

$$D_N^{EST} = \min\{[t_i] \mid w(t_i) = 0, i \le N\} = \pm_N^- \tag{2}$$

In case that all N samples happen in the interval [0,D] the estimate D_N^{EST} remains equal to the initialization value 1.

C. Active Inactive Time Algorithm, AITA

This algorithm is a combination of the previous solutions. By considering both the maximum between the $[t_i]$ less than D and the minimum between the $[t_i]$ greater than D, we observe that the error is uniformly distributed between these two thresholds; the simplest choice is therefore to derive an estimation of the duty cycle D, after having gathered N samples, as the mean between $\pm_N^+$ and $\pm_N^-$:

$$D_N^{EST} = \frac{\pm_N^+ + \pm_N^-}{2} \tag{3}$$

D. Count Active Algorithm, CAA

In order to implement the *Count Active Algorithm* algorithm introduced by (Bhatti, Denneau, & Draper, 2005) we observe that the duty cycle estimate after N samples is the ratio between the number of high level signal samples and the total amount of collected samples, as expressed by the following Equation:

$$D_N^{EST} = \frac{\#\{t_i \mid w(t_i) = 1, i \leq N\}}{N} \tag{4}$$

E. Metrics

A good metric to evaluate the performance of each algorithm could be the error between the actual duty cycle and the estimated one, after N samples and for a value of actual duty cycle D (Papoulis & Pillai, 2002; Kay, 1993) this metric is expressed by the following random variable μ_D :

$$\mu_D = \mid D - D_N^{EST} \mid$$

We observe that with ATA and ITA techniques the order relation between D and D_N^{EST} is known a-priori, so the absolute value operator would not be necessary.

We call with $\overline{\mu_D}$ its mean value with respect to the variable D_N^{EST} for a fixed value of D:

$$\overline{\mu_D} = E[\mu_D]$$

To have an idea about the data scattering with respect to the mean value we can consider the variance of the μ_D :

$$\tilde{A}_{\mu_D}^2 = E[(\mu_D - \overline{\mu_D})^2]$$

Let us remark that from the computation point of view all the algorithms have about the same complexity and memory usage. CAA needs to remember the number of occurrences until the last run, while ATA and ITA need to store the maximum and the minimum collected values. AITA needs the double of information, but in all cases the evaluation is trivial and processor surely has enough space to realize any of these approaches.

3. NUMERICAL EVIDENCE

We have built a simple simulator that implements the four cited algorithms (III-A, III-B, III-C, III-D), in order to test the behavior of the new proposed algorithms and to compare their performances with an already existent solution (Bhatti, Denneau, & Draper, 2005) based on a random sampling approach.

The results presented in this section have been obtained as a mean of 10000 realizations, by verifying a good degree of convergence of the performance metrics. Each single test has been started with t_0 uniformly distributed in the interval [0, 1].

A. Impact of the Interarrival Time PDF

In order to perform simulations we have to specify a probability density function for the interarrival time of the samples. To investigate the impact of the choice of the specific PDF function describing the interarrival time process, we present in this subsection the results concerning the average error ε obtained by implementing in the simulator two different PDF:

- An exponential function $f_g\left(\frac{3}{4}\right) = »e^{-»\frac{3}{4}}$, with mean $E[g] = 1 / »$, i.e., a mean number of λ samples are expected in a period; the choice of exponential PDF comes from its simplicity and because it represents rare events;

- The gamma function, with parameter b and c: $f_g(\xi) = \frac{c^b}{(b-1)!}\xi^{b-1}e^{-c\xi}$

- The mean value of the interarrival time, E[g], is equal to the ratio b/c. When b=c=1 the gamma function becomes the exponential PDF with λ=1.

Figure 2 plots the average error ε of the four algorithms obtained with three different options for the λ parameter of the exponential PDF: λ = 1, λ = 200, and λ = 1/200 (correspondent to the mean values of the interarrival time g respectively: E[g] = 1, E[g] = 1/200 and E[g] = 200). Figure 3 plots the average error ε of the four algorithms obtained with three different options for the b and c parameter of a gamma PDF: the case b = 2 and c = 2, that gives a E[g] = 1; the case b = 400 and c = 2, that gives a E[g] = 200; finally the case b = 2 and c = 400, that gives a E[g] = 1/200. We observe that in cases (b = c = 2) and (b = 400, c = 2) we obtain the same results obtained with exponential distributed interarrival times with parameter λ = 1 or λ = 200, while in case of (b = 2, c = 400) the result is almost the same of the case λ = 200 with exponential interarrival time. Therefore we can conclude that the behavior of the average error

ε depends on the mean value of the interarrival time, E[g], and not on the specific PDF function describing the random variable g. All the other simulations presented in the rest of the paper refer to exponential distributed interarrival times.

B. Performance as a Function of the Actual Duty Cycle

Figure 4 shows the trend of the error $\overline{\varepsilon_D}$ after N=30 samples as a function of D and for different value of the parameter λ. We can observe that for $» \leq N$ the trend is the same for every duty cycle the AITA algorithm performs better than the other three.

As λ increases, for example we have plotted in the same Figure the cases λ = 60 and λ = 100, we can distinguish three intervals: for small value of D (for the values of λ considered here, around D < 0.1) the lowest error is obtained by using the ATA algorithm, for high value of D (for the values of λ considered here, around D > 0.9) the lowest error is given by the ITA algorithm while in the intermediate interval the best solution is represented by the AITA.

C. Impact of the λ Parameter

We focus the attention on the behavior of the error ε as a function of the number of collected samples. We remember that, in correspondence any value of N, this metric is calculated as the mean value between the errors εD obtained after N samples with various values of D spanning the [0, 1] interval.

Figures 2 plots ε as a function of N, where N varies from 1 to 1000, by considering exponential sampling processes characterized by three different λ parameters: λ = 1, λ = 200, and λ = 1/200 (correspondent to the mean values respectively: E[g] = 1, E[g] = 1/200 and E[g] = 200. We call with B the ratio N/l that is the mean time necessary to collect N samples. In all the new proposed

Figure 2. Average error ε as a function of the number of collected samples N, when λ = 1, λ = 1/200 or λ = 200

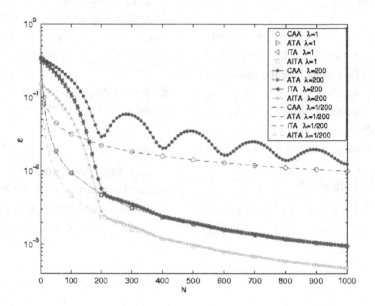

Figure 3. Average error ε as a function of the number of collected samples N . The interarrival time is described by a gamma P DF with parameters b and c: the plotted curves are related to the values (b = c = 2), (b = 400, c = 2) and (b = 2, c = 400)

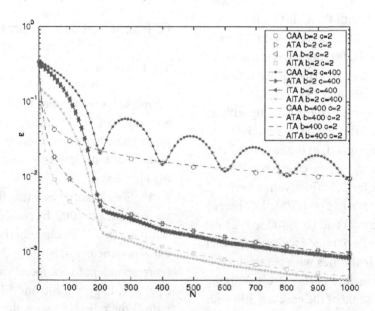

Figure 4. Error εD after N = 30 samples as a function of D and for different value of the λ parameter

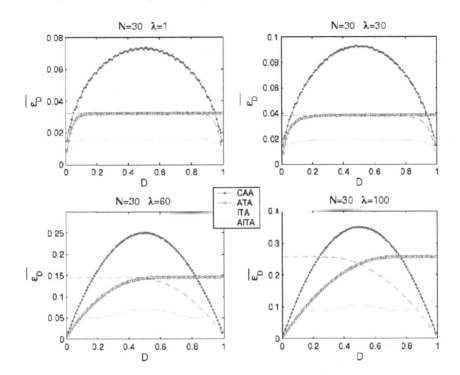

algorithms, ATA, ITA and AITA, we have verified with various simulations that the value of E[g] does not affect the error behavior as a function of N, provided that the number of collected samples N allows exploring at least a time equal to a whole period, i.e., provided that the parameter B be greater than 1. For example, suppose to have N = 200: since E[g] = 1/λ, the same error is obtained with λ = 1 (where we meanly observe 200 periods with one sample each), with λ = 200 (where we meanly observe one period containing 200 samples) or with all the intermediate possibilities 1 < λ < 200.

The error substantially increases if we do not collect enough information about the whole period, i.e., if B < 1, where, even if we collect a great amount of samples N, these are all concentrated in only a fraction of one single period. This is the case shown in Figure 2 when λ = 200: we meanly expect 200 samples for each period, so evaluating the duty cycle with N < 200 we perform an

estimation based on information about only a fraction of a period.

Note that curves with λ = 1 and λ = 1/200 have a very similar error, confirming what we have previously stated: since these cases are related to B > 1 and N > 1, if E[g] = 1 (λ = 1) we observe N periods containing meanly one sample, otherwise if λ = 1/200, i.e., E[g] = 200, we have N samples occurring meanly every 200 periods; in both the situations we nevertheless have the possibility to collect information related to the whole period.

CAA shows a different behavior. We have verified with various simulations that with values of λ ≤ 1 the results are independent of the actual value λ: for example in Figure 2 the curves related to λ = 1 and λ = 1/200 are perfectly overlapped. When λ > 1 the mean error ε shows an oscillatory behavior strictly dependent of the number of collected samples and the value λ: in fact this oscillation presents minimums in correspondence of value of N multiple of λ, i.e., when

B is a multiple of the signal period, since we are able to collect meanly λ samples in a time length of one period. As shown in Figure 5 the same trend is found also for the metric $\overline{\mu_D}$: the figure plots the results of $\overline{\mu_D}$ for value of duty cycle D between 0 and 0.5 since the trend of the curves in the interval between 0.5 and 1 is symmetric, so for example the plot in case of D=0.9 is perfectly overlapped with the curve related to D=0.1;we can observe that the oscillations are in correspondence of D=0.5 and they decrease as much as the value of D differs from 0.5. The points of minimum and maximum of the oscillations clearly depends on the initial instant of observation of the phenomenon, as shown in Figure 6, where curves of $\overline{\mu_D}$ with D=0.5 for some different values of the initial instant t_0 have been plotted: in these cases each simulation started with an initial point t_0 as indicated in the legend of the Figure. No matter what the initial t_0 is, we observe that the error always has a minimum when N is a multiple of l, since in correspondence of these values of N we are estimating the duty cycle by meanly observing a number of N/λ entire

time periods; as much as N differs from these values instead the estimate is based on a time length that includes partial interval of a signal period, where in case the signal is high this overestimates the duty cycle while in case the signal is low it underestimate the duty cycle, giving origin to the observed oscillations. By averaging the results obtained with these different t_0 we obtain a curve with the same trend of the curve related to D = 0.5 in Figure 5, where each simulation trial started from an initial point uniformly distributed inside the interval [0, 1]. By observing Figure 6 we can therefore conclude that the average trend behaves as the case of $t_0 = 0$: the samples collected after N = 200 meanly are situated at the beginning of the next period, where the signal is high, so they tend to overestimate the duty cycle, causing an increase in the mean error, that decreases again as more information about the whole period are collected, i.e., as N increases until N = 400, that almost corresponds to the end of the second period of the signal. These oscillations tends to disappear as much as N increases and are more stressed as much as λ is high, as shown in Figure 7.

Figure 5. Average error εD as a function of the number of collected samples N for CAA algorithm, with λ = 200 and different values of D

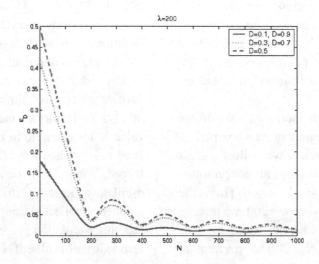

Figure 6. Average error εD as a function of the number of collected samples N for CAA algorithm, with D = 0.5, λ = 200 and different values of the starting instant t₀

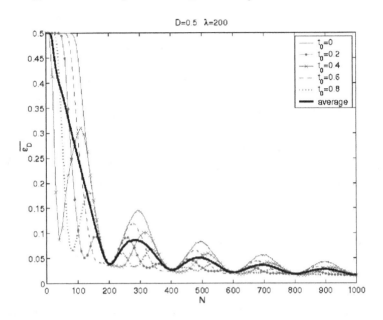

Figure 7. Average error εD as a function of the number of collected samples N for CAA algorithm, with D = 0.5 and different values of λ

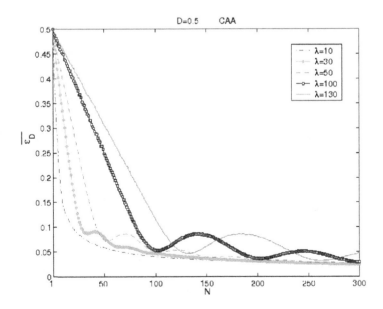

D. Mean Performance: Comparisons

Having specified the impact of the parameter $E[g]$ on the expected error, we can compare the performances of the four mentioned algorithms as a function of N and by considering $\lambda = 1$. Results are re-plotted in Log Log scale in Figure 8, in order to better highlight the error trends and the gap between different methods.

ATA, ITA and AITA algorithms show a considerable gain with respect to the CAA solution, in terms of number of samples necessary to obtain a duty cycle estimate with a desired accuracy.

Both ATA and ITA algorithms meanly show the same behavior and perform worse than the AITA one, due to the halves number of processed samples intrinsic in the single side algorithms.

Note that the error trend slope of ATA, ITA and AITA are equal and higher than CAA, resulting a generic uniform benefit with respect to algorithm (Bhatti, Denneau, & Draper, 2005). By observing the Figure 8 we can note that, for higher values of N, the mean error with ATA, ITA and AITA algorithms follow the same trend as the function 1/N, while the mean error with CAA shows a trend similar to $1/\sqrt{N}$. In case of $\lambda > 1$, where the CAA presents some oscillations, these trends are nevertheless confirmed by the curve envelope.

Meanly N = 3 samples give the knowledge of a duty cycle with an error $\varepsilon = 10^{-1}$ with the AITA, versus the N = 10 required by the CAA; N = 50 samples give the knowledge of a duty cycle with an error $\varepsilon = 10^{-2}$ with the AITA, compared to the N = 100 required by the ATA or ITA and the N = 1000 required by CAA; with N = 500 AITA can measure a duty cycle with an error $\varepsilon = 10^{-3}$.

4. MEMORY OF THE SAMPLING PROCESS

The sampling process we have considered until now is a renewal process described by the succession of the instants where we are going to collect the samples, defined as:

$$t_i = t_{i-1} + g_i = \sum_{n=1}^{i} g_n$$

Figure 8. Average error ε as a function of the number of collected samples N, with $\lambda = 1$

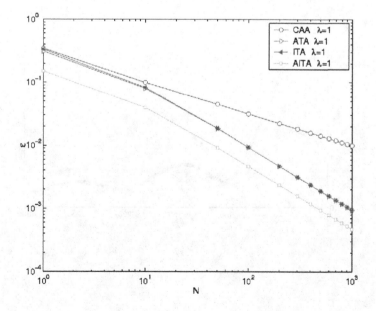

this means that for each index i we are taking into account all the previous interarrival times, i. e., the whole history of the process. This mechanisms results in a process with N memory, i.e., with a memory equal to the total number of collected samples used to evaluate the estimate of the duty cycle. In the rest of the paper we refer to this model with the term $M\,EM_N$ to remember that is a process with memory length equal to N .

In order to investigate what the actual memory of the sampling process is, we introduce in the following subsections some other processes and we investigate how these new introduced models can effectively catch the behavior of the original sampling process.

A. M EMγ Process

The first model we introduce is described as follows:

[ti] = [ti−1 + gi]

if i mod γ ≠ 0 [ui + gi] = ui

if i mod γ = 0

where ui is a random variable uniformly distributed in the interval [0, 1]. The equivalence [ui + gi] = ui is due to the fact that the clipped sum of two independent random variables, one of which is uniform in [0, 1], is uniform in [0, 1]. This process presents a memory length equal to the parameter γ: in fact, every γ samples, the state of the sampling process is canceled and the next samples ti starts from a previous point that is uniformly chosen in the period interval [0, 1]. We refer to this process with the term M EMγ to evidence that is a process with memory γ. The model M EMγ with γ = N obviously coincides with the original sampling process M EMN . We notice that the case with γ = 1 refers to a memory-less process, since for each i the condition (i mod γ = 0) is always satisfied.

In Figure 9 we have plotted the curves of the mean error as a function of the number of collected samples N, for the original process M EMN

Figure 9. Comparison between the error εD obtained with the original sampling process M EMN and various models M EMγ , with γ = 1, 3, 5, 10, 20, 30. The Figure refers to ATA algorithm, D = 0.5 and λ = 30

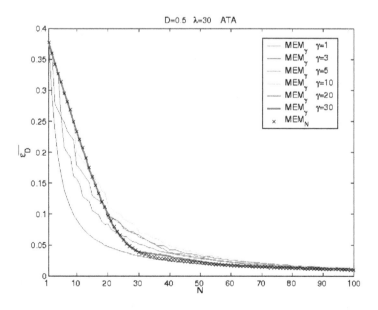

and for the processes M EMγ with different values of the memory length γ. The curves have been obtained by means of simulations and by referring to ATA and to a duty cycle D = 0.5. Same results have been obtained also with ITA and AITA and with different values of the actual duty cycle. The interarrival time g is modeled as an exponential random variable with $f_g\left(\frac{3}{4}\right) = »e^{-»\frac{3}{4}}$ and λ = 30. The curve related to a M EM30 process is clearly overlapped with the curve related to the original sampling process with N memory, for each value of the variable N: this shows that a sampling process with a λ exponential interarrival time has a memory length γ = λ. We observe that when N ≥ λ, i.e., when the burst coefficient B ≥ 1, the curves of the processes M EMN and M EM$_λ$ coincide with the curve of the memoryless process M EM1: this shows that, at least in the tested cases, the algorithms behave as if the samples had been collected at independent time instants.

B. M EM$_{TH}$ Process

We therefore consider the following process:

$$[t_i] = [t_{i-1} + g_i]\ \text{if}\ i \leq TH$$

$$[u_i + g_i] = u_i\ \text{if}\ i > TH$$

that presents a memory length equal to λ only for the first λ collected samples and then continues by considering the next samples independent; we could refer to this process with the term M EM T H since it takes into account the memory only for the samples collected before a certain threshold T H, that here we have taken equal to the parameter λ. Figure 10 shows that M EM T H with T H = λ perfectly overlaps the trend of the original process M EM$_N$: the curves have been obtained with simulations by considering exponential interarrival times with λ = 30, D = 0.5 and the ATA algorithm. Same results have been obtained also with ITA and AITA and with different values of the actual duty cycle.

In case of CAA instead, as the Figure 11 shows, the process M EMγ with γ = λ quite follows the intrinsic oscillations of the original process but tends to overestimate the error in correspondence of the maximum of the oscillations, while the M

Figure 10. Comparison between the error εD obtained with the original sampling process M EMN and the model M EM T H with threshold T H = λ. The Figure refers to ATA algorithm, D = 0.5 and λ = 30

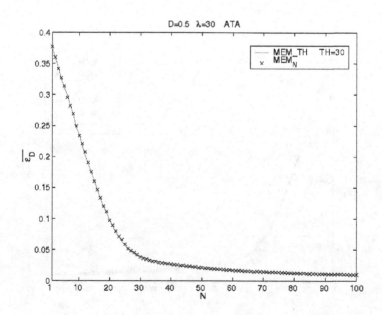

Figure 11. Comparison between the error εD obtained with the original sampling process M EMN , the model M EMγ , with γ = λ, and the model M EM T H with threshold T H = λ for the CAA algorithm. The Figure refers to the parameters λ = 50 and D = 0.5

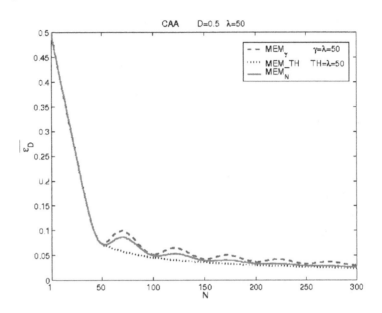

EM T H with T H = λ process can not precisely follow the intrinsic oscillations of the original process, it tends to underestimate the actual error and therefore can catch his behavior only when N is high enough.

We can therefore conclude that when the burst coefficient B ≥ 1 for ATA, ITA and AITA and λ ≤ 1 or N >> λ for CAA, we can describe the original sampling process by referring to a more trivial one, M EM T H with T H = λ, that consider the samples as independent after the threshold N = T H = λ. In VII we will develop an analytical model describing the sampling activities of the four algorithms that exploits this hypothesis of independence of the samples under the mentioned conditions.

5. PDF EVOLUTION OF A QUANTIZED SU OF RANDOM VARIABLES

In order to develop an analytical framework defining the expression of the mean error for a spe-

cific duty cycle D, $\overline{\varepsilon_D}$, its variance $\sigma^2_{\varepsilon D}$, and the average error ε for ATA, ITA and CAA we introduce in this section an important result concerning the behavior of the PDF of a quantized sum of random variables.

Note that the absolute instant of arrival of the i-th sample, expressed as $t_i = t_{i-1} + g_i$ can also be written as the sum of all the i interarrival times, i.e., as the sum of i independent random variables:

$$t_i = \sum_{n=1}^{i} g_n .$$

The quantity $x_i = [t_i] = t_i - \text{Floor}(t_i) = [\sum_{n=1}^{i} g_n]$ is therefore a quantized sum of random variables and it is a periodic random variable of period 1. It is possible to demonstrate that the succession x_i weakly converges to a random variable uniformly distributed in [0, 1]. We remember that the Moment Generating Function M GF of a random variable v is defined as:

$$\psi_v = \mathcal{F}^{-1}\left[f_v\right](\omega) = \mathcal{F}\left[f_v\right](-\omega) = E[e^{2\pi j \omega v}]$$

where $\mathcal{F}$ is the Fourier transform function.

Given the condition about the Moment Generating Function MGF of *ti*, ψ_{t_i},

$$\lim_{i \to \infty} \sum_{k=1}^{\infty} |\psi ti\ (k)| = 0$$

then the succession xi weakly converges to a Random Variable x uniformly distributed in [0,1].

To proof that, we firstly calculate the Cumulative Distribution Function C DF of the random variable x = [t], indicated with F_x ; x is obtained as the positive fractional part of the real number t; this operation is known with the term mantissa and is a periodic function of period 1. By remembering the trend of the mantissa function, the function F_x can be easily calculated as follows

$$F_x(\xi) = P(x < \xi)$$

$$= \sum_{k=0}^{\infty} P(k < t < k + \xi)$$

$$= \sum_{k=0}^{\infty} (F_t(k + \xi) - F_t(k))$$

where the sum is related only to positive indexes since the real variable *t* can assume only positive values since it represents absolute temporal instants. The Probability Density Function *P DF* of x, $f_g(\xi)$ is therefore:

$$f_x(\xi) = \chi_{[0,1]}(\xi) \frac{\partial F_x}{\partial \xi}(\xi)$$

$$= \chi_{[0,1]}(\xi) \sum_{k=0}^{\infty} f_{ti}(\xi + k)$$

(6)

where the function $\chi_{[0,1]}$ is defined 1 inside the interval [0,1] and null outside.

By recalling the (6) we can define the PDF of the succession x_i a follows:

$$f_x(\xi) = \chi_{[0,1]}(\xi) \sum_{k=0}^{\infty} f_{ti}(\xi + k)$$

where the P DF f_{ti} is obtained as the convolution of i PDF related to the independent variable g_n that constitute the sum t_i:

$$f_{ti}(\xi) = (f_{g1} * \ldots * f_{gi})(\xi)$$

By going on the MGF we obtain:

$$\psi_{xi}(\omega) = \psi_0(\omega) * \left[\psi_{ti}(\omega) \sum_{k=0}^{\infty} e^{j2\pi k\omega}\right]$$

$$= \psi_0(\omega) * \left[\psi_{ti}(\omega) \sum_{k=0}^{\infty} \delta(\omega - k)\right]$$

And we define

$$\psi_0(\omega) = \frac{\sin(\pi\omega)}{\pi\omega}$$

By recalling the convolution definition and by exploiting the properties of the Dirac function δ we obtain the following expression:

$$\psi_{xi}(\omega) = \int_{-\infty}^{\infty} \psi_0(\omega - \xi) \psi_{ti}(\xi) \sum_{k=0}^{\infty} \delta(\xi - k) d\xi =$$

$$\sum_{k=0}^{\infty} \int_{-\infty}^{\infty} \psi_0(\omega - \xi) \psi_{ti}(\xi) \delta(\xi - k) d\xi =$$

$$\sum_{k=0}^{\infty} \psi_0(\omega - k) \psi_{ti}(k) = \psi_0(\omega) + \sum_{k=1}^{\infty} \psi_0(\omega - k) \psi_{ti}(k)$$

We can evaluate the following expression:

$$|\psi_{xi}(\omega) - \psi_0(\omega)|$$

$$= \left|\sum_{k=1}^{\infty} \psi_0(\omega - k) \psi_{ti}(k)\right| \le \sum_{k=1}^{\infty} |\psi_0(\omega - k) \psi_{ti}(k)| \le \sum_{k=1}^{\infty} |\psi_{ti}(k)| \to 0$$

Where we have exploited the fact that $\psi_0(\omega)$ is a non negative function, since it is the antitransform of a function that never assumes negative values, therefore $\psi_0(\omega) \leq \psi_0(0) = 1$ and where the last evanescence is given by the initial condition 5. With this we know that for each ω the function $\psi_{xi}(\omega)$ converges to the $\psi_0(\omega)$ and that the random variable x_i weakly converges to the variable x which PDF is

$$f_x(\xi) = \mathcal{F}[\psi_0](\xi) = \chi_{[0,1]}(\xi)$$ as stated before.

Figure 12 shows an example of the convergence of the PDF $f_x(\xi)$ to the uniform function in the interval [0, 1] as the number of collected samples i increases, by starting from interarrival times exponentially distributed and characterized by the parameter $\lambda = 5$.

Figure 13 plots the mean error εD for a sampling process $t_i = t_{i-1} + g_i$ with the variable g uniformly distributed in [0, 1] and for some sampling processes with exponentially distributed

interarrival times ($f_g(\xi) = \lambda e^{-\lambda \xi}$) with different values for the λ parameter: as much as the number of samples N increases, all the curves related to different interarrival time distributions converge to the curve related to the uniformly distributed interarrival time.

As an example the simulations shown in this Figure refer to a duty cycle D = 0.5 and to the ATA algorithm but this overlapping trend has been also obtained with all other possible values of duty cycle and with ITA and AITA algorithms; in case of CAA the trend is shown in Figure 14, where we find again the collapse of the curves into the one related to the uniform interarrival time process but we observe the need of a greater number on samples N in order to obtain this overlapping, due to the presence of the aforementioned oscillations.

This property of the PDF of the samples x_i allows to describe the original process with a more trivial one based on uniformly distributed samples.

Figure 12. Probability density function of the random variables x_i for different values of the collected samples i; the interarrival times are described by an exponential PDF with parameter $\lambda = 5$

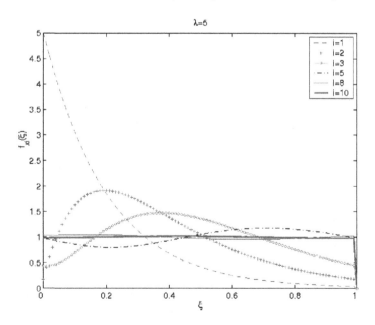

Figure 13. ATA. Comparison between a sampling processes with exponentially distributed interarrival times, with λ = 1, 25, 50, 100, and a sampling process with uniformly distributed interarrival times

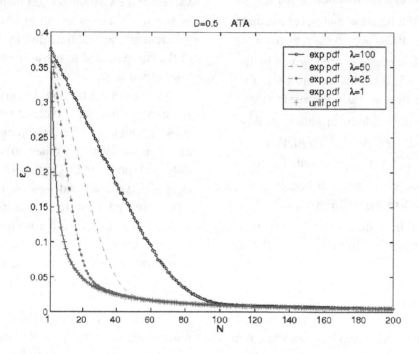

Figure 14. CAA. Comparison between a sampling processes with exponentially distributed interarrival times, with λ = 1, 30, 50, 100, and a sampling process with uniformly distributed interarrival times

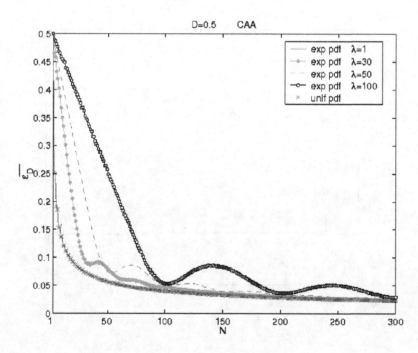

6. ANALYTICAL FRAMEWORK WITH INDEPENDENT UNIFORMLY DISTRIBUTED SAMPLES

In this section we describe a mathematical evaluation defining the expression of the mean error for a specific duty cycle D, $\overline{\varepsilon_D}$, and its variance $\tilde{A}^2_{\mu D}$ and the average error e for ATA, ITA, AITA and CAA, valid for every value of N. This model is based on the results evidenced in the previous sections: independent samples uniformly distributed in [0, 1] described by the uniform memoryless process M EM1.

A. ATA

If $f_{\alpha_N^+}$ is the PDF of α_N^+, then the performance $\overline{\varepsilon_D}$ with N samples can be evaluated as:

$$\varepsilon_D(N) = \int_0^D (D - \xi) f_{\alpha_N^+}(\xi) d\xi + D P_{N_{[D,1]}} \quad (7)$$

The first term of the sum in (7) refers to all the possible estimate of duty cycle ξ after N samples while the second term of this sum takes into account the initialization of this algorithm, that fixes the estimate $D_N^{EST} = 0$ in case all the samples occurred in the interval [D,1]: in this case the error is equal to D and $P_{N_{[D,1]}}$ is the probability that all the N samples occur in the interval [D,1], where the signal is low.

The PDF can be calculated by re $f_{\alpha_N^+}(\xi) = \dfrac{\partial F_{\alpha_N^+}(\xi)}{\partial \xi} = N(1 - D + \xi)^{N-1}$ ferring to the CDF,

$$F_{\alpha_N^+}(\xi) = \sum_{q=1}^N P(E_q) = \sum_{q=1}^N \binom{N}{q} [F_u(\xi)]^q \ [1 - F_u(D)]^{N-q}$$
$$= (1 - D + \xi)^N - (1 - D)^N$$

In fact, the probability to have $\alpha_N^+ < \xi$ corresponds to the sum of the probabilities of the events E_q with q ranging from 1 to N, where the event E_q is defined as {q samples in the interval [0,ξ] and the other N-q samples in the interval [D,1]}. Since all the variable $[t_i]=u_i$ are independent, by supposing that q observations over the N possible ones fall before D, we can calculate that the probability of the event E_q is given by the product of these two probabilities: probability that q observations are before ξ and probability that the other N-q are greater than D; that is the product $\binom{N}{q} \xi^q (1 - D)^{N-q}$, where the binomial term takes into account that given N objects there are $\binom{N}{q}$ distinct subsets of cardinality q and for each one the probability of occurrence is the same, i.e., $\xi^q (1 - D)^{N-q}$. The probability density function is obtained as follows:

$$f_{\alpha_N^+}(\xi) = \frac{\partial F_{\alpha_N^+}(\xi)}{\partial \xi} = N(1 - D + \xi)^{N-1}$$
$$(8)$$

The probability $P_{N_{[D,1]}}$, that corresponds to the probability of the event E_0={q=0 samples in the interested interval [0,ξ] and all the N samples in the interval [D,1]}, is calculated as follows:

$$P_{N_{[D,1]}} = (1 - F_u[D])^N = (1 - D)^N$$

We can therefore calculate the mean error $\overline{\varepsilon_D}$:

$$\overline{\varepsilon_D} = \int_0^D (D - \xi) f_{\alpha_N^+}(\xi) d\xi + D(1 - D)^N = \frac{1 - (1 - D)^{N+1}}{N + 1}$$
$$(9)$$

It is trivial to see that $\overline{\varepsilon_D} \to 1 / N$ when $\to \infty$.

Note that obviously the following equivalence is verified, for every D, ξ and N:

$$\int_0^D f_{\alpha_N^+}(\xi)\, d\xi + (1-D)^N = 1$$

Where the term $(1-D)^N$ needs to be taken into account to correctly close all the events space, i.e., all the events {q samples in $[0,\xi]$ and N-q samples in $[D,1]$, with $1 \leq q \leq N$ }, obtained by integrating the variable x between 0 and D, and the event {N samples in $[D,1]$} represented by the term $(1-D)^N$.

The variance is:

$$\sigma_{\varepsilon D}^2 = E\left[(D-\xi)^2\right] - \eta_{\varepsilon D}^2$$
$$= \int_0^D (D-\xi)^2 f_{\alpha_N^+}(\xi)\, d\xi + D^2 (1-D)^N - \eta_{\varepsilon D}^2$$
$$= \frac{2(1+N)[1-(1-D)^{N+1}(1+D+DN)]}{(2+N)(1+N)^2} - \frac{(2+N)[1-(1-D)^{N+1}]^2}{(2+N)(1+N)^2}$$

The average error e can be calculated as follows:

$$\varepsilon = \int_0^1 \frac{1-(1-D)^{N+1}}{N+1}\, dD = \frac{1}{2+N}$$

and also for this metric it is easy to demonstrate that when $N \to \infty$ the trend of ε behaves as the ratio $1/N$.

Figures 15 and 16 confirm the good agreement of the analytical framework with the simulation trend.

B. ITA

The analytical model related to the ITA follows an approach similar to that explained for the ATA one. If $f_{\alpha_N^-}$ is the PDF of α_N^-, then the performance $\overline{\varepsilon_D}$ with N samples can be evaluated as:

$$\overline{\varepsilon_D}(N) = \int_D^1 (\xi-D) f_{\alpha_N^-}(\xi)\, d\xi + D P_{N_{[0,D]}} \qquad (10)$$

Figure 15. ATA. Comparison between the mean error εD obtained through simulations of the original process M EMN with exponential interarrival times characterized by λ = 1 and with the analytical framework based on independent uniformly distributed samples

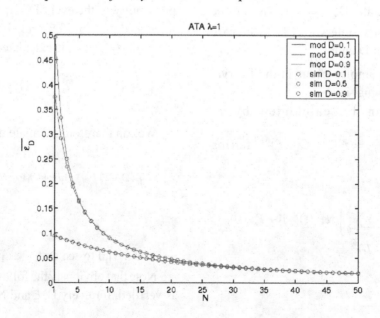

Figure 16. ATA. Comparison between the variance σ^2 obtained through simulations of the original process M EMN with exponential interarrival times characterized by $\lambda = 1$ and with the analytical framework based on independent uniformly distributed samples

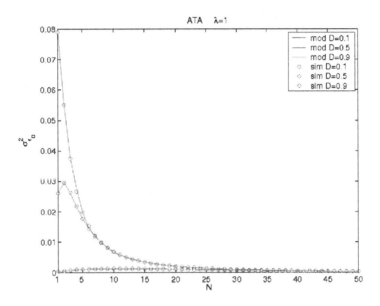

In this case the CDF can be calculated as follows:

$$F_{\alpha_N^-}(\xi) = P\left[\alpha_N^- < \xi\right]$$

$$= 1 - P\left[\alpha_N^- > \xi\right] = 1 - \sum_{q=1}^{N} P\left(H_q\right)$$

$$= 1 - \sum_{q=1}^{N} \binom{N}{q} \left[1 - F_u(\xi)\right]^q \left[F_u(D)\right]^{N-q}$$

The probability PN[0,D], that correspond to the probability of the event $H_0 = \{q = 0$ samples in the interested interval $[\xi, 1]$ and all the N samples in the interval $[0, D]\}$, is calculated as follows:

$$P_{N_{[0,D]}} = F_u[D]^N = D^N$$

We observe that the function C DF for ITA is equal to (1- the function C DF of ATA with D instead of $(1 - D)$ and with $(1 - \xi)$ instead of ξ). We find this similarity in all other expressions; in particular, the final expressions of the functions

PDF, $\overline{\varepsilon_D}$ and $\sigma_{\varepsilon D}^2$ for ITA can be obtained from the ones of ATA by exchanging each other the terms D and (1-D) and the terms ξ and (1-ξ).

The probability density function is:

$$f_{\alpha_N^-}(\xi) = N(1 + D - \xi)^{N-1} \tag{11}$$

The mean error is:

$$\overline{\varepsilon_D} = \frac{1 - D^{N+1}}{N + 1} \tag{12}$$

The variance is:

$$\sigma_{\varepsilon D}^2 = \frac{2\left(1 + N\right)\left[1 - D^{N+1}\left(2 - D + N(1 - D)\right)\right]}{(2 + N)(1 + N)^2}$$

$$- \frac{(2 + N)\left[1 - D^{N+1}\right]^2}{(2 + N)(1 + N)^2}$$

Note that obviously the following equivalence is verified, for every D, ξ and N:

The average error ε coincides with the ε evaluated in the ATA algorithm. Also in this case it is easy to demonstrate that when $N \to \infty$ the trend of the metric εD and of ε behaves as the ratio $1/N$.

Figures 17 and 18 confirm the good agreement of the analytical framework with the simulation trend.

C. AITA

For simplicity we call here $\alpha_N^+ = \eta$ and $\alpha_N^- = \beta$. Three cases can happen:

A. All the N samples are collected in the interval $[0, \eta]$:this event happens with a probability $P_A(\eta) = \eta^N$ and the error in this case is equal to abs(D-(η+1)/2) since the minimum α_N^- remains initialized value, 1;

B. All the N samples are collected in the interval $[\beta,1]$:this event happens with a probability $P_B(\beta) = (1-\beta)^N$ and the error in this case is equal to abs(D-β/2) since the maximum α_N^+ remains initialized value, 0;

C. Q samples fall in the interval $[0,\eta]$ and the other (N-q) samples in the interval $[\beta,1]$, where q=1,...N: this event happens with a probability

$$P_C(\eta,\beta) = \sum_{q=1}^{N} \binom{N}{q} \eta^q (1-\beta)^{N-q};\text{ in this}$$

case the error is equal to $\left| D - \dfrac{\eta+\beta}{2} \right|$.

We derive the *P DF* related to each of this events:

$$f_a(\eta) = \frac{\partial P_A(\eta)}{\partial \eta} = N\eta^{N-1}$$

$$f_b(\beta) = -\frac{\partial P_B(\beta)}{\partial \beta} = N(1-\beta)^{N-1}$$

$$f_c(\eta,\beta) = -\frac{\partial^2 P_C(\eta,\beta)}{\partial \eta \partial \beta} = N(N-1)(1+\eta-\beta)^{N-1}$$

The error $\overline{\varepsilon_D}$ can be calculated as follows:

Figure 17. ITA. Comparison between the mean error εD obtained through simulations of the original process M EMN with exponential interarrival times characterized by λ = 1 and with the analytical framework based on independent uniformly distributed samples

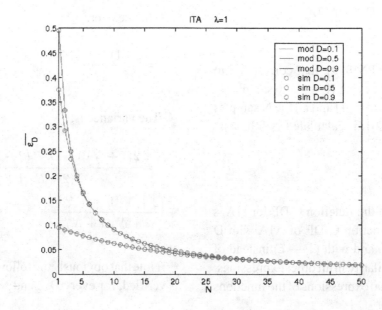

Figure 18. ITA. Comparison between the variance σ² obtained through simulations of the original process M EMN with exponential interarrival times characterized by λ = 1 and with the analytical framework based on independent uniformly distributed samples where, as a specula case of the event Eq for ATA, here we define the event Hq ={q samples in the interval [ξ, 1] and the other N — q samples inside the interval [0, D]}

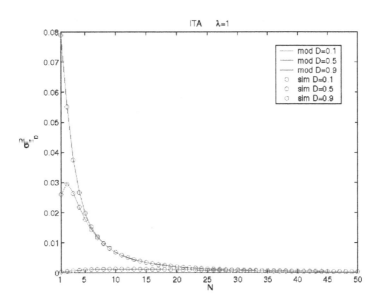

$$\overline{\varepsilon_D} = \int_0^D \left| D - \frac{\eta+1}{2} \right| f_a(\eta)\, d\eta$$

$$+ \int_D^1 \left| D - \frac{\beta}{2} \right| f_b(\beta)\, d\beta$$

$$+ \int_0^D \int_D^1 \left| D - \frac{\eta+\beta}{2} \right| f_c(\eta,\beta)\, d\eta\, d\beta$$

Figure 19 confirms the good agreement of the analytical framework with the simulation trend.

D. CAA

Having a signal w(t) with duty cycle D, the probability of the event {sample in correspondence of high logic level} by following the sampling process $t_i - u_i - x_i$ is equal to D and therefore the probability of the event {sample in correspondence of low logic level} is equal to 1 — D. The random variable xi has a mean equal to D and a variance equal to D(1 — D). After N independent trials the estimate of the error is k/N if the event {sample in correspondence of high logic level} has occurred k times. The probability of having an error |D –k/N| is the probability of having k high level samples in a total amount of N samples; this is obtained thanks to the Bernouilli's result concerning repeated trials: the probability of the event {k high logic level samples in a any order} after N trials is:

$$\binom{N}{k} D^k (1-D)^{N-k} \tag{13}$$

The absolute value operator in the error expression is needed since the estimate of the duty cycle calculated with this algorithm can be greater or less than the actual value *D*. The mean error εD is calculated as the sum of all the possible errors weighted by their probabilities:

Figure 19. AITA. Comparison between the mean error εD obtained through simulations of the original process M EMN with exponential interarrival times characterized by λ = 1 and with the analytical framework based on independent uniformly distributed samples

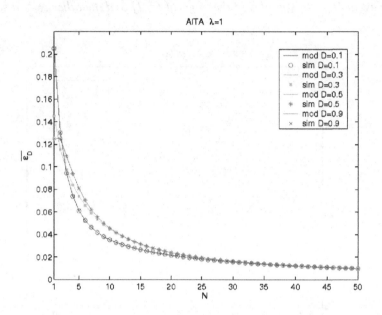

$$\varepsilon_D = \sum_{k=0}^{N} \left| D - \frac{k}{N} \right| \binom{N}{k} D^k (1-D)^{N-k}$$

$$= \sum_{k=0}^{ND} \left(D - \frac{k}{N} \right) \binom{N}{q} D^k (1-D)^{N-k}$$

$$+ \sum_{k=ND+1}^{N} \left(\frac{k}{N} - D \right) \binom{N}{k} D^k (1-D)^{N-k}$$

We prove here that for high values of N the mean error tends to zero like the function $1/\sqrt{N}$. When N is high we can apply the De Moivre-Laplace theorem, that allows to approximate the Bernouilli Equation (13) with a Gaussian function, opportunely scaled with average $m_N = ND$ and variance $\sigma_N^2 = ND(1-D)$, where m_N and σ_N^2 are obtained as the sum of the averages and variances of each of the N random variables x_i due to the independence of the variables x_i:

$$\binom{N}{k} D^k (1-D)^{N-k} \cong \frac{1}{\sqrt{2\pi ND(1-D)}} e^{-\frac{(k-ND)^2}{2ND(1-D)}}$$

We substitute this approximation in the mean error definition:

$$\overline{\varepsilon_D} \cong \sum_{k=0}^{N} \left| D - \frac{k}{N} \right| \frac{1}{\sqrt{2\pi ND(1-D)}} e^{-\frac{(k-ND)^2}{2ND(1-D)}}$$

$$\cong \int_0^N \left| D - \frac{k}{N} \right| \frac{1}{\sqrt{2\pi ND(1-D)}} e^{-\frac{(k-ND)^2}{2ND(1-D)}} dk$$

By applying the variable substitution h=k/N we obtain:

Figure 20. CAA. Comparison between the mean error εD obtained through simulations of the original process M EMN with exponential interarrival times characterized by λ = 1 and with the analytical framework based on independent uniformly distributed samples

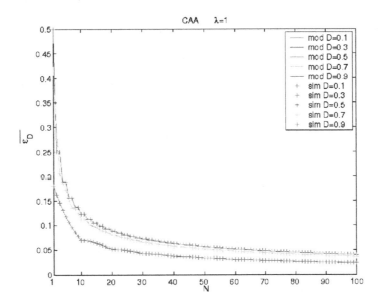

Figure 21. CAA

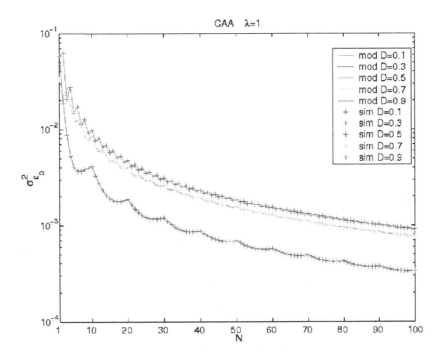

$$\overline{\varepsilon_D} \cong N \int_0^1 |D-h| \frac{1}{\sqrt{2\pi ND(1-D)}} e^{-\frac{N(h-D)^2}{2D(1-D)}} dh$$

$$= \frac{N}{\sqrt{2\pi ND(1-D)}} \left[\int_0^D (D-h) e^{-\frac{N(h-D)^2}{2D(1-D)}} dh + \int_D^1 (h-D) e^{-\frac{N(h-D)^2}{2D(1-D)}} dh \right]$$

$$= \frac{ND(1-D)\left[2 - e^{-\frac{(1-D)N}{2D}} - e^{-\frac{DN}{2(1-D)}} \right]}{\sqrt{2\pi ND(1-D)}} \quad N \to \infty \quad \sqrt{\frac{2D(1-D)}{\pi N}}$$

The variance σ_N^2 is:

$$\sigma_N^2 = \sum_{k=0}^N \binom{N}{k} \left(D - \frac{k}{N} \right)^2 D^k (1-D)^{N-k} - \overline{\varepsilon_D}^2 = \frac{(1-D)D}{N} - \varepsilon_D$$

Figures 20 and 21 confirm the good agreement of the analytical framework with the simulation trend.

REFERENCES

Bhatti, R. Z., Denneau, M., & Draper, J. (2005, August). Duty cycle measurement and correction using a random sampling technique. In *Proceedings of the 48th IEEE International Midwest Symposium on Circuits and Systems* (pp. 1043-1046).

de Jong, P. C., & Toth, F. N. (n. d.). *Measuring duty cycles with an Intel MCS-51 microcontroller*. Retrieved from http://www.smartec.nl/pdf/appsmt01.pdf

Gallager, R. G. (1996). *Discrete stochastic processes*. Boston, MA: Kluwer Academic.

Kay, S. M. (1993). *Fundamentals of statistical signal processing: Estimation theory*. Upper Saddle River, NJ: Prentice Hall.

Lach, J., Evans, D., McCune, J., & Brandon, J. (2003). Power-efficient adaptable wireless sensor networks. In *Proceedings of the Military and Aerospace Programmable Logic Devices International Conference*.

Lan, S., Qilong, M., & Du, J. (2008, December 21-22). Architecture of wireless sensor networks for environmental monitoring. In *Proceedings of the International Workshop on Education and Technology Training and the Workshop on Geoscience and Remote Sensing* (pp. 579-582).

Moragrega, A., Ibars, C., & Geng, Y. (2009, June 11-12). Energy efficiency of a cooperative wireless sensor network. Palma de Mallorca.

Papoulis, A., & Pillai, S. U. (2002). *Probability, random variables and stochastic processes* (4th ed.). New York, NY: McGraw Hill.

Rao, R., Vrudhula, S., & Rakhmatov, D. N. (2003). Battery modeling for energy aware system design. *IEEE Computer, 36*, 77–87.

Spiegel, M. (1975). *Schaum's outline of theory and problems of probability and statistics*. New York, NY: McGraw Hill.

Taddia, C., & Mazzini, G. (2006). Fast algorithms for duty cycle measurement with random sampling technique. In *Proceedings of the International Conference on Wireless Communications and Mobile Computing*, Vancouver, Canada.

Taddia, C., Mazzini, G., & Rovatti, R. (2010, September 23-25). Duty cycle measurements under non controlled sampling: Part I. In *Proceedings of the 48th Midwestern Symposium on Circuits and Systems* (pp. 1043-1046).

Taddia, C., Mazzini, G., & Rovatti, R. (2010, September 23-25). Duty cycle measurements under non controlled sampling: Part II. In *Proceedings of the 48ᵗʰ Midwestern Symposium on Circuits and Systems* (pp. 1043-1046).

Vigorito, C. M., Ganesan, D., & Barto, A. G. (2007). Adaptive control of duty cycling in energy-harvesting wireless sensor networks. In *Proceedings of the 4ᵗʰ Annual Conference on Sensor, Mesh, and Ad Hoc Communications and Networks*, San Diego, CA (pp. 21-30).

332

Compilation of References

Aaronson, S., & Arkhipov, A. (2001). *The computational complexity of linear optics.* Retrieved from http://www.scottaaronson.com/papers/optics.pdf

Adamczyk, J., Chojnacki, R., Jarzqb, M., & Zielinski, K. (2008). *Rule Engine Based Lightweight Framework for Adaptive and Autonomic Computing* (LNCS 5101, pp. 355-364).

Adve, S., et al. (2002). The Illinois GRACE Project: Global Resource Adaptation through CoopEration. In *Proceedings of the Workshop on Self-Healing, Adaptive, and self-MANaged Systems.*

Agarwal, M., Bhat, V., Liu, H., & Matossi, V. (2003). Automate: Enabling autonomic applications on the grid. In *Proceedings of the Fifth Annual International Autonomic Computing Workshop on Active Middleware Services* (pp. 48-57). Washington, DC: IEEE Computer Society.

Agrawal, D., Lee, K. W., & Lobo, J. (2005). Policy-based management of networked computing systems. *IEEE Communications Magazine, 43*(10), 69–75. doi:10.1109/MCOM.2005.1522127

Agrawal, S., Bruno, N., Chaudhuri, S., & Narasayya, V. (2006). AutoAdmin: Self-Tuning Database Systems Technology. *A Quarterly Bulletin of the Computer Society of the IEEE Technical Committee on Data Engineering, 29*(3), 7–15.

Aguilera, M. K., Mogul, J. C., Wiener, J. L., Reynolds, P., & Muthitacharoen, A. (2003). Performance Debugging for Distributed Systems of Black Boxes. In *Proceedings of the 19th ACM Symposium on Operating Systems Principles* (pp. 74-89).

Aida, K., Futakata, Y., & Tomotaka, O. (2006). Parallel branch and bound algorithm with the hierarchical master-worker paradigm on the grid. *Transactions on High Performance Computing Systems, 47*(12), 193–206.

Akyildiz, I. F., Su, W., Sankarasubramaniam, Y., & Cayirci, E. (2002). Wireless sensor networks: A survey. *Computer Networks: The International Journal of Computer and Telecommunications Networking, 38*(4), 393–422.

Akyildiz, I. F., Vuran, M. C., Akan, O. B., & Su, W. (2005). Wireless sensor networks: A survey revisited. *Computer Networks Journal, 38*(4), 393–422. doi:10.1016/S1389-1286(01)00302-4

Al Hanbali, A., Ibrahim, M., Simon, V., Varga, E., & Carreras, I. (2008, October). A survey of message delivery protocols in mobile ad hoc network. In *Proceedings of the INTERPERF Conference*, Athens, Greece.

Aly, S. G., & Elnahas, A. A. (2008). Sustained service lookup in areas of sudden dense population. *Wireless Communications and Mobile Computing, 8*, 61–74. doi:10.1002/wcm.427

Appleby, K., Fakhouri, S., Fong, L., Goldszmidt, G., Kalantar, M., Krishnakumar, S., et al. (2001). Oceano-SLA based management of a computing utility. In *Proceedings of the 7th IFIP/IEEE International Symposium on Integrated Network Management*, Seattle, WA (Vol. 5).

Arcangeli, J.-P., Leriche, S., & Pantel, M. (2004). Development of flexible peer-to-peer information systems using adaptable mobile agents. In *Proceedings of the DEXA Workshops* (pp. 549-553).

Armbrust, M., Fox, A., Griffith, R., Joseph, A. D., Katz, R., & Konwinski, A. (2010). A view of cloud computing. *Communications of the ACM, 53*(4), 50–58. doi:10.1145/1721654.1721672

Association of Radio Industries and Businesses. (2007). *ARIB Standard, Service Information for Digital Broadcasting System*. Retrieved December 14, 2009, from http://www.arib.or.jp/english/html/overview/doc/6-STD-B10v4_4-E1.pdf

Atzori, L., Iera, A., & Morabito, G. (2010). The Internet of things: A survey. *Computer Networks, 54*, 2787–2805. doi:10.1016/j.comnet.2010.05.010

Austin, T., & Bertacco, V. (2005). Deployment of better than worst-case design: solutions and needs. In *Proceedings of IEEE International Conference on Computer Design (ICCD)* (pp. 550-555).

Aversa, R., Di Martino, B., & Venticinque, S. (2009). Distributed agents network for ubiquitous monitoring and services exploitation. In *Proceedings of the 7th IEEE/IFIP International Conference on Embedded and Ubiquitous Computing* (Vol. 1, pp. 197-204).

Avizienis, A., Laprie, J. C., & Randell, B. (2001). *Fundamental concepts of dependability* (Tech. Rep. No. 1145). Paris: LAAS-CNRS.

Avizienis, A. (1985). The N-version approach to fault-tolerant software. In []. Washington, DC: IEEE Computer Society.]. *Proceedings of the IEEE Transactions on Software Engineering, 11*(12), 1491–1501. doi:10.1109/TSE.1985.231893

Aydin, H., Melhem, R. G., Mossé, D., & Mejía-Alvarez, P. (2004). Power-Aware Scheduling for Periodic Real-Time Tasks. *IEEE Transactions on Computers, 53*, 584–600. doi:10.1109/TC.2004.1275298

Bacon, D. (2008). *Self-correcting quantum computers (part II)*. Retrieved from http://scienceblogs.com/pontiff/2008/08/selfcorrecting_quantum_compute_1.php

Bae, J.-H., Lee, K.-O., & Park, Y.-Y. (2006). MONETA: An embedded monitoring system for ubiquitous network environments. *IEEE Transactions on Consumer Electronics, 52*(2), 414–420. doi:10.1109/TCE.2006.1649658

Bai, Y., & Ito, M. (2006). A study for providing better quality of service to VoIP users. In *Proceedings of the 20th International Conference on Advanced Information Networking and Application* (pp. 799-804). Washington, DC: IEEE Computer Society.

Bai, Y., & Ito, M. (2007). A new technique for minimizing network loss from users' perspective. *Journal of Network and Computer Applications, 30*(2), 637–649. doi:10.1016/j.jnca.2006.01.003

Bako, B., Borchert, A., Heidenbluth, N., & Mayer, J. (2006). Linearly ordered plugins through self-organization. In *Proceedings of the International Conference on Autonomic and Autonomous Systems* (p. 8). Washington, DC: IEEE Computer Society.

Balakrishnan, M., Birman, K., Phanishayee, A., & Pleisch, S. (2007). Ricochet: Lateral error correction for time-critical multicast. In *Proceedings of the Fourth Usenix Symposium on Networked Systems Design and Implementation* (pp. 73-86). New York, NY: ACM Press.

Balakrishnan, M., Pleisch, S., & Birman, K. (2005). Slingshot: Time-critical multicast for clustered applications. In *Proceedings of the Fourth IEEE International Symposium on Network Computing and Applications* (pp. 205-214). New York, NY: ACM Press.

Ballagny, C., Hameurlain, N., & Barbier, F. (2007). Endowing software components with autonomic capabilities based on modeling language executability. In *Proceedings of the 1st Workshop on Model-driven Software Adaptation* (pp. 55-60).

Bari, F., & Leung, V. C. M. (2009). Architectural aspects of automated network selection in heterogeneous wireless systems. *International Journal of Ad Hoc and Ubiquitous Computing, 4*(5), 282–291. doi:10.1504/IJAHUC.2009.027478

BeanAir. (2010). *BeanDevice TH version datasheet*. Retrieved from http://www.beanair.com/English-docs/Flyer%20BeanDevice%20TH.pdf

Behzadana, A. H., Aziz, Z., Anumbab, C. J., & Kamata, V. R. (2008). Ubiquitous location tracking for context-specific information delivery on construction sites. *Automation in Construction, 17*(6), 737–748. doi:10.1016/j.autcon.2008.02.002

Bekooij, M., Moreira, O., Poplavko, P., Mesman, B., Pastrnak, M., & Meerbergen, J. V. (2004). Predictable embedded multiprocessor system design. In []. New York: Springer.]. *Proceedings of the Software and Compilers for Embedded Systems*, *3199*, 77–91. doi:10.1007/978-3-540-30113-4_7

Belding-Royer, E., Sun, Y., & Perkins, C. E. (2001). *Global connectivity for IPv4 mobile ad hoc networks*. Retrieved from http://tools.ietf.org/id/draft-royer-manet-globalv4-00.txt

Ben Hamida, A. (2010). *AxSeL: Un intergiciel pour le déploiement contextuel et autonome de services dans les environnements pervasifs*. Unpublished doctoral dissertation, INSA de Lyon, Villeurbanne, France.

Ben Hamida, A., Le Mouël, F., Frénot, S., & Ben Ahmed, M. (2008). A graph-based approach for contextual service loading in pervasive environments. In R. Meersman & Z. Tari (Eds.), *Proceedings of the Federated International Conferences of On the Move to Meaningful Internet Systems*, Monterrey, Mexico (LNCS 5331, pp. 589-606).

Bender, P., Black, P., Grob, M., Padovani, R., Sindhushayana, N., & Viterbi, A. (2000). CDMA/HDR: A bandwidth-efficient high-speed wireless data service for normadic users. *IEEE Communications Magazine*, *38*(7), 70–77. doi:10.1109/35.852034

Benini, L., Bogliolo, A., & De Micheli, G. (2000). A survey of design techniques for system-level dynamic power management. *IEEE Transactions on Very Large Scale Integration Systems*, *8*, 299–316. doi:10.1109/92.845896

Bernardeschi, C., Fantechi, A., & Simoncin, L. (1994). Formal reasoning on fault coverage of fault tolerant techniques: A case study. In K. Echtle, D. Hammer, & D. Powell (Eds.), *Proceedings of the First European Dependable Computing Conference* (LNCS 852, pp. 77-94).

Berners-Lee, T. (1998). *Uniform resource identifiers (URI): Generic syntax*. Retrieved from http://www.ietf.org/rfc/rfc2396.txt

Berthold, J., Dieterle, M., Loogen, R., & Priebe, S. (2008). Hierarchical master-worker skeletons. In P. Hudak & D. S. Warren (Eds.), *Proceedings of the 10th International Symposium on Practical Aspects of Declarative Languages* (Vol. 4902, pp. 248-264). New York: Springer.

Bhatti, R. Z., Denneau, M., & Draper, J. (2005, August). Duty cycle measurement and correction using a random sampling technique. In *Proceedings of the 48th IEEE International Midwest Symposium on Circuits and Systems* (pp. 1043-1046).

Bondavalli, A., Chiaradonna, S., Cotroneo, D., & Romano, L. (2004). Effective Fault Treatment for Improving the Dependability of COTS and Legacy-Based Applications. *IEEE Transactions on Dependable and Secure Computing*, *1*(4), 223–237. doi:10.1109/TDSC.2004.40

Borkar, S. (2005). Designing Reliable Systems from Unreliable Components: The Challenges of Transistor Variability and Degradation. *IEEE Micro*, *25*(6), 10–16. doi:10.1109/MM.2005.110

Bosman, P. A. N. (2005). Learning, anticipation and time-deception in evolutionary online dynamic optimization. In *Proceedings of the workshops on Genetic and evolutionary computation* (pp. 39-47). ACM: New York.

Bouchenak, S., De Palma, N., Hagimont, D., & Taton, C. (2006). Autonomic management of clustered applications. In *Proceedings of the IEEE International Conference on Cluster Computing*, Barcelona, Spain.

Boulding, K. E. (1956). General systems theory - the skeleton of science. *Management Science*, *2*(3), 197–208. doi:10.1287/mnsc.2.3.197

Bracciali, A., Brogi, A., & Canal, C. (2005). A formal approach to component adaptation. *Journal of Systems and Software*, *74*(1), 45–54. doi:10.1016/j.jss.2003.05.007

Briot, J.-P. (2005). Foreword. In Choren, R., Garcia, A., Lucena, C., & Romanovsky, A. (Eds.), *Software Engineering for Multi-Agent Systems III (LNCS 3390)*.

Broch, J., Maltz, D., & Johnson, D. (1999). Supporting hierarchy and heterogeneous interfaces in multi-hop wireless ad hoc networks. In *Proceedings of the IEEE International Symposium on Parallel Architectures, Algorithms, and Networks*, Perth, Australia (pp. 370-375).

Brodnik, A., & Munro, J. (1994). Membership in constant time and minimum space. In J. van Leeuwen (Ed.), *Proceedings of the Second Annual European Symposium on Algorithms* (LNCS 855, pp. 72-81).

Broll, G., Rukzio, E., Paolucci, M., Wagner, M., Schmidt, A., & Hussmann, H. (2009). Perci: Pervasive service interaction with the Internet of things. *IEEE Internet Computing*, *13*(6), 74–81. doi:10.1109/MIC.2009.120

Brooks, D., & Martonosi, M. (2001). Dynamic thermal management for high-performance microprocessors. In *Proceedings of the Seventh International Symposium on High-Performance Computer Architecture* (pp. 171-182).

Broto, L., Hagimont, D., Stolf, P., de Palma, N., & Temate, S. (2008). Autonomic management policy specification in Tune. In *Proceedings of the ACM Symposium on Applied Computing*, Fortaleza, Ceara, Brazil (pp. 1658-1663).

Brown, A., Kar, G., & Keller, A. (2001). An Active Approach to Characterizing Dynamic Dependencies for Problem Determination in a Distributed Environment. In *Proceedings of the IEEE/IFIP Symposium on Integrated Network Management* (pp. 377-390).

Brun, Y., & Ernst, M. D. (2004). Finding Latent Code Errors via Machine Learning over Program Executions. In *Proceedings of the 26th Conference on Software Engineering* (pp. 480-490).

Bruneton, E., Coupaye, T., Leclercq, M., Quéma, V., & Stefani, J.-B. (2006). The fractal component model and its support in java: Experiences with auto-adaptive and reconfigurable systems. *Software, Practice & Experience*, *36*(11-12), 1257–1284. doi:10.1002/spe.767

Bruneton, E., & Riveill, M. (2001). An architecture for extensible middleware platforms. *Software, Practice & Experience*, *31*(13), 1237–1264. doi:10.1002/spe.412

Brynjulfsson, B., Hjalmtysson, G., Katrinis, K., & Plattner, B. (2006). Autonomic network-layer multicast service towards consistent service quality. In *Proceedings of the 20th International Conference on Advanced Information Networking and Applications* (pp. 494-498). Washington, DC: IEEE Computer Society.

Burleigh, S., Torgerson, L., Fall, K., Cerf, V., Durst, B., & Scott, K. (2003). Delay-tolerant networking: An approach to interplanetary internet. *IEEE Communications Magazine*, *41*(6), 128–136. doi:10.1109/MCOM.2003.1204759

Buyya, R., Yeo, C. S., Venugopal, S., Broberg, J., & Brandic, I. (2009). Cloud computing and emerging IT platforms: Vision, hype, and reality for delivering computing as the 5th utility. *Future Generation Computer Systems*, *25*(6), 599–616. doi:10.1016/j.future.2008.12.001

Cabri, G., Ferrari, L., Leonardi, L., & Zambonelli, F. (2005). The laica project: Supporting ambient intelligence via agents and ad-hoc middleware. In *Proceedings of the 14th International Workshop on Enabling Technologies: Infrastructure for Collaborative Enterprise* (pp. 39-46). Washington, DC: IEEE Computer Society.

Capit, N., Da Costa, G., Georgiou, Y., Huard, G., Martin, C., Mounié, G., Neyron, P., et al. (2005). *A batch scheduler with high level components*. Arxiv preprint.

Caporuscio, M., Carzaniga, A., & Wolf, A. (2003). Design and evaluation of a support service for mobile, wireless publish/subscribe applications. *IEEE Transactions on Software Engineering*, *29*(12), 1059–1071. doi:10.1109/TSE.2003.1265521

Cappello, F., Caron, E., Dayde, M., Desprez, F., Jegou, Y., Primet, P., et al. (2005). Grid'5000: a large scale and highly reconfigurable grid experimental testbed. In *Proceedings of the 6th IEEE/ACM International Workshop on Grid Computing*, Seattle, WA (pp. 99-106).

Cardenas, A. A., Baras, J. S., & Seamon, K. (2006). A Framework for the Evaluation of Intrusion Detection Systems. In *Proceedings of the IEEE Symposium on Security and Privacy* (pp. 63-77).

Caron, E., & Desprez, F. (2006). DIET: A Scalable Toolbox to Build Network Enabled Servers on the Grid. *International Journal of High Performance Computing Applications*, *20*(3), 335–352. doi:10.1177/1094342006067472

Carreras, I., Tacconi, D., & Miorandi, D. (2007, October). Data-centric information dissemination in opportunistic environments. In *Proceedings of the International Conference on Mobile Adhoc and Sensor Systems*, Pisa, Italy (pp. 1-3).

Carreras, I., Chlamtac, I., De Pellegrini, F., & Miorandi, D. (2007). BIONETS: Bio-inspired networking for pervasive communication environments. *IEEE Transactions on Vehicular Technology*, *56*(1), 218–229. doi:10.1109/TVT.2006.883762

Cauvet, C., & Semmak, F. (1999). La réutilisation dans l'ingénierie des systèmes d'information: Etat de l'art. In *Génie Objet: Analyse et conception de l'évolution d'objet*. Paris, France: Hermés.

Cefriel. (n. d.). *Cefriel: Forging innovation*. Retrieved from http://www.cefriel.it/

Chae, S., & Kano, N. (2005, September). *A location system with RFID technology in building construction site*. Paper presented at the ISARC 22nd International Symposium on Automation and Robotics in Construction, Ferrara, Italy.

Chaintreau, A., Hui, P., Crowcroft, J., Diot, C., Gass, R., & Scott, J. (2006, April). Impact of human mobility on the design of opportunistic forwarding algorithms. In *Proceedings of INFOCOM*, Barcelona, Spain.

Chakravorty, R., & Ottevanger, H. (2002). Architecture and implementation of a remote management framework for dynamically reconfigurable devices. In *Proceedings of the 10th IEEE International Conference on Networks* (pp. 375-381).

Chan, P., & Abramson, D. (2001). NetFiles: A novel approach to parallel programming of master/worker applications. In *Proceedings of the 5th International Conference and Exhibition on High Performance Computing in the Asia-Pacific Region (HPC Asia 2001)*, Queensland, Australia. Retrieved December 14, 2009, from http://messagelab.monash.edu.au/Publications

Chandy, M., Etzion, O., von Ammon, R., & Niblett, P. (2007). *DROPS 07191 summary – event processing*. Paper presented at the Dagstuhl Seminar on Event Processing, Schloss Dagstuhl, Germany, David, P.-C., & Ledoux, T. (2006). An aspect-oriented approach for developing self-adaptive fractal components. In W. Löwe & M. Südholt (Eds.) *Proceedings of the 5th International Symposium on Software Composition* (LNCS 4089, pp. 82-97).

Chang, Y., Lander, L. C., Lu, H. S., & Wells, M. T. (1993). Bayesian Analysis for Fault Location in Homogenous Distributed Systems. In *Proceedings of the 12th Symposium on Reliable Distributed Systems* (pp. 44-53).

Chang, K.-D., Chen, C.-Y., Chen, J.-L., & Chao, H.-C. (2010). Challenges to next generation services in IP multimedia subsystem. *Journal of Information Processing Systems, 6*(2), 129–146. doi:10.3745/JIPS.2010.6.2.129

Chantem, T., Dick, R. P., & Hu, X. S. (2008). Temperature-aware scheduling and assignment for hard real-time applications on MPSoCs. In *Proceedings of the conference on Design, automation and test in Europe* (pp. 288-293). New York: ACM.

Chebaro, O., Broto, L., Bahsoun, J. P., & Hagimont, D. (2009). Self-TUNe-ing of a J2EE clustered application. In *Proceedings of the 2009 Sixth IEEE Conference and Workshops on Engineering of Autonomic and Autonomous Systems*, San Francisco (pp. 23-31).

Chen, J., & Kuo, C. (2007). Energy-Efficient Scheduling for Real-Time Systems on Dynamic Voltage Scaling (DVS) Platforms. In *Proceedings of Intl. Conference on Embedded and Real-Time Computing Systems and Applications (RTCSA)*.

Chen, M. Y., Kiciman, E., Fratkin, E., Fox, A., & Brewer, E. (2002). Pinpoint: Problem Determination in Large, Dynamic Internet Services. In *Proceedings of the IEEE/ IFIP Conference on Dependable Systems and Networks* (pp. 595-604).

Cheng, X., Dale, C., & Liu, J. (2008). Statistics and social network of youtube videos. In *Proceedings of the IEEE 16th International Workshop on Quality of Service*, Enschede, The Netherlands.

Chillarege, R., Biyani, S., & Rosenthal, J. (1995). Measurement of Failure Rate in Widely Distributed Software. In *Proceedings of the 25th Symposium on Fault-Tolerant Computing* (pp. 424-433).

Chillarege, R., Bhandari, I., Chaar, J., Halliday, M., Moebus, D., & Ray, B. (1992). Orthogonal Defect Classification-A Concept for In-Process Measurements. *IEEE Transactions on Software Engineering, 18*(11), 943–956. doi:10.1109/32.177364

Choi, B.-J., & Lajos, H. (2001). Optimum mode-switching assisted adaptive modulation. In *Proceedings of the Global Telecommunications Conference* (pp. 3316-3320).

Claremont, B. (1992). *Understanding the Business Aspects of Software Migration*. Migration Specialties.

Constantinides, K., Plaza, S., Blome, J., Zhang, B., Bertacco, V., Mahlke, S., et al. (2006). BulletProof: A Defect-tolerant CMP Switch Architecture. In *Proceedings of the of Intl. Symposium on High Performance Computer Architecture (HPCA)* (pp. 3-14).

Cornea, R., Dutt, N., Gupta, R., Krueger, I., Nicolau, A., Schmidt, D., & Shukla, S. (2003). FORGE: A Framework for Optimization of Distributed Embedded Systems Software. In *Proceedings of International Parallel and Distributed Processing Symposium.*

Cosemans, S., Dehaene, W., & Catthoor, F. (2008). A 3.6pJ/access 480MHz, 128Kbit on-Chip SRAM with 830MHz boost mode in 90nm CMOS with tunable sense amplifiers to cope with variability. In *Proceedings of the Solid-State Circuits Conference* (pp. 278-281). ESSCIRC.

Costa, P., et al. (2007). The RUNES middleware for networked embedded systems and its application in a disaster management scenario. In *Proceedings of the 5th Annual IEEE Int. Conf. on Pervasive Computing and Communications.*

Courcelle, B. (2011). *Graph structure and monadic second-order logic, a language theoretic approach.* Retrieved from http://www.labri.fr/perso/courcell/Book/TheBook.pdf

Create-Net. (2008). *U-Hopper: User centric - heterogeneus opportunistic middleware.* Retrieved from http://u-hopper.create-net.org

Crepaldi, R., Casari, P., Zanella, A., & Zorzi, M. (2006). Testbed implementation and refinement of a range-based localization algorithm for wireless sensor networks. In *Proceedings of the Third International Conference on Mobile Technology, Applications & Systems* (Vol. 270, p. 61).

Cristian, F. (1991). Understanding Fault-Tolerant Distributed Systems. *Communications of the ACM, 34*(2), 56–78. doi:10.1145/102792.102801

Crossbow Technology. (2009). *Iris OEM datasheet.* Retrieved from http://bullseye.xbow.com:81/Products/Product_pdf_files/Wireless_pdf/IRIS_OEM_Datasheet.pdf

D'Haeseleer, S. (2008). *DB 3.1: Detailed requirement-based functional specification of gateway: Part 1: Private network (Tech. Rep. No. MUSE IST-6thFP-507295).* Brussels, Belgium: MUSE.

Das, S. R., Perkins, C. E., & Royer, E. M. (2000, March). Performance comparison of two on-demand routing protocols for ad hoc networks. In *Proceedings of the IEEE Conference on Computer Communications*, Tel Aviv, Israel (pp. 3-12).

David, J. S., Schuff, D., & St. Louis, R. (2002). Managing your total IT cost of ownership. *Communications of the ACM, 45*(1), 101-106. doi:http://doi.acm.org/10.1145/502269.502273

David, P.-C., & Ledoux, T. (2006). An aspect-oriented approach for developing self-adaptive fractal components. In W. Löwe & M. Südholt (Eds.), *Proceedings of the 5th International Symposium on Software Composition* (LNCS 4089, pp. 82-97).

Davis, H., & Miller, R. (2009). *Power management for Mica2 motes.* Retrieved from www.cs.etsu.edu/

De Florio, V., & Blondia, C. (2005). A System Structure for Adaptive Mobile Applications. In *Proceedings of the IEEE International Symposium on a World of Wireless, Mobile and Multimedia Networks 2005 (WOWMOM 2005)*, Giardini Naxos, Italy.

De Florio, V., & Blondia, C. (2007). Reflective and Refractive Variables: A Model for Effective and Maintainable Adaptive-and-Dependable Software. In *Proceedings of the 33rd Euromicro Conference on Software Engineering and Advanced Applications (SEEA 2007)*, Luebeck, Germany.

De Florio, V., & Blondia, C. (2008). A survey of linguistic structures for application-level fault tolerance. *ACM Computing Surveys, 40*(2), 6.

De Florio, V., Deconinck, G., & Lauwereins, R. (1997). An application-level dependable technique for farmer-worker parallel programs. In B. Herzberger & P. Sloot (Eds.), *Proceedings Of the High-Performance Computing and Networking International Conference And Exhibition. Lecture Notes in Computer Science* (Vol. 1225, pp. 644-653). Berlin: Springer Verlag.

de Jong, P. C., & Toth, F. N. (n. d.). *Measuring duty cycles with an Intel MCS-51 microcontroller.* Retrieved from http://www.smartec.nl/pdf/appsmt01.pdf

de Saint-Exupery, A. (2009). *Internet of things: Strategic research roadmap.* Retrieved from http://ec.europa.eu/information_society/policy/rfid/documents/in_cerp.pdf

Deavours, D. D., Clark, G., Courtney, T., Daly, D., Derisavi, S., & Doyle, J. M. (2007). The mobius framework and its implementation. *IEEE Transactions on Software Engineering, 28*(10), 956–969. doi:10.1109/TSE.2002.1041052

Demirbas, M. (2004). *Scalable design of fault-tolerance for wireless sensor networks.* Unpublished doctoral dissertation, Ohio State University, Columbus, OH.

DeRoure, D., & Sure, Y. (2006). Semantic grid - The convergence of technologies. *Journal of Web Semantics, 4*(2), 82–83. doi:10.1016/j.websem.2006.03.004

Dietterich, T. (1995). Overfitting and undercomputing in machine learning. *ACM Computing Surveys, 27*(3), 326–327. doi:10.1145/212094.212114

Dobing, B., & Parsons, J. (2006). How UML is used. *Communications of the ACM, 49*(5), 113. doi:10.1145/1125944.1125949

Dobson, G., Lock, R., & Sommerville, I. (2005). Qosont: A qos ontology for service-centric systems. In *Proceedings of the 31st EUROMICRO Conference on Software Engineering and Advanced Applications* (pp. 80-87). Washington, DC: IEEE Computer Society

Dong, X., Hariri, S., Xue, L., Chen, H., Zhang, M., Pavuluri, S., & Rao, S. (2003). Autonomia: an autonomic computing environment. In *Proceedings of the 2003 IEEE International Performance, Computing, and Communication Conference* (pp. 61-68).

Dunklau, R., & Frénot, S. (2009). *Proposal for a suspend/resume extension to the OSGi specification* (Tech. Rep. No. RR-7060). Le Chesnay, France: INRIA.

Duraes, J., & Madeira, H. (2006). Emulation of Software Faults: A Field Data Study and a Practical Approach. *IEEE Transactions on Software Engineering, 32*(11), 849–867. doi:10.1109/TSE.2006.113

Dyakonov, M. I. (2006). *Is fault-tolerant quantum computation really possible?* Retrieved from http://www.ee.sunysb.edu/~serge/ARW-5/ABSTRACTS/DyakonovAbs.pdf

Eclipse. (2010). *Equinox platform.* Retrieved from http://www.eclipse.org/equinox/

Edmonds, T. (2002). Pervasive Adaptation for Mobile Computing. In A. Hopper & S. Hodges (Eds.), *Proceedings of the 15th International Conference on Information Networking (ICOIN'01).*

Elnahrawy, E., Li, X., & Martin, R. (2004). The limits of localization using signal strength: A comparative study. In *Proceedings of the First IEEE International Conference on Sensor and Ad Hoc Communications and Networks* (pp. 406-414).

Equinox Aspect. (2008). Retrieved from http://www.eclipse.org/equinox/incubator/aspects/index.php

Ernst, D., Kim, N. S., Das, S., Pant, S., Rao, R., Pham, T., et al. (2003). Razor: A Low-Power Pipeline Based on Circuit-Level Timing Speculation. In *Proceedings of the Intl. Symp. on Microarchitecture (MICRO-36).*

Etter, R., Costa, P., & Broens, T. (2006). A Rule-Based Approach Towards Context-Aware User Notification Services. In *Proceedings of the IEEE International Conference on Pervasive Services 2006*, Lyon, France (pp. 281-284).

Eyer, M. K. (2003). *PSIP: Program and system information protocol.* New York: McGraw-Hill.

Fall, K. (2003, March). A delay-tolerant network architecture for challenged internets. In *Proceedings of the ACM SIGCOMM Conference on Applications, Technologies, Architectures, and Protocols for Computer Communications*, Karlsruhe, Germany (pp. 27-34).

Farail, P., Gaufillet, P., Canals, A., Le Camus, C., Sciamma, D., Michel, P., et al. (2006). The TOPCASED project: a toolkit in open source for critical aeronautic systems design. In *Proceedings of the European Congress on Embedded Real Time Software*, Toulouse, France (pp. 54-59).

Fischer, W. (2004). *Digital television: a practical guide for engineers.* Berlin: Springer Verlag.

Flaviu, C. (1993). Automatic reconfiguration in the presence of failures. *Software Engineering Journal, 8*(2), 53–60. doi:10.1049/sej.1993.0009

Fleury, E., & Frénot, S. (2003). *Building a JMX management interface inside OSGi* (Tech. Rep. No. RR-5025). Le Chesnay, France: INRIA.

Flissi, A., Dubus, J., Dolet, N., & Merle, P. (2008). Deploying on the Grid with DeployWare. In *Proceedings of the 2008 Eighth IEEE International Symposium on Cluster Computing and the Grid (CCGRID)* (p. 177-184).

Forrest, S., Hofmeyr, S. A., Somayaji, A., & Longstaff, T. A. (1996). A sense of self for Unix processes. In *Proceedings of the IEEE Symposium on Security and Privacy* (pp. 120-128).

Foster, I. T., & Iamnitchi, A. (2003). On death, taxes, and the convergence of peer-to-peer and grid computing. In M. F. Kaashoek & I. Stoica (Eds.), *Proceedings of the Second International Conference on Peer-to-Peer Systems II* (LNCS 2735, pp. 118-128).

Foster, I., Kesselman, C., & Tuecke, S. (2001). The anatomy of the grid: Enabling scalable virtual organizations. *International Journal of High Performance Computing Applications, 15*(3), 200. doi:10.1177/109434200101500302

Frei, A., & Alonso, G. (2005). A Dynamic Lightweight Platform for Ad-Hoc Infrastructures. In *Proceedings of the Third IEEE International Conference on Pervasive Computing and Communications* (pp. 373-382). Washington, DC: IEEE Computer Society.

Frénot, S., & Royon, Y. (2005). Component deployment using a peer-to-peer overlay. In A. Dearle & S. Eisenbach (Eds.), *Proceedings of the Third International Working Conference on Component Deployment*, Grenoble, France (LNCS 3798, pp. 33-36).

Frénot, S., Ibrahim, N., Le Mouël, F., Ben Hamida, A., Ponge, J., Chantrel, M., et al. (2010). ROCS: A remotely provisioned OSGi framework for ambient systems. In *Proceedings of the Symposium on Network Operations and Management*, Osaka Japan (pp. 503-510). Washington, DC: IEEE Computer Society.

Frénot, S., Royon, Y., Parrend, P., & Beras, D. (2008). Monitoring scheduling for home gateways. In *Proceedings of the Symposium on Network Operations and Management*, Salvador de Bahia, Brazil (pp. 411-416). Washington, DC: IEEE Computer Society.

Gacs, P. (1986). Reliable computation with cellular automata. *Journal of Computer and System Sciences, 32*(1), 15–78. doi:10.1016/0022-0000(86)90002-4doi:10.1016/0022-0000(86)90002-4

Gaertner, F. (1999). Transformational approaches to the specification and verification of fault-tolerant systems: Formal background and classification. *Journal of Universal Computer Science, 5*(10), 668–692.

Gaeta, M., Ritrovato, P., & Salerno, S. (2003). Elegi: The European learning grid infrastructure. In *Proceedings of the 3rd LeGE-WG Workshop.*

Gallager, R. G. (1996). *Discrete stochastic processes.* Boston, MA: Kluwer Academic.

Ganapathi, A. (2005). *Why does Windows Crash?* Berkeley, CA: Berkeley University.

Garlan, D., Cheng, S. W., Huang, A. C., Schmerl, B., & Steenkiste, P. (2004). Rainbow: Architecture-based self-adaptation with reusable infrastructure. *Computer, 37*(10), 46–49. doi:10.1109/MC.2004.175

Geilen, M. C. W., Basten, T., Theelen, B. D., & Otten, R. H. J. M. (2005). An Algebra of Pareto Points. In *Proceedings of International Conference on Application of Concurrency to System Design (ACSD)* (pp. 88-97).

Geoffray, N., Thomas, G., Muller, G., Parrend, P., Frénot, S., & Folliot, B. (2009). I-JVM: A java virtual machine for component isolation in OSGi. In *Proceedings of the International Conference on Dependable Systems and Networks*, Estoril, Portugal (pp. 544-553).

Georgiou, Y., Leduc, J., Videau, B., Peyrard, J., & Richard, O. (2006). A tool for environment deployment in clusters and light grids. In *Proceedings of the Second Workshop on System Management Tools for Large-Scale Parallel Systems,* Rhodes Island, Greece (Vol. 4).

Gheorghita, S. V., Basten, T., & Corporaal, H. (2008). Application Scenarios in Streaming-Oriented Embedded-System Design. In *IEEE Des. Test.* (Vol. 25, pp. 581-589). Washington, DC: IEEE Computer Society Press.

Gheorghita, S. V., Palkovic, M., Hamers, J., Vandecappelle, A., Mamagkakis, S., & Basten, T. (2008). System Scenario Based Design of Dynamic Embedded Systems. *ACM Transactions on Design Automation of Electronic Systems*, 14.

Giorgino, T., Tormene, P., Maggioni, G., Capozzi, D., Quaglini, S., & Pistarini, C. (2009). Assessment of sensorized garments as a flexible support to self-administered post-stroke physical rehabilitation. *European Journal of Physical and Rehabilitation Medicine*, 45(1), 75–84.

Gkantsidis, C., & Rodriguez, P. (2005). Network coding for large scale content distribution. In *Proceedings of the 24th Annual Joint Conference on INFOCOM* (Vol. 4, pp. 2235-2245).

Google. (n. d.). *Geolocation API.* Retrieved from http://code.google.com/apis/gears/api_geolocation.html

Gouardères, G., Mansour, S., Nkambou, R., & Yatchou, R. (2005). The grid-e-card: Architecture to share collective intelligence on the grid. *Applied Artificial Intelligence*, 19(9-10), 1043–1073. doi:10.1080/08839510500304108

Goux, J. P., Linderoth, J., & Yoder, M. (2000). *Metacomputing and the master-worker paradigm.* Retrieved December 14, 2009, from http://www.cs.wisc.edu/condor/mw/papers.html

Grace, P., Coulson, G., Blair, G., & Porter, B. (2005). Deep middleware for the divergent grid. In G. Alonso (Ed.), *Proceedings of the ACM/IFIP/USENIX International Conference on Middleware* (LNCS 3790, pp. 334-353).

Grant, S. (2005). Clear e-portfolio definition: A prerequisite for effective interoperability. In *Proceedings of the First International ePortfolio Conference.*

Gray, J. (1985). *Why Do Computer Stop and What Can Be Done About It?* (Tech. Rep. No. 85.7). Tandem.

Groenevelt, R., Nain, P., & Koole, G. (2005). The message delay in mobile ad hoc networks. *Performance Evaluation*, 62(1-4), 210–228. doi:10.1016/j.peva.2005.07.018

Groeseneken, G. (2005). Recent Trends in Reliability Assessment of Advanced CMOS Technologies. In *Proceedings of the IEEE Intl. Conf. on Microelectronic Test Structures* (Vol. 18, pp. 81-88).

Grondin, G., Bouraqadi, N., & Vercouter, L. (2006). MaDcAr: An abstract model for dynamic and automatic (re-)assembling of component-based applications. In I. Gorton, G. T. Heineman, I. Crnkovic, H. W. Schmidt, J. A. Stafford, C. Szyperski, & K. Wallnau (Eds.), *Proceedings of the 9th International SIGSOFT Symposium on Component-Based Software Engineering*, Vasteras, Sweden (LNCS 4063, pp. 360-367).

Grottke, M., & Trivedi, K. S. (2007). Fighting Bugs: Remove, Retry, Replicate, and Rejuvenate. *IEEE Computer*, 40(2), 107–109.

Gruber, T. R. (1993). Towards principles for the design of ontologies used for knowledge sharing. *International Journal of Human-Computer Studies*, 43(5-6), 907–928. doi:10.1006/ijhc.1995.1081

Gu, Y., Chakraborty, S., & Ooi, W. T. (2006). Games are up for DVFS. In *Proceedings of the 43rd Annual Design Automation Conference (DAC '06)* (pp. 598-603). New York: ACM.

Guessoum, Z. (2000). A multi-agent simulation framework. *Transactions of Computer Simulation*, 17(1), 2–11.

Gui, N., De Florio, V., Sun, H., & Blondia, C. (2008). *A framework for adaptive real-time applications: The declarative real-time OSGi component model.* Paper presented at the the 7th Workshop on Adaptive and Reflective Middleware (ARM), Leuven, Belgium.

Gui, N., De Florio, V., Sun, H., & Blondia, C. (2009a). An architecture-based framework for managing adaptive real-time applications. In *Proceedings of the Euromicro Conference on Software Engineering and Advanced Applications* (pp. 502-507).

Gui, N., De Florio, V., Sun, H., & Blondia, C. (2009b). ACCADA: A framework for continuous context-aware deployment and adaptation. In R. Guerraoui & F. Petit (Eds.), *Proceedings of the 11th International Symposium on Stabilization, Safety, and Security of Distributed Systems* (LNCS 5873, pp. 325-340).

Guinard, D., Trifa, V., Karnouskos, S., Spiess, P., & Savio, D. (2010). Interacting with the SOA-based Internet of things: Discovery, query, selection, and on-demand provisioning of web services. *IEEE Transactions on Service Computing*, 3(3), 223–235. doi:10.1109/TSC.2010.3

Hagimont, D., Stolf, P., Broto, L., & De Palma, N. (2009). Component-Based Autonomic Management for Legacy Software. *Autonomic Computing and Networking*, 83-104.

Hall, R. S., & Cervantes, H. (2004). Challenges in building service-oriented applications for OSGi. *IEEE Communications Magazine*, *42*(5), 144–149. doi:10.1109/MCOM.2004.1299359

Hanano, H., Murata, Y., Shibata, N., Yasumoto, K., & Ito, M. (2009). Video ads dissemination through wifi-cellular hybrid networks. In *Proceedings of the International Conference on Pervasive Computing and Communications* (pp. 1-6).

Hancke, G. P., Markantonakis, K., & Mayes, K. E. (2010). Security challenges for user-oriented RFID applications within the "Internet of things.". *Journal of Internet Technology*, *11*(3), 307–313.

Hao, Z., & Zhang, M. (2010). Management optimization of tangible goods for e-commerce logistics process in Internet of things era. In *Proceedings of the International Conference on on Management and Service Science.*

Harlan, R. C. (2003). Network management with Nagios. *Linux Journal*, (111), 3.

Hashimoto, S., Kojima, F., & Kubota, N. (2003). Perceptual system for a mobile robot under a dynamic environment. In *Proceedings of the IEEE International Symposium on Computational Intelligence in Robotics and Automation* (pp. 747-752).

Hayes, B. (2008). Cloud computing. *Communications of the ACM Journal*, *51*(7), 9–11..doi:10.1145/1364782.1364786

He, T., Huang, C., Blum, B., Stankovic, J., & Abdelzaher, T. (2003). Range-free localization schemes for large scale sensor networks. In *Proceedings of the 9th Annual International Conference on Mobile Computing and Networking* (pp. 81-95).

Hennessy, J. L., & Patterson, D. A. (2003). *Computer architecture: a quantitative approach*. San Francisco: Morgan Kauffmann.

Herssens, C., Faulkner, S., & Jureta, I. J. (2008). Context-driven autonomic adaptation of SLA. In A. Bouguettaya, I. Krueger, & T. Margaria (Eds.), *Proceedings of the 6th International Conference on Service-Oriented Computing* (LNCS 5364, pp. 362-377).

Hightower, J., & Borriello, G. (2001). A survey and taxonomy of location system for ubiquitous computing. *IEEE Computer*, *34*(8), 57–66.

Hodges, W. (2001). *First-order model theory.* Retrieved from http://plato.stanford.edu/entries/modeltheory-fo/

Hoffert, J., & Schmidt, D. (2009). Maintaining QoS for publish/subscribe middleware in dynamic environments. In *Proceedings of the 3rd International Conference on Distributed Event-based Systems* (pp. 1-2). New York: ACM Press.

Hoffert, J., Gokhale, A., & Schmidt, D. (2009). Evaluating transport protocols for real-time event stream processing Middleware and applications. In *Proceedings of the 11th International Symposium on Distributed Objects, Middleware, and Applications* (pp. 614-633).

Hoffert, J., Schmidt, D., & Gokhale, A. (2010a). Adapting and evaluating distributed real-time and embedded systems in dynamic environments. In *Proceedings of the 1st International Workshop on Data Dissemination for Large Scale Complex Critical Infrastructures* (pp. 23-28). New York, NY: ACM Press.

Hoffert, J., Schmidt, D., & Gokhale, A. (2010b). Adapting distributed real-time and embedded pub/sub middleware for cloud computing environments. In I. Gupta & C. Mascolo (Eds.), *Proceedings of the ACM/IFIP/USENIX 11th International Middleware Conference* (LNCS 6452, pp. 21-41).

Hoffert, J., Mack, D., & Schmidt, D. (2010). Integrating machine learning techniques to adapt protocols for QoS-enabled distributed real-time and embedded publish/subscribe Middleware. *Network Protocols and Algorithms*, *2*(3), 37–69. doi:10.5296/npa.v2i3.429

Hoffmeyer, J., Il-Pyung, P., Majmundar, M., & Blust, S. (2004). Radio software download for commercial wireless reconfigurable devices. *IEEE Communications Magazine*, *42*(3), 26–32. doi:10.1109/MCOM.2004.1273771

Holzmann, G. J., & Joshi, R. (2008). Reliable software systems design: Defect prevention, detection, and containment. In B. Meyer & J. Woodcock (Eds.), *Proceedings of the First IFIP TC 2/WG 2.3 Conference on Verified Software: Theories, Tools, Experiments.* (LNCS 4171, pp. 237-244).

Hong, X., Gerla, M., Pei, G., & Chiang, C. C. (1999). A group mobility model for ad hoc wireless networks. In *Proceedings of the 2nd International Workshop on Modeling, Analysis and Simulation of wireless and mobile systems* (pp. 53-60).

Hong, S., Kim, D., Ha, M., Bae, S., Park, S. J., Jung, W., & Kim, J. (2010). SNAIL: An IP-based wireless sensor network approach to the Internet of things. *IEEE Wireless Communications, 17*(6), 34–42. doi:10.1109/MWC.2010.5675776

Houssos, N., Gazis, V., & Alonistioti, N. (2003). A Novel Mechanism for Mobile Service Adaptation. In *Proceedings of the 57th IEEE Vehicular Technology Conference*.

Hsieh, H.-Y., & Sivakumar, R. (2004). On using peer-to-peer communication in cellular wireless data networks. *IEEE Transactions on Mobile Computing, 3*.

Huang, Q., Freedman, D., Vigfusson, Y., Birman, K., & Peng, B. (2010). Kevlar: A flexible infrastructure for wide-area collaborative applications. In I. Gupta & C. Mascolo (Eds.), *Proceedings of the ACM/IFIP/USENIX 11th International Middleware Conference* (LNCS 6452, pp. 148-168).

Huang, Y., & Gannon, D. (2006). A comparative study of web services-based event notification specifications. In *Proceedings of the International Conference on Parallel Processing Workshops* (pp. 7-14). Washington, DC: IEEE Computer Society.

Huang, Y., Jalote, P., & Kintala, C. (1994). Two Techniques for Transient Software Error Recovery. In *Proceedings of the Workshop on Hardware and Software Architectures for Fault Tolerance: Experiences and Perspectives* (pp. 159-170).

Huebscher, M. C., & McCann, J. A. (2008). A survey of autonomic computing—degrees, models, and applications. *ACM Computing Surveys, 40*(3), 1–28.. doi:10.1145/1380584.1380585

Hui, P., Yoneki, E., Chan, S.-Y., & Crowcroft, J. (2007, August). Distributed community detection in delay tolerant networks. In *Proceedings of the 2nd ACM/IEEE International Workshop on Mobility in the Evolving Internet Architecture*, Kyoto, Japan (p. 7).

Husain, S., Alonso, T., Midani, M., & Jung, K. (2008). Remote device management of WiMAX devices in multi-mode multi-access environment. In *Proceedings of the IEEE International Symposium on Broadband Multimedia Systems and Broadcasting* (pp. 1-14).

Ibrahim, M., Nain, P., & Carreras, I. (2009, June). Analysis of relay protocols for throwbox equipped DTNs. In *Proceedings of the 7th International Symposium on Modeling and Optimization in Mobile, Ad Hoc and Wireless Networks*, Seoul, Korea (pp. 1-9).

Ibrahim, N. (2008). *Spontaneous integration of services in pervasive environments*. Unpublished doctoral dissertation, INSA de Lyon, Villeurbanne, France.

IEEE Standards Association. (2003). *802.15 WPAN Low Rate Alternative PHY Task Group 4a*. Retrieved from http://www.ieee802.org/15/pub/TG4a.html

Inamura, T., Inaba, M., & Inoue, H. (2000). *User adaptation of human-robot interaction model based on Bayesian network and introspection of interaction experience*. Paper presented at the the IEEE/RSJ International Conference on Intelligent Robots and Systems.

International Telecommunication Union (ITU). (2005). *Internet reports 2005*. Retrieved from http://www.itu.int/osg/spu/publications/internetofthings/

Intille, S., Bao, L., Munguia Tapia, E., & Rondoni, J. (2004). Acquiring in situ training data for context-aware ubiquitous computing applications. In *Proceedings of the Conference on Human Factors in Computing Systems* (pp. 1-8).

Ioannidis, I., Carbunar, B., & Nita-Rotaru, C. (2005). High throughput routing in hybrid cellular and ad-hoc networks. In *Proceedings of the International Symposium on the World of Wireless Mobile and Multimedia Networks* (pp. 171-176).

Iqbal, M., Li, S., Wang, X. H., & Ellis, T. S. (2009, October 12-14). Bandwidth calculation scheme to provide cross layer rate adaptive admission control in wireless mesh networks. In *Proceedings of the Conference on Next Generation Wireless Systems*, Melbourne, Australia.

Iqbal, M., Shancang, L., Wang, X. H., & Ellis, T. (2009). A QoS scheme for multimedia multicast communications over wireless mesh networks. *IET Communications, 4*(11), 1312–1324. doi:10.1049/iet-com.2009.0413

Iqbal, M., Wang, X. H., & Wertheim, D. (2009). Reliable multimedia multicast communications over wireless mesh networks. *IET Communications, 4*(11), 1288–1299. doi:10.1049/iet-com.2009.0134

Iqbal, M., Wang, X. H., Wertheim, D., & Zhou, X. (2009). SwanMesh: A multicast enabled dual-radio wireless mesh network for emergency and disaster recovery services. *The Journal of Communication, 4*(5), 298–306.

Irmert, F., et al. (2007). Towards Runtime Adaptation in a SOA Environment. In *Proceedings of the 4th ECOOP Workshop on Reflection, AOP and Meta-Data for Software Evolution.*

Jagadeesh, R. P., Bose, C., & Srinivasan, S. H. (2005). Data Mining Approaches to Software Fault Diagnosis. In *Proceedings of the 15th IEEE Workshop on Research Issues in Data Engineering: Stream Data Mining and Applications* (pp. 45-52).

Jain, S., Fall, K., & Patra, R. (2004, March). Routing in a delay tolerant network. In *Proceedings of the ACM SIGCOMM Conference on Applications, Technologies, Architectures, and Protocols for Computer Communications*, Portland, OR (pp. 145-158).

Jalali, A. A., & Nadimi, V. (2006). A Survey on Robust Model Predictive Control from 1999-2006. In *Proceedings of the International Conference on Computational Intelligence for Modelling, Control and Automation* (p. 207). Washington, DC: IEEE Computer Society.

Java Community Process. (n. d.). *JSR82: Javatm apis for bluetooth.* Retrieved from http://jcp.org/aboutJava/communityprocess/final/jsr082

Jelger, C., & Noel, T. (2006). Algorithms for prefix continuity in IPv6 ad hoc networks. *Ad Hoc & Sensor Wireless Networks, 2*(2).

Jelger, C., Noel, T., & Frey, A. (2004). *Gateway and address autoconfiguration for ipv6 adhoc networks.* Retrieved from http://tools.ietf.org/html/draft-jelger-manet-gateway-autoconf-v6-02

Jet Propulsion Laboratory. (n. d.). *Nasa Mars rover.* Retrieved from http://marsrover.nasa.gov

Ji, X., & Zha, H. (2004). Sensor positioning in wireless ad-hoc sensor networks using multidimensional scaling. In *Proceedings of the Twenty-Third Annual Joint Conference of the IEEE Computer and Communications Societies* (Vol. 4, pp. 2652-2661).

Johanson, P., Larsson, T., Hedman, N., Mielczarek, B., & Degermark, M. (1999). Scenario-based performance analysis of routing protocols for mobile ad-hoc networks. In *Proceedings of the 5th Annual ACM/IEEE International Conference on Mobile Computing and Networking*, Seattle, WA (pp. 195-206).

Jonquet, C., Dugenie, P., & Cerri, S. A. (2008). Agent grid integration language. *Multiagent and Grid Systems, 4*(2), 167–211.

Jonsson, U., Alriksson, F., Larsson, T., Johansson, P., & Maguire, G. Q., Jr. (2000). MIPMANET - Mobile IP for mobile ad hoc networks. In *Proceedings of the 1st ACM International Symposium on Mobile Ad Hoc Networking and Computing.*

Joshi, K. R., Hiltunen, M. A., Sanders, W. H., & Schlichting, R. D. (2005). Automatic Model-Driven Recovery in Distributed Systems. In *Proceedings of the 24th IEEE Symposium on Reliable Distributed Systems* (pp. 25-36).

Jrv, O., Aasa, A., Ahas, R., & Saluveer, E. (2007). Weather dependence of tourist's spatial behavior and destination choices: case study with passive mobile positioning data in Estonia. In Matzarakis, A., de Freitas, C. R., & Scott, D. (Eds.), *Developments in tourism climatology.* Milwaukee, WI: International Society of Biometeorology.

Jung, S., Lee, U., Chang, A., Cho, D.-K., & Gerla, M. (2007). Bluetorrent: Cooperative content sharing for bluetooth users. *Pervasive and Mobile Computing, 3*, 609–634. doi:10.1016/j.pmcj.2007.06.003

JXTA. (2003). *Project jxta v2.0.* Retrieved from http://www.jxta.org

Kagal, L., Berners-Lee, T., Connolly, D., & Weitzner, D. J. (2006). Using semantic web technologies for policy management on the web. In *Proceedings of the AAAI Conference on Artificial Intelligence* (pp. 1337-1344).

Kaiser, G., Parekh, J., Gross, P., & Valetto, G. (2003). Kinesthetics eXtreme: an external infrastructure for monitoring distributed legacy systems. In *Proceedings of the Autonomic Computing Workshop Fifth International Workshop on Active Middleware Services*, Seattle, WA (pp. 22-30).

Kalai, G. (2005). *Thoughts on noise and quantum computation.* Retrieved from http://www.ma.huji.ac.il/~kalai/QN.pdf

Kalai, G. (2007). *How quantum computers can fail.* Retrieved from http://www.ma.huji.ac.il/~kalai/QQT.pdf

Kang, S.-S., & Mutka, M. (2004). Efficient mobile access to internet data via a wireless peer-to-peer peer network. In *Proceedings of the 2nd Annual Conference on Pervasive Computing and Communication* (pp. 197-205).

Kang, J. M., Ju, H.-T., & Choi, M.-J., Won-ki Hong, J., & Kim, J.-G. (2009). OMA DM-based remote software fault management for mobile devices. *International Journal of Network Management, 19*(6), 491–511. doi:10.1002/nem.724

Kang, K., Song, J., Kim, J., Park, H., & Cho, W.-D. (2007). USS monitor: A monitoring system for collaborative ubiquitous computing environment. *IEEE Transactions on Consumer Electronics, 53*(3), 911–916. doi:10.1109/TCE.2007.4341565

Karl, E., Blaauw, D., Sylvester, D., & Mudge, T. (2006). Reliability modeling and management in dynamic microprocessor-based systems. In *Proceedings of the 43rd annual conference on Design automation* (pp. 1057-1060). New York: ACM.

Kay, S. M. (Ed.). (1993). *Fundamentals of statistical signal processing: Estimation theory.* Upper Saddle River, NJ: Prentice Hall.

Kempe, J. (2006). *Approaches to quantum error correction.* Retrieved from http://www.bourbaphy.fr/kempe.ps

Kephart, J. O., & Chess, D. M. (2003). The vision of autonomic computing. *Computer, 36*(1), 41–50. doi:10.1109/MC.2003.1160055

Kephart, J., & Chess, D. (2003). The vision of autonomic computing. *Computer, 36*(1), 41–50. doi:10.1109/MC.2003.1160055

Keutzer, K., & Orshansky, M. (2002). From Blind Certainty to Informed Uncertainty. In *Proceedings of the Intl. Workshop on Timing Issues in the Specification and Synthesis of Digital Systems (TAU)*.

Khanna, G., Laguna, I., Arshad, F. A., & Bagchi, S. (2007). Distributed Diagnosis of Failures in a Three Tier E-Commerce System. In *Proceedings of the 26th IEEE Symposium on Reliable Distributed Systems* (pp. 185-198).

Kiczales, G., Lamping, J., Mendhekar, A., Maeda, C., Videira Lopes, C., Loingtier, J.-M., & Irwin, J. (1997). Aspect-Oriented Programming. In *Proceedings of the European Conference on Object-Oriented Programming (ECOOP)*, Finland.

Kim, B. C., Lee, J. Y., Lee, H. S., & Ma, J. S. (2003). An ad-hoc routing protocol with minimum contention time and load balancing. In *Proceedings of the IEEE Global Telecommunications Conference* (pp. Vol. 1, 81-85).

Kim, S., Whitethead, E. J., & Zhang, Y. (2008). Classifying Software Changes: Clean or Buggy? *IEEE Transactions on Software Engineering, 34*(2), 181–196. doi:10.1109/TSE.2007.70773

Kirn, S. (2002). Ubiquitous healthcare: The OnkoNet mobile agents architecture. In M. Aksit, M. Mezini, & R. Unland (Eds.), *Proceedings of the International Conference on Objects, Components, Architectures, Services, and Applications for a Network World* (LNCS 2591, pp. 265-277).

Kiselev, I. (2002). *Aspect-Oriented Programming with AspectJ.* Indianapolis, IN: Sams.

Kon, F., & Campbell, R. H. (1999). Supporting Automatic Configuration of Component-Based Distributed Systems. In *Proceedings of the USENIX Conference on Object-Oriented Technologies and Systems*, San Diego (Vol. 5, p. 13).

Kon, F., Costa, F., Blair, G., & Campbell, R. (2002). The case for reflective middleware: building middleware that is flexible, reconfigurable, and yet simple to use. *Communications of the ACM, 45*(6), 33–38.

Krishnaswamy, D., Pfeifer, T. et al. (2007). OMA DM based remote RF signal monitoring of mobile devices for QoS improvement. *Real-Time Mobile Multimedia Services*, 76-87.

Krutisch, R., Meier, P., & Wirsing, M. (2003). The agent component approach, combining agents, and components. In M. Schillo, M. Klusch, J. Müller, & H. Tianfield (Eds.), *Proceedings of the First German Conference on Multiagent System Technologies* (LNCS 2831, pp. 1-12).

Ku, D. C., & De Micheli, G. (1991). Constrained resource sharing and conflict resolution in Hebe. *Elsevier Integration, the VLSI journal, 12*, 131-165.

Kubiatowicz, J., Bindel, D., Chen, Y., Czerwinski, S., Eaton, P., & Geels, D. (2000). Oceanstore: An architecture for global-scale persistent storage. *ACM SIGARCH Computer Architecture News, 28*(5), 190–201. doi:10.1145/378995.379239

Kulkarni, S. S., & Ebnenasir, A. (2005). Adding fault-tolerance using pre-synthesized components. In *Proceedings of the Fifth European Dependable Computing Conference* (pp. 72-90).

Lach, J., Evans, D., McCune, J., & Brandon, J. (2003). Power-efficient adaptable wireless sensor networks. In *Proceedings of the Military and Aerospace Programmable Logic Devices International Conference*.

Lacouture, J., & Aniorté, P. (2008). Compaa: A self-adaptable component model for open systems. In *Proceedings of the 15th IEEE International Conference on Engineering of Computer-Based Systems* (pp. 19-25). Washington, DC: IEEE Computer Society.

Lacouture, J., & Mansour, S. (2007). E-portfolio, an auto-adaptable grid service with components using peer-to-peer agents. In *Proceedings of the 4ᵗʰ International Conference on Grid Engineering and Management*, Leipzig, Germany (pp. 51-65).

Lan, S., Qilong, M., & Du, J. (2008, December 21-22). Architecture of wireless sensor networks for environmental monitoring. In *Proceedings of the International Workshop on Education and Technology Training and the Workshop on Geoscience and Remote Sensing* (pp. 579-582).

Langendoen, K., & Reijers, N. (2003). Distributed localization in wireless sensor networks: A quantitative comparison. *Computer Networks: The International Journal of Computer and Telecommunications Networking, 43*(4), 499–518.

Leal, W. (2001). *A foundation for fault tolerant components.* Unpublished doctoral dissertation, Ohio State University, Columbus, OH.

Lee, J., Kim, D., Garcia-Luna-Aceves, J. J., Choi, Y., Choi, J., & Nam, S. (2003, April). Hybrid gateway advertisement scheme for connecting mobile ad hoc networks to the Internet. In *Proceedings of the 57th IEEE Semiannual Vehicular Technology Conference*, Jeju, Korea (pp. 191-195).

Lee, S. J., & Gerla, M. (2001). Dynamic load-aware routing in ad hoc networks. In *Proceedings of the IEEE International Conference on Communications*, Helsinki, Finland (pp. 3206-3210).

Lee, Y. J., & Riley, G. F. (2005, March 13-17). A workload-based adaptive load-balancing technique for mobile ad hoc networks. In *Proceedings of the IEEE Wireless Communications and Networking Conference* (pp. 2002-2007).

Leeman, M., Leeman, M., De Florio, V., & Deconinck, G. (2003). A flexible library for dependable master-worker parallel programs. In A. Clematis (Ed.), *Proceedings of the Eleventh Euromicro Conference on Parallel, Distributed and Network-Based Processing* (pp. 299-307). Washington, DC: IEEE Computer Society.

Lee, U., & Magistretti, E. (2008). Dissemination and harvesting of urban data using vehicular sensing platforms. *IEEE Transactions on Vehicular Technology, 99*, 1.

Lee, U., Park, J.-S., Lee, S.-H., Ro, W. W., Pau, G., & Gerla, M. (2008). Efficient peer-to-peer file sharing using network coding in manet. *Journal of Communications and Networks, 10*, 422–429.

Legendre, F., Lenders, V., May, M., & Karlsson, G. (2008, September). Narrowcasting: An empirical performance evaluation study. In *Proceedings of the Third ACM Workshop on Challenged Networks* (pp. 11-18).

LeJOS. (2009). *Java for LEGO mindstorms.* Retrieved from http://lejos.sourceforge.net/

Leung, L. F., Tsui, C. Y., & Hu, X. S. (2005). Exploiting Dynamic Workload Variation in Low Energy Preemptive Task Scheduling. In *Proceedings of the conference on Design, Automation and Test in Europe* (Vol. 1, pp. 634-639). Washington, DC: IEEE Computer Society.

Li, M., Bougard, B., Novo, D., Van Thillo, W., Van der Perre, L., & Catthoor, F. (2008). Adaptive SSFE Near-ML MIMO Detector with Dynamic Search Range and 80-103Mbps Flexible Implementation. In *Proceeding of IEEE GLOBECOM*.

Lim, H.-J., Park, S.-H., & Chung, T.-M. (2008). u-MoDEM: Ubiquitous mobile device environment manager based on OMA-DM. In *Proceedings of the 10th International Conference on Advanced Communication Technology* (pp. 283-287).

Lippert, M. (2004). AJEER: An AspectJ-Enabled Eclipse Runtime. In *Proceedings of Conference on Object Oriented Programming Systems Languages and Applications (OOPSLA '04)*, Vancouver, Canada. New York: ACM.

Lippert, M. *(2008). Aspect weaving for OSGi. In* Proceedings of Conference on Object Oriented Programming Systems Languages and Applications, Companion to the 23rd ACM SIGPLAN conference on Object-oriented programming systems languages and applications.

Littlewood, B., & Strigini, L. (2000). Software Reliability and Dependability: A Roadmap. In *Proceedings of the ACM Conference on The Future of Software Engineering* (pp. 175–188).

Liu, C., & Wu, K. (2005). Performance evaluation of range-free localization methods for wireless sensor networks. In *Proceedings of the IEEE International Conference on Performance, Computing, and Communications* (pp. 59-66).

Liu, C., Wu, K., & He, T. (2004). Sensor localization with ring overlapping based on comparison of received signal strength indicator. In *Proceedings of the IEEE International Conference on Mobile Ad-hoc and Sensor Systems* (pp. 516-518).

Liu, Y. (2006). Create stable neural networks by cross-validation. In *Proceedings of the International Joint Conference on Neural Networks* (pp. 3925-3928). Washington, DC: IEEE Computer Society.

Liu, H., & Parashar, M. (2006). Accord: A programming framework for autonomic applications. *IEEE Transactions on Systems, Man, and Cybernetics, 36*(3), 341–352. doi:10.1109/TSMCC.2006.871577

Lorentz, A. (2005). Agent-based ubiquitous user modeling. In L. Ardissono, P. Brna, & A. Mitrovic (Eds.), *Proceedings of the 10th International Conference on User Modeling* (LNCS 3538, pp. 512-514).

Lundstrom, L. (2006). *Understanding digital television: an introduction to DVB systems with satellite, cable, broadband and terrestrial TV distribution*. Focal Press.

Luo, H., Ramjee, R., Sinha, P., Li, L., & Lu, S. (2007). The design and evaluation of unified cellular and ad hoc networks. *IEEE Transactions on Mobile Computing, 6*(9), 1060–1074. doi:10.1109/TMC.2007.1035

Ma, J., Liao, J., & Zhu, X. (2008). Device management in the IMS. *Journal of Network and Systems Management, 16*(1), 46–62. doi:10.1007/s10922-007-9092-7

Manevitz, L. M., & Yousef, M. (2002). One-Class SVMs for Document Classification. *Journal of Machine Learning Research, 2*, 139–154. doi:10.1162/15324430260185574

Mansfeld, Y., & Ya'acoub, K. (2004). Patterns of tourist destination-choice and travel behavior among members of the urban and rural arab community of israel: A comparative study of haifa and ibilin. *GeoJournal, 35*(4), 459–470. doi:10.1007/BF00824356

Mao, G., Fidan, B., & Anderson, B. D. O. (2007). Wireless sensor network localization techniques. *Computer Networks: The International Journal of Computer and Telecommunications Networking, 51*(10), 2529–2553.

Marin, C. A., & Mehandjiev, N. (2006). A classification framework of adaptation in multi-agent systems. In *Proceedings of the Conference on Cooperative Information Agents* (pp. 198-212).

Massie, M. L., Chun, B. N., & Culler, D. E. (2004). The ganglia distributed monitoring system: design, implementation, and experience. *Parallel Computing, 30*(7), 817–840. doi:10.1016/j.parco.2004.04.001

Maymounkov, P., & Mazieres, D. (2003). Rateless codes and big downloads. In *Proceedings of the International Workshop on Peer-to-Peer Systems*.

Mesman, B., Timmer, A. H., Van Meerbergen, J. L., & Jess, J. A. G. (1999). Constraint analysis for DSP code generation. *IEEE Transactions on Computer-Aided Design of Integrated Circuits and Systems, 18*(1), 44–57. doi:10.1109/43.739058

Meyer, D., Leisch, D., & Hornik, K. (2003). The support vector machine under test. *Neurocomputing, 55*(1-2), 169–186. doi:10.1016/S0925-2312(03)00431-4

Mihic, K., Simunic, T., & De Micheli, G. (2004). Reliability and Power Management of Integrated Systems. In Proceedings of the Dependable System Design (DSD).

Miklas, A. G., Gollu, K. K., & Saroiu, S. Gummadi, K. P., & de Lara, E. (2007, September). Exploiting social interactions in mobile systems. In *Proceedings of the 9th International Conference on Ubiquitous Computing*, Innsbruck, Austria.

Millonig, A., & Gartner, G. (2009). Ways of walking - developing a pedestrian typology for personalised mobile information. In Gartner, G., & Rehrl, K. (Eds.), *Location based services and telecartography II: From sensor fusion to context models* (pp. 79–94). Berlin, Germany: Springer-Verlag. doi:10.1007/978-3-540-87393-8_6

Milojicic, D. S., Kalogeraki, V., Lukose, R., Nagaraja, K., Pruyne, J., Richard, B., et al. (2002). *Peer-to-peer computing* (Tech. Rep. No. HPL-2002-57R1). Palo Alto, CA: Hewlett-Packard.

Mochocki, B., Hu, X. S., & Quan, G. (2007). Transition-overhead-aware voltage scheduling for fixed-priority real-time systems. *ACM Transactions on Design Automation of Electronic Systems, 12*, 11. doi:10.1145/1230800.1230803

Mohammed, H. K., Tripathi, R., & Kant, K. (2006). Performance of adaptive modulation in multipath fading channel. In *Proceedings of the 8th International Conference on Advanced Communication Technology* (pp. 1277-1282).

Monson-Haefel, R., & Chappell, D. (2000). *Java message service*. Sebastopol, CA: O'Reilly Media.

Moraes, R., Duraes, J., Barbosa, R., Martins, E., & Madeira, H. (2007). Experimental Risk Assessment and Comparison Using Software Fault Injection. In *Proceedings of the 37th IEEE/IFIP Conference on Dependable Systems and Networks* (pp. 512-521).

Moragrega, A., Ibars, C., & Geng, Y. (2009, June 11-12). Energy efficiency of a cooperative wireless sensor network. Palma de Mallorca.

Muldoon, C., O'Hare, G., Phelan, D., Strahan, R., & Collier, R. (2003) ACCESS: An agent architecture for ubiquitous service delivery. In *Cooperative Information Agents VII*, (LNCS 2782, pp. 1-15).

Musolesi, M., & Mascolo, C. (2007). Designing mobility models based on social network theory. *ACM SIGMOBILE Mobile Computing and Communication Review, 11*(3).

Nain, P., Towsley, D., Liu, B., & Liu, Z. (2005). Properties of random direction models. In *Proceedings of the 24th Annual Joint Conference of INFOCOMM* (Vol. 3, pp. 1897-1907).

Neglia, G., & Zhang, X. (2006, September). Optimal delay-power tradeoff in sparse delay tolerant networks: A preliminary study. In *Proceedings of the SIGCOMM Conference on Challenged Networks*, Pisa, Italy (pp. 237-244).

Ngatman, M., Ngadi, M., & Sharif, J. (2008). Comprehensive study of transmission techniques for reducing packet loss and delay in multimedia over IP. *International Journal of Computer Science and Network Security, 8*(3), 292–299.

Nguyen, X., & Rattentbury, T. (2003). *Localization algorithms for sensor networks using RF signal strength* (Tech. Rep. No. CS252). Berkeley, CA: University of California.

Niblett, P., & Graham, S. (2005). Events and service-oriented architecture: The OASIS web services notification specifications. *IBM Systems Journal, 44*(4), 869–886. doi:10.1147/sj.444.0869

Nicolai, M., Behrens, N., & Yoneki, E. (2006, March). Wireless rope: An experiment in social proximity sensing with bluetooth. In *Proceedings of the PerCom Conference*, Pisa, Italy.

Noel, V., Arcangeli, J.-P., & Gleizes, M.-P. (2010). Component-based agent architectures to build dedicated agent frameworks. In *Proceedings of the International Symposium on From Agent Theory to Agent Implementation*, Vienna, Austria (pp. 483-488).

Nordström, E., Gunningberg, P., & Tschudin, C. (2010). *Design of Internet connectivity for mobile ad hoc networks*. Retrieved from http://user.it.uu.se/~erikn/papers/adhoc-internet.pdf

Novo, D., Bougard, B., Lambrechts, A., Van der Perre, L., & Catthoor, F. (2008). Scenario-Based Fixed-point Data Format Refinement to Enable Energy-scalable Software Defined Radios. In *Proceedings of Design, Automation, and Test in Europe (DATE'08)*.

Nwana, H. S., & Heath, M. (1996). Software agents: An overview. *The Knowledge Engineering Review, 11*(3), 1–40. doi:10.1017/S026988890000789X

Oommen, P. (2001). A framework for integrated management of mobile-stations over-the-air. In *Proceedings of the IEEE/IFIP International Symposium on Integrated Network Management* (pp. 247-256).

Oreizy, P., Gorlick, M. M., Taylor, R. N., Heimbigner, D., Johnson, G., & Medvidovic, N. (1999). An Architecture-Based Approach to Self-Adaptive Software. *IEEE Intelligent Systems, 14*(3), 54–62. doi:10.1109/5254.769885

OSGi Alliance. (2008). *OSGi Service Platform* (Release 4.1).

Papanicolaou, A., Wang, H., Miranda, M., Catthoor, F., & Dehaene, W. (2008). Reliability Issues in Deep Deep sub-micron technologies: time-dependent variability and its impact on embedded system design. In *Proceedings of VLSI-SoC, Research Trends in VLSI and Systems on Chip* (Vol. 249/2008). New York: Springer.

Papatheodorou, A. (2001). Why people travel to different places. *Annals of Tourism Research, 28*(1), 164–179. doi:10.1016/S0160-7383(00)00014-1

Papoulis, A., & Pillai, S. U. (2002). *Probability, random variables and stochastic processes* (4th ed.). New York, NY: McGraw Hill.

Parashar, M., Liu, H., Li, Z., Matossian, V., Schmidt, C., Zhang, G., & Hariri, S. (2006). AutoMate: Enabling Autonomic Applications on the Grid. *Cluster Computing, 9*(2), 161–174..doi:10.1007/s10586-006-7561-5

Pardo-Castellote, G. (2003). OMG data-distribution service: Architectural overview. In *Proceedings of the 23rd International Conference on Distributed Computing Systems* (pp. 200-206). Washington, DC: IEEE Computer Society.

Park, J. C., & Kasera, S. (2005). Enhancing cellular multicast performance using ad hoc networks. In. *Proceedings of the Wireless Communications and Networking Conference, 4*, 2175. doi:10.1109/WCNC.2005.1424854

Parnas, D. (1972). On the criteria to be used in decomposing systems into modules. *Communications of the ACM, 15.*

Parrend, P. (2008). *Modèles de Sécurité logicielle pour les plates-formes a` composants de service (SOP).* Unpublished doctoral dissertation, INSA de Lyon, Villeurbanne, France.

Parrend, P., & Frénot, S. (2006). *Secure component deployment in the OSGi(tm) release 4 platform* (Tech. Rep. No. RT-0323). Le Chesnay, France: INRIA.

Parrend, P., & Frénot, S. (2007a). *Java components vulnerabilities - an experimental classification targeted at the OSGi platform* (Tech. Rep. No. RR-6231). Le Chesnay, France: INRIA.

Parrend, P., & Frénot, S. (2007b). Supporting the secure deployment of OSGi bundles. In *Proceedings of the International Symposium on a World of Wireless, Mobile and Multimedia Networks*, Helsinki, Finland (pp. 1-6). Washington, DC: IEEE Computer Society.

Parrend, P., & Frénot, S. (2008a). Classification of component vulnerabilities in java service oriented programming (sop) platforms. In M. R. V. Chaudron, C. Szyperski, & R. Reussner (Eds.), *Proceedings of the 11th International Symposium on Component-Based Software Engineering*, Karlsruhe, Germany (LNCS 5282, pp. 80-96).

Parrend, P., & Frénot, S. (2008b). Component-based access control: Secure software composition through static analysis. In C. Pautasso & E. Tanter (Eds.), *Proceedings of the 7th International Symposium on Software Composition*, Budapest, Hungary (LNCS 4954, pp. 68-83).

Parrend, P., & Frénot, S. (2008c). *More vulnerabilities in the Java/OSGi platform: A focus on bundle interactions* (Tech. Rep. No. RR-6649). Le Chesnay, France: INRIA.

Parrend, P., & Frénot, S. (2009). Security benchmarks of OSGi platforms: Towards hardened OSGi. *Journal of Software Practice and Experience, 39*(5), 471–499. doi:10.1002/spe.906

Patterson, D. W. (1998). *Artificial neural networks: Theory and applications*. Upper Saddle River, NJ: Prentice Hall.

Patwari, N., Hero, A. O. III, Perkins, M., Correal, N. S., & O'Dea, R. J. (2003). Relative location estimation in wireless sensor networks. *IEEE Transactions on Signal Processing*, *51*(8), 2137–2148. doi:10.1109/TSP.2003.814469

Pearlman, M. R., Haas, Z. J., Sholander, P., & Tabrizi, S. S. (2000). On the impact of alternate path routing for load balancing in mobile ad hoc networks. In *Proceedings of the 1st ACM International Symposium on Mobile Ad Hoc Networking & Computing*, Boston, MA (pp. 3-10).

Pelusi, L., Passarella, A., & Conti, M. (2006). Opportunistic networking: Data forwarding in disconnected mobile ad hoc networks. *IEEE Communications Magazine*, *44*(11). doi:10.1109/MCOM.2006.248176

Perkins, C. E. (1996). *IP encapsulation within IP*. Retrieved from http://tools.ietf.org/html/draft-ietf-mobileip-ip4inip4-00

Perkins, C. E., Royer, E. M., & Das, S. R. (2008). *Ad hoc on demand distance vector routing*. Retrieved from http://tools.ietf.org/html/rfc3561

Pieter-Jan, P. (2010). *An adaptive OSGi robotic application*. Unpublished doctoral dissertation, University of Antwerp, Belgium.

Pietilainen, A.-K., & Diot, C. (2009, June). Experimenting with opportunistic networking. In *Proceedings of the MobiArch Conference*, Kraków, Poland.

Pillai, P., & Shin, K. G. (2001). Real-time dynamic voltage scaling for low-power embedded operating systems. In *Proceedings of the eighteenth ACM symposium on Operating systems principles* (pp. 89-102). New York: ACM.

Pippenger, N. (1990). Developments in the synthesis of reliable organisms from unreliable components. In *Proceedings of the Symposia in Pure Mathematics* (Vol. 50, pp. 311-324).

Podgurski, A., Leon, D., Francis, P., Masri, W., Minch, M., Sun, J., et al. (2003). Automated Support for Classifying Software Failure Reports. In *Proceedings of the 25th Conference on Software Engineering* (pp. 465-475).

Poellabauer, C., Abbasi, H., & Schwan, K. (2002). Cooperative run-time management of adaptive applications and distributed resources. In *Proceedings of the tenth ACM international conference on Multimedia* (pp. 402-411).

Poldner, M., & Kuchen, H. (2008). On implementing the farm skeleton. In []. New York: World Scientific Publishing.]. *Proceedings of the International Workshop on High-Level Parallel Programming and Applications*, *18*(1), 117–131.

Pollin, S., Mangharam, R., Bougard, B., Van Der Perre, L., Moerman, I., Rajkumar, R., & Catthoor, F. (2007). *MEERA: Cross-Layer Methodology for Energy Efficient Resource Allocation in Wireless Networks*. IEEE Trans. on Wireless Communications.

Preparata, F. P., Metze, G., & Chien, R. T. (1967). On the Connection Assignment Problem of Diagnosable Systems. *IEEE Transactions on Electronic Computers*, *16*(6), 848–854. doi:10.1109/PGEC.1967.264748

Presser, M., Barnaghi, P. M., Eurich, M., & Villalonga, C. (2009). The SENSEI project: Integrating the physical world with the digital world of the network of the future. *IEEE Communications Magazine*, *47*(4), 1. doi:10.1109/MCOM.2009.4907403

Ramani, S., Trivedi, K. S., & Dasarathy, B. (2001). Performance analysis of the CORBA notification service. In *Proceedings of the 20th IEEE Symposium on Reliable Distributed Systems* (pp. 227-236). Washington, DC: IEEE Computer Society.

Randell, B. (1975). System structure for software fault tolerance. In []. Washington, DC: IEEE Computer Society.]. *Proceedings of the International Conference on Reliable Software*, *10*(6), 437–449. doi:10.1145/800027.808467

Randell, B., Xu, J., & Zorzo, A. (1996). Software fault tolerance in object oriented systems: approaches, implementation and evaluation. In *First year report of Design for Validation* (pp. 213–226). DeVa.

Rao, R., Vrudhula, S., & Rakhmatov, D. N. (2003). Battery modeling for energy aware system design. *IEEE Computer*, *36*, 77–87.

Ratanchandani, P., & Kravets, R. (2003). A hybrid approach to internet connectivity for mobile ad hoc networks. In *Proceedings of the IEEE Conference on Wireless Communications and Networking*, New Orleans, LA (pp. 1522-1527).

Rellermeyer, J. S., & Alonso, G. (2007). Concierge: A service platform for resource-constrained devices. In *Proceedings of the European Conference on Computer Systems* (pp. 245-258). New York, NY: ACM Press.

Riehle, D., Buschmann, F., & Martin, R. C. (1998). *Pattern languages of program design 3*. Reading, MA: Addison-Wesley.

Riva, O. (2006, November). Contory: A middleware for the provisioning of context information on smart phones. In M. van Steen & M. Henning (Eds.), *Proceedings of the 7th International Conference of Middleware*, Melbourne, Australia (LNCS 4290, pp. 219-239).

Riva, O., & Toivonen, S. (2007). The dynamos approach to support contextaware service provisioning in mobile environments. *Journal of Systems and Software*, *80*(12), 1956–1972. doi:10.1016/j.jss.2007.03.009

Rosenschon, M., Mänz, T., Habermann, J., & Rakocevic, V. (2004, March). Performance analysis of Internet gateway discovery protocols in ad hoc networks. In *Proceedings of the IEEE Conference on Wireless Communications and Networking* (pp. 120-125).

Royon, Y. (2007). *Environnements d'exécution pour passerelles domestiques*. Unpublished doctoral dissertation, INSA de Lyon, Villeurbanne, France.

Royon, Y., Frénot, S., & Le Mouël, F. (2006). Virtualization of service gateways in multi-provider environments. In I. Gorton, G. T. Heineman, I. Crnkovic, H. W. Schmidt, J. A. Stafford, C. Syzperski et al. (Eds.), *Proceedings of the 9th International Symposium on Component-Based Software Engineering*, Stockholm, Sweden (LNCS 4063, pp. 385-392).

Royon, Y., & Frénot, S. (2007). Multiservice home gateways: Business model, execution environment, management infrastructure. *IEEE Communications Magazine*, *45*(10), 122–128. doi:10.1109/MCOM.2007.4342834

Ruiz, P. M., & Gomez-Skarmeta, A. F. (2005). Adaptive gateway discovery mechanisms to enhance internet connectivity for mobile ad hoc networks. *Ad Hoc & Sensor Wireless Networks*, *1*, 159–177.

Salehie, M., & Tahvildari, L. (2009). Self-adaptive software: Landscape and research challenges. *ACM Transactions on Autonomous and Adaptive Systems*, *4*(2), 14–55.

Sandeep, A., Sangita, M., & Vasudevan, V. (2004). Universal manager: Seamless management of enterprise mobile and non-mobile devices. In *Proceedings of the IEEE International Conference on Mobile Data Management* (pp. 320-331).

Sanz, C., Prieto, M., Papanikolaou, A., Miranda, M., & Catthoor, F. (2006). System-level process variability compensation on memory organization of dynamic applications: a case study. In *Proceedings of International Symposium on Quality Electronic Design* (pp. 376-382). Washington, DC: IEEE Computer Society.

Sarker, R. A., & Newton, C. S. (2007). *Optimization modelling: a practical approach*. Boca Raton, FL: CRC Press. doi:10.1201/9781420043112

Satoh, I. (2004). Software agents for ambient intelligence. In *Proceedings of the International Conference on Systems, Man and Cybernetics* (pp. 1147-1152). Washington, DC: IEEE Computer Society.

Schmidt, D. C. (2000). GPERF: A perfect hash function generator. In Martin, R. (Ed.), *More C++ gems* (pp. 461–491). Cambridge, UK: Cambridge University Press.

Schmidt, D. C., Stal, M., Rohnert, H., & Buschmann, F. (2000b). *Pattern-oriented software architecture: patterns for concurrent and networked objects* (*Vol. 2*). New York, NY: John Wiley & Sons.

Schollmeier, R. (2001). A definition of peer-to-peer networking for the classification of peer-to-peer architectures and applications. In *Proceedings of the First International Conference on Peer-to-Peer Computing.* (pp. 101-102). Washington, DC: IEEE Computer Society.

Scowen, R. S. (1993). Extended BNF-a generic base standard. In. *Proceedings of the Software Engineering Standards Symposium*, *3*, 6–2.

Sebastiani, F. (2002). Machine Learning in Automated Text Categorization. *ACM Computing Surveys, 34*, 1–47. doi:10.1145/505282.505283

Serafini, M., Bondavalli, A., & Suri, N. (2007). On-Line Diagnosis and Recovery: On the Choice and Impact of Tuning Parameters. *IEEE Transactions on Dependable and Secure Computing, 4*(4), 295–312. doi:10.1109/TDSC.2007.70210

Seshadri Sastry, K., & Prasad Babu, M. S. (2010). Adaptive modulation for OFDM system using fuzzy logic interface. In *Proceedings of the IEEE International Conference on Software Engineering and Service Sciences* (pp. 368-371).

Seyler, F., & Aniorté, P. (2004). A model driven integration process to manage component interoperability. In *Proceedings of the Conference on Software Engineering Research and Practice* (pp. 104-110).

Shang, Y., Ruml, W., Zhang, Y., & Fromherz, M. P. J. (2003). Localization from mere connectivity. In *Proceedings of the 4th ACM International Symposium on Mobile Ad Hoc Networking & Computing* (pp. 201-212).

Sharrock, R., Khalil, F., Monteil, T., Stolf, P., Aubert, H., Cocccetti, F., et al. (2009). Deployment and management of large planar reflectarray antennas simulation on grid. In *Proceedings of the 7th international workshop on Challenges of large applications in distributed environments*, Munich, Germany (pp. 17-26).

Shelton, C., & Koopman, P. (2003). Using architectural properties to model and measure graceful degradation. In R. de Lemos, C. Gacek, & A. Romanovsky (Eds.), *Proceedings of the Conference on Architecting Dependable Systems* (LNCS 2677, pp. 267-289).

Shen, G. C., & Liu, B. W. (2010). Research on application of Internet of things in electronic commerce. In *Proceedings of the International Symposium on Electronic Commerce and Security* (pp. 13-16).

Shi, Z., Dolwin, C., Steinke, B., & Droege, A. (2007). A OMA DM based software defined radio proof-of-concept demonstration platform. In *Proceedings of the IEEE 18th International Symposium on Indoor and Mobile Radio Communications* (pp. 1-5).

Shin, J., Chung, Y., Sun Ko, K., & Ik Eom, Y. (2008). Design and implementation of the management agent for mobile devices based on OMA DM. In *Proceedings of the 2nd International Conference on Ubiquitous Information Management and Communication.*

Shin, J., Zyuban, V., Hu, Z., Rivers, J. A., & Bose, P. (2007). A Framework for Architecture-Level Lifetime Reliability Modeling. In *Proceedings of the 37th Annual IEEE/IFIP International Conference on Dependable Systems and Networks* (pp. 534-543). Washington, DC: IEEE Computer Society.

Shnayder, V., Hempstead, M., Chen, B., Werner Allen, G., & Welsh, M. (2004). Simulating the power consumption of large-scale sensor network applications. In *Proceedings of the 2nd International Conference on Embedded Networked Sensor Systems* (pp. 188-200).

Sicard, S., Boyer, F., & De Palma, N. (2008). Using components for architecture based management. In *Proceedings of the 30th International Conference on Software Engineering* (Vol. 1-2, pp. 101-110).

Siddiqui, F., & Zeadally, S. (2006). Mobility management across hybrid wireless networks: Trends and challenges. *Computer Communications, 29*(9), 1363–1385. doi:10.1016/j.comcom.2005.09.003

Simoens, P., Deboosere, L., De Winter, D., De Turck, F., Dhoedt, N., & Demeester, P. (2006). Optimization Models for Application Migration to Support Mobile Thin Clients. In *Proceedings of EuroNGI Workshop.*

Smith, E. A. (2005). Communities of competence: New resources in the workplace. *Journal of Workplace Learning, 17*, 1. doi:10.1108/13665620510574423

Song, J.-H., Wong, V., & Leung, V. C. M. (2003, April 22-25). Load-aware on-demand routing (LAOR) protocol for mobile ad hoc networks. In *Proceedings of the 57th IEEE Semiannual Vehicular Technology Conference* (pp. 1753- 1757).

Spiegel, M. (1975). *Schaum's outline of theory and problems of probability and statistics.* New York, NY: McGraw Hill.

Srinivasan, J., Adve, S. V., Bose, P., & Rivers, J. A. (2004). Impact of Technology Scaling on Lifetime Reliability. In *Proceedings of the Intl. Conf. on Dependable Systems and Networks (DSN)*.

Srinivasan, J., Adve, S. V., Bose, P., & Rivers, J. A. (2005). Exploiting Structural Duplication for Lifetime Reliability Enhancement. In *Proceedings of the Intl. Symp. on Computer Architecture (ISCA)*.

State, R., Fester, O., & Zores, B. (2004). An extensible agent toolkit for device management. In *Proceedings of the IEEE/IFIP International Symposium on Network Operations and Management Symposium* (pp. 845-858).

Stavrou, K., & Trancoso, P. (2007). Thermal-aware scheduling for future chip multiprocessors. *EURASIP Journal on Embedded Systems*, 40–40.

Steinke, B., & Strohmenger, K. (2007). Advanced device self management through autonomics and reconfigurability. In *Proceedings of the 16ᵗʰ Mobile and Wireless Communications Summit* (pp.1-4).

Sterritt, R., & Bustard, D. (2003). Autonomic Computing - a means of achieving dependability? In *Proceedings of the 10th IEEE International Conference and Workshop on the Engineering of Computer-Based Systems*, Huntsville, AL (pp. 247-251).

Stiemerling, M., & Kiesel, S. (2009). A system for peer-to-peer video streaming in resource constrained mobile environments. In *Proceedings of the 1ˢᵗ Workshop on User-Provided Networking: Challenges and Opportunities* (pp. 25-30).

Su, J., Scott, J., Hui, P., Crowcroft, J., de Lara, E., Diot, C., et al. (2007, August). Haggle: Seamless networking for mobile applications. In J. Krumm, G. D. Abowd, A. Senevirante, & T. Strang (Eds.), *Proceedings of the 9ᵗʰ International Conference on Ubiquitous Computing*, Innsbruch, Austria (LNCS 4717, pp. 391-408).

Sullivan, M., & Chillarege, R. (1991). Software Defects and Their Impact on System Availability - A Study of Field Failures in Operating Systems. In *Proceedings of the 21st Symposium on Fault-Tolerant Computing* (pp. 2-9).

Sun, H., De Florio, V., Gui, N., & Blondia, C. (2007). Global Adaptation Framework for Quality of Experience of Mobile Services. In *Proceedings of the 2007 IEEE Three-Rivers Workshop on Soft Computing in Industrial Applications*.

Sun, H., De Florio, V., Gui, N., & Blondia, C. (2010). The missings ones: Key ingredients towards effective ambient assisted living systems. *In the Journal of Ambient Intelligence and Smart Environments, 2,* 1-12.

Sun, Y., Belding-Royer, E. M., & Perkins, C. E. (2002). Internet connectivity for ad hoc mobile networks. *International Journal of Wireless Information Networks, 9*(2), 75–88. doi:10.1023/A:1015399632291

Tack, N., Lafruit, G., Catthoor, F., & Lauwereins, R. (2005). A content quality driven energy management system for mobile 3D graphics. In *Proceedings of the IEEE workshop on Signal Processing Systems Design and Implementation*.

Taddia, C., & Mazzini, G. (2006). Fast algorithms for duty cycle measurement with random sampling technique. In *Proceedings of the International Conference on Wireless Communications and Mobile Computing*, Vancouver, Canada.

Taddia, C., Mazzini, G., & Rovatti, R. (2010, September 23-25). Duty cycle measurements under non controlled sampling: Part I. In *Proceedings of the 48ᵗʰ Midwestern Symposium on Circuits and Systems* (pp. 1043-1046).

Tan, F., Ardon, S., & Ott, M. (2007). UbiStore: Ubiquitous and opportunistic backup architecture. In *Proceedings of the Fifth Annual IEEE International Conference on Pervasive Computing and Communications*, White Plains, NY (pp. 71-78).

Tan, L., & Wang, N. (2010). Future internet: The Internet of things. In *Proceedings of the International Conference on Advanced Computer Theory and Engineering* (pp. 376-380).

Tarkoma, S., & Raatikainen, K. (2006). *State of the art review of distributed event systems* (Tech. Rep. No. C0-04). Helsinki, Finland: University of Helsinki.

Tock, Y., Naaman, N., Harpaz, A., & Gershinsky, G. (2005). Hierarchical clustering of message flows in a multicast data dissemination system. In *Proceedings of the International Conference on Parallel and Distributed Computing Systems* (pp. 320-326).

Tu, M. T., Griffel, F., Merz, M., & Lamersdorf, W. (1998). A plug-in architecture providing dynamic negotiation capabilities for mobile agents. In *Proceedings of the Second International Workshop on Mobile Agents* (pp. 222-236).

Tucek, J., Lu, S., Huang, C., Xanthos, S., & Zhou, Y. (2007). Triage: Diagnosing Production Run Failures at the User's Site. In *Proceedings of the 21st ACM SIGOPS Symposium on Operating Systems Principles* (pp. 131-144).

Vahdat, A., & Becker, D. (2000). *Epidemic routing for partially connected ad hoc networks* (Tech. Rep. No. CS-2000-06). Durham, NC: Duke University.

Vaidya, N. H., & Pradham, D. K. (1994). Safe System Level Diagnosis. *IEEE Transactions on Computers*, *43*(3), 367–370. doi:10.1109/12.272443

van der Spek, S. (2009). Mapping pedestrian movement: Using tracking technologies in Koblenz. In Gartner, G., & Rehrl, K. (Eds.), *Location based services and telecartography II: From sensor fusion to context models* (pp. 95–118). Berlin, Germany: Springer-Verlag. doi:10.1007/978-3-540-87393-8_7

Van Renesse, R., Birman, K. P., & Vogels, W. (2003). Astrolabe: A robust and scalable technology for distributed system monitoring, management, and data mining. [TOCS]. *ACM Transactions on Computer Systems*, *21*(2), 164–206. doi:10.1145/762483.762485

Venkatachalam, V., & Franz, M. (2005). Power Reduction Techniques for Microprocessor Systems. *ACM Computing Surveys*, *37*(3), 195–237. doi:10.1145/1108956.1108957

Vienne, P., & Sourrouille, J.-L. (2005). A middleware for autonomic QoS management based on learning. In *Proceedings of the 5th International Workshop on Software Engineering and Middleware* (pp. 1-8). New York, NY: ACM Press.

Vigorito, C. M., Ganesan, D., & Barto, A. G. (2007). Adaptive control of duty cycling in energy-harvesting wireless sensor networks. In *Proceedings of the 4th Annual Conference on Sensor, Mesh, and Ad Hoc Communications and Networks*, San Diego, CA (pp. 21-30).

Vogel, A., Vasudevan, B., Benjamin, M., & Villalba, T. (1999). *C++ programming with CORBA*. New York: John Wiley & Sons, Inc.

von Neumann, J. (1956). Probabilistic logic and the synthesis of reliable organisms from unreliable components. In C. E. Shannon & J. McCarthy (Eds.), *Automata studies* (pp. 43–98). Princeton, NJ: Princeton University Press.

Wakikawa, R., Malinen, J., Perkins, C., Nilsson, A., & Tuominen, A. (2006). *Global connectivity for IPv6 mobile ad hoc networks*. Retrieved from http://tools.ietf.org/html/draft-wakikawa-manet-globalv6-05

Wang, X. H., Iqbal, M., & Zhou, X. (2008, May 30-31). Design and implementation of a dual-radio wireless mesh network testbed for healthcare. In *Proceedings of the 5th International Conference on Information Technology and Applications in Biomedicine*, Shenzhen, China.

Wang, H., Miranda, M., Papanikolaou, A., Catthoor, F., & Dehaene, W. (2005). Variable tapered pareto buffer design and implementation allowing run-time configuration for low-power embedded SRAMs. *IEEE Trans. VLSI Syst.*, *13*(10), 1127–1135. doi:10.1109/TVLSI.2005.859480

Wang, M., & Li, B. (2007). R2: Random push with random network coding in live peer-to-peer streaming. *IEEE Journal on Selected Areas in Communications*, 25.

Weber, D. G. (1989). Formal specification of fault-tolerance and its relation to computer security. *ACM SIGSOFT Software Engineering Notes*, *14*(3), 273–277. doi:10.1145/75200.75240doi:10.1145/75200.75240

Weinstein, Y. (2007). *A universal operator theoretic framework for quantum fault tolerance*. Paper presented at the First International Conference on Quantum Error Correction.

Wenger, E. (2000). Communities of practice: The key to knowledge strategy. In Lesser, E. L., Fontaine, M. A., & Slusher, J. A. (Eds.), *Knowledge and communities*. Boston, MA: Butterworth Heinemann. doi:10.1016/B978-0-7506-7293-1.50004-4

Whitney, M. G. (2009). *Practical fault tolerance for quantum circuits*. Unpublished doctoral dissertation, University of California Berkeley, Berkeley, CA.

Wiegand, T., Sullivan, G. J., Bjontegaard, G., & Luthra, A. (2003). Overview of the H.264/AVC video coding standard. *IEEE Transaction on Circuits and Systems for Video Technology, 13*(7).

Wiljakka, J., Soininen, J., Sundquist, J., & Sipilä, T. (2004). IPv6 enabling IMS-based peer-to-peer services in 3GPP and 3GPP2 cellular networks. *Journal of Internet Technology, 5*(2), 67–73.

Wing, R. (2006). RFID applications in construction and facilities management. *ITcon, 11*, 711–721.

Wireless Sensors. (2010). *SB110-T datasheet*. Retrieved from http://www.wirelesssensors.com/pdf/WSI%20SB110-T%20v4.5.pdf

Xu, J., Kalbarczyc, Z., & Iyer, R. K. (1999). Networked Windows NT System Field Data Analysis. In *Proceedings of the Pacific Rim Symposium on Dependable Computing* (pp. 178-185).

Yan, B., & Huang, G. W. (2009). Supply chain information transmission based on RFID and Internet of things. In *Proceedings of the International Colloquium on Computing, Communication, Control and Management* (pp. 166-169).

Yang, P., Wong, C., Marchal, P., Catthoor, F., Desmet, D., Verkest, D., & Lauwereins, R. (2001). Energy-Aware Runtime Scheduling for Embedded-Multiprocessor SOCs. *IEEE Des. Test., 18*, 46–58. doi:10.1109/54.953271

Yeo, I., Liu, C. C., & Kim, E. J. (2008). Predictive dynamic thermal management for multicore systems. In *Proceedings of the 45th annual conference on Design automation* (pp. 734-739).

Yi, Y., Kwon, T. J., & Gerla, M. (2001). A load aWare routing (LWR) based on local information. In *Proceedings of the 12th IEEE International Symposium on Personal, Indoor and Mobile Radio Communications*, San Diego, CA (Vol. 2, pp. 65-69).

Yoon, H., Kim, J., Tany, F., & Hsieh, R. (2008). On-demand video streaming in mobile opportunistic networks. In *Proceedings of the 6th Annual International Conference on Pervasive Computing and Communication* (pp. 80-89).

Yu, L., Li, X. M., Zhong, J., & Xiong, Y. N. (2010). Research on the innovation of strategic business model in green agricultural products based on Internet of things (IOT). In *Proceedings of the International Conference on e-Business and Information System Security* (pp. 1-3).

Yuan, C., Lao, N., Wen, J. R., Li, J., Zhang, Z., Wang, Y. M., et al. (2006). Automated Known Problem Diagnosis with Event Traces. In *Proceedings of the EuroSys ACM Conference* (pp. 375-388).

Zhang, L., Zhao, Z., Shu, Y., Wang, L., & Yang, O. W. W. (2002). Load balancing of multipath source routing in ad hoc networks. In *Proceedings of the IEEE International Conference on Communications* (Vol. 5, pp. 3197-3201).

Zhang, X., Kurose, J., Levine, B. N., Towsley, D., & Zhang, H. (2006, September). Study of a bus-based disruption tolerant network: Mobility modeling and impact on routing. In *Proceedings of the Mobicom Conference*, Montreal, QC, Canada (pp. 195-206).

Zhang, Y., Parikh, D., Sankaranarayanan, K., Skadron, K., & Stan, M. (2003). *HotLeakage: A Temperature-Aware Model of Subthreshold and Gate Leakage for Architects* (Tech. Rep. No. CS-2003-05). Charlottesville, VA: University of Virginia, Deptartment of Computer Science.

Zhao, W., Ammar, M., & Zegura, E. (2005, April). Controlling the mobility of multiple data transport ferries in a delay-tolerant network. In *Proceedings of the IEEE Annual Joint Conference INFOCOM*, Miami, FL (pp. 1407-1418).

Zhe, M., & Catthoor, F. (2007). *Systematic Methodology for Real-Time Cost-Effective Mapping of Dynamic Concurrent Task-Based Systems on Heterogeneous Platforms.* New York: Springer.

Zheng, A. X., Lloyd, J., & Brewer, E. (2004). Failure Diagnosis Using Decision Trees. In *Proceedings of the 1st IEEE Conference on Autonomic Computing* (pp. 36-43).

Zhou, X., Wang, X. H., Iqbal, M., & Yan, L. (2009). A handheld mobile device for wireless mesh networks in healthcare. In *Proceedings of the 2nd IEEE International Symposium on IT in Medicine & Education*, Jinan, China (pp. 1070-1073).

Zschaler, S. (2004). Formal specification of non-functional properties of component-based software. *Software and Systems Modeling*, *9*(2), 161–201. doi:10.1007/s10270-009-0115-6

About the Contributors

Vincenzo De Florio obtained his "Laurea in Scienze dell'Informazione" (MSc, Computer Science) from the University of Bari (Italy, 1987) and his PhD in Engineering from the University of Leuven (Belgium, 2000). He was researcher for eight years and part-time professor for three years with the University of Leuven. He is currently a researcher with the Performance Analysis of Telecommunication Systems (PATS) research group at the University of Antwerp, where he is responsible for PATS' branch on adaptive and dependable systems. Vincenzo De Florio is also a researcher of IBBT, the Flemish Interdisciplinary Institute for BroadBand Technology. He published about seventy reviewed research papers, fifteen of which are in international research journals, and the book "Application-layer fault-tolerance protocols," edited by IGI Global. He is Co-Chair of workshop ADAMUS (the third Workshop on Adaptive and DependAble Mobile and Ubiquitous Systems, http://www.adamus.ua.ac.be), and Editor-in-Chief of the *International Journal of Adaptive, Resilient and Autonomic Systems*.

* * *

Philippe Aniorté is Professor in Computer Science at the University "Pau et Pays de l'Adour" (UPPA) – France since 2006. He is entitled to supervise research since 2004 when he defended his HDR (Habilitation à Diriger des Recherches, specific French grade) at UPPA. His Ph.D. Thesis was defended in 1990 at the University "Paul Sabatier" (UPS) - Toulouse - France. He teaches in Bayonne at the Institute of Technology (IUT), in the Computer Science Department, since 1990. As a researcher he works in the Computer Science Laboratory at UPPA (LIUPPA). Since 2009, he is at the head of this laboratory who counts with 60 members. He works in the team called MOVIES which is mainly dedicated to Software Engineering. More precisely, he deals with engineering of complex heterogeneous distributed systems based on reuse. His approach is in keeping with the recent trends to develop software and systems. During several years based on the "component" paradigm promoted by the Object Management Group (OMG), his works have addressed the "agent" paradigm to deal with adaptability, and more recently the "service" paradigm. His current researches deal with a MDE (Model Driven Engineering) approach for the design and the implementation of complex systems by managing "multi-paradigm modeling". Since several years, the field of experimentation of its works is mainly e-learning and e-training.

Rocco Aversa is Associate Professor in Computer Science at the Department of Information Engineering of the Second University of Naples. His research interests are in the area of parallel and distributed systems. The research themes include: mobile agents in the distributed computing; simulation tools for performance analysis of parallel applications; innovative middleware software to enhance the Grid and

Cloud computing platforms. Such scientific activity is documented on scientific journals, international and national conference proceedings. Rocco Aversa participated to various research projects supported by national organizations and in collaboration with foreign academic institutions. In 2005 he was appointed in the board of the directors of the consortium "Centro Regionale Information e Communication Technology" as the representative of the Second University of Naples.

Chris Blondia obtained his Master in Science and Ph.D. in Mathematics, both from the University of Ghent (Belgium) in 1977 and 1982 respectively. In 1983 he joined Philips Belgium, where he was a researcher in the Philips Research Laboratory Belgium (PRLB). Between August 1991 and end 1994 he was an Associate Professor in the Computer Science Department of the University of Nijmegen (The Netherlands). In 1995 he joined the Department of Mathematics and Computer Science of the University of Antwerp (UA), where he is currently a Full Professor and head of the research group "Performance Analysis of Telecommunication Systems" (PATS - www.pats.ua.ac.be). The group is member of the Flemish Interdisciplinary institute for Broad Band Technology (IBBT) (www.ibbt.be). His main research interests are related to performance evaluation of communication systems. He is editor of the Journal of Network and Computer Applications and of the International Journal of Electronics and Communications. He is co-founder of the spin-off company Wishbone (www.wishbone.be).

Laurent Broto received his Ph.D. from the University Paul Sabatier in 2008. After a postdoctoral stay at Oak Ridge National Laboratory – TN - USA, he was recruited as Associate Professor in computer science at the Polytechnic National Institute of Toulouse (France).

Iacopo Carreras is a Technical Group Leader at CREATE-NET, Italy. He received a PhD in Computer Science and M.Sc degree Telecommunications Engineering from the University of Pisa, Italy, in 2001 and 2007, respectively. From 2001 to 2003 he worked as software engineer at Netikos (Telecom Italia Group). In 2003, he joined the iNSPIRE (Networking and Security Solutions for Pervasive Computing Systems: Research & Experimentation) group at CREATE-NET research center. His research interests span the areas of pervasive and mobile computing, autonomic networking with a specific focus in the areas of performance evaluation, biologically-inspired paradigms, large-scale networks and complex systems.

Gabriella Carrozza was born in Naples, Italy, July 17th, 1981. She graduated cum laude in Computer Science Engineering at the "Federico II" University of Naples (UoN), Italy, in 2005. From 2005 to 2008 she has been Ph.D. student in Computer Engineering at UoN. She is mainly interested into the dependability of off-the-shelf based safety critical systems, especially in the field of air traffic control, as well as on software faults diagnosis for such systems. Gabriella Carrozza is currently employed at the SESM (Sistemi Evoluti per la Sistemistica e i Modelli) consortium as research project manager, in the field of dependable systems and open source software in the embedded system domain. She has been serving in the Program Committees of international workshops in this field, as well as a reviewer for several international conferences in the dependable computing community. She is currently involved as project leader into the SESAR European programme.

Francky Catthoor received a Ph.D. in Electrical Engg. from the K.U.Leuven, Belgium in 1987. Since then, he has headed several research domains in the area of architectural methodologies and system synthesis for embedded multimedia and telecom applications, all within the SSET division at IMEC, Leuven, Belgium. His current research activities mainly belong to the field of system-level exploration, with emphasis on data storage/transfer and concurrency exploitation, both in customized and programmable (parallel) instruction-set processors.

Han-Chieh Chao is a jointly appointed Professor of the Department of Electronic Engineering and Institute of Computer Science & Information Engineering, National Ilan University, I-Lan, Taiwan. He also holds a joint professorship of the Department of Electrical Engineering, National Dong Hwa University, Hualien, Taiwan. His research interests include High Speed Networks, Wireless Networks and IPv6 based Networks and Applications. He received his MS and Ph.D. degrees in Electrical Engineering from Purdue University in 1989 and 1993 respectively. Dr. Chao is also serving as an IPv6 Steering Committee member and Deputy Director of R&D division of the NICI Taiwan, Co-chair of the Technical Area for IPv6 Forum Taiwan. Dr. Chao is an IEEE senior member, IET and BCS Fellows.

Chi-Yuan Chen received the M.S. degree in electrical engineering from National Dong Hwa University, Hualien, Taiwan, in 2007. He is currently working toward the Ph.D. degree in electrical engineering at National Dong Hwa University. He is a student member of IEEE and ACM. His research interests include wireless networking, communication networks, and network security.

Jiann-Liang Chen was born in Taiwan on December 15, 1963. He received the Ph.D. degree in Electrical Engineering from National Taiwan University, Taipei, Taiwan in 1989. Since August 1997, he has been with the Department of Computer Science and Information Engineering of National Dong Hwa University. Prof. Chen joins the Department of Electrical Engineering, National Taiwan University of Science and Technology, as a full professor and Vice Dean now. His current research interests are directed at cellular mobility management, digital home network and personal communication systems.

Yuh-Shyan Chen received the B.S. degree in Computer Science from Tamkang University, Taiwan, R. O. C., in June 1988 and the M.S. and Ph.D. degrees in Computer Science and Information Engineering from the National Central University, Taiwan, R. O. C., in June 1991 and January 1996, respectively. Since 2006, he has been a Professor at the Department of Computer Science and Information Engineering, National Taipei University, Taiwan. Prof. Chen now serves as Editor-in-Chief of International Journal of Ad Hoc and Ubiquitous Computing, Regional Editor (Asia and Pacific) of IET Commuications, and Editorial Board of Telecommunication System Journal, EURASIP Journal on Wireless Communications and Networking, International Journal of Communication Systems, Mobile Information Systems, and Journal of Internet Technology. His paper wins the 2001 IEEE 15th ICOIN-15 Best Paper Award. Prof. Chen was a recipient of the 2005 Young Scholar Research Award, National Chung Cheng University, R.O.C.. His recent research topics include wireless communications and mobile computing, and next-generation personal communication system. Dr. Chen is a senior member of the IEEE Communication Society.

Chun-I Fan was born in Tainan, Taiwan. He received his M.S. degree in Computer Science and Information Engineering from National Chiao Tung University, Taiwan, in 1993, and the Ph.D. degree in Electrical Engineering at National Taiwan University in 1998. From 1999 to 2003, he was an associate researcher and project leader of Telecommunication Laboratories, Chunghwa Telecom Co., Ltd., Taiwan. In 2003, he joined the faculty of the Department of Computer Science and Engineering, National Sun Yat-sen University, Kaohsiung, Taiwan to be an assistant professor. He had been an associate professor from 2006 and a full professor from 2010. He won the Dragon Thesis Award from Acer Foundation and Best Thesis Award from Institute of Information & Computing Machinery in 1999, Best Student Paper Awards in National Conference on Information Security 1998 and 2007. He also was the editor-in-chief of Information Security Newsletter, Chinese Cryptology and Information Security Association. He served as program co-chair, international advisor, and program committee members of many international conferences. His current research interests include applied cryptology, information security, wireless and mobile communication security, and he has published over 100 papers in journals, books, and conference proceedings.

Flavio Frattini is graduated in Computer Engineering at Università di Napoli (UoN) Federico II (Italy). He is Research Fellow at Consorzio Interuniversitario Nazionale per l'Informatica (CINI), and since July 1, 2010 also at Institute of High Performance Computing and Networking (ICAR) of Italian National Research Council (CNR). His research is related to Wireless Sensor Networks (WSN), in particular localization algorithms for WSN, Fuzzy Inference Systems, Mobile Systems and various aspects of Distributed Systems.

Stéphane Frénot is associate professor at the Center for Innovation in Telecommunication and Integration of Services (CITI Lab.), Telecommunications Department of the National Institute for Applied Sciences of Lyon (INSA Lyon, France). He leads the Amazones (AMbient Architectures: Service-Oriented, Networked, Efficient and Secured) INRIA team. His main interests are middlewares, component instrumentation, component security, deployment and management, constrained devices and specially home gateways.

Aniruddha Gokhale is an Associate Professor in the Electrical Engineering and Computer Science Department, and a Senior Research Scientist at the Institute for Software Integrated Systems (ISIS) both at Vanderbilt University. At ISIS/VU, he manages a vibrant research group comprising a mix of several graduate students and staff engineers. His primary research interests are in blending software engineering with systems to solve challenging systems problems, notably in the area of cyber physical systems. In this space he focuses on real-time middleware optimizations, model-driven engineering of component-based applications, deployment and configuration issues, and distributed resource management. He has led DARPA, NSF and industry funded projects involving modeling and middleware solutions, networking solutions, and distributed dynamic resource management. He has been awarded the NSF CAREER award. His research has led to the open source CoSMIC (www.dre.vanderbilt.edu/cosmic) model-driven engineering project at Vanderbilt.

Ning Gui (BSc, 1999; MSc, 2002) received his BS degree in information engineering from Central South University (China) in 1999, and his master's in Computer Science from the same University in 2002. From 2002 to 2006, he worked as lecturer in the Central South University. He is currently a PhD candidate of University of Antwerp, PATS Research Group and a research assistant for the IBBT (Institute of Broad Band Technology). His research interests include adaptive software architecture, service component model especially on embedded system. Ning Gui has published more than 20 reviewed research papers. He also serves as program committee member for several international conferences and reviewer for several journals.

Daniel Hagimont is Professor at Polytechnic National Institute of Toulouse and a member of the IRIT laboratory, where he leads a group working on operating systems, distributed systems and middleware. His current research addresses the design and implementation of an autonomic management system for distributed software infrastructures. Daniel Hagimont received a Ph.D. from Polytechnic National Institute of Grenoble in 1993. After a Postdoc at the University of British Columbia, Vancouver, in 1994, he joined INRIA Grenoble in 1995. He took his Professor position in Toulouse in 2005.

Joe Hoffert recently received his Ph.D. in the Department of Electrical Engineering and Computer Science (EECS) at Vanderbilt University. His research focuses on Quality of Service (QoS) support for the infrastructure of the Global Information Grid (GIG). He is currently involved with the evaluation of the Object Management Group's (OMG) Data Distributed Service (DDS), a publish and subscribe service supporting a wide array of real-time and other QoS properties. While previously working for Boeing (St. Louis), he was involved with model-based integration of embedded systems as well as with virtual and constructive simulations. He has been designing and developing distributed systems for over 15 years. He received his B.A. in Math and Computer Science from Mount Vernon Nazarene College, Mt. Vernon, OH in 1986 and his M.S. in Computer Science from the University of Cincinnati, Cincinnati, OH in 1990.

Muddesar Iqbal is working as a Director of Faculty of Computer Science and Information Technology, at University of Gujrat, Pakistan. He started his research in the area of wireless mesh network at Kingston University on MSc level in 2006. Later in 2007 he was upgraded to PhD on receiving EPSRC studentship and completed his PhD in the year 2010. Dr. Iqbal has taught British Computer Society (BCS), Association of Business Executive (ABE) courses at several Institutes in London. He has received ABE appreciation award for tutoring the prize winner in computer fundamentals modules in 2006. He also received Foreign Expert Certificate from State Administration of Foreign Experts Affairs, People's Republic of China in 2008. He won another Award of Appreciation from ABE UK for tutoring the prize winner in Information System Project management module, in 2010. He has published several papers in the area of wireless networks targeting its application in healthcare and emergency and disaster recovery.

Jérôme Lacouture obtained his M.S. degree in Cognitive Science from the University of Bordeaux 2, France in 2004, and the Ph.D. degree in computer science from the University of Pau et des Pays de l'Adour, France in 2008. He has joined the Laboratory of Analysis and Architectures of Systems (LAAS-CNRS), for a first postdoctoral position on the adaptability management for autonomous mobile group communication. He is actually a Post-Doc on cooperative management of systems in the SMAC

(Cooperative Multi-Agent Systems) team at the Institute of research of Informatics of Toulouse (IRIT) supported by the RTRA-STAE (Réseau Thématique de Recherche Avancée "Sciences et Technologies pour l'Aéronautique et l'Espace). His research interests include adaptive distributed architectures, self-adaptation, service oriented computing, component and agent paradigms, and semantic aspects.

Mieke Leeman received her master's degrees in engineering and in artificial intelligence at the Katholieke Universiteit Leuven, Belgium. In the course of these studies, she co-developed RAFT-net, a reliable and fault-tolerant framework for parallelizing master-worker applications, which was presented at PDP 2003. Her main focuses and interests are on software design, parallel and distributed computing, optimizations, networking, video systems and video analysis, operating systems. She started her career at T&T Solutions, Belgium, as an analyst-programmer of automated services. Her video experience originates from her former position as video processing software engineer at Vigitec, Belgium. She worked on a system for analyzing video content in the surveillance domain. Currently she holds the position of software engineer at Cisco, where she designs and develops embedded software for video-content-processing devices. She also contributes to the management and continuous improvement of the test environment of these devices.

Rahul Malik is a Ph.D. student in the Department of Computer Science, University of Illinois. His research is about video processing, HCI, and camera placement/management.

Jose Manuel Camacho was born in Madrid, Spain in 1984. He received the Telecommunication Engineering degree in 2008 and the Master's Degree in Telematics in 2010 from the University Carlos III of Madrid, Spain (UC3M). Since 2009, he holds a Ph.D. student position at the Telematics department of UC3M and recently in 2010 has actively participated in the TRILOGY research project founded by the European Commission, conducting research activities in the field of multi-path routing protocol design, implementation and validation.

Leo Marcus has been a Research Scientist at The Aerospace Corporation since 1980. After receiving his Ph. D. in Mathematics (Model Theory) from the Hebrew University of Jerusalem in 1975 he taught at the University of California, Santa Barbara and Los Angeles campuses, and worked at USC Information Sciences Institute. His research in computer science related topics has ranged from formal methods (program verification) to computer security, security architectures, cryptography, fault tolerance, and quantum information science.

Beniamino Di Martino is full Professor at the Second University of Naples (Italy), affiliated with Dept. of Information Engineering. He is author of 6 international books and more than 150 publications in international journals and conferences. He participated to various research projects supported by national and international organizations. He acted as evaluator of international scientific projects. He is editorial board member and chair of international journals. His research interests include: Automated Program Analysis and Transformation, Semantic based Information Retrieval, Semantic Web and Semantic Web Services, Compiler Techniques for High Performance Cluster and Grid Computing, Mobile and Intelligent Agents, Parallel Computing and Architectures,Reverse Engineering, Image analysis.

Gianluca Mazzini was born in Bologna, Italy, on January 3, 1968. He received the Laurea degree in Electronic Engineering (with honors) and the Ph.D. in Electronic Engineering and Computer Science from the University of Bologna, Bologna, Italy, in 1992 and 1996, respectively. In 1996 he joined the University of Ferrara, Italy, where he currently is an Associate Professor of Telecommunications. He teaches Telecommunication Networks; Internet and UMTS; Telecommunication Network Laboratory; Internet Security; Digital Transmission Systems; and Multimedia Communications. His research interests are related to: spread spectrum communications; application of chaotic system to telecommunications; non-linear dynamical system modeling; next generation of cellular/ambient systems; wireless LAN architectures, routing and protocols; sensor networks; Internet mobile computing; and routing and security. He is author or co-author of more than 200 papers. He is an IEEE senior member.

Daniele Miorandi is the head of the iNSPIRE Area at CREATE-NET, Italy. He received a PhD in Communications Engineering from Univ. of Padova, Italy, in 2005, and a Laurea degree (summa cum lauda) in Communications Engineering from Univ. of Padova, Italy, in 2001. He joined CREATE-NET in Jan. 2005, where he is leading the iNSPIRE (Networking and Security Solutions for Pervasive Computing Systems: Research & Experimentation). His research interests include bio-inspired approaches to networking and service provisioning in large-scale computing systems, modelling and performance evaluation of wireless networks, prototyping of wireless mesh solutions. Dr. Miorandi has co-authored more than 90 papers in internationally refereed journals and conferences. He serves on the Steering Committee of various international events (WiOpt, Autonomics, ValueTools), for some of which he was a co-founder (Autonomics and ValueTools). He also serves on the TPC of leading conferences in the networking field, including, e.g., IEEE INFOCOM, IEEE ICC, IEEE Globecom. He is a member of IEEE, ACM and ICST.

Thierry Monteil is assistant professor in computer science at INSA of Toulouse and researcher at LAAS-CNRS. He has a Doctorate in parallel computing and Certified Engineer Degree in computer science and applied mathematics. He works on parallel computing (LANDA parallel environment), Grid resources management (AROMA project), computer and network modeling, autonomous policies to improve performance on distributed applications and parallelization of large electromagnetic simulation. He has managed a SUN center of excellence in the field of grid and cluster for network applications and a Cisco academy.

Frédéric Le Mouël is associate professor in the National Institute for Applied Sciences of Lyon (INSA Lyon, France), Telecommunications Department, Center for Innovation in Telecommunication and Integration of Services (CITI Lab.) (2004-). He is also member of the AMbient Architectures: Service-Oriented, Networked, Efficient, Secure research group at INRIA (Amazones Team). He holds a master's degree in Languages and Operating Systems (1997) and a Ph.D. degree in Computer Science and Telecommunications (2003) from the University of Rennes 1, France. His dissertation focused on an adaptive environment for distributed executions of applications in a mobile computing context. His main interests are service-oriented architectures and middleware, specifically in the fields of dynamic and autonomic configuration, adaptation, composition, orchestration of services. He is specially studying these topics in the domains of constrained and mobile devices in ambient intelligent environments.

Satyakiran Munaga received masters degree in VLSI Design Tools and Technology from Indian Institute of Technology Delhi, India in 2002. He is a research scholar at Philips Research, Eindhoven from Sept'01-Nov'01, research associate at IISc Banaglore and IIT Delhi from Feb'02-May'04, and design engineer at Intel, Bangalore from Jun'04-Sept'05. Since Oct'05 he is part of IMEC's Technology aware design team and also a PhD candidate at the University of Leuven, Belgium. His research intertests include design and control of reliable, low-power, and real-time electronic systems in advanced IC technologies.

Klara Nahrstedt is a Professor in the Department of Computer Science, University of Illinois. Her research is about Quality of Service, Multimedia networking for wired and wireless network, Tele-immersive system.

Michele Di Natale is Dean of the Engineering Faculty at the Second University of Naples. He is full Professor of Hydraulic Works. His research activities deal with scientific and technical issues relating to water, with particularly reference to the management of water resources, water supplies and drainage networks, protection hydrogeology of the area and the processes of coastal dynamics. He participates in a number of national and international research projects. He also developed an intense activity as a technical consultant of national and international companies, by taking part in the execution of important hydraulic engineering works in different parts of the world.

Roberto Natella received the M.Sc degree cum laude in Computer Science Engineering from the University of Naples Federico II in 2007. He was research fellow at Consorzio Interuniversitario Nazionale per l'Informatica (CINI) within the framework of the COSMIC project. He is currently a Ph.D. student at the University of Naples Federico II. His research interests include operating systems and software dependability, and in particular novel methodologies for dependability assessment based on software fault injection.

Julien Ponge is an Associate Professor in Computer Science and Engineering at INSA de Lyon, a leading engineering school in France. He teaches in the Department of Telecommunications, Services and Usages while he does his research activities as part of the CITI Laboratory / INRIA in the Amazones group. Prior to joining INSA-Lyon, he obtained a PhD in Computer Science and Engineering from Université Blaise Pascal, Clermont-Ferrand, France, as well as a PhD under cotutelle agreements from the University of New South Wales, Sydney, Australia. He was also a temporary lecturer at ISIMA, the computer science and engineering school of Université Blaise Pascal. His current research interests cover middlewares, service-oriented architectures, next-generation software distribution and deployment.

Lisardo Prieto was born in Madrid, Spain in 1981 and received the Technical Computer Science Engineering [Systems] degree in 2007 from the Complutense University of Madrid, Spain (UCM) and the Computer Science Engineering [AI] degree in 2010 from the University Carlos III of Madrid, Spain (UC3M). He is currently a researcher and teaching assistant in the UC3M, currently researching about interdomain multi-path routing protocols. He has been involved in several international research projects related with protocol design, protocol engineering, network management, advanced networks and multimedia systems. Some of the recent research projects funded by the European Commission in which he has participated are: TRILOGY and MUSE. He has also participated in national research projects (in Spain) such as CONPARTE.

Stefano Russo is Chairman of the Curriculum in Computer Engineering at Università di Napoli (UoN) Federico II (Italy), Deputy Head of the Department of Computer and Systems Engineering (DIS), and Director of the "C. Savy" Laboratory of CINI. He graduated cum laude in Electronic Engineering at UoN in 1988, and received the Ph.D. in Electronics and Computer Engineering in 1993. He became assistant professor in 1994, associate professor in 1998, and professor in 2002. He leads the MOBILAB research group on distributed and mobile systems at DIS (www.mobilab.unina.it). He has published over 100 scientific papers in these research fields.

Guillaume Salagnac is an associate professor in the Information Technology department of INSA-Lyon University, and a member of the CITI research laboratory, in the INRIA Amazones research group. He holds a PhD (2008) from Grenoble University, where he studied real-time automatic memory management for embedded Java applications. After that, he was a post-doctoral researcher at the CSIRO ICT Centre in Brisbane, Australia, where he worked on high-level programming for Wireless Sensor networks. His current research interests lie in the area of programming languages and operating systems for embedded platforms.

Douglas C. Schmidt is a Professor at Vanderbilt University and the Deputy Director of Research and Chief Technology Officer at the Software Engineering Institute. He has published 9 books and more than 450 technical papers covering a wide range of software-related topics, including patterns, optimization techniques, and empirical analyses of object-oriented frameworks and domain-specific modeling environments that facilitate the development of DRE middleware and mission-critical applications running over data networks and embedded system interconnects. Dr. Schmidt has also led the development of ACE, TAO, CIAO, and CoSMIC for the past two decades. These technologies are DRE middleware frameworks and model-driven tools used in many domains, including aerospace, datacom/telecom, financial services, medical engineering, and massively multiplayer online gaming. Dr. Schmidt received B.S. and M.A. degrees in Sociology from the College of William and Mary and an M.S. and a Ph.D. in Computer Science from the University of California, Irvine.

Rémi Sharrock holds a Certified Engineering degree in Networks and Telecommunications from INSA Toulouse. He obtained his M.S. in 2007 from the National Polytechnic Institute of Toulouse. He is now a Ph.D. student in grid computing and applications.

Patricia Stolf is an assistant professor since 2005. She teaches computer sciences at Toulouse University. She obtained a Ph.D. in 2004 in the LAAS-CNRS laboratory on Tasks scheduling on clusters for remote services with quality of service. She is a member of the IRIT laboratory and currently working in the field of autonomic computing for high performance applications on grids. Her research interests are large-scale distributed systems such as grid computing, resources management, scheduling and distributed algorithms. She is involved in different national research projects and also participates in the european COST project IC0804 "Energy Efficiency in Large Scale Distributed Systems", she investigates how to improve energy consumption in autonomic systems.

Hong Sun (BSc, 2004; MSc, 2006) received his degree in information engineering from Southeast University (China) in 2004, and his master's in electronics from University of York (UK) in 2006. He is currently a PhD candidate of University of Antwerp, PATS Research Group and a research assistant for the IBBT (Institute of Broad Band Technology). His research interests include ambient assisted living, adaptive system, service oriented architecture and semantic service matching. Hong Sun has published more than 20 reviewed research papers. He received the 'IBM PhD Fellowship 2009-2010'; and was also the winner of "FITCE.be Young ICT Personality 2008' competition'. He is a board member of the IEEE CIS Society, Benelux Chapter Board, and he also serves as program committee member for several international conferences. Hong Sun is expected to receive his PhD degree in May, 2010, and will join AGFA Healthcare since June, 2010.

Chiara Taddia was born in Argenta (FE), Italy, on February, 21st 1979. She received her Dr Eng Degree in Electronic Engineering on December, 18th 2003 from the University of Ferrara, with the thesis "Retransmission Mechanisms for Wireless Sensor Networks". On January 2004 she started her Ph.D research activities with the TLC GROUP in the Department of Engineering of the University of Ferrara. On March 20, 2007, she defended her P.h.D thesis "Resource Allocation in Wireless Networks". From February 2007 to September 2008 she collaborated with TLC group at the University of Ferrara, as a PostDoc researcher. Since October 2008 she works with the R&D of Lepida SpA. Since 2007 she teaches Multimedia Communications at the University of Ferrara.

Salvatore Venticinque is Assistant Professor at Department of Information Engineering of the Second University of Naples. He is adjunct professor in "Computer Programming" and "Computer Architecture" in regular courses. He is involved in research activities dealing with Parallel, Grid an Cloud computing, Pervasive and Ubiquitous Computing, Mobile Agents programming for distributed systems. He is author of several publications in international journals, books, and conferences in collaboration with international research organizations and academic institutions. He has participated to research projects supported by national and international organizations. He is chair and committee member of several international conferences and scientific board.

Francisco Valera was born in Ciudad Real, Spain in 1974 and received the Telecommunication Engineering degree in 1998 from the Technical University of Madrid, Spain (UPM) and the Ph.D. in Telecommunications in 2002 from the University Carlos III of Madrid, Spain (UC3M). He is currently a tenured associate professor in the UC3M and he has published over 50 papers in the field of advanced communications in magazines and congresses. He has been involved in several international research projects related with protocol design, protocol engineering, network management, advanced networks and multimedia systems. Some of the recent research projects funded by the European Commission in which he has participated are: TRILOGY, MUSE, E-NEXT or E-NET. He has also has participated in the scientific committee, organization and technical review in different national and international conferences (like IEEE Networks, IEEE Communication, Elsevier Computer Communications, IEEE Infocom or IEEE Globecom).

Long Vu is a Ph.D. student in the Department of Computer Science, University of Illinois. His research is about content distribution in mobile peer-to-peer networks, multimedia peer-to-peer streaming, and distributed systems.

Qiyan Wang is a Ph.D. student in the Department of Computer Science, University of Illinois. His research is about security and privacy for multimedia peer-to-peer streaming systems and distributed systems.

Xinheng Wang is currently a senior lecturer in wireless communications in College of Engineering of Swansea University with research interests in wireless mesh and sensor networks, software defined radio and their applications in healthcare.

Tin-Yu Wu currently works as an assistant professor in the Department of Electrical Engineering, Tamkang University, Taipei, Taiwan. He received his M.S., and Ph.D. degrees in the Department of Electrical Engineering, National Dong Hwa University, Hualien, Taiwan in 2000 and 2007 respectively. His research interests focus on the next-generation Internet protocol, cloud computing and wireless networks.

Andrea Zanardi received his degree in Electronic Engineering with Computer Science specialization in 1992 from the University of Padua, Italy. From 1995 he has been working as software engineer and software architect for Telecom Italia taking part in the implementation and design of the fault management OSSs for the TI access and backbone data networks. In 2006 he joined Create-Net where he has been working in a research project funded by a major US industry related to the use of GMPLS in optical networks.

Hui Zhang received her Bachelor's degree in Environmental Engineering in the School of Automation in University of Electronic Science and Technology of China (UESTC) in 2008. From Sep. 2008 to Jan. 2010, she studied Control Theory and Control Engineering as a postgraduate student in University of Electronic Science and Technology of China (UESTC). Currently, she is a research student in College of Engineering in Swansea University to study telecommunications. Her research interests include automatic network management, mobile device automatic management and reconfiguration.

Index